BHAVABHŪTI'S

# MĀLATĪMĀDHAVA

**With the Commentary of Jagaddhara**

*Edited with*
*a literal English Translation,*
*Notes and Introduction by*

**M.R. KALE**

MOTILAL BANARSIDASS PUBLISHERS
PRIVATE LIMITED • DELHI

*Third Edition: 1967*
*Reprint: Delhi, 1983, 1997*



*Also available at:*

MOTILAL BANARSIDASS

41 U.A. Bungalow Road, Jawahar Nagar, Delhi 110 007
8 Mahalaxmi Chamber, Warden Road, Mumbai 400 026
120 Royapettah High Road, Mylapore, Chennai 600 004
Sanas Plaza, Subhash Nagar, Pune 411 002
16 St. Mark's Road, Bangalore 560 001
8 Camac Street, Calcutta 700 017
Ashok Rajpath, Patna 800 004
Chowk, Varanasi 221 001

PRINTED IN INDIA

BY JAINENDRA PRAKASH JAIN AT SHRI JAINENDRA PRESS,
A-45 NARAINA INDUSTRIAL AREA PHASE I, NEW DELHI 110 028
AND PUBLISHED BY NARENDRA PRAKASH JAIN FOR
MOTILAL BANARSIDASS PUBLISHERS PRIVATE LIMITED,
BUNGALOW ROAD, DELHI 110 007

# INTRODUCTION.

## I The Sanskrit Drama.

( *Abridged from our introduction to the Sâk.* )

Rûpaka* is the general name in San. for a dramatic composition which belongs to the class of दृश्य Kâvyas. It is divided into ten classes, *viz.*, नाटकं सप्रकरणं भाणः प्रहसनं डिमः । व्यायोग-समवकरौ वीथ्यंकेहामृगा इति ॥ The three principal elements constituting a drama are वस्तु the Plot, नेता the Hero ( with or without the Heroine ), and रस the sentiment. *Vastu*, also called इतिवृत्त, is of two kinds-आधिकारिक or that which relates to the principal characters and प्रासंगिक, also called पताका, or accessary, which helps and furthers the main topic and is concerned with characters other than the Hero and the Heroine. Next we have what is called Prakarî—an episodical incident of limited duration and minor importance which also assists the progress of the plot. There are three other elements constituting the plot. These are बीज or the seed, *i. e.* the circumstance or the circumstances from which the plot arises, बिन्दु or the drop, which connects one part of the story with another, and Kârya or the ultimate object. Thus the five essential constituents of the plot are बीजबिन्दुपताकाख्यप्रकरीकार्यलक्षणाः ।

The five stages of enterprise or the object wished to be gained ultimately, called Arthaprakritis, are—आरम्भ यत्न प्राप्त्याशा नियताप्ति फलागमाः । These names are self explanatory. The five essentials of the plot in combination with the five stages form what are technically called the five Sandhis:—अर्थप्रकृतयः पञ्च पञ्चावस्थासमन्विताः । यथासंख्येन जायन्ते मुखाद्याः पञ्चसंधयः ॥ The names of the five Sandhis are मुख, प्रतिमुख, गर्भ, अवमर्श and निर्वहण ( also called उपसंहृति ). For the meaning and scope of these Sandhis see Technical Remarks. For other particulars see our Intro. to Sâk. or Vik. or D. R. The subject matter is further divided into three kinds:—सर्वश्राव्यं or प्रकाशं, अश्राव्यं or स्वगतं and नियतश्राव्यं ( what is fit to be heard by select persons only ). The last is of two kinds जनान्तिक and अपवारितक. See notes.

---

* रूप्यतेभिनयैर्यत्र वस्तु तद् रूपकं विदुः ; नाटकाद्यैर्दशविधम् । D. R.

## NETA' OR THE HERO.

The hero must be one well brought up, decorous, munificient, clever, of sweet address, &c. See Jag. p. 11, नेता विनीतो &c. Heroes are of four kinds, Dhîrodâtta, Dhîralalita, Dhîras'ânta and Dhiroddhata. The hero of the present play is Dhîrapras'-ânta. See. Technical Remarks. Each of these heroes is again of four sorts, *viz.* दक्षिण or gallant, शठ or sly, धृष्ट or bold and अनुकूल or devoted to the heroine only. The Nâyikâ or heroine who must have qualities answering to those of the hero is of three kinds, *viz.* स्वीया ( wife of the Hero, as Sîtâ in the Uttar.) अन्या or परकीया ( as a maiden who is in the power of another, her parents &c. ) and सामान्या a common woman. For her assistants a Heroine may have a सखी, दासी, धात्रेयी or so.

## 3 RASA OR SENTIMENT.

*Rasa* is that lasting impression or feeling produced to his overwhelming delight in a man of poetic suceptibility by the proper action of the *Vibhâvas* and *Anubhâvas* as well as the *Sâtvika* and the *Vyabhichâribhâvas**. Bhâva ( भाव ) or feeling is the complete pervasion of the heart by any emotion, whether of pleasure or pain, arising from the object under sight. Vi-bhâva ( विभाव ) or an Excitant is that which being perceived nourishes the main sentiment. It is divided into *Alambana*, that which is, as it were, the support or substratum of the Rasa—the person or thing with reference to which a sentiment arises—such as the Hero or the Heroine, and *Uddîpana* or what enhances ( adds to the development of ) the sentiment, such as the moon, the beauties of the vernal season &c., decorations &c., of the principal characters, in the case of Sṛingâra. *Anubhâva* is the outward manifestation of the internal feeling through the eyes, face &c. The Sâtvika or natural *bhâvas* are a subdivision of the *Anubhâva*. They are usually mentioned as eight in number—स्तम्भप्रलयरोमांचाः स्वेदो वैवर्ण्यवेपथू । अश्रुवैस्वर्यमित्यष्टौ । The *Vyabhi-châris* or the Accessaries are those bhâvas which are not strictly confined to any *Rasa*, but which serve as feeders to the pre-vailing sentiment and strengthen it in different ways. † *Sthâyi-*

---

* विभावैरनुभावैश्च सात्त्विकैर्व्यभिचारिभिः । आनीयमानः स्वाद्यत्वं स्थायिभावो रसः स्मृतः ॥ सुखदुःखादिकैर्भावैर्भावस्तद्भावभावनम् । ज्ञायमानतया तत्र विभावो भावपोषकृत् । आलम्बनोद्दीपनत्वप्रभेदेन स च द्विधा । अनुभावो विकारस्तु भावसंसूचनात्मकः ॥

† विरुद्धैरविरुद्धैर्वा भावैर्विच्छिद्यते न यः । आत्मभावं नयत्यन्यान्स स्थायी लवणाकरः ॥

*bhâva* ( स्थायिभाव ) or the permanent Sentiment of a composition is one—the ocean melting all salt into water—which, not being interrupted by any sentiment contrary or akin to its nature occurring at intervals, converts all of them into its own nature. Now a *Rasa* would prove contrary to another if the आश्रय or substratum of both were the same. But as अङ्गि ( Principal ) and अङ्ग ( subordinate ) a रस may be mixed with one or more of others.

There are eight Sthâyibhâvas, रति, हास, शोक, क्रोध, भय, जुगुप्सा and विस्मय on which are based respectively the eight sentiments, शृङ्गार The Erotic, हास्य The Comic, करुण The Pathetic, रौद्र The Furious, वीर The Heroic, भयानक The Terrible, बीभत्स The Loathsome, and अद्भुत The Marvellous. Of these eight sentiments शृङ्गार and हास्य, वीर and अद्भुत, बीभत्स and भयानक and रौद्र and करुण are akin to each other, as they proceed from the same condition of the mind. As we are concerned with the Erotic alone, that being the prevailing sentiment in the present play, we will say something about it here. शृङ्गार is mainly divided into विप्रलम्भ or Love in separation, and संभोग or Love in union. The Former, the Dasarûpaka subdivides into two kinds, अयोग the Non-consummàtion of marriage, and विप्रयोग the Separation of the lovers deep in love ( after marriage ). The former which arises from the dependent position of one or the other of the parties or through distance or through the intervention of adverse fate, has ten stages, अभिलाष, चिन्ता &c. mentioned in the com.; the latter occurs through मान, प्रवास or some such cause. संभोग is when the two lovers are in the enjoyment of each other's company, engaged in looking at each other, kissing each other &c.

## 4. THE GENERAL CONDUCT OF THE NA'TAKA.

Every dramatic piece opens with a prelude or prologue ( प्रस्तावना ) itself introduced by what is called the *Nándi*. This Nándi according to some must suggest the gist of the whole plot. The Sûtradhára may sometimes retire after the recital of the Nándî, in which case, another actor called स्थापक ( for he establishes as it were the topic of the play ) takes his place. In the prelude, which may begin with a brief allusion to the poet's literary attainments, his genealogy &c., the Sutradhára or the Sthápaka suggests the subject in the form of the Bîja, or by a simple beginning, or by naming the character just to enter as in the present play. He must please the audience with sweet songs descriptive of some season and couched in the

Bhàrati vriti. The प्रस्तावना is of two kinds-(1) प्ररोचना as in the Rat., and (2) आमुख in which the Sutradhára holds conversation with the actress or his assistants bearing on the subject to be introduced. This latter is of three kinds of which one is प्रयोगातिशय (as in this play). When the entry of the character to enter is directly indicated in the words there he enters, that is Prayogatis'aya.

The prelude being over, the piece is commenced being hereafter arranged and exhibited in the manner indicated in the three foregoing sections. The whole matter should be well determined and divided into Acts and Scenes. The principal sentiment should be शृङ्गार or वीर (or sometimes करुण), others being introduced as conducive to its development. Nothing should be introduced in the play which either misbeseems the Hero or is discordant with the main sentiment. An act must not be tiresomely long, should be full of *Rasa* and introduced by *Vis'kambhaka,* &c. according to necessity. Its close is marked by the exit of all characters. Such incidents as journeys, massacres, wars &c. should not be represented in a play; they may only be indicated. The death of the Hero must never be exhibited. This accounts for the somewhat monotonous character of Sanskṛt plays and the absence of tragedies in Sanskṛt.* The play should end, as it began, with a benediction or prayer, called the Bharatavákya, which is generally repeated by the principal personage in his character as भरत or member (of the theatrical Co.) and contains an expression of their wishes for general prosperity and happiness.† The Unity of

* Wilson observes—They (the Hindu plays) never offer a calamitous conclusion, which, as Johnson remarks, was enough to constitute a Tragedy in Shakespear's days; and although they propose to excite all the emotions of the human breast, terror and pity included, they never effect this object by leaving a painful impression upon the mind of the spectator. The Hindus in fact have no Tragedy,......The absence of tragic catastrophe in the Hindu dramas is not merely an unconscious omission; such catastrophe is prohibited by a positive rule. The conduct of what may be termed the classical drama of the Hindus is exemplary and dignified. Nor is its moral purport neglected; and one of their writers declares, in an illustration familiar to ancient and modern poetry, that the chief end of the Theatre is to disguise, by the insidious sweet, the unpalatable but salutary bitter of the cup.

† भरतवाक्यं नटवाक्यम्। प्रस्तावनानन्तरं नटवाक्या भावादत्र भरतवाक्यमित्युक्तिः। Rághavabhatta on Śak.

interest or action must be maintained throughout. As regards the language to be used in a piece, the Hero and the higher characters speak in Classical Sanskṛt, while female and other minor characters speak in the different Prákṛta dialects. The student will see from the foregoing sketch, that the characteristic peculiarities of the Indian drama are mainly three (1) its peculiar structure; (2) absence of the distinction between Comedy and Tragedy; and (3) the diversity of language to be spoken by the characters.

The above mentioned general characteristics of a Nátaka belong with certain modifications to the other divisions of the Rûpaka as well. Of these we are here concerned with Prakarana only. The plot of a प्रकरण should be fictitious and drawn from real life in a respectable class of society. The Hero must be of the धीरप्रशान्त kind. The Heroine may be a maiden of a noble family, or a courtesan. The most appropriate sentiment is the Erotic. Gamblers and other low characters should be introduced. There should be ten acts. The Màl. Màdh. and the Mṛch, belong to this species. For other particulars see Technical Remarks.

## II THE POET,

### His Life, Works and Poetry.

It is a matter for some satisfaction that Bhavabhûti has not left us altogether in the dark about himself, and therefore we have not to pour forth the usual complaint of Sans. critics about the absence of any reliable information about a poet's life, and which we had occasion to make when writing about his great predecessor, Kálidàsa. In his introduction to the present play and to the Mv. he gives some account of himself and his family, which, meagre as it is, saves the antiquarian from one kind of difficulty. But as regards the time in which he flourished he is silent and to determine his date we must look for information in other quarters. We will begin first by giving the reader a short sketch of the life of the poet as given by himself in this and his other plays.

Bhavabhûti was the scion of an illustrious family which traced its descent back to the sage Kaśyapa. His ancestors, who were the followers of the Taittirîya branch of the Black Yajurveda and ever kept the fivefold sacred fire, lived in a town named Padmapura, in the county of Vidarbha, now called the Berars. Their surname was Udumbara. They were the performers of such higher sarifices as Vajapeya, Somayága &c. and drank the Soma. Profoundly learned in the various branches of knowledge then in vogue among the Bráhmaṇas, they led a holy life and were never remiss in the discharge of the duties that are incumbent upon householders. Those eminent Bráhmaṇas applied themselves zealously to the study of the Vedic lore solely with a view to gain correct knowledge and not as a weapon to disarm the contrávertialist. And they employed the emoluments of their priestly profession in the construction of such works of public utility as wells by the wayside, tanks and others of the kind. In short, their life on earth was perfectly holy—one that eminently fitted them for permanent residence in heaven.

In a family with such illustrious ancestors was born one, Mahákavi by name. Bhavabhûti was fifth in decent from him. His grand-father's name was Gopálabhatta, that of his father Nîlakantha and of his mother Játukarnî. Bhavabhûti's deep scholarship and versatile genius had also won for him the distinguishing title of 'Shrikantha.' According to the commentators this was the poet's proper name; he came to be called Bhavabhûti after he composed the famous lines तपस्वी कां गतोऽवस्थां &c. (See Sans. Intro.). But the words भवभूतिर्नाम in the introductory part of the three plays show that this is not correct. Bhavabhûti was a profound scholar. Well-versed in the Vedas and the Upanishads, he knew grammar and very probably the Mimámsa (although he does not directly mention it), as his ancestors were great performers of sacrifices and was an adept in the Yoga and Sánkhya systems of philosophy.* (See I. 7 of the present play). He was also well grounded in the Uttaramîmámsa or Vedánta as propounded by Bàdaráyana and possibly by the venerable Śankaráchárya†, as he alludes to the Vivarta theory in his Uttar. (III, 47; IV, 15). We learn from the Mahávîracharita that the name of his Guru was Jnánanidhi, lit.-'The repository of knowledge.' And our poet probably derived all his knowledge, especially that of

* The poet gives ample proofs of his thorough acquaintance with the various subjects mentioned above. His allusion to the Vairája (Uttar. II. 12) and the Asûrya lokas (Act IV *Idem*, Janaka's speech) show that he knew the Upanishads well. That he knew even the practical side of the Yoga is apparent from the 5th Act of this play and the 3rd of the Mv.

† This is a disputed point. Dr. Bhándarkar thinks that by Bhavabhûti's Vivarta we are to understand परिणाम.

the Upanishad philosophy from this Guru. To his literary attainments, Bhavabhûti joined a powerful memory, a wonderful genius and a keen perception which characterise a first class poet and dramatist.

Although patronised by a king ( see below ) Bhavabhûti does not appear ever to have basked in the sunshine of royal favour so far as to have been in affluent circumstances or to have come in closer contact with a royal court. For, had he been acquainted with courtlife like his predecessors Kâli. and Bâna, he would have given us fine and exact descriptions of a royal court and its surroundings, courtly etiquette, &c. Nor does he appear to have been very popular in his own time like Kâli.* Otherwise he could not have complained of the apathy of the people towards him ( see I. 6 ) and depended upon future generations for an appreciation of his works and poetic genius. Perhaps that was not the age for the drama. The style of writing approved of by critics like Dandin and elaborated by poets like Bhâravi and Bâna had caused a revolution in men's ideas about poetry and as such style was suited to Kâvyas, or prose works, these better appealed to the taste of the Pandits and commended themselves to their approval and naturally the drama declined. For very few dramas were written during the interval that separates Bhava. from Kâlidâsa.

His date.

The first quarter of the 8th ( or the last quarter of the 7th ) century of the Christian era may be assigned as the date of our poet, as shown by Dr. Bhândarkar. From a śloka in the Râjatarangini* it is known that Bhavabhûti was patronised by Yaśovarman, king of Kanouj.† Again, a certain poet, Vâkpatirâja by name, who was also in the service of Yaśovarman and his court poet, refers to our poet in eulogistic terms in his work called the Gaudavaho, as one to whom he was indebted for some poetic conceptions and modes of expression.‡ Coupling these two facts

* The austerity of Bhavabhûti's style, his lack of humour, his insistent grandeur, are qualities which prevent his being a truly popular poet. Dr. Ryder, Intro. to Mṛch.

† कविवाक्पतिराजश्रीभवभूत्यादिसेवितः । जितो ययौ यशोवर्मा तद्गुणस्तुतिबन्दिताम् ॥

‡ भवभुइजलहिनिग्गयकव्वामयरसकणा इव फुरन्ति । जस्स विसेसा अज्जवि विअडेसु कहाणिवेसेसु ॥ भवभूतिजलधिनिर्गतकाव्यामृतरसकणा इव स्फुरन्ति । यस्य विशेषा अद्यापि विकटेषु कथानिवेशेषु ॥

and after discussing the various questious at issue the learned Doctor comes to the conclusion that Vákpatirája must have written his work between 733 A. D. and 753, the approximate date of Yaśovarman's death, since he mentions in it the annular eclipse of August 14th, 733 A. D. If Vák. then lived in the 2nd quarter of the 8th century, Bhavabhûti must have flourished in the first. See preface to Dr. Bhá.'s Ed. of the play, pp. 17-18. This shows that Bhavabhûti comes after Báṇa and accoounts for the latter's not referring to him in the long list of his predcessors, such as Kálidas'a, Pravarasena and others, mentioned by him in his introduction to the Harshacharitá.

His Works.

Bhavabhúti's fame as a poet rests on his three plays (the only works known to be his as yet), *viz.* the Málatîmádhava, the Mahávîracharita and the Uttarará macharita. It is impossible to conceive that a gifted poet like Bhavabhúti could not have written at least a poem or two like Kálidása's Raghu. or Megh., although his special leaning was towards the drama. This is clear from the speech of the Sûtradhâra at p. 8 (भवभूतिर्नाम कविर्नि सर्गसौहृदेन भरतेषु &c.) There are, however, two ślokas* quoted in Śárgadhara's Paddhatî (See Dr. Bha.'s ed. p. 9) and two in Gadádharabhatta's Rasikajivana, according to the Nir. Ed. (Intro.) from Bhavabhúti's works. This shows that Bhavabhúti might have written some other work or works but now lost to us or not discovered yet. Dr. Bhándárkar, however, comes to the conclusion that he did not. Perhaps the poet's earthly career was abruptly cut short.

To turn to the dramas now, Mál. Mád. appears to be the poet's first composition, Mv., the second, and Uttar., the last. For this chronological order there is no historical evidence as such but internal evidence there is. We base our conclusion on the following points :—(1) In the first place like every first attempt the Mâl. Mâd. displays an admixture of excellences and defects, however small the number of the latter may be. The plot, although well conceived, suffers from a sort of clumsiness

* One of these is :—
निरवद्यानि पद्यानि यदि नाट्यस्य का क्षतिः । भिक्षुकक्षाविनिक्षिप्तः किमिक्षुर्नीरसो भवेत् ॥ Those in the Ras. are :—

अलिपटलैरनुयातां सहृदयहृदयज्वरं विलुम्पन्तीम् ।
मृगमदपरिमललहरीं समीर किं पामरेषु रे किरसि ॥
किं चन्द्रमाः प्रत्युपकारलिप्सया करोति गोभिः कुमुदावबोधनम् ।
स्वभाव एवोन्नतचेतसां सतां परोपकारव्यसनं हि जीविनम् ॥

( see General remarks further on ), and the *denouement* is faulty to some extent. (2) In its prelude the poet speaks of his great literary attainments with a glow of pride and indirectly hints that he possesses the great powers and the necessary qualifications of a dramatist ( see sl. s. 4, 7. ) which he would not have done had this not been his first work. Again the metres of the opening stanzas, the fondness for long compounds and out-of-the-way words, a conscious attempt to introduce matter from the Nyâya, Yoga and other philosophies, evince the irresistible desire on the part of an erudite scholar, fresh from his Guru's home, to show forth his learning somehow. This desire appears to be less and less intense in the other two plays. (3) The sl. वश्यवाच: कवेर्वाक्यं ( I. 4 ) in Mv. shows that that play was the second production of our poet, as he speaks more confidently of himself in it than in the Mâl. Mâd., a confidence due to his previous attempt having been successful. He also speaks more favourably of his audience in the Mv. The śloks—कल्याणानां &c., wherein he himself invokes, although indirectly, the favour of the deity to grant him the powers of a first class poet ( which he does not do in the other two plays ), and भूम्ना रसानां &c., wherein he gives his audience an idea of what a play ought to be like, also point to the same conclusion. The sl. ये नाम केचिदिह &c. need not be supposed, as shown in the notes, to refer to the possibility of our poet's first play being unfavourably received by his audience. In fact, his successful attempt to write the Mál. Mád. must have led the poet to say वश्यवाच: &c., and its reflex in the Uttar., यं ब्राह्मणमियं देवी वागवश्येवानुवर्तते &c. (4) We cannot reasonably suppose the poet to have taken up Rámá's early history once, then to have set aside the work of completing it for a time, written the Mál. Mád., and to have resumed it afterwards. Moreover Bhav. is supposed to have written the Vth Act of the Mv. upto sl. 46; again there are two versions of the last two Acts. This want of proper finish also shows that it could not have been the first work of the poet. ( 5 ) Sanskrit dramatic poets have always given the greatest prominence to शृंगार and a new poet, striving to gain popularity, can hardly be supposed to go out of the way and treat Vîrarasa first. It is a general rule that passionate love, such as is found depicted in the present drama, appeals to a person earlier in life than bravery or other serious qualities of the mind. Sṛngára, Vîra, and Karuna–is the natural order of the Rasas, and it agrees well with the three plays if arranged as Mál.

Mád., Mv. and Uttararámacharita. (6) The fame of his great predecessor, Káli, must have induced the poet to write a love play first. He had to establish his reputation as a great poet and hence his effort to imitate Káli. in the 9th Act of this play, both in sentiment and style and therein to rival him successfully in his own element. This imitation is inexplicable after the confidence he is supposed to have gained in his powers according to the theory that Mv. was his first work. Thus it is abundantly clear that Bhavabhûti must have begun his career as a dramatist with this play.*

We can refer but briefly to his other two plays here. The Máhavîracharita is a historic play based on the early history of Ráma's life as related in the Rámáyaṇa—from his boyhood to his return to Ayodhyá after the Lanká war and Sîtá's rescue. To suit his purpose the poet has made considerable alterations in the original story. The principal sentiment is Vîra or heroism. 'The same loftiness of sentiment' remarks Prof. Wilson, 'excellence of picturesque description and power of language, which mark the Uttar. and Mál. Mád., are the characteristics of the Vîracharita.' And if the style is less elegant or harmonious, and the expression less felicitous, it is because the poet so meant it on account of the subject chosen—'Wherein the mighty deeds of great men will be chivalrous and awe-inspiring and the language vigorous and stern and yet sonorous and prolific in sense.'† 'As a poem,' Prof. Wilson further on remarks "it ranks worthily with the other works of the same author, and as a play ( although inferior to the other two ) is infinitely superior to others in which the same subject is treated by less skilful hands."

The third play of the poet is the Uttararámacharita or 'the latter part of Ráma's life.' It is the poet's master piece. It was this drama which at once placed Bhavabhûti in the very first rank of Sans. poets. In it is dramatised one particular incident in Ráma's life after his rescue of Sîtá and his return to Ayodhyá from Lanká, *viz.*, Sitá's abandonment. The story only serves the poet as a nucleus, while all the incidents, which cluster round it and produce such wonderful dramatic effect,

* Perhaps the earliest of the works is the Mahávîracharita, but the evidence for this is uncertain, and there is no reason to assign it definitely to an earlier date than the Málatimâdhava. Dr. Keith.

† महापुरुषसंरम्भो यत्र गम्भीरभीषणः । प्रसन्नकर्कशा यत्र विपुलार्था च भारती ॥

are the creation of the poet's genius. In this play Bhav. has done his best to depict the sentiment of *Karuna* or pathos with a success scarcely achieved by any other poet of classic India that preceded or succeeded him. It is in connection with this play that the anecdote about Káli.'s having called it superior to even his own plays, related by Dr. Bhándarkar ( see his introduction to Mál. Mád. p. 11 ) is told. With regard to this play Prof. Wilson remarks—The style is equally vigorous and harmonious as that of the Mál. and Mádh ; several of the sentiments found in that play also recur in this; and the general character of the two dramas, notwithstanding the difference of their subjects, offers many analogies. We have the same picturesque description and natural pathos in both.

Bhavbhûti as a *Poet.*

We now come to the question of assigning his proper place to Bhavabhûti in Sans. Literature. As dramatic writers, Sûdraka, and Kálidása alone press upon our notice as his rivals—and these indeed are the three greatest names in the classical drama of India. " So different are these men " remarks Dr. Ryder, " and so great, that it is not possible to assert for any one of them such supremacy as Shakespeare holds in the English drama. " The Mṛchchhakatika is placed chronologically before Śákuntala by Sans. critics, and not without reason. The plot of the drama is strikingly unorthodox. The author does not draw upon the storehouse of stories-the Puránas, as is done by many other Sans. poets, for his plot. He seems to have struck out his own independent line and have composed a drama from the incident or incidents observed in actual life. He has dispensed with the orthodox Vidûśaka, the ever-recurring and hence stale replica of an original invented to tickle the groundlings. There is something original and fresh about his Maitreya. The funny element introduced to feed the prevailing tragic element is not the clumsy, stilted humour, sanctioned by holy usage. In fact the character of Śakára stands probably alone in Sans. literature. Fun consisting of play on words abounds in Sans. literature. But the comic element that sees the grotesque in nature, that smiles at the incongruities and contrasts with a relish, is entirely absent in it. And excepting the Cheta and Vita, or the thief in it, or the scene between Śyála, captain of the city guards and the fisherman in Śak , there is not much of humour in the dramas of these great poets, in the English sense of the word.

If Kálidása comes after Śûdraka ( which he probably does although we do not find his name mentioned along with those of Bhása and Saumilla in the Mál. ) we find him drawn back to the Scholastic fold again. For although gifted with creative faculty of no ordinary type, although full of inspiration, fresh images and novel conceptions, he bends his powers back upon the old stories though he renders them attractive and beautiful, so as to strike as new. His was thus the power of a new creative imagination curtailed and limited ( though to a very small extent, as far as his Śak. at least is concerned ) by the Scholasticism of his time. One is sometimes sorry that he did not write out a purely original drama–not that he is the less original because he has not written an original drama. Chronologically Bhav. comes the last of the three. A greater interval of time perhaps separates Bhavabhûti from Kàli. than that which separates Káli. from Sûdraka. Sûdraka's play, although written in Sans., has a cosmopolitan character. Káli. and Bhav. are essentially Hindu poets. As masters of constructive art Sûdraka and Káli. bear comparison to each other. As far as variety, the delineation of male characters as drawn from the different strata of the society and humour are concerned Śûdraka excels both, Káli. and Bhavabhûti. But in other respects the latter two far outshine him. In the words of Dr. Ryder-Sudraka cannot infuse into mere language the charm which we find in Kâli. or the majesty which we find in Bhavabhûti. In fact these two poets may be considered as the greatest dramatists in Sanskrit.

In Bhav. we have an instance of an attempt at another revolt against the Scholastic way ( see Gen. remarks ). He has to defy his contemporaries and has to appeal to generations yet unborn for a proper modicum of praise and a fair estimate of his poetic powers. As a creator of new incidents ( although Bâna is superior to either in this respect ) and of an original story he stands comparison with Sûdraka alone. As a student of human nature he is not equal to his master (Súd.) and in the skill of arranging the incidents and working out the *denouement* he is far surpassed by him and even by the author of the Mudrârakshasa. But here must end all comparison between Śûdraka and Kâli. and Bhavabhûti. As a poet Bhav. holds an almost equal rank with Kâlidâsa. He possesses the various requisites for a truly great poet, a creative imagination, playful fancy, power to appreciate the sublime and the beautiful and a very high power of characterisation. His style is chaste and his thoughts majestic. And he adapts language in a wonderful manner to the sentiment to be expressed (*Cf.* II. 6, III. 9. &c. ). He has a deep insight into the soft places of the human heart and considerable knowledge of its workings. He is essentially a poet of stirring passion and has brought out pathos and tenderness most successfully. The lyrical element predominates over the other elements in his writings. He can interprete nature in her grandeur, her awful solitude, her cataracts, dense forests, and mountain regions, with a masterly style and felicity of expression. Nature in her littleness or softer beauties appeals to him not at all or but very lightly. His love is intense but not natural, expressed, not suggested, is more a conception than a reality. His characters storm and weep, do not brood and languish. He has no humour or does not indulge in any; his own temperament did not fit him for that. He has tried to depict all the Rasas, not excluding *Bîbhatsa* and *Adbhuta* with more or less success but is grand only in the Vîra and Karuṇa. His language is majestic and dignified but in many places pedantic and pretentious—not at all suited to convey his thoughts in a lucid manner or to please the audience. His pedantry is without elegance as Bâna's is full of unexpected surprises. However, he is not stilted like Dandin, if he has none or very few of the graces of Bâna. Love of an elaborate style has spoiled the prose part of his writings. The use of bewildering compounds and obscure words is extremely unsuited to quick retorts or vigorous conversation and serves rather to retard the effect than help it on. Let us now compare Bhav. with Kâlidâsa.

## BHAVABHÛTI AND KA'LIDA'SA.

( Almost reproduced from our intro to Śakun. )

As already remarked Kâli. and Bhav. are the two greatest dramatic poets of classical India. Although separated from each other by no less than seven centuries, they so much resembled each other in spirit that in a few years they came to be regarded as contemporaries and rivals of each other * And

° With reference to Kâlidâsa he holds a position such as Aeschylus holds with reference to Euripides. He will always seem to minds that sympathise with his grandeur the greatest of Indian poets; while by other equally discerning minds of another order he will be admired, but not passionately loved. Dr. A. W. Ryder, Intro. to Mrch. p. YVI.

they have both justice done them by the voice of discerning critics. Although as a poet on the whole we may place Kâlidâsa above Bhavabhûti, as a dramatic poet the palm is certainly disputed with him by the latter. Nay, the tide of opinion among the Pandits once ran so high as to decidedly declare in favour of Bhavabhûti, as the author of the Uttararâmacharita[*]. Kâli. is justly called 'the Grace of Poetry,' Bhavabhûti 'the Master of loquence.' Both are most original poets, gifted with genius of the highest order. Both are masters of the natural style of poetry and both are equally happy in their choice of words. True that Bhavabhûti's style is rather elaborate and in a few places marked by long compounds, but in that the poet was unconsciously yielding to the tendency of his age. If Kâlidâsa has more fancy and imgaination, Bhavabhûti is more sentimental and passionate. Kâlidâsa excels in depicting the sentiment of Love ( शृंगार ) while Bhavabhûti is in his element when depicting the sentiment of Pathos ( करुण ) and Heroism ( वीर ). Neither, however, is much inferior to the other in depicting what may be called the others' *forte*. As Dr. Bhândârkar remarks, 'the former *suggests* or *indicates* the sentiment which the latter *expresses* in forcible language. In the words of Sanskrit critics Kâlidasa's *Rasa* is conveyed or *Abhivyakta* by the *Lakshya* or *Vyangya* sense of words, while Bhavabhûti's is conveyed by the *Vâchya* sense.' Kâlidâsa's may be described as the synthetical method of poetry as opposed to Bhavabhûti's which is analytical. We shall give a few quotations in illustration of what we have said above. When Dushyanta sees Śakuntalá after love has wounded his heart, he simply says—'अये लब्धं नेत्रनिर्वाणं' p. 17, ( see also our note on this ) but compare Bhavabhûti, Mal. Mád. where Mâdhava says—हन्त पुण्यवानस्मि यदहमतर्कितोपनतदर्शनोल्लासितलोचनयानया—अविरलमिव दाम्ना पौण्डरीकेण नद्धः &c. III. 16. Here the feeling is the same but the different forms of it are described.

Compare the scene between Dushyanta and Śakuntalá when left alone with what Mádh. says when Málati embraces him in the disguise of her friend लवङ्गिका—

एकीकृतस्त्वचि निषिक्त इवावपीड्य
 निर्भुग्नपीनकुचकुड्मलयानया मे ।
कर्पूरहारहरिचन्दनचन्द्रकान्त-
 निष्यन्दशैवलमृणालहिमादिवर्गः ॥

---

[*] *Cf.* the memorable line. उत्तरे रामचरिते भवभूतिर्विशिष्यते ।

*Cf.* also, as an instance of Bhavabhûti's forcible style, the first effect produced on Mádhava on seeing Málati. He says—परिच्छेदातीतः सकलवचनानामविषयः &c. I. 30.

Compare further the meeting of Dushyanta and Śakuntalâ. ( p. 82 भवतु । मोक्ष्यामि &c. ) with that of Mádhava and Málati—( ततः प्रविशतः &c. ) माधवः—( सानन्दम् ) दलयति परिशुष्यत् &c. निश्चोतन्ते स्तुनतु &c. VIII. 1, 2. Again he says—अयि निरनुरोधे—जीवयन्निव &c. and दग्धं चिराय मलयानिलचन्द्रपादैः &c. VIII. 3, 4.

Space does not permit us to give here more illustrations. As Dr. Bhândârkar remarks, Bhav. might have modelled the love of Mádh. and Mál. on that of Dushyanta and Śakuntalâ. But the love of Mâdhava is more ætherial than that of Dushyanta and perhaps Bhavabhuti as a poet is more ætherial than Kâli-dâsa. Bhavabhûti's delineation of the sentiment of pathos is simply unparallelled ( *cf.* the general opinion of the Pandits कारुण्यं भवभूतिरेव तनुते ).* The characters of Kâlidâsa seldom make us weep; Bhavabhuti's do. Bhav. rarely makes any attempt at wit; while Kâli. does though to a limited extent. As a poet of nature and as a describer of the picturesque he is not inferior to Kâlidâsa. Natural scenery, however, as it is, without the fantasies it gives rise to, alone appeals to him. Kâli. would be more attracted by its suggestiveness. *Cf.* in this respect Bhav.'s descriptions of the दण्डक forest, the cemetery and the river Godâvarî, with Kâli's. descriptions of the Gandhamâdana (Vik.). Himâlaya, Kum. I and the confluence of the Ganges and Yamunâ ( Ragh. XIII ). The plays of Kâlidâsa on the whole do not much aim at giving a realistic picture of the life of the society of his time; Bhavabhúti's do. The characters of Káli-dása are more romantic and idealistic in their conception, those of Bhavabhúti more realistic and varied.

---

# III. THE PLAY.

## 1. THE PLOT.

THE PRELUDE—**After the benediction the poet gives a brief account of himself and then introduces to the audience the characters just to enter on the stage.**

---

* Marâthi students will do well to read Mr. Chiplunkar's essay on the two poets.

## ACT 1.

### Scene 1. Kâmandakî's convent.

Kámandakî and Avalokitâ speak of the desired match between Mâlatî and Mádhava in furtherance of a solemn engagement made by their fathers when students that they would join their children in wedlock. Kâmandakî, who had secret instructions to bring about the much coveted connection, feels encouraged to pursue her plans on learning from Lavangiká that love has struck root in the heart of Mâlatî, as she often saw Mâdhava passing by the street that fronted her mansion and that Mālatî had actually drawn his likeness to dispel her love-longing. Lavangiká takes the wise step of handing over Mádh.'s likeness to Mandârikâ from whom it was expected to find its way to Mádhava himself. Avalokitâ tells Kâmandakī how, she too, in anticipation of the wishes of the latter, has induced Mâdhava to go to the grove of Kâma where a fair was to be held and so he might see Mâlati. The conversation then incidentally turns upon Saudâminî, a former pupil of Kâmandakī, and they talk of her attainment of miraculous powers by the practice of Yoga. They also wish that they could bring about the union of Makaranda, Mádhava's friend and Madayantikà, Nandana's sister.

### Scene II. The Grove of Ka'ma.

Kalahamsaka, Mádh.'s servant, goes with the portrait drawn by Màlati to the Madana garden and sits there waiting for Mádh. and Makaranda. Maka. who also goes to the same garden in search of his friend, finds him there but much changed in appearance and he at once guesses what the matter might be. On meeting Mádhava he asks him the cause of his despondent mood. Mádh. confesses to him his love for Màlatî, telling him how at the very first sight she had made a complete conquest of his heart. Málati betrays signs of a consuming passion for some fortunate youth, as Mádhava at first supposes, but the subsequent behaviour of Màlatî and her companions shows that he is the actual object of her love. Nay, Lavangiká, Málatî's confidante, approaches Mádh. and apparently praising the wreath which Mádh. was then weaving, tells him in enigmatical terms that his union with Màlatī would be the most desirable thing. She then takes away from him the Bakula-wreath on which her mistress had set her heart. Maka. thinks that this is encouragement enough and asks Mádhava to be hopeful. Kala., who overhears them now approaches the two friends and offers Mádhava's portrait delineated by Málatî, which clears up all doubts in the matter. Makaranda asks Mâdhava to paint Málatī by the side of his picture which Mádhava does, although with some difficulty. Mandáriká comes at this time and takes away the picture-board. The act ends with a description of Mádhava's love pangs.

---

## ACT II.

Interlude—After the meeting in the Madana-garden Málatî's passion grows intense and consequently her love-torment becomes more unbearable. And to make matters worse she is affianced to Nandana by her father at the instance of the King.

### SCENE I. THE WHITE HOUSE.

Conversation between Mâlatî and Lavangiká. Málatī takes from Lavangiká the chaplet of *Bakula* flowers woven by Mádhava. Lavangiká tells Málatī how Mádhava, too, is cruelly smitten with love and shows her portrait drawn by him. Màlatî looks at it, reads the stanza subscribed by Mádhava and expresses her wish that all should be well with the youth. She, however, feels her own anguish grow more poignant and describes her state to Lavangikâ. The latter insinuates Love marriage but Mâlatî, true to her instincts, rejects the proposal, saying that she would rather die than do any thing unworthy of a maiden of noble extraction.

### SCENE II. PLACE THE SAME.

Káma. comes with her pupil Avalo. to see Málatî and expresses her anxiety on her account on beholding her sad condition. She then tells her how she is betrothed to Nandana by her father, tries, by using cunning words, to create in her mind distrust about his doings and disgust for Nandana, eulogises Mádhava and by shrewd allusions to the espousal of Śak. by Dushyanta and other historical matches of that kind, prepares her mind for a marriage by self choice.

---

## ACT III.

### SCENE I. BHURIVASU'S MANSION.

Conversation between Fuddharakshitá and Avalokitá—Madhava is induced to go to the Kusumákara garden where Mál. also was to go. Budhara. seizes every occasion to create in Madhayantiká's heart a feeling of love for Mak. and succeeds in her object so far as to make her long for a sight of him.

### Scene II. The Garden.

Kám. first enters the garden and in her soliloquy describes the change she has wrought in Mál.'s thoughts. Mál. and Lav. follow her. Mâdh., too, enters unobserved and watches their movements as they are engaged in culling flowers. As he now sees Mál. with the eyes of a lover, she appears more charming to him—the inflamer of his passion and the sovereign balm to his eyes. Kám. asks. Mál. to desist from plucking flowers any more as she finds her exhausted and when they had all sat down, describes to her Mádh.'s love-affected condition in very pathetic terms. Lav. replies by giving her an equally touching picture of Mál.'s sad plight. Kám., expresses her anxiety regarding Mádh.'s wellbeing. Here the talkers are rudely startled by a voice announcing a tiger's escape from his cage, describing the terrible havoc made by the monster and asking men to save their lives as best as they can. Buddh. suddenly enters in alarm and asks them to save her friend, Madyantiká, then attacked by the tiger. All rush forth to the scene, and are glad to see Mak. come to the rescue; but their momentary joy changes to pain when they see Mak. faint by the wound inflicted by the tiger, although the beast falls under Mak.'s stroke. Mada. supports her gallant rescuer as he leans on his sword. Mádh., too, swoons away.

## ACT IV.

### Scene—The Same Continued.

The two lovers soon recover and the party is again engaged in conversation when a messenger enters and tells Madayantiká that the king has given Màl. to Nandana, her brother, with Bhûrivasu's implied consent and asks her to come away to share in her brother's joy. This news fills Mádh. and Mál. with despair. Maday., who was deep in love with Mak., as shown by the loving glances she had been casting at him, expresses her joy at the wished-for connection and departs. Kám. cheers up Mál. and Mádh. by explaining to them the real import of Bhûri.'s enigmatical words which really meant that the king had power over *his* daughter alone ( and not *his*-Bhûrivasu's ) and encourages Mádh. further by assuring him that she would bring about his marriage with Mál. even at the cost of her life. Kám. is called away by the queen, with Mál., who departs with a heart heavy with anguish. Mádhava, full of despair, resolves on a desperate expedient and enters the city with Mak., having waded through the confluence of the Pára and the Sindhu.

## ACT V

### SCENE I. THE VICINITY OF THE CREMATION GROUND.

Kapálakundalá enters and after describing her journey through the air by the power of Yoga, says that the maiden wanted by her Guru for being offered to Karálá was to be found in the neighbouring city and that she would proceed to look for her. Before she starts, however, she notices Mádhava advancing towards the burning ground.

Mádhava now appears on the scene, describes in a soliloquy the deep impression made by Mal.'s charms on his mind and expresses his vehement desire to see her. He then calls out to the goblin host haunting the cemetary and offers human flesh for sale. As he walks on, he describes the wild sports and the ghastly meal of the fiends and finally reaches the river skirting the burning ground, when, all on a sudden, a plaintive voice falls on his ears.

### SCENE II. KARÂLÂ'S TEMPLE.

Aghoraghanta and Kapálakundalá are discovered making preparations to offer up Málatî to Chámundâ whom they praise in a style and metre suitable to the terrific nature of the Goddess. They ask Málatî to say her last prayers and think of the person most loved by her. She professes her love for Mádhava. On recognising her voice Mádh. rushes forth and interposes himself between Aghoraghanta and Mâlatī. As some hot words are exchanged between the two, Aghora. and Mâdh. leading to a scuffle, the voice of Kâmandakî is heard outside asking the soldiers in search of Mál. to surround the shrine of Chamundá as the place where Mál. could, in all certainty, be found. This fills Aghor. and Kapál. with alarm; the two combatants ply on their swords with increased energy with the sesult that Aghoraghanta falls and thus meets with a doom he so richly deserved.

---

## ACT VI.

### SCENE I.

Kapálakundalá enters and expresses her resolve to wreak vengeance upon Mádh. for having slain her Guru. In the meantime a voice behind the curtains announces the celobration of Mál.'s marriage, asks all those concerned to be ready to receive the bridegroom's party that was approaching and conveys to Málatî her mother's bidding in accordance with Káma.'s injunctions to repair to the temple of the town-deity that all obstacles should be warded off. Kapâl. is glad to hear this as she might find an opportunity, in the bustle of the marriage, to carry out her wishes.

SCENE II. THE INSIDE OF THE TEMPLE.

Mádh. and Mak., stationed in the interior of the temple, observe Mâlatî coming and are greatly struck with the princely wealth of Bhûrivasu, as evinced by the gorgeous dresses and the glittering jewel-ornaments worn by Mál.'s attendants and relatives. Kám., Mál. and Lavangiká now enter and give vent to their feelings. A servant now enters bringing with him the bridal dress and ornaments to be worn by Málatî in the presence of the deity and delivers them over to Kámandakî. Mál. and Lav. then enter the interior of the temple at the bidding of Kám. who stays behind under the pretext of examining the ornaments. Mâl. in her utter despair opens her heart to Lav. in the hearing of Mádh. and Mak., telling her how deeply she loved Mádh. and how life would be hateful to her any more under the circumstances, declares her resolve to put an end to her wretched existence and asks her to assist her in carrying out that resolve. As she falls at Lavangikás feet the latter beckons to Mádh. to come and stand in her place which he readily does. The supposed Lav. then asks Mál. to embrace her. Mál. gladly complies with this request, addresses a long speech to her friend, and as a last token of friendship, wishes to put the Bakula wreath—the only object dearest to her as woven by her chosen lord—round her neck. But when proceeding to do so she discovers her mistake and starts back in confusion. Mâdh. then tells her that his love-torment was none the less intense than hers, and that the knowledge that she too loved him was the only means by which he could support life. Seizing this opportunity Mak. and Lav. suggest a love marriage. Mál. shudders at the idea when Káma. suddenly makes her appearance, cheers up Mál. and asks Mádh. to accept Mál. as a gift from the God of Love. This done, she asks Mak. to put on Mál.'s bridal dress and get married to Nandana under that disguise. She then directs Mádh. and Mál. quickly to repair to her own sanctuary where preparations were already made by Avalokitá to celebrate their nuptial ceremony, which they do accordingly.

## ACT VII.

### Scene I. Nandana's Mansion.

Buddharakshitá enters and tells how cleverly Mak. maintained Mál.'s disguise and how after the celibration of the marriage and their coming to the bridegroom's house, poor Nandana was deceived and offended by the supposed Málatî.

### Scene II. Place—The Same.

Mak. and Lavan. are disclosed. Mak. pretends to be asleep. Buddh. and Maday. now enter, the latter with the object of chiding Mál. for her rude behaviour towards her brother. Lav. and Bud. cleverly lay the blame on Nandana. Mada. tries to defend her brother by saying that even if Nandana was the offender, the cause was to be sought in Mál 's too much talked of love for Mádhava. Lava. and Budh. then cunningly turn the conversation on Mak. and elicit from Maday. a confession of her love for Makaranda. They work up her mind for a Gándharva marriage! Mak then throws off his disguise and appearing in his true character takes hold of Maday.'s hand, addressing her lovingly. Lava. then asks them to go, under cover of the night's darkness, to where Mál. and Màdh. had already gone. The party then leaves for Kám.'s dwelling by a private passage.

---

## ACT. VIII.

### Scene I. Place-the Grove near Ka'm 's Dwelling.

Mâl. and Mádh. are discovered seated on the margin of a well after an evening bath, some day in the sultry season. Avalokitá joins them. Mâl. is very reserved, and shy and is taken to task by Avalokitá for refusing to take part in the conversation and thus denying to Mádh. even the pleasure of hearing her speech. The conversation turns on Mak. and Mada., and Mádh. expresses his diffidence as to Bud.'s success in her undertaking. Ava. sets his doubts at rest and asks him what reward he would give if some one were to tell him of Maday.'s being won.

As they are thus talking they hear the sound of approaching foot-steps and presently Bud., Lav. and Maday., accompanied by Kal., come up in confusion and apprise Mádh. of their being surprised by the city police and Mak.'s single-handed fight with them. On hearing this Mádh., after having addressed a word of encouragement to Maday., runs with Kal. to his friend's rescue. Mál. sends Ava. and Budh. to Kám. to tell her of Mak.'s adventure with the police and also despatches Lava. after her lord to caution him to be careful in his fight.

SCENE II. PLACE–THE SAME.

Kapál. now enters, snatches away Mál. thus left alone, and flies with her off to the mountain Srpaîrvata, wishing to put her to a cruel death. After a while Kal. returns and expresses his gratification at the happy issue of the affray. Màdh. and Mak., too, return after a time after being honoured by the King, pleased at their extraordinary valour, wishing to communicate the happy news to their beloveds. They meet Ava. and Lav. who were searching for Mál., but to their anxious enquiries the latter had no satisfactory answer to give. Mak suggests that Mál. might have gone to Káma.'s abode and to it, full of misgivings, they all direct their foot-steps.

---

## ACT IX.

PADMA'VATI AND ITS NEIGHBOURHOOD.

Saudáminî arrives at Padmávati, wishing to find out Mâdh. and to cheer him up with the news that Mál. was quite safe. Struck by the beauty of the scenery of the place she describes it and then starts on her mission.

SCENE I.

Màdh. and Mak. make their appearance. Mak. bewails the irony of fate that had reduced them to such a miserable plight. Mádh. gives vent to his grief caused by Mál.'s sudden disappearance although Mak tries in vain to divert his mind. The beauty of the landscape and the setting in of the rainy season so intensify Mádh.'s grief that he actually swoons. Mak. is alarmed on his friend's account and bursts into sad lamentations. Mádh. regains consciousness and driven almost to the verge of insanity, addresses a cloud in touching terms and asks it to compose his beloved in case it saw her and to tell her about his own sad state. Next he sees the form of Mâl. apportioned in the forest, goes on addressing his prayers for news about her to peacocks, cuckoos, monkeys, elephants &c. but finds them unheeded, calls out to Mak., soliciting an embrace from him and swoons again. Mak. now pours fourth the most pathetic laments and bereft of his friend wishes to throw himself into the Pâtâlâvatî. Saudâminî suddenly appears and prevents him from taking that step by telling him that Mâl. was quite safe and that she had a token from her. The two then hasten to Mâdh.'s rescue who regains consciousness just as they approach him As Mâdh. addresses the wind, Sau. drops the Bakula wreath into his hands. She then comforts the two friends by telling them how Kapâl. had carried Mâl. away with the intention of putting her to death but how she rescued her. She then flies up into the sky with Mâdh., and Mak. goes away in search of Kâm. to communicate to her the happy news.

---

## AOT X.

Kâmandakī, Lavangikâ and Madayantikâ lament the loss of Mâl. and resolve to put an end to their lives by throwing themselves from the top of a hill that was girt by the Madhumatî. At this critical moment they suddenly see a flash like that of lightning, followed by Mak. and learn from him that that was the work of a Yoginî ( Sau ). Just at the time a voice behind the curtains announces that Bhúrivasu, unable to bear Mâl.'s separation, was approaching the mountain Suvarnabindu with intention to cast himself into fire. This is followed by a wailing cry from Mâl. who asks her father to desist from the rash act. Now appears Mâdh. bearing in his arms Mâl. who is in a trance. He tells them how he came there from the mountain Sriparvata with Sau. They then call upon her to come to their rescue once more. At this time a shower from the clouds calls back Mâl. to her senses and the whole party hear the voice of Saud. from behind the curtains announcing how Bhûrivasu was turned back, when just about to throw himself into the fire, by her words. At the conclusion of her speech the Yoginî is seen descending from the sky. All rejoice. Kâm. raises up and embraces Mâl. as she falls at her feet. Sau., too, now comes up and bows to Kâm. as her old pupil. Mádh. and Mak. now find with wonder that their benefactress was none other than Kâm.'s beloved pupil, Saudâminî. Kâm. praises Sau. for what she had done. Sau. now delivers a letter from the King, written in the presence of Bhûrivasu and addressed to Mâdhava, containing not only his approval of the two secret marriages but his entire satisfaction with the sons-in-law. As they are thus talking, Avalokitâ, Buddharakhsitâ and Kalahamsaka come and join them. Kâm. expresses her satisfaction at the happy turn of events, but Sau. remarks that happier still must be considered the fulfilment of the long cherished desire of the two ministers to have their children united in wedlock. This remark as much takes Mál. by surprise as it does Mâdh. and Mak. Kâm., however, explains matters and all is well that ends well.

---

## 2. THE SOURCES OF THE PLAY.

For the plot of the मालतीमाधव in its barest outlines, Bhavabhûti is indebted to the बृहत्कथा, as for the plots of his other two dramas he is indebted to the Rāmāyaṇa. The बृहत्कथा is now lost to all appearances but there are two abridgements of it in Sanskrit, the बृहत्कथामञ्जरि by क्षेमेन्द्र, and the कथासरित्सागर by सोमदेव. The following two stories* from the last mentioned work will show that Bhavabhûti must have got the material for the plot of the मालतीमाधव from the Bṛhatkathá then in existence. The idea of selling human flesh to the ghosts of the cemetery also the poet has got from the same work; *cf.* Katha.—अपश्यन्पूर्वदृष्टां तां स्त्रियं तन्नपुरान्तये । उपायमेकं बुबुधे स महामांसविक्रयम् । तरुपाशाद्गृहीत्वाथ शवंबभ्राम तत्र सः । विक्रीणामो महामांसं गृह्यतामिति घोषयन् ॥ V. 2. 182-3. स कूपादुद्गतोऽपश्यंस्तदर्थप्राप्तिमन्यथा । पणायितुं महामांसं श्मशानं प्राविशन्निशि ।......गृह्णातु कश्चिद्विक्रीणे महामांसमितिब्रुवन् ॥ XVIII. 2. 53, 54.

In the town of शोभावती in the Kalinga country lived a Bráhmaṇa of the name of यशस्कर with his wife and an only son. Owing to a terrible famine he had to leave his country; he went to विशाला, and fixed his residence there. His son, who had now come of age, was studying at the house of a learned *guru* in the town, where among many others like himself, he formed an intimate friendship with one, Vijayasena, a Kshatriya youth. This Vijayasena had a sister named मदिरावती. Once she went to the house of her brother's *guru*, where she and the youthful son of यशस्कर, her brother's friend, saw each other only to fall in love immediately. Thereafter the Brâhmaṇa youth was invited by Vijayasena to his house; for his mother's curiosity to see him was aroused by मदिरावती,s report. There he was very kindly and hospitably received by his friend's mother, and besides he had there the gratification of receiving, as a present, a garland of Malati-flowers, from the nurse of मदिरावती. The same nurse also intimated to him, in equivocal terms, how deeply her young

---

* Written for this ed. by Prof. Shembavanekar M. A. of the St. Xaviers college, Bombay.

mistress loved him, and entreated him to bring the matter to a speedy end by marrying her. In the meanwhile, however, a certain Kshatriya youth of noble descent made an offer for Madirâvati's hand and got her father's consent. The day of the marriage approached, and the disappointed lover—the son of यशस्कर—found solace only in one thing: he tried to hang himself from the branch of a tree. But fortunately for him he was saved from that peril by a man, who also was a disappointed Brâhmaṇa lover, like himself. This stranger then consoled and put him into the proper mood by relating to him the story of his own disappointment. He was an inhabitant of the Nishâdha country. In his wanderings he came to Shankhapura the ladies of which town had gathered at the lake Shankhahrada to take a bath. There he beheld a lovely maiden collecting flowers in a Mâdhavî bower. They fell in love with each other at first sight, and as the maiden began to go home, the youthful stranger followed her. Before she could reach her home, however, an elephant rushed out into the street, spreading consternation among the towns-folk. The lover had here a lucky chance of saving his beloved and of embracing her too. Before long, however, her attendants and a crowd of people gathered round her, and she was taken home in the bustle, the stranger being left ignorant of her name or address. Sadly disappointed he then wandered a long time till at last he came to the spot, where Madirávatî's lover had all but accomplished suicide.

Just as the two lovers have finished their sad tales, मदिरावती comes to the temple of Kâmadeva, at a little distance from them, as is customary for the girls to do before the wedding. At this, her lover—the son of यशस्कर—is advised by his friend to conceal himself behind the shrine and watch the proceedings. They both then go into the temple and stand carefully hidden behind the idol. Splendidly attired as a bride of rank. मदिरावती enters into the temple leaving outside her retinue, and disclosing her heart to Kâmadeva, prays to him to unite her with the Brâhmaṇa youth in the next birth at least, if not in this. This done, she attempts to put an end to her life by means of her upper garment. Suddenly her lover—the son of यशस्कर—comes forward from behind, rescues her from the peril, and escapes with her by a hind door. His friend then takes the upper garment and veil of मदिरावती, and disguised as मदि, joins the party outside. The time being evening, the disguise proves successful. The counterfeit bride, on returning home, is surrounded by a number of young girls and ladies. Strangely enough, the same girl, whom this stranger, now disguised as मद्दि० had seen at the lake of Shankhapura, happens to be a friend of the real मद्दि० and she comes there to bid her farewell that night. As she thrusts aside the veil of her friend, she is startled to discover under that veil a person far more important and dearer to her than the beloved मद्दिरावती. In an instant their resolve is formed. In another instant they stealthily pass by a side-door, walk the whole night, and at day-break find themselves in a forest at some distance from the town. Lastly they get married in an *agrahâra* or monastery. ( See Kalthe. XIII. 1. ).

The second story is known as the story of विदूषक, and Bhavabhuti has made use of it for the incidents embodied in the fifth Act of the मालतीमाधव.

Once king आदित्यसेन of Ujjaini returned to the town at nightfull, after a terrible riding experience. But then the city-gates being closed, he tried to obtain shelter for the night in a monastery, situated at no great distance from the cemetry of the town. The timid Bràhmaṇas of the monastery took him for an obnoxious night-farer, and began to rudely address him, when विदूषक, who, though a Brâhmaṇa by caste, had all the qualities of a Kshatriya, stepped in and knowing the stranger to be some great man from his appearance, received him politely and accorded him a splendid hospitality. Next morning the king entered his capital, and in gratitude for the services of विदूषक, made a grant of a thousand villages to his monastery, and retained him as his own Purohita in the town. In course of time, however, there were quarrels among the Brâhmaṇas thus suddenly enriched by the king's generosity, for the sake of supremacy. They conveniently forgot that for their present greatness they were indebted to विदूषक. He, however, showed only a supreme contempt for the meanness of the other Brâhmaṇas, and remained indifferent, when one day there came a mendicant Bráhmaṇa, of remarkable outspokenness. This latter reproved the swollen upstarts of the monastery, as indeed they deserved, and proposed to them to have recourse to a trial of strength, to settle the point of supremacy. " There are " said he " three corpses hanging on the gallows in the cemetary; whosoever among you dares to cut and bring their noses at midnight, shall be your acknowledged leader. " The swollen upstarts naturally evaded the trial, while विदूषक stood to it. He took his sword, given to him by the god

Agni, went to the burning ground at mid-night, and not with standing the terrible spirits, performed the heroic feat. As he was about to return he found a man sitting on a corpse and muttering *mantras* to acquire superhuman powers. When he gained his desideratum, he repaired to the temple of Kātyāyanī near by. विदूषक, who was secretly watching his actions, also followed him there. The fierce Kāpālika grimly implored a boon from the goddess, when there came the voice that he would have it if he gave the goddess the daughter of king आदित्यसेन as a victim. Immediately he mounted the corpse animated by a Vetâla ( goblin ), made an aerial flight to the palace, and returned with the princess. As he was about to slaughter her, the brave विदूषक suddenly stepped in, and with one sure stroke of his sword struck off his head. He was then directed by the same invisible voice to carry the princess home riding the same animated corpse. विदूषक did accordingly and the next morning he was discovered in the apartment of the princess by the surprised maids. When the king was informed of this he investigated the whole matter, and convinced of Vidushaka's heroic defence of his daughter, and of her love for him, settled their marriage. ( See Kathá. III. 4-105-203 ).

A comparison of the plot of the Mál. with these two stories will show that though the poet got the various elements from these he has dexterously handled them and worked them into a shapely whole with the true skill of a master dramatist. Dr. Keith says—" The main love-story occurs in the Kathá. and in that collection we find the motifs of the sacrifice of a maiden by a magician and the offering of flesh to the demons to obtain their aid. But the credit is due to Bhava of combining them in an effective enough whole and of producing in Act V a spectacle at once horrible and exciting. He has also improved his authorities in detail; the escaped tiger replaces the more conventional elephant; and the intrigue is more effectively welded by making Madayantikâ, the sister of Nandana, the king's favourite. "

### 3. GENERAL AND CRITICAL REMARKS.

The Màlatimâdhava, like the Abhijnánas'akuntala, is a love play, or rather a dramatic romance It is not, however, the poet's master piece. It ranks second to the Uttar. in which Bhav.'s powers as a poet have reached their culminating point. Bhavabhúti was, by the natural temperament of his mind or the reverses of fortune he had to experience during the early part of his life, better fitted for the Karuṇa Rasa than for Sṛngâra, and hence he could not write a love play with equal success. The plot of the Mâl. Mâd. is not based on any historical event but is, as already remarked, a work, for the most part, of the poet's fancy. It was this that gave a free scope to the poet's creative power and enabled him to dispense with the minute and over-elaborated rules of Indian Dramaturgy. The language throughout is highly elegant, vigorous and bold where necessary, very beautiful and tender in its conversational parts and though impassioned rarely vulgar. It is sublime in its poetical portions. The monotony of the plot is relieved by such events as the escape of the tiger from the cage, the ghaslty scenes in the cemetery and the mid-night revelry of the ghosts and the fight with the police men. The play is embellished with no less than 238 s'loks in 24 different metres which are highly musical. It is to be noted, however, that there is not a single stanza in Prákrit in the whole work. The poet shows great skill in selecting proper metres to express particular feelings. The play also contains many pithy sayings. The similes, although not always happy, are often good and sometimes forcible.

A distinguishing feature of the present play is the union of two events, the marriage of the principal Hero and the Heroine and that of Makaranda and Madayantikâ.* These two events are so cleverly conceived and skilfully interwoven that they look like the parts of a connected whole, thus giving variety to the plot without detriment to its unity. The poet shows great constructive skill in contriving a love marriage between Mak. and Maday., the sister of Nandana, the bridegroom elect of Málatî. By this he awakens interest in the audience and paves the way for the pacification of Nandana and the king. The incidents of the story' remarks Wilson, 'are varied and some of them highly dramatic. They are rather diffusely spread out, but they are all essential to the *denouement,* the concurrence of all parties in the union of the lovers'. Dr. Bháudârkar thinks that the events subsequent to the scene in the cemetery look like clumsy appendages and not like parts of a whole, and that

*The fervour of attachment which unites the different personages of the drama so indissolubly in life and death, is creditable to the national character Unless instances of such disinterested union had existed, the author could scarcely have conceived, much less depicted, it. *Wilson.*

the poet represents Kapâlakundalâ as carrying away Mâl. simply to give him an opportunity to display his power of depicting the feelings of a man in Viraha. This censure, coming as it does from such an high authority, is only partly just. That the poet has a strong desire to show his power of delineating the love-lorn condition of a lover we admit; we also concede that the poet wants the Kalidâsian skill of arranging the incidents into a shapely whole. But we fail to see how the subsequent events do not naturally arise out of what precedes. If fault is to be found with the arrangement of the play the same may be said of the fifth Act. It is also brought in simply for the purpose of depicting the Adbhuta and Bibhatsa Rasas. It could also have been omitted without interfering with the continuity of the plot. It is quite natural for Kapâlakundala to burn with indignation and seek to avenge the insulting death inflicted by Mâdh. on her Guru. Unflinching devotion to one's Guru, whatever his profession or creed, is a characteristic of the Indian religious students. The events of the 7th and 8th Acts are also necessary to carry the plot to its legitimate end, *viz* the conclusion of the two marriages without any hitch and the removal of the King's anger. It can also be seen that the poet's boast expressed in the words अस्ति वा कुतश्चिदेवं भुतं महाद्भुतं प्रकरणं ( p. 216 ) is not altogether unjustified. He has shown considerable skill in keeping Bhurivasu, the man who really sets the whole machinery in motion, behind the screens so much so that even Mâl. knows the real truth only when the final catastrophe is nearly reached. The interest once awakened is well borne up. The principal characters are gathered together in the last Act and placed in a very critical state and the fate of almost every person is made to depend on the solution of one mystery, viz. Mal.'s safety.

Another point which redounds to the credit of our poet is that his heroes know of one love only. Mâdh. and Mak. are in this respect superior to Dushyanta, Purúravas, Vatsarâja or Udayana, and others. For this reason the usual love intrigues and the clever but often unsuccessful subterfuges employed by heroes find no place in Bhav.'s plays. This accounts also for the absence of the Vidu, the hero's accomplice in love matters, in his plays. The loves of Mâl. and Mâdh., although vehement, are pure and restrained by a proper sense of personal dignity and honour.*

---

* The following quotation from H. H. Wilson will be of interest:— The heroine of this drama is loved as a woman: she is no goddess

It is rather strange that the poet should have chosen persons professedly of a different faith and religious character from his own to bring about the main issue of the piece Kam. was probably selected as the least likely to rouse any suspicion in the heart of the King or Nandana about her taking any part in the plan that was being hatched behind the curtains to defeat their object. The characters although not much varied are well sustained. Mâdh. is bold and faithful in his love to the last Mâl., although powerfully affected by love, does not allow her passion to override her good manners and sense of family honour. Mak. is brave and sincere in his love for Mádh. for whom he lives or dies. The ascetic, a worthy disciple of Chânakya in policy, is firm-minded and unerring in her designs and persevering and cautious in their execution. Lav., Avalokitâ and Buddha., display a charming mixture of shrewdness and affection, faithfulness and perseverance, while Saudâmini's benevolence and magnanimity are well contrasted with Kapâlakundalá's selfishness and malignity.

It now remains for us to point out the defects.† These are very few and are more than counterbalanced by the merits. The first and foremost of these is the use of long and often puzzling compounds and obscure words. In a few places the style is laboured and borders on obscurity. The third and the seventh Acts are disfigured by descriptions which are needlessly pushed to a monstrous length, viz., those of Mâl.'s love

---

in the estimation of her lover, and although her glances may inflame, no hint is given that her frowns can kill. At the same time Madhava's passion is as metaphysical as need be, and

Mâlati alone,
Heard, felt, and seen, possesses every thought,
Fills every sense, and pants in every vein.

The passion of Mâlati is equally intense with that of Juliet; but her unconquerable reserve, even to the extent of denying her utterance to him she loves more than life, is a curious picture of the restraint to which the manners of Hindu women were subjected, even whilst they were in enjoyment, as appears from the drama, of considerable personal freedom.

† The over elaborated and fantastic style of Bhavabhúti, especially in the Mâl. Mâdh., has produced a result so artificial and purely literary, that Mr. Grierson declares:—'I do not believe that there ever was even a Pandit in India who could have understood, say, the more difficult passages of Bhavabhúti at first hearing, without previous study.' Frazer, Lit. His. of India.

pangs, the havoc made by the tiger, and Maday.'s sad plight due to love-torture—descriptions which are really an outrage on the rules of good style. We have already remarked that the *denouement* is faulty to a certain extent. In his zeal to give us masterly descriptions the poet did not attend to the proper grouping together of the different incidents. His observance of the canons of Dramaturgy also accounts for this. The number of the Acts could have been also reduced. The 3rd and the 4th Acts could have been well amalgamated and 6th, 7th and 8th reduced to two. For the same reason he has also failed to do justice to his hero. For, some of the positions in which the Nâyaka is placed do not revert to his credit. According to some the use of preternatural agency is a defect. But that is not our opinion. We have shown in our notes that the agency employed is neither superhuman nor supernatural. It is quite within the competancy of man to gain powers such as those mentioned in the 5th and 9th Acts. Again when judging of the merits or faults of ancient great poets, we must not apply to their works the modern criteria of judgment or apply them at least very cautiously. We must take into account the tastes and tendencies of the times in which they lived. Looked at in this light, the use of long compounds &c. cannot be regarded as a blemish. In this the poet only yielded to the tendency of the age in which he lived. Perhaps these were regarded as beauties by the Pandits of those times whose opinions are condensed in the remarks of Dandin—ओजः समासभूयस्त्वमेतद्गद्यस्य जीवितम् । दाक्षिणात्यानां—Lengthy compounds which constitute a vital force form the very life of prose, as also of verse in the case of the Gaudas, &c. Perhaps the audience for which Bhav. wrote was accustomed to such sort of compounds and grasped the meaning more readily than we can do now.

## 3. TECHNICAL REMARKS.

The Málatimádhava belongs to that division of dramatic compositions which is termed 'Prakaraṇa.' The subject matter of a Prakaraṇa must be drawn from worldly life and a work of pure invention * Love should be its predominant sentiment,

* अथ प्रकरणे वृत्तमुत्पाद्यं लोकसंश्रयम् । अमात्यविप्रवणिजामेकं कुर्याच्च नायकम् ॥ धीरप्रशान्तं सापायं धर्मकामार्थतत्परम् । शेषं नाटकवत्संधिप्रवेशकरसादिकम् ॥ नायिका तु द्विधा नेतुः कुलस्त्री गणिका तथा । क्वचिदेकैव कुलजा वेश्या वापि द्वयं क्वचित् ॥

See also भरत quoted by Jag. pp. 10, 11.

and the hero must either be a Bráhmaṇa (as in Mrich.), a person of a ministerial rank (as in the present play), or a merchant (as in Pushpabhushita) and of the kind called *Dhira-pras'ánta* (bold and pacific). The heroine may be a woman of family (कुलस्त्री), or a courtesan (गणिका) or both. The Prak. is called शुद्ध according to Bharata (see Jag. p. 10) in the former case and संकीर्ण in the latter. The acts should not be less than five and more than ten. In all other respects it coincides with a Nátaka (see sec. I). We shall find that all these conditions are, in the main, fulfilled in the Mál. Mád.

The Vastu (also called इतिवृत्त) or plot of this drama is two-fold. (1) Principal (मुख्य) and accessary (प्रासंगिक). The principal relates to the love of Mádhava and Málati, the chief hero and the heroine. The accessary refers to the love of Makaranda and Madayantiká, the hero and the heroine of the Pataká. This Patâká runs through the whole of the play. The hero of a Patáká is called Pi'thamarda.

The Bija or seed from which the present plot arises is the promise made to each other by Bhurivasu, the minister of the king of Padmávati and Devarâta, the minister of the king of Vidarbha, when still students, in the presence of Kâmandakî, then their school-mate, afterwards a Buddhistic ascetic, that in case one got a son and the other a daughter, they would join them in matrimonial alliance. This Bija is slightly indicated by the words of Kàm. अपि नाम तयोः कल्याणिनोः &c. and the sl. विवृण्वतेव &c, p. 13. The आरंभ 'beginning or setting on foot of the enteprise is indicated in प्राणैस्तपोभिरनवा &c. I. 9.

For the five Sandhis, see p. 1.

The Mukhasandhi (having 12 angas) which is a combination of *Bija* and *A'rambha* and in which the seed is sown, so to speak, with its various Rasas (as in यद्विस्मयास्तिमित &c. I. 19.), comprises the events of the first two Acts. *viz.* the first sight of Mâlati, the incidents of the Bakula-wreath and Mâdhava's portrait drawn by Mâlati, the love pangs of Mādhava and Màlati, and the cunning speeches of Kâmandaki calculated to intensify Málati's love for Mâdhava.

The Pratimukhasandhi (which has 13 angas) is a combination of *Bindu* and *Prayatna*. It takes up the 3rd and 4th acts, and indicates a further sprouting up of the Bija. Bindu is the development of some incident which maintains the continuity of the plot and helps on its progress. It is here, the desire of Mâdhava to see Màlatî caused by his love for her which grew ever more by the contrivances of Kâmandakî and her pupil Avalokitâ, and the incident of the tiger &c. The effort is indicated by तत्सर्वथा संगमनाय यत्नः &c. (IV. 5 p. 90 ). Its chief events are the conversation of Kámandakî with Mâlatî in the hearing of Mâdhava, the tiger's attack on Madayantikâ, the swooning of Mâdhava and his recovery at the words of Mâlatî, the message with regard to Mâlatî's betrothal to Nandana by the king, the shrewd insinuations of Kâmandakî at the proposed match and the despair of the two lovers

The Garbhasandhi ( having 12 angas formed by the union of the Pata'ká and Prâptyâśá or the hope of success ), spreads over the fifth, the sixth and the seventh Acts. In it the plot attains further development both under encouragement and resistence (the attainment and the non-attainment of the desired object). Its chief events are the scenes in the cremation ground, the scene at the temple of Kara'lá and the fall of Aghoraghanta beneath the sword of Ma'dhava, the marriage of the supposed Ma'latî with Nandana, the secret marriage of Màlatî and Mâdhava, and the elopement of Makaranda with Madayantikâ.

The Avamarshasandhi (having 13 angas ) consisting of the union of the Prakarî and Niyata'pti or the certain attainment of the end, which, however, is yet postponed by fresh impediments and disappointments, fills up the 8th and the 9th Acts. Its chief events are Makaranda's falling in with the city-guards and Madh.'s and Mak.'s fight with them, Mal'.s being carried away by Kapa'lakudalà, and the consequent despair of Mâdh and Mak., and the timely appearance of Saudâminî'.

The Nirvahaṇa Sandhi ( which has 14 angas )—the final converging of all events towards the one goal, forms the subject matter of the 10th Act. Its principal events are the rescue of Ma'latî by Sauda'mini', the union of Mâl. and Mâdh. and of Maday. and Mak. and the king's consent to their marriages with Nandana's approval.

## 4. THE TIME REQUIRED BY THE EVENTS OF THE PLAY.

It is (very) difficult to fix exactly the period of time required by the events represented in the play. The whole action seems to occupy a period of about three months—probably a little less. The events of the first two acts occupy one day. The action commences, at the earliest, on the first of the bright half of Chaitra, as Mâdhava is represented to have gone to the grove of Madana to witness the Madana festival (see Avalokita's speech on page 18). And the Madana festival is celebrated in Chaitra. According to a Com. on Va'tsya'yana's Ka'masûtras this festival is held on the 1st of Chaitra. It probably thus began and ended on the 5th. Prof. Wilson, in his notes on Ratna'valī, says, it was celebrated on the 13th and 14th of the bright half of Chaitra, while according to M. Williams it was celebrated on the full moon-day of Chaitra. When Makaranda meets Màdhava, it is about noon; as appears from the words of Mak. सखे ललाटंतपस्तपाति तपनः &c. p. 23. The conversation lasts for an hour or so and the sun is in the middle of the sky, exactly overhead, when the two friends rise to go home (see p. 41 Mak.'s speech). The events of the 2nd Act, too, happen in the latter part of the same day, as is clear from the conversation of the maids in the Praveśaka. They terminate with the talk between Kâm. and Mâl. and Lavangikâ in the evening (see Sl. 12). A period of about a month and a half intervenes between the events of the first two Acts and those of the 3rd. And taking into consideration Mâlati's extreme modesty, such a period is necessary for the changes wrought in her feelings by Káman. as expressed in the words नीता कतिपयाहेन सखीत्रिंश्रंभसेव्यताम् (III. 1.). It is the 14th of the dark half probably of Vaiśákha on which the business of the third Act begins. Mádh. and Mak. are in a trance at the close of the Act, and they regain conciousness at the beginning of the 4th Act. The events of the 4th Act, therefore, happen on the same day. Mádh. on hearing the news that Mal.'s marriage with Nandana was almost settled on account of the king's interference utterly despairs of the hand of Mâl., goes to the cemetery at nightfall and passes the night there in the hope that the tenants of the cremation ground might, at least, favour him. In the meanwhile Ma'l. is taken away by Kapálakundalá to the temple of Kara'lâ to be offered as a victim to that goddess on the same night. These events which form the subject matter of the 5th Act take place on the night of the same day. (*Vide* Lav.'s speech on p 135). Thus the events of the 3rd, 4th and 5th Acts occupy one day and one night.

An interval of about a fortnight must be reckoned as separating the occurrences of the 6th Act from those of the 5th—a period necessary for Ma'l. to recover from the effects of the rude shock she had received by being suddenly carriad to the cemetery. Mâl's marriage with Nandana must have been fixed for some day early in the dark half of Jyeshtha, probably the 3rd or 4th day. And the marriage of the supposed Mâl. with Nandana takes place on that day. The covert marriage of the real Mâl. with Mâdh. described in the 6th Act also takes place on the same day. The incidents mentioned in the 7th and the 8th Acts occur some four days after. For at the commencement of the 7th Act, we are told that the bridegroom's party returned that day, with the bride to Nandana's house. And the bridegroom is generally entertained for four days by the bride's father. So that that must have been the 7th or 8th day of the dark half of Jyeshtha. And this conclusion is based on the following facts. When the real character of Mak. is revealed to Mand. and their love marriage determined upon, they are asked to repair to Kâmandakî's dwelling under cover of the dense darkness (See sl. 3, p. 158) of the midnight. On the same night Mâl. and Mâd., too, are described as having taken their evening bath, so pleasant in the days of Grishma (See p. 161, निर्वर्तितग्रीष्मदिवसावसान &c.). From the 1st sloka of the 8th Act it appears that the moon was just rising then. And the fight between Mak. and Mâd. and the city guards was witnessed by the king when the moon was brightly shining. So it was pitchy dark when Mak., and Maday. left Nandana's house; the fight continued for some time and by that time the moon was high up in the sky. This can be possible only on the 7th or 8th of the dark half of a month. Thus it is clear that the events of the 7th and 8th Act must have happened on the 7th or 8th day of the dark half of Jyeshtha. The incidents which form the subject matter of the last two Acts must have happened on the following day. Mâl. was borne away by Kapâlakundalâ just after midnight. Mâdh. and Mak. must have searched for her the whole of the following morning. When Sau. comes to look for Mâdh. it is mid-day ( See p. 178 अये कथं मध्याह्न &c. ) and that must be the mid-day of the same day, as Sau. must have started in search of Mâdh. just after her rescue of Mâl. from Kapâlakundalâ's hands. All these events could easily be thrown back by one full month, but for the mention of the setting in of the rainy season and the fall of the first shower. Thus we conclude that the events of the 9th and 10th Acts must have occurred on the 9th of the dark half of Jyeshtha.

## 5 CHARACTERS OF THE CHIEF DRAMATIS PERSONAE.

### KA'MANDAKÎ.

The most conspicuous personage in the play is certainly Kâmandakî, a Buddhist female mendicant, who, as Bhûrivasu's chief agent and trusted friend, holds the threads of the plot in her hands. Actuated by nothing but a pure feeling of friendship for Bhûrivasu and Devaráta, and a sincere desire to promote the well-being of their children, she works, heart and soul, to lead to a successful termination the cause she had espoused and to it she subordinates even the observance of her religious rites (see Avalokitá's speech on p. 13). Fully. conscious of her diplomatic skill, Kám., at the very outset, outlines the course of action she had chalked out for herself in the words बाहुः सर्वाकारप्रगुणा &c. (p. 20), and the success she finally attains shows that this was no idle boast. She acts as the tender-hearted foster-mother to Mâl., nay, she is more than a mother to her even. In her is centered all her joy; (*cf.* Mak.'s speech मालती मालतीति मोदते भगवती का. p. 36). How deeply she loved Mál. appears from her readiness to put an end to her life when the latter was taken away a second time by Kapálakundalá and she was unable to get the slightest inkling about her whereabouts. Assisted by her pupil, Avalokitá, and her friend Buddharakshitá, Kám. tries to beget in Mál.'s heart a love for Mádh., which she seizes every opportunity to foster by giving her a lively description of Mâdh.'s youth, personal charms and accomplishments, arranges secret meetings, cunningly suggests the course to be adopted by narrating love stories of old, and thus prepares Mâlatî's mind (तथा विनयनम्रापि &c. III. 1) for a marriage by self-choice. At the same time she takes good care to create in Mál. an extreme disgust for Nandana. She offers consolation to the two lovers when driven to the verge of despondency, after love had wounded the minds of both equally, and tries to keep up their spirits by holding forth hopes of a successful future, to bring about which she would not mind the loss of even her life. (See IV. 5). When Mál. was kidnapped by Kapál. she leads the search for her and rightly suspecting the hand of Aghoraghanta in the matter asks the men to surround the temple of Karálá.

The news that the king had given away Mál. to Nandana came like a thunderbolt on the two lovers who thought that

Kám 's efforts could then be little expected to be crowned with success. But Kám. could see Bhûrivasu's real meaning through the enigmatical words used by him in his reply to the king. She rises equal to the occasion and finding no other remedy to frustrate Màl.'s marriage with Nandana, takes the bold step of asking Mak. to assume the disguise of Mál. by putting on her wedding garments and ornaments; and the incident is so well planned and managed under her guidance and advice and with such dexterity, that poor Nandana is thrown off his guard and finally finds himself completely balked. She is less active in the last four acts where her place is taken by her former pupil Saudâmini, who rescues Mâl., cheers up Mâdh. with the news that Mâl. was alive and finally reunites the two lovers but only through her regard for Kâm. Thus it will be seen that Kâm. ably acquits herself of the onerous duties of a *Nisrishtârtha dúti* which she had willingly taken upon herself to discharge.

---

MA'DHAVA.

Mádhava, the Hero of the play, is what a Dhiraśânta* Nâyaka ought to be. He has most of the generic qualities of the hero, as described by writers on dramaturgy. He is young, modest, munificient, of sweet address, eloquent, of illustrious lineage, intrepid, and above all, indebted in no small measure to nature for an external which at the very first sight deeply wounded the heart of Mâlati. Excepting these general qualities, however, there is nothing special about him to rouse our admiration for him. Perhaps the stringent rules of dramaturgy ( which require the hero of a Prak. to be possessed of ordinary qualities only ) prevented our poet from investing him with a character that would make the nearest approach to Râma or place him on a level even with Dushyanta.

He falls a helpless victim to love at the very first sight of Mâl. He is not able to resist its influence at all even for a moment, though his extreme youth is some justification for this. He takes the desperate step of selling even human flesh to the infernal tenants of the cemetery in the hope of gaining their help. The only redeeming trait in his character is his

---

* सामान्यगुणयुक्तस्तु धीरशान्तो द्विजादिकः । D. R. According to Jag. Mâdh. belongs to the Dhirodâtta class; ( see p. 11 अयममात्यत्वाद्धीरोदात्तो नायकः । ) But this does not appear to be the case; Bhavabhûti, at least, does not depict his character as such. See General Remarks.

deep love for Mâlati. It is the rich exhuberance of his passion, which continues to the last, that secures our sympathy for him. Hazlitt's description of Romeo exactly applies to him, if we substitute Mâdh.'s name for his–"Mâdhava is abstracted from everything but his love and lost in it. He is himself only in his Mâlatî; she is his only reality, his heart's true home and idol. The rest of the world is to him a passing dream." *Cf.* Mádhava's soliloquy at the beginning of the fifth Act. Mâdhava's passion is more intense than Romeo's. It is rather metaphysical, as, Prof. Wilson calls it. Bhav. is supremely happy in describing it here. It is the intensity of his passion, coupled with its purity and innocense, that makes us even forgive him for his visit to the cemetery.

---

## MA LATI.

Malati, the Heroine of the play, is a very fine picture of a maiden of high birth. True, that in sublimity of character she is inferior to Sîtá or even to Śakuntalá But to portray her as such was not the poet's object. He did not wish either to paint her in the grandeur of married life or to show us how she would have borne its good or ills. His object wos simply to depict her as a maiden in whom passion is just enkindled but which is restrained by a charming reserve and sweetened by girlish innocene—to unite in one ideal picture purity of heart and intensity of passion, a high sense of family honour and dignity of manners. Here is a character which is full of sincerity and sweetness—there is nothing affected or conquettish about it.

She has the prettiest countenance and a symmetry of form which at once make conquest of the heart of the Hero, who calls her the very goddess of beauty ( I. 20 ). We shall now point out, with references to the text, some of the noble traits of her character as brought out by the poet. She is tender-hearted, loving and extremely modest, (तथा विनयनम्रापि &c. p. 64). She is so noble-minded that even Kâm. knows that she would not stoop to any act that would reflect discredit on her ( अत्युदार-प्रकृतिर्मालती । तन्निपुणं &c. p. 20 ). Although deeply wounded by the shafts of Love she does not like the very idea of a love-marriage without the consent of her parents; ( *cf.* अयि साहसोपन्यासिनि अपेहि &c. p. 51 ). She would rather die than tarnish the honour of her family, which she prizes above all earthly things, by a rash marriage. She also loves her father ( whom she calls श्लाघ्य ) and her mother of noble extraction ( अमलान्वया ) too tenderly to think of such a step. ( See ज्वलतु गगने &c. p. 51.). She has wonderful mastery over herself and keeps her passion always under check. Even after her marriage with Mâdh., she is the same modest, reserved and unassuming girl that she was before. (See Intro. 8th Act). Twice in imminent risk of life she excites our sympathy which deepens as the plot progresses and all interest centres round her as the situation grows more tragic in the last four Acts.

---

### MAKARANDA.

Makaranda, the play-mate of Mâdhava from childhood and the Hero of the Patâkâ, is an inseparable associate of his friend in all that he does and stands by him in weal or woe. After he had elicited from Mâdh. a confession of his love for Mâlatî, he interested himself in his behalf and even ran the risk of personating himself as Mâl. in the sham marriage arranged by Kâm. with Nandana, only to make his friend happy. His lamentations in the Ninth Act bear ample testimony to his sincere and deep love for Mâdhava. Life to him was a burden and the world a wilderness when without Mâdhava. Like his friend, he, too, is bold, loving, intrepid and ready to save another's life even at the cost of his own (as shown by his rescue of Maday. from the clutches of the tiger ( Act III ), and his gallant fight with the city-guards ( Act VIII ). He is thus a type of sincere friendly affection and chivalrous enterprising.

---

### AVALOKITA', BUDDHARAKSHITA', LAVANGIKA' AND SAUDA'MINÎ.

Avalokitâ, Kâm.'s pupil, Buddharakshitâ, and Lavangikâ, Mâlati's friend, all take part in the love-intrigue, set on foot by Kâmandakî, and the success attained by the latter is, in no small measure, due to the fidelity with which they serve her and the energetic efforts they make to further the holy dame's plans. They are all very shrewd, affectionate, skilled in the use of enigmatical language and though artful yet looking natural in their conversations. Saudâminî, however, claims our admiration all the more, since the service she renders to Mâl. and Mâdh. is quite disinterested. There was no motive to induce her to exert herself in their behalf save that she had been an old pupil of Kâm., who, she knew, had interested herself in their well-being. How she came to know this, the poet does not tell us, but he tells us that the solemn agreement to marry their children to each other was made by the two ministers in her presence ( अस्मत्सौदामिनिसमक्षं &c. p. 14 ) and that she had attained wonderful powers ( समासादिताश्चर्यमंत्रसिद्धिप्रभावा ). So it must have been by her superhuman power that she knew every thing. Sau. makes good use of the miraculous powers she had acquired by the practice of Yoga and directing the whole course of events from a tragic to a blissful end, wins the thanks of all.

Aghoraghanta and Kapâlakundalâ are painted in colours which fit in well with their shocking practices.

## ABBREVIATIONS USED IN THE WORK.

A. Dic.—Apte's Dictionary.
A. G.—Apte's Guide to San. Composition.
Ab. Śak. or Śak.—Abhijnànaśákuntala of Kâlidása
Chhàn'—Chhàndogyopanishad.
Bg.—Bhagavatgîtà.
Bhag. or B. P.—Bhágavata Purana.
Com.—Commentator; com.—Commentary.
Comp., *Cf.*—Compare.
Comp.—Compound.
Das.—Daśakumáracharita.
D. R.—Daśarúpaka.
Hito.—Hitopadeśa.
Kàv.—Kàvyaprakàśa.
Kâv. Prad.—Kàvyapradîpa.
Kâd.—Kâdambarî.
Kaiv. U.—Kaivalyopanishad.
Kathâ.—Kathâsaritságar.
Kathop.—Kathopanishad.
Kum.—Kumárasambhava.
Mv.—Mahávîrachandra.
Mál.—Málavikâgnimitra.
Meg.—Meghadûta.
Mṛch.—Mṛchchhakatika.
Mud.—Mudrárákshasa.
Mund. Up.—Mundakopanishad.
M. W.—Monier Williams.
Nág.—Nágánanda.
Pán.—Pánini.
Priy.—Priyadarśiká.
Ragh.—Raghuvams'a.
Rat.—Ratnávalî.
S. D. or Sah. D.—Sáhityadarpaṇa.
Sid.—Siddhántakaumudi.
Udár.—Udârarághava.
Uttar.—Uttararámcharita.
Vis. P.—Vishṇu-Puráṇa.
Vik.—Vikramorvas'îya.
Sve. Up.—Śvetàsvataropanishad.
Vats. K.—Vatsyayana's Kámasûtras.
Other abbreviations can be easily understood.

## DRAMATIS PERSONÆ.

—:o:—

### MALES.

MÂDHAVA—The son of Devarâta, minister of the king of Vidarbha, the Hero.

MAKARANDA—His friend, lover of Madayantikâ, sister of Nandana.

KALAHAMSAK—Màdhava's servant.

NANDANA—A favourite of the king of Padmávatî.

BHURIVASU—Minister of the king of Padmàvatî and father of Málatî.

DEVARÂTA—Father of Màdhava, and minister of the king of Vidarbha.

AGHORAGHANTA—A votary of Chámundà.

The Sovereign of Padmávatî ( alluded to ).

### FEMALES.

MA'LATÎ—Daughter of Bhûrivasu, the Heroine of the play.

MADAYANTIKA'—The sister of Nandana and Màlati's friend who falls in love with Makaranda.

KA'MANDAKÎ—A Buddhist ascetic, Màlatî's governess.

LAVANGIKA'—Foster sister of Màlatî.

SAUDA'MINÎ, BUDDHARAKSHITA', AVALOKITA' } Disciples of Kamandakī.

MANDA'RIKA'—An attendant of Kàm., beloved by Kalahamsa.

KAPA'LAKUNDALA'—A disciple of Aghoraghanta.

# उपोद्घातः ।

**भवभूतेः सम्बन्धाद्भूधरभूरेव भारती भाति ।**
**एतत्कृतकारुण्ये किमन्यथा रोदिति ग्रावा ॥**

—गोवर्धनः ।

यद्यप्यस्य कवेरितिवृत्तं साकल्येन न क्वाप्युपलभ्यते तथाप्यनेन महाकविना स्वविरचितमालतीमाधवमहावीरचरितोत्तररामचरिताख्यप्रबन्धत्रयस्य प्रस्तावनास्वात्मनो वंशादेर्वर्णनमल्पमात्रमपि तावत्कृतमस्तीति सर्वथा न जिज्ञासूनां वैरस्यप्रसङ्गः । तथाहि । दक्षिणापथे विदर्भेषु पद्मपुरनाम्नि नगरे केचित्तैत्तिरीयाः काश्यपाश्चरणगुरवः पंक्तिपावनाः पञ्चाग्नयः सोमयाजिनः उदुम्बरोपाभिधाना ब्रह्मवादिनो द्विजा वसन्ति स्म । तद्वंशे महाकविर्नाम वाजपेययाजी कश्चिद्विप्रो बभूव । तस्मात्पञ्चमः पुरुषः सुगृहीतनाम्नो भट्टगोपालस्य पौत्रः पवित्रकीर्तेर्नीलकण्ठस्यात्मसंभवो भवभूतिः । अस्य जननी ज ( जा )- तुकर्णी गुरुश्च ज्ञाननिधिर्नाम यथार्थनामा । पितृकृतं श्रीकण्ठ इति नाम बिभ्रदप्ययं केषांचिन्मतेन ' तपस्वी कां गतोवस्थामिति स्मेराननाविव । गिरिजायाः स्तनौ वन्दे भवभूतिसिताननौ ॥ ' इति पद्यरचनोत्तरमपरेषां मतेन ' साम्बा पुनातु भवभूतिपवित्रमूर्तिः–' इति श्लोकरचनानन्तरं भवभूतिरिति नाम्ना लोके प्रथां गतः । कान्यकुब्जाधिपतेर्यशोवर्मणः संसदि भवभूतिरासीदिति—' कविवाक्पतिराजश्रीभवभूत्यादिसेवितः । जितो ययौ यशोवर्मा तद्गुणस्तुतिबन्दिताम् ॥ ' इति राजतरङ्गिणीस्थश्लोकाज्ज्ञायते । यशोवर्मा च ख्रिस्ताब्दीयसप्तमशतके बभूव । तथा च तदानींतनेन केनापि वाक्पतिराजनाम्ना कविना सगौरवमात्मनो ग्रन्थे भवभूतेर्नामनिर्देशः कृतः स च अष्टमशतक आसीत् । अतोऽष्टमशतकारम्भः सप्तमशतकापरार्धं वा भवभूतेः समय इति प्रतीयते । अतितीक्ष्णमतिरयं कविः सोपनिषत्सु वेदेष्वधीती सांख्ययोगतर्कमीमांसादिशास्त्रेषु कृतावगाहनोपि प्रतिभाशाली साहित्यशास्त्रस्य सकलं रहस्यमाकलयदिति सर्वपथीनमतिमत्त्वमस्य स्फुटमेव ॥

एतत्कविकृतमालतीमाधवमहावीरचरितोत्तररामचरिताख्यरूपकत्रयं विहाय नान्यः कोपि प्रबन्धोनेन प्रणीतः संप्रत्युपलभ्यते । तथापि शार्ङ्गधरपद्धतौ–' निरवद्यानि पद्यानि यदि नाट्यस्य का क्षतिः । भिक्षुकक्षाविनिक्षिप्तः किमिक्षुर्नीरसो भवेत् ॥ ' इति पद्यं गदाधरभट्टप्रणीते रसिकजीवने ' अलिपटलैरनुयातां सहृदयहृदयज्वरं विलुम्पन्तीम् । मृगमदपरिमललहरीं समीर किं पामरेषु रे किरसि ॥ ' ' किं चन्द्रमाः प्रत्युपकारलिप्सया करोति गोभिः कुमुदावबोधनम् । स्वभाव एवोन्नतचेतसां सतां परोपकारव्यसनं हि जीवितम् ॥ ' ( र. जी. प्र. ३ । २२, १९५ ) इति पद्यद्वयं च भवभूतिनाम्ना समुद्धृतं लभ्यते । अतोनेन कविना विरचितोऽन्यः कोपि रूपकप्रबन्धः काव्यग्रन्थो वासीदुत तत्कृतानि सुभाषितान्येतान्याहोस्विदन्यः कोपि भवभुतिरेतेषां पद्यानां निर्मातेति सांप्रतं निर्णेतुं न पार्यते । तथापि भवभूतिर्नाम कविर्निसर्गसौहृदेन भरतेषु वर्तमानः ' इति सूत्रधारोक्तेर्यं नाम केचिदिह नः प्रथयन्त्यवज्ञामिति कव्युक्तेश्च केपि

नाटकप्रबन्धा अनेन प्रणीताः कालवशं प्राप्य प्रणष्टाः स्युरिति कल्पयितुं शक्यम् । 'शृङ्गारवीरकरुणा–' इति क्रममनुरुन्धानेनानेन कविना मालतीमाधवं शृङ्गाररसप्रधानं महावीरचरितं वीररसप्रधानमुत्तररामचरितं च त्रिभूत्तमगुणं करुणरसप्रधानं व्यरचि । यद्यप्यस्य काव्येषु विशेषतो मालतीमाधवे समासभूयस्त्वमुपलभ्यते तथापि वैदर्भीरीति-माश्रित्यैवैतानि लिखितानि । तथाहि–'श्लेषः प्रसादः समता माधुर्यं सुकुमारता । अर्थव्यक्तिरुदारत्वमोजःकान्तिसमाधयः । इति वैदर्भमार्गस्य प्राणा दशगुणाः स्मृताः॥' इति दण्डयुक्ता गुणा अस्य प्रबन्धेषु यथायथमुल्लसन्ति । तत्र प्रधानान्कविरेवाह 'यत्प्रौढित्वमुदारता च वचसां यच्चार्थतो गौरवम् । इत्यादिना । नाटककृदित्ययं कविर्न केवलं कालिदासेन तुलामारोहति किंतु–' उत्तरे रामचरिते भवभूतिर्विशिष्यते '–इति पण्डितानामभ्युपगमो नासमञ्जस्यपर इति भाति । तथा च कालिदासीयप्रबन्धेषु क्वचिदुपलभ्यमानः सचेतसां वैरस्यापादकः पुनरुक्तिदोषो भवभूतिकृतिषु प्रायो न दृश्यते । अपि चेदृश्यस्य कवेर्वाक्चातुरी रसोन्नयनपाटवं च यद्वश्यवाचः कवेर्वाक्यम् । इति, यं ब्राह्मण मियं देवी वागवश्येवानुवर्तते । इति च ब्रुवतोस्य कवेः–' भूतार्थव्याहृतिः साहि नात्मश्लाघा महात्मनः । ' इति को न ब्रूयात्सहृदयः । किं बहुना महाकवेरावश्यकाः सर्वे गुणाः प्रतिभादयो भवभूतौ संभूय स्थिता इति प्रतीमः ॥

अनेन कविना रूपकत्रयं विरचितमित्युक्तं प्राक् । तत्र मालतीमाधवं प्रकरणम् । तल्लक्षणं तूक्तमेव टीकाकृतेति नात्र पुनरुक्ततामापाद्यते । अस्मिन्संभोगशृङ्गारोङ्गी । स च विप्रलम्भपूर्वक एव । अन्ये वीराद्भुतकरुणबीभत्सादयोङ्गभूताः । तत्र-अत्रान्तरे किमपि ( अं. १–२६ ) इत्यत्र नायकस्य रागोदयः । अलसवलितेत्यत्र च कटाक्षैरुक्तरूपैरनुभावैस्तत्कारणस्य काष्ठां प्राप्तस्य माधवविषयस्य रतिभावस्य तत्समुचितव्यभिचारिणां च प्रतीतेर्माधवस्याप्यपहृतमित्यादिना मालत्यनुरागगोचरगाढानुरागतन्नियतव्यभिचारितत्तदुचितानुभावप्रतीतेर्युगपदन्योन्यालम्बनशृङ्गाररसध्वनिः । अत एव बीजस्य परस्परानुरागरूपस्यात्रैव परिन्यासः । एवमन्येप्यर्थास्तत्र तत्रोह्याः । यत्तु मध्ये विच्छेदो मध्ये उद्दीपनं पुनर्मध्ये विच्छेदः पुनरुद्दीपनं तदङ्गिरसपरिपोषापेक्षयैव । अन्येऽर्था वीराद्भुतबीभत्सादयो रसाश्च टीकाकृता तत्र तत्र निर्दिष्टा द्रष्टव्याः । अन्यच्च किंचिदनुक्तमप्यूह्यमिह विस्तरभयान्नोच्यते । अस्य प्रकरणत्वाद्दशाङ्काः । इतिवृत्तं च कविकल्पनानिर्मितमतीव सहृदयहृदयचमत्कारीति युक्तमेव कविराह–अस्ति वा कुतश्चिदेवं महाद्भुतं विचित्ररमणीयोज्ज्वलं महाप्रकरणमिति । अस्मिन्विदूषकप्रतिनायिकाभावः प्राकृतपद्याभावश्च विशेषः । एतत्सर्वमन्यच्च वक्तव्यमाङ्गलभाषोपनिबद्धप्रस्तावनायां विस्तरत उक्तमिति विरम्यतेत्र । शिवं भूयादध्येतुरध्यापकस्य च ॥

मो. रा. काळे.

# MÂLATÎMÂDHAVA.

## ACT I.

### Prologue.

May the shakings of the head of Vináyaka accompanied with *Chîtkâras* (sounds expressive of fear, &c.) long protect you!-the shakings (which were occasioned) at the time of the vehement dance of Śiva (the trident-holder), as the lord of serpents, with his body contracted, entered the front aperture of his nostril through the fear of Kártikeya's peacock that was attracted by the sound of the tabor joyfully beaten with his hands by Nandi, and which made the directions resound with the (buzzings of the) swarms of bees flying up from his temples. (1)

Moreover,

May the matted hair of the Lord of creatures (Śiva), from which the waters of the Mandákinî are trickling from the obstructing string of skulls lying crosswise on the crest, the splendour of which is intermingled with the lightning-like lustre of the eye on his fore-head, the charming crescent of the moon on which is mistaken for the tender spire of a *ketaka* and the mass of which is tied up with the encircling creeperlike (flexible) bodies of serpents, grant you protection! (2)*

---

*** Additional sls. Moreover,**

**May the waves of the river on S'iva's head protect you!—the waves which, falling upon the rows of his teeth, are shattered as they roll along with a splash, which make a gurgling sound as they rush through the ravines and caves of his nostrils, eyes, and ears, which are torn into spray as they dash against his cheek-joints and which swell again as they wind their way through the cavernlike skull of Brahmâ.**

**And further.**

**May the third eye of Purâri, which consumed Madana, of the tawny hue of whose lids the whole assemblage of lightnings**

(*After the Benediction.*)

MANAGER—Away with prolixity. (*Looking forth*) Ah, the divine luminary, the lamp (illuminator) of all the divisions of the world, has risen for the most part. I will adore him. (*Bowing.*)

O thou whose manifestation is the universe, thou art the abode of auspicious splendours ; be pleased, O glorious one, and put in me (endow me with) the resources of a leader in a preeminent degree ; O lord of the world, destroy whatever sin I, humble that I am, might have committed ; O divine one, vouchsafe to me every kind of blessing for the attainment of supreme good. (3)

(*Looking towards the tiring room.*) Ho Mârisha, the auspicious theatrical preliminaries have been well gone through ; and a large conclave of men residing in different quarters has gathered here on the occasion of the fair of the divine Kálapriyanátha. And I am orderd by the assembly of the learned that I should amuse them by the representation of some novel play. Why then are the actors indifferent ?

(*Enter* PA'RIPA'RSHVAKA.)

ACTOR—Sir, we are not aware of a dramatic piece possessing the merits mentioned by the audience.

SÛTRA —Màrisha, what are those merits which the respectable, learned and the venerable Bráhmaṇas speak of?

ACTOR—Representations profound (too difficult for ordinary people to understand) on account of the excess of sentiments delineated ; (an interchange of) actions charming on account of affection ; daring acts fully assisting the progress of love ; interesting conversations and cleverness in speech. (4)

SÛTR.—Ah, I remember then.

ACT.—What may it be, sir ?

SÛTR.—There is, in the southern region, in the province of Vidarbha, a city named Padmapura. There dwell

---

**appears to be a particle, in which, slightly opened, the sacrificer in the shape of Kâla (the destroyer) offered an oblation of the universe and the corners of which make a hissing sound on account of the streams of nectar dropping down from the crescent on his crest heated by the flames, grant you protection ! !**

certain Bráhmaṇas, of the race of Kaśyapa and followers of the Taittirīya branch of the Yajurveda, who are the teachers of Brâhmaṇa-guilds, Panktipâvanas*, worshippers of the five fires, observers of religious vows, drinkers of Soma (*i.e.*, performers of Soma sacrifices), known by the family name of Udumbara and expounders of the philosophy of Brahma.

They, Vedic scholars, perpetually devote themselves to manifold holy studies for ascertaining truth (and not with the object of gaining victory in disputation), acquire wealth for the performance of sacrificial rites and the construction of works of public utility (and not for luxury), are anxious to lead a conjugal life for progeny (and not for carnal pleasures) and care for life only for the performance of religious austerities (and not for enjoyment). (5)

The grandson of a section of this illustrious family, the revered Bhatta Gopala, of auspicious memory, and the son of Nīlakaṇtha of pure fame, whose appellation is Bhatta Srīkantha, but who is better known as Bhavabhûti, the son of Játûkarnî and a poet, has, out of his natural friendship with actors, handed over to us a composition of his own, containing most of the above-named qualities. Wherein we find this dexterous statement :—

Those, who indeed speak ill of us (depreciate our efforts) in this matter, know something that is inexpressible; this attempt is not for them. There will be born, (or) there is, some one of similar tastes with me; for, time is unlimited and the earth is wide. (6)†

---

* Taking precedence at dinner parties or purifying men sitting in a line with them at dinner parties. See notes.

† After this—

Say, then, to the actors, that the play might be performed, that they should quickly begin the concert and put on their costumes. As to the mention of the poet's merits he himself has said—

What excellence of me will not be proclaimed by my mention of the merits of the good, of me whose preceptor is the venerable Jnánanidhi, true to his name?

Again,

What avails it to speak of the study of the *Vedas* and the knowledge of the *Upanishads*, and of the Sánkhya and the Yoga philosophies? They are of no use in dramatic compositions. If one has felicity and richness of expression (command of language) and depth of meaning, then that alone serves as an index to one's scholarship and poetic excellence. (7)

I am, therefore, prepared to exhibit by representation before the divine Kálapriyanâtha, the play entrusted to us by our esteemed friend, the revered Bhavabhûti, entitled 'Málatîmàdhava' and composed by him. Let all the actors then be ready to accomplish my object by proper acting.

ACTOR.—(*Recollecting*) This order of your honour shall be obeyed. Your honour, however, has assigned to each of the actors that part only which befits him. And your honour is cast for the first character, that of Kâmandakí, the old Buddhistic female mendicant, while I am to assume the role of Avalokitá, her disciple.

SUTRA.—What then?

ACT.—Then how is the assumtion of the part of Mádhava, the hero of the piece and the lover of Málatî, to be A?

SU'TR.—It will be very appropriate after the entrance of Makaranda and Kalahamsa.

ACT.—Let us then wait upon the audience with the performance of the same piece.

SUTR.—Very well. Here am I turned into Kámandakî.

ACT.—And I into Avalokitâ.

(*They turn round and exeunt*).

END OF THE PROLOGUE.

---

(*Enter* KA'MANDAKI' *and* AVALOKITA' *in red costumes*).

KA'M.—Daughter, Avalokitâ.

AVA.—Your commands, revered Mistress.

KA'M.—Can the much coveted match between the blessed Málatî and Mádhava, the offspring of Bûrivasu and Devaráta, take place? (*Gesticulating the twitching of the left eye, with joy.*)

My (left) eye, as if cognisant of my inward feelings, throbs and auguring a blissful issue becomes *dakshina* (*right*, kind or favourable) although *vâma* (*left*, unfavourable). (8)

Ava.—Great, indeed, is the uneasiness of your reverence's mind on this account! It is extremely wonderful that minister Bhûrivasu should employ in such a wearisome matter your reverence who wears tattered vestments and lives on the dole of alms only. (And strangely enough) you too apply to it your soul that has broken through the shackless of worldly life.

Ka'm.—Say not so, daughter.

That his honour appoints me to such a duty is the fruit of his friendship; it is the outcome (*lit.* essence) of his regard for me; and if by my religious austerities or (even) at the expense of my life the cherished object of my friend is accomplished I shall have fulfilled the purpose of my existence. (9)

Ah, do you not know that all of us living in different quarters had gathered together for the purpose of education? Then in the presence of Saudâminî and myself a solemn declaration was made by Bhûrivasu and Devarâta that they should necessarily join in wedlock their offspring. And it is a wise step that the noble Devaráta, the minister of the king of Vidarbha, has taken in sending from Kundinapura to Padmàvatî here his son, Mádhava, to receive instructions in the logical (*nyâya*) philosophy.

On the one hand he has called back to his dear friend's memory the plighted betrothal of their children, while on the other he has presented his son, possessing uncommon merits, to the public that he may be endeared (to all); (or, that he may be aquainted with the ways of the world). (10)

Ava.—Why then does the minister not bestow Málatî on Mâdhava of his own accord, but impels your reverence to bring about a stolen marriage?

KA'M.—Nandana, the king's pleasure-companion, asks her hand through his royal master. A direct refusal, therefore, will lead to displeasure, while this course is safe. (11)

AVA.—My wonder is all the greater (at this); for the minister appears from his indifference not to know even the name of Mádhava.

KA'M.—It is dissimulation, daughter.

It is necessary for him to conceal his intentions from Málatî and Màdhava, particularly because they are open-hearted in consequence of their youthful age. ( 12 )

Another consideration is—

The report of the mutual love of the two children has become universal; and it is to our advantage; for the king and Nandana could thus be deceived. (13)

Mark you,

A clever man, outwardly acting in an extremely pleasant manner and to all appearances, covers even the minutest points that might give to others a clue to his plans; and remaining indifferent and overreaching all the people by his devices, encompasses his own ends, single-handed, and observes silence. (14)

AVA.—I, too, acting to your instructions make Mádhava, on one pretex or another, pass by the royal road adjoining the mansion of Bhûrivasu.

KA'M.—I am already told by Lavangiká, Málatî's foster-sister,

That Málatî, stationed at the lofty window of the top-most room of her mansion, having again and again beheld Mádhava, constantly passing by the high road close by, like Rati (beholding) Kâma himself in a new form, and her longing growing intense, has been pining away with her limbs extremely languished. (15)

AVA.—It is so. She also had drawn a portrait of Mâdhava for her diversion; and the same has just been placed to-day into the hands of Mandârikà by Lavangikâ.

KA'M.—(*Musing*) Lavangiká has done well. For Kalahamsaka, Màdhava's attendant, loves that Mandârikâ, the female servant of the monastery; and it is her object that by this means it may come to pass that the portrait may find its way to Mádhava to serve as an introduction (to the work—the kindling of mutual love).

Ava.—I have this morning sent Mádhava too, having roused his curiosity, to the Makaranda garden where the festival in honour of Madana has commenced. I hear that Málatî is to go there, so that the two lovers might see each other.

Ka'm.—Good, daughter, good. By this your zeal in my object you remind me of my former pupil, Saudáminî.

Ava.—Revered lady, that Saudámini who has now attained miraculous power has been practising the vow of a Kápálika on Śriparvata.

Ka'm.—Whence is this information?

Ava.—There is in this city in the great cemetery the deity Châmundá, called Karàlá.

Ka'm.—There is, who, adventurers say, delights in the sacrifice of animals of various kinds.

Ava.—There comes every evening one, Kapálakundalà by name, possessing miraculous power, and the disciple of a skull-bearing practiser of charms, named Aghoraghanta, a night-ranger, who has come from Shrīparvata and who dwells in a forest not far off. From her I got the news.

Ka'm.—Everything is possible in Saudáminī.

Ava.—Enough of this. Revered lady, if Makaranda, Mádhava's companion and his friend from child-hood can marry Madayantiká, the sister of Nandana, then we shall have done another agreeable service to Mâdhava.

Ka'm.—I have already charged her friend Buddharakshitiá to look to that.

Ava.—Your reverence has done well.

Ka'm.—(*Pondering*) Get up then. Having learnt the news about Mádhava, let us repair to Màlati herself.

(*They both rise.*)

Ka'm.—(*Thinking*) Mâlatî is of a lofty character; therefore the business of the agent-having-full-charge-of-an-affair must be skilfully arranged. Under any circumstances—

May the blessed one gladden him, nobly-born and of a lovely form, as the autumnal moon-light does the well-formed lovely lotus; may the youth be perfectly happy (*lit.*, have his wishes fulfilled); may the excellent working of the Creator, efficient in producing merits so eminently befitting each other, bear fruit and be charming! (16). [*Exeunt*].

END OF TME VISHKAMBHAKA.

(*Enter* KALAHAMSA *with a picture-board and other materials*).

KALA.—Where can I find my lord, Mâdhava, who has upset the gravity of Mâlatî's heart by the graces of his form which equals the pride of the god of love? (*Walking forth*) I am weary and so will repose myself in the garden for a while and then see master Mâdhava, the delight of Makaranda. (*He enters and sits down.*)

(*Enter* MAKARANDA).

MAK.—Avalokitá told me that Mâdhava had gone to the garden of Madana. Well, thither shall I go. (*Walking forth and seeing*) Happily my friend is coming this way. (*Marking.*) But his

Gait is slow, his look vacant, his frame not in good trim (lit. has lost its grace) and his breathing accelerated. What may this be? Or what else can it be? The command of the god of love wanders (unobstructed) over the world; youth is succeptible and the various objects (in the world) which are charming and sweet, shake off the firmnesss (of mind). (17)

(*Enter* MA'DHAVA *as described above.*)

MA'D.—(*To himself*).

Having long dwelt on her with a countenance lovely like the moon, my heart, which has suddenly overcome shame, set aside good manners, uprooted fortitude and has its power of discrimination blunted, returns to me but with difficulty. (18)

What marvel!

That heart of mine which in her presence was benumbed with astonishment, from which every other feeling had vanished and which was stupified with joy as if from a plunge into nectar, now writhes as if touched by live-coal. (19)

MAK.—(*Approaching.*) Dear Mádhava, here, here.

MA'D.—(*Walking forth.*) Oh, my dear friend Makaranda!

MAK.—Friend, Mádhava, the sun is so hot as to scorch the forehead. Let us, therefore, sit for a while in this garden.

MA'D.—Just as my friend likes. (*They both walk forth*).

KAL.—(*Seeing them.*) What! Master Mádhava adorns this very garden of the young Bakula trees, accompanied by Makaranda. I will then show him this picture of himself—the balm to the eyes of Málatî tormented with the pangs of love. Or let him for a while enjoy the pleasure of repose.

MAK.—We shall therefore sit underneath this very Kánchanára tree which has perfumed the garden by the cooling and fragrant perfume of the filaments of its flowers which have blown up. (*They do so*).

MAK.—Dear Mádhava, now as you have returned from the fair in the Madana garden, attractive on account of the great festival celebrated by all the fair of the city, I see you, I think, altogether changed. Have you fallen a little within the range of the shafts of Cupid?

MA'D.—(*Hangs down his face thorough shame.*)

MAK.—(*Smiling.*) Why then do you stand thus with the sweet lotus of your face drooping down? See,

It is, indeed, he, the mind-born god, of well known power, who affects equally the ordinary creatures governed by the *Rajas* and *Tamas* qualities, the Creator of the universe and the supreme God; on no account, therefore, should there be any concealment on your part through bashfulness. (20)

MA'D.—Friend, why shall I not tell it? Listen. My curiosity being excited by Avalokitâ, I went to the temple of the god of love. There having strolled about and enjoyed the scene I sat down, through fatigue, near the basin of a young *bakula* tree growing in the court-yard and beautiful on account of its charming ornaments in the shape of the clusters of buds thickly covered over with a whole swarm of bees gathering together, being attracted by the agreeable odour of the scent of wine spreading about. Having gathered the full-blown flowers of the tree which had thickly fallen down of themselves I began to weave a garland, charming on account of skilful arrangement. Then there came, having issued from the interior of the temple, a maiden, who was as it were the moving banner of the god of love proclaiming his victory over the world, whose bright and pretty dress skilfully adjusted gave indication of her virginity, whose form was very noble, and who was attended by very highly accomplished maids (or who had a very splendid train of attendants).

She is the guardian deity of the treasure of beauty, or the abode of the store of the essence of loveliness: and certainly, O friend, the moon, ambrosia, the lotus-stalks, moonlight and the like, were her material causes and the god of love her creator. (21)

Then she, being solicited by her loving attendants who had an eager desire for the sport of gathering the flowers that hung in thick clusters (upon the ground), came to the very spot of the Bakula tree. And I observed in her the effects of a consuming passion that appeared to have been growing for many days for some very fortunately-born youth. For, her

Body was as languid as a crushed lotus-stalk; she was led to do things with great difficulty only by the importunities of her attendant maids; and her cheek, palish-white like the newly-cut piece of the tusk of an elephant, possessed the beauty of the moon without the spot. (22)

And she, from the first time I saw her, causing extreme (*lit.* that cannot be exceeded by another) delight to my eyes like a pencil formed of nectar, entirely drew my heart to her just as a magnetic needle attracts iron. In short—

This (my) heart became attracted to her without having regard to the cause, that I should be subjected to the great calamity in the shape of a series of harrowing torments (or continued affliction). Mostly it is the all-powerful goddess Destiny that dispenses good or evil to creatures. (23)

**Mak.**—Friend Mâdhava, that it is affection and that it should depend upon some visible cause—this is contradictory. Mark,

Some internal cause binds together objects; affection does not, indeed, depend upon external causes; for the day-lotus blooms at the rise of the sun, and the moon-stone becomes wet when the moon rises. (24)

What next ?

**Ma'd.**—Then,

With the sportive movements of their eye-brows, having said 'this is he' and having looked at me as if they recognised me, her friends, adept in reading each other's feelings, cast glances at me sweet with the nectar of their smiles. (25)

Mak.—( *To himself* ) What, recognition too !

Mad.—Then they playfully turned back, setting into agitation the rows of their bracelates by the loud clapping of their lotus-like hands, and giving rise to a musical sound by the sweet chiming of the little bells attached to their waist-bands, mingled with the gentle clank of their anklets sounding agreeably to the movements of their feet graceful like the sportive gait of impassioned royal swans when frightened, and pointed to me with the grace of their shoot-like ( delicate ) fingers, saying "Daughter of our lord, we are favoured by fortune ; for here is some one of some one."

Mak.—( *To himself* ) Oh, it is the out-break ( manifestation ) of great pre-conceived love.

Kal.—( *Listening* ) What ! It is a conversation about ladies the subject matter of which is sentimental and pleasing !

**Mak.**—What ensued ?

M'ad.—And now there was manifested that victorious teaching of the god of love on the part of the lotus-eyed maiden, of a nature indescribable, the wonderfulness of which transcended the power of speech, in which there appeared the sweet confusion caused by amor, which disclosed several emotional changes caused by love and which annihilated fortitude. (26)

And then,

'I became the object of her varied glances, steady and expanded, with the arched (*lit.*, creeper-like) eyebrows upturned, glistening and half-closed, stretched at the corners and somewhat contracted when they met my eyes.' (27)

By those

Side glances of the lovely-eye-lashed one, which were, slow, turned sideways, pretty, affectionate, steady and dull, and in which the pupils brightened on account of the internal wonder growing more and more, my helpless heart was snatched off, pierced, swallowed up and uprooted. (28)

Though I was thus subdued by this disclosure of the feelings which could be inferred as proceeding from love of her who was bewitching to the heart in every way, I, wishing to conceal my agitation, somehow finished the remaining portion of the garland of *bakula* flowers which I had already commenced. Afterwards, as the guards, mostly consisting of eunuchs armed with cane-staves and weapons, gathered together, the moon-faced one mounted a she-elephant and graced the road leading to the city.

And then, while going, by her having eyes with graceful eye-lashes, whose face with the neck repeatedly turned backwards resembled a lotus with its stem twisted, a side glance steeped in nectar and venom was planted deep in my heart. (29)

From that time forward,

Some internal affection, which is past exact determination, which baffles all power of expression, which again was never before experienced by me, and which is impenetrable owing to the great infatuation growing in strength on account of the total destruction of discrimination, stupifies and afflcts me simultaneously. (30)

Moreover,

Although an object is before me I cannot discern it correctly; and even with regard to things familiar to me my remembrance (of them) becomes unplesant on account of its incorrectness; the fever of my torment cannot be allayed in a cool lake or by the moon; and my mind being void of fixity wanders about and presents visionary objects. (31)

KAL.—Certainly some maiden has strongly attracted him. May she be Màlatî herself?

MAK.—( *To himself* ) Oh the overpowering attachment ! Shall I then divert my friend from it ? Or rather,

" Let not the self-born god ( Kâma ) infatuate you ; let not thy judgement be thickly over-clouded with impure passion ".–this and the like advice is verily of no avail. For Kâma and budding youth have already exerted their influence. (32)

( *Aloud* ) Does my friend know her family and name ?

MA'D.—Listen, friend. At the time she mounted the she-elephant, one from her large multitude of friends, a courtesan, lagged behind and having approached me in the course of gathering the flowers of the young *bakula* tree saluted me and thus addressed me, apparently referring to the garland of flowers (referring to love under cover)–Noble one, on account of the thread being well run this your agreement of flowers is beautiful ; (The union of you two-Mâlatî and Mâdhava-noble minded ones, is charming on account of your virtues so well befitting each other) ; and our mistress has a curiousity for this (garland, love); wonderful skill as regards the arrangement of flowers is a novelty to her ( the operation of the god of love is wonderful and quite new in her case ); therefore, let skill gain its end ; let the beauty of creation of the maker have its fruit ; and let this, while it is fresh, aquire the high value of resting round the neck of our mistress ( let the skill of the Creator in fashioning you two have its object accomplished ; let the beauty of creation of the Creator bear fruit ; and let this person, *i. e.* you, full of love, attain the high position of clasping our mistress at the neck ).

MAK.—Oh the cleverness of speech !

MA'D—She, being questioned by me, said—'She is the offspring of the minister Bhûrivasu, Mâlati by name ; I am the daughter of her nurse, Lavàngikâ by name, and a favourite of my mistress.

KAL.—What is her name he said ? Mâlatî ? Favourably, indeed, has the venerable flower-arrowed god exerted his influence. So we have gained our object.

MAK.—That she is the daughter of the minister Bhûrivasu, we cannot too highly regard her ( or we cannot be too highly honoured ). Moreover, her reverence Kâmandakî always speaks with delight of Mâlatî. ( *To himself* ) And there is the report that the king solicits her for Nandana.

Ma'd.—Being importuned by her I took off the garland of the *bakula* flowers from my neck and gave it to her. She, on her part, setting a high value on it, although it was unevenly woven in one part owing to the distraction caused by my gazing on Màlatî's face with eyes ardently fixed upon it, accepted it saying that it was a great favour. Afterwards when she had disappeared in the great throng of the citizens who moved about at the close of the fair, I came back.

Mak.—Friend, this is a happy event, since Màlatî too has betrayed her love. And it is quite clear that her love, previously grown intense and indicated by such signs as the pallidness of her cheeks and others, was with reference to you. But I do not know this, where my friend was seen by her before. Verily noble maidens like her who have their heart attached to one person do not look with loveful eyes at others ( or have love awakend in them at the sight of another ).

Moreover,

The words of her friends addressed to her glancing at each other—'Here is some one of some one,' as well as the enigmatical (double-meaning) speech of her foster-sister are indications of her pre-conceived love. (33)

Kak.—( *Approaching.* ) And this too. ( *With these words he shows the picture-board.* )

( *Both look at it.* )

Mak.—Kalahamsaka, who drew this likeness of Mâdhava ?

Kak.—She who has robbed his heart.

Mak.—Mâlatî ?

Kal.—Yes.

Ma'd.—Friend Makaranda, your conjecture has almost proved true.

Mal.—Kalahamsaka, from whom did you get this ?

Kal.—I got it from the hands of Mandârikâ. And she in her turn had it from Lavangikâ.

Mak.—And what did Lavangikà say was the object of Mâlatî in delineating the picture of Mâdhava ?

KAL.—The diversion of her longing.

MAK.—Dear Mâdhava, take consolation by all means. You too, of noble extraction, are the object of the desire ( *lit.* the friend *i. e.* the fulfiller, of the tie of desire ) of her who is the moon-light to your eyes; therefore, oh friend, there is no doubt as to your union, in which both, Fate and the god of love, are exerting themselves. ( 34 )

The form of her who has affected you must be worth seeing; therefore paint Mâlatî just here.

MA'D.—As my friend likes. Bring me then the picture-board and the brushes.

[ Makaranda *brings them.* ]

MA'D.—( *Drawing* ) Friend Makaranda,

The flood of tears again and again obstructs the function of my eyes; my body becomes paralysed owing to the dulness brought on by my picturing her in my mind; and when I proceed to paint her, this my hand, at once perspiring, has its fingers excessively shaking on account of incessant tremor. What can I do? ( 35 )

Still I am trying. ( *Finishing the drawing after a long time shows it.* )

MAK.—( *Observing carefully the picture.* ) Proper, indeed, is your honour's attachment. ( *Admiringly* ) What! A S'loka too written here being composed in a short time! ( *Reads it.* )

There are various other objects in the world, the new digit of the moon, and others, victorious and sweet by nature, which exhilarate the mind. But when she, the moon-light to my eyes, fell within the range of my eyes, that was to me the only occasion of exquisite delight in my life. ( 36 )

( *Enter in haste* Mandârikâ. )

MAN.—Kalahamsaka, you are overtaken by tracking your footsteps. ( *Seeing* Mâdhava *and* Makaranda, *bashfully* ) What, these two, magnanimous ones, also here! ( *Approaching.* ) I salute you.

BOTH—Mandârikâ, sit down here.

MAN.—( *Sitting down.* ) Kalahamsaka, bring me the picture-board.

KAL.—Take this.

Man.—( *Looking at it.* ) Kalahamsaka, who has drawn here Màlatî and for what purpose ?

Kal.—He who was delineated by Mâlati and with the same object.

Man.—( *Joyfully.* ) Thanks to Fate! The skill of the Creator has shown its fruit now.

Mak.—Oh Mandárikà, is what your lover says with respect to this matter true ?

Man.—Noble one, it is so.

Mak.—Where then did Mâlatî see Ma'dhava before?

Ma'd—Lavangiká says,—while she was standing at the window.

Mak.—Friend, verily we frequently pass just by the road lying close to the maasion of the minister. .So it is proper.

Man.—The noble ones should permit me, so that I may commnnicate this good work of the revered god of love to my dear friend, Lavangiká.

Mak.—Time requires you to do this.

[ Mandâriká *exit with the picture-board.* ]

Mak.—Friend, the divine sun, with his fiercely burning rays, adorns the mid-part of the day. Come then, let us go home. ( *They rise and walk about.* )

Ma'd.—This I think of ( now ).

By the rolling of the streams of perspiration-water the saffron paintings on the cheeks of the charming-eyed one lose ( leave no trace of ) the skill of the courtesan-maids in tracing divers ornamental figures in the morning. ( 37 )

Moreover,

O breeze, charged with ( *lit.* friend of ) the fragrance of the thick floral juice trickling from the calyces of the *kunda* flowers gaping on accouut of the opening buds, touch every part of my body after having gently embraced that fair one with tremulous eyes. ( 38 )

Mak.—( *To himself* ).

Alas! How does the resistless god of love, cruel on account of the woeful change he has worked in a shor time, smite Màdhava, who has a tender body, just as the malignant fever that attacks elephants, terrible by the fearful changes it speedily brings about, smites a young elephant. ( 39 )

Therefore the revered Kàmandakī is our resort in this matter.

MA'D.—( *To himself.* ) Wonderful !

I see her having a countenance resembling a golden lotus pretty and blown up, and with eyes directed to me and then turned slantingly away, moving here and there, before me, behind me, inside and out of me, and all round. (40)

(*Aloud*) Friend, in my case, now

Some destructive burning fever rages through the body; a powerful stupor robs the senses of their power of perception and my heart, bearing increased torment, and restless, burns internally and also becomes one with her. (41)

[ *Exeunt Omnes* ]

END OF THE FIRST ACT NAMED BAKULAVÎTHÎ.

## ACT II.

(*Then enter two* Servant-girls.)

FIRST—Friend, what were you talking about with Avalokitá in the vicinity of the Music hall?

SECOND—Friend, the whole affair in the grove of Madana was communicated to the revered Kámandakî, as I heard, by that Makaranda, the dear friend of Màdhava.

FIR.—What then?

SEC.—Then her reverence desirous of seeing the daughter of our master sent Avalokità to ascertain the news. I too told her that the daughter of our master was in a closet accompained by Lavangikà.

FIR.—Friend, Lavangikâ, saying that she wanted to gather the *bakula* flowers did not return from the grove of Madana itself. Has she returned now?

SEC.—Yes. And just as she was returning, our mistress took her by the hand and forbidding the attendance of the servants, ascended the upper terrace.

FIR.—Surely she is diverting herself with a talk about the magnanimous one.

SEC.—(*Breathing a sigh.*) Whence can she find amusement? Her passion will undoubtedly reach its climax by this closer interview of to-day. And to make matters worse, just in the morning the king, soliciting the daughter of our lord for Nandana, was told by the minister—

FIR.—What?

SEC.—That the king was the master of his (own) daughter. So I think that Málatí's passion for Mádhava has certainly become a dart to her heart for life.

FIR.—Would that her reverence (Kâmandaki) would show some of her superhuman power in this case.

SEC.—You, having extravagant fancies, come away.

(*They turn round and exeunt.*)

END OF PRAVESA'KA.

---

(Mâlatî, *full of longing and* Lavangikâ *are discovered seated*)

MA'L.—Well, friend, what next?

LAV.—Then the noble one handed over to me this garland of *bakula* flowers. (*She gives her the garland.*)

MA'L.—( *Takes it and observing, with joy* ) Friend, the weaving is uneven in one part.

LAV.—As for its want of beauty in this respect you are at fault.

MA'L.—How do you mean?

LAV.—Since by you, he, with a body glossy-blue like the Durvâ grass, was unnerved in that manner.

MA'L.—Dear friend Lavangiká, you are disposed to offer comfort under any circumstances.

LAV.—Friend, what has the 'desposition-to-comfort' to do here. Verily, I say, he too was seen with her own eyes by my dear friend, as he looked cleverly' on account of his creeperlike eye-brows imitating the graceful motions of the bow of the bodiless one (Kâma), being made to dance in the play of the movements (of the pupil) upto the long borders, slow by reason of rising wonder, with eyes which possessed the beauty of full-blown white lotuses agitated by a gentle breeze, and which, though fixed downward under the pretext of weaving the *bakula* garland already commenced, were, perforce, expanded.

MA'L —(*Clasping* Lavangiká.) Yes, my dear friend; but are those playful gestures of the noble-minded one, calculated to mock a person in his company for a short while, natural, or are they as my dear friend thinks them to be?

LAV.—( *Smilingly and with an air of disapprobation.* ) You too were made to dance without musical accompaniment by your nature only; were you?

MA'L—(*Smiling, bashfully*) Well, what more ?

LAV.—Afterwards when he was hidden from view on account of the great throng of citizens returning (from the fair) I went to the house of Mandâriká. For I had left the picture-board with her this morning.

MA'L.—With what intention ?

LAV.—A follower of Mâdhava, Kalahamsaka by name, loves her. She would show it to him. This was my object. And then Mandáriká communicated to me some agreeable news.

MA'L—( *To herself* ) Surely that Kalahamsaka must have shown the picture to his master. (*Aloud.*) What was it that pleased you, friend ?

LAV.—This your portrait indeed, calculated to soothe for a moment one whose heart is being burnt by the insufferable torment caused by vehement longing for an unattainable object, one that is afflicted and that causes affliction. ( *She shows her the picture*).

MA'L.—(*Observing it closely, with delight.* ) Oh the distrust of my heart yet, by which even such consolation I regard as a mere deception. What, characters too ! (*She reads the stanza*—There are various objects in this world &c ; *and with delight.*) Very noble one, verily your words appear by their sweetness, similar to your form; your sight again, though charming for the time, is terrible in consequence of the continued torment it causes afterwards. Fortunate, indeed, are those girls who do not see you or having seen you are mistresses of their hearts. ( *Weeps*).

LAV.—Friend, can you find no comfort even thus ?

MA'L—How possibly ?

LAV.—Because that person, on whoss account you, drooping like a fading Navamáliká flower, pine away like a tender *leaf of Aśoka*, plucked off from its stem, even he is made to know by the revered god of love the unbearableness of anguish.

MA'L.—May that magnanimons person be happy! As for myself, consolation is beyond hope. (*Tearfully*) More particularly to-day, my dear friend, ( *speaking in Sanskrit* )

The torturing affection of my heart incessantly spreads ( through my body ) like virulent poison, blazes like fire without smoke when stirred up, and like violent fever preys upon each and every limb. My father is not able to protect me, nor my mother nor yourself. (1)

LAV.—Thus, indeed, does the meeting of good persons give pleasure in their presence but becomes insufferable owing to the pain it causes in their absence. Moreover, must it be said that you are greatly tormented to-day on having obtained a closer view of him, when after you saw him for a short time from the window, the condition of your body was such that the rising full-moon became to you a fire blazing very briskly and your life was in danger on account of the merciless operation of Káma?

And now, my dear friend, we know this much that a union with a noble lover, befitting great love, is the laudable fruit of desires that are unattainable in this world of the living.

MA'L.—Away friend, you, to whom Málatí's life is dear and who suggest a daring act. Or I alone am to blame in this matter who, degraded by immodesty, again and again looked (at him) with a heart the supporting firmness of which was kept up with difficulty and which was quite lost to all shame. Still, my dear friend, ( *again having recourse to Sanskrit* )—

Let the moon with all the digits blaze in the sky night after night. Let *Madana* burn; what harm will he do me further than death? As for myself, my noble father, my mother descended from a pure race, and my unblemished family are dear to me; neither this person nor my life. (2)

LAV.—( *To herself* ) What is the remedy in this case now?

( *Enter partially a female* Doorkeeper.)

This revered Kámandakî here–

BOTH—What, her reverence!

FEM. D. k.—has come desirous of seeing the daughter of our lord.

BOTH.—Why delay her then ?

[*Exit* Pratikâri. MAL. *hides the picture*].

LAV.—(*To herself*) A thing very desirable has happened.

(*Enter* Kâmandakî *and* Avalokitâ)

KA'M.—Commendable, friend Bhûrivasu, commendable! The reply given by you that the king was lord over your (his *own*) daughter is unopposed to (your welfare in) either world. Moreover, from to-day's events in the Madana-grove I infer that revered Fate too is favourably disposed. The wonderful turn (arrangement) of affairs in the matter of the *bakula* garland and the picture-board gives rise to singular gratification Mutual love is certainly the highest blessing in connubial connection. And Angiras has declared himself to the same effect—Prosperity attends her for whom the heart and the eye (of the bride-groom) have an attachment.

AVA.—Here is Mâlatî.

KA'M.—(*Observing*).

Having limbs extremely emaciated, graceful like the interior of a living plaintain tree, giving delight to the eyes like the moon with only a single digit left, and reduced to a condition lamentable on account of the burning heat of the fire of love, this blessed one pleases our mind and also causes it to tremble. (3)

Moreover,

Possessing a face the cheeks of which are pallid and dusty she looks all the more charming : for triumphant is the influence of love, graceful when operating on a person of happy birth. (4)

Verily she is enjoying the union with her lover pictured by her mind. For

The tie of her lower garment is loosened ; her lower lip is quivering ; her arms are drooping ; she is perspiring ; her eye is glossy, pleasing, a little contracted, affectionate and pretty ; her lims are motionless ; her bud-like breasts are heaving continuously ; the hair on her broad cheeks is standing erect ; and there is stupor and consciousness. (5) (*Approaches*).

( Lavangikâ *moves* Málati. *Both rise* ).

MA'L.—Revered one, I bow to you.

KA'M.—Noble maiden, may you obtain the fruit of your desire !

LAV.—Here is a well-prepared seat; your reverence should sit down.

( *All sit down* )

M'AL.—Is it all well with your reverence ?

KA'M.—( *Sighing* ) Well enough.

LAV.—( *To herself* ) This is but the prelude to the drama of deception. ( *Aloud* ) Your reverence's speech is quite unusual the breath being choked ( sticking ) in the throat rendered dull by the heavy flow of tears being suppressed. What can be the cause of this disconsolation ?

KA'M.—Indeed, this very attachment ( to you ) which is opposed to the tattered weeds I wear.

LAV.—How possibly ?

KA'M.—Oh, do you too not know—

That this body here, the virtuous missile of the god of love, the receptacle ( or cause ) of natural graces, but lamentable on account of its gift to ( union with ) an unworthy husband, will have all its supreme excellences rendered fruitless ? (6)

( Mâlatî *gesticulates distraction of the mind.*)

LAV.—Yes; it has so come to pass that all the people blame the minister for having given Málatî to Nandana in compliance with the words of the king.

MA'L.—( *To herself.* ) How is it that my father has made an offering of me to the king ?

KA'M.—Wonderful !

How has he set this on foot without any regard to merits ! Or whence can there be affection for their offspring in those whose minds are well-versed in crooked policy ! This is, however, the sole object that the monarch's companion-in-pleasures should be his friend by this gift of his daughter. (7)

MA'L.—( *To herself.*) The king's pleasure weighs heavy with my father and not Málatî !

LAV.—It is as your reverence says. Otherwise how can it be that the minister did not hesitate in the case of that bride-groom, ugly-looking and past youth.

MA'L.—( *To herself.* )Alas! I am undone, luckless that I am, by the thunder-bolt of the calamity that is about to fall on me.

LAV.—Therefore be pleased, O revered one, and save my dear friend from this living death. She is your daughter, too.

KA'M.—O simple-minded one, what can my revered self do in this case? Generally their sires and Destiny have power over daughters. As to what men, adept in historic lore, say with reference to S'akuntalâ, daughter of Kaus'ika, having loved Duhyanta, the heavenly nymph Urvasî having bestowed her affection on Purûravas, and Vàsavadattá espousing Udayana, although betrothed by her father to king Sanjaya,—all that looks like rashness and therefore this course can not be recommended. By all means,

Let the minister be happy by giving his daughter, on purpose, to the king's dear friend and counsellor; and let this girl also be united with that ugly person, like the bright digit of the moon with a shrouding comet. ( 8 )

MA'L.—(*Tearfully to herself.*) Alas father ! All powerful must be the desire for pleasures, since you too are thus disposed towards me !

AVA.—Your reverence has tarried here long. I say that noble Màdhava is indisposed.

KA'M.—We shall just go. Dear daughter, permit me to go.

LAV.—(*Aside.*) Dear Mâlatî, now we shall know the origin (family) of that high-souled person, from her reverence.

MA'L.—(*Aside.*) Friend, I too long to hear it.

LAV.—(*Aloud*) Who is this youth, called Mádhava, for whom your reverence has such an affectionate regard?

KA'M —It is a long story and one with which we are not immediately concerned.

LAV.—Still your reverence should tell it, and so favour us.

KA'M—Listen. The king of Vidarbha has a minister, Devaràta by name, who is the crest jewel of the whole circle of eminent statesmen and whom, of a greatness holy and laudable to the whole world, and your father's fellow student, your father himself kuows as to who he is and what sort of a man he is. Moreover,

Men like him are rarely born in this world, who fill to their extremes the quarters with their pure fame, who are the abode of mighty exploits, the results of meritorious deeds, whose greatness is incomprehensible and who are the store of all blessings. (9)

MA'L.—(*Aside*) Friend, my father, indeed, always remembers him whose name the revered lady has uttered.

LAV.—Friend, men whe know those times say that they studied together.

KA'M.—From him, as from the Rising-mountain, arose an only child, like the moon, charming with the spreading lustre of virtues, possessed of arts (like digits) and the source of great delight, to those who have eyes, in this world. (10)

LAV.—(*Aside*) Would that it is Màdhava !

KA'M.—He, the abode of learning and lovely like the full autumnal moon, has come here, having left his home though young; he, who being in sight, the windows of the town appear to be full of blue lotuses on account of the glances of the ladies, unsteady through excitement. (11)

And here he has been studying the Nyàya-lore, along with Makaranda, his friend from childhood. This is he, Madhava by name.

MA'L.—(*Joyfully, apart*) Did you hear, friend?

LAV.—(*Aside*) What can the Párijàta spring from, if not from the ocean !

(*The sound of the conch behind the Scenes*)

KA'M.—Oh the great delay ! For now,

First breaking off the seal of sleep, easily induced at the termination of love quarrels, of the pairs of (the Chakravàka) birds now filled with anxious thoughts, and then assuming magnitude (on account of its reverberations) in the expansive vaults of mansions, it is the sound of the evening conch that is spreading loudly in the sky. (12)

Let us get up then. (*They rise.*)

MA'L.—(*Aside*) What ! Papa has offered me as a present to the king ! My father, indeed, sets a high value on the king's pleasure and not on Mālatī. (*With tears.*) Alas, father, you too act thus towards me! So triumphant must be the thirst for pleasures. (*Joyfully.*) What, that blessed one is very high born! Properly did my friend say—where can the Pārijātaka spring from except from the ocean? Oh that I should behold him again!

LAV.—Avalokitā, here, here. Let us descend by these stairs.

KA'M.—(*Aside*) Maintaining an attitude of indifference well have I lightened the burden of a go-between-taking-the-whole-responsibility-on-herself, with regard to Mālatī. For,

I have produced in her a dislike to another husband, and a suspicion about her father's doing; I have pointed out to her the course to be pursued by narrating historical instances and incidentally praised the greatness of the dear boy both as regards his noble birth and personal accomplishments; now, indeed, it remains (for me) to bring about an intimate acquaintance between them.

[ *All walk about and exeunt.* ]

END OF THE 2ND ACT, STYLED 'DHAVALAGRHA'.

## ACT III.

(*Enter* BUDDHARAKSHITĀ').

BUD.—(*Walking about and looking into the sky.*) O Avalokitā, do you know where the revered lady is?

AVA.—(*Entering.*) O Buddharakshitā, are you gone mad? It is for a long time that her reverence has been attending upon Mālatī excepting the time for begging alms.

BUD.—Well; but, where have you been (all this while)?

AVA.—I was sent by her reverence to (the presence of) Mādhava, with a message to the effect that he should go to the garden called Kusumākara (the Treasure of flowers) attached to the temple of S'ankara and wait in the dense cluster of the red *aśoka* trees on the border of the *kubjaka*-bower. And Mādhava has gone there accordingly.

BUD.—With what object has Mādhava been sent there?

AVA.—To-day being the 14th day of the dark half of the month, Málatī will go to the temple of S'ankara with her reverence. Then the revered dame herself will take Màlataî, accompained by Lavangiká, to the same *Kusumâkara* garden, with the object that she (Málatî) should gather flowers with her own hands to worship the god saying that in that way her good fortune would be enhanced, and thus they might meet. But where are you going to now?

BUD —I am called by my dear friend Madayantiká who too goes to the very temple of S'ankara. I will, therefore, go to the same place after having paid my respects to her reverence.

AVA.—And what is your success in the affair entrusted to you by her reverence?

BUD.—By the command of the holy dame, I, indeed, have produced in my dear friend Madayantiká an intense love for Makaranda, though unseen, by telling her—he is this sort and that sort of man-in the course of various confidential talks; and it is now her ardent wish that she should see him.

AVA.—Well done, Buddharakshitá, well done. Come, let us go. (*Exeunt*)

END OF PRAVES'AKA.

---

(*Enter* KA'MANDAKI')

KA'M.—Though Málatî is so much bent down with modesty, yet by adopting remedies I have made her, in the course of a few days, fit to be served with the confidence that is reposed in a friend. (1)

For now,

In my absence she becomes uneasy at heart but brightens in my presence; she delights in being alone (with me), replies to me with affection and follows my will; and at the time of my going, clinging to my neck and stopping me again and again, she bowingly solicits my immediate return with oaths. (2)

And this is the stronger ground for hope in her case. When she hears the historical tales of S'akuntalá and others introduced in conversations relating to other matters, she, with her body resting in my lap, remains for a long time absorbed in meditation. (3)

To-day, therefore, I will proceed with what is to be done next in the presence of Mâdhava. (*Looking towards the curtains.*) Dear daughter, come here.

(*Enter* MA'LATI' *and* LAVANGIKA').

MA'L.—(*Soliloquises*) What, Papa......again (see p. 22).

LAV.—Friend, here this breeze from the Kusumâkara garden embraces you, the breeze which is delightful on account of the odour of the opened Champaka flowers, the petals of which have been reft asunder by the contact of the active swarms of bees that have flown from the tops of the fragrant mango trees resounding with the mingled notes of the cuckoos sweetly warbling in the act of playfully eating the blossoms filled (*lit.* very wet) with the sweet honey, and the touch of which is cool like sandal paste to your sweet moon-like face bristling with the ambrosial drops of perspiration brought on by the slow gait of the movement of your feet uneven and faltering, owing to the weight of the thighs rendered dull as they have to bear the expansive hips fleshy like those of an elephant. Come then, let us enter.

(*They walk forth and enter*)

(*Enter* MA'DHAVA.)

MA'D.—(*Joyfully.*) Oh, her reverence has come. Verily she, appearing before my beloved, cheers up the mind of me who have been burnt with the heat of passion, just as lightning that precedes a shower does the heart of the young peacock oppressed with heat. (4)

(*Looking*) Ah, there is also Mâlatî accompanied by Lavangikâ !

Wonderful ! the mind of me, who am nobly born (जात्य) being again and again benumbed in the presence of the spotless moon of the face of the lotus-eyed one, experiences a fluid condition by its being melted, just as the excellent moon-stone of a mountain undergoes fluidity by its chilliness being acted upon by the clearly shining moon. (5)

Now Málati looks more graceful.

By her limbs which are drooping and dull, thus having the grace of a garland of crushed *champaka* flowers, she inflames the fire of love, intoxicates the heart and gratifies the eye. (6)

MA'L.—Friend, let us gather flowers in this arbour of the *Kubjakas*.

MA'D.—By me with the hair standing erect on my hearing the first words of my beloved, is now imitated the majestic condition of the Kadamba tree putting forth buds the moment it is sprinkled over with the fresh water of a row of clouds. (7)

LAV.—Friend, let us do so. (*They gesticulate the plucking of flowers.* )

MA'D.—The teaching of her reverence is fraught with countless wonders.

MA'L.—Friend let us pluck flowers from another arbour too.

KA'M—( *Embracing* Malati. ) Desist, O child, desist. You are fatigued. For,

Exhaustion causes your speech to falter, makes every one of your limbs droop down, gives birth to drops of perspiration sparkling on your moon-like face and causes the closing of your eyes in every way, oh beautiful-eye-browed one, it acts as charmingly upon you as the sight of your lover. (8)

(Mâlati *looks bashful.*)

LAV.—Your reverence has observed well.

M'AD.—A very pleasant joke.

KA'M·—Sit down then. I wish to tell a tale.

(*All sit down*).

KA'M.—(*Raising the chin of* Mâlati.) Listen to this wonderful story, O blessed one.

MA'L.—I am all attention.

KA'M.—There is a youth, named Màdhava, already incidetally mentioned by me, who, like you, is the second tie of my heart.

LAV.—We remember that.

KA'M.—Verily he, being uneasy at heart ever since the

day of the fair in the Madana garden, has become almost helpless by bodily torment. To be more clear,

Since he takes no delight in the moon or in ( the company of ) affectionate persons, he, very firm-minded as he is, discloses painful internal anguish ; and though naturally his limbs are darkish like the Priyangu, he has a body gracefully palish and extremely emaciated, and (yet) appears charming. (9)

LAV.—So much was said by Avalokitâ hastening away your reverence at that time—that Mâdhav suffered bodily ailment.

KA'M.—In the mean time I heard that Mâlatî was the cause of his love-distraction. I, too, have come to the same conclusion. For,

Certainly this moon-like face must have fallen within the range of the eyes of the high-souled one, since the mind of him, as yet unaffected, has been agitated being tossed about by longings, like the water of the ( otherwise ) serene ocean ruffled by waves ( at the appearance of the moon ). (10)

MA'D.—Oh the clearness of introduction ; oh the effort to raise (me) to greatness ! Or rather,

Definite knowledge of the S'âstras, natural (power of ) comprehension, eloquence, practised skill in speech, knowledge of the proper opportunity, and readiness of wit—these qualifications lead to the accomplishment of the desired object in undertakings. (11)

KA'M.—Hence, it is not that he will not expose himself to some danger, disgusted with his life as he is ; for he,

With his frame languishing, fixes his eyes on the young mango tree bearing blossoms and having cuckoos warbling in it ; throws his body across the path of the wind charged with the odour of the *bakula* flowers ; and through the love of being burnt often resorts to the rays of the moon to court death, with an only fresh lotus leaf protecting him. (12)

MA'D.—Quite unparalleled and unusual ( *lit.* not followed or resorted to by any one else as yet ) is the way of speaking of her reverence.

MA'L.—( *To herself.* ) He is in a very painful condition.

**Ka'm.**—The poor boy who is thus tender by nature has never experienced such torment before. For it is even possible for him to suffer death.

**Ma'l.**—(*Aside*) Friend, I am alarmed by her reverence apprehending some mishap on my account to him who is an ornament to the whole world. So what shall I do in this case?

**Ma'd.**—Fortunately I am favoured by her reverence.

**Lav.**—Since your reverence has spoken thus I say–The daughter of our lord too, having many a time obtained a sight of him who graced for a short while the entrance of the road adjoining her mansion, makes her servants painfully anxious, though appearing more charming on account of the pangs of love indicated by the grace of her limbs beautiful like the stalk of a young lotus-plant touched by the rays of the sun. She does not take delight in diversions and arts, but simply passes the day with her broad (or round) cheek resting on her beautiful lotus-like hand. Moreover, she becomes uneasy by the wind blowing from the borders of the garden attached to the mansion, agreeable by the trickling of the honey of full-blown lotuses, and wafting a mass of the drops of honey of the Kunda and Mâkanda flowers slightly opened.

And since my dear friend obtained the pleasure of a meeting with him, which was charming on accouut of the various amorous actions of him who graced the grove of Madana, looking like the revered god of love himself assuming a bodily form in order to witness the glory of his own festival, in which their budding youth was made highly precious by fitting and uninterrupted love, in which curiosity was quickened by the disappointment caused to their hearts on the occasion of avoiding the meeting of each other's glances, which was pleasing owing to tremor, horripilation and perspiration produced in the limbs rendered dull by fear and numbness then manifested, and which brought delight to her friends, she has been pining away from that time, like a young lotus-plant which comes in contact with the rays of the moon but for a moment, experiencing a change of condition, terrible on account of the excessive bodily torment resulting from the still more unbearable mental anguish.

Still I find that when she enjoys the company of her lover as he is pictured by her in her mind for a short while, she is cooled like the earth when sprinkled over with a heavy shower of rain-water, by which she—bearing a pretty lotus-like countenance rendered more graceful by the lustre of the rows of her pearly teeth shining forth from her throbbing lovely lips, having clusters of the continuous tears of joy quivering on her beautiful cheeks covered with the hair thickly standing on end, with the blue lotus-like eyes half closed, unctuous, raised up and having their pupils slightly expanded, fixed and slow, and engaging with the new-crescent-like broad forehead charming on account of the drops of perspiration appearing thickly upon it,—becomes one whose girlhood is suspected by her clever friends in their minds. Moreover, she passes the night sleeplessly wearing a necklace of the moon-gems oozing by being touched by a stream of the excessively cool rays of the moon and (lying) on a bed formed of lotus-leaves serving as wet sheets, brought for the purpose by the multitude of her female companions busily engaged in such occupations as gently rubbing her with the plantain leaves rendered uneven by being besmeared with a thick mass of sandal juice made cooler with a great quantity of camphor. When she gets relief-giving sleep with great difficulty, the red-lac-dye falls off from her tender feet being loosened by perspiration, her garment gets loose on account of the throbbing of the upper part of her plump thighs, she places as a covering-fold her trembling creeper-like hands on her breasts ruffled with hair and heaving unequally (or forcibly) on account of her forcible respiration swelling like waves in her agitated bosom; and when waking suddenly and casting about her anxious glances she beholds the bed empty, she closes her eyes in a swoon that comes over her, and even when the swoon is removed by the efforts of her confused friends, her life is confined to the long sighs that escape from her and thus she makes persons like us wish for the termination of their life first, owing to our inability to know what to do, and restricts our efforts simply to the act of censuring the foul play of irresistible fate.

Let your reverence, therefore, see how long this fearful operation of Love will continue without producing a bad effect on limbs which are extremely tender on account of their being endowed with exquisite beauty; also what effect these fore-parts of the nights will have on her, the enveloping darkness of which has been entirely dispelled by the clear moon-light waving about and mellow like the cheeks of the Kerala ladies, flushed (*lit.* made red like a leaf ) with the glow of anger in the love-quarrels with their lovers; and further that these long nights of the vernal season, that wash the court-yard of heaven with the water of the moonlight, bright and shining like the flood of the surging milky ocean, that fill the faces of the ten quarters with the breezes from Malaya, heavy and slow owing to their being impregnated with the effusion of the copious odour arising from their forcibly coming in contact with the perfume-laden *pâtala* and *bakula* flowers, will lead to fearful consequences.

KA'M.—Lavangikà,

If her attachment has him for its object then clearly this is the result of her power to appreciate merits; but my mind, though delighted at the thought, is torn asunder by her frightful condition. (13)

MA'D.—Proper, indeed, is the anxiety of her reverence.

KA'M.—Oh calamity!

This naturally graceful form here is truly the sole essence of tenderness, and as truly also, this five-arrowed god is unmerciful (towards her); and the season too happens to be one which is adorned by the delightful light of the moon and in which the mango blossoms are shaken by zephyrs blowing from the Malaya mountain. (14)

LAV.—And be it further known to your reverence that this picture-board containing the likeness of Mâdhava, and this *bakula* garland (*shows it removing the garment covering the bosom of* Mâlatî) worn round the neck as being interwoven with his own hands by him, are the life (*i.e.*, means of sustaining the life) of my dear friend.

MA'D.—(*Earnestly*)

Thou hast gained a victory in this world, dear Bakula garland, since thou, becoming the sportive banner (proclaiming the excellence) of her expansive breasts, pretty and yellowish-white like a ripened lotus stock, hast become her darling. (15)

(*A confused noise behind the curtains; all listen. Again behind the curtains*)—

Ye people that live in the temple of Śankara! This wicked tiger here is playing the part of the enraged god of destruction; the tiger, the form of whose body is fierce on account of the pomp of the formidable banner in the shape of his thick and long tail waving high in the exercise of natural sports regained by his breaking through the restraint of the chain with which he was tied in the cage which was forcibly smashed and thrown open by him in consequence of the union of unbearable anger and fury brought about by the pride of the prime of youth, whose cavern-like mouth is horrid on account of jaws harsh like a saw, making a grating sound by the noise made in breaking the hard bones from out of the bodies of many creatures gluttonously devoured the very moment he got out of the convent, who has frightened and put to flight so as to seek some safe asylum the whole multitude of men by the wide-spreading (*lit.*, the magnitude of the) echo of the continuous sound of his deep and hoarse growl swelling in his cheeks and proceeding from the interior of his cavern-like throat filled with a quantity of the flesh of the many horses and men felled down after being crushed with a slap of paw, as terrible as the mighty stroke of the thunderbolt, and the line of whose track has become muddy with the blood flowing from the mangled bodies of animals cruelly torn by being struck with his weaponlike sharp claws. Save, therefore the life of my dear friend, Madayantikà.

(*Enter in perplexity* Buddharakshitâ).

Help, help, this Madayantiká here, my dear friend and the sister of the minister Nandana, is being attacked by the tiger, all her attendants being either killed or put to flight.

M'AL.—Lavangikâ, Oh the great calamity!

MA'D.—( *Rising in great confusion* ) Buddharakshitâ, where is he?

MA'L.—( *Seeing* Mâdhava, *with joy and trepidation, to herself.*) What! He too here!

MA'D.—(*To himself.*) Ah, I am blessed, since by her with her eyes brightened at my unexpected sight, I am

Closely bound as if with a garland of lotuses, bathed as if with an overflowing stream of milk, as if wholly swallowed up with her expanded eyes, and sprinkled over perforce, as it were, by a dense nectar-laden cloud. (16)

BUD.—Noble one, here, indeed, at the entrance of the street, outside the garden.

(Mâdhava *walks forth with stately steps.*)

KA'M.—Child, show your valour without being rash (*i.e.*, acting cautiously).

MA'L.—(*Aside.*) Lavangikâ, alas, alas! A peril, no doubt.

(*All walk forth in haste* )

MA'D.—(*Looking forward with disgust*) Ah,

The path of the tiger looks frightful, having mangled (or, a number of) trunks turned upside down, a little astir and covered over with the net work of entrails adhering to each other, snapped and cut to pieces, and with ankle-deep mud mixed with blood. (17)

Oh, the peril!

We, alas! are at a great distance, while the maiden is within the reach of the brute.

ALL.—Alas, Madayantikâ!

KA'M. and MA'D.—( *With joy and wonder* ).

How now, Makaranda, having come from somewhere and snatched a sword from a man struck down by the beast, has interposed himself quite unexpectedly!

OTHERS.—Bravo! noble youth, bravo!

KA'M. ann MA'D.—(*With alarm*) He is struck forcibly by the beast !

OTHERS.—A great calamity ! !

KA'M. and MA'D.—(*With joy*) the monster is killed. (18)

OTHERS.—(*Joyfully.*) Fortunately the evil is averted !

KA'M—(*Feelingly.*) What ! My boy, Makaranda, bleeding profusely on account of the wound inflicted by the tiger's nails and standing motionless being upheld by the sword and supported by Madayantiká in confusion, appears to reel !

OTHERS.—Woe, woe ! The noble one languishes, owing to the hard strokes (deep wounds).

MA'D.—What ? He faints ! (*To* KA'M.) Revered lady, save me.

KA'M.—Dear boy, you are very nervous. Come then, let us attend to him.

(*All walk forth and exeunt*)

(END OF ACT III, STYLED S'A'RDULAVIDRA'VANA.)

## ACT IV.

(*Enter* Makaranda *and* Màdhava *insensible, supported by* Madayantikâ *and* Lavangiká, Kám. *bewildered,* Malati *and* Budharakshitá).

MAD.—Revered lady, be gracious and save this noble youth, who feels compassion for the distressed and who risked his life for the sake of Madayantikâ.

OTHERS.—Alas, alas ! What are we to see here !

KA'M.—(*Sprinkling water from her gourd-pot over both*) Now, do you fan my dear boys with the ends of your garments.

(M'al. *and others do accordingly*).

MAK.—(*Reviving and looking about*) Friend, you are very timid ; what is this ? I say, I am well.

MAD.—(*Rejoicingly.*) Oh joy, now the full moon in the form of Makaranda has risen.

MA'L.—(*Placing her hand on the forehead of* Mád.) Noble one, you are to be congratulated ; I say the noble

Makaranda has quite come back to life having regained consciousness.

MA'D.—(*Reviving.*) Friend, adventurer, come, come. (*He embraces him.*)

KA'M.—(*Smelling both on the head*) Thank God, my boys are restored to life.

OTHERS.—We are highly delighted at this.

(*All exhibit joy.*)

BUD.—(*Apart*) Friend, Madayantiká, this is he.

MAD.—Friend, I already knew that this was Mádhava, and that this too was that person.

BUD.—Do you think that I told you the truth ?

MAD.—Verily perons like you do not fix their affection on unworthy objects. (*Looking at* Màdhava) Friend, the rumour about the love of Màlatî for this noble one is pleasing. (*Again looks longingly at* Makaranda *alone*).

KA'M.—(*To herself*) Pleasant and blissful is this meeting of Madayantikà and Makaranda brought about by fate. (*Aloud.*) Makaranda, my boy, how did revered Fate lead you, of long life, here to be the means of saving the life of Madayantikà ?

MAK.—To-day I heard some news in the city and fearing that the mental anguish of Màdhava would increase thereby, I hastened back being informed by Avalokitâ of the Kusumàkara-garden-affair, and on my way saw this noble girl fallen-within-reach of the tiger's leap.

(MA'L. *and* MA'D. *reflect.*)

KA'M.—(*To herself*) The gift of Màlati must have been an accomplished fact. (*Aloud.*) Dear Mâdhava, Mâlatî has felicitated you on the recovery of your friend. So this is the fit occasion to present a token of affection.

MA'D.—Revered lady, verily this (Màlatî),

Since she, out of her goodness, brought me back to my senses from the trance in which I lay on account of the swoon of my friend, who was wounded by the tiger, has a right to accept my heart as well as my life by way of a free-will-present. (1)

LAV.—This favour, indeed, is accepted by my dear friend.

MAD.—(*To herself.*) This magnanimous person knows how to speak at the proper time in a manner weighty and charming.

MAL.—(*To herself*) What possibly can be the cause of his (Mád.'s) distraction that Makaranda has heard?

MAD.—Friend, what is the news that would add to my affliction?

A MAN.—(*Entering*) Child Madayantiká, the minister Nandana, your elder brother, sends you word:—To-day the King came to our house and having shown great confidence in Bhûrivasu and favour to us, himself offered Málatî. Come then; let us enjoy the great happiness.

MAK.—Friend, this is the news.

(MAL. *and* MAD. *act changing of colour.*)

MADA.—(*Joyfully embracing* Málatî.) Dear Málatî, you have been my dear friend and sister ever since we played together in the dust owing to our residence in the same city; and now you have become the ornament of our house.

KAM.—Dear daughter, Madayantikà, I congratulate you on your brother's getting Màlatî.

MAD.—This is by the power of your blessings. Friend Lavangiká, our wishes are gratified now that we have obtained you.

LAV.—Friend, must this be said even to us?

MAD.—Dear Buddharakshitâ, let us now celebrate the marriage festival. (*They rise*).

BUD.—Friend, come; let us go.

LAV.—(*Aside*) Revered lady, as there are exchanged between Madayantikâ and Makaranda these glances, which are charming on account of their hearts being filled to over-flowing with wonder and joy, which are graceful owing to their fortitude being shaken, and which resemble garlands of full blown blue lotuses, so I think they have formed a union by their minds.

KAM.—(*Smilingly.*) Surely these are repeatedly enjoying the delight of a mental union by an interchange of looks. For,

Their sight plainly and quickly tells this; the sight which is dull on account of the eyes being turned sideways a little, in which the corners are contracted, which is steady and half-closed in consequence of the rise of the emotion of love, in which the eye-brows are a little curved, which is glossy owing to the enjoyment of internal delight, and in which the eyelashes are motionless owing to stupor and the eyes (gracefully) squinted. (2)

MAN—Child, Madayantikâ, this way, this way.

MAD.—(*Aside.*) Dear Budharakshitâ, can I see again this lotus—eyed one, the preserver of my life ?

BUD.—If fate be favourable. [*Exeunt with the man.*

MA'D—(*Aside.*)

Let the thread of hope fragile like a lotus-fibre, snap after a long time ; let the powerful disease in the form of mental affliction spread without limit ; let the yoke of restlessness settle undisguisedly upon me ; let fate be happy and let the god of love gain his end. (3)

Or rather,

This is the merited result in the case of me who, while fate was unfavourably disposed, longed for a person whose love was equal (to mine) but who was difficult to be obtained. Still her face which resembled the morning moon, with its lustre fading at the time when she heard of her being given away, burns me internally. (4)

KA'M.—(*To herself*) Mádhava, who has thus become exceedingly disconsolate, pains me ; and child Mâlatî too, being full of despair, lives in distress. (*Aloud.*) Màdhava, my boy, I ask you—Did you ever cherish the hope that Bhûrivasu himself would give us Mâlatî ?

MA'D—(*Bashfully.*) No, never.

KA'M—Your situation is none the worse then.

MAK.—Revered one, now she has been given away and this causes apprehension.

KA'M.—I am surely aware of the rumour. This much however, is publicly known, that when the monarch solicited Màlatî for Nandana, Bhûrivasu said that the king had power over *his* daughter.

MAK.—So it is.

KA'M.—Now the man told us that the king himself gave Mâlatî to-day. Now my son, the transactions of human affairs are based on speech ; on speech depend the causes leading to meritorious or wicked acts ; every thing is dependent on speech. And that speech of Bhûrivasu too is of a misleading nature. Mâlatî is not certainly the king's *own* daughter. Nor is it a rule of established religious custom that kings have a right to give away another's daughter. Therefore this should not be thought of. And how do you think me, my son, to be heedless ? See—

May not that evil overtake even enemies which is to be feared in your or her case; therefore, I must make an effort even at the cost of my life to bring about the union by any means. (5)

MAK.—What your reverence says is well and reasonable. Moreover,

O revered lady, your compassion (or affection) for these children moves your heart although detached from worldly life; and hence is actively set forth your effort so opposed to the usual practices of a life of renunciation; but again destiny also prevails. (6)

(*Behind the curtains*).

O reverd Kâmandakî, the queen here requests you to come quickly with Màlatî.

KA'M.—Child, get up. (*All rise.*)

(Mâl. *and* Màd. *look at each other with feelings of sorrow and affection.*)

MA'D.—(*To himself*) Alas, so far, indeed, is Mâdhava's connection in this world with Mâlatī. Oh pity !

Fate, having at first, like a friend disposed to give happiness, manifested an unmixed favourableness, but again becoming ruthless by the sudden reverse, enhances the anguish of the mind. (7)

MA'L.—(*Aside.*) Noble one, the delight of the eyes, you are seen for the last time.

LAV.—Woe, woe ! The minister has placed the life of our dear friend in jeopardy.

MA'L.—(*Soliloquises.*) The fruit of my desire for life has now ripened (*i.e.*, the purpose of my existence has ended); the cruelty of my father too has been fully proved by his merciless conduct; and a result worthy of the cruel beginning of wicked fate has been ensured; whom then shall I blame, luckless that I am? A forlorn creature, whom shall I approach as my protector?

LAV.—Friend, this way, this way.

(*Exeunt with* Kámandakî).

MA'D.—(*To himself*) Surely it is a mere consolation that her reverence holds forth to Màdhava, being apprehensive on account of her natural affection. (*With dejection.*) Oh misfortune! The blissful result of my life is suspended in doubt. What shall I do now? (*Musing.*) I see no other remedy than selling human flesh. (*Aloud*) Friend Makaranda, are you pining for Madayantiká?

MAK.—Just so.

This touches my:: mind, that she, with eyes as unsteady as those of a frightened fawn one year old, on beholding me covered with fresh (*lit.* bleeding) wounds, embraced me, not caring for her upper garment which was slipping off, with limbs that were steeped in nectar as it were. (8)

MA'D.—The dear friend of Buddharakshitá is not unattainable to you. Moreover,

How can she, having embraced you who protected her at the time of death by killing the tiger, find pleasure in some one else? Besides the glances of the lotus-eyed one were long directed towards you, steady and charming on account of the affection manifested towards you. (9)

MAK.—Get up then Having bathed at the junction of the Pàrâ and the Sindhu, we shall enter the town itself. [*They rise and walk forth*].

MA'D.—This is the confluence of the mighty streams; the confluence,

The banks of which are crowded with ladies who have emerged (from the stream) just after their bath, the depressed and prominent parts of whose bodies are clearly visible owing to the close-fitting wet garments and who have placed their hands cross-wise (*like Svastikas*) on their prominent and full breasts that possess the beauty of bright pots of gold. (10) (*Exeunt omneses*)

END OF ACT IV STYLED 'SÁRDŪLAVIKRAMA,'

## ACT V.

(*Enter by a heavenly path* Kapálakundalà, *in a terrific and brilliant apparel.*)

KAP.—Glorious is the Lord of energies, who is surrounded by the *Saktis* (or endowed with potentialities), whose self is situated in the midst of the circle of the sixteen veins (or in the middle of the circle of the ten veins, the principal among the six circles of organs), who, when his form is realised in the mind confers miraculous power on those who know how to do it, and who is sought after by those desirous of eternal felicity (or, super-human power) with unwavering (concentrated) minds (1)

Here have I now,

Come, mentally beholding by the power of abstraction the Supreme Spirit in the form of S'iva, eternal, placed in the circles of the six parts of the body mystically touched (with the recitation of the several *mantras*) and manifested in the heart-lotus, without experiencing any fatigue from my flight on account of my drawing off the five elements from the body by the gradual filling up of the veins with wind (so as to create a propelling force within), and dividing the clouds in the sky before me. (2)

Moreover,

The velocity of my journey along the surface of the sky, in which are resounding the harsh bells as the garland of skulls which is tossed up and down strikes against them, imparts to me a charming frightfulness to the fullest extent. (3)

Also,

The mass of my matted hair though tied together by a tight knot shakes forcibly moving in all directions; the bell attached to my *Khatvâ* (a sort of club) moving circuitously makes a piercing sound, prolonged by its continuous tinkle, and the howling wind, the cause of the incessant tinkling of the bells and resounding through the hollows of the lines of the bare skulls of dead bodies, shakes upwards the banners. (4)

(*Walking forth, looking forward and perceiving the smell.*) Here is the temple of *Karâlâ* in close proximity of the spacious cemetery-ground, which is indicated to be in front of me by the smoke of the funeral piles having the smell of garlic fried with the old oil of the *nimba* seeds, where I have to gather together to-day a special collection of the materials of worship by the command of my preceptor, Aghoraghanta, who has completed the course for the attainment of miraculous power by incantations. And the preceptor has said to me :— Dear daughter, Kapàlakundalà, to-day is to be offered to the goddess, *Karâlâ*, the jewel of womankind promised before, and that it is found out in this city. I must, therefore, look for the damsel. (*Looking forth with curiosity.*) But who is this, of a very grave and lovely form, with his curly hair tied up and sword in hand, that is stepping into the cemetery ground ? He who,

Though darkish like the petal of a blue lotus, has a body pale all round ; who stepping gracefully looks majestic and has a countenance like the moon ; and whose left hand, with human flesh flashing in it, from which coagulated blood is dropping down and which indicates his adventurous spirit, robs him of gentility. (5)

(*Marking him closely.*) Ah ! It is Màdhava, the vendor of human flesh, and the son of Kàmandakî's friend. But what have I to do with him ? Well, I will attend to my business. The hour of eve has almost passed away. For now,

The horizon all round is being shrouded by the spreading masses of darkness as if by rows of the bunches of the *Tamâla* blossoms; the earth appears to sink into nascent waters by its bounds (being dimmed) ; and in these forests the night, even at the very commencement, thickens its darkness resembling an immense mass of smoke spread and whirled about all round by the violence of a whirl-wind. (6)

(*Walks about and exit.*)

END OF THE VISKAMBHAKA.

---

(*Enter* Màdhava *as described.*)

MAD.—(*Wishfully.*)

Would that those various amorous actions of the charming-eyed one, sweet by nature, pleasing through affection, proceeding from love and disclosing intense passion developed by familiarity, were again manifested towards me! Actions in which, even when they are merely pictured by imagination the mind falls into a state of absorption which is full of joy and in which the functions of the external senses are suspended. (7)

Moreover,

May I obtain the (pleasure of being in close) embrace with her body, with my face placed by my beloved at the root of her ear and there being contact of her breasts rendered fragrant by the constant presence of the garland of *Bakula* flowers woven by me and worn by her in disparagement of even the pearl-necklace! (8)

Or, this is too remote (for me to think of). This only I long for—

I may once more behold that face of her, the auspicious abode of the god of love, which is, as it were created by means of the quintessences extracted from a number of the digits of the new moon, and which having come within the range of sight, all delights as if commingling give rise to the highest bliss and the joy of the eyes becomes an introduction to the sentiment of love. (9)

Truly speaking (however), there will not be the slightest difference in my condition by my seeing her. For, indeed, the continuation of the production of the knowledge in the form of the remembrance of my beloved, kept up by the ceaseless awakening of the impression generated by (*lit.*, which has derived its birth from) the former close perception, and with its stream unobstructed by other cognitions at variance with it, makes my inmost spirit one with her on account of the identity of my subjective senses with her (or, on account of the likeness of the inward image or internal state to her). For,

That beloved of mine is fixed in my mind as if she were melted in it, or mirrored in it, or painted on it, or sculptured out from it, or planted in it, or united with it by adamantine glue, or deeply buried in it, or nailed to it by all the five shafts of Cupid, or sewed to it by a network of the threads of continuous recollections. (10)

(*A mixed noise behind the scenes*).

MAD.—(*Hearing*.) Oh the great frightfulness of the cemetery-ground with crowds of fiends boldly figuring about ! For in it,

The darkness, hideous by its extent and thick on account of its unctuous mass which hems in from all sides (the funeral pyres), displays to advantage their brilliancy; while the ghosts, the goblins and others, frantic with joy and engaged in their wild and confused sports, are making one universal clamour by their mingled *kilakila* sounds. (11)

Let it be. In the mean-while I will call out to them. (*Aloud*.) Ye demons and spirits that haunt the cemetery, I am going to sell human flesh, which is undefiled by a weapon, real (or, acceptable to you), and taken from the limbs of men ; take this, take this. (12)

( *Noise behind the scenes again*. )

MAD.—What ! Just after my announcement, the charnel-ground seems to be in motion all round, noisy with the indistinct and tumultuous uproar of the formidable demons stalking about on all sides and crowded with the goblins that are making their appearance. Wonderful !

The sky is being filled with the faces of the fiery-mouthed spirits flitting about, whose lank and long bodies are scarcely visible–faces from which fire is blazing forth on account of the horrible opening of their mouths with the corners stretched to the borders of the ears, which are thick-set (or, frightful) with the points of their fangs, and whose hair, eyes, eye-brows and thick beards look like clusters of the flashes of lightning. (13)

Moreover,

Here I see the goblin-host all round, feeding the wolves howling hoarsely with the refuse of human flesh that drops down as it is half nibbled off at random, with thighs as long as date trees, with gaunt skeletons consisting of the cage (framework) of bones, firm by the knots of sinews spreading all over the body and wrapped in black skins. (14)

(*Casting a glance about and smiling*.) Oh the manner of the goblins ! For these,

With their pale and long bodies, having opened their

cavern-like mouths, terrible on account of their lolling broad tongues, present the appearance of burnt-up old *Rohina* trees with their hollows frightful owing to the large serpents moving in them. (15)

(*Walking forth and looking.*) Oh fie ! Yonder is just a loathsome scene.

Having first torn off again and again the skin and then having eaten the flesh readily obtained from such parts as the shoulders, the hinder parts, the back, and the thighs &c., having a horrid stink and augmented on account of the great swelling, a goblin with a meagre frame, taking out the muscles, entrails and eyes and exhibiting his teeth, is eating leisurely (lit., without disturbance) the raw flesh found in the bones and even that in the difficult places (*i.e.*, the crevices, joints of the bones) of the skeleton lying in his lap. (16)

Moreover,

The eaters of the dead bodies, dragging from the numerous funeral piles the corpses although enveloped in smoke, the marrow in which is being seasoned by the boiling in the bones which are being moistened by heat, and having bared the thigh-bone, the flesh of which is dropping down on account of its being roasted, which is detached from the joints, and which is hanging loosely on either side, are drinking the streams of (liquified) marrow issuing forth from it being in close contact with them. (17)

(*Smiling*) Oh the evening merriment of the females of the goblins ; For,

These females of the evil spirits, who have formed their auspicious bracelets (or wreathes for the wrists or necks) of entrails, who have worn the prominent ear-ornaments of red lotuses in the form of the hands of women, who have hastily put on the garlands of heart-lotuses, and who have applied the marks of saffron in the form of thickened red blood, are drinking, in the company of their husbands, being in full spirits, the wine of the marrow in the bones in the cups of skulls.(18)

(*Walking forth and repeating again,* I am going to sell &c,) What wonder ! the ghosts have vanished, all their horrible pastimes having ceased at once. Oh the dastardliness of the evil spirits! (*Walking forth and looking despondingly*). I have surveyed all round the region of the cemetery. And now there is before me,

The river on the other side of the cemetery, with its banks formidable by reason of their being filled with the fierce cries of the howling jackals mingled with the hootings of the masses of owls crying in the hutlike bowers, and making a fearful splashing sound as its current rushes forth dashing against the banks* in consequence of the free course of its water being obstructed by the pieces of the mouldering skulls fallen into it. (19)

(*Behind the curtains*)

Ah heartless father! This person here, your means of pleasing the mind of the king, is going to be destroyed.

MA'D—(*Hearing the sound, with emotion.*)

The sound by itself is sharp and sweet like the note of a frightened ospray; it attracts my mind and bursts upon the ears as one familiar to them; my heart, being pierced internally, whirls about; every limb fails me; and the torpor of the body causes my gait to falter. What means all this! What can it be? (20)

The piteous sound that is rising up appears to come from the temple of Karâlâ. Verily it is the scene of horrible deeds such as this. (21)

Well, I will see. (*Walks forth*)

(*Enter* Kapâlakundalâ *and* Aghoraghanta *engaged in worshipping the goddess, and* Mâlatî dressed *as a victim.*)

MA'L.—Alas, pitiless father, here is the person, you meant as an offering to the king's pleasure, going to be destroyed! Ah mother, with a heart full of affection, you are undone by the foul play of destiny; oh revered Kàmandakî, to whom life consists of Mâlatî and who have left off all other pursuits for the sole purpose of bringing about the good of Mâlatî, your affection has made you experience grief after a long time. Alas. dear friend Lavangikâ, I have become one to be seen by you in dreams only.

---

* Or with the reading पय:संरोधि (of Jag.)—dashing against the banks and obstructing the path of those wishing to cross it on account of the pieces of, &c.

**MA'D.**—Alas, it is the same charming-eyed one. Now all doubt is cleared up. I, therefore, wish that I should assist her while she is alive. (*He walks forth hastily.*)

**KA'PA'LIKAS.**—O goddess Châmundâ, our reverential bow to you.

We venerate your sport (of dancing) in which the stability of this part of the universe is disturbed on account of the shaking of the Tortoise whose back-bone is pressed down by the heavy pressure of the earth suddenly bending down in consequence of the vigorous planting of your foot (or the placing of the *nishumbha**), in which the seven oceans are thrown into the cavity of your mouth which rivals Pàtâla (in expanse) and the excellence of which is manifested by its giving delight to the assembly of the attendants of S'iva (or the excellence of which gives delight, &c.). (22)

Moreover,

Oh goddess, may the dance of you two be for our welfare and joy—the dance, in which your praise is commenced by the various creatures terrified by the fierce and loud laughter of the rows of skulls revived by the dropping upon them of the nectar flowing from the moon pierced by the strokes of the nails protruding from the skirts of the elephant-hide moved about; in which the mountains are hurled off by your spreading arms tossed about and frightful on account of the uprise of the poisonous flames issuing forth from the broad hoods widely extended in consequence of the firm pressing of the armlet-like coils of the bodies of hissing black serpents; in which the divisions of the universe are connected by the fiery circle, as of a fire-brand, traced out by your whirling head rendered frightful by its being covered over with the mass of flames issuing from the eye tawny on account of the fire blazing in it; in which the constellations of the stars are tossed about by the flapping of the banner attached to the lofty point of your club, and which brings delight to S'iva who is pleased at heart by the close embrace of Gauri appalled by her ears being stunned by the clapping of the hands of the frantic *veta'las* and the delighted ghosts and goblins. (23)

**MA'D**—(*Looking*) Oh fie ! What calamity !

---

* A kind of weapon.

This is that same daugher of Bhûrivasu, like that of god Vasu, who, the timid one, having fallen into the clutches of these infidels engaged in impious acts, like a timid fawn into those of wolves, and wearing garments and garlands dyed with red-lac, now lies in the jaws of death ! Alas ! Woe, woe ! calamity ! What ruthless act of fate is this ! (24)

KAP—Good girl, now think of him who has been your beloved in this world ; cruel death speeds you on to-day.

MA L.—Alas, dear Màdhava, this person should live in your memory, though departed to the other world. Surely that person is not dead whom a beloved person remembers.

KAP.—Oh pity ! The poor girl is attached to Mádhava.

AGHOR—(*Raising his sword.*) Be it what it may. I will kill her.

Divine Châmundâ, accept this offering vowed to you at the commencement of the rite for making the *mantras* efficacious, and now placed before you. (25)

(*Proceeds to kill her*)

MA'D.—(*Rushing forward and snatching* Mâlatî *away with his arm*) Ha, villain, away. Wretch of a Kâpàlika, thou art foiled !

MA'L—(*Seeing him unexpectedly.*) Let the noble one save me. (*Embraces* Mâdhava.)

MA'D—Noble maiden, fear not, fear not.

Here before you is that friend of yours for whom you, having set aside all hesitation in the hour of death, declared your affection in words freely spoken. O fair-bodied one, forbear this trembling ; let this wicked one now taste here the fruit of his sin recoiling upon him (lit. resulting adversely). (26)

AGHOR—Ha ! who is this sinful wretch that has become an obstacle to us ?

KAPA'L—Revered sir, this is that same Mâdhava, the object of her love, the son of Kâmandakî's friend and a vendor of human flesh.

MA'D.—(*Tearfully*) Noble one, how comes this ?

MA'L.—(*Summoning courage after a long time*) Noble one, I too know nothing. I am aware of this much only, that I slept on the upper terrace and awoke here. But how do you come to be here ?

MA'D.—(*Feeling shame*).

Tormented by the vehement desire that my life should be blessed by my accepting your lotus-like hand, I, wandering in the cemetery for selling human flesh, heard your cries, O timid one, and came here. (27)

MA'L—(*To herself*) How now, regardless of himself, he is thus wandering for my sake only!

MA'D—O wonder, this is what is called strange chance! For now,

How will the mind of me, who, through good luck, found my beloved and snatched her away from the range of the descent of the sword of the vile wretch, like the digit of the moon entering into the jaws of Ràhu, fare (now), as it is distracted through fear, melted with pity, agitated by astonishment, inflamed with wrath and brightened with joy? (28)

AGHOR.—O thou, Bráhmana's brat,

In the manner a deer moved with pity for his mate in the clutches of a tiger, thou art fallen, O wicked one, into the hands of me who delight in killing and who* am engaged in the act of offering a human sacrifice; I will, therefore, please the mother of all creatures (the earth) with your own body streaming with a mass of blood gushing forth from the wounds in the trunk, the head being severed with a stroke of my sword. (29)

MA'D—Miscreant, basest of infidels,

How art thou prepared to deprive life of its balmy essence, to rob the three worlds of their jewel, to deprive the people of their light, to make death the only resort of her relatives, to humble the pride of the god of love, and to make the creation of the eyes of men fruitless, and the world a dreary wilderness? (30)

Moreover, O sinful wretch,

Let this arm (of mine) fall, like the untimely rod of Yama, on the head of thee that hast raised thy weapon to strike a body which experiences fatigue even by the strokes of the tender S'irîsha flowers sportively cast at her in their fondness for jokes by her loving friends. (31)

*Or who am in a place (केतन) which is the seat of offering human sacrifices.

AGHOR.—Ha, villain, strike, and surely thou wilt breathe no more.

MA'L—Be pleased, my adventurous lord. This accursed wretch is, indeed, very terrible. Have mercy on me (lit. save me) and desist from this perilous deed.

KAPA'L—Revered sir, be careful and despatch this perjured soul.

MA'D. & AGHOR.—(*To* Màl. and Kapàl. *respectively*) O timid one,

Compose (lit. have courage in) your heart; the villain dies; in a fight with a deer has any one ever experienced a mishap to the lion whose thunder-bolt-like claws cleave the peak-like temples of elephants ? (32)

(*Noise behind the scenes; all listen; again behind the scenes.*)

Ho soldiers that are in search of Mâlatî, this venerable Kámandakī here, who is cheering up minister Bhūrivasu and whose intellectual vision is ever unobstructed, enjoins you to surround the temple of Karâlâ.

This terrible and extraordinary deed cannot be the act of any one else but Aghoraghanta, nor does the object appear to be any other than an offering to Karâlá. (33)

KAPA'L.—Holy sir, we are surrounded.

AGHOR.—Now is the need for a more energetic effort.

MA'L.—Oh father, oh revered lady !

MA'D—Well, I will place Málatî secure in the company of her relatives and then kill him in their presence. (*Sending* Mâl. *in another direction he walks forth.*)

MA'D. & AGHOR.—(*Addressing each other*) O villain,

Let this sword scatter piecemeal every one of your limbs, the sword noisy with the sound caused by its coming in contact with the joints of your hard bones, having its quickness for a moment arrested by its cutting the tough muscles, and playfully moving among the fleshy parts (of your body) as among balls of mud. (34)

(*Exeunt all*).

END OF ACT V STYLED 'THE DESCRIPTION OF THE CEMETERY !

## ACT VI.

( *Enter* Kapâlakundalâ. )

KAP.—O wicked one, accursed Mâdhava, who killed my preceptor on account of Mâlatî, though I was mercilessly striking you at that time, you took no notice of me as I was a woman. (*Angrily*) You shall, therefore, necessarily experience the effect of Kapàlakundalà's wrath.

Whence can there be repose for the destroyer of a serpent to bite whom the female serpent, with the sense of injury rankling in her heart, having the points of her fangs keen and dreadful with the effusion of venom, is ever wakeful (watch ful of an opportunity)? (1)

(*Behind the curtains.*)

Ho kings, act according to the directions of the elders in the matter of duties to be performed; let the holy Bràhmaṇas recite (the *mantras*) in a way pleasing to the ear; let there be diverse movements accompanied by various songs for auspicious purposes; the entrance of the procession of the bridegroom, which is near at hand, urges (all) to speed. (2)

The wife of the minister acting upon the instructions of the revered lady commands that before the relations arrive, Mâlatî should go to the temple of the guardian deity of the town for (to secure) the unobstructed completion of the auspicious ceremony. Moreover, she should wait there for her followers who will take with them special decorations.

KAP.—Well. I will depart from this place which is crowded with thousands of people and door-keepers, busily engaged in the preparations for the nuptials of Mâlatî, and seriously devote myself to doing injury to Màdhava. (*Exit*.)

END OF THE VIS'KAMBHAKA.

---

( *Enter* Kalahamsaka. )

KALA.—I am commanded by lord Mâdhava, stationed along with Makaranda in the inner shrine of the Town-deity, that I should see whether Málati has set out for the procession or not. I will, therefore, delight him.

( *Enter* Màdhava *and* Makaranda. )

M'AD.—To-day, indeed, will end, in either way, this continued love-torment of mine, which was growing ever since the day on which I saw Màlati first, and which was carried to its extreme by the actions of the deer-eyed one indicative of deep love, whether the device of the revered lady leads to a blissful result or otherwise. (3)

MAK.—How can the diplomacy of Her Reverence, of acute intellect, fail?

KAL.—(*Approcahing*) Master, good luck awaits you. Màlatî has set out in procession.

MA'D.—Can it be true?

MAK.—Friend, why do you ask doubtingly. She has not only set out but is quite at hand. For,

The sound of thousands of deep-sounding auspicious drums, which resembles the peal of a train of clouds scattered by the wind, deprives us, all at once, of the power of hearing any other sound. (4)

Come then; let us see (the procession) from the latticed window. (*They do so*).

KAL.—See, see, my lord. The numerous white umbrellas first meet our sight, bearing the grace of white lotuses with prominent stalks thickly set in the lake of the broad surface of the sky having for its waves the rows of banners streaming on high as they are played upon by the wind of the *chauries* charmingly moving like royal swans flying up. And now appear the female elephants, clanking with the sound of the collections of golden bells that are tinkling, and mounted by bevies of courtesans that are giving rise to a confused noise by singing aloud the sweet auspicious songs uttered indistinctly in consequence of the expanse of the orbs of their cheeks being filled with rolls of betel-leaves chewed sportively, and are decorating the surface of the sky with the beaming rays of various jewel-ornaments resembling the fragments of Indra's bow. (*Mâdhava and Makaranda see with curiosity.*)

MAK.—Covetable, indeed, are the riches of Bhûrivasu. For,

The directions covered all round to their ends with the quivering circles of the rays of gems, shooting upward; having their mass variegated with the throbbing rays of gold, and therefore looking as if mingled with the lustre of the wings of the Chása birds flying about, appear as if they have the rain-bows displayed therein or as if they are vested with coverings of China silk with pictures interwoven in it. (5)

KAL.—What! Her (Málatí's) attendants have stood at a (respectful) distance forming into a circle according to the line marked out with their cane-staves variegated with bright gold and silver leaf and lowered down in haste by the body of numerous waiters; and here has Màlatī advanced some distance, possessing the beauty of the digit of the new moon, her beautiful form pale and lean, adorning the night-like she-elephant that wears the beautiful Star-garland-ornament (like the constellations of stars) dangling about and has a face dyed with a thick paint resembling the ruddy twilight, and looking graceful by being looked at by all the people raising their faces in curiosity.

MAK.—Friend, see, see.

Like some young creeper that has put forth flowers but is withering at the core, this beauteous maiden who adorns the ornaments by her pale and emaciated limbs and has worn flowers, bears the charming grace of the marriage festival and at the same time manifests the deep anguish of the heart rising up. (6)

Wonderful! The female elephant is made to kneel.

MA'D.—(*With joy*) What! Having descended she is already making hitherwards with Her Reverence and Lavangikâ.

(*Enter* Kâmandakî, Mâlatî *and* Lavangikâ.)

KA'M—(*Joyfully; aside.*)

May the disposer of all things bless us with the successful performance of the charming (desired) rite; may the gods bring about a result exceedingly pleasing; may I attain my object by the children of my dear friends being married; and may this effort wholly bear fruit and lead to a blissful end! (7)

MA'L.—(*To herself*) By what means shall I now find an opportunity to seek the rest which death brings? But even death flies further from the unlucky when they pray for it.

LAV.—(*To herself*) Greatly distressed, indeed, is my dear friend on account of this favourable delusion!

(*Enter with a box in hand*)

A FEM. DOOR-KEEPER—Revered lady, the minister sends word that Màlatî should be adorned in the presence of the deity with this bridal dress and ornaments sent by the king.

KA'M.—The minister says well. The place is indeed propitious. Therefore show the things.

DOOR-KEEPER—This is the corset of white silk; this red silken garment to serve as the mantle; these are the sets of ornaments to suit the different parts of the body; this, the necklace of pearls; this is sandal and this, the chaplet of white flowers.

KA'M—(*Aside.*) Verily Madayantikà will behold a lovely figure in child Makaranda (thus decorated). (*Aloud, accepting*) Well, say to the minister that it will be done as he directs.

DOOR-KEEPER—As Your Reverence commands. (*Exit*)

KA'M.—O Lavangikâ, do you enter the inner shrine with dear Málatī.

LAV.—Now, where will Your Reverence be?

KA'M.—I too will, in the meanwhile, examine, scientfically in private, the excellence of the gems in the ornaments. [*Exit.*

MA'L.—(*To herself*) Now I have for my attendant Lavangikà alone.

LAV.—This is the door of the temple. Let us therefore enter. (*They enter*)

MAK.—Friend, let us wait here concealed by this pillar. (*They do so*).

LAV.—Friend, this is the perfumed unguent for the body; and these are the garlands of flowers.

MA'L.—What of them ?

LAV.—Friend, you are sent here by your mother with the object that you should worship the deities at the commencement of the auspicious marriage rite for the attainment of good fortune.

MA'L.—Why do you again and again torture me, an unlucky creature, in a manner insufferable on account of its piercing the vital parts when my mind is already burnt by the grief consequent on the result of the evil pastime of fate that has set on foot something terrible.

LAV.—Now what do you mean to say ?

MA'L.—The same that a person, whose luck is opposed to a wish the object of which is unattainable, says.

MAK.—Friend, did you hear ?

MA'D.—I did, and yet my heart is not satisfied (*i.e.* longs to hear yet more).

MA'L—(*Embracing* Lavangikà.) My true sister, loving friend, Lavangikà, this your dear friend here, about to die, having embraced you in a manner worthy of the confidence that has grown in consequence of your unceasing favours ever since the time of her birth thus requests you. "If I am to be favoured by you, bear me in your heart and behold the lotus-like face of the esteemed Màdhava, sweet with joy and the sole auspicious object, being the chosen abode of the goddess of gracefulness in her entirety." (*Weeps.*)

MA'D.—Friend, Makaranda,

Fortunately have I heard the nectar-like words which cause the faded flower of life to bloom, give rise to satisfaction, enchant all senses, produce delight and form the sovereign elixir for my heart. (8)

MA'L.—So manage it that that sort of excellent body of that person, the presever of my life, will not be emaciated through affliction on hearing of my end; also that he will not grow weary of life even after a long time, making it consist simply of remembrances and talks about me, after I shall have become a tenant of the other world only. Thus favoured by her friend will Mâlati become blessed.

MAK.—Alas, something exceedingly heart-rending is begun.

MA'D.—

Having heard the extremly piteous and yet charming lamentation caused by infatuation brought on by kindliness, of the fawn-eyed one who is distracted at heart on account of despair, I experience the affliction caused by disconsolation and anxiety and also excessive delight. (9)

LAV.—Ah you, your evil is averted. I will hear no more of this.

MA'L.—Friend, you love, indeed, the life of Málatî but not Málatî herself.

LAV.—Friend, what do you mean by saying so ?

MA'L.—(*Pointing to herself*) Because having kept up my life by arranging your speeches is such a way as to hold forth hopes to me, you have made me go through this extremely loathsome procedure. Now my desire is simply this—that I should destroy myself since I have sinned against that lord by having belonged to another. My dear friend, therefore, should not oppose me in my purpose. ( *She falls at her feet*).

MAK.—This is the climax reached by love.

(Lavangiká *betokens* Mádhava *to approach*).

MAK.—Friend, go and take Lavangikâ's place.

MA'D.—I am made powerless by agitation.

MAK.—This is the nature (sign) of approaching good fortune.

(Mád. *noiselessly advances and stands in* Lavangiká's *place*).

MA'L.—Friend, favour me by giving your assent.

MA'D.—O simple one, forego this desire for adventure; O plantain-thighed one, give up this rashness: my heart is unable to bear the distressful pain of your separation. (10)

MA'L.—Friend, you cannot disregard Mâlatî's prostration.

MA'D—(*Joyfully*) What can I say, O you causing the terrible pangs of separation ? Do as you wish; O you with beautiful hips, embrace me (11)

MA'L.—( *With joy*.) How has she favoured me ! (*Rising*)

Here I embrace you. My eyes being suffused with tears, I cannot, however, see my friend. (*Embracing, with delight*) Friend, the touch of your body, being as thrilling as that of a ripened lotus and unusual, cools me to-day. (*With tears.*) Moreover, with your joined hands placed across your brow, respectfully say to that person at my request 'I, unlucky that I am, did not for a long time feast my eyes by looking at my will at the orb of the moon of your face that surpasses (or, possesses) the grace of the beauty of a blooming lotus. With vain hopes I bore up my heart the root of which was being undermined by the irresistible anguish incessantly increasing. I have again and again endured bodily torments which distressed my friends on account of their extremely unbearable course. I have, with great difficulty, outlived such a series of evils as the rays of the moon, the breezes from Malaya and others. But now I have become full of despair.' You too, my dear friend, should always remember me and this *bakula* garland also, which is charming on account of its being woven with his own hands by the esteemed Mâdhava, should be considered by my dear friend as not different from Mâlati and should be ever worn on the heart. (*She removes the garland from her neck but when putting it on the bosom of Madhava withdraws and stands trembling through agitation.*)

MA'D.—(*Apart.*) Thank God !

By her with bud-like breasts, stout and compactly grown, is sprinkled upon my skin,as it were, after being got together and squeezed, the class of such things as camphor, pearl necklaces, yellow sandal, oozings of the moon-stones, Sáivala, lotus-fibers, snow and the like. (12)

MA'L—(*To herself*) Oh ! Màlatī has been deceived by Lavangikà.

MA'D—O you who know only the anguish of your heart but are ignorant of the torment of another, here are you taken to task.

Have I not passed the days in which I suffered from the violent fever in the shape of intense bodily heat, in which my anguish was diverted by a fancied union with you, and in which life was sustained by the knowledge of your love? (13)

LAV.—Friend, you are blamed as you deserved.

KAL.—Oh, how charming and full of sentiment is this arrangement of incidents!

MAK.—Noble maiden, thus it is.

Certainly this person passed so many days, supporting himself somehow, knowing that you loved him; having obtained the favour of accepting your hand with the auspicious thread tied round it, let him rejoice for a long time and have his desire fulfilled. (14)

LAV.—Magnanimous one, will this person, who, even at heart, did not disapprove of the bold step of accepting him herself, now wait for the hand to be adorned with the auspicious marriage thread-bracelet?

MA'L.—Oh fie, she insinuates something opposed to the ways of maidens of honour.

KA'M—(*Entering*) Daughter, you timid one, what is this?

(MA'L. *trembling embraces* KA'M.)

KA'M.—(*Raising her chin*) Dear child,

This is that youth, very much beloved, whose eye for you and for whom your eye, first conceived love; whose heart to you and to whom your heart was then solely attached; and whose body on your account and on account of whom your body became emaciated: give up this hesitation, O fair-faced one, towards him; let the wishes of Kâma be fulfilled. (15)

LAV.—Revered lady, verily he is a desperado, who, wandering over the cemetery-ground on the fourteenth day of the dark half of the month, did a very desperate act and also prevented the atrocious deed from being committed by the fierce and huge hand of the monstrous infidel. It was this that made my dear friend tremble.

MAK.—(*To himself*) Well done, Lavangikâ, well done. Opportunely, indeed, is the double connection of great love and obligation suggested!

MA'L.—Oh my father, oh mother!

K'AM.—My boy

MA'D.—Command me.

KA'M.—This Mâlatī, the only jewel-like offspring of the minister Bhûrivasu, the toes of whose feet are coloured with the pollen in the flowers of the garlands on the heads of all the tributary princes, is given to you by the Creator who takes delight in uniting together two persons worthy of each other, by the god of iove and by myself. (*Weeps*).

MAK.—Then the kind favour of Your Reverence has gratified our wishes.

MA'D.—But why these tears on the part of Your Reverence ?

KA'M.—(*Wiping off the tears from her eyes with the end of her garment.*) I request the blessed one—

MA'D.—Rather command me.

KA'M.—The affection of people like you is charming in the end; and I too am to be respected by you for various reasons: therefore, in my absence, O dear son, do not in any respect cease to be kind towards this fair-faced one. (16) (*Proceeds to prostrate herself*).

MA'D.—(*Preventing her.*) Oh, on account of affection the event transgresses (makes her transgress) the proper bounds !

MAK.—Revered lady,

That she is sprung from a noble race, that she gives delight to the eyes, that she has fully proved her intense love and that she is illustrious with merits; any one of these is a powerful attraction in itself; and to add to these, she has been thus endeared to you; what more should I say then ? (17)

KA'M.—Dear Mâdhava.

MA'D.—Your commands.

KA'M.—Dear daughter.

MA'L.—Your Reverence may command.

KA'M.—

The husband to women and the lawful wife to men are the dearest objects, friends (or, dearest friends), all relatives put together, all things that the heart covets, a treasure and life itself; let this be mutually known to my dear children. (18)

MAK.—Just so.

LAV.—It is as Your Reverence has said.

KA'M—My son, Makaranda, having put on this bridal dress meant for Màlatî get yourself wedded. (*She hands over the box.*)

MAK.—As Your Reverence commands. Just retiring behind the painted curtain I will make my toilet. (*Does accordingly.*)

MA'D.—Your Reverence, this is an exceedingly hazardous procedure for my friend and fraught with many perils.

KA'M.—Ah, who are you to interfere in this matter ?

MA'D —Your Reverence herself knows it.

MAK.—(*Entering, smilingly*) Friend, I am transformed into Mâlatî.

(*All look at him, full of amazement and curiosity.*)

MA'D.—(*Embracing* Mak., *jestingly.*) Your Reverence, blessed, indeed, must be Nandana to covet a bride like this.

KA'M.—Màlatî and Màdhava, my dear children, leaving this place and passing by the avenue of trees, repair to the garden behind our sanctuary, that the auspicious marriage rite might be performed. There Avalokità has well gathered together all the necessary things for the nuptial ceremony. And again (or, very greatly),

Will those quarters, fenced with the hedges of waving Màtulunga trees, in which the areca-trees, bowed down with the load of fruit, are covered with numerous betel-creepers with their leaves of a palish hue like that of the cheeks of the grown up ladies of Kerala affected with great anxiety, and which are musical with the songs of the birds delighted by eating the Kamkoli fruit, do you an agreeable service. (19)

Having gone you should wait just there until the arrival of Makaranda and Madayantiká.

MA'D.—(*With joy.*) The attainment of one blessing is happily followed by the acquisition of another.

KAL.—If fortune favours, this too will be accomplished.

MAK.—How can you doubt this ?

LAV.—Did my dear friend hear ?

KAM.—My son Makaranda, child Lavangikâ, we start now from here.

MA'L.—Friend, must you go, too?

LAV.—(*Smiling*) It is meet in the present case that we should stay away (not accompany you).

(*Exeunt* KA'M., LAV. *and* MAKARANDA.)

MA'D—Here shall I now,

Distressed by the heat of summer in the shape of love, seize with my hand her (Málatí's) hand, which has the tender stalk-like arm horripilated from the root and the petal-like fingers of which are wet (with perspiration), just as an elephant oppressed with the heat of love-like summer plucks off with his trunk from some lake a red lotus with its armlike stalk covered from its root with the downy filaments and having its finger-like petals wet. (20)

( *Exeunt omnes* )

END OF ACT VI ENTITLED 'MALATYUPAHA'RA'.

## ACT VII.

( *Enter* BUDDHARAKSHITA. )

BUD.—So far so good. Makaranda, wedded to Nandana who was imposed upon by the beautiful and well-fitted disguise of Malatî was well taken care of in the mansion of the minister, Bhûrivasu, according to the instructions of her reverence. To-day we too came to the residence of Nandana. Her reverence then took leave of Nandana and went home. Now this evening time, in which the whole body of servants is busily engaged in celebrating the untimely *Kaumudi* festival in the shape of the entrance of the bride into the house of her husband, will be favourable to the execution of our plans. It was now that the son-in-law, as he, his passion inflamed, besought again and again his wife, that he should approach her as a husband, with prostrations at her feet, but afterwards proceeded to do violence, was severely repulsed by Makaranda. Then he, his words faltering through rising excitement, exasperated and exceedingly grieved, and his eyes rolling through intoxication, declared on oath that he would have no more to do with the wanton girl and left the inner apartment. So seizing this occasion I will get in Madayantiká and unite her with Makaranda. [ *Exit.*

PRAVESA'KA.

—o—

( *Then are discovered* Makaranda *in* Màlati's *attire on a couch and* Lavangikà. )

MAK.—Lavangikà, do you think that the scheme of her reverence entrusted to Budharakshità will succeed ?

LAV.—Why should the noble one entertain a doubt as to that ? Or why waste words ! Since I hear the tinkling of the foot-ornaments I feel sure that Buddharakshità has brought Madayantiká under that pretext. Therefore covering yourself with your mantle lie down like one asleep. (Mak. *does accordingly.*)

( *Then enter* Madayantikâ *and* Buddharakshitá, )

MAD.—Friend, is my brother really offended by Málatî ?

BUD.—Just so.

MAD.—Oh the most unfortunate thing ! Come ; let us take the cross-tempered Màlati to task. (*They walk forth.*)

BUD.—This is her chamber-door. (*Both enter in.*)

MAD.—Dear Lavangikâ, it appears that your dear friend is fast asleep.

LAV.—Friend, come ; do not rouse her from slumber; for after being long vexed she has just slept, having given up her anger a little. Do you, therefore, gently sit here on the border of the couch.

MAD.-(*Sitting down.*) Friend, this saucy girl gets vexed ?

LAV.—How can she possibly fret having obtained for her husband your brotherr so skilled in the means of winning the confidence of a maiden newly married, beautiful, of a clever and sweet address, loving and dispassionate ?

MAD.—Buddharakshità, see. We too are censured on the contrary.

BUD.—It may be on the contrary or not on the contrary.

MAD —How, pray ?

BUD.—Inasmuch as she did not respect her husband though prostrate at her feet, in that *she* is to blame on account of her fault of bashfulness ; and *you*, my dear friend, inasmuch as the something unbecoming that there was in the speech of your brother who was made to forget his nobility by the embarrassment brought on by his failūre in his violet advance, coutrary (to usage) in the case of a newly married bride. (*Resorting to Sanskrit*) Moreover, " Women who are of the nature of flowers should be gently approached. But if they are forcibly approached by (husbands) who have not yet gained their confidence, they at once come to dislike a union ". So declare the writers on erotic science.

Lav.—(*Tearfully*) In every house men wed maidens of gentle birth. But no one, indeed, burns, with the fire of speech, simply because he has the power, a high-born maiden of a simple and gentle nature, unoffending and acting under the influence of bashfulness. Verily these are the great indignities, like barbs implanted into the heart, which make residence in the husband's house hateful, and which are painful to remember throughout life ; indignities on account of which relatives condemn the birth of a girl.

Mad.—Buddharakshitâ, my dear friend Lavangikâ seems to be sadly grieved. Very great must be the offence which my brother's words have given her.

Bud.—Quite so. I heard that he said ' I will have no more to do with thee (Màlatî), a libidinous girl. '

Mad.—(*Stopping her ears.*) Oh the breach of decorum ! Oh the inadvertency ! Friend, Lavangikâ, I am unable to show you my face even. Yet I am going to say (to you) something because I can (or, I have a right to) do so.

Lav.—This person is at your disposal.

Mad.—Let alone the question of my brother's perverseness or impropriety of conduct. But you too must please him now by conforming to his wishes since he is the husband. Morever, do you not know the ground of the blame he cast upon her by a taunt expressed in words of censure unbecoming in a gentleman ?

Lav.—How possibly should we not know it when it was (actually) expressed in words !

Mad.—The talk of the people had reached its climax as regards the spontaneous affection which Mâlati had betrayed for the magnanimous Mádhava. It is, indeed, this that has been thus telling. Therefore, my dear friend, act in such a way that this strong belief of the husband in something wrong (on Mâlatî's part) will be entirely eradicated from his heart. Otherwise, be it known, that a great evil will result. For girls, who are unflinchingly cruel, afflict the heart of men by such ill-placed affection. Say not to her that Madayantiká has counselled thus.

Lav.—Ah you heedless girl, beguiled by absurd rumours, I will not talk with you.

Mad.—Friend, be pleased ; or rather I will not leave you addressed indistinctly (*i. e.* I will explain matters fully to you). We know for certain that to Màlatî life consisted solely of Màdhava. Who did not mark the form of Mâlatî, which presented a singular beauty brought on by the languor of the limbs graceful like the developed blade of the *Ketaki*, and the life of which was kept up simply by her wearing round her neck the *Bakula* garland woven with his own hands by Màdhava, and of Mâdhava looking charming being wan and pallid like the disk of the morning moon? Moreover, did not you too notice their meeting glances, when on that day they met at the entrance of the *Kusumâkara* garden, glances in which there were brilliant gestures in consequence of the motion of the charming pupils being slow owing to the abundant play of the lotus-like eyes dilated and fully opened through curiosity and shining sportively, and which were charming and sweet, on account of the skill imparted by the thorough-going instruction of that dancing master, the god of love ? Did you not also mark the hearts which had, as it were, the ties of their roots torn off, of the two, the beauty of whose persons faded away on account of the great agony produced the very moment they heard the news of Mâlatî being given away to my brother? Moreover, I remember something more too.

Lav.—Now, what is that something more ?

Mad.—That Mâdhava, prompted by the skilful words of the revered dame placed both, his heart and life by offering them as presents, in the hazard of being accepted, of her own accord, by Màlatî, who greeted him with the agreeable news of the coming to consciousness again of that magnanimous one, the preserver of my life. And you yourself, O Lavangikâ, said just there that the favour was accepted by your friend.

LAV.—Friend, who was that magnanimous person? I have forgotten that.

MAD.—Remember, remember, friend: he, the preserver of my life, a disinterested friend; and having huge arms like pillars, who, appearing on the scene when on that day I, helpless that I was, fell into the clutches of the Destroyer in the shape of the formidable, ferocious beast, saved me having run the risk of offering up his own body, the sole essence of the whole world. He, who, with his bosom, huge, fleshy, lofty and expansive, scarched by the (monster's) hard jaws, and therefore surpassing (or resembling) a garland of full-grown *japâ* flowers torn into shreds, for my sake bore, with a heart wholly overpowered by pity, the thunder strokes of the sharp claws of the extremely ferocious tiger, and killed the monster of the savage beast.

LAV.—Ah, Makaranda!

MAD.—(*Joyfully.*) Dear friend, what, what do you say

LAV.—Why, I say it was Makaranda.

(*Smilingly touches her body and resorting to Sanskrit.*)

Granted that we are as you represent us to be. What can I say to that? But how comes it that this person, a maiden of high family, pure and guileless, suddenly has become unnerved in the course of conversation and assumed the form of the bud-covered Kadamba? (1).

MAD.—(*Bashfully*) Friend, why do you laugh at me? I own that the mention of the name and the remembrance, in coversations, of that person, who exerted himself in that manner, reckless of himself, and conferred upon me a great obligation by forcibly rescuing me from the jaws of Death, soothe me. Moreover, you too saw with your own eyes the noble youth, who discarded this highly precious world simply for the sake of Madayantika, as an effusion of perpiration flowed forth from his body of which he was made unconscious as the sharp pain of his wounds began to be felt, as he closed the pair of the dark lotus as of his eyes in a swoon, supporting with fortitude the burden of his body on the prop of his sword resting on the ground. (Madayantikā *manifests perspiration and other emotional effects*).

BUD.—(*Touching her body.*) The body of my dear friend has taken its resolve.

MAD.—( *Bashfully* ) Away with you, my dear. I am affected by the confidential talk of my friend.

LAV. Friend, Lavangikā, we too know what inference to draw. Be, therefore, pleased and desist from this dissimulation. Come, let us enjoy the happiness in a manner befitting a conversation based on mutual confidence.

BUD.—Friend, Lavangikā speaks well.

MAD.—I am at my friends' disposal now.

LAV.—Friend, if so, then tell us how you pass your time.

MAD.—Listen, my dear friend. On account of the confidence produced by Buddharakshitā's special liking (for him) my heart was, at first, filled with an axious desire and curiosity (to see him) risen to overflowing. Then having obtained, through the will of fate, a sight of him, I had my life (as it were) forced away on account of the heart boiling being heated by the irresistible and terrible pangs of love. With my servants afflicted on account of the unsufferable pangs caused by the fierce heat of the fire of love flaming through the whole body and spreading in a manner inexperienced before, and rendered shaky in consequence of the anguish increased by the words of Buddharakshitā opposed to the solace to be obtained from death easily procurable by my simply giving up all hope (of union), I have been experiencing a changed condition of life.

And stupefied by the intoxication caused by my longings I behold that person in my fancies and dreams. He too, my dear friend, looks intently at me for a long time in a manner in which he appears to reel under the powerful influence of wine, as it were, in the course of the dance of his loveful eyes which are unsteady, rolling about and expanding on account of the wonder gaining upon him for a while. Moreover, he addresses me as 'my love Madayantikà' filling the cavities of my ears with his deep, loud and grave voice faltering and hoarse like the note of a swan with his throat rendered astringent * by the lotus filaments eaten. And then immediately he frightens me causing my heart to heave and palpitate forcibly through flurry by committing the indecorous deed of laying hold on the skirt of my upper garment fluttering on my throbbing bosom.

And as I hastily cast off the garment and prepare to go away, covering my budding breasts with the fold of my arms which resemble full grown lotus-stalks at the very moment, but have my motion backward hindered by my robust thighs being fettered by the displaced waist-band falling disorderly, he laughs at me although I reprove him, with my heart rendered stern by uneasiness caused by the flush of temporary anger brought on by his persistent efforts † (or, after a great deal of painstaking), as he knows the full extent of my feelings conveyed to him by the superfluous casting of loving glances. Then, my dear friend, locking me up in his doubly folded strong arms and making me quite powerless by firmly (lit. ruthlessly) pressing me to his broad chest decked with large ornamental figures in the shape of the marks left by the scratches from the hard claws of the tiger, he, with his lotus like face clever in fixing its smiles upon the different parts of my face which become contracted, raised and motionless in consequence of his laying his hand on my braid, dishevelled as I turn away my head in flurry, and acting in a manner in keeping with his indecorous audacity, solicits from me something that should not be asked for me the beauty of whose body is made hearily (entirely) to thrill agreeable touch of his throbbing and contracted nether lip as he long imprints it upon the root of my left check, and whose eyes roll about slowly on account of the frenzy brought on by the unpleasant excitement caused by the rising joy and trepidation.

---

* According to Jag. 'fragrant.' † Or after Dr. Bhandarkar 'by most careful efforts.'

Having thus experienced all this as passing before my eyes, my dear friend, I suddenly awake and consider, in my wretchedness, the world of the living as a dreary wilderness.

LAV.—(*Laughing*). Tell me distinctly, dear Madayantikà, whether at that time your + + + observed by Buddharakshità, her eyes brightening as she smiles affectionately and sportively, is covered or not with the bedsheet, that the servants might not see it.

MAD.—O you who are in the habit of cracking nonsensical jokes, away with you.

BUD.—Friend, Madayantikà, the dear companion of Mâlati, of course, knows to talk in this fashion only.

MAD.—Don't deride Màlati in this way, friend.

BUD.—Dear Madayantikâ, I will now ask you something, if you will not betray the secret.

MAD.—Friend, have I also been guilty of a breach of friendly trust that you should say so? Dear friend, Lavangiká and you are now my heart.

BUD.—If Makaranda meets your eyes again by some chance what will you do?

MAD.—I will allow them a long feasting as they will be entirely rivetted motionless on each of his limbs.

BUD.—And if driven by love he makes you, the inflamer of his passion, his lawful wife by a choice-marriage, as Krishna did Rukminī, the mother of Káma (Pradyumna), how would you act?

MAD.—(*Sighing*) What, you simply hold out such a hope to me!

BUD.—Tell me, friend.

LAV.—Friend, her deep breathings that betray the agitation of her heart have already answered for her.

MAD.—Friend, what power have I over this my person, which he purchased by his own body, rescuing it from the jaws of the ferocious tiger, and which has therefore been enslaved to him!

Lav.—That is (an answer) worthy of the nobility ( of your character ).

Bud.—(I hope) you will bear these words in mind.

Mad.—Holloa, the drum announcing the lapse of the second watch is being beaten! I will then first of all reprove Nandana and beseeching him by falling at his feet get him reconciled to Mâlatî.

(*She rises and wishes to go.* Makaranda *discloses his face and seizes her by the hand.*)

Mad.—Dear Mâlatī, are you awake?

( *Looking with joy and trepidation.* )

Oh, this is something else altogether?

Mak.—

O you with plantain-like thighs, banish your fear; your waist is not able to bear the throbbing of your weighty breasts. This your slave, the bestowal of the favour of your love upon whom was thus declared by you, has been familiar to you in your fancied enjoyments. (2)

Bud.—(*Raising the face of* Madayantikà, *and speaking in Sanskrit.*)

This is the dearly-loved one, solicited (by you, or whom you surrounded) with a thousand desires; and this house of the minister has some of its inmates asleep * (*i. e.* not watchful); the darkness is pitchy; do the wished for thing just through gratitude; come silencing your jewelled anklets by drawing them up; let us go. (3)

Mad.—Dear Buddharakshitá, where are we to go to now?

Bud —There where Màlatî is.

Mad.—Has Málati taken the bold step?

Bud.—Yes. Moreover, you say—(*She repeats* ' *what power have I &c.*'). (Madayantiká *sheds tears.*)

Bud.—Noble youth, my dear friend has, of her own accord, bestowed herself upon you.

Mak.—

Today have I gained a glorious victory; what else (have

* While others are quite drunk.

I to wish for )! This is the jubilee day of my youth which has borne fruit; I, for whom the fish-bannered god being favourably disposed has upheld this yoke of friendship (*i. e.* undertaken the task of a friend). (4)

Then going out by this side-door let us be off. ( *They step gently* ).

MAK.—Oh, how charming does the royal road look in the stillness of midnight! Moreover, now,

The wind having rolled about in the topmost rooms and through the lofty windows of the mansions and coming back fraught with the strong aroma of old wine, perfumed by the garlands and strongly scented with the repeatedly accumulated smell of camphor, indicates young men's being in the company of newly married wives. (5)

[ *Exeunt omnes.*

END OF ACT VII STYLED 'THE DECEPTION OF NANDANA.'

## ACT VIII.

( *Enter* Avalokitá. )

AVA.—I have paid my respects to the revered lady who has returned from the residence of Nandana. I will now go to Màlatî and Mádhava. (*She walks on*). Here they are gracing the stone-slab on the margin of the well after having taken their summer-bath. I will then approach them. [*Exit.*

END OF THE PRAVES'AKA.

(*Enter* Malatî *and* Mâdhava *seated and* Avalokitâ.)

MA'D.—( *With joy.* ) The beauty of midnight, the great friend of Cupid, is in youth ( full vigour). For,

The rising early light of the moon, palish-white like the withering full-grown leaf of the palm tree, is chasing away the mass of darkness, as if the dense pollen of the *ketaka* flowers, rising upwards by the force of the wind, were gently moving in the sky. (1)

( *To himself* ). How shall I win over the wayward Mâlatî? Well, I shall try this, first. (*Aloud*) Dear Mâlati, to cool the heat of summer, I have been saying something to you who are the more cooling on account of your fresh evening ablution. Why do you then, without reason, misunderstand me?

Fair damsel, whilst these drops are yet falling from your tresses, whilst the interval between your budding breasts is till moist, and whilst your soft tender frame is yet blooming with bristling hair, be pleased, and give a close embrace at least once. (2)

O you unrelenting one,

Lay your arm round my neck instilling new life into me as it were, with the drops of perspiration breaking upon it through excitement and therefore possessing the beauty of a necklace of moonstones bedewed with water when kissed by (under the influence of) the lunar rays. (3)

Or rather, this is too much for me to think of. But how it is that this person is not worthy of even sharing your conversation?

As for refreshing my body with an embrace, though it has been scorched for a long time by the Malaya breezes and the lunar beams, well, it was not done; but you who have the voice of a Kinnara, let my ear which has been pained by the cooings of the impassioned cuckoos, drink your heart-ravishing speech. (4)

Ava.—( *Advancing* ) Ah you irresolute girl (lit. one not carrying out one's intentions), when Mâdhava was away from you for a moment you were disconsolate and would say to me—" My lord tarries; how long would it be before I see him, so that (when I see him) setting aside all my timidity and gazing on him in a manner to forget the interruption of a twinkle, I will thus speak unto him—do you favour me with a double embrance" and this is the outcome of all that?

(Mâlatî *eyes her with an air of reproof* )

Ma'd.—( *To himself.* ) Oh the all-grasping skill of the principal disciple of her reverence! Oh her inexhaustible store of elegant expressions! ( *Aloud* ) My love, is what Avalokitâ says true?

Ma'l.—(*Shakes her head.*)

MA'D.—I conjure you by my life and by that of Lava. and Avalokitâ if you do not tell it in actual words.

MA'L.—I do not know anything. (*After this half-said, she gesticulates shame*).

M'AD.—Oh, how charming is her unfinished and therefore unintelligible speech! (*Observing on a sudden*) Avalokitá, what is this?

The bright cheek of the fawn-eyed one is washed on a sudden with tears, wherein the moon, having implanted his ray like a lotus-stalk ( -tube ), shines as if desirous of drinking the nectar of her beauty worthy to be drunk in mouthfuls. (5)

AVA.—Friend, why do you weep in a manner slow in consequence of the tears gushing forth in a stream?

MA'L.—Friend, how long shall I have to endure the pain of my dear friend Lavangikâ's absence? I cannot get even any news about her.

MAD.—Avalokitá, what can it be?

AVA.—Being put in mind of Lavangikâ, by your own mention of her in the oath, she now yearns to learn some intelligence about her.

MA'D.—Why, just now I have sent Kalahamsaka there, asking him to go secretly and ascertain how matters stand at the house of Nandana. (*Hopefully.*) Avalokita, can it be that the endeavour of Buddharakshita with regard to Madayantika be crowned with success?

AVA—Whence should your noble self cherish a doubt? Magnanimous one, when Mâlatî informed you of the blissful event of the recovery from swoon of Makaranda, decorated with the scratches from the tiger's nails, you, inspired by Her Reverence, made her a present of your heart along with your life. If any one now felicitates you upon your acquisition of Madayantikâ, what reward will he get?

MA'D.—You have asked me the proper question. (*Looking at his bosom.*)

Here is the garland of the flowers of the beautiful Kesara tree that adorns the grove of Kâma, the witness of the deep attachment produced in me by the first sight of Mâlatî.

Which, when taken to her by her dear friend, she honoured affectionately, because I had wreathed it, with a place on her weighty, bud-like and expanding stout breasts, but which when her nuptial ceremony drew near, she, losing all hope of me, presented to me as her all in all, mistaking me for Lavangikâ. ( 6 ).

AVA.—Dear Mâlatî, this wreath of *bakula* flowers is highly prized by you; so be on your guard, that it does not suddenly pass into another's hands.

MA'L.—My dear friend's advice is welcome.

AVA.—What ! It is something like the sound of foot-steps.

MA'D.—(*Looking towards the curtains.*) Ah, here comes Kalahamsaka.

MA'L—Fortune favours you ; Madayantikâ is won.

M'AD.—(*Embracing her joyfully.*) This highly pleases us. (*Removes the Bakula-wreath from his neck and presents it to her*).

AVA.—Surely Buddharakshitâ has acquitted herself well of the honourable task imposed upon her by Her Reverence.

MA'L.—(*With joy.*) Thank Heaven, my dear friend Lavangikâ too comes. (*She rises*).

(*Enter* Kalahamsaka, Madayantikâ, Buddharakshitâ and Lavangikà *in agitation*).

ALL—To the rescue; let the noble one go to the rescue. Makaranda was attacked by the city guards in the middle of the way; so we were sent here with Kalahamsaka who met us just at the time.

KALA —As we heard a great uproar while on our way here, I think another hostile party must have appeared on the scene (the guards must have been reinforced).

MA'L. and AVALO—Alas ! alas! Happiness and distress mingling together have simultaneously fallen to our lot.

MA'D.—Dear Madayantikâ, you are welcome; come here. You have honoured our house. Surely he is that same (Makaranda). Why is your ladyship uneasy ? That he has been assaulted by many is a matter of small moment with my friend.

In an adventure, that paw of his, formidable by its rattling nails, is the friend of the lion having an ardent longing for deeds of matchless valour,—that paw which alone has the power to break the bones in the head of the lordly elephant whose face is moistened with the ichor exuding from his opening temporal hollows. (7)

I, too, will be close by my dear friend displaying his valour with heroic boundings.

[ *He walks with fierce strides and exit with* Kalaha. ]

AVA, LAV. & BUD.—We hope the mighty youths would return unharmed !

MA'L.—Friends, Avalokitá and Buddharakshitâ, go hastily and acquaint the revered lady with this accident. And you too, my dear Lavangikà, lose no time in telling my lord that if at all they (Maka. and he) have any tender feeling for us they should not be wreckless in their movements.

[ *Exeunt* Lav. Ava. and Buddharakshitá. ]

MAL.—Alas ! Alas ! I know not how time (this interval) is to pass away. Well, I will wait looking at the road by which my dear friend Lavangiká is to return. [ *She walks forth. With apprehension*] My right eye throbs inauspiciously. (*Sits down.*)

(*Enter* Kapâlakundalâ).

KAPA'L.—Ah, wretch, stay.

MA'L —( *In dismay.* ) Alas, my lord. ( *Here she is struck dumb.*)

KAPA'L.—(*With a grim smile.*) Oh, cry on.

Where is that lover of thine, the slayer of ascetic people ? Let that paramour of a girl, thy husband, protect you. Why dost thou flutter like a wild quail frightened at the swoop of the hawk ? Surely thou hast fallen into my clutches after a long time. (8)

I will take her to Sris'aila and having cut her piecemeal will inflict upon her an agonising death. [ *Exit snatching away* Mâlati. ]

MAD.—I too will follow Màlatî. ( *Walking forth.* ) Dear Málatî.

(*Enter* Lavangikâ)

LAV.—Friend Madayantiká, I am Lavangiká.

MAD.—Did you see the noble youth ?

LAV.—No, I did not. Just as he reached the door of the garden-compound, he heard a tumultuous noise, and darting forth defiantly and fiercely with long strides stretching with great force his huge legs, disappeared amidst the opposing force. Upon this, hapless that I am, I returned, and heard (on my way back) in every house the doleful exclamations.—'Ah warlike Màdhava, alas Makaranda, thou daring spirit'-of the citizens who were so completely enamoured of their merits. And it is rumoured that the great king too, having heard of the abduction of his ministers' daughters, had his feelings of jealousy and contempt roused and at once despatched a numerous troop of chosen foot-soldiers, and that. stationed on the top of his palace, he has been watching the course of events by the light of the moon.

MAD.—Alas ! I am undone, an ill-starred creature !

LAV.—Friend, but where is Màlatî !

MAD.—She, indeed, went first to watch your way back. Since that I have not seen her. Can it be that she has entered the avenue of trees in the garden ?

LAV.—Friend, let us quickly go in search of her. My friend is exceedingly timid. With such a crisis at hand she will not be able to bear herself up. [*They quickly move forward.*) Dear Màlatî, I say dear Màlatī ! [*They wander here and there.*]

[*Enter* Kalahamsaka *in high spirits* ]

KAL.—Thank Heaven ! We have escaped safe from the hard and close fight. Heyday ! Meseems I yet behold before me the congregated host of the enemy, which appeared frigthful in the gleaming light of the moon reflected all round from the polished blades of the sharp-edged swords brandished in close proximity with each other (or, incessantly), which appeared like the stream of the Jamuna lashed into heaving waves by a sportive move of the plough tossed about forcibly with his formidable and long hands by Balarâma when under the influence of the intoxication of wine, and the clamorous shouts of which spread through the entire vault of heaven as the antagonistic warriors retreated, losing heart, on account of the panic spread among them by the fierce and nimble Makaranda bounding about (or, darting upon them) in a wild and fearful manner. I also remember how my master, Màdhava, performed the extraordinary martial feat of moving on the road cleared of [ or, inasmuch as he cleared the road of ] the entire force of the enemy which was fiercely routed, by inflicting wounds upon it with the various weapons which he snatched from the hands of the soldiers who staggered as their bony frames were shattered with his formidable thunderbolt-like arms.

Oh the king's regard for merits ! For sending the door-keeper from the top-terrace of the palace he got the evil of hostility averted by the use of mild words, cast affectionate looks again and again at the moon-like faces of Màdhava and Makaranda when brought before him, and on learning from me of their noble descent, he showed exceptional and great respect to them. He then asked in sweet tones Bhûrivasu and Nandana, whose faces were darkened with the ink of rising jealousy and chagrin, if they were still dissatisfied with their sons-in-law who were an ornament to the whole world, noble-minded and amiable by their fresh youth and excellent qualities, and setting them right on that point retired to the inner apartment.—But here are Mádhava and Makaranda coming this way. I too go to comm nicate the matter to Her Reverence. ( *Exit.* )

( *Enter* Mádhava *and M*akaranda ).

Mak.—Oh the truly mighty valour of dearest Mádhava, surpassing that of all men ! For,

As he, having first fallen on the warriors, smote them in a manner in which their skeletons were shattered on account of their joints having given way by being crushed with his arms, and then displayed his valour having snatched their weapons, his path to the ocean of fight, strewed with large heaps of struggling trunks, became in its front frightful by the lines of foot-soldiers rooted ( to the ground, or paralysed with terror) on either side. (9)

MA'D—Rather this is a matter for regret. Lo!

The men who drank even to-day in their midnight-revels the liquor, thickly penerated by the rays of the moon, after it was drunk in mouthfuls by their beloveds, embracing them in sport—even they now proclaim by their bodies whose bones have been smashed by the heavy blows from your huge arms, that worldy men are, for the most part, in a woeful plight on account of their frailty. (10)

The goodness of the king, however, is worth remembering; for though offenders, he treated us as if we had given him no offence. Come away now. I wish to hear the account, related in detail, of how Madayantikà was won, in Màlatî's presence. For,

As you will be telling it, our friend ( Madayantiká ) will bend down the lily of her face, with the eyes motionless through rising shame and turned away as they would meet the tremulous side-glances cast by smiling Málatî. (11)

( *They walk forth.* )

This is the enclosure of the garden.

(*They enter it.* )

MA'D.—What, the region of the tank is quite deserted!

MAK.—Friend, surely being distracted by anxiety on our account they might be diverting themselves by wandering here and there in the dense part of this very garden. Come then, let us look for them. ( *They both walk on.* )

LAVANGIKA' & MADAYATIKA' —Friend Málatî! (*Seeing them suddenly, with joy.* ) Fortunately do we see the noble youths again all safe and sound.

MA'D. & MAK.—Ladies, where is Màlatî ?

BOTH.—Whence can Màlatî be here ! We, hapless that we are, were deceived by the sounds of your foot-steps.

MA'D—Ladies, somehow my heart breaks into a thousand pieces. Speak out distinctly.

The internal soul of me who am thinking of evil only befalling the lotus-eyed one is fluttering within me forcibly and continuously ; my left eye is, indeed, throbbing; and here are your painful words: alas! I am entirely undone. (12)

MAD.—When your noble self went from here she despatched Avalokitá and Buddharakshità to the revered lady and then sent Lavangikà after you telling her to warn you against rashness. Then feeling uneasy she started ahead to watch her return. I followed, but could see nothing of her. Afterwards as we were looking for her in the interstices of the shrubs we saw you.

MAD.—Alas, dear Málati!

Something, something do I fear which is far from auspicious. Have done with jest; O wrathful one, I am pining for you. If you (only) desire to test me I have already stood the test. Beloved one, speak to me. My heart being unhinged reels within me; you are ruthless. (13)

BOTH—Ah dear friend, where are you?

MAK.—Friend, why do you yield to dejection without ascertaining the fact?

MA'D.—Do not you too know how she acts in her timidity when not at ease on account of her love for Mádhava?

MAK.—True; but it is possible to suppose that she might have gone to Her Reverence. Come then let us look for her there.

BOTH.—This, too, is possible.

MA'D.—May it be so! [ *He walks on.* ]

MAK.—( *Musing, to himself.* )

Whether our friend ( Málatí ) has gone to the residence of the revered lady or not; whether she will come to us alive or not—such doubts haunt me; for happiness, such as (springs from) the company of kinsfolk, of friends and of those we love, is as fleeting as the flash of lightning. (14)

[ *Exeunt Omnes* ]

END OF ACT VIII ENTITLED 'MA'LATYAPAHA'RA'.

# ACT IX.

( *Enter* Saudâminî ).

SAU.—Here have I, Saudáminî, arrived at Padmávatî, having flown up from the divine S'riparvata. Now I will approach Mádhava, who, separated from Málatî and unable to bear the sight of familiar spots, has left his home and is now staying with his friends in a region full of large valleys, hills and woods. Oh, I have soared so high as to take a bird's-eye-view of the whole scene chequered with mountains, towns, hamlets, rivers and forests. (*Looking back.*) Excellent! Excellent!

Under the cover of the girdle of the broad rivers, the Pârà and the Sindhu, with their pellucid waters, Padmâvatî appears to possess the sky, as it were, fallen down after being torn off by being rubbed against her lofty mansions, temples, and the turrets of town-gates. (1)

Moreover,

Here comes in sight the Lavanà, with its series of graceful ripples, the rows of whose border woods, attractive on account of their having the Uḷapa grass, so coveted by cows with calf, greatly delight the country-folk at the advent of the rainy season. (2).

(*Looking in another direction.*) This is the cataract of the holy Sindhu which has cleft the surface of the earth.

This its wild roar, awful like the peal of dense fresh clouds pregnant with water, and spreading through the caverns of the adjacent mountains, becomes comparable to (resembles) the deep hollow sound of Ganes'a's throat. (3).

These sylvan mountain tracts, fragrant with the ripened *bilvas* and covered with woods chiefly consisting of the sandal, As'vakarṇa, Kesara and the Pátalá trees, vividly call to my mind the mountains of the southern forests with their extensive table-lands, glistening and resounding with the Godavàrî, as it rushes through the deep caverns overgrown with large arbours, gloomy-looking on account of their being screened with the clumps of the Taruna, * the Kadamba and the Jambu trees.

---

* Or, young ( तरुण ) Kadamba &c.

And here is the ( *linga* ) of the divine lord of Bhava'nî, self-existent ( lit not set there by man ) and conferring sanctity on the confluence of the Madhumatî and the Sindhu, which is called Suvarṇabindu. (*Bowing.*)

My homage to thee, divine one, the author of creation; victory to thee, the glorious one, the granter of all boons; and the store of the Vedas; conquer thou, whose tiara is the glittering moon; be triumphant, O destroyer of Madana; all glory to thee, the primeval progenitor (or preceptor) ! ! (4)

(*Preparing to go.*)

This mountain, Bṛhadas'man by name (or, with its large rocks), gives delight to my eyes, with its lofty summits darkened by the new clouds, noisy with the mingled notes uttered by the peahens through hilarity and presenting a charming appearance by its trees with their chequered birds' nests. (5)

Moreover,

Here, deepened by their echoes, the growls of the young bears living in the caves, swell in magnitude; and the smell of the exudations from the joints of the Sallaki trees torn off by the elephants, cool, pungent and astringent, gains in strength. (6)

(*Looking upwards.*) Ah, it is mid-day. For here now

Leaving the Káshmarî tree the Koyashitika bird (the lapwing) repairs to the Kṛtamâla, which has got fresh leaves; the blue jays run to the reservoir of water, touching with their beaks the pods of the As'mantaka creepers ( or, the tops of the As'mantaka trees) along the bank; the gallinules lie hiding themselves in the hollows of the trunk of the Tinis'a tree; and underneath cry the wild cocks in response to the cooings of the pigeons in their creeper-nests. (7)

Well then. I will seek out Mádhava and Makaranda and finish the business as set on foot. [ *Exit.*

END OF VIS'KAMBHAKA.

---

( *Enter* Mâdhava *and* Makaranda ).

MAK.—( *Sighing pitiably.* )

Alas ! On account of the adverseness of fortune here are we weltering in a woeful plight being quite helpless (*lit.*

not able to do anything ) like beasts; a plight in which the mind being tossed about (by doubts) neither cherishes hope nor gives it up, but nevertheless plunges into the dense darkness of bewilderment. (8)

MA'D—Alas, dear Málatí ! where are you ! How have you disappeared all of a sudden, without our knowing the truth about your real fate, in such a strange way ? I say, heartless one, be pleased; come to me.

O you to whom Mádhava was dear, why are you unkind to me ? Surely I am the same ( Mádhava ) whom formerly your hand, with the charming wedding string-bracelet put on ( by you ) of your own motion, delighted as if it were a great festival incarnate. (9)

Friend Makaranda, such intense love is difficult to be found in this world.

With limbs tender like fresh flowers she long bore the burning fever of love consuming her incessantly and rising in violence every moment; then she resolved to relinquish life like straw : and what is more than this, that she performed the desperate act of offering her hand to me ? (10)

Moreover,

Do you remember how she, before the celebration of the marriage rite, feeling all hope of union with me gone, displayed her internal feeling of love with weepings, which paralysed her senses, and which were piteous, and helpless as if they proceeded from a cut in the vital parts, in such a manner that even I had my mind tossed about by distraction ? (11)

(*In agitation.*) Oh pity !

My heart, whose anguish is intense, bursts but is not split in twain; my languid frame suffers stupefaction but parts not with consciousness; the fire within inflames the body but does not reduce it to ashes entirely; fate strikes cutting at the vital parts but cuts not off life. (12)

MAK.—Friend, the fierce sun burns irresistibly like fate; and such is the condition of your body. Let us, therefore, sit here for a while near this lotus lake. For here,

The breeze, charged with odour rendered strong by its being mixed with the stream of honey flowing from the bed of the young high-stalked lotuses and slow on account of the spray of the particles of waves rolling in front, will refresh you. (13)

(*They move on and sit down.*)

MAK.—(*To himself.*) Well, I will thus divert his attention. (*Aloud.*) Dear Mádhava,

Enjoy, in the intervals of the trickling down and the gushing forth of the tears, these spots in the lake with their broad-stemmed lotuses waving being shaken by the wings of the Mallikáksha birds singing through passion, and with their beauty never deserting them. (14)

(Mâdhava *rises in a phrensy.*)

MAK.—What! He has risen absent-mindedly and is going away! (*He sighs and follows him*). Friend, take heart. See, see,

The water of the rivulets flowing through the ravines is charged with the scent of the cane-flowers. Clusters of Yûthikâ and Mâlatî ( kinds of Jasmine ) buds have bloomed all round. And the clouds spreading on the peaks of the mountains have formed a canopy for the frantic dance of the peacocks on summits smilling with the opening *kutaja* flowers, ( 15 )

Moreover,

The extensive mountain tracts present the beauty of the Kadamba trees majestic by the display of their blossoms thick-set on account of their opening; the directions are darkened with the trains of clouds; the banks of rivers and brooks (or, of the streams of rivers ) are lined with Ketakas, charming by the tender shoots springing up, and the row of woods is smiling with the scent-bearing flowers of Śilîndhras and of the Lodhra trees. ( 16 )

MA'D.—I see these, friend. But the beauty of the forest and mountain scenes is such as I cannot enjoy now. But what is this ? ( *Tearfully* ) Or what else can it be !

Those days have now come, in which the rows of clouds have the mellow blue of the pieces of saphires shaken off by the blast of a strong eastern gale odoriferous with the fragrance of full-blown *Arjuna* and *Sarja* flowers, which bear the sweet smell of the earth wetted by showers, and which are charming on account of the blending of the departing summer and the commencing rains. (17)

Ah my love, Mâlatî,

How can I behold the quarters in which numerous clouds are floating up, dark like the young *Tamâla* trees in which the particles of fresh water are wafted by cool breezes, which display the rain-bow and which are resounding with the cries of love-maddened peacocks? (18)

(*Acts being distressed by sorrow*).

MAK —Some inexplicable change of state, exceedingly terrible, has overtaken my friend now. (*Tearfully*) But I that play the part of adamant have been seeking diversion. (*With a sigh.*) Our hope for Màdhava has thus well-nigh faded away.

(*Observing with alarm.*) What! He has fainted! (*Looking towards the sky.*) Málati, Mâlati, what more, you are relentless.

On account of your longing for him, you, who disregarded your kinsmen, did the desperate deed. What course of conduct is this, friend, so far removed from mercy, that you have adopted towards this your unoffending lover? (19)

What! He does not revive yet. Alas! I am robbed by fate.

Mother, mother! my heart breaks; my frame gives way; I consider the world blank; I burn within with unceasing flames; my internal soul, afflicted and writhing with pain (or exhausted), plunges into dense darkness; stupefaction overtakes me from all sides; what am I, a hapless being, to do? (20)

Alas! Oh hard lot!

He, the Kaumudi–festival to the heart of his kinsmen, the lovely moon to the eyes of Màlatî, and the joy of Makaranda–even he, the ornament to the mortal world now passes away! (21)

Ah, friend Mádhava,

You were the sandal juice to my limbs, autumnal moon to my eyes, the very joy of my heart and extremely amiable; by robbing me all of a sudden of you, as of my life, the Destroyer has made me wretched. (22)

(*Touching him.*)

Ruthless one, favour me with your glance bright with a smile; O exceedingly cruel one, give me a reply; O you who loved Makaranda, how is it that you do not think your companion to be attached to you ? (23)

(Mâdhava *regains consciousness*).

MAK.—(*With a sigh of relief.*) This new cloud with the deep bright hue of a fresh polished *râjapatta* ( a diamond of inferior kind) calls back my friend to life by a shower of water-drops. Fortunately he has recovered.

MA'D.—Whom then shall I send as a messenger to my beloved in this wilderness ? (*Looking up*). Good, good !

A new cloud, dark like the full blown *tamâla* flower and assuming fantastic shapes above, is spreading upon the top of the mountain to the north of the river which stumbles with its gentle ripples through the bowers of the Jambu trees dark with their loads of ripened fruit. (24)

( *Rising in haste and looking up with folded hands* ).

Gentle cloud, does lightning, thy beloved companion, embrace thee ? Do the Chátakas, welcome (to thee) by the affection they manifest, wait upon thee ? Does the eastern wind gladden thee by its gentle touches; and does the rainbow bearing beauty on all sides become thy prominent mark ? (25)

(*Listening*) Ah, he consents (to my addressing him) with a low rumble closely followed by the sweet notes of the peacocks with necks outstretched and delighted at the echo reverberating through the caverns. I will then proffer my request. Revered cloud,

If in thy free rambles over the world thou chancest to see my beloved, first cheer her up and then tell her of the sad plight Mâdhava is in; in telling it thou shouldst not snap, to any great degree, the thread of hope; for that alone somehow sustains the life of the long-eyed one. (26)

( *With joy* ) Ah, he has set out. I shall go elsewhere then. (*He moves.*)

MAK.—(*With alarm.*) How is it that the Ráhu of infatuation now attacks the moon of Màdhava. O father, O mother, O revered lady, help, help. Behold the condition of Mâdhava.

MA'D.—Fie, what a calamity !

Evidently my beloved is killed and severally distributed in the forest—her complexion being given to the fresh *lodhra* flowers, her eyes to the fawns, her gait to the elephants and her modest demeanour to the creepers. (27)

Alas, my dear Málatí!

MAK.—Accursed heart, why dost thou not burst somehow and part into two, when my friend, the abode of virtues, dear-loved, the lord of my life and of intimate friendship from our playing in the same dust, has been suffering mental and bodily torment on account of separation from his beloved? (28)

MAD—Verily the Creator's formation of objects in this world may easily have similitude. Well; I will do this. (*Aloud.*) Ye animals that tenant the woods of the mountain, having offered my respects to you I solicit the favour of your listening to me for a moment.

Have you, living here, seen a damsel of high birth, naturally graceful in all her limbs? Or do you know what has become of her? Hear from me, friends, her age; she is in that stage wherein love acts with full force in the heart but with a charming reserve on the body (its effects on the body are not fully discernible). (29)

Alas! Oh pity!

With his plumage raised in the frantic dance, the peacock drowns my voice by his cries; with his pupils rolling through intoxication the Chakora approaches his mate through inward joy; the black-faced ape smears the cheek of his female with the pollen of flowers; whom should I request? Every where begging is certainly out of season. (30)

And this monkey having raised the face of his beloved imprints a kiss upon it—the face which has its tiny teeth tinged with the red of her lips and its temple-region reddish like the Kâmpillaka flowers, and so resembling a pomegranate burst open and red when ripened. (31)

Here is an elephant with his trunk resting on the shoulder of his beloved. How is it that here too I am ill-timed!

Scratching with the point of his tusk his consort who has contracted her eyes on account of the scratching sensation, fanning her with the pleasing winds from the ears flapped in alternate succession, and feeding her with the half-chewed new sprouts of the Sallaki, this happy wild elephant has been practising close familiarity. (32)

(*Looking in another direction.*)

But this elephant does not utter a moderately deep grunt when the clouds are rumbling; he does not eat morsels of S'aivala, collecting it from the adjacent lake; and his face is miserable as the bees that cling to it are silent being dejected at the lack of frontal juice: surely he is pining, being afflicted with separation from his dear mate. (33)

It is no use troubling him. Here is another, the lord of a herd of rutting elephants, the sound of whose pleasant and deep grunt is being heard by his delighted mate and who, having entered the lake which is scented and made viscous by the profuse exudation from his fleshy temples having an odour sweet and cooling like that of numerous fresh-blown Kadamba flowers, is sporting, scattering all round the mass of the leaves and the stalks, fibres, roots, tender sprouts, and the leaves of beds of lotuses torn up, spreading about a mist of spray from the waves dashing against each other by being set in motion by the beautiful and harmonious play of his ears going on unceasingly, and spreading terror among the ospreys and the cranes. Well, I will address him. Noble lord of elephants, thy youth is commendable; thou hast also the skill to please thy beloved. Still, (there is this), ( *Disapprovingly.* )

Whenever she finished her repast of lotus-stalks torn off sportively thou gavest her mouthfuls of water scented with the opening lotuses; thou gavest her a bath with thy trunk scattering a shower of spray: granted all this; but at its close thou didst not affectionately hold over her the umbrella of a lotus-leaf with a straight stalk. (34)

How is it that he departs in a manner disagreeable on account of his treating me with contempt. Ah, I am simply a fool since I act towards this forest-rover in a manner befitting my friend, Makaranda. Alas dear friend!

Fie upon this distressful life which I thus pass without thee (lit. alone); fie upon that beauty which is not appreciated and enjoyed by thee; accursed is the day also which dawns upon me without thee; and fie upon that delusive joy which springs from something else (than thee)! (35)

MAK.—Oh! the impression of genuine affection, dormant on account of the stupefaction wrought by insanity, has been re-awakened by some excitant, and he thinks I am not near him. (*Stepping before him*) Here is the unhappy Makaranda standing by your side.

MA'D.—Dear friend, come and embrace me. As to my love Málatî, I am past all hope and am quite knocked up. (*He faints.*)

MAK.—(*Joyfully.*) Here do I come to the lord of my life. (*Looking at him pitifully.*) Woe me! The moment he felt a longing for my embrace he swooned away. Let me then have done with any more fond hope of life. That I have entirely lost my friend is the reasonable conclusion (now). Alas, friend!

All that fear which my heart, feverish with anxiety caused by love, ever entertained tremblingly, although without any cause, in anticipation of your misfortunes, has now suddenly disappeared. (36)

Friend, better are those past moments in which I had the pleasure of seeing you alive although in a pitiable condition like that. But now,

On your departure the body is a burden to me; life an adamantine nail; the quarters are blank; the senses without purpose; time painful, and the world void of interest all round. (37)

(*Musing*) Why do I live then? Simply that I should witness the end of Màdhava? Well. Falling into the Pàtalávatî from the peak of this mountain I will anticipate Màdhava in death. (*He walks forth a little; then turning back with pity and looking*) Pity, oh pity!

This is that bodily frame resembling in complexion a blue lotus, even by very closely embracing which I never felt satiated, and which, the glances of Màlatî, full of dalliance consequent on dawning love and brightening with wonder, drank in at one time. (38)

Strange! How could this body possess at an early age such a store of noble qualities! Dear Mádhava,

The moment the spotless moon waxed full with all its digits it entered the jaws of Râhu; no sooner did the cloud become compact and ready to burst it was scattered by the force of the wind; just as the stately tree bore fruit it was consumed by a wild fire: (thus) did you fall a prey to death just as you became the crest jewel of the world. (39)

I will then clasp my dear friend even though in this state. And it was the very thing solicited by him. ( *Having embraced him.* ) Ah friend Màdhava, the repository of spotless lore, the preceptor of (or eminent by) virtues, the self-chosen lord of Màlatî's life, and one whose moonlike face gladdened the faces of Kámandakī and Makaranda, this is Makaranda's lat embrace in this life, solicited by you in your last moments. Friend, do not at all think that Makaranda will now live even for a moment longer.

Having drunk the suck of our mothers in company, on account of our living together from the time of birth, it is unbecoming in you, O you with a lotus-like countenance, alone to drink the libation of water offered to you after death by your kinsmen. (40)

( *He leaves him sorrowfully and moves about.* ) Here is the Pátalâvatī below. Divine river,

May I have my birth in the same place where my friend will be born; may I be his associate again ! (41)

(*He wishes to throw himself down.*)

(*Enter in a hurry* Saudàminî).

SAU.—(*Holding him back.*) Dear son, have done with this rash act.

MAK.—(*Looking at her*) O, who are you ? Why do you obstruct me ?

SAU.—Long-lived one, are you Makaranda ?

MAK.—Leave me. I am that same wretch.

SAU.—Dear boy, I am a Yoginî and have with me a memento from Málatî. (*She shows him the wreath of Bakulaflowers.*)

MAK.—( *With a sigh of relief and pitiably.*) Revered lady, does Málatî live ?

SAU.—Yes, she does. But my dear boy, has the worst befallen Màdhava? I am alarmed that you are determined upon this desperate step.

MAK.—Revered lady, quitting him just in his swoon, I came here disgusted with the world. Come then, let us quickly repair to him. (*They move rapidly.*)

MA'D.—(*Reviving*) Oh, I am brought back to my senses by some one. (*Musing*) Surely this is the work, without any regard to my condition, of this gale wafting the drops of water from the fresh clouds.

MAK.—(*Looking at him.*) Thanks to Heaven, my friend has regained consciousness.

SAU.—The build of the body of both agrees with what Mâlatî told me.

MA'D.—Divine Eastern wind,

Whirl about the clouds charged with water; delight the Chátakas; impel the peacocks to utter their notes with necks outstreched; and develop the Ketakas; but when a lovelorn man dispels his anguish by falling into a swoon, what object dost thou seek, oh ruthless one, by afflicting him with the malady of consciousness? (42)

MAK.—A good service has been done by the wind that enlivens all creatures.*

MA'D.–Divine wind, still I will address thee this request.

Bear my life along with the pollen of the collection of blooming Kadamba flowers thither where my beloved is; or give me something that has been cooled by contact with her body: for thou art my final refuge. (43)

(*He bows with folded hands*)

---

* Moreover,

These breezes of the rainy season, charged with the fragrance of the Ketaka flowers, kissing the faces of the town-matrons under colour of agitating their flowing curls which roll over them (the faces) and delightful with (or, bearing along) the hummings of the swarms of bees rolling in the flowery dust in the cavities of the opened Kadamba buds, torment those in separation.

Sau.—This is, indeed, the proper time to offer him the token of recognition.

(*She drops into his hands the Bakulu-wreath.*)

Ma'd.—(*With emotion, amazement and joy.*) Strange! This is the wreath of the flowers of the Bakula tree in the yard of the temple of Káma, which, woven by me, was fondled on her lofty bosom by my beloved. (*Marking it with joy.*) What doubt about this? For, here is the very same part of it which, although it was unevenly woven and had its flowers badly arranged, as I tried to conceal the intense curiosity caused by emotion at the sight of her pretty moonlike face, gave joy to Lavangikà. (44).

(*Rising in joy and excitement.*) Dear Màlatî, here I will find you out. (*With an air of anger.*) O you who shut your eyes to my condition,

Life is passing out, as it were; O fair one, my heart is giving way, as it were; my limbs are, as if, burning; and darkness seems to shoot forth from all sides; this is, forsooth, the occasion for speedy help and not for joking; give then bliss to my eyes and be not cruel to me. (45).

(*Surveying all quarters, in despair.*) Whence can there be Mâlatî here! (*Addressing the Bakula-wreath.*) O Bakula wreath, the dear companion of my beloved, thou art my benefactor. Welcome to thee!

At a time, when, O dear friend, the pangs of love-torture, irresistible and agonising on account of the evil of the fierce burning of the body, became unbearable, thy close contact, which almost equalled my embrace, became the most efficient means of saving the life of the blue-lotus-eyed one. (46).

(*Marking it, dolefully.*)

Painfully do I remember those thy transferences to my neck and to that of the lovely-eyed one on various occasions, which inflamed the fever of love mingled with joy, which were enlivening on account of deep love and which were the marks of affection. (47).

(*He places it on his bosom and faints.*)

MAK —(*Approaching and fanning him*) Friend, take heart, take heart.

MA'D.—(*Recovering*) Makaranda, don't you see how, all of a sudden, I have obtained from some source this *Bakula*-wreath, the token of (or, which bears with it) Màlatí's love ? What do you think then as to where this comes from ?

MAK.—Friend, this revered lady here, an adept in the practice of Yoga*, has brought this Málatí's keep-sake.

MA'D.—(*Looking at her, piteously and with folded hands.*) Noble lady, be gracious and tell me if my beloved lives.

SAU.-Cheer up, son, cheer up. She lives, the blessed one.

MA'D. and MAK.—(*Taking heart.*) Revered lady, if so, then tell us what all this means.

SAU.—Formerly, as the story goes, Aghoraghanta was slain by Mádhava in the temple of Karálá, as he, sword in hand, was offering up Málati.

MA'D.—(*In excitement.*) Revered lady, desist, desist. I know the whole thing now.

MAK.—Friend, how so ?

MA'D.—Friend, what else can it be ? Kapálakundalá has gratified her wish.

MAK.—Revered lady, is it so ?

SAU.—It is as my son has understood it.

MAK.—Oh hard lot !

If the autumnal moonlight blended with a bed of lilies for giving rise to the quality of beauty, then let the good deed remain: but what fatality is this that an unseasonable line of clouds should have parted them. (48).

MA'D,—Alas, dear Málatí ! Oh pity ! You found yourself in a very dreadful situation.

Lotus-faced one, in what sad plight you must have been when in the grasp of Kapálakundalá, like a digit of the moon seized by the ominous Ketu (or, shrouded by the tail of a comet). (49).

Venerable Kapálakundalá,

---

* Or, who has got miraculous power by the practice of Yoga.

That creation (of God) ought to be treated with respect; do not act demoniacally; be propitious: the natural place of a sweet-smelling flower is fixed on the head; and not under crushing pestles. (50)

SAU.—Son, do not be excited.

She would have done the execrable deed if I had not bee… there, an obstacle in her way; she is, indeed, exceedingly cruel. (51)

BOTH.—(*Bowing.*) Your Reverence has done us a great favour. Tell us, then who you are that have thus proved to us a relative.

SAU.—You will know this, to be sure. (*Rising.*) Here do I now,

Put forth, for your good, the miraculous power to bear one away, the result of my application to Yoga, incantations, mystic diagrams, penance and attendance on the preceptor. (52)

(*Exit with* MA'DHAVA.)

MAK.—Wonderful wonderful !

A frightful blending of darkness and lightning obstructing the function of the eye appeared for a moment and then disappeared.

(*Observing, with alarm.*)

How is it that my friend is not here ? What is this ? (*Pondering.*) Or what else can it be !

All powerful is this mistress of the Yogis by her might. (53)

(*With surmise.*) I am now quite at a loss to know whether this is a desirable thing or an evil.

Moreover,

My heart which is not a little astonished, which has forgotten th previous occurrences, which is overwhelmed with the fever caused by the appearance of a fresh danger, and whose bewilderment disappears and thickens upon it at one and the same moment, experiences a state which is a mixture of joy and sorrow. (54)

I will then seek her reverence who has come to this dense forest in company with our friends and apprise her of this event. [*Exit.*

END OF ACT IX, STYLED 'THE APPEARANCE OF SAUDA'MINÎ.

## ACT X.

(*Enter* KA'MANDAKI', LAVANGIKA' *and* MADAYANTIKA')

KA'M.—(*Pitiably and with tears.*) Ah child Mâlati, who graced my lap, where are you ? Give me a reply.

Those various acts of yours whose charm grew every moment ever since the time of your birth, as well as your endearing words, sweet and gentle, as they are called back to memory, burn the body and rend the heart. (1)

Moreover, daughter,

I remember your lotus-like countenance, when you were a child, with its random cries and smiles, with a few tender, tiny and budlike teeth shining therein, and with its faltering, unintelligible and sweet lispings. (2)

THE OTHER TWO—(*Tearfully*) Ah dear friend, charming with the bright moon of your face, whither are you gone ? What fate, the result of perverse destiny has, in your loneliness, overtaken your body which is as tender as a S'irîsha flower ? Noble Mâdhava, the world has been such with you that great joy visited you only to vanish the next moment.

KA'M.—(*With greater grief.*) Alas, dear children !

This your union, which brought joy with it and which was delightful on account of fresh love, was smitten by the violent blast of Destiny like that of Lavali and Lavanga (by a violent storm). (3)

LAV.—(*Dejectedly*) Accursed heart that art adamantine, thou art cruel in every way. (*She beats her heart and falls down.*).

MAD.—Dear Lavangikà, I say cheer up but for a moment.

LAV.—Friend, what can I do ? My life, as if immovable by being indelibly fixed with adamantine glue does not leave me.

KA'M.—Child Mâlatî, from birth Lavangîkà has been dearest to you Why don't you take pity on the poor girl whose life is about to pass away ? For she,

Abandoned by you of a bright complexion, your loving friend, whose face is gloomy, does not shine out like the oily wick of a lamp with its point black when bereft of the flame. (4)

And how do you, blessed one, leave Kámandakî? You, ruthles child, your limbs were developed just by the warmth of my weeds.

Ever since the time you were weaned, by me, you, with an engaging face, were made to play like a doll of ivory, then taught good manners, reared up, and united to an accomplished husband supremely eminent among men: you ought, therefore, to have a greater affection for me than even for your mother. (5)

(*Despondently.*) Moon-faced one, now I have lost all hope.

I, whose fortune is reversed, did not see your suckling son lying in your lap, with his face engaging by his cause-less smiles and with white mustard seeds placed on his crest and fore-head. (6)

LAV.—Revered lady, be gracious. I am now wearied by bearing (the burden of) my life. I will, therefore, precipitate myself from the top of this mountain and find relief thereby. Your Reverence should give me such a blessing that I shall see my beloved friend at last in my next life.

KA'M.—Oh Lavangikà, Kàmandakî too will not live any longer in separation from the dear daughter. Equal is this our pang of anguish. Moreover,

If owing to the diversity of actions there is no union (after death), let it not be: but the quitting of life has this fruit that all suffering is annihilated. (7)

LAV.—Just as you say. (*All rise.*)

KA'M.—(*With a compassionate look.*) Child Madayantikà.

MAD.—What is your command? That I should take the lead? I am ready to attend (to your bidding).

LAV.—Friend, be good enough and desist from killing yourself. You must not, indeed, forget this person.

MAD.—(*With an angry look.*) Avaunt! I am not your slave.

KA'M.—Alas, the poor girl has formed her resolve.

MAD.—(*To herself.*) Lord Makaranda, my homage to you.

LAV.—Revered lady, this is the precipitous peak of the mountain with its skirts hallowed by being begirt by the Madhumatî.

KA'M.—Away with delay now in our present purpose. (*All are ready to fall down.*)

(*Behind the scenes.*)

Wonderful ! What marvel !

A terrible admixture of darkness and lightning thwarting the perceptive power of the eye appeared for a moment and then vanished.

KA'M.—(*Looking, with joy mingled with amazement.*) What ! My dear boy is here ! Then what can this be ?

MAK.—(*Entering.*) What else can it be ? Predominant is this mistress of Yoga by her greatness. (8)

(*Behind the curtains.*)

What an appalling throng of men ?

On hearing of the end of Mâlatî, Bhûrivasu, his heart filled with disgust for the pleasures of the world and also for his life, is coming to Suvarṇabindu resolved upon throwing himself into fire: we are, therefore, done up. (9)

MAD.—and LAV.—Unexpectedly we have the prospect of a meeting with Mâlatī and Mâdhava and as unexpectedly this dire calamity !

KA'M. and MAK.—Oh joy ! Oh, fie; what pity ! Wonderful, strange !

What ! Is this a simultaneous fall of sword-blades and of a shower of the streams of sandal juice ? or is this a rain of nectar, without clouds, intermixed with streaks of fire ? (10)

To-day, Fate represents a mixture of the elixir of life with poison, a blending of light and darkness, and a combination of thunderbolts and lunar rays. (11)

(*Behind the curtains.*)

Alas, father, hold, hold, I long to see your lotus-like face. Be gracious and gladden me. How, on my account, do you cast yourself off who are the sole auspicious lamp of a family, spotless and renowned in all the space encircled by the mountain Lokâloka ? But I, ungenerous that I was, had thought you to be without sympathy.

KA'M—Alas, daughter,

No sooner have you been recovered by a strange chance as if from a second birth than there has appeared this fresh calamity to smite you like the planet (Ràhu) appearing to devour the digit of the moon. (12)

OTHERS—Alas, dear friend !

(Enter Mâdhava *bearing* Málatî *who is in a swoon.*)

MA'D.—Painful ! Oh what a hard lot !

When she had somewhat survived (the effect of) her isolation she has encountered danger from quite a different quarter. Who possibly can shut the gates of a creature's destiny when ready to operate ? (13)

MAK.—(*Entering hurriedly, to* Mâdhava) Friend, but where is that Yoginî ?

MA'D.—Starting from S'riparvata I lighted down here rapidly just with her. But after the doleful words of the forester uttered the very moment, I have not seen her. (14)

KA'M. and MAK.—(*Beseechingly, looking in mid-air.*) Noble lady, save us once more. Why have you become invisible ?

MA'D and LAV.—Dear Malati, we call out to you, dear Málati.—(*With trepidation.*) Help, revered lady ! Her heart has ceased to beat owing to her breathing being long suppressed. Alas minister ! Alas dear friend ! Both of you have become the cause of each other's death.

KA'M.—Ah dear child, Málatî.

MA'D.—Ah my love !

MAK.—Alas, dear friend !

(*All faint but recover.*)

KA'M—(*Looking upwards.*) How is it that this stream of water bursting down as if from a cloud suddenly torn asunder refreshes us !

MA'D.—(*With a sigh of relief*) Ah, Máláti has come back to her senses. For,

Her heart, as it beats with the returning respiration, makes her breasts throb; her lovely eyes regain their natural expression; and then, owing to the termination of the swoon, her face, brightening up, shines like a lotus when at dawn its beauty returns to it. (15)

( *Behind the scenes.* )

Bhurivasu who was ready to rush into the massive fire,

disregarding the king who fell at his feet with Nandana, at once falls back at my words, filled with intense joy and amazemet. (16)

MA'D. and MAK —( *Looking up, joyfully* ) Revered lady, we congratulate you.

That Yoginî descends from the sky parting the cloud, of whom this shower of nectareous water in the form of words surpasses the shower of water from the clouds. (17).

KA'M.—Welcome, welcome is this to us!

MA'L.—Fortunately have I come to life again after a long time.

KA'M.—( *With tears of joy* ) Come, come, daughter, Màlatî.

MA'L.—What! Your reverence (here)! (*She falls at her feet with these words* ).

KA'M.—(*Raising and embracing her, and smelling her on the head* ).

Live daughter; give life to him whom you prize as much as life; let your friends also live; and enliven me and your dear friend with your limbs cooling ( as if ) by contact with snow. (18).

MA D.—Friend Makaranda, now ( life in ) this mortal world has become acceptable (worth living) to Màdhava

MAK.—( *With joy* ) It is just so.

MAD. and LAV.—Dear friend, you whose sight ( again ) was past all hope, honour us with an embrace.

MA'L.—My dear friends! ( *She embraces them* ).

KA'M.—Dear sons, what is this ( how did all this come to pass ) ?

MA'D and MAK.—Revered lady,

Subjected to affliction by the evil in the form of Kapâlakundalâ's wrath,* we have been rescued from the calamity by this venerable lady with a resolute effort. (19)

KA'M.—How comes this to be the consequence of Aghoraghanta's being slain!

MAD. and LAV.—Oh wonder! How charming is the final issue brought about by Fate, though repeatedly cruel.

( *Enter* Saudâminî ).

SAU.—( *Approaching* ) Venerable Kámandakî, here bows to you that old pupil of yours.

---

* Or ( if व्यापद्: be taken as ab. sing. qualifying कृच्छ्रात् ,) from the calamity in which affliction was caused to us &c. we have been &c.

KA'M.—Ah, it is the good Saudáminí !

MA'D. and MAK.—( *In amazement* ) How strange !

This is Saudáminí, the first pupil of her reverence and an object of her favour ! Every thing is now explained.

KA'M.—Come, come, thou that possessest a store of merit arising from thy gift of life to a number of persons. What a pleasure it is to see thee after a long time ! Gladden my body, although it is filled with great delight, oh treasure of friendliness, with an embrace and desist from obeisance. (20)

Moreover.

Thou alone whose attainment of miraculous power is inviolable art adorable to the world by acts of this nature which surpass (even those of) the *Bodhisatvas*: thou (the plant of ) whose conduct, with its seed laid in our former familiarity has (thus) yielded its wealth of fruit. (21)

MAD & LAV.—Is this the noble Saudâminî ?

MA'L.—Yes. She, indeed, loving us owing to her connection with the revered lady, reproved Kapâlakundalá, took me to her lodging and there ministered to my comfort with an affection not different from that of her reverence. Nay, she bent her course hither with the keepsake of the *Bakula* wreath and preserved you all.

MAD & LAV.—Our younger preceptress has been very gracious to us.

MA'D. & MAK.—Oh, how marvellous !

Even the gem that grants all desires of the heart requires the exertion of the manifestation of a wish ( on one's part); but this noble lady, methinks, worked this wonder without a solicitation. (22)

SAU.—( *To herself.* ) Oh, their extreme goodness makes me blush. ( *Aloud.* ) Revered mistress, here is a letter addressed to Màdhava, of long life, written in Bhûrivasu's presence by the king, the lord of Padmâvatí, with the approval of the over-joyed Nandana. (*Hands over the letter.*)

KA'M.—( *Takes it and reads* ) All hail to you ! ! The king thus sends you his greeting—

We are greatly pleased with thee, our son-in-law, foremost of the meritorious and the praiseworthy, of noble descent, with all calamities surmounted and magnanimous. And in token of our pleasure and to give thee delight, we, to-day, bestow Madayantikâ upon thy beloved friend though already united to him by her affection. (23)

( *To Mâdhava* ) Hear, my son.

MA'D.—I have heard it. Now all my wishes are attained.

MA'L.—Fortunately the dart of apprehension has been removed from my heart.

LAV.—Now all the desires of the noble Màdhava and Mâlatî, without exception, have borne fruit.

MAK.—( *Looking forth.* ) Oh! Here come Avalokitá and Buddharakshitá, accompanied by Kalahamsaka, dancing in the transport of joy.

( *Enter* Avalokitâ, Buddharakshitá *and* Kalahamsaka).

ALL.—( *Dancing in a variety of ways, they approach* Kâmandakî *and say with a bow* )—

Glory to you, the treasure of (all these) achievements. ( *To* Mâdhava ) Victory to you, Mádhava, the delighter of Makaranda; full moon*, we offer our felicitations to you ( or, fortune smiles upon you ).

( *All look smilingly* )

LAV.—Who is not filled with glee on this occasion for rejoicing in every way ?

KA'M.—Just so. Has there ever been an affair ( a Prakarana ), full of such incidents, so exceedingly wonderful, varied, charming and ennobling ?

SAU.—This is all the more charming in this that the cherished object of the ministers, Bhûrivasu and Devaráta, regarding the alliance of their children, has been accomplished in the long run.

MA'L.—( *To herself* ) How does she mean !

M'AD. & MAK.—( *With eager curiosity* ) Revered lady, the course of events is one way, while the words of the noble lady imply another.

LAV.—( *Aside.* ) Revered lady, what is to be said ?

KA'M.—( *To herself* ) Now all our anxiety is removed on account of Nandana being won over to our side

---

* Or, moon that have waxed full ( *i. e.* gained all your ends. )

through our connection with Madayantikâ. ( *Aloud* ) Sons, not indeed is the course of events the other way. In the days of pupilage a solemn agreement was made by the two ( ministers ) in the presence of us and of Saudâminî, that they would necessarily unite in wedlock their children. It was the anger of the King and of his minister that was thus shunned.

MA'L.—Oh the concealment !

MA'D. & MAK.—Marvellous ! Triumphant are the plans of the great which conceal the object in view but lead to blissful results.

KA'M.—Boy,

The happy union of you two, of long life, which had been cherished by the mind just from the beginning, has been accomplished by our merits and my efforts; the pains of my two disciples too have been rewarded; also the union of your dearest friend with his beloved has been effected beyond the shadow of a doubt; and delight has been brought to the king and Nândana: if there be any thing more that you wish for, let that also be declared. ( 24 )

MA'D.—( *Bowing with joy.* ) Revered lady, is there any object further than this to be wished for ! Still, let there be this by the favour of your revered self :—

May the good, rid of all evil occurrences, be ever happy; may kings guard the earth ever abiding by law ; may the clouds, ever send down their showers on the earth in season by the merit ( of the people ); and may the subjects, highly delighting in the conversation ( or society ) of their relatives, kinsmen and friends, be in affluent circumstances ( lit. enjoy pleasures ) ! ! !* (25)

[ *Exeunt Omnes.*

END OF ACT. X

End of the play 'MA'LATÎ MA'DHAVA',

---

* Instead of this some Mss. read:—

May good ( *v. l.* prosperity ) attend all the worlds; may the multitudes of creatures be devoted to the benefit of others; may evil disappear; and may the people be happy in all respects ! !

# NOTES.

## Act I.

P. 1 **मालतीमाधवम्**—Explain मालत्या सहितः माधवः मालतीमाधवः तमधिकृत्य कृतं नाटकमभेदोपचारात्तथा.

**सानन्दं**—Adv. to विशति; joyfully because he readily found a hole to hide himself in; or with Jag., it may be taken ( and which is perhaps better as this avoids अस्थानस्थपददोष ) with नन्दिहस्ता०. **नन्दी**—The principal attendant and door-keeper of Śiva. *Cf.* Kum. III. 41. The name, however, is applied to different attendants of Śiva; *cf.* आद्यः कनकनन्दी च गिरिकाख्यो द्वितीयकः । सोमनन्दी तृतीयस्तु विज्ञेया नन्दिनस्त्रयः ॥ **मुरजरवाहूत**—The sound of the tabor is mistaken for the rumbling of clouds on hearing which peacocks are said to scream and dance in joy. *Cf.* संगीतमृदंगध्वनितेषु केकाशङ्कया ......मयूरमुखानि स्थगयति । Kád. मृदङ्गशब्दापगमादलास्याः (क्रीडामयूराः) Ragh. XVI. 14; see also 64. **अग्ररन्ध्र**—अग्रं च तद्रन्ध्रं च. This is a Karm. comp. and must be so dissolved, the two, अग्र and रन्ध्र, being related to each other as अवयव and अवयविन् and thus there being सामानाधिकरण्य; see our note on अग्रहस्त Śak. p. 92; or on Kum. V. 63 and *cf.* Malli. on the same or on Kir. V. 29. It is equivalent to रन्ध्राग्रं the forepart of the nostril ( which is put for the whole नासारन्ध्रं ). **भोग**—the hood or the body. **उड्डीन**—p. p. of डी with उत्. **विधुतयः**—Shakings, rapid or forcible movements. There is no idea of fear. Gaṇapati shook his trunk simply to get rid of the unwelcome obstruction into his nose. The entrance of the serpent and his being shaken off refer by implication to public calamities and their being warded off by Gajánana's favour. According to the Com. Trip. the fig. in the stanza is Kávyalinga. For the figures उक्तिपोष and जाति noticed by Jag., see com. Jag. finds in some of the epithets allusions to the monsoon &c. to be described later on.

P. 2. **आपीड**—A garland worn on the crown of the head. 'शिखास्वापीडशेखरौ' Amara. Lit. a garland closely woven. **संकुल**—as the skulls dipped into the water it overflowed ( कपालैः संकुलं &c. as Jag. takes it ). Or with Trip. कपालेषु संकुलं, अतएव गलत् तत्पूरणादधःस्रवत् &c. ). Water trickled down from the skulls as they were filled with it. **विद्युत्प्राय०**—Better dissolve विद्युत्प्रायं यद्...पुटज्योतिः &c. **केतकशिखा०**—*Cf.* J.'s remarks. The केतक is one of the flowers not offered to Śiva but the poet seems to have forgotten it. **संदिग्ध**—The crescent of the moon is mistaken for a tender Ketaka flower. The close resemblance between the two causes such an illusion. The fig. is संदेह ( or संशयोपमा as Dandin calls it ) Mark the root sense; cf. our note on भ्रूपेर्जालविनिःसृतैर्वलभयः संदिग्धपारावताः । Vik. III. 2. जूट—The mass of. Trip. remarks:—अत्र रूपकसंदेहानुविद्धा स्वभावोक्तिरलंकारः । अत्रेश्वरस्य जटाजूटालंकृतस्य प्रशान्ताकारप्रतीतेर्धीरशान्तः कथानायकः सूचितः । जटा इति कर्तृबहुत्वेन नायकनायिकाबहुत्वम् , भूतेशस्येत्युपसर्जन्येन जटा इति स्वातन्त्र्येण नायकस्य स्वप्रयोजननिर्वाहेऽन्यपारतन्त्र्यम् , कामन्दक्यादितपस्विनीजनस्येव तत्कार्यनिर्वहणनिरन्तरोद्योगित्वं सूचितमिति मनाक्काव्यार्थसमुन्मेष ऊह्यः ॥

On the ingenuity of those commentators who detect hidden references to some minute details described further on in the play, Trip. has this rather severe comment:—एताभ्यां श्लोकाभ्यां जलधरसमयप्रारम्भः सूच्यते । तस्य निर्वहणसंधौ वक्ष्यमाणत्वात् । मुखसंधिसूचितस्यैव निर्वोढव्यत्वात् । तत्र कपोलेत्यनेन बलाकावलिः, जलक्षरणेन वृष्टिः, विद्युदित्यनेन च विद्युत् , केतकशिखेत्यनेन केतकोद्गमः, भुजगवलयबद्धजटापटलत्वेन जलदोदयः, मुरजध्वानेन गर्जितशब्दः, कौमारबर्हीति मयूरहर्षश्च सूच्यत इति केश्चिद्व्याचक्ष्यते । तदेतच्छब्दशक्त्या प्रतीयतेऽर्थशक्त्या वेति त एव जानन्ति । नन्वेते शब्दाः प्रकृतार्थनियन्त्रिता अपि शक्त्यन्तरबलादन्वितमर्थान्तरं प्रत्याययन्तीति कस्यचिद्व्युत्पन्नस्य प्रतीतिः । अर्थोऽपि प्रकृता नैतादृशस्यार्थान्तरस्य प्रतीतौ समर्थोऽनुभूयते सहृदयैः । कथांशानामेव निर्वहणे निरूप्यमाणानां मुखसंधौ सूचननिर्बन्धः । न तु तत्र वक्ष्यमाणस्य सर्वर्तुवनवर्णनादेरपि । नैषोऽर्थः कवेर्विवक्षागोचरोऽपि । तस्मान्नायं ध्वनिमार्गविदां पन्थाः ॥

दन्तश्रेणिषु &c.—This is a Prakshipta sloka. The Com. Trip. also remarks ' दन्तश्रेणिषु ' इत्यादिश्लोकद्वयं प्रक्षिप्तमिति पूर्वैरव्याकृतमपि क्वचित्पुस्तकेषु दृष्टत्वादस्माभिर्व्याख्यायते ॥ The sl. describes the universal form ( विराट्स्व० ) of Śiva. दन्त०संग०—The whole should have been compounded; it is a सापेक्षत्वेपि गमकत्वात्समासः. दन्तश्रेणिषु संगलन्त्यः कलकलसहितेन व्यावर्तनेन ( by their rolling along ) व्याकुलाः thrown into commotion. नासाश्च लोचनानि च कर्णाश्चैव कुञ्जाश्च कुहराणि च तेषु; Karm. उद्गतः गद्गदः यस्मिन्कर्मणि तथा ध्वानिनः ध्वननशीलाः । मन्थि—Joints or cheek-bones. चूडास्रवन्ती—The Ganges. ब्रह्मकपाल०—an allusion to the severance of Brahman's head by Śiva. उल्बण—swelling into a mass, appearing prominent. स्वभावोक्तिः अलंकारः Trip.

पक्ष्माली०—This sl. looks like Bhavabhûti's and is so quoted by Śár., as remarked by Dr. Bhandarkar. ईषद् &c—ईषत् विघटितं मुकुलं यस्य slightly opened. अर्चिः &c.—अर्चिर्भिः निष्टप्तः यः चूडाशशी तस्माद्गलितः यः सुधासारः तेन झंकारिणौ कोणौ यस्य. As the flames rose up all round, the crescent on the crest was heated and nectar trickled down from it on the corners of the eye तार्तीयीकं—तृतीयमेव ता०; so द्वैतीयीक, द्वितीय. ' तीयादीकक् स्वार्थे वाच्यः' Vartt. on Pân. V. 3. 48. पुरारिः ( more usually called त्रिपुरारि, त्रिपुरान्तक &c. )—Śiva who destroyed the cities of gold, silver and iron built by Maya for the demons in heaven, in mid-air and on the earth. See Mah. Bhá. VII. 203, 62-77. **मदनप्लोषणं**—For the story see Kum III. 64-72; उदात्तालंकारः Trip.

These two ślokas form what is technically called नान्दी, which also constitutes the usual *Mangala* which is necessary for the unimpeded completion of a poetic composition. For the def. of नान्दी see com. p. 2. On the efficacy of Mangala *cf.* Patanjali's Mah. Bhá.—मङ्गलादीनि हि शास्त्राणि प्रथन्ते वीरपुरुषकाणि च भवन्त्यायुष्मत्पुरुषकाणि चाध्येतारश्च सिद्धार्था यथास्युः ।

P. 4. **नान्द्यन्ते**—The question as to the propriety and meaning of this stage direction has been fully discussed in the com., and by us elsewhere. ( See Śak. or Vikra. ); the stanza forming the *Mangala* is placed first as remarked by the Com.; *cf.* in this respect the Sûtra of Páṇ. वृद्धिरादैच्, where वृद्धि being an auspicous word is placed first. **सूत्रधारः**—See com.; some explain the term as नर्तनीयकथासूत्रं प्रथमं येन सूच्यते । रङ्गभूमिं समासाद्य सूत्रधारः स उच्यते ॥ The term seemes to have originally arisen out of the shows of puppets which must have preceded the Drama, the exhibitor of the shows holding the threads and moving the puppets as he desired. **उदितभूयिष्ठः**—The greater part of the disc of the sun was visible above the horizon. *Cf.* सद्मभूयिष्ठा द्रविणराशयः Ragh. IV. 70. दग्धभूयिष्ठं वनं; अभिरूपभूयिष्ठा परिषद् Śak. Prelude.—**दीप**—is more poetical than दीपक, the lamp of the whole world; *cf.* जज्ञे विवस्वाञगदेकदीपः । Udár. I. 8. Mark the alliteration. **उपतिष्ठे**—The Atm. by the Vártt. उपाद्देवपूजासङ्गतिकरण०; see Sid. Kau. on Pán. I. 3. 25.; or according to Trip. by पथ्याराधनयोश्च ( I will propitiate ).

P. 5. **विश्वमूर्ते**—'सूर्य आत्मा जगतस्तस्थुषश्च' इति श्रुतेः । Tripurári. **धुर्यां लक्ष्मीं**—धुरि साधुः धुरं वहतीति वा धुर्या तां the wealth of mental power and means leading to the successful conduct of business; hence the glory of success as a leader ( here of a dramatic party ); 'the power or resources of a leader.' Dr. Bhân. **अथ**—इह *V. l.* 'in the present undertaking'-would be a better reading. Mark the appropriateness of the terms लक्ष्मी and देव. All the epithets of the sun in this stanza are aptly chosen. **यद्यत्**—तत्—here तत् refers collectively to all that is indicated by यद्यत्. This stanza is quoted in Kâv. P. VII. to show that the correlative ( where it refers to a thing in its generic form ) need not be repeated although the relative may be repeated ( referring to a thing in all its specific forms ). **भद्रं भद्रं**—The repetition may refer to the totality of good ( every kind of blessing ), or the first भद्र may be taken as an adj., meaning 'excellent, of the best kind;'

see com ; मङ्गलानुबन्धीनि मङ्गलानि प्रयच्छेत्यर्थः remarks Trip. भूयसे मङ्गलाय–for supreme bliss. See the commentator's remarks. The final object of the drama is the attainment of the triad of human objects, धर्म, अर्थ and काम ( कार्यं त्रिवर्गः D. R. ), and thereby prepare the way for the fourth, *viz*. Moksha. रङ्गमङ्गलानि— the theatrical preliminaries; see com. कालप्रिय०—The proper form is कालप्रियानाथ ( as in the Maha. ch. ); the shortening of the आ of प्रिया may be explained by ङ्यापोः संज्ञाछन्दसोर्बहुलम् । Pán. VI. 3. 63. ०वास्तव्यः—वसतीति residing in. The affix तव्य here indicates the agent, by the Vártt. वसेस्तव्यत्कर्तरि णिच्च । प्रकरण-does not appear to be used in its technical sense here but merely in that of a play. विद्वत्परिषद्—the audience composed of appreciative men. ( परितः सीदन्त्यस्यामिति परिषद् ).

P. 6. भावः—The Sútradhára is technically so addressed. भूम्ना–Excess, according to Jag; प्राचुर्येण......। अनेन रसैकप्रवणत्वं प्रबन्धस्य जीवितभूतो गुणो दर्शितः । Trip. रसानां—the principal sentiment and its accessaries. प्रयोगः—delineation, development. औद्धत्यं— Adventurousness, bold steps taken, such as Mak.'s killing the tiger, the selling of human flesh by Mádh, and his encounter with Aghoraghanta in Act V, Makaranda's personating Málatî, the secret marriage of Mak. and Mada., &c. They help the growth of love and hasten the final catastrophe. कामसूत्रं—See Jag. कामः अनुरागः स एव वर्तिष्यमाणसर्वकार्यबीजभूतत्वात्सूत्रमिव सूत्रम् । Trip.; or कामस्य सूत्रमिव सूत्रं; सूत्र properly a thread; hence metaphorically (by लक्षणा) the various incidents leading to the development of love. Perhaps there is a reference here to Vâtsyáyana's work of the same name, some of the principles laid down in which the poet follows further on.

P. 7. पद्मपुरं—is not the same as पद्मावती as remarked by Jag. but is situated somewhere near Chandrapura or Chándá in the Central Provinces. तैत्तिरीयिणः—*V. l.* followers of the Taittiriya *Sákhá* of the Krishṇayajurveda; तित्तिरिणा प्रोक्तं छन्दः तैत्तिरीयं तदधीयते इति तैत्तिरीयाः is the form directly got from the Sûtra 'तित्तिरिवरतन्तु—' Pán. IV. 3. 102, and has therefore been adopted in the text ( which is also Trip.'s reading ). The form तैत्तिरीयिन् is inaccurate as इन् is not available in this case. This is probably formed on the analogy of काश्यपिन् or शौनकिन् ; or we must add the मत्वर्थीय इन्—तैत्तिरीयं स्वाध्यायत्वेन विद्यते एषाम्. चरण—followers of a particular branch of the Veda, a Vedic-guild; see com. पंक्ति०—पंक्तिं पावयन्तीति । Bráhmaṇas so holy by their Vedic studies and purity of conduct that by their very presence they can purify a whole पंक्ति ( men sitting in the same line with them to dine );

*cf.* Manu III. 183.—अपाङ्क्त्योपहता पंक्तिः पाव्यते यैर्द्विजोत्तमैः । तान्निबोधत कार्त्स्न्येन द्विजाग्र्यान्पंक्तिपावनान् ॥ also 184; see Jag. also. **सोमपीथिन्**—Also ०पीतिन्; सोमस्य पीथं or पीथः अस्यास्तीति; पीथ-थं is a Vedic word formed fr. पा + थ an Unádi aff; ( Un. II. 7. ). The आ is changed to ई by घुमास्था—Pán. VI. 4. 66.

**श्रोत्रियः**—छन्दः अधीते, irregularly formed from छन्दस्; see Pán. V. 2. 84. **इष्टं**—एकाग्निकर्म हवनं त्रैतायां यच्च हूयते । अन्तर्वेद्यां च यद्दानमिष्टं तदभिधीयते ॥ **पूर्त**—Charitable works such as digging wells, &c. वापीकूपतडागादिदेवतायतनानि च । अन्नप्रदानमारामाः पूर्तमित्यभिधीयते ॥ These are enjoined on every mortal; see Manu IV. 226. **दारान०**—पुत्रार्थं क्रियते भार्या पुत्रः पिण्डप्रयोजनः । इति स्मरणात्; *cf.* प्रजायै गृहमेधिनाम्.' Ragh. I. 7. The com. Trip. notices the fig. Parisankhyá in this Śloka.

P. 8. **तदामुष्यायणः**—Now the Sûtra. proceeds to mention the name and family of the poet according to Bharata's dictum प्रसाद्य रङ्गं विधिवत्कवेर्नाम च कीर्तयेत् । Nat. V. 154; *cf.* also Sáh. D. रूपकस्य कवेराख्यां गोत्राद्यपि स कीर्तयेत् । VI. 28. अमुष्य ख्यातस्य पुत्रः आमुष्यायणः; fr. अमुष्य and the aff फक् ( आयन्. ). There is अलुक् of the gen. by the Vártt. आमुष्यायणामुष्यपुत्रिकामुष्यकुलिकेति च । One born of him, the well-known one; hence a descendant or scion of an illustrious family. प्रख्यातात्पितुरुत्पन्न आमुष्यायण उच्यते । Ratnamála. **सौहृदेन**—Though सौहार्द presents no difficulty of grammar ( that being directly got from the Sûtra हृद्भग—Pán. VII. 3 19. see com. ) and is more usual, सौहृद is by no means of rare occurrence; *cf.* यत्सौहृदादपि जनाः शिथिलीभवन्ति Mrch. I. 13; also Vik. I. 9.; सौहृदादपृथगाश्रयामिमां Utt. I. 45. Jag. thus accounts for the form. In interpreting a Sútra we must take the words just as they are stated ( प्रतिपदोक्त ); in the present case it is the word हृद् substituted for हृदय that takes Vṛddhi and not the independent word हृद्, that we have in सौहृद्; or by the Paribháshá संज्ञापू० ( *i. e.* the operation of a rule stated using a संज्ञा such as गुण, वृद्धि &c., is optional ) there is no उभयपदवृद्धि. See com. for the full discussion. Vámana in his Káv. Sûtras derives the word from सुहृदय—सौहृददौर्हृदशब्दावाणि हृद्भावात् । V. 2. 83. The com. कामधेनु on the Sûtra says—शोभनं हृदयं यस्य दुष्टं हृदयं यस्य इति विग्रहसिद्धाभ्यां सुहृदयदुर्हृदयशब्दाभ्यां भावार्थे हायनान्तयुवादिभ्योऽण् इत्यणिकृते सति हृदयस्य हृल्लेखयदण्लासेषु इति हृदादेशे तद्धितेष्वचामादेः इत्यादिवृद्धौ च सत्यां सौहृददौर्हृद शब्दौ सिद्धौ । **भरताः**—stage players, actors; भरतस्य मुनेः शिष्याः; भरत + अण्; there is no Vṛddhi of the initial vowel as it is a संज्ञा.

**वाचोयुक्ति**—वाचः युक्तिः an aluk comp.; see the Vártt on Pán. VI. 3. 21, quoted in the com.; a dexterous or skilful arrangement of words, a clever declaration or remark. See Dr. Bhándárker's notes.

नः—dramatic writers. इह—in this matter, *viz.* writing dramas; perhaps the drama had got into disodour with the Pandits when Bhav. was just rising. किमपि—Something inexpressible; inexpressible on account of its supreme greatness, excellence &c.; or littleness, worthlesness. Both the senses seem to be intended here ( see com. ), though the word is generally used in a good sense. In either way the expression is ironical. Mark the maxims quoted by Jag. नहि बधिरे &c. नहि संम्राज &c. उत्पत्स्यते &c.—is equivalent to य उत्पत्स्यते तं प्रति एव यत्नः. Here the relative and correlative can be easily got from the context and so are omitted. The stanza is cited in the K. P. as an instance of such an omission. निरवधिः, विपुला—The significance of these epithets is explained in the com.

P. 9. उपनिषदां—The Upanishads are the philosophic portions of the Vedas. They teach *Brahmavidyá,* the true nature of Brahma and the cosmos. The word is thus derived by the Vedantists :—उपनिपूर्वस्य क्विप्प्रत्ययान्तस्य षद्लृ (सद्) विशरणगत्यवसादनेषु इत्यस्य धातोः ( *i. e.* of सद् with उप and नि ) उपनिषदिति रूपम् । तत्र उपशब्दः सामीप्यमाचष्टे । तच्च संकोचकाभावात्सर्वान्तरे प्रत्यगात्मनि पर्यवस्यति । निशब्दो निश्चयवचनः । That which certainly destroys primal ignorance by giving a correct knowledge of Brahma and cuts off the bonds of wordly existence. गर्भजन्मजरारोगाद्यनर्थपूगं निशातयति परं वा ब्रह्म गमयति अविद्यादिसंसारकारणं चात्यन्तमवसादयति इत्युपनिषद् उपनिपूर्वस्य सदेरेवमर्थश्रवणात् । Saṃkaráchárya. Others derive it fr. सद् with उपनि ' to sit close to' and it means the secret knowledge got from the Guru by sitting close to him; and secondly the works setting forth such knowledge.

सांख्यस्य—Sámkhya is the system of philosophy developed and propounded by Kapila. It comes from Samkhyá ( संख्यया निर्वृत्तं; अण् *i. e.* अ ); it is the proper enumeration of the true principles, which, according to the Sáṃkhyas, are 25. A correct knowledge of these, leading to the discrimination of Purusha from the other 24 *tatvas*, effects *Moksha*. The primary principles are two, *viz.* Pradhâna, otherwise called Prakriti, and Purusha. Purusha takes no part in the creation of the world but is a passive looker on. The whole universe is the development of Prakriti constituted by the three qualities सत्व, रजस् and तमस् equally balanced, which evolves 23 other principles ( मूलप्रकृतिरविकृतिर्महदाद्याः प्रकृतिविकृतयः पञ्च । षोडशकस्तु विकारो न प्रकृतिर्न विकृतिः पुरुषः ॥ Sám. Ká. 3).

The chief feature of this philosophy is that it does not consider God as the creator and the ruler of the world. See A. Dic. and our notes on Kum. II. 13.

योगस्य—The Yoga philosophy, another of the six Dars'anas, (regarded as a further development of the Sáṃkya philosophy) is attributed to Patanjali. It admits the principles of the Saṃkhyas but adds one more, Isvara, to the list. This Isvara is क्लेशकर्मविपाकाशयैरपरामृष्टः पुरुषविशेषः ( Pat. Yog. I. 24 ) while मोक्ष (कैवल्य ) is attained सत्वपुरुषयोः शुद्धिसाम्ये (Yog. III. 55; see also 50). Its chief aim is to teach the means by which the individual soul can be united with the Supreme spirit, and many elaborate rules are given for the proper practice of *Yoga* or abstract meditation.

तत्कथनेन किं—*i. e.* To mention these will be simply pedantic. The poet, however, does imply that he was well-versed in all the afore-mentioned Śástras. प्रौढत्वं—Power of expression, felicity of speech; it is the art of expressing one and the same idea in a condensed form ( laconically ) or *Vice versa*; see. com. उदारता—richness of expression, command of language. अर्थगौरवं-Depth of meaning, the art of making words express a manifold and charming sense. See com. Herein the poet states his qualifications to write a drama. We must not consider this as pedantry, as a writer was obliged to make such a statement in those days when manuscript copies of a book were the only means of circulation and people were not tempted to make such copies unless an author was known to be a man of extraordinary ability and merits.

P. 10. प्रकरण—One of the ten Rûpakas. The special features of a Pra. are—The story should be imaginary and must be human. Love should be the principal sentiment. The hero must be of the kind धीरप्रशान्त 'firm and patient.' For other particulars see Intro. and Technical Remarks. कुशीलवाः—Amara gives कुशीलव as a synom. of चारण a bard; but it seems here to mean a singer, or an actor. Bha D. derives this as कुत्सितं (because they are whimsical and sing well only when they are in a mood to do so ) शीलमस्त्येषां, व being added by अन्यत्रापि दृश्यते Vártt. on Pán. V. 2. 109; or as कुत्सितं शीलं वान्ति, क ( अ ) being added to वा.

संगीतप्रयोगेण—संगीत properly means the triple symphony of song, instrumental music and dancing or pantomimic representation; गीतं वाद्यं तथा नृत्यं ( or नृत्तं ) त्रयं संगीतमुच्यते । By *lakshaṇâ* it sometimes signifies one of these. Here it must be taken to mean '*acting*', to suit the actor's reply—या यस्य युज्यते भूमिका &c. **वर्ग्यः**—वर्गे भवः one belonging to the same class or company; here an actor; वृन्दभेदाः समैर्वर्गः । Amara. **सौगत**—a follower of Sugata or Buddha. **अधीते**—Lit. has been practising; *i. e.* it has been assigned to.

P. 11. **वर्णिकापरिग्रहः**—वर्णिका is colour or paint necessary for the change of form ( रूपान्तर or भूमिका ); hence by *lakshaná* 'a character or part'. **मालती, माधव**--Mark how the names ( also मकरन्द, कलहंसक &c. ) are adopted from nature. They are all significant terms. See also com.

P. 12. **तत्प्रयोगात्**—तत् of course refers to प्रकरणं ( मा० वं नाम ) p. 10. **कामन्दकी, अव०**—Mark the derivations. The former knows all the intricacies of the policy taught by Kâmandaka; the latter is scrupulously *watchful* of the good of those in whom her mistress is interested. This way of announcing the entrance of a *pátra* is called प्रयोगातिशय. **नेपथ्यं**—Dress.

P. 13. **अपि नाम**—expresses hope, expectation; it is likely that, I wish that. The expression is of frequent occurrence; *cf. infra* p. p. 24, 34, 59, 61, &c. **आन्तरज्ञेन**—Knowing the inward feelings of persons. The left eye, as if knowing the uneasiness of Kâma.'s mind throbbed and dispelled her anxiety and hence Kâma. regards this as a kindly act on the part of the eye. This is the view of Jaga. and the Com. Tripurári. *Cf.* अन्तर्गतं प्राणभृतां हि वेद सर्वं भवान्भावमतोभिधास्ये । Ragh. II. 43. Dr. Bhándákar takes आन्तरज्ञ to mean 'knowing the interior or hidden secret of things' rather than of Káma., remarking that the eye does not tell what passes in Káma.'s mind but what the result will be. But in this case इव must be taken with विवृण्वता and thus becomes inappropriate; for the eye does not as if declare but *does* declare.

**वामकेनापि दाक्षिण्यं**—Virodhâbhâsa. Mark the double *entendre* on the words वामक and दाक्षिण्य. The former means (1) left; and (2) perverse, unfavourable; the latter (1) the state of being the right; and (2) the state of being well disposed, favourableness, courteousness or kindliness. So there is a double Virodha ( *i. e.* between left and right and perverse and auspicious ) The apparent antithesis is removed by taking दक्षिण to mean favourable in the first case and वाम in the sense of left in the second.

**चीर० पिण्डपात**—For the meanings of these see com.;-**परिग्रहां**—Who should, therefore, be least expected to take interest in worldly matters. **संसारावग्रह**—The chains or fetters of worldly life.

P. 14. विधेयविषये—In the matter of what is to be done; or to the office of an agent. अस्मत्सौदामिनी०—Trip. takes अस्मत् separately as ab. pl., saying अस्मत् एव मत्कारितैव and remarks—मम च सौदामिन्याश्च समक्षमिति व्याख्यानमनुपपन्नम् । स च देवदत्तश्च ताविति त्यदादीनि सर्वैर्नित्यमित्येकशेषप्रसङ्गात् । द्विपर्यन्तादीनामेव त्यदादित्वामिति तु त्यदाद्यत्वमात्रनिरासार्थम् । आन्वीक्षिकी—आन्वीक्षिकी दण्डनीतिस्तर्कविद्यार्थशास्त्रयोः । Amara; fr. अन्वीक्षा + इक ( ठञ् ) by प्रयोजनम् । Pân. V. 1. 107 + ई; प्रत्यक्षपरोक्षाभ्यामीक्षितस्यार्थस्यानु पश्चादीक्षणमन्वीक्षा सा प्रयोजनं यस्याः सान्वीक्षिक्यनुमानविद्या न्यायदर्शनवैशेषिकादिका । com. on Kâman II. 7, 1 The knowledge of this philosophy is indispensable to a politician; for it is प्रदीपः सर्वविद्यानामुपायः सर्वकर्मणाम् । आश्रयः सर्वधर्माणां विद्योद्देशे प्रकीर्तिता ॥ Vâts. on Gau. Nya. sû. I. 1. कुण्डिनपुर—The ancient capital of Vidarbha, probably the modern Beder. पद्मावती—the scene of the play. General Cunningham considers this as identical with the modern Narwar in Mâlvâ, situated on the river Sind corresponding to the Sindhu of the play. But from what the poet says about its position at the end of the fourth act, and again at the beginning of the ninth, Dr. Bhândârkar thinks that as the town was situated at the confluence of the rivers Pârâ and Sindhu, Narwar could hardly have been the ancient Pad. since it it situated about 25 miles above the confluence of the Sind and Parbati. The sight of the ancient town, therefore, must be looked for somewhere nearer. See. Dr. Bhândarkar's notes. प्रयोचनार्थम्—That he may endear himself to the world by being acquainted with its manners and ways; hence to know how to act in the world, to gain worldly experience; see Jaga:; or as Dr. Bhândarkar takes it 'for being seen and liked by the people.' प्रकटीकृतः—sent into the world at large. The fig. is समुच्चय.

P. 15. तां याचते &c.—Notice the alliterations in this line. नर्मसुहृत—This shows why the king was easily induced to interfere on behalf of Nandana. नरपतेः and नृपमुखेन ( न श्लाघ्यवरगुणेन ) are significant: the former implies that he, as king, could command; the latter suggests absence of such merits in Nandana as Màdhava has ( and hence the necessity to move the king to exert his influence in his favour ). निरपेक्षता—indifference, absence of any reference to him. विवृत०—'Who have given indication of their love for each other. भाव feeling, love; hence also 'the seat of love;' the heart. बालत्वात्—बालश्च बाला च बालौ तयोर्भावः ; hence ignorant of the art of dissimulation. बाल्यमिह प्रथमयौवनं Trip. आर्यः &c.—cf. Trip. तथा सति अकुण्ठितोत्साहयोस्तयोः स्वत एवाभिमतसंघटनं सिध्येत् । अन्यथा गुरुजनेन

विदितमस्मच्चापलमिति लज्जया तदुद्योगभङ्गादभिलषितः कृतकपरिणयो न निष्पद्येतेति भावः । **अनुरागप्रवादः**—अत्र नायकयोरन्योन्यानुरागस्य बीजस्योपन्यासादुपक्षेपो नाम मुखसन्धेरङ्गमुक्तं भवति । Trip.

P. 16. **बाह्यैः** &c.—This is the crooked policy, first chalked out and practised by Cháṇakya, which appears to be much in vogue in the times of Bhavabhûti, Daṇḍin &c. Bhavabhûti, though he appears from his Mál. Mád. to be an admirer of the policy, does not make his hero commit homicide without extreme provocation and just cause, nor is Kámandakî's policy stained with bloodshed, as in the case of some of the *Kumaras* of the Daśakumáracharita.

**प्रगुण**—may mean (1) honestly, excellently, favourably ( to his designs ); प्रकृष्टा गुणा यस्मिन्कर्मणि तद्यथा तथा च रमणीयं च; or (2) exceedingly. Further on ( sl. 16 ) it means 'worthy, befitting.' **विद्वान्**—'one adept in policy.' The figure in this sl. is समुच्चय.

**तेन** &c.—On one pretext or another, suggesting several reasons. **वचनोपन्यासेन**—उपन्यास a statement or proposal made before a person; hence वचनो० proposal or pretext to go out.

**गाढोत्कण्ठा**—may also be taken as part of the comp. ०लुलितैः as Jaga. does; but taken separately it better explains why Mála. pines ( ताम्यति ). **उत्कण्ठा**—Great uneasisness or pain of mind caused by love being not gratified (by postponement of marriage, &c.); it is defined as रागे त्वलब्धविषये वेदना महती तु या । संशोषणी तु गात्राणां तामुत्कण्ठां विदुर्बुधाः ॥ See Meg. II. 23. **ललित०**—*v. l.* see com.; it rather means ललितं यथा तथा लुलितैः gracefully crushed or drooping. ललितं लुलितं ( unnerved or spiritless condition ) येषां will also do. This change in Mála. is marked by Mâdhava also ; see sl 22 below. The word लुलित frequently occurs in Bhava.; *cf. infra* III. 6. IV. 3. Uttara. I. 24, &c. This stanza is quoted in the D. R. with the reading लुलितललितैः as an illustration of youthful persons serving as the Vibhávas of रति or lo·e, the Stháyîbhâva of शृङ्गार. **अङ्गकैः**—Here the affix क which expresses pity ( by ' अनुकम्पायां ' Pán. V. 3. 76; for her limbs were reduced to a pitiable condition ) indicates the greatness of her emaciation which, in its turn, suggests that her love-longing is great. *cf.* ताम्यति युवतिसार्थकः; Rat. I. 14. This sl. is quoted in the K. P. as an illustration of the aff. क suggesting विप्रलम्भशृङ्गार–अत्रानुकम्पाव्यङ्ग्येन सौकुमार्येण दुःखासहिष्णुत्वद्वारा विप्रलम्भोत्कर्षः । Uddyota. ताम्यति indicates उद्वेग. अत्र मालत्या माधवविषयोनुरागः प्रथमावस्थेति मन्तव्यम् । Trip. Fig.—Jaga. says अत्रोत्प्रेक्षा विशिष्टस्यैव । The words साक्षात् and नवं favour this view; or it may be taken as an Up-má.

P. 17. बाढम्—Yes, it must be so. तया &c.—Here we have two sentences the first. ending with लिखितं. यतः तया—V. l. Since she had drawn; this will connect the first sentence with बाढं; but then अपि will have no force विनोद्—dispelling of her longing.

P. 18. तन्निर्गेन—By this channel or means, medium; घटेत-supply एवं or यत् after this. It may come to pass that. उपोद्घाताय—To form an introduction to the business we have set ourselves about. This shows that Kala. and Mandá. were in the secret. This explains why Kala. took the picture-board with him when in search for his master; see p. 33. Jaga. reads उपोद्घातेन—There being an occasion for it. अभिप्रायः—i. e. of Lavangiká (and not of Avalok. as Jaga. remarks). अभियोग—Close or zealous application to, energetic pursuit of. समा०—समासादितः आश्चर्यो मन्त्रसिद्धया प्रभावः यया. प्रभाव superhuman power such as that of flying through the air, becoming invisible, producing any thing at will, &c.; see Ragh. V. 52; प्रभावनिर्मितेन भूर्जपत्रेण: Vik. II. p. 47.

श्रीपर्वत—Also called Śriśaila–the mountain of Śrî or Lakshmî, is a holy place still visited by pilgrims, near the Krishṇa river, in the Karnul Zilla, about 120 miles from Hyderabad. The temple of Mallikárjuna is on a small hill in its neighbourhood. कापालिकव्रतम्—The vow or practice of the Kápâlikas. They were a sect, so called from the garlands of human skulls (which they also used and still use as vessels for eating and drinking purposes) they wore, who worshipped Bhairava (Śiva in his terrific form) and Chámundá. They even offered human sacrifices to propitiate their favourite deity, Kâlî. They renounced the world and wore loathsome things on their persons, thus presenting a hideous appearance. The mountain Śriśaila was their rendezvous. They were adepts in the science of mesmerism which they used for evil purposes and were called, for that reason, the followers of the left hand order. They are still to be seen and are much dreaded by the people on account of their wicked and cruel practices. The student will get a good idea of their dress and common practices from the poet's introduction to his fifth Act. See also Dr. Bhând.'s notes.

चामुण्डा—Chandiká, Chámundá, &c. are the names of Pârvatî in her terrific form.* *Cf.* the well known sloka descriptive of

* Châmundá was an emanation of the goddess Durgá sprung from her forehead to encounter the demons Chanda and Munda. Having slain the demons, she bore their heads to her parent goddess, who told her that having slain Chanda and Munda she should thenceforth be

Châmundâ—ऊर्ध्वकेशि विरूपाक्षि मांसशोणितभोजने । तिष्ठ देवि शिखाबन्धे चामुण्डे ह्यपराजिते ॥

P. 19. साहसिक—See com.; fr. साहस + टक् ( इक ) adventurous spirits. साधक—one wishing to attain miraculous power by securing the efficacy of spells.

P. 20. उदार—The same as उदात्त noble, dignified.-प्रकृतिः—and so not likely to listen to any proposal that would reflect discredit on her or to do any thing derogatory to the dignity of her family Hence the necessity for being cautious in dealing with her. निसृष्टार्थदूती—A messenger or go-between who acts on her own responsibility, the full management of a business being entrusted to her. निसृष्टः त्वमेव वेत्सि कार्यभारमिति अर्थः कार्यभारो यस्याम् । तदुक्तं—रूढानुरागयोर्यूनोरभिलाषं मनोगतं । ज्ञात्वा ताभ्यामनादिष्टा तद्पेक्षितसिद्धये । या प्रवर्तेत सा प्रोक्ता निसृष्टार्थेति कोविदैः ॥ Trip. *Cf.* निसृष्टार्थो मितार्थश्च ( who has the management of a particular piece of business and whose powers are therefore limited ) तथा शासनवाहकः ( a mere executor of commands ) । सामर्थ्यात्पादतो हीनो दूतस्तु त्रिविधः स्मृतः ॥ Kâm. XIII. 3. For some of the qualifications of such a go-between, see III. 11.

कल्पः—कल्पते अनेन that by which one is able to gain one's end; hence business, schemes, the procedure to be adopted. सूत्रयितव्यः-should be systematically arranged or well planned.

प्रगुण—Worthy, befitting. The figures in this śl. are उपमा in the 1st line, सम ( ध्वनित ) and क्रियासमुच्चय. For the idea in the last two lines comp. परस्परेण स्पृहणीयशोभं न चेदिदं द्वंद्वमयोजयिष्यत् । अस्मिन्द्वये रूपविधानयत्नः पत्युः प्रजानां वितथोऽभविष्यत् ॥ Ragh. VII. 14.

विष्कम्भकः—See com.; The D. R. defines it as वृत्तवर्तिष्यमाणानां कथांशानां निदर्शकः । संक्षेपार्थस्तु विष्कम्भो मध्यपात्रप्रयोजितः ॥ ( I. 59. ); it is an interlude at the beginning of an Act briefly indicating the events, past and those to follow. It is called शुद्ध when carried on by one or more minor ( मध्य ) characters and mixed ( मिश्र ) when carried on by minor and low characters ( नीचमध्यम ).

तुलित—Weighed, equalled. तुलितः मकरध्वजस्य ( रूपविषयकः ) गर्वो येन तादृग् यो रूपविभ्रमः the grace of beauty, तेन &c. चित्रफल०—We have adopted this reading because Kala. further on ( p. 37 ) shows the picture-board to Mâdhava with his form painted on it. माहात्म्यं-magnanimity, hence gravity, firmness.

P. 21. असौष्ठवं—( सुष्ठु इत्यस्य भावः सौष्ठवं ) Void of loveliness or grace; not in good trim ( Dr. Bhân. ). कन्दर्पाज्ञा-Mark the

---

known on earth as Châmundâ. She is also termed Kâlî from her black colour and Karâlâ or Karâlavadanâ from her hideous countenance. Wilson.

derivation ( कं दर्पयामि &c., whom shall I intoxicate &c.: see Apte's Dic ; or कुत्सितः दर्पः यस्मात् who quells the pride of all ). Hence the word is peculiarly appropriate here. **ललित०**—ललित heart-bewitching; मधुर gratifying the outer senses. The figures of speech in this śl. are—कारणसमुच्चय and a kind of अप्रस्तुतप्रशंसा ( as instead of विशेष, सामान्य is put forth ). This Śloka is cited in the D. R. (II. 51) as an instance of नर्मस्फोट which is defined as नर्मस्फोटस्तु भावानां सूचितोल्परसो लवैः । The partial unfolding of the Hero's love by slight indications ( of feeling ). अत्र गमनादिभिर्भावलेशैर्माधवस्य मालत्यामनुरागः स्तोकः प्रदर्श्यते ।

P. 22. **इन्दु०**—Dissolve इन्दुरिव सुन्दरं मुखं यस्याः । **व्यपवर्तते**—returns; *cf.* व्यपवर्तत एष बालवीरः &c. Uttar. V. 8. where it means returns, *i. e.* desists from. **अकाण्डे**—All at once—goes with विजित्य &c. The fig. in this is Sâra or Climax, the stupifaction of mind being the ultimate result.

P. 23. **विस्मय**—( caused by the sight of uncommon beauty ) is the permanent feeling of अद्भुतरस. **आनन्दमन्द**-Drunken with, rendered dull by. **व्यथमानमास्ते**—Keeps writhing, suffers torture. The figure in this sl. is Kâvyalinga. Sl. quoted in D. R. along with 29 as an instance of विधान, one of the 12 *Angas* of Mukhasandhi; इत्यनेन मालत्यनुरागस्य समागमहेतोर्बीजानुगुण्येनैव माधवस्य सुखदुःखकारित्वाद्विधानम् । It is the working of the *Bija* in such a way as to cause pleasure and pain to the Hero, so as to advance the growth of *love* which leads to the final union. See D. R. I. 28. ( विधानं सुखदुःखकृत् ).

**ललाटंतपः**—See com.; before the aff. खश् ( अ ) the preceding word used prepositionally as the object of the verb to which it is added takes the augment मुम् ( म् ).

**विश्राम**—This is grammatically not correct; it should be विश्रम; विश्राम इत्यपाणिनीयं Sid. Kau. on Pân. VI. 3. 122. But the word has become *rûdha* even with great poets ( *cf.* विश्रामो हृदयस्य यत्र &c., Uttar. I. 30; विश्रामं लभतामिदं &c. Ab Śak. II. 6 ) and may be explained as विश्रम एव विश्रामः on the analogy of प्रज्ञ एव प्राज्ञः ।

P. 24. **कषाय**—Sweet, fragrant. **अन्यादृशं**—'आ सर्वनाम्नः' Pân. VI. 3. 91. Pronouns change their final vowel to आ ( dropping the final consonant if there be any ) before the affixes दृश-श् and वत्. अन्य इव पश्यति तम्. **अपि नाम**—अपि joined with नाम is used to express hope likelihnd, &c. when the speaker expects that a certain thing would happen; *cf.* अपि नाम रामभद्रः पुनरपीदं वनमलङ्कुर्यात्, Uttar II. p. 54; अपि नाम कुलपतेरियमसवर्णक्षेत्रसंभवा स्यात् । Śak. I. p. 23.

See *supra* p. 13. **मुग्ध**—pretty, or with Jag. 'vacant'. **अन्येषु**—ordinary. **रजस्तमसा०**—*i e.* men and animals ( as characterised by the two qualities ) respectively.

P. 25. **उल्लसित**—Rising or spreading out. **मदिरामोद०**—Sweet like the aroma of wine; if we dissolve the comp. as ०मोदेन मधुरः ( see Jag. यद्वा &c. ) then *cf.* विकसति बकुलः सीधुगण्डूषसेकात् ( by being sprinkled over with mouthfuls of wine by women ); ०आकृष्टं मिलच्च यद्‌लिपटलं तस्य संकुलेन ( संकुल a mixed crowd, confused mass; *cf.* p. 36 l. 15.) आकुलिता covered; or संकुलं यथा तथाकुलिता thickly covered. **विकसितानि कु०**—Sir Dr. Bhândârkar omits विकसितानि but it is necessary to exclude the faded flowers. **अङ्गन**—according to Jag. the word must be written with a final न and not ण; see com. **मुग्ध**—pretty, befitting girls. **०प्रकृतिः**—of a very noble disposition or demeanour; or 'make', as Dr. Bhândarkar takes it.

P. 26. **रामणीयक०**—रमणीयस्य भावो रामणीयकम् । योपधाद्गुरूपोत्तमाद्वुञ् । Pân. V. 1. 132. The aff. ( अक ) is added in the sense of भाव or कर्मन् to words having a penultimate य् preceded by a long syllable; similarly अभिधानीयकम्; but क्षत्रियत्वम्.

**सौन्दर्यसार**—The quintessence of beauty; *cf.* रूपोच्चयेन मनसा विधिना कृता नु । Ab. Śak. II. 9; and सर्वोपमाद्रव्यसमुच्चयेन यथाप्रदेशं विनिवेशितेन &c. Kum. I. 49. **इन्दुसुधा०**—इन्दु is used to account for her lovely face, सुधा her sweet speech or general charms, मृणाल her tender hands, ज्योत्स्ना her complexion, &c. The figure in the first two lines is ससंदेह and in the last two अतिशयोक्ति.

**महाभाग०**—महाभागधेयाद् महाभागधेयेन वा जन्म यस्य; or महद्भागधेयं यत्र तादृशं जन्म यस्य ।

P. 27. **परिमृदित०**—The comparison to the juicy and tender lotus-stalks, crushed ( or withering under the influence of heat &c. ) is very happy: *cf.* परिमृदितमृणालीदुर्बलान्यङ्गकानि Uttar. I. 24; Kum. V. 29. **अङ्ग**—जात्यभिप्रायेणैकवचनम् ।

**अभिनव०**—अभिनवः यः करिदन्तच्छेदः तद्वत्पाण्डुः. कान्तः is the reading of the K. P. पाण्डु of the Pradipa. Mr. Zalkikar ( K. P. IV. ). however, remarks-छेदपाण्डुरिति पाठस्तु न रुचिरः बहुपुप्राचीन पुस्तकेषु तथा-पाठाभावात् पाण्डुता व्यज्यते इति सकलटीकाविरुद्धत्वाच्च । But Bhav. might have got the idea from सद्यःकृत्तद्विरददशनच्छेदगौरस्य तस्य । Meg. I. 62, and so might have written पाण्डु. The fig. in the 3rd line is निदर्शना. Sl. quoted in K. P. IV. as containing the Anubhâvas, such as शरीरम्लानि, विषयपराङ्मुखत्व, पाण्डुता &c. which together with the Vibhâvas such as मालतीमाधवौ, मदनोद्यान &c. and the व्यभिचारिs such as निर्वेद, ग्लानि &c. which can be easily gathered from the context, give rise to शृङ्गार ( अभिलाषविप्रलम्भ. )

**अमृतवर्तिर्नयनयोः**--*Cf.* इयं गेहे लक्ष्मीरियममृतवर्तिर्नयनयोः । Uttar. I. 38. **अयस्कान्त०**--*Cf.* Kum. II. 59 ( अयस्कान्तेन लोहवत ); the simile shows that the influence was both unseen and irresistible.

**आसक्तं**--attached; p. p of सञ्ज् with आ. **प्रायः शुभं च** &c.--indicates the poet's faith in the workings of Destiny. **सर्वंकषा**--Lit. rubbing against or touching every thing; all powerful; by ' सर्वकूलाभ्रकरीषेषु कषः ।' Pân. III. 2. 42; कूलंकषा नदी, अभ्रंकषो वायुः &c. The fig. is अर्थान्तरन्यास.

P. 28. **निमित्त** &c.--व्यपेक्षा is particular (विशेषेण अपेक्षा) expectancy or dependence; व्यपेक्षया सहितः सव्य०; निमित्तेन सव्यपेक्षः; Mak. corroborates the statement of Mâd. that his mind was drawn by some influence which was irresistible. He says ' That it is love and that it should depend on some external cause is contradictory;' *i. e.* love cannot depend on external causes. This sentence and the following sl occur in Uttar. ( VI. 12; p. 158 ).

**व्यतिषजति**--joins, connects or links together. **उपाधि**--outward conditions, external causes such as beauty of person, nobility of birth, &c.

**सभ्रूविलासं**--With the play of their eye-brows. **सप्रत्यभिज्ञं**--प्रत्यभिज्ञया सहितं यथा । प्रत्यभिज्ञा नाम पूर्वानुभूतस्य पुरोवर्त्यैक्यावगाहिनी धीः । सा च परबुद्धित्वान्न मया प्रत्यक्षीकृता किंतूत्प्रेक्षिता इति इव शब्देन द्योतयति । Trip. Cons.--तस्याः सखीजनेन मामवलोक्य सप्रत्यभिज्ञमिव सोयमिति सभ्रूविलासमीरयित्वा &c. **भावः**--भावोभिप्रायवस्तुनोः इति हैमः ।

P. 29. **प्रत्यभिज्ञा**--see Jag.; सः (तत्ता) अयं ( इदंता ) देवदत्तः (विशिष्टं) इति ज्ञानम्. **उत्ताल०**--उत्तालाः forcibly struck याः करकमलतालिकास्ताभिः तरला वलयावल्यो यस्मिन् कर्मणि तद्यथा तथा । उत्त्रस्तमत्तकलहंसानां विभ्रम इव अभिरामं यच्चरणसंचरणं तेन रणरणायमाना मञ्जवो ये मञ्जीरास्तेषां रसितेन अनुविद्धः यः...रणत्कारस्तेन मुखरं यथा स्यात्तथा । विभ्रम graceful steppings, sportive movements; तालिकाः striking together the palms.

P. 30. **सरस०**--सरसश्चासौ रमणीयश्च तादृशः अनुबन्धः अस्य विद्यते । From अनुबन्ध् + इन्. The rule न कर्मधारयान्मत्वर्थीयः is, as remarked by Dr. Bhandarkar, disregarded in Prákṛit. अनुबन्ध a connected story.

**वाग्विभव**--power of speech or description. **विभ्रम०**--चित्तवृत्त्यनवस्थानं शृङ्गाराद्विभ्रमो मतः । A state of confusion of the mind, or actions indicative of such a state, caused by the feeling of love. **सात्त्विक**--सत्त्वेन निर्वृत्ताः सात्त्विकाः ( fr. सत्त्व + ठक् ). Satva is that particular state of the mind which makes it readily yield to any emotion. **०विकार**--These are *bhâvas* or feelings inasmuch as they directly proceed from Satva; and Anubhávas inasmuch as they are the outward manifestations of the internal feelings; see D. R. IV. 4-6; Sàh. San. p. 45, see also Jag.

**आचार्यकं**—आचार्यस्य कर्म; see note on रामणीयक p. 26. **विजयि**—i. e. सर्वत्राप्रतिहतप्रसरं whose operation is unobstructed every where; all-triumphant. **मान्मथं**—मन्मथस्येदं sprung from मन्मथ; मत् चेतना consciousness, reason, judgment; fr. मन्+क्विप् (०) न् being dropped and त् added; मथनीति मथ: the destroyer; मतो मथः मन्मथः; the god of love.

**स्तिमित** &c.—Śl. quoted in the D. R. and S. D. as containing an instance of विलास ( तात्कालिको विशेषस्तु विलासोऽङ्गक्रियादिषु D. R. ). **प्रतिनयन०**—प्रतिगतं नयनं तस्य निपातः तस्मिन् । **विविधं**—विविधा विधा यस्मिन्कर्मणि. The fig. is परिकर according to Trip.

P. 31. **अलस**—may be taken as an adj. or an adv.; see Jag. **स्मेर**—beaming, smiling; fr. स्मि+र ( added ताच्छील्ये or कर्तरि ) by नमिकम्पिस्म्यजसकमहिंसदीपो रः; so नम्रः, कम्प्रः tremulous; अजस्रं सन्ततमित्यर्थः, कम्र, हिंस्र and दीप्र. **अशरणं**—helpless, powerless to resist the action of the glances. **पक्ष्मलाक्ष्याः**—पक्ष्मले अक्षिणी यस्याः सा पक्ष्मलाक्षी तया. पक्ष्माणि मनोहराणि सन्त्यस्येति पक्ष्मलं having beautiful eyelashes; fr. पक्ष्मन्+ल ( च् ) a मतुप् aff. added to words of the सिध्मादि group of which पक्ष्मन् is one. **कटाक्षः**—कटौ अतिशयितौ अक्षिणी यत्र; or कटं गण्डम् अक्षति इति । Fig. A shade of सार. Trip. remarks अत्र कटाक्षैरुक्तरूपैः ( मालत्याः ) अनुभावैस्तत्कारणस्य काष्ठां प्राप्तस्य माधवविषयस्य रतिभावस्य तत्समुचितव्यभिचारिणां प्रतीतेः माधवस्याप्यपहृतमित्यादिना मालत्यनुरागगोचरगाढानुरागतन्नियतव्यभिचारितदुचितानुभावप्रतीतेर्युगपदन्योन्यालम्बनशृङ्गाररसध्वनिः ।

P. 32. **अभिसन्धि**—secret purpose of the heart; intention. **विधेयीकृतः**—brought into its power completely subdued.

P. 33. **आवृत्त०**—आवृत्तं वृन्तं यस्य; ०पत्रेण सदृशं ०निभं; स्युरुत्तरपदे त्वमी । निभसंकाशनीकाशप्रतीकाशोपमादयः । Amara; these words are used only as the latter members of comp.s in this sense ( i. e. सदृश ). **यान्त्या** &c.—This device is frequently resorted to by Sans. poets. *Cf.* दर्भाङ्कुरेण चरणः क्षत इत्यकाण्डे...आसीद्विवृत्तवदना च विमोचयन्ती । Śák. II. 12; प्रियमाचरितं लते त्वया मे गमनेऽस्याः क्षणविघ्नमाचरन्त्या । यदियं पुनरप्यपाङ्गनेत्रा परिवृत्तार्धमुखी मया हि दृष्टा ॥ Vik. I. 16. व्यावृत्यैव सितासितेक्षणरुचा... यद्दृष्टोस्मि तया मुनेरपि पुरः &c. Nâg. II. 2.

Śl. Quoted in the D. R. along with 19 as an instance of विधान ( see notes on that śl. ), and again as indicative of अन्योन्यानुराग. Fig. उत्प्रेक्षा.

**परिच्छेद**—definite or accurate knowledge about; exact nature. Śl. quoted in K. P. IV. to show that a preposition also may suggest some charming sense, Rasa &c., as प्र does here the विप्रलम्भशृङ्गार by indicating that the destruction of विवेक was complete, and the effect of love therefore very great; and again in Ull. X. as an instance of Virodha or apparent antithesis between two *Krityas*, stupifaction and tormentation. *Cf.* Uddyota—प्रशब्देन समूलोन्मूलनलक्षणः प्रकर्षस्तेन मोहप्रकर्षस्तेन च रागातिशयस्तेन च विप्रलम्भातिशयो व्यंग्यः । अत्र विरोधः विरहवैचित्र्येण कालभेदात्तत्परिहारः ( the two effects being considered as produced at two different times ).

P. 34. अतथाभावः—तथा सत्यस्य भावः the state of being the real thing, reality; न तथाभावः not being that ( *i. e.* correct ) अतथा०. न संताप०—च्छेदः—This is what Mâd. expects to be the possible result as he had no time yet to try either. निद्रा०—So great is the agitation that my mind cannot be fixed on one particular object. आलिखति–lit. draws lines, touches against different objects; hence entertains visionary thoughts. *Cf.* किमपि हृदयेनालिखन्ती; Mṛch. II. Fig. क्रियासमुच्चय.

अभिष्वंग—intense love, overpowering affection. अभिषङ्ग—*V. l.* will have the same meaning. ( See p. 147 ).

मलीमस—मलः अस्यास्ति; fr. मल + ईमस (showing possession; a *matub* aff. ), by Pân. V. 2. 114. ०घना—thickly covered with foul passion; hence unable to perceive things properly. जृम्भित—जृम्भ् properly to yawn or open; hence to extend, to stretch; जृम्भित stretched, enhanced.

अन्वयः—अन्वीयते इति what is connected successively; hence a line, a family.

P. 35. अन्यतमा--तम added to अन्य has the sense of one of many, though अन्य is not actually mentioned among the words that take the termination. अन्यतरान्यतमशब्दौ अव्युत्पन्नौ स्वभावाद्द्विबहुविषये निर्धारणे वर्तेते । Sid. Kau. कुसुमापीड—(1) A dexterously woven garland or wreath of flowers; (2) god of love. सुश्लिष्टगुण—(1) A well-arranged string; सुश्लिष्टः गुणः यत्र तस्य भावस्तत्ता तया; and (2) merits befitting each other; सुश्लिष्टाः गुणाः यत्र. सुमनसां–(1) flowers; (2) noble minds. संनिवेशः–(1) excellent or beautiful arrangement; (2) union. कुसुमेषु &c.--कुसुमेषु नव व्यापारः ( skilful working ), तस्याः ( to her ) अभिनवः exciting curiosity, awakening her interest; (2) कुसुमेषुव्यापारः the working of the god of love (is new in her case.) निर्माण—act of weaving, workmanship; (2) creation. विधातुः—(1) of you, the weaver of the wreath; (2) the Creator. सरसः—(1) fresh; (2) full of love. एषः--the chaplet; (2) yourself. Fig. श्लेष. According to Trip. this is an instance of पताकास्थान.

P. 36. धात्रेयिका—a foster-sister धात्र्याः अपत्यं स्त्री धात्रेयी सैव धात्रेयिका; by affixing क स्वार्थे before which the preceding ई is shortened. See Pân. VII. 4 14. अपर्याप्तिर्बहुमानस्य—The honour cannot be too high ( for her ); her greatness is unbounded; or it may mean-no honor can be too high or sufficiently great for Mádhava, that she, the daughter of the minister, should have fastened her affection on him. **अभिनिविष्टया दृशा**—goes with तामेव **बहुमन्यमाना** she, ardently or fixedly looking at it, thought highly of it just as it was, &c. **विहस्ततया**—विगतौ हस्तौ यस्य ( one who has lost his hand· *i. e.* the power of ) स विहस्तः तस्य भावस्तत्ता तया; owing to my hands being unnerved or shaky. *Cf.* विहस्तीकृतः *infra* p. 46. **०भागां तां**—Dr. Bhând. reads भागान्तां the end of a part of which; or the पदच्छेद may also be भागां तां, म् being changed to न् before त.

**यात्राभङ्ग०**—may also be dissolved as यात्रायाम् अभंगेन प्रचलितस्य ( moving in a thick mass ). **सुश्लिष्टं** &c —The event has well fallen out; it is a happy coincidence. **चक्षूरागिणः**—having the love of the eyes; fixing loveful glances on; expresses the first stage of love; *cf.* notes on VI. 15.

P. 37. **अन्योन्य०**—Who exchanged glances. **संभिन्न** lit. meeting or mingling together ( without the idea of withdrawal); *cf.* for this sense मधुमतींसिन्धुसंभेदः p. 177. Cons—सखीनां निवेदितं धात्रेयिकायाः वचश्च तस्यास्त्वयि प्रागनुरागचिह्नम् . Fig. समुच्चय.

**इदं च**—Kal.'s speech is so introduced as to fit in with and look like a continuation of Mak.'s speech; इदं च चित्रं तस्या अनुरागचिह्नम् ।

P. 38. **सुजन्मा**—Because possessed of such amiable qualities, both of the mind and person; *cf.* सुजातं. *supra* sl. 16. It may also be taken with मालती by देहलीदीपकन्याय. **बन्धुः**—बन्धुचन्द्रकुलः; see trans.; आश्रयः Trip. **कृताभियोग**:—has been energetically exerting himself; अभियोग is an effort with close application or with all one's might. Fig.—कारणसमुच्चय.

**बाष्पपूर**:—*Cf.* मम नयनयोरुद्बाष्पत्वं सखे न भविष्यति । Vik. II: 10. **जडिमन्**-Benumbing sensation, heaviness. Fig.—क्रियासमुच्चय.

P. 39. **जयिनः**—Lit. triumphant, victorious; *i. e.* सर्वोत्कर्षशालिनः preeminent by their excellence as charming objects. S'loka quoted in the D. R. as representing love which has joy for its soul ( प्रमोदात्मा रतिः ) and in the K. P. VII as an instance of self-contradiction ( व्याघात or व्याहतत्वं ). Here Mâdhava who speaks disparagingly of such delightful objects as moon-light, the digit of the moon, &c., compares Mâl. to moonlight and thus there is contradiction; अत्रेन्दुकलादयो यं प्रति अप्रशस्य( तुच्छ ) प्रायाः स एव चन्द्रिकात्वमुत्कर्षार्थमारोपयति इति व्याहतत्वम् । The Udyota has this on the first two lines:—ये नवेन्दुकलादयः । आदिना चन्द्रिकापद्मादिपरिग्रहः । भावास्ते जगति जयिनः न तु ममेत्यर्थः । ये अन्ये मनो मदयन्ति तेपि जगन्त्येव प्रकृतिमधुराः । लोका एव तान्प्रकृतिमधुरत्वेन व्यवहरन्तु न त्वहं व्यवहरिष्य इति भावः । Fig.-See Jag. अतिशयोक्त्यलंकार. Trip. It may probably be प्रतीप.

P. 40. विज्ञानं :—Practical knowledge or skill in shaping things; see Jag: *cf* मोक्षे धीर्ज्ञानमन्यत्र विज्ञानं शिल्पशास्त्रयोः । Amara; 'विज्ञानं कार्मणे ज्ञाने' इति हैमः ।

P. 41. कपोलकु०—The Com. connects this with परिजनवारसुन्दरीणां but without propriety. It does not seem natural that Mád. should be thinking of Málatî's maids instead of Málatî herself. He also speaks of the paintings on the cheeks (and not on those parts of the body on which married women have them) which a maiden has no objection to have. पत्ररेखाः—पत्राकाराः रेखाः पत्ररेखाः (a comp. of the शाकपार्थिवादि class); ornamental figures traced on the cheeks, the bosom &c. of women. Fig. अप्रस्तुतप्रशंसा as the Kárya or effect is stated instead of the cause.

P. 42. अनवग्रहः—नास्ति अवग्रहो यस्य without impediment or restraint; uncontrolled, irresistible. वैकृतविवर्त०—वैकृत disturbance, affection; तस्याचिरेण विवर्तः sudden change; the affection quickly taking a serious turn, तेन दारुणः. कूटपाकलः—A kind of malignant fever resulting from the disturbance of the three bodily humours and attacking elephants. Trip., thus comments on this—कूटेन कपटेन अकस्मादागत्य तस्मिन्नेव निपातयतीति कूटपाकलः । यथाभिहन्यात्कूटेन मृगयूथं वनेचरः । तथा पातात्मको नागं हन्ति वै कूटपाकलः ॥ केचित्कूटीभूय संघीभूय दोषत्रयेण जनितो ज्वरविशेष इति व्याचक्षते । अनेनोन्मादावस्था सूचिता । उपमालंकारः ।

उन्मीलन्मु०—उन्मीलन्तश्च ते मुकुलाश्च तैः कराला ये कुन्दकोशास्तेभ्यः प्रश्चोतन् &c. नताङ्गी a woman with a stooping body (on account of the weight of the breasts, &c.); hence beautiful; or नत may also stand for उन्नत (being its उपलक्षण), and may mean उन्नतानताङ्गी (the same as बन्धुरगात्री Ragh. XIII. 47) with some parts elevated and others depressed; hence with the limbs properly or symmetrically developed; beautiful. स्पृशाङ्गमङ्गं &c.—For a similar idea, *cf.* शक्यमविरलमालिंगितुं पवनः Sâk. III. 5; आलिङ्ग्यन्ते गुणवति मया ते तुषाराद्रिवाताः पूर्वं स्पृष्टं यदि किल भवेदङ्गमेभिस्तवेति । Meg. II. 47; and *infra.* IX. 43. Trip. remarks गन्धवन्धो इत्यनेन विलापगत्या मदनावस्था दर्शिता ॥

This is an Ankávatára (see Jag.) which occurs when the actors indicate the business of the succeeding Act at the close of the proceding Act, the two being thus connected; (अङ्कावतारस्त्वङ्कान्ते पातोङ्कस्याविभागतः । D. R.).

उद्बद्ध &d.—कनकाब्जेन (for, an ordinary lotus would not suit) सदृशं कनकाब्जनिभं; see *supra*, note on शतपत्रनिभं p. 33.

आसक्त &c.—See Jag; or rather आसक्ता (fixed on me) च तिर्यगपवर्तिता च दृष्टिर्यस्य यत्र वा ।

P. 43. **ग्राहकत्वं**--*i. e.* स्वस्वविषयग्रहणशक्तिः power of perception **प्रमोह** :—सुखदुःखादिजनितो मोहश्चित्तस्य मूढता इत्युक्तरूपः । Trip. **रणरणकः**— Constant uneasiness of the mind caused by love. **विभ्रत्** &c.— Jag.'s reading is विभ्रदावर्ति गात्रं, but it does not give a good sense, as the body cannot with propriety be spoken of as आवर्ति ( wandering or whirling about ). Fig. क्रियासमुच्चय.

---

# ACT II.

P. 44. **हला**--Indec. is used in addressing a friend. हण्डे हञ्जे हलाह्वाने नीचां चेटीं सखीं प्रति । Amara. **परिसर** :--परितः सरन्त्यत्र; surrounding ground, environs. **मन्त्रयन्ती**—Better read मन्त्रयमाणा.

P. 45. **उपर्य०**--उपरितनः अलिन्दकः; अल्यते भूष्यते इति (fr. अल् + इन्द) अलिन्दः; अलिन्द एवालिन्दकः a terrace near the door of a house; प्रघाणप्रघणालिन्दा बहिर्द्वारप्रकोष्ठके । इत्यमरः । **कल्पं**--कलयति चेष्टामिति । **प्रभवति निजस्य**--See p. 52. **अपि नाम**—would that, I hope that (implying the fulfilment of wish ; see *supra* p. ).

P. 46. **प्रवेशकः**—See Jag.; like the विष्कं० ( see notes p. 12 ) a प्रवे० also is an interlude designed to indicate the events that have occurred between two acts and that cannot be introduced in an Act on account of their multiplicity. It is carried on by low characters ( servants, &c. ). The D. R. ( I. 60 ) defines it as तद्वदेवानुदात्तोक्त्या नीचपात्रप्रयोजितः । प्रवेशोऽङ्कद्वयस्यान्ते शेषार्थस्योपसूचकः ॥ Hence it is clear that a Pra can never introduce the 1st Act.

**अपराद्धाः**--used in an active sense ( with the gen. or the loc. of the person offended ); *cf.* कस्मिन्नपि पूजार्हेपराद्धा शकुन्तला । Śak. VI. p. 88; अपराद्धोस्मि तत्रभवतः कण्वस्य; *ibid* VII. p. 200. **दूर्वाश्यामल**—having the sheen of the Dûrvá grass. It is but meet that माधव ( a name of Krishṇa ) should be described as श्यामवर्ण. **सर्वथाश्वासनशीला** &c.—You are by disposition given to encouraging or cheering up a person; that is all ; you say this simply to please me. I do not think I am so fortunate as to attrat Mádhava by my charms. Mâl. says this out of modesty although she knew that that must have been the fact.

P. 47. **मन्दमारुतो०**—उद्वेल्लत् ( waving, dancing ) पुण्डरीकं नस्येव विभ्रमः engaging beauty, charm, grace ययोः. **विजृम्भमाण** &c.— विस्मयेन स्तिमितः; दीर्घाश्च ते पर्यन्ताश्च तेषु या परिवर्तना तस्याः सैव वा विलासः । now see Jag.; विजृम्भमाणेन ततः तेन ( विभ्रमेण ) विदग्धं यथा स्यात्तथा. **आम्**— अम्मो (वितर्के) is a better reading. **विप्रलम्भ०** —deceiving; misleading .

Jag. reads विप्रलम्भितकाः; but it is not a good translation of विप्पलनम्भइत्तका, as that does not give the intended meaning directly as वचितृकाः does. The reading विप्रलम्भकाः, as remarked by Dr. Bhân., shows that a derivative of the root in an active sense is required here.

P. 48. **त्वमपि** &c.—नर्तितासि—You too were &c.; were you not? Lav. means–If your agitation was natural (and not due to Mad.'s sight) then Mád.'s too may be supposed to be natural. **सन्तापितस्य**—refers to Mádhava. **सन्तापकारिणः**—*i. e.* causing torment to Málatî.

P. 49. **अनासङ्गः**—Want of confidence. आसंग–lit. close application or adherence to a thing (from सञ्ज् with आ to be closely attached, fixed; *cf.* आसज्यमानेक्षणः Sak. III. 24; आससंज भयं तेषां Bhatti. XIV. 104); close contact, as in (पङ्कजं) सशैवलासङ्गमपि प्रकाशते; Kum. V. 9; पतनिवलयासङ्गसंजातपाशः। Śak. I. 30; deep attachment to; *cf.* त्यक्त्वा कर्मफलासङ्गं Bhag. IV. 23. Hence अनासङ्ग want of deep attachment or close union.; *i. e.* indifference or unconcern; hence the result of it; absence of consolation;—my heart will not cheer up even now.

**नवमालिका०**—The delicate frame of a fair woman is often compared to the Nav. flower which forms one of the arrows of the god of love; *cf.* येन नवमालिकाकुसुमपेलवा त्वं &c. Śák. I p. 19. also II. 1. **निःसहा**—निः न सहते असौ; or निर्गतः सहः (power to bear or to resist) यस्याः।

P. 50 **मनोरागः तीव्रं**—Some take this adverbially. But it is better to take it as an adj. as it preserves symmetry. **तातः प्रभवति**—Because he will have to conform to the wishes of the king and give her in marriage to Nandana. The fig. is what Dandin calls Málopamá. Sl. quoted in the Káv. Pra. VIII. to show that Alankáras, such as Upamà and others, heighten Rasa (as विप्रलम्भशृङ्गार here) by adding to the beauty of the sense; अत्र विषमिवेत्यादिरुपमा। सा चार्थमलंकुर्वाणा रसमुत्कर्षयति। विषमिवेत्युपमावशेन विसर्पणादेरतिशयप्राप्त्या विप्रलम्भोत्कर्षात्। Kàv. Prad.

**प्रत्यक्ष०**—प्रत्यक्षे सौख्यं दातुं शीलं येषाम्। **सविशेष०**—सविशेषं यथा तथा समिद्धो यः हुतवहस्तद्वदाचरन्पूर्णचन्द्रस्योदयो यस्याः।

P. 51. **सविशेषदर्शनं**—a closer view. **किमत्र भणितव्यम्**—*i. e.* it is but natural that you should thus pine for him. **आघनीयं** &c.—This is a covert hint to Màlatî to have recourse to the Gándharva marriage.

**साहसो०**—Màlatî understands the gist of Lav.'s speech and takes her to task for the suggestion. **दुःख** &c.—धीरत्वमेव धीरत्वस्य

वावष्टम्भः (support) धीर०; दुःखेन व्यवस्थापितः धीरत्वावष्टम्भो यस्य । Read after this हृदयेन which has been accidentally omitted. दुर्विनय-लघ्वी—indicates her high sense of family honour. The reading दूरविजृम्भमाण &c. means—mean or frivolous owing to excessive (*lit.* high-grown) immodesty or ill-manneredness ( दूरं विजृम्भमाणो योऽविनयस्तेनलघुकं ); or a heart with excessive दुर्विनय (०दुर्विनयो यत्र) and लघुक (लघुकं च). दूरविलीयमानलज्जात्वेन *V. l.*—दूरं विलीयमाना लज्जा यस्याः तस्याः भावः दूरविलीयमानलज्जात्वं तेन owing to my sense of shame having vanished far off.

ज्वलतु &c.—Sl. quoted in the D. R. and S. D. as an instance of धैर्य which is defined as चापलाविहता ( undisturbed by rashness ) धैर्यचिद्वृत्तिराविकत्थना ( in which one does not mention one's good qualities ). Fig. व्यतिरेक ( only a shade of ).

P. 52. एषा भगवती कामन्दकी—This serves as a fortuitous reply to क उपायः; this is, therefore, a Patàkàsthâna. See S. D. VI. 45. उभयलोका०—See Jag.; निजस्य (1) his *i. e.* Bhúrivasu's; (2) his own *i. e.* the king's ( and not Bhûrivasu's ).

P. 53. व्यतिकरसंविधानं—व्यतिकर lit. what is mixed or connected; hence, an affair;—the happy event or the incidents of; or व्यतिकर combination; as Jag. takes it. This word occurs frequently in the present play; see p. p. 65, 118, 152, 176 &c. There may also be a secret reference to the poet's skill in inventing the two incidents.

इतरे०—इतरेतरस्मिन्ननुराग इतरे०. दारकर्मन्—दाराणां कर्म marriage; तादर्थ्ये समासः । *cf. infra* VI. 18. आङ्गिरस् name of a sage, to whom several hymns of the Ṛg. Veda are ascribed. One of the seven sages and the ten Prajápatis and a law-giver. For other particulars see Apte's Dic. अनुबन्धः—strong attachment. One of the Mss. consulted by Dr. Bhánd. reads निबन्धः for अनुबन्धः, which also means the same (नितरां बन्धः), or after Dr. Bhán. 'binding, enchainment, attachment.' This reading is preferable. No Gṛhyasûtra of Angiras, however, is known. The words quoted here as from Angiras occur in A'pastaba's Gṛhyasûtra, where they are said to state the view of some ( एके ). Vijnâneswara while commenting on Mitá. I. 53. quotes the passage as from Apa. ( कान्तां कमनीयां वोढुर्नयनानन्दकारिणीं-' यस्यां मनश्चक्षुषोर्निबन्धस्तस्यामृद्धिः' इत्यापस्तम्बस्मरणात् । ) but does not say that it is the view of some one quoted by A'pastamba. Vatsyâyana also quotes the passage in his Kámasûtras—यस्यां मनश्चक्षुषोर्निबन्धस्तस्यामृद्धिर्नेतरामाद्रियेतेत्येके । Kâm. III. I. 14.

निकामं—&c इयं नः कल्याणी &c. -*cf.* शोच्या च प्रियदर्शना च मदनाक्लिष्टेयमालक्ष्यते । Sák. III. 8. कलाशेषा मूर्तिः &c.—कलाशेषा यस्याः A digit of which has remained; is the moon of the fourteenth day of the dark half of the month rather than of the second day of the bright half, as the reference here is to its क्षामत्व; *cf.* प्राचीमूले तनुमिव कलामात्रशेषां हिमांशोः । Meg. II. 29; and आक्लिष्टाबिम्बशोभाधरस्य नयनोत्सवस्य शशिन इव &c. Nag. II. 8. **नवनोत्सवकरी**—*cf. infra* VI. 17; Priya. III. 7. The fig.s are Upamâ and Virodha.

**परिपाण्डु**—may also be read separately as an adj. qualifying आननं. **पांसुल**—dusty ( पांसवोऽस्य विद्यन्ते; fr. पांसु + ल ) on account of the want of attention to personal decorations, clealiness &c. *cf.* परिपाण्डुदुर्बलकपोलसुन्दरं दधती विलोलकबरीकमाननम् । Uttar. III. 4. **ललितो विधिः**--Graceful operation or working. *Cf.* for the same idea differently expressed न तु ग्रीष्मस्यैवं सुभगमपराद्धं युवतिषु । Sák. III 7. **रमणीयज॰**—रमणीयं charning, pleasing, जन्म यस्य; because of a charming exterior and rare qualitics of the heart. *cf.* सुजातं I. 16, and सुजन्मा. I. 34.

**संकल्प**—thought, mental act.

**विषादः**—drooping condition. **मसृण** &c.-मसृणं च तन्मधुरं च तदाकेकरं च &c. आकेकर-half-closed, with the pupil turned towards the corner; *cf.* दृष्टिराकेकरा किंचित्स्फुटापाङ्गे प्रसारिता । मीलितार्धपुटालोके ताराव्यावर्तनोत्तरा ॥ Malli. on Kir. VII. 53. आ समन्तात् के मूर्ध्नि करीतुं नेत्रतारां शीलमस्य ( आ, क the head, कृ+अच् ). **उत्प्रबन्धः**-Continuous ( उद्गतः प्रबन्धः continuity अस्य ). **गण्डाभोगे**—on her large cheeks. For the different Bhâvas see com.

P. 54—**कुशलमिव—इव** 'something like,' implying that she was not entirely happy ( there being something to disturb her happiness ). **कपटनाटकस्य**—Because it was Kâmandakî's object to show to Mâlatî that all her uneasiness was due on her account. Lavangikâ's speech is meant to make this clear.

P. 55. **स्तम्भ**—stopping, checking. **अन्यादृशं**--see p. 24. **परिचय**-*i. e.* with Mâlatî.

**जैत्रं** -जेतुं शीलमस्य तद् जेतृ, तदेव जैत्रं; जेतृ + स्वार्थे अण् ( अ ). Habitually conquering; ever victorious. **सहजविलास** &c.—विलास is क्रिया शृङ्गारभावजा, an action under the influence of love; such as dalliance, playful movement, smiling &c.; and as these add beauty to the person, it means 'grace, beauty;' *cf.* इदं किलाव्याजमनोहरं वपुः &c. Śak. I. 17. **अनुचितवर** &c.-*cf.* ( शकुन्तला ) मा कस्यापि हस्ते पतिष्यति Sák. II. p. 55.

**वैचित्त्यम्**--विगतं चित्तं यस्यास्तस्या भावः; embarrassment, distraction. Trip. reads वैचित्र्यं which he explains as वैलक्षण्यम् । **नाटयति**--This stage direction is, of course, for the actor; Mâl. was simply विचित्ता. **उपहासीकृतास्मि**--Mark the significance of the च्वि aff.; she thinks that she was treated as no better than an ordinary chattel by her father. See com. and p. 107 ( नरेन्द्रचित्ता &c. )

**आश्चर्यम्**—This is a remark on Lav.'s speech. Kâm. seizes this opportunity to prejudice Mâl.'s mind against her father although she knew that he too had the same object at heart. Here begins the कपटनाटक spoken of above, in which Lav. and Budh. are also to take an active part.

P. 56. **कृतोपत्य** &c.—By this Kâm. insinuates that Mâl. may also be justified in going against the wishes of a father who pays so little heed to his daughter's well-being. **निष्णातः**—Lit. one who has dived deep *i. e.* to the bottom; hence who knowss all about a thing; well-versed, skilled in; the **स्** is changed to **ष्** in this sense by Pân. VIII. 3. 89, quoted in the com. **इदं**—*i. e.* यदुत मित्रं भवत्विति इदम्. **ऐदंपर्यं**—Object, purpose; lit. इदं परं यस्मिन् that of which this is the main point or chief object; तस्य भावः the state of being the chief object. Jag. takes this as merely equivalent to इदंपरं on the analogy of चातुर्वर्ण्यं=चतुर्वर्णाः । But the word इदंपर is not found in the group चातुर्वर्ण्यादि which is also not an आकृतिगण. It must, therefore, be taken as an abstract noun.

**राजाराधनं खलु** &c., **हा हतास्मि** &c.—Note the progressive effect on Mâl.'s mind produced by Kâm.'s and Lav.'s speeches. **आज्ञातम्**—remarked, observed. **जीवितमरणात्**—जीवितमेव मरणं तस्मात् ।

P. 57. **यच्च किल**—Mark the subtle way in which Kâm suggests to Mâl. that she too should pursue the same course; also how she begins, henceforward, to carry out the policy set forth by her in the words बाह्यः सर्वाकार &c. ( I. 14 ) and तन्निपुणं निभृतार्थ-दुर्विकल्पः मन्त्रयितव्यः ( p. 20 ); *cf.* śl. 13, further on. In fact the whole of this scene is most ingeneously conceived and artistically worked out. **कौशिकी**—being the daughter of Kauśika ( Viśvâmitra ). The poet refers here to कौशिक rather than to काश्यप probably because the former was a cruel father ( inasmuch as he left his daughter uncared for ).

**वासवदत्ता**—Daughter of Mahâsena, also called Chandamahâsena, king of Ujjayinî. She was so called because she was born by Indra's favour. *Cf.* ततस्तं नृपतिं स्वप्ने तुष्टो वक्ति स्म वासवः । प्राप्स्यस्यनन्य-सदृशीं मत्प्रसादात्सुतामिति ॥ दत्ता मे वासवेनैषा तुष्टेनेति स भूपतिः । नाम्ना वासवदत्तां तां तनयामकरोत्तदा । Kathâ. XI. 76,79. Shriharsha in his Rat. calls her the daughter of Pradyota, and Kâli. also does the same in his Meg. I. 24. ( प्रद्योतस्य प्रियदुहितरं वत्सराजोऽत्र जह्रे । ). So प्रद्योत was another name of Mahâsena. **आख्यान**—historical tales. According to Kathâsaritsâgara, Chandasena himself wished to bestow his daughter in marriage on Udayana, king of the Vatsa country. ( See Tranga X. 7-8 ). Sanjaya is not mentioned there.

**साहसाभासं**—What looks like an act of wantonness ( but is not really so, and hence such a step may be taken ). And so this reading is preferable. **साहसकल्पं**—*V. l.* almost equal to an adventure or a wanton act; a rash deed.

**कार्यात्**—( कार्यमुद्दिश्य ) to gain his end; having a purpose in view. **दुर्दर्शनेन**—This is purposely put in to show that the minister simply means to sacrifice his daughter to gain his own ends.

**सास्रं**—shows that Kám.'s speech has the desired effect on Málatî. **जनान्तिकम्**—Speech, which is meant to be heard by a particular character, is of two kinds, जना० and अपवारितक; जनान्तिक is that which is said by a character turning to another hiding the rest with the hand with its three fingers extended so as to resemble three banners (त्रिपताककरेणान्यानपवार्यान्तरा कथाम् । अन्योन्यामन्त्रणं यत्स्याज्जनान्ते तज्जनान्तिकम् ॥ D. R. ). **अपवारित** is that which a character secretly communicates to another by turning aside; रहस्यं कथ्यतेन्यस्य परावृत्यापवारितम् ।

P. 58. **अप्रास्ताविकी**—प्रस्तावे भवा or प्रस्तावस्येयं ( arising out of, relating to, the matter in hand, relevent ) प्रास्ताविकी; fr. प्रस्ताव and aff. इक with the fem ई; न प्रा० अप्रा०; irrelevant. Hereby Kám. wants apparently to show that she is not much interested in Mádhava. **समग्र०**—प्रशस्ताः धुर्यपुरुषाः धुर्यपुरुषप्रकाण्डानि ( Nityasam. ); समग्राणि च तानि &c. तेषां चक्रं तस्य चूडामणिः। **सतीर्थ्य**—समानतीर्थे ( the same Guru ) वासीति (सतीर्थ्यः) यत्प्रत्ययः । Sid. Kau. समान is changed to स by 'तीर्थे ये । Pân. VI. 3. 87. तीर्थे उत्तरपदे यादौ प्रत्यये विवक्षिते समानस्य सः स्यात् । Sid. Kau. **सातीर्थ्यात्**—*V. l.* सातीर्थ्य सहाध्ययनं Trip.

**व्यतिकरित**—व्यतिकर एषां संजातः ते व्यतिकरिताः; व्यतिकरिताः दिगन्ता येषां ( and not यैः ). So we should have translated this as ' Whose spotless glory &c. **ऊर्जस्वल**—अतिशयितं ऊर्ज एषां विद्यते; fr. ऊर्जस्+ वल (न्); according to some ऊर्ज + वल the स् coming in irregularly ( निपातनात् ); mighty. **अकलित**—Trip. reads अगणित. **केतनं**—We have translated this after Jag. who takes it in the sense of निवास residence. But the poet is not likely to repeat ideas in the same sl. ( he has already used स्थानं ). So it is better to take it in the sense of 'a mark, a harbinger of ( bringing in their train blessings ). चिह्नभूताः Trip. केतनं—केत्यते ज्ञायतेऽनेन fr. कित् + अन (करणे). Fig. अप्रस्तुतप्रशंसा ( विशेषे प्रस्तुते सामान्योक्तिरूपा ).

P. 59. **ततः** &c.—बालचन्द्रः—(1) बालश्चासौ चन्द्रश्च; (2) बालः चन्द्र इव. स्फुरित० and **कलावान्** apply both to the young moon and the boy. (1) स्फुरितगुणा with its brightness well shining out द्युतिः lustre तया सुन्दरः; (2) see Jag. नयनवतां महोत्सवस्य हेतुः. Sl. quoted in the D. R. as containing the characteristics of a धीरशान्त hero ( see Intro. ) Fig. Upamâ ( श्लेषोपमागर्भो रूपकालंकारः Trip. ).

**विद्याधारः**—विद्याया आधारः the treasure of learning; or धारयतीति धारः ( धृ + अण् ) the holder or possessor of; विद्यायाः धारः. **०चन्द्रमधुरः**—०चन्द्रवद् मधुरः. **कुवलयित**—कुवलयानि एषां संजातानि इति कु०नि वातायनानि यस्य. *Cf.* कुवलयितगवाक्षां लोचनैरङ्गनानां Ragh. XI. 93; also VII. 11. Fig. उपमा in the 2nd line and उत्प्रेक्षा in the last two.

P. 60. **आन्वीक्षिकी**—(अनु श्रवणोत्तरमीक्षणं परीक्षणं अन्वीक्षा सा प्रयोजनमस्याः ) seems to mean here Nyàya or the logical philosophy originally propounded by Gotama. It also means अध्यात्मविद्या. See note on the same, p. 14. **स एष माधवो नाम**—Trip. remarks that the passage beginning with ( निःश्रस्य ) कुशलमिव and ending with this constitutes what is called a पताकास्थान. **सखि कुतो** &c.—*cf.* Sák. III. सागरमुज्झित्वा कुत्र वा महानद्यवतरति ।

**उपात्तोत्कम्पानां, अवाप्तो०**—which are trembling ( at the thought of the approaching separation ). **विहगमिथुनानां**—It is not necessary to restrict the expression to the pairs of Chakra. birds, as done by Jag.; the उत्कण्ठा might have been caused in the birds by their being suddenly roused from sleep also. **प्रथमतः**—Because the sound reached the trees or the aviaries first which were lower than the vaults of the mansions. **सौधः**—सुधा लेपः ( white-wash or paint, plaster ) अस्यास्तीति, सुधया लिप्त इति वा; fr. सुधा + अ ( अण् which occasions Vriddhi of the penultimate vowel ). **निकुञ्ज**—a bower; hence what resembles such a bower; a vault. See p 62. Fig. स्वभावोक्ति.

P. 61. **कथं** &c—How turns it out that the great one &c. She means to say that now there would be no objection to him on that score too were she to think of choosing him.

**विचिकित्सा**—Jag. translates this by 'censure, dislike,' but it is premature. It simply means संशय or doubt ( lit. thinking differently or in various ways about a thing ) fr. कित् संशये with the desi. स् added according to Pan. III. 1 5. विचिकित्सा तु संशयः । Amara. *Cf.* येयं प्रेते विचिकित्सा मनुष्ये अस्तीत्येके नायमस्तीति चैके । Kathop. I. 20. So it means here misgivings as to her father' desire to promote his daughter's real welfare. Trip. says—विचिकित्सा आप्तत्वसंदेहमूलं वैमुख्यम् । यद्वात्स्यायनसूत्रं..... अन्यथा पितॄणां दोषानभिप्रायविरुद्धान्प्रतिपादयेदिति मातापित्रोश्च गुणानभिज्ञतामनपेक्षतां लुब्धतां शठतां चपलतां बान्धवानां प्रतिपादयेदिति पूर्वसूत्रादनुषज्यते । **पुरावृत्तो०**-Trip. quotes Vàtsyáyana—याश्चान्या अपि समानजातायाः कन्याः शकुन्तलाद्याः स्वरुच्या भर्तारं

प्राप्य मोदन्ते स्म ताश्चारताः प्रदर्शयेत् । स्तुतं &c.-Cons.-वत्सस्य यदभिजननः यत्र गुणतः माहात्म्यं तत्स्तुतं &c. Trip. again quotes Vát.—तस्याः स्वरुच्या नायकगुणान्भूयिष्ठान् परिवर्णयेत् । अथ खलु विधेयः &c.—This is also Trip.'s reading. परिचय-familiarity or close acquaintance. This is preferable to Jag.'s विधिविधेयः. For, a woman of Kám.'s self-reliance and diplomatic skill is not likely to refer to fate or depend upon its working. Herein she undoubtedly gives an indication of what her future policy will be. This is clear from her words further on ( p. 65. )—तदद्य माधवसमक्षमुत्तरमुपक्रमिष्ये । Fig. कारणसमुच्चय. Trip. notices in this Sl. करण, one of the Angas of Mukha Sandhi ( करणं प्रकृतारम्भः ).

---

## ACT. III

—:o:—

P. 62. कोपि—What a long time, &c. ( क इव what-like *V. l.* has also the same meaning ). Jag.'s rendering कोऽप्यकालः ( some unreasonable length of time—when she should not have been properly with her ) does not give good sense. He was probably misled by the reading को विअकालो । ( व्यकालः ). *Cf.* कोपि कालस्तस्या आगत्य गतायाः Rat. III. p. 60.

पिण्डपातवेलां &c.—We think वर्जयित्वा means here 'excepting.' It appears from the words of the poet पिण्डपात ( and not भिक्षापात ) that Kám was with Mâl. for sometime before noon and that she must have gone away before noon to beg for 'food.' This meeting of Kâm and Mál. takes place several days after the first meeting of Mâdh. and Mál. as is clear froms Kám.'s words नीता कतिपयाहेन &c. sl. 1.

कुञ्जक—&c.०—निकुञ्जस्य परिसरे &c; or after Jag. ०निकुञ्जाः परिसरे यस्य (surrounded, fenced round by ) तादृशः अशोकगहनस्य. निकुञ्ज is a place covered over with creepers; hence a bower ( निकुञ्जकुञ्जौ वा क्लीबे लतादिपिहितोदरे । Amara ). For different senses *cf.* II. 12. IX. 3.

P. 63. कृष्णाच०—which is sacred to Śiva. भगवत्या समं—The reading जनन्या समं though it looks natural is abandoned as we have further on भगवत्येव नेष्यति. एवं किल &c.—*i. e.* स्वहस्तकुसुमावचयकृतेन देवताराधनेन. परोक्षानुरागः—as a preliminary step to चक्षूरागः.

P. 64. प्रविशति—*i. e.* on the border of the *Kusumâkara* garden. विनयनम्रा—Lit. bowed down with modesty, exceedingly modest; or humbly yieding ( acquiescing in what I would say ) through modesty and hence not giving out her real thoughts. कतिपय०—कतिपयानामह्नां समाहारः कतिपयाहः तेन;–होभिः is against Pán. although Jag. tries somehow to defend it. Although कतिपय is not a numeral, still, as it is mentioned among the संख्या nouns in Pan. V. 2. 51, it may be regarded as a संख्या noun by the ज्ञापक प्रमाण *i. e.* a reason indirectly leading to the conclusion that कतिपय is a संख्या (कतिपयशब्दस्य असंख्यात्वेपि अत एव ज्ञापकात् डुत् Sid. Kau,) 'Besides', remarks Dr. Bhándarkar, "कतिपयाहेन occurs in Sáñkhyáyana's Śrautasûtra (पुरस्तादेव कतिपयाहेन होता प्रेङ्खफलकमुत्पाटयति। XVII 1. 2.) कतिपयाहस्य in Mbh. V. 180. 18. (ततः कतिपयाहस्य तच्छ्रुत्वा भरतर्षभ) and a similar comp. कतिपयरात्रं in Śak. (II. p. 59), so that there is no question that कतिपयाह is correct according to Pánini".

वैचित्यं—State of being uneasy; mental disquietude, listlessness. वाचं—Jag. reads द्रायं (Fr. द्रा + य; *cf.* प्रीतिद्रायः p. 84. which is Jag.'s reading for ०द्रानस्य). Here Jag.'s first meaning is preferable; this shows that he too would have preferred वाचं. There is no reason why Mál. should give presents to Kámandakî. वाच अनुवर्तते attends to me; follows my advice; it is not to be taken with गमनसमये as Jag. does. शपथैः याचते—adjures me to return. Fig. स्वभावोक्ति and कारकदीपक.

साधीयः—Better *i. e.* stronger. Mark the root-meaning of साधु-साध्नोत्यर्थम्; fr. साध् + उ (Unádi aff.) lit. leading to the accomplishment of an object.

शाकु०—शकुन्तलाया अयं शाकुन्तलः स आदिर्येषाम्. इतिहासवादान्—इतिहासः–इतिह इति पारम्पर्यार्थे अव्ययं तदास्तेऽस्मिन्; or fr. इतिह + आस (perf. अस्) thus it was. It merely means 'a past event'; इतिहासः पुरावृत्तं Amara; and has not got its technical meaning here. इतिहाससम्बधिनः वादाः (narrations; accounts) तान्. चिन्ता—musing; a reverie; she is lost in thought as to what course she should adopt.

P. 65. उत्तरं—Further steps, the future course, the line of action to be followed next (*i. e.* परिचयविधानं &c. as indicated in II. 13–अथ खलु विधेयः परिचयः).

मधुर &c.—मधुरमधुरसेन आर्द्रार्द्राः very juicy या मञ्जर्यस्तासां कवलनमेव केलिः &c., see Jag. कलः—Uttering indistinct but sweet notes. सहकारः—सह कारयति मेलयति द्वंद्वं; a kind of mango the blossoms of which have a very agreeable smell and which, therefore, is a favourite haunt of young couples. सहकारोतिसौरभः। Amara. चटुल—nimble. चञ्चरीक—a bee. कराल—rugged, uneven.

मराल०—मरालस्य इव मांसलः (fleshy, lusty) यः जघनपरिणाहः (*i. e.* परिणाहि जघनं stout thighs). विसंष्ठुलः स्खलितश्च or विसंष्ठुलं यथा तथा

स्खलितः यश्चरणसंचारः &c. विसंष्ठुल fr. स्था with वि and सम् and aff. उल. स्वेद०–There is some difficulty about taking this comp; सुधाबिन्दु० must be taken as an adj. qualifying स्वेदशीकर; but as such it ought to precede it. The comp. must, therefore, be taken, after Dr. Bhándárkar as—शीकराश्च ते सुधाबिन्दूयमानाः ( सुधाबिन्दव इवाचरन्तः ) च ( Pán. II. 2 38 ); Or as a Bah. of the आहिताग्नि class; शीकराः सुधाबिन्दूयमाना यस्मिन्. Or it should be explained as स्वेदशीकरैः सुधाबिन्दुमानिवाचरंश्चासौ मुग्धमुखचन्द्रश्च, the मत् being dropped before the affix य by विन्मतोर्लुक् by Pán. V. 3. 65. The reading स्वेदशीकर-सुधाबिन्दूज्ज्वल presents no difficulty of grammar.

P. 66. **प्रथमं**—must be taken as प्रियायाः प्रथमं 'before my beloved' and not with करोति, as Jag. has done. It corresponds to पुरस्तात् in the 2nd line. **संतापः**—The heat of the sultry season.

This constitutes the Bindu according to Trip.; माधवस्य मालती-दर्शनाभिलाषो द्वितीयाङ्कगतमालतीवृत्तान्तनन्दनवृत्तान्तविच्छेदे प्राप्ते पुनर्दर्शनहेतुत्वेनाच्छे-दकारणत्वाद्बिन्दुः । He also remarks that the contents of the 3rd and 4the Acts form the Pratimukha Sandhi. See Introd.

**आश्चर्यं** &c.—Cons. महीधरस्य जात्येन चन्द्रमणिना इव मम मनसा जडि-मानमेत्य द्रवमयो विकारः संधार्यते &c. **जात्येन**—See Jag. जातौ भवेन high born, excellent; with चन्द्रमणि, pure, fine. **जाड्येन** v. l. through its dulness. The fig is शाब्दी पूर्णा उपमा.

P. 67. **ज्वलयति** &c.—परिमृदित crushed ( though fresh and not faded ) and hence ललित charming, attractive. **लुलित**—*V. l.* drooping, spiritless. This is not a good reading as there remains nothing to support the first line. Fig. कारकदीपक.

**घनराजि** &c.—क्षण may also mean उत्सव; for the idea *cf.* मरुत्नवाम्भःप्रविधूतसिक्ताः कदम्बयष्टिः स्फुटकारकैव । Uttar. III. 42; also Kum. III. 68; त्वत्संपर्कात्पुलकितमिव प्रौढपुष्पैः कदम्बैः । Meg. 26. Fig. I. उपमा.

P. 68. **स्खलयति** &c.–Fig. कारकदीपक. and a trace of समुच्चय. **स्रंसयति**—संभ्रयति *V. l.* on this Trip. thus comments:—अस्मिन्पाठे वल्लभालोकनेन तुल्यमिति सहोक्तिनिर्वाहकं वल्लभालोकनस्य कर्तृत्वेन प्रक्रान्तस्य परित्यागेन कर्त्रन्तरस्वीकारात् । न च व्यङ्ग्यत्वादस्यार्थस्यायमदोष इति वाच्यम् । तुल्यमिति सहार्थतुल्यशब्दबलादुभयोरपि वाच्यत्वेन व्यङ्ग्यत्वाभावात् । वल्लभालोकनजानितानुभावा-भिव्यक्तो हि शृङ्गारो व्यङ्ग्यः । न तु वल्लभालोकनव्यापारः । तस्मात् 'स्रंसयति' इति पाठः श्रेयान् ।

**सुभ्रु**—although against Pàn. is often used by poets; *cf.* विमानना सुभ्रु कुतः पितुर्गृहे । Kum. V 43. and Malli. on it and our note thereon. The correct form is सुभ्रूः; कथं तर्हि हा पितः क्वासि हे सुभ्रु ( Bhatti VI. 11. ) इति भट्टिः । प्रमाद एवायमिति बहवः Sid Kau. **खेदः**—*cf.* मनःशरीरयोः खेदः क्रियातिशयतः श्रमः । Trip. **वल्लभालो०**—*i. e.* वल्लभकर्म-

केन्नालोकनेन the sight of (*i. e.* thy seeing) thy lover. वल्लभमवलोकयन्त्या येनुभावास्ते श्रमवशात्त्वयि दृश्यन्त इति नर्मगर्भोक्तिः । Trip. The other sense वल्लभकर्तृकालोकनेन (thy being seen by thy lover) is also hinted at as Jag. shows. किंच वल्लभकर्तृकावलोकनजनिता एवैते भावा न श्रमप्रभवाः । तेन विलोकयन्तं वल्लभमजानानाया अपि ते तत्कटाक्षसंस्पर्शमात्रेण चन्द्रकान्तस्येव चन्द्रकरसंपर्कमात्रेणैवंविधो विकार इत्यहो ते गाढानुरागित्वमिति प्रतिपाद्यां मालतीं प्रति अपह्नवातिशयोक्तिध्वनिः । Trip. सहोक्तिदीपकयोः संकरः Trip.

**हृदयंगमः**—हृदयं गच्छतीति; गम् + खच् (*i. e.* अ, before which a nasal comes in). **आज्ञप्तम्**—remarked, said. Mark the uses of the words आज्ञप्तं and विज्ञप्तं which are often used without the idea of command or request being actually present but as mere formal expressions when something is said by a superior person to one who is inferior to him and *Vice versa.* **चित्रं**—Lit. that would excite interest. **सुभगे**—The word is very appropriate here. It means (1) you are fortunate (भग fortune) to hear such an account; (2) you for whom I am making a good effort (भग–प्रयत्न).

P. 69. **परवान्**—Rendered helpless, overpowered by. **यावदशृ॰**—यावद् is अवधारणे I did hear, or I heard as much as. **यद्** &c.—यद् यस्माद् आनन्दं न भजते तत् तस्मात् (on that account). **विषम**—extreme, severe, trying. **क्षामं क्षामं**--अनेन काश्यं नामावस्थोक्ता । Fig. अनुमानविरोधयोः संसृष्टिः । Trip.

**उत्कलिका**—(1) Longing; (2) waves. यथा पयोनिधेः पय इन्दुदर्शनादेव क्षुभ्यति न तूष्णीमेवं माधवमनःक्षोभेपि त्वन्मुखेन्दुदर्शनमेव निमित्तमिति कार्यात्कारणमनुमीयते इत्यर्थः । Fig. A combination of अनुमान and उपमा the former adding charm to the latter. In the Upamá the following are compared—मनः and पयः; माधव and महोदधि; वदनं and उत्कलिका–longing and also waves. वदनेन्दु involves a रूपक (वदनमेवेन्दुः) रूपकोपमाभ्यामङ्गाङ्गिभावेन संकीर्णमनुमानमलंकारः । Trip.

**उपन्यासस्य**—see *supra* p. 18. **शुद्धिः**—Clearness or the proper way of. इष्टविषयप्रस्तावनप्रकारस्य शुद्धिः पूर्वापरविरोधाद्विदोषराहित्यम् । or अक्लिष्टता as Jag. takes it.

**अभ्यस्तगुणा**—गुणाः प्रसादमाधुर्यादयः । Trip. **कामदुघाः**—कामान् दुहन्तीति fr. काम + दुह् + अ, ह् being changed to घ् by दुहः कब्घश्च Páṇ. III. 2. 70. Stanza quoted in the D. R. as evidencing the qualities necessary for the Hero's or Heroine's accomplice. Fig. कारणसमुच्चय.

P. 70. **धत्ते चक्षुः** &c—Construe मृत्यवे बालचूते चक्षुः धत्ते &c. The tender mango sprouts &c. are the inflamers of passion, which, by intensifying his suffering, might hasten death and thus put an end to his torment. अत्रैकस्मिन्मृत्युलक्षणे कार्ये कुसुमितबालसहकारदर्शनादिक्रियाणां बह्वीनां साधनत्वेन समुच्चितत्वात्समुच्चयालंकारः । यदाह गुणक्रियायौगपद्यं

समुच्चयः । इति । Trip. **दाहप्रेरणा**—For the burning effect produced by the rays of the moon *cf.* मुञ्चन्त्येते हिमौघं नखरजनिकराः पश्च किं सोपि-दाहीं; Priya. III. 11; also Śak. III. 3.

**अक्षुण्णः**—Lit. Not trodden by any one before; unusual, one originating with her, quite unique. **दुष्करं करोति**—suffers excruciating pain; hard is his lot. *Cf.* Śàk. IV. दुष्करमहं करोमि p. 107.

P. 71. **भीतायिता**—P. p. p. of भीतायते. Here the aff. य cannot be taken in the sense of आचार ( as Jag. has it ) which it usually expresses; here it must be taken in the sense of करण ( making one to be) by शब्दवैरकलहाभ्रकण्वमेघेभ्यः करणे Pán. III. 1. 17. ( एभ्यः कर्मभ्यः करोत्यर्थे क्यङ् स्यात् Sid. Kau. ) भीतं करोति भीतायते । Dr. Bhàn. however, considers this as the p. p. p. of the den. or cau verb. भीतयति frightens or alarms. So भीताविद्दा should better have been translated by भीतिता or भायिता. See the whole question fully discussed by the learned Doctor. Trip. reads तस्य मर्त्यलोका... शङ्कमानाभूताविष्टेव &c. which avoids the difficulty; but the reading is not appropriate. **मुग्ध**—tender. **कन्द**—The bulbuous stalk.

**अभिनन्दति**—takes interest or delight in, welcomes. *Cf.* नाहार-मभिनन्दति Kád. I. p. 104. **केलिकलाः**—केलीश्च कलाश्च amorous sports and the fine arts; or केलीनां कलाः the parts *i. e.* sports even in part, in the least; or कला skill in. Trip. reads कलाक्रीडाः. This indicates अरति ( due to love-longing ).

**कमलायमान**—The palm spread out like a lotus. पर्यस्त—fully resting on. **ईषत्**—ind. a little. **उत्ताम्यति**—उद्दीपनविभावनाजनितवेदना-तिशयोक्तिः । Trip.

P. 72. **निजमहो**०—निजमहोत्सव एवाभ्युदयः निजमहोत्सवस्याभ्युदयो वा तस्य दर्शनार्थं प्रतिपन्नं रूपं येन । **अनुरूपा**०—रूपस्य सदृशो योग्यो वा अनुरूपः; अनुबध्यते इति अनुबन्धः; fr. अनुबन्ध् and aff. अ ( घञ् ); what is fastened upon another, a succession; here love fastened upon love, *i. e.* uninterrupted or continuous course of love; *cf. infra* Sl. 13 p. 76; and *ante* मनश्चक्षुषोरनुबन्धः p. 53. अनुरागस्यानुबन्धो यस्मिन्. **वञ्चना**—eluding, avoiding. **विविध**०—This and the other comp. expressions may also be taken as adverbs; विभ्रमैरभिरामं यथा तथा; महार्घीकृतो यौवनारम्भो यस्मिन्कर्मणि तद्यथा तथा &c. **समुल्लसित**०—०साध्वसाद्यः स्तंभस्तेन मन्थरेषु अवयवेषु प्रतिलग्ना ये स्वेदपुलकोत्कम्पास्तैः सुन्दरम् । **आयास**—torment, affliction. **बालकमलिनी**—The young sun-lotus. **प्रम्लायति**—The moon has no attraction for the Kamalinî. So the similarity extends only to this much that both fade away and that both obtain a momentary view of.

P. 73. **निर्मीयमाण**०—मुहूर्त एव मुहूर्तमात्रं, मु० हृदये विनिहितः निर्मीयमाणः ( created by fancy, pictured to the mind ) वल्लभसमागमो यया ।

**उच्छलत्** &c.--उच्छलन्ती या दन्तमौक्तिकपंक्तिकान्तिः तया &c. **निरन्तरो—** &c.--निरन्तरं यथा तथा उल्लसिताः ( risen up ) ये पुलकास्तैः पक्ष्मलौ ( hairy; fr. पक्ष्मन् properly an eyelash + ल showing possession ) यौ कान्तौ कपोलौ तयोः घूर्णमानः &c. ईषद्विकसिता निष्पंदा मन्दा च तारा यत्र तादृशे उत्ताने मसृणे नेत्रनीलोत्पले यत्र । **कौमारभावा०**.—कौमारमेव भावः कौमारभाव..

P. 74. **उद्दाम** &c.—उद्दामं excessively शिशिरः यः &c; or उद्दामः ( very great ) चासौ शिशिरश्च यः ०निकुरम्बः । **चुम्बित**—Jag. takes it as equivalent to चुम्बन ( भावे क्तः; Pán. III. 3. 114 ); or निकुरम्बेन चुम्बितः ( kissed, *i. e.* acted upon ) अत एव प्रवृत्तः निष्यन्दः यस्य तादृग् यः चन्द्रमणिहारः &c. शिशिर is without propriety and should have been omitted. **प्रचुर** &c.—०च्छटासारनिकरेण ( a thick sprinkling or paint of) दन्तुरितानि ( rendered rugged or uneven ) पत्राणि &c. **संवाहन**—applying to (Jag.); or gently rubbing or fanning with; *cf.* IX. 25. Trip. reads-प्रचुर...बालकदलीपत्रशयना पादसंवाहनादि...... जलार्द्रतालवृन्तोन्निद्रेव &c. **प्रस्रस्त**—loosened, dissolved. **उद्वान्त**—means here 'given out' and so there is no objection to its use ( as there is no ग्राम्यतादोष or vulgarism); *cf.* निष्ठ्यूतोद्गीर्णवान्तादि गौणवृत्ति व्यपाश्रयम् । अतिसुन्दरमन्यत्र गाम्यकक्षां विगाहते ॥ Dandin K. D. I. 95.

P. 75. **पीवरो०**—०मूलेन विसंवादितं ( lit. made to disagree with, loosened ) नीविबन्धनं यस्याः । **उच्छ्वस्य** &c.—न्तरे उत्तरङ्गा ये निश्वासाः तेषां वशेन विषमं यथा तथा उच्छ्वसन्तौ यौ पक्ष्मलौ पयोधरौ तयोरुपरि &c. **प्रतिबोध०**—वेलायां विसर्जिता प्रेरिता या उद्विग्ना दृष्टिस्तस्याः &c: ससंभ्रमः यः सखीजनस्तस्य प्रयत्नेन प्रतिपन्नः यः मूर्च्छाविच्छेदस्तस्य समये संगलिताः ( which escaped her ) ये &c. Trip. reads णीसासजणिदजीविदासा ( निश्वासजनितजीविताशा ) ०वृदं. **दुर्वारदैव** &c.—shows their utter helplessness to do anything for palliating her suffering.

**लावण्य** &c.—लावण्यं भूयिष्टं यस्मिन्यस्य वा तादृक् यन्निर्माणं ( frame, form; or creation; fashioning of ) तेन पेलवेषु । **दारुण०**-दारुणं यथा तथा विजृम्भितस्तस्य यद्वा दारुणं विजृम्भितं यस्य ।

P. 76. **रमणकेलि०**--रमणेन सह यः केलिकलहः तत्र यः कोपस्तेन जनितो य उपरागः ( a red tinge or glow; for a different sense see p. 189 l. 2; *cf.* also आताम्रतां कोपोपरागजनितां तु मुखेन्दुबिम्बे Rat. III. 14. ) तेन पल्लवितः ( made like a tender leaf; reddened ) यः केरली-( The Kerala ladies are described as possessing very fair and transparent cheeks; *cf. infra* VI. 19. ) कपोलस्तद्वत् कोमला ( the comparison indicates the early moon-rise ) उद्वेलन्ती या विमला चन्द्रिका तया उद्दामं ( forcibly, entirely ) यथा तथा दलितं तिमिरावरणं येषु. Here the word उद्दाम is out of place as it goes against कोमलोद्वे०; but the poet's fondness for long comp.s makes him use such words in more places than one.

**उल्लसित** &c.—उल्लसितः यः दुग्धसिन्धुपूरः तद्वद्धवला &c. **परिमलित**—संजातः परिमलो येषां endowed with perfume; this is preferable to

Jag.'s rendering. संवलन mixing with; मसृण agreeable to touch; मांसल heavy; परिमलितपाटलामुकुलानां निर्मथनं (crushing i. e. forcibly coming in contact with them) तेन बहलः यः परिमलोद्गारः (effusion, rising up) तेन यत्संवलनं तेन मसृणः मांसलः (lit. augmented) च यः &c. परिणाहः--विशालता i. e. the long summer nights (of course to love-affected persons).

यदि &c. गुणज्ञतायाः—Hereby Kám. suggests that Mâl.'s love is not only not ill-placed but that it is bestowed on the proper person and also has her approval. विदीर्यते &c—By this she suggests that Mâl. might have her sympathy and help in any step that she would take. Fig विरोध.

P. 77. हृल्लासः--disquietude, anxiety; हृदय is changed to हृद् when followed by लास by हृदयस्य हृल्लेखयदण्लासेषु। Pán. IV. 3. 50. हृदयोद्वेगः v. l.-dejection or disquietude of the mind. प्रमादः— An evil, a calamity (resulting from neglect or carelessness). See further on p. 79. l. 16; 81 l. 6; 189. l. 5. &c., and cf. अहो महान् प्रमादः Uttar. III. p. 74.

प्रकृति &c.—चलित &c. The southerly breeze, the mango blossoms and the moon are the exciters of passion and as such form the paraphernalia of Cupid. Fig.--A combination of विषम and समुच्चय (कारण).

जितमिह &c.—Cf. the similar address to the bee by Dushayanta in Sák, I. 21. परिणत०—परिणतः यः बिसकाण्डस्तद्वत् पाण्डू च तौ मुग्धौ च स्तनौ तयोः परिणाहे विलासस्तस्य वैजयन्ती. Fig. (Kávyalinga according to Trip. and) रूपक.

P. 78. यौवन &c.—संभृतौ waxed strong, दुर्विषहौ च तौ अमर्षरोषौ &c; शृंखलानिरोधस्य प्रतिभंगः तेन संकलिताः प्राप्ता (resumed) ये निजलीलाविलासाः तत्र विलसन् यो बहल उत्तुंगश्च लाङ्गूलः स एव विकटवैजयन्तिका तस्या डम्बरेणोड्डामरः; now see Jag. डम्बर display, pomp. डामर frightful, terrific; see V. 3. सतृष्णं voraciously, greedily. चपेट—The extended palm of the hand; (पाणौ चपेटप्रतलप्रहस्ता विस्तृताङ्गुलौ Amara); hence a smart slap. मोटन or आमोटन fr. मुट्। 1 P. or 10 P. A to crush. जाङ्गलं—(जंगले भवं) properly the flesh of the forest animals such as the deer, &c. उद्गार--coming up (of the flesh forced in). गल्लूरणः—Trip. retains this and says गल्लूरणशब्दः मांसभक्षणसमयकुपितशार्दूलजातिप्रयुक्तं कण्ठगर्जितम्। Cf. Ger. gellen; Eng. Yell. संदर्भः—विपुलत्वं Trip.; or it may mean continuity; continuous sound. निष्ठापितः—निष्ठा the last boundary (Jag.); or निर्भयं स्थानं तत्पर्यन्तं गमितः made to go to some safe place. विद्रावित V. l. put to flight. (so as to disappear). कर्पर—a kind of weapon (resembling a karpara). कर्दमित—कर्दमः अस्य संजातः। उल्लसित--Brightened, animated.

P. 79. **विनिहत०**—*i. e.* some were killed, others were put to flight. **अतर्कितो०**—अनाकिंतं यथा तथोपनतं &c. **प्रमादः**—see *anti* p. 77.

P. - 80. **अविरलमिव**-&c.-Mâl. looked at Mâdhava steadfastly and with eyes dilated. The white portion of the eye, therefore, being prominent it is compared to a white lotus, milk &c, and her continuous and steadfast gaze to a garland of lotuses, a stream of milk &c. *cf.* द्वितीययेव पुण्डरीकमालया दृष्टया संभावयन्ती भुवननाथम् । Kâr. p. 211. When the pupil, however, in its quick play, is alone prominent, the eye is compared to a blue lotus and a series of such glances to a garland of blue lotuses. **दाम्ना**—दामत्वं च कटाक्षाणां पंक्तिभूयाविरलनिपातनात् । नद्धत्वेन निष्क्रियत्वमात्मनो दर्शयन् स्तम्भाख्यं सात्विकभावमभिव्यनक्ति । See p. 86 l. 17. **सिक्तः**—अनेन धारासारन्यायेन कटाक्षप्रवृत्तेर्लोलाख्यो दृष्टिव्यापार उक्तः । यथा—धारावाहिकसंचारो यस्य तल्लोलमुच्यते । Trip. Fig. Malotprekshâ a series of Utprekshâs.

P. 81. **संसक्त** &c.—संसक्तानि च तानि त्रुटितानि......अन्त्रजालानि तैर्व्याकीर्णश्चासौ स्फुरन्तश्च ते अपवृत्ताश्च रुण्डखण्डा यत्र तादृक् च । **कीलाल०**—कीलालस्य व्यतिकरेण मिश्रणेन ( rather than संघेन as Jag. has it ). **गुल्फदघ्न०**—गुल्फः प्रमाणमस्य. Fig. Svabhâvokti.

**क्रम**—The distance covered by the leap of a wild beast. **च पशुना**—परशुना *v. l.* then the cons. is दंष्ट्रायुधः परशुना दृढं हतः प्रमथितश्च. But this reading will not do, as it leaves no room for the cry अत्याहितं अत्याहितं.

P. 82. **अत्याहितं**—(अत्यन्तमाधीयते तन्निवारणार्थं मनो दीयते अस्मिन्). Lit. that which requires a great effort of the mind to ward it off, hence, a great calamity.

Kám. & Mâd.—**सहर्षं**—because the tiger was killed and so Mak. was past danger. **निश्चलः**—standing firm ( and not falling down ). **तदेहि तावत्पदग्रामः**—As the subject matter of the next Act is thus introduced here this is what is technically called Ankávatâra (अङ्कावतारस्त्वंकान्ते पातोङ्कस्याविभागतः । The fourth Act is thus a continuation of the 3rd.

## ACT IV.

P. 83. The fourth Act, as already remarked, is a sequel of the 3rd and the two could have been well amalgamated but for the exigencies of the Prakaraṇa which must have ten Acts.

**ततः प्रविशतः** &c. We should rather have read मदयन्तिकामालतीभ्यां as Trip does. Kâm. might have purposely asked Mâl. to support

Mâd. and the latter, although modest and reserved, could not have refused to do so at such a critical time. Besides Kâm. who was trying to intensify Mâl.'s passion for Mâd. had not as yet given the slightest indication of her knowledge to the latter of her love for Mâdhava, so that we can expect Mâl. to comply the more readily with her request. Again further on, it is Mâl. who addresses a speech to Mâdh. ( महाभाग &c.). In that speech we have omitted the words सखि लवङ्गिके and adopted the reading महाभाग instead. For there is no reason why Mâl. should address the speech to Lav. who was not directly interested either in Mâdh. or Maka.; *cf.* Trip माधवस्यापि मित्रव्यसनेन प्रमुग्धत्वान्मालत्या संनिहितयावलम्बनं द्रष्टव्यम् । माधवस्य ललाटे हस्तं दत्त्वेत्यङ्गसंस्पर्शेनामृतासेचनकल्पेन झटिति प्रमोहमपसारयितुं ललाटे हस्तनिक्षेपः । न चैतावता मालत्या धाष्टर्यमाशङ्कनीयम् । ईदृशे विपत्समये सर्वत्र सर्वेषामुचितोपकारकरणस्य लोके धाष्टर्यतयानुद्भावनात् ।

**प्रतिबुद्धं**—(1) shone brightly; (2) come back to his senses. The comparison to the full moon indicates that her heart thrilled with delight at his sight पूर्णचन्द्रत्वारोपणेन स्वचित्ताह्लादकत्वादनुरागप्रकर्षं सूचयति Trip.

P. 84. **अयमपि स जनः**—Mad., as a well bread Hindu maiden does not utter Mak.'s name as she loves him now. **ऊर्जित**—properly 'powerful, mighty'; hence excellent, blissful, &c. **वत्स मकरन्द** &c.—construe आयुष्मान्...हेतुः कथं सन्निधापितः sent as the saviour. **वृत्तेन—वृत्तान्तेन** *v. l.* the news must be about the gift of Mâlatî. **सुहृद्बुध्या**—बुद्धि coming back to consciousness, recovery.

P. 85. **पूर्णपात्र**—Properly a vessel or dish filled with such articles as clothes, ornaments &c. kept for being freely carried away by relatives or servants on festive occasions, such as the birth of a son, &c.; *cf.* कदा मे तनयजन्ममहोत्सवानन्दनिर्भरो हरिष्यति पूर्णपात्रं परिजनः Kâd. p. 106.; hence any thing seized on such occasions or a present made to one bringing some happy news. *Cf.* तस्योत्तरीयं पूर्णपात्रं जहार Kâd. p. 123. हर्षादुत्सवकाले यदलंकारांशुकादिकम् । आकृष्य गृह्यते पूर्णपात्रं स्यात्पूर्णकं च तत् ॥ See also com.

P. 86. **भरित**—presents some difficulty of grammar, as भृत is the p. p. p. of भृ; see the question discussed in the com. Trip. who omits एदे (एते) reads the passage as हृदयभरितोद्गमाद्रि...सुन्दरघूर्णितधीरपर्यन्तमनोहराः ( ०नन्दाभ्यां सुन्दरं यथा तथा घूर्णिता धीरा आकारगोपनार्थमवलम्बितधैर्याः पर्यन्तमनोहराश्च)...नीलोत्पलमांसलच्छवयः &c. **दलितनीलोत्पल** &c.—*cf.* अनिलचलितकुवलयदामदीर्घैः दृष्टिपातैः Kad. p. 153; see *supra*. p. 80, note on अविरलमिवदाम्ना &c.

P. 87. **मनोरथ** &c.—मनोरथेन निर्वृतः समागमः ययोः । **ईषत्ति०**—For the cons. see com. **०विषमं**—Jag. says मन्दं dull; rather as Trip.

takes it-विषमं वक्रं । वक्राख्योयं शृङ्गारदृग्विकारः । यथा—चलितोपाङ्गसंचारो यत्र तद्वक्रमुच्यते । कुणित०—Trip. explains कुणितं प्रान्ते अपाङ्गदेशे भागत्रयेण संकुचितमित्यर्थः । पुरस्त्रिभागसंकोचे प्रेम्णा तत्कुणितं भवेत् । लुलितं—Trip. reads ललितं which he explains as प्रेमार्द्रमन्तर्विकसत्तारं ललितमीरितम् । आकेकराक्षम्—आके मूर्ध्नि करितुं संचारयितुं नेत्रतारां शीलमस्य । अचिरं—may also be taken as an adj. to दृष्टं meaning unsteady. Fig. Anumána.

This speech of Kám. does not accord well with her holy character. Perhaps the poet, led by his zeal to give us an exact picture of a love-stricken person, forgot that he was putting the speech into the mouth of a female ascetic, how-so-ever devoted to worldly concerns she might have been.

P. 88. भिदुरः—capable of being broken, fragile; see Jag.; the affix उर is similarly added to विद् and छिद्; विदुर, छिदुर. Pán. III. 2. 162. पारिप्लवधुरा—धुर् implies excess ( उत्कर्ष ). For in this case the torture of his mind would be greater. स्वास्थ्यं—Because it has gained its end now and has no more to trouble itself about thwarting my object. कृतकृत्यश्च—*Cf.* भवतु पञ्चबाणः कृती । Vik. II. 11. The fig. is समुच्चय. एकस्मिन्कार्येऽनेककारणसमुच्चयात् समुच्चयालंकारः । Trip.

Sl. 4. Fig. काव्यलिङ्ग in the first two lines and आर्थी उपमा and विरोधाभास in the last.

P. 89. दत्तपूर्वा—She has been already given to another ( and Mádh. cannot try to get her from Bhûrivasu now. ) अदत्तपूर्वा *V. l.* She was not given before ( and so there was no cause for anxiety ) but now she is. The former is evidently better.

वाक्प्रतिष्ठानि—वाचि प्रतिष्ठा the being based on येषां. पुण्या० व्यवस्थिताः—पुण्यापुण्यहेतवो व्यवस्थाः &c. *V. l.* ( See foot note ). The arrangements of the affairs of all men which cause merit and demerit dipend ( आयतन्ते ) on speech.

अनृतात्मिका—अनृतम् आत्मा यस्याः of the nature of untruth *i. e.* not supported by truth. This is explained in the next two sentences. If he means 'The King is lord over his ( the king's ) daughter', then Mal. is not his daughter. If he means—The king is lord over his ( Bhurivasu's ) daughter, then this statement has no sanction from religious law. Trip. says छलात्मिका *i. e.* intended to mislead, not really meaning what it apparently means. उपचारोक्तिचातुर्येणापाततः सत्यत्वप्रतिभासेपि विचार्यमाणे परमार्थतो मिथ्याभूतैव । Trip. अविमर्शितव्यम्—should not be thought over; you should not attach any weight to this matter. Bhûrivasu cannot be bound by what he has said. विमर्शितव्यम् *V. l.* will have nearly the same meaning; it means—the matter must be thought over before we accept the truth of it. *i. e.* we should not take his words as true unless so proved by facts. विमर्शितव्यं or र्धनीयं—*V. l.* means "Should be borne, not contended against, as it is inoffensive". Dr. Bhánd अविचिकित्स्यं *V. l.*—not deserving to be criticised अव्यवस्थितं—*V. l.* not well settled or proper.

P 90. **सपत्नेषु**—सपत्न an enemy; सपत्नीव (one a cowife) like सपत्नः irregularily formed being so mentioned by Pán in त्यन् सपत्ने IV. 1. 145. **संगमनाय यत्नः**—Trip. remarks.— इयं च यत्नाख्या द्वितीयावस्था । यथा—अपश्यतः फलप्राप्तिं यो व्यापारः फलं प्रति । परं त्वौत्सुक्यगमनं स यत्न इति कथ्यते ॥ **प्रसक्तः**—Lit. forcibly (प्रकर्षेण) attached (सक्तः); hence set forth continuously or in earnest; or uninturrupted.

P. 91. **प्रकटस्य** &c.—प्रकटोप्यसुखप्रदः *V. l.* **एकरसां**—Lit. of one flavour; एको रसो यस्याः hence uniform, unmixed. **अकाण्ड**—नास्ति काण्ड उचितावसरो यस्य. काण्ड—a division or portion of time; hence proper time; अकाण्डे abrupt विवर्तनं turning away, a sudden adverse turn or course (विरुद्धा वृत्तिः प्रातिकूल्येन व्यवहरणं) &c. **प्रविशिनष्टि** &c.— बधिरह्यो विशिनष्टि मनोरुजम् । *V. l.* See Uttar. IV. 15.

**निर्व्यूढं**—fully carried out, proved. *Cf.* निर्व्यूढस्तेऽपत्यस्नेहः Uttar. I. p. 29; and *infra* निर्व्यूढः संभावनाभारो बुद्ध. p. 166; for other senses *cf.* VI. 17. and p. 152 (मुहूर्तनिर्व्यूढाविस्म). **दारुणसमारम्भ**—Fate began by producing in Mâl. intense love for Mâdh. which tormented her much and now had made her miserable for ever. Mâdh. also says the same; *cf. supra* sl. 4. 7. **कापालिकत्वं**—Lit. the vow or course of life of the Kápálikas (who are known to kill young girls and women); hence cruelty. This foreshadows Mâl.'s being carried away by Kap.; see Jag. Trip. also remarks अनेन पश्चमाङ्ककृत्यं च किंचित्सूचितम् ।

P. 92. **महामांसविक्रयात्** &c.—Mádh. in his despair hopes, by this means at least, to propitiate some spirit of the cemetery and so to gain his object. See Jag. This shows his utter desperateness.

**त्रस्तैकहायन** &c.—एकः हायनः यस्य स एकहायनः । त्रस्तः एकहायनः कुरङ्गस्तस्य &c. such a dear is mentioned as it is more easily frightened; अनेन दृष्टेरतितरलता सूचिता । The line occurs in Uttar. (ऊद्वृष्टेः &c. III. 28). **अमृत** &c.—Fig. उत्प्रेक्षा.

**बुद्धरक्षिताप्रियसखी**—a हेतुगर्भविशेषण. She, the dear friend of Bud., must naturally follow her advice and acquiesce in all she tells her to do. So you may rest sure that the latter will exert her influence and induce Mad. to marry you. **प्रमथ्य**—&c.— This is the first reason why she should choose you alone; (she must repay your obligation). **परिष्वङ्गं लब्ध्वा**—This is the second

हेतु. Having once come in contact with your body, she, a nobly born maiden, cannot offer herself up to any other man. रमताम्—used in the sense of the Poten. but is more forcible. व्यक्तस्नेह &c —See Jag. or व्यक्तः यः स्नेहः तेन &c. Fig. Anumâna. Sl. quoted in Śârgadhara's Paddhati under the heading ग्रीष्मसमयस्वभावाख्यानम्.

P. 93. पारा—वरदा Trip. See IX. 1. संभेद—Confluence, junction. *Cf* मधुमतीसिन्धुसंभेद p. 177; हर्षोद्वेगसंभेदः ( mixture ) p. 167, आलोकतिमिरसंभेदम् X. 11. निबिडित—p. p. p. of the den. from निबिड. रुचिर०—रुचिरकनककुम्भस्य श्रीः विद्यते येषां; रुचिर may also qualify श्री. आभोग—expanse; extent, हस्तस्वस्तिकाभिः—*i. e.* they crossed their hands, ( which, therefore, looked like a स्वस्तिक ) and placed them on their bosoms. हस्तौ स्वस्तिकमिव हस्तस्वस्तिकं; तानि हस्तस्वस्तिकानि । Fig. तत्क्षणस्नानोत्थितवधूस्वभावोक्तिः ।

---

# ACT V.

P. 94. आकाशयानेन—Passing through the air or along the aerial path. Here यान may mean 'journey, or a path ( यात्यत्र; या+अन added अधिकरणे ) and not a vehicle. Those having superhuman power could travel through space; *cf.* ततः प्रविशत्याकाशयानेनोर्वशी. Vik. p. 41. See also notes on sl. 4. and Remark. भीषणोज्ज्वलवेषा—This is described in the 3rd and 4th Ślokas.

षडधिक &c.—For the cons. see Jag. The best way of taking the comp. is षड्भिरधिका दश षोडश नाड्यः तासां चक्रं a circular case or envelope formed by the sixteen Nâdîs. षोडश नाड्यात्मकं चक्रं कण्टबिलवर्ति अनाहताख्यम् । Trip.

According to the Yoga-Śâstra there are 72000 veins and arteries in the body ( 101 encircling the heart; see Jag. ) through which the vital air passes. Of these ten are principal.* These

---

*The following extract from the Yogarahasya given by Dr. Bhând. may also be usefully read—क्रियाशक्त्या विना क्वापि ज्ञानशक्तिर्न दृश्यते । तेनेदं ज्ञानशक्त्यर्थं कृतं वेश्म (the human body) क्रियामयम् ।। चतुर्विंशतिभिस्तत्त्वैः क्रियाशक्तिरचेतना । ज्ञानशक्त्या युता वापि लभ्यते चेतनावती ।। सर्वज्ञोपि शिवस्तत्र शक्तिसङ्गेन मोहितः । नात्मानं न परं वेत्ति विचेष्टति तदिच्छया ।। प्राणापानमयी शक्तिः षट्चक्राधारसंयुता । शान्तं शिवं वशीकृत्य वर्तते कामकारतः । आधारः कन्दमित्युक्तं स्वाधिष्ठानं च जन्मभूः । नाभिस्तु मणिपूराख्यं हृदयं विद्ध्यनाहतम् ।। विशुद्धिः कण्ठ इत्युक्तमाज्ञाचक्रं भ्रुवोन्तरे । आधारो हि चतुर्भिन्नः स्वाधिष्ठानं च षड्दलैः ।। दशाभिर्मणिपूराख्यं द्वादशैस्तु अनाहतम् । विशुद्धिः षोडशैर्भिन्नैराज्ञाचक्रं द्वयेन तु ।। कालाग्निरुद्र आधारे शक्तिः कुण्डलिनी तथा । आनन्दाख्या स्वधिष्ठाने शक्त्या

together with six others, more prominent than the rest, make up the total of sixteen referred to here. Their names are:— इडा च पिङ्गला चैव सुषुम्णा चापरा स्मृता । गान्धारी हस्तिजिह्वा च पूषा यशस्विनी तथा ॥ अलम्बुषा कुहूश्चैव शङ्खिनी दशमी स्मृता । तालुजिह्वेभजिह्वा ( लोलजिह्वेभजिह्वा ) च विजया कामदापरा ॥ अमृता बहुला नाम नाड्यो वायुसमीरिताः ॥ Even out of these the most important are three *viz.*, Id'a, Pingala and Sushumná, through which the breath flows. The Idà, passing through the left side of the spinal cord reaches the left nostril and the Pingalâ, running through the right side joins the right nostril. The Sushumná passes through the middle of these and reaches the crown of the head. इडा नासापुटे वामे पिङ्गला दक्षिणे भवेत् । सुषुम्णा तालुभित्त्वैव ब्रह्मद्वारं प्रवर्तिता ।

. The other way of taking the comp. which is suggested by Jag. ( and which Dr. Bhándarker prefers ) is षड्भिः चक्रैः अधिकं यद् दशनाडीचक्रं ( इडाच……शङ्खिनी दशमीस्मृता ॥ एतन्नाडीमहाचक्रं ज्ञातव्यं योगिभिः सदा । Yogachūdamaņi Upanishad ) &c., *i. e.* (who resides) in the midst of all the seven Chakras that compose the body. But as षट् cannot be grammatically connected with चक्र, we have recourse to लक्षणा and understand by षट् षट् चक्राणि. Jag. understands by the षट्च० the six centres of activity, *viz.* the ear, the navel, the heart, the throat, the palate and the centre of the eyebrows. The *Chakras* usually mentioned are—चक्राणि च योगशास्त्रे—चतुर्दलं स्यादाधारे स्वाधिष्ठाने च षड्दलम् । नाभौ दशदलेपेतं सूर्यसंख्यदलं हृदि ॥ कण्ठे स्यात्षोडशदलं भ्रूमध्येऽशीतिसंमितम् । सहस्रदलमाख्यातं ब्रह्मरन्ध्रं तु पंकजम् । एतानि सप्त पद्मानि चक्रस्थानि प्रचक्षते ॥ नाडीचक्रात्मककमलानां नाड्य एव दलानि । Trip. The other explanation of this given by Jag. is also admissible.

**हृदि विनिहितरूपः**—हृदि विनिहितं रूपं यस्य तथा सन् whose form being realised or manifested in the heart ( by meditation ); or रूपं येन whose form reposes or rests in the heart-lotus ( हृत्पद्मे ); *cf.* अथ यदस्मिन्ब्रह्मपुरे दहरं पुण्डरीकं…तस्मिन्यदन्तस्तदन्वेष्टव्यं &c. Chhân. Up. हृत्पुण्डरीकं विरजं…विचिन्त्य मध्ये विशदं विशोकम् । अचिन्त्यमव्यक्तमनेकरूपं शिवं प्रशान्तममृतं ब्रह्मयोनिम् ॥ Kaiva. Up. ईश्वरः सर्वभूतानां &c. ( See Jag. ) Bg. XVIII. 61. Trip construes तद्विदां ( तादृगात्मस्वरूपदर्शिनां योगिनां ) हृदि विनिहितरूपः सन् &c.

---

कामाख्यया सह । नाभौ ब्रह्मा हृदि श्रीशः कण्ठे रुद्रो व्यवस्थितः । ईश्वरोलाम्बिकायां च तदूर्ध्वे च सदाशिवः ॥ ज्योतिः स्थानानि चैतानि षट् चक्राणि जगुर्बुधाः ॥+ + + द्वासप्ततिसहस्राणि कन्दान्नाडयो विनिर्गताः । प्रविश्य नाभिदेशेषु सर्वाङ्गेषु ततो गताः ॥ + + + एताः प्राणवहा ज्ञेयाः प्रधानाः दश नाडिकाः ॥ इडा नासापुटे वामे पिङ्गला दक्षिणे भवेत् । सुषुम्णा तालुभित्वैव ब्रह्मद्वारं प्रवर्तिता ॥ सरस्वती च जिह्वायां गान्धारी वामकर्णके । दक्षिणे हस्तिजिह्वाख्या पूषा वामे च लोचने ॥ अलम्बुषा दक्षिणे स्याद्गुदद्वारे कुहूर्भवेत् । आब्रह्मरन्ध्रान्मार्गेण ब्रह्मरन्ध्रस्य शङ्खिनी ॥

अविचलितमनोभिः—With the mind not swerving from the object of contemplation; *i. e.* the mind unflinchingly resting on it. This implies ध्यान which Patanjalî defines as प्रत्ययैकतानता the continuous ( and unobstructed ) perception of the object of contemplation by the mind restrained from all activities. *Cf.* Bg. तत्रैकाग्रं मनः कृत्वा &c. VI. 12-14., Vik. I.1. अन्तर्यश्च मुमुक्षुभिर्नियमितप्राणादिभिर्मृग्यते &c.

परिणद्धः शक्तिभिः—परिणद्धः equipped or endowed with. The Śaktis or the potentialities by which God acts are three, *viz.* ज्ञान, इच्छा and प्रयत्न or क्रिया as mentioned by Jag.; hence the sole creator of the world. शक्तिनाथ—The lord of the Śaktis, Bràhmî, Máheśvari and others ( see Jag. ) who attend upon Śiva as Bhairava. If, however, परिणद्ध be taken in the sense of 'Surrounded or encircled by' ( *cf.* पुनर्भवं परिगतशक्तिरात्मभूः Śak. VII. 35 ), by शक्तिभिः must be understood the eight goddesses above mentioned as done by Jag. and then शक्तिनाथ would mean thelord of the Siddhis, Mahimà and others ( see Jag. ) *i. e.* not only possessing them but having them in his gift ( सिद्धिदः ); or शक्तिनाथ might mean the lord of P'arvatî.

In this sl. Śiva is described as the Supreme Being from whom the whole universe emanates. See Dr. Bhândárkar's notes. This sl. is quoted in the K. P. VII. as an illustration of the doctrine that the use of words not familar to readers, which usually constitutes a fault in a composition ( called अप्रतीतत्व unintelligibility ), becomes a merit when the speaker, who knows the meaning of the technicalities used, uses them in a soliloquy. अत्र नाडीचक्रादिपदानां केवलयोगशास्त्रप्रसिद्धत्वादप्रतीतत्वमपि स्वात्मविमर्शने न दुष्टत्वं किंतु गुणत्वमित्याहुः ।

P. 95. नित्य—the ever-lasting one; नियमेन भवः fr. नि + त्य; (or it may mean 'always', if construed with न्यस्त; प्रतिदिने जपोपक्रमसमये Trip. ) न्यस्त०—mystically touched. न्यास properly means 'the placing in or implanting of' by repeating particular *mantras* and touching the six parts mentioned by Jag. ( or, the six *Chakras* referred to in the previous sloka ). निहितं—placed therein by means of meditation. उदितं—manifested, risen to view. लयवशात्—लय is complete absorption into or identity with the object of contemplation, effected when the stage of Samâdhi is reached. This is done by means of ध्यान ( see above ) तदेवार्थमात्रनिर्भासं स्वरूपशून्यं समाधिः । Yog. III. 2,3. By Samâdhi here is meant that condition in which the mind is called off from the multitudinous concrete objects in the world and is concentrated and focused on one object. This is called Asmitá Samâdhi, a division of ( संप्रज्ञात समाधि. )

**अभ्यागता**—*i. e.* Come through space. When the power of concentration of the mind has reached a very high degree of perfection, a Yogî can move through space by concentrating his mind on such light objects as cotton and being quite one with them, and on the relation of the body to space (कायाकाशयोः सम्बन्धसंयमाल्लघु तुलसमापत्तेश्चाकाशगमनम् । Pat. Y. S. III. 41. See remark on this śl. below. Trip. takes लयवशात् with अभ्यागता which appears to be better. न्यस्तषडंग......शिवरूपिणमात्मानं पश्यन्ती अहं I who always behold the soul in the form of Śiva......have come here by the force of contemplation &c.; *cf.* Trip लयवशात् ऊर्ध्वमाकृष्टस्य वायोस्तेषु तेषु नाडीनिवेशेषु वृत्तिनिरोधो गगनगमनहेतुभूतो योगशास्त्रप्रसिद्धो लयः । तद्वशाद्धेतोः ।

**नाडीनामुदयक्रमेण**—By forcing the breath through the principal Nâdîs in proper order to create a propelling force in the body. **पञ्चामृताकर्षणात्**—By drawing off the five grosser elements, which is necessary to make the body light and capable of floating in air. This is what is called the dematerialisation of the body. The elements are called अमृत here because they are permanent. नाडीनां पार्थिवाप्याग्नेयवायव्यनाभसाख्यानां पञ्चभूतप्रकृतिकानां नाडीविशेषाणामुदयसाम्यावस्थानिरोधानक्रमेण तत्तद्भूताकर्षणसाधनेन जगतां यान्यारम्भकाणि पञ्च अमृतानि न म्रियन्ते नात्यन्तं विनश्यन्ति कार्यकारणरूपेण सर्वदावस्थानादित्यमृतानि तेषां &c. Trip.

**विघटयन्ती**—as she forced her way through them. **अग्रे**—Jag. reads अग्रेभुवः lying before. Trip. reads अग्रेनभः as an adv. comp. ( नभसः अग्रे ). **नभोम्भोमुचः**—नभःसम्बन्धिनः अम्भोमुचः.

The above description of Kapálakundalâ's flight through the sky is not a myth. Not to mention the mighty sages of old, such as Srimad Vyâsa and others, the venerable Śankarácbárya and many other Yogis of modern times are described as having, achieved such a feat. This is what is technically called 'Levitation.' It is a process of Hatha Yoga by means of which a Yogi can make his body buoyant by Will-power and remain seated in air or pass through it. With the Indian Yogins this is an inward process and the result may be attained without any external help or mesmeric means. It is accomplished by the breath being well controlled and regulated ( technically called Prânâyáma ). When a Yogi knows perfectly the art of levitating himself and thereby is able to overcome the force of gravitation, he can transfer his body through space. This, however, will require a supreme effort of the will which must be developed to the highest degree. When a Yogi transports his body through space he also has to dematerialise it and when he arrives at his destination, he regains his former condition by Will-force. The Indian ascetics practised this art not for performing wonderful feats, but as a preparatory step to spiritual enlightenment. For when a proper degree of spiritual progress is reached by means of Prâṇâyáma, the purified mind becomes fit to imbibe knowledge of the highest order.

P. 96. **उल्लोल** &c.—उल्लोला tossed up कपालानां कण्टमाला तस्याः संघट्टेन striking against क्वणिताः कराला: harsh किंकिण्यः यस्मिन् येन वा । **रमणीय०**—रमणीयश्चासौ डामरश्च तस्य भावः the state of being charming and awful.

**विष्वग्वृत्तिः**—विष्वक् in all directions वृत्तिः movement यस्य. **संस्कार**—the effect produced by the first striking causing a continuation of the sound. **उत्तालः**—howling, or strong, violent. **कुहरेषु**—the cavities ( सरन्ध्रकुहरेषु Trip. ). Fig. स्वभावोक्ति.

P. 97. **पुराण** &c.—तैलेन अक्तं च तत्परिभुज्यमानं च यद् रसोनं तस्येव गन्धः येषाम्. **रसोन**—रसे ऊन्यते त्यज्यते; or see Jag. **श्मशानवाट**—the extensive cemetery ground. Although वाट is generally used in the sense of a 'path' ( see Jag. ), it means here 'what is encircled; hence the spacious ground. **पूजासंभार**—collection of the materials of worship.

**ललितचरणन्यासः**—This reading is preferable to विकटन्यासः. Because (1) the epithets in the first two lines refer to all that is graceful in him while in the last two lines the poet alludes distinctly to his *Vikatatva*; with the reading विकट these will be inappropriate. (2) Mâdhava's natural gait was graceful and his entrance shows that he was not so much thinking of selling flesh as of his beloved and so there was nothing to disturb his natural mode of walking; (3) न्यास in the sense of देहन्यास, general appearance or shape, is unusual. Fig. in the first two lines there is Upamá ( आर्थी पूर्णा समासगा ).

P. 98. **व्योम्नः पर्यन्ताः**—The skirts of the sky; the horizon all round. **तापिच्छ**—The tamala tree. **वात्या**—वात + य in the sense given in the com.; य is added in this sense to पाश, तृण, धाम and other words, by पाशादिभ्यो यः । Pân. IV. 2. 49; so पाश्या, तृण्या &c. **स्फीत**—p. p. of स्फाय् 1. A. to swell &c. The Figs of speech in this. śl. are उत्प्रेक्षा and विरोध ( in the last line ).

**प्रेमार्द्राः** &c.—Herein Mâd. wishes to witness the several actions of Mâl. under the influence of the different feelings worked up in her by the different stages of love, viz. an affection ( प्रेम ) produced at first sight, growing into love and finally developing into intense affection owing to familiarity. **प्रणयस्पृशः**—Trip. explains प्रणय as उपचारैर्मिथो यूनोर्यद्बाह्याभ्यन्तराभिधैः । प्रेम नीतं प्रकर्षं चेतस तत्र प्रणयः स्मृतः ॥ **चेष्टाः**—कटाक्षक्षेपणगात्रविक्षेपादयः; it is premature to say संभोगे चुम्बनादयः

( as Jag. does ). **रोधी**—Obstructing, paralysing. **आशंसापरि०**—*Cf.* दुःखं याति मनोरथेषु तनुतां संचिन्त्यमानेष्वपि । Pray. III. 5. Sl. quoted in the K. P. and Sah. Dar. as an instance of *Abhilásha* (a desire for union) a kind of Vipralambha Sṛngára or love not yet consummated by union or thwarted by separation.

P. 99. **अतिमुक्त०**—See Jag.; ( surpassing pearls *i. e.* a pearl-necklace, more precious than a pearl-necklace ); the other sense ( अतिविरला ) given by Jag. is not good. Trip. who reads अतिमुक्तकस्र० says अतिमुक्तकैः वासन्तिकाकुसुमैरन्तरान्तरा निवेशितैर्ग्रथिता. But this is not correct, as the garland was woven entirely of the Bukula flowers. अविमुक्तं *v. l.* means-not left off, continuously worn. Jag.'s objection to this reading is that it is redundant when we have सततावियाव in the next line. But this objection does not count much. **०र्पितस्तनम्**—Jag. takes this as an adv., as his reading in परिवृत्ति for परिवर्तम्; with our reading this must be taken as an adj. qualifying परिवर्त. **०ताननं**—is similarly to be taken as an adj. to परिवर्त Jag. after taking ०ताननं as an adv. proposes to take it as an adj. ( तानन: ) qualifying अहं but with माधव it looks awkward. **तदङ्क**—is preferred to तदङ्क० after Dr. Bhánd. as Mádh. would perfer to have an embrace of the whole person rather than rolling on her lap. **प्रियया**—goes with विनिवेशित. **कर्णजाह**—जाह is added in the sense of ' the root of ' to कर्ण, अक्षि, नख, मुख and other words; see Pán. V. 2. 24. **०तानन:**—The reading ०ताननं ( see Jag. विनिवेशितमाननं यत्र ) would be better as being in harmony with the other two adjectives.

**दूरे तावत्** &c.—For मनोरथानामगतिर्न विद्यते ।

**भूमन्**—( Fr. बहु + इमन् the इ being dropped ) greatness, high magnitude. परं भूमानं the highest pitch, supreme bliss ( a Vedantic term applied to Bramhan. *cf.* यो वै भूमा तत्सुखं; भूमात्वेव विजिज्ञासितव्यः... ...यो वै भूमातदमृतं &c. Ch. han up. VII. 23, 24 forms an introductio to. **प्रस्तौति**—gives rise to ( Trip. ). Jag.reads प्रस्नौति continuoly gives ).

**बालेन्दु०**—बालेन्दोः कलंकराहित्यसौकुमार्यमनोहरस्य प्रतिमासमेकैकक्रमेणोत्पाद्यमानाः कलास्तासां &c. Trip. Fig. Samádhi according to Jag.; अतिशयोक्ति, उत्प्रेक्षा and रूपक, according to Trip who remarks—एते वाच्यालंकाराः । प्रसिद्धसुखसाधनाभावेऽपि कारणान्तरादेव तत्समस्तसुखोत्पत्तेर्विभावना संभूयेवेत्यत्र व्यज्यते । नेदं मुखमितरशरीरवद्भौतिकोपादानकं किं त्वन्यदेव लोकोत्तरमस्योपादानमित्यपह्नवः । कलङ्कशून्यसारांशनिर्मितत्वादस्य चन्द्रमण्डलाधिक्यप्रतीतेर्व्यतिरेकः । चन्द्रादेरप्युपमानत्वायोग्यत्वादन्यस्य चाभावादस्येदमेवोपमानमित्यनन्वयश्च यद्बालेन्दुकलेत्यत्र व्यज्यत इत्यादि निरूपणीयं सहृदयैः ।

P. 100. **यत्सत्यं** &c.—His awakened memory places a vivid image of his beloved before his mind's eye which enraptures his soul, as though she were bodily present before him, and hence he remarks–but truly or to tell the truth &c.' Now he explains how that is the case. सातिशय &c—सातिशयः lit. excessive, that could make a deep impression, close, यः प्राक्तन. उपलम्भः (direct knowledge, or perception) तस्मात्संभावितं आत्मनः जन्म येन तादृशः संस्कारस्य । सातिशय is necessary to account for the impression being deep which alone would cause स्मृति. This passage requires a knowledge of some of the technicalities of Nyáya. उपलम्भ is the same as अनुभव one of the two divisions of *Buddhi*; the other being स्मृति ( See Tarkasang. ); अनुभव is direct cognition or knowledge, the first obtained from the direct sight of an object. स्मृति is defined as संस्कारमात्रजन्यं ज्ञानं, *i. e.* knowledge arising from an impression alone; in other words it is ' recalled knowledge. ' संस्कारस्य—Samskâra is of three kinds; but the one meant here is भावनाख्य संस्कार ( अनुभवजन्या स्मृतिहेतुर्भावना ) *i. e.* the impression first formed when a thing is seen. This Samskàra when roused by any cause leads to Smṛti. प्रत्ययान्तरैः—अन्ये प्रत्ययाः प्रत्ययान्तराणि तैः. प्रत्यय—cognition, perception. अतिरस्कृत—Lit. not hidden or obscured; not overpowered, or obstructed. अन्तर्वृत्तिसारूप्यतः—अन्तर्वृत्तेर्मालतीगोचरायाः स्मृतिरूपायाः अन्तः करणवृत्तेः सारूप्यं ( सरूपस्य भावः ) मालत्याकारकारितत्वं तस्मात् । Trip. The internal state or condition being one with her, having assumed the form of her image. This passage ( The sentence मम हि प्राक्तनोपलम्भ &c. together with the following śloka is quoted in the D. R. as containing an instance of स्मृति one of the thirty three व्यभिचारिभावs (see Introd. I) and is again referred to under IV 34. as an illustration of the definition of a Sthàyîbháva or permanent feeling, which predominating over all other feelings makes them subservient to itself. Here रति, the स्थायी भाव of शृङ्गार, predominates over the बीभत्सरस (बीभत्सरसेन मालत्यनुरागस्यातिरस्कारो ममाहि...इत्यनेनोपनिबद्धः । ).

लीनेव &c.—An instance of the forcible style of Bhav. वज्रलेप–a kind of cement, things glued by means of which are as difficult to separate as a diamond. Three or four ways of preparing it are given in Varáhamihira's Bṛh Sam. chap, 57.

P. 101. कीलित—fixed with a nail, pinned down; p. p. of कील् बन्धे 1 P. चिन्तासंतति ( continuous thought about her ) एव तन्तुजालं; each effort of the mind to continue the thought is compared to a thread. The Fig. is a series of उत्प्रेक्षाs ( with a trace of Sára ). This śl. and the preceding passage are again quoted in the D. R. as an instance of Smṛti one of the

Vyabhichâribhâvas or accessories, *i. e.* feelings not restricted to any particular permanent sentiment ( Sthâyîbhâva ) but serving as feeders to it.

P. 102. **प्रगल्भमान**—Getting bold; stalking boldly. **कौणप**—कुणपं a dead body भक्षयितुं शीलमस्य; a demon or goblin; fr. कुणप + अण् Pân. IV. 3. 120.

**पर्यन्त** &c.—पर्यन्तं प्रतिरोद्धुं शीलमस्य; now see Jag; or पर्यन्तप्रतिरोधी यो मेदुरः चयस्तेन । मेदुर ( fr. मिद् + उर added ताच्छील्ये; Pân. III. 2. 161 ) thick, dense ( which substitute for unctuous in the trans. ) स्त्यान—p. p. of स्त्यै. **संसक्त**०—Jag.'s संसक्ता कुलेन केलिः &c. appears to be farfetched. **उत्ताल**—may mean 'hideous or hurried;' see Jag.; *cf.* sl. 4 and pp. 29, 103 &c. **कटाः**—शवाः dead bodies; Jag. or rather कटपूतनाः a kind of goblin ( feeding on dead bodies ). Jag. remarks कटानां शवानां शब्दकरणं वेतालाधिष्ठानात्. **संराविणं**—सर्वतो विसृत्वरमाक्रोशं a cry spreading all round; fr. रु to cry, with सं + इनुण् ( इन् ) by अभिविधौ भावे इनुण् Pân. III. 3. 44. The alliterations in this sl. can be easily noticed.

P. 103. **अशस्त्रपूतं** &c.—not hallowed or sanctified by a weapon ( correct the trans. accordingly ) and which, therefore, is quite acceptable to you. The ghosts cannot touch the flesh of a warrior cut down with a sword while fighting face to face with his enemy and thereafter gone to heaven; see. Jagr.'s remarks. शस्त्रपूतं हि पवित्रत्वात्पिशाचैः स्प्रष्टुमशक्यम् । उक्तं हि कापालिकागमे-अशस्त्रसंच्छिन्नमयोषिदीयं ( not of a female ) नृमांसमार्द्रं गलदस्त्रबिन्दु यत् । Trip. **गृह्यतां गृह्यतां**—The repetition shows his earnestness, since such a thing is rare and may not be obtained again.

**उत्तालः**—Huge, formidable or of a monstrous height. **भूतसंकटः**-भूतैः संकटः ( close packed or over-crowded with ); संकट fr. कट् with सम् to cover + अच्; or सम् + कट added स्वार्थे by Pân. V. 2. 92. **अभ्यर्ण**—p. p of अर्द् with अभि, when the sense is neither very long nor very near. Pân. VII. 2. 25; otherwise अभ्यर्दित. **विसंकटैः**—The more usual form is विशंकट; fr. वि meaning extensive and शंकट added स्वार्थे; Pân. V. 2. 28. Lit. large; hence closely filled with; or formidable, frightful. **निकाश**—( also नीकाश ) expresses likeness or resemblance when at the end of a compound; *cf.* स्युरुत्तरपदे त्वमी । निभसंकाशनीकाशप्रतीकाशोपमादयः । Amara.

**लक्ष्यालक्ष्य**—now visible, now invisible ( owing to the darkness and the extreme thinness of their bodies ); or dimly visible. लक्ष्य is got by adding य ( ण्यत् ) by ऋहलोर्ण्यत् Pân. III. 1. 124 and लक्ष by adding अ ( घञ् ) कर्मणि लक्ष्यते इति; see Jag. **उल्कामुख**—see Jag. who says शृगालभेदाः. The poet Harsha also describes such jackals as frequenting a great cemetery; *cf.* वक्त्रोद्वान्ताः पतन्त्यच्छिभिति-शिखिशिखाश्रेणयोऽस्मिञ्शिवानां Nag. N. 18. kinds of ghosts; Trip. This śl. is an instance of the अद्भुतरस.

P. 104 **अक्रम०**—अक्रमेण कृतो यः ग्रासस्तस्मादर्धभुक्तैः । **विघस**—remnant of food; विशिष्टैरद्यते; fr. अद् with वि + अप (अ) before which अद् is changed to घस्. **०दघ्न०**—खर्जूरद्रुमः प्रमाणं यस्याः तादृशी जङ्घा यस्य । स्नायुग्रन्थिभिः घनानि; now see Jag. **रोहिणानां**—चन्दनानां Trip. Jag. identifies this with the रोहित tree.

**आस्यगर्त**—गर्तमिवास्यम् । उपमितसमासः । अत एव आस्यसाम्यात्तद्वाचिलोपे लुप्तोपमा । Trip. **चलदजगर** &c.—The fig. here is निदर्शना. चन्दनग्रहणं तेषां स्वभावतः पुष्पादिशून्यत्वान्नीरसत्वादजगरादिसमाश्रयत्वाच्चास्यगर्तस्य कोटरेण चलन्त्या रसनाया अजगरेण साधर्म्यं विवक्षितम् । तेन निदर्शनमलंकारः । न हि अन्यगतां श्रुतिमन्यो दधातीति चन्दनतरुगतद्युतेः पिशाचेष्वसंभवात्किचन्धनतयार्थाद्बिम्बप्रतिबिम्बभावेनोपमेयत्वाद्याक्षेपात् । Trip.

P. 105. **उत्कृत्यो०**—In this and the following two Ślokas the poet has very successfully delineated, as he himself remarks, ( हन्त बीभत्समेव &c. ), the Bîbhatsarasa and this śl. is quoted as a stock instance ( मूर्धाभिषिक्तमुदाहरणं ) of this Rasa in K. P., D. R. and S. D. आर्तः पर्यस्तनेत्रः and उत्सेध for उच्छोफ are the readings found in some editions of the K. P. **उत्कृत्यो०**—Jag. reads निर्भिद्योत्कृत्य. **उच्छोफ**—swelling; fr. शु 1 conj. to go + फ; also शोथ. **पूतिः**—पूयते इति पूतिः fr. पूय् to stink and ति; उग्रा पूतिर्येषां तानि । **रङ्कः**—a beggar. **प्रेत०**—a wretched goblin **स्थपुट**—तिष्ठतीति स्थं; fr. स्था + क ( अ ); स्थं पुटमत्र; what is unevenly raised, elevated and depressed. The description here gives rise to जुगुप्सा which leads to the Bîbhatsarasa.

**निष्टाप**—ईषत्ताप of Jag. does not seem proper as little heat is not sufficient to make the marrow come out. *Cf.* Trip. निःशेषेण तापो निष्टापस्तेन सम्यक्कांपनं । निःशब्दपानासेचनमित्यत्रासेचनमीषत्सेचनं तद्व्यतिरिक्तेनासेचनेनेषत्वविधानान्निष्टापेन इति षत्वम् । निष्टप्तं रक्ष इत्यादौ निःशेषतापस्यैव विवक्षितत्वात् । **०दस्थ्नः**—must be taken as acc. pl. as qualifying कायान् and as such is grammatically incorrect, as Jag. also remarks; see com. The context ( भूयसीभ्यः &c. ) requires the plural ( कायान् ) no doubt. So it is probable that the poet forgot the rule under poetic impulse. Or, rather than make the poet guilty of inadvertency, we should adopt the reading ०कायात् proposed by Jag. and found in one of his Mss. by Dr. Bhândârkar, changing संसक्तधूमान् into संसक्तधूमात् which removes the difficulty. For, all the adjectives then become ablatives and ०दस्थ्नः, as abl. sing., is quite correct. The cons. then becomes ०दस्थ्नः, ०मेदसः संसक्तधूमादपि प्रेतकायात् जंघानलकं कृत्वा &c. In this case, however, the adj. संसक्तधूमात्

becomes inappropriate as there can be no smoke about the body when dragged away from the pyre. The reading °दस्रः though grammatically correct will not do as there can be no blood in the dead body. Or अस्थ्नः may be taken as gen. singular and connected with कथन—अस्थिसम्बन्धि यत्कथनं तेन परिणमन्मेदः येषु तान्.

उत्पक्कं &c.—Well-boiled अत एव स्रंसि &c. See Jag. संधेर्मुक्तमत एव उभयतः प्रचलत् moving about; qualifies जंघानलकं. Jag. takes प्रचलत् with सन्धि treating the whole as a comp. word. निष्कुष्य—निश्चूष्य *V. l.* having sucked up. पूर्वश्लोके मांसभक्षणस्योक्तत्वादत्र पानक्रियावर्णनेन बीभत्सरसपरिपोषः ।

P. 106. प्रादोषिकः—प्रदोषे भवः (प्रदोष + इक). पिशाचाङ्गनाः—The word अङ्गना, which means a woman with beautiful limbs प्रशस्तानि अङ्गानि अस्याः ( अङ्गात्कल्याणे इति नः ), is not well chosen here.

स्त्रीहस्त०—स्त्रीहस्ता एव रक्तोत्पलानि तान्येव व्यक्तानुत्तंसान् बिभ्रतीति । सहसा—in haste, as they were anxious to join the company of their lovers. शिरसा *v. l.* ought to be taken to mean—Tying and wearing on their heads. हृत्पुण्डरीके *v. l.* is bad as there is nothing left to tell us what the garlands were made of as in other cases. ( अन्त्रैः &c. ). शोणित &c.—शोणितपङ्क एव कुंकुमं तज्जुषन्तीति । पिबन्ति—इत्येकदेशवर्ति सावयवं रूपकम् । पिशाचानां संभोगनायकत्वस्य तदङ्गनानां तन्नायिकात्वस्य च अन्यारोपणाभावादर्थात्प्रतीतेः । आन्त्रैः कल्पितमङ्गलप्रतिसरा इत्यत्र तु परिणाम । आन्त्रप्रतिसरत्वस्य प्रकृतोपयोगित्वेनारोपणात् । In this s'l. we have संभोगशृङ्गार. The s'l., therefore, is cited in D. R. as an illustration of the doctrine that two sentiments, although represented independently, do not mar the beauty of a composition, provided one serves to heighten the other or both contribute to the development of a third, as in the present case the Sṛngâra and the Bîbhatsa give rise to Hásya ( हास्यरसैकपरत्वमेव ). *Cf.*, however, Trip —अत्र प्रियतमैः सह मधुपानप्रवृत्तस्रक्चन्दनाद्यलंकृतनायिकाप्रतीतेः संभोगशृङ्गाररसः प्रतीयमानः प्रधानस्य चार्थभूतस्य बीभत्सरसस्याङ्गमिति रसवदलंकारश्च । अङ्गाङ्गिभावापत्तेश्च शृंगारबीभत्सयोर्विरोधपरिहारः ।

P. 107. बिभीषिका०—बिभीषिका what frightens or scares away; Desi. noun from भी; *cf.* केयमद्य बिभीषिका; Uttar. IV. 28. तस्याः प्रकाराः—terror inspiring ways, or manners. निःसत्त्वता—want of innate strength or sustaining power. सनिर्वेदम्—Because he could not find one who would take the flesh from him and grant his desire. विचितः—अन्विष्टः searched; Jag 's व्याप्तः is unwarranted. इयंपुरतः—The river that formed the boundary of this cemetery on the other side.

गुञ्जत् &c.—कुञ्जाः कुटीराः huts इव कुञ्जकुटीराः गुञ्जन्तः कु० रेषु कौशिकाः owls तेषां घटाः तासां ( गुञ्जन्तीनां कौशिकघटानां वा ) घूत्कारैः संवलिता

( mixed ) याः क्रन्दतां फेरवाणां ( jackals ) चण्डाः डात्कृतयः ताभिः भृतः &c. Jag. takes the first part as a Dwandwa—घूत्काररूपं संचारितं ( sound ) च......डात्कृतयश्च ताभिः &c. the portion गुञ्जत्कु...... घूत्कार occurs in Uttar. II. 29 also. प्राग्भार—the forepart; for different meanings, *cf.* sl. 29, IX. 15. अन्तःशीर्ण &c. see Jag.; ०कर्करैः यः पयःसंरोधः the obstruction of water तेन कूलंकषः ( dashing against the banks ) यः स्रोतोनिर्गमः ( or,—कषं स्रोतस्तस्य निर्गमः ) &c. The current dashed against the banks because it was obstructed by &c. तरःसंरोधि *V. l.* ( तरसः वेगस्य संरोधः अस्यास्तीति तरःसंरोधि स्रोतः, or रोधी ०निर्गमः. These are better readings than Jag.'s तरत्सं० (which must be explained as he does–करङ्कश्च तरत्संरोधी च, तरत् meaning things floating on the surface of the water ), as there is nothing to explain why the current is कूलंकष; तरत् is also without propriety. Trip., who reads अन्तःकीर्ण० says ०कर्परेषु तरत् ( floating across ) अत एव संरोधोस्यास्तीति संरोधि यत्स्रोतः &c. कूलंकष— See note on सर्वंकषा p. 17. पारेश्मशानं—श्मशानस्य पारे Avy. comp.; see Jag.

P. 108. उपकरण—a tool; mark the sarcasm in the use of the word. श्रोत्रसंवाद—संवाद agreement, correspondence, similarity; *cf.* अस्य मुखं सीतायाः मुखचन्द्रेण संवदति Uttar. श्रोत्रं metaphorically means श्रोत्रगृहीतशब्द ' a voice heard before; एति—strikes the ear as one familiar to it before. देह( गात्र )स्तम्भः—The paralysis or torpor of the body deprived the feet of their free motion; and hence स्खलयति गतिं. देहोत्कम्पः—*V. l.* has not much propriety after विह्वलत्यङ्गमङ्गम्. The figures of speech in this sl. are उत्प्रेक्षा and क्रियासमुच्चय in the last two lines.

कृतवध्यचिह्ना—For these see sl. 24. p. 111.

P. 109. कल्याणसाधन०—साधनमेव एकं तदर्थं मुक्तः &c.; ०नैकसुख ( शुभ ) *V. l.*—साधनमेव एकं सुखं यस्मिन् तादृशः सकलः व्यापारः यस्याः; साधनमेव एकं शुभं तस्मिन् एव वा व्यापारो यस्याः । Whose entire business consists in or is directed to the accomplishment of the one good act, *viz.* &c.

निशुम्भ—Hard pressing, the firm planting of ( the foot ) in a particular way in the act of dancing; see Jag. and the quotation from Bharata. उत्क्षिप्ता—&c.—पातालस्य प्रतिमल्लं ( properly an antagonist of equal strength, a rival; hence equal to; fr मल्ल् 1 A. to hold, to be strong; *cf.* for the root sense, ameliorate, multitude ) यद्गल्लविवरं &c. Although the use of गल्ल is considered as vulgar by rhetoricians, put in the mouth of a heretic it is a merit, as remarked by Trip.—यद्यपि गल्लपदं केवलं लौकिकसंकेतसिद्धत्वाद्ग्राम्यमित्युक्तं तथापि पाषण्डोक्तौ गुणत्वमेव ग्राम्यस्य न दोषत्वम् । यदाह-अधमप्रकृत्युक्तिषु

प्राप्यत्वं गुणः । व्यक्तिषद् हेतुना व्यक्ता ऋद्धिः यस्य; or after Jag. नन्दिता नीलकण्ठस्य शिवस्य परिषद् येन तच्च तद् व्यक्तर्द्धि च ।

**प्रचलित**--For the metre, see appendix. Here the goddess, in her terrific form, is described as identical with Śiva performing the Tándava dance and having the same apparel ( such as the elephant-hide ), decorations ( such as the necklace of skulls, the coiling serpents, &c. ) and attributes. **करिकृत्ति**—The hide of the elephant-demon killed by Śiva and therefore worn by him as a trophy. **चञ्चत्**—moving. For the comp. see Jag.; प्रचलिता या करिकृत्तिः तस्याः पर्यन्ते चञ्चन्तः flashing, moving about ये नखाः &c. अट्टहासेन त्रसतां भूरीणां भूतानां प्रवृत्ता स्तुतिर्यस्मिंस्तत् । His second way यद्वा प्रचलितकरिचर्मरूपो अवधिर्यत्र तत् । पश्चात्कर्मधारयः does not look good.

P. 110. **श्वसद्** &c.—श्वसन्तश्च ते असित ( black ) भुजंगाश्च तेषां भोगा लक्षणया भोगवेष्टनानि ( coilings ) एवाङ्गदग्रन्थयः तेषां निष्पीडनेन स्फारं यथा तथा उत्फुल्लन्त्यः फणाः पीठानीव ( a Karm. comp. ) तेभ्यो निर्यद्विषज्योतिषः उज्जृम्भणेन ( flashing forth, uprising ) उड्डामर: ( formidable ) चासौ व्यस्तः ( tossed irregularly ) च विस्तारिदोष्णां ( spreading arms; *cf.* संकोचेनैव दोष्णां मुहुरनुपततः सर्वलोकातिगानां । Mud. I. 2. ) खण्डस्तेन पर्यासिताः (scattered all round) क्ष्माधरा: mountains यस्मिन् । **ज्वलद्**०—for comps. see com.; छटा the mass of flames issuing forth; साट the extent ( of the glare of flames ). **भ्रमि**--As she moved rapidly round, a circle of light was traced by her head. उत्तुङ्गं यत्खट्वाङ्गं तस्य कोटौ (attached to the extremity or point ) यः ध्वजस्तस्योद्धून्या &c. उद्गताः तालादुत्तालाः formidable, terrific or frantic; *cf.* above sl.s 4, 11, and *supra* I. p. 29 l. 2. उत्तालाश्च ते वेतालाश्च; प्रमुदिताश्चते कटपूतनाश्च उत्तालवेतालाश्च तेषां तालेन तालैर्वा स्फुरन्तौ कर्णौ यस्याः सा अनः संभ्रान्ता &c.; see com. **ताल**—may also mean the beating of hands. हृष्यन्मनः यस्य स चासौ त्र्यम्बकश्च तं; see Jag. अरिष्टये *V. l*—रिष्टि evil, injury; fr. रिष् 1. 4. P. to injure, to kill **अरिष्ट**—safety, welfare.

P. 111. **प्रमादः**—Misfortune, calamity; or carelessness ( on the part of Bhúrivasu and Málatí's guards ). **न्यस्तालक्तक**०— A victim or a person about to be put to death was made to wear a red garland ( either of red flowers or dyed red ), a red garment, had marks of red sandal made on the body-see Mṛch. X. 2 ( दत्तकरवीरदामा ), 5 ( सर्वगात्रेषु विन्यस्तै रक्तचन्दनहस्तकैः ), &c. एतद्रक्तांशुकयुगलं परिधायारोह वध्यशिलाम् । Nág. IV. p. 79. **पाखण्ड**—is curiously derived as पा ( the order established by Vedic law—पालनाच्च त्रयीधर्मः पाशब्देन निगद्यते ) खण्डयति ( overthrows. ) इति. **वसोः**— brought in for alliteration. Or rather, we may understand by Vasu 'Kubera' as then the simile will be a ppropriate. *Cf.* Mak.'s remarks on Bhûrivasu's wealth, p. 122. Fig. Upamá.

P. 112. तपस्विनी—Properly one practising penance and so deserving protection; hence any one deserving or requiring help, one in a pitiable condition. पूजां—*i. e.* the principal offering, Mâlatî. प्रकोष्ठ—Read प्रकोष्ठेन. Trip. reads खड्गं प्रकोष्ठेन विक्षिप्य (having thrust aside Aghor.'s sword with his fore-arm ) which seems to be more probable from Mâl.'s next speech. If प्रकोष्ठे be the reading the meaning will be having shielded Mâl. with the fore-arm.

प्रलाप०—प्रलापे निरर्गलं यथा तथा ( without restraint, unreservedly *i. e.* having thrown off all reserve ; in a speech freely uttered ). त्वया प्रकटितः निजः स्नेहः यस्मिन्. This is the proper explanation. प्रलाप may also mean विलाप lamentation. The first two lines refer to the open and unrestrained way in which Mál, when about to be put to death, avowed her loves for Mádhava as was natural. The reading प्रलापनिरर्गलप्र०—also must be explained as above Jag. seems to read प्रतापनिरर्गलः or ल०. He also notices the reading in the text. The reading मुक्ताशङ्कः......प्रलापनिरर्गलः ( and Jag.'s explanation as well as Trip's interpretation as प्रलापऽनर्थकवचोजल्पने इदानीमेवैनं संहरिष्यामीत्येवंरूपो निरर्गलो निष्प्रतिबन्धः &c. ) is quite out of place The adj. as referring to Mâl. is peculiarly happy. If taken with Mâdh., as done by the Com.s, it loses its beauty. The reading प्रताप० has no propriety. It looks awkward to make Mâdh. boast of his own prowess. प्रतीपविपाकिनः—प्रतीपं यथा तथा विपाकोस्य bearing a result adverse to him.

P. 113. अन्तरायः—Fr. अन्तः or अन्तर् and इ or अय् to go and aff. अ ( घञ् or अच् ). उपर्यलिन्दं—The acc. by अकर्मकधातुभिर्योगे देशः कालो भावो गन्तव्योऽध्वा च कर्मसंज्ञक इति वाच्यम् । Sid. Kau.; *e. g.* कुरून् स्वपिति ( an instance of देश ), मासमास्ते ( of time ), गोदोहमास्ते, क्रोशमास्ते । अभिनिवेश—Earnest or strong desire, ardent longing; see *infra* p. 127. परेत—Fr. पर ( the outer world ) or परा and इत. *Cf.* English 'gone for good'. आत्मनिरपेक्षः—Because he exposed himself to the terrors of the cemetery.

P. 114. काकतालीयं—काकताल + ईय (छ); यदृच्छिकं काकगमनं तालपतनं च तद्दिव । इवे प्रतिकृतौ इति इवार्थप्रकरणे कुशाग्राच्छः इत्यतश्छ इत्यनुवर्तमाने समासाच्च तद्विषयादिति तच्छब्देनेवार्थः परामृश्यते । इवार्थविषयात्समासादिवार्थे छो भवतीति सूत्रार्थः । Trip. See Pân. V. 3. 106. काकता० means any unexpected and sudden occurrence.

राहोः चन्द्रकलां—A digit or part of ( the full ) moon entering ( about to enter ). The simile is extremely happy. It well brings out the extreme cruelty and wickedness of Aghor. and the extreme delicacy of Mâlatî. दस्यु—a wicked man. It is a word of Vedic origin, and is probably connected with दास the destroyer of the good, fr. दस् to destroy, to kill. In Vedic literature दस्यु means an evil spirit, hence a cruel man, a thief &c. The aborigins of India were called Dasyus or Dâsas by the Aryans.

**आतङ्कात्**—Through mental fear. This was due to the thought that had he been late by a single minute a great calamity might have ensued. भय is defined as—भयं चित्तस्य वैक्लव्यं रौद्रसंजनितं विदुः। **चेतः कथं वर्तताम्**—He did not know what the state of his mind was going to be. For it had become the acting point of a variety of feelings. There is a blending of the Sthâyîbâvas of भयानक, करुण, अद्भुत and रौद्र with that of शृङ्गार here. आतङ्क indicates भयानक विस्मय, अद्भुत ( being its स्थायी भाव ) and क्रोध रौद्र. क्रोध is defined as प्रतिकूलेषु तैक्ष्ण्यस्य प्रकर्षः क्रोध इष्यते । मुदा विकसितं indicates शृंगार. The different Rasas here, which are the Angas, heighten शृङ्गार which is Angî. *Cf.* Trip. एते रसा अङ्गभावापत्यैव दूरतो निरस्तपरस्परविरोधाः प्रधानरसापेक्षयाऽविरोधाः प्रधानरसपरिपोषापेक्षया न्यूनरसपरिपोषत्वेन श्लाघनीयौचित्यानिबन्धनाव्यतिकराख्यया शोभनाख्यया च मेलनगतया शृङ्गारेण सह संकीर्त्यन्ते । **यथाह**—समकालसमुत्पन्नैस्त्रिभिर्द्वाभ्यामथापि वा । रसश्चेद्व्यतिकीर्येत समव्यतिकरः स्मृतः ॥ विरोधे मित्रशत्रूणां रसानां संकरेपि च । महिम्ना शोभते स्वेन यः स शोभन ईरितः ॥ Fig.—a mixture of Kávyalinga, Upam and Kriyásamuchchaya.

**व्याघ्राघ्रात**—आघ्रात is appropriate when used with व्याघ्र which is derived as विशेषेण आजिघ्रतीति. **केतनजुषः**—केतन an indispensable act, or a place, a house ( I who am in a place known for ); or a distinguishing mark ( I who am known for my offering &c. ) **गोचरं**—गाव इन्द्रियाणि चरन्त्यत्र । Pân. III. 3. 119. Properly range or the distance covered by the senses, especially the eyes; hence scope, power, influence, &c. *Cf.* अपि मनागवतीर्णोस्मि रतिरमणबाणगोचरतां p. 24, where the original sense of गो is dropped altogether.

P. 115 **असार** &c—Because she is सौन्दर्यसारसमुदायनिकेतन; also because she was created out of the essences of the best and the most beautiful things in the world ( I. 20 ). **परिमुषितरत्नं**—Even Kapa. calls her स्त्रीरत्न p. 97. **निरालोकं**—because she is the only moonlight to the eyes; (*cf.* I. 34, 36). **मरणशरण**—as proved by the incidents of the 8th and 9th Acts. **अदर्पं कन्दर्पं**—For she is his जगद्विजयवैजयन्तिका ( p. 25 ) and his जैत्रमस्त्रं ( p. 15. ). **जननयन०**—For she is the only object worth seeing ( विलोचनचन्द्रिका ); *cf.* माढव्य अनवाप्तचक्षुःफलोसि येन त्वया दर्शनीयं न दृष्टम् । Śak. II. p. 51. Fig. अप्रस्तुतप्रशंसा ( कारणे प्रस्तुते कार्यस्योक्तिः ) । Also साध्यवसाना अतिशयोक्ति ( रूपकातिशयोक्ति according to Kuv. ) *Cf.* Trip-अत्र विषयनिगरणेन मालत्यां सकलसंसारैकसारवस्तुत्वस्य अध्यवसितत्वात् 'निगीर्याध्यवसानं तत्प्रकृतस्य परेण यत्' इत्युक्तलक्षणाध्यवसितप्रयत्नातिशयोक्तिः ।सिद्धवन्निर्दिष्टाया व्यवसायक्रियायाः सर्वत्रान्वयात्क्रियादीपकं च वाच्यालंकारौ । चन्दनचामी-

करादीनां न वस्तुतः सारत्वं किंतु पामरजनप्रसिद्ध्यैव । इयमेव सारभूतेत्यपह्नवः । सर्वसारवस्तूपमानानि यानि तेभ्योऽपि सारभूतेयमेवेति व्यतिरेकश्च व्यङ्ग्याविति सर्वत्र द्रष्टव्यम् । अत्र ( अस्मिन्पद्ये ) चैकेन वाक्येनोत्कर्षप्रतिपादनात्तस्यैव वाक्यान्तरैरपि प्रतिपादनादार्थं पौनरुक्त्यमाशङ्क्य रसाक्षिप्तवक्त्रा तस्यैवार्थस्य प्रौढोक्तिवैचित्र्येण गम्भीरविशेषणोपादानान्न पौनरुक्त्यमिति भोजराजः परिजहार । यथाह—'विशेषणं तु पूर्वोक्तं यदि भूयोऽपि कीर्त्यते । तदेकार्थं रसाक्षिप्तं तत्तस्मात्तु न दूष्यते ॥' इति । छेकानुप्रासोऽत्र शब्दालंकारः ।

P. 116. **प्रणयि॰**—प्रणयिन्यः सख्यः प्रणयिसख्यः तासां सलीलः परिहास प्रणयि॰ परिहासः तस्मिन्रसः तेन अधिगतैः । **शिरीषमृदु**—which is extremely delicate and ought not to cause the least pain; this indicates her extreme delicacy. **यमदण्ड इव**—As required by his extremely hard-heart. Sl. cited in the K. P. as an instance of the Fig. Kàvyalinga, where several words express the हेतु of some act, as the words तत्र वपुषि वधाय शस्त्रमुपक्षिपतः here do of the fall of Màdh.'s hand on Aghoraghanta.

**परित्रायस्व मां**—This he would do by turning back from the combat as suggested. For any mishap to Màdh. would be worse than death to her. See Jag.

**प्रमादः**—does not mean here carelessness but rather its result, a calamity, mishap. See *supra* p 81 l. 1 and notes. **कूट**—the elevated or projecting part, top, peak. **कुट्टाक**—habitually splitting; fr. कुट्ट् + आक ( षाकन् added ताच्छील्ये by 'जल्पभिक्षकुट्टलुण्टवृङः षाकन्' Pân. III. 2. 155. अत्र क्षुद्रविपक्षपक्षे मम प्रमादो न संभवतीति तदसंभवलक्षणे वाक्यार्थे हरेः प्रमादासंभवलक्षणो वाक्यार्थोऽध्यारोप्यमाणः सारङ्गवधे सिंहस्य प्रमादसंभवेन ममाप्येतद्वधे प्रमादसंभावनेप्युपमानोपमेयभावं परिकल्पयतीति निदर्शनालंकारः । न चात्र श्लेषभ्रान्तिः कर्तव्या । वाक्यद्वयस्यैव युगपदुभाभ्यां पाठात् । Trip.

P. 117. **अप्रतिहत॰**—प्रज्ञागति is the power of the intellect to reach a thing; *i. e.* of penetration; unobstructed *i. e.* unerring perception; who sees things in their proper light. This is meant to show that Kám. was on the right scent and her instructions could safely be carried out. This reading is better than Jag.'s ॰प्रतिज्ञा whose declaration is unobstructed, not amiss *i. e.* true.

**दारुण**—Heart-rending; frightful; दारयति चित्तमिति; fr. दॄ and the Uṇâd aff. उन ( III. 53 ) which is also added to कॄ ( करुण ) and वॄ ( वरुण ).

P. 118. **कठोरा॰**—कठोरास्थिग्रन्थिभिः यः व्यतिकरः मिलनं ( coming in contact with, clashing against ) तेन यः रणत्कारः तेन मुखरः । **खर॰**—खराणां ( hard, touch ) स्नायूनां छेदेन क्षणं विहितः वेगस्य व्युपरमः cessation यस्य । **निरातंकं**—Lit. without anxiety or hesitation; hence moving freely. बीभत्सोपस्कृतो रौद्ररसो व्यज्यते । Trip. Fig. स्वभावोक्ति and उपमा.

Wilson Remarks—The Hindu theatre is as particular as the French in prohibiting the exhibition of death upon the stage.

## ACT. VI.

P. 119. Sl. 1 अमुक्तानुशया—अनुशय, fr. शी with अनु meaning to lie close to ( the mind ), means the state of lying close to the mind—being the subject of constant thought or pondering over; hence its two principal meanings are (1) intense enmity, deep hatred; and (2) repentance, sorrow, regret &c 'अथानुशयो दीर्घद्वेषानुतापयोः । Amara. Here it means hatred, ill feeling rankling in the heart ( due to Kapa.'s constantly brooding over Agor.'s slaughter); *cf.* अभिधाय तदा तदप्रियं शिशुपालोनुशयं परं गतः । Sis. XVI. 2. It is more often used, however, in its second sense; see *infra*. p. 172. *cf.* Sák. अनुशयदुःखायेदं हतहृदयं संप्रति विबुद्धं । VI. 7. See VII. 25 also; इतो गतस्यानुशयो माभूदिति । Vik. IV. p. 102. The fig. of speech here is अप्रस्तुतप्रशंसा ( तुल्ये प्रस्तुते तुल्यस्याभिधाने ). There is also a shade of निदर्शना according to Trip. who remarks—अस्मद्गुरुवधपातकस्य मयि बद्धवैरायां जाग्रत्यां कुत सुखमित्येव वाक्यार्थे तदवश्यमित्यादिवाक्योक्तवाक्यार्थान्तरसंभवद्वस्तुसंबन्धात्मकमुपमानोपमेयपरिकल्पितं निदर्शनालंकारच्छाययाध्यारोपयन्नाह शान्तिरिति ।

भो राजानः—Cons. कर्तव्येषु संचरत्वं proceed, act. नानावचन०—०निवह may mean a song.

जन्ययात्रा—जनीं वधूं वहन्ति प्रापयन्तीति जन्याः; irregularly derived fr. जन्या by affixing य; 'संज्ञायां जन्या' Pāṇ. IV. 4. 82. तेषां यात्रा journey *i. e.* procession. चेष्टयतां—Let it be acted, *i. e.* let *Suvâsinîs* act by repeating &c.

P. 120. नगरदेवतागृहं &c.—Wilson remarks—It was customary also amongst the Greeks for the intended bride to pay her adoration to some divinity before her marriage, usually to Diana; but at Athens no virgin was allowed to be married before worshipping Minerva, who, as in the present instance, was the tutelary deity of the city.

अविघ्नमङ्गलाय—अविद्यमानः विघ्नः यस्मिन् तच्च तन्मङ्गलं ( the marriage ceremony ) च तदर्थम् । यथा may also be connected with गृहीत० having put on a special dress as suited to the position or rank of each. प्रतीक्ष्यताम्—be awaited. We should have preferred the reading प्रतीक्षताम्—Let the persons wait, be in readiness to start. प्रतिष्ठतां *v. l.*—also will do. मालतीविवाह०—परिकर्माणि (the various functions in connection with ) सत्वरैः प्रतीहारैः जनसहस्रेण च &c. अभिनिविष्टा—assiduously engaged in or occupied with.

P. 121. समकरन्देन &c.—The reading माहवसआसवत्तिणा मअरन्देण ( which makes Mak. send Kala. ) should have been noticed.

**आयासप्रबन्ध**—आयासानुबन्ध continuous ( course of the ) torment. **भयान्तः खलु**—For he would either be happy or put an end to his life. **सुमेधसः**—शोभना मेधा यस्यास्तस्याः. मेधा is changed to मेधस् after नञ् ( अ ), दुस् and सु ( अमेधाः, दुर्मेधाः ) by नित्यमसिच्प्रजामेधयोः । Pán. V. 4. 127.

**जीमूत**—जीवनस्य मूतः पटबन्धः; a comp. of the पृषोदरादि class. **०नुकृतिः**—The fig. is Upamá. रसितस्यानुकृतिरस्यास्तीति । **मङ्गल०**—मङ्गलार्था मृदङ्गाः । अन्ये शब्दाः शब्दान्तराणि तेषां ( Nityasamása ).

P. 122. **उत्पतित०**—उत्पतिताश्च ते राजहंसाश्च तेषामिव यः विभ्रमस्तेनाभि० चामराणां समीरणेनोद्वेलन्ती या कदलिकावली तया तरङ्गितं गगनमेव सरोवरं तत्र निरन्तराणि उद्दण्डानि च तानि पुण्डरीकाणि तेषां विभ्रमम्. **सविलास** &c.—सविलासं यथा तथा कवलिता ताम्बूलवीटिका ( the roll of betel leaves with the areca nut, catcheu, cardamoms, &c. ) तया पूरितः कपोलमण्डलस्याभोगस्तस्य व्यतिकरेण ( owing to ) or तेन यः व्यतिकरः ( coming in contant with ) तेन स्खलितं यन्मधुरं च तद् मङ्गलोद्गीतं च तेन बद्धः कोलाहलः यैः । विविधाश्च ते रत्नालंकाराश्च तेषां किरणावलीभिः विडम्बिताः ये महेन्द्रचापस्य विच्छेदाः ( portions of ) तैः विच्छुरितं ( inlaid or chequered with ) नभस्थलं यैः । उत्कणद्यत्कनकस्य किंकिणीनां जालं &c.

**प्रेङ्खत्**—&c.—Construe प्रेङ्खन्तः भूरयः विविधाः ( such as those of rubies, emeralds, sapphires, &c. ) मयूखा एव मेचका मयूखमेचकाः तेषां चया येषु तैः अत एव उन्मेषिचाषच्छदच्छाया ( the lustre of the wings of ) संवलितैः इव विवर्तिभिः ( moving here and there ) उन्मुखमणिज्योतिर्वितानैः प्रान्तेषु पर्यावृता दिशः व्यक्ता० का इव भवन्ति &c. भूरि in the sense of gold is unusual. Change the trans., therfere, as—The directions... variegated with the pea-cock-eye-like rays of various kinds flashing about &c ; Or after Dr. Bhândarkar, प्रेङ्खद्भिः भूरिमयूखमेचक-( मयूखानां मेचकाः तेषां ) चयैः इव उन्मेषि०वलितैः इव as two Utprekshás on ज्योतिर्वितान. The reading मयूर for मयूख is better as it makes the sense clear.

P. 123. **आखण्डलः**—आखण्डयति भेदयति पर्वतान् the cleaver of mountains, Indra. **चीनांशुक**—Silk-cloth, simple or of a diversified colour, seems to have been imported in India from a very ancient time. Káli. makes mention of it in his Sâk. ( I. 34 ) and Kum VII. 3. **प्रस्तार**-what is spread out, a covering, a sheet. Fig Utpreksha.

**ससंभ्रम०**—ससंभ्रमं यथा तथा अनेकप्रतिहाराणां मण्डलेन आवर्जिताः ( pointed downward ) याः उज्ज्वल...पत्रैः विचित्राः वेत्रलताः ताभिः परिक्षिप्तया रेखया रचितं ( formed along the line drawn &c.) मण्डलं येन । The staves were mounted in thin gold and silver leaves intermingled and hence they were विचित्र. With the reading पङ्क for पत्र the staves must be taken to be gilt with gold and silver. **बहल**—०निकर एव सन्ध्यारागः; पक्षे

निकर इव यः सन्ध्यारागः तेन उपरक्तमुखे घूर्णन्ती नक्षत्रमाला सैवाभरणं तद्धारिणीं. Here the she-elephant is likened to the night on account of her black-colour and huge form; the Sindûra applied to her forehead takes the place of the twilight, being the colour which is first seen. **नक्षत्रमाला**—in the case of the she-elephant—A necklace of 27 pearls or an ornaments for elephants. **०मनोहरापाण्डुर** &c.—the two may also be read as one word. दृश्यमाना मनोहरा आपाण्डुरा परिक्षीणा च देहशोभा यस्याः सा. Trip. reads शोभाविभाविताऽनङ्गवेदना । **मालती**–To keep up the metaphor the poet should have said मालतीप्रथमचन्द्रलेखा. The moon reduced to a digit is a coveted object of sight. *Cf.* ( प्रजाः तं ) नेत्रैः पपुस्तृप्तिमनाप्नुवद्भिर्नवोदयं नाथमिवौषधीनाम् ॥ Ragh. II. 73; also VIII. 65. A woman emaciated by love-longing and thereby looking more lovely is often compared to such a moon. **प्रसृता**—The word occurs several times in this play; see p. p. 154, 170, 174 &c.

P. 124. **इयमवयवैः** &c.—अलंकृतमण्डना–*Cf.* आभरणस्याभरणं...प्रत्युपमानं वपुरतस्याः । Vik. II. 3. **बाला लतेव**—the fig. is Upamâ. इव and अन्तः are in wrong places. The cons. is बाला लता इव अन्तः परि०. **वरारोहा**-वरः आरोहः यस्याः । **सहर्षम्**—At the thought of her plans being near their fruition. **विधाता**—The disposer of all things (and therefore able to grant the prayer ). **शिवतातिः**—शिवं करोतीति शिवतातिः; Pân. IV. 4. 144. quoted in the com.; see *infra* p. 201.

P. 125. **अभिमतमिति**—because if it would come it would be showing favour. **अनुकूलविप्रलम्भः**—The *Vipralambha* meant is the delusion under which Mâlatî was allowed to labour by Kâm, that she was going to be wedded to Nandana, while she was really brought there for being secretly married to Mâdhava, and so the विप्र० was to be अनुकूल. Jag. has missed the point. **आभरणसंयोगाः**—Articles of decoration to be worn together, ( संयोज्यन्ते संयुज्य धार्यन्ते इति ) sets of ornaments; *cf.* अलंकारसंयोगाः Mud. II. p. 59; fr. संयुज् + अ ( घञ् ) कर्मणि.

P. 126. **रमणीयं हि** &c.–*i. e.* when decked with the dress and ornaments sent for Mâlati. **एवमित्युच्यतां**—एवं very well, all right; so it will be done. ओम् *v. l.* also means the same thing ( अनुमतौ ).

P. 127. **निव्वेदद्दूसहं**—मम्मच्छेदद्दूसहं ( मर्मच्छेददुःसहं ) v. l. Trip. ( असंतोषः ) **च**—and yet, but. **दुर्लभाभिनि०**—दुर्लभः ( दुर्लभे वा ) अभिनिवेशो यस्य तादृशो यो मनोरथस्तेन विसंवदत् &c. **अभिनिवेश**—The being firmly or uncontrollably fixed upon something, hence a strong desire ( see *supra* V. 27 ), ardent longing, deep love; *cf.* बलवान्खलु मेऽभिनिवेशः Śak. III., p. 69; also 72. ईदृश एव तत्राभिनिवेशः Vik II. p 36; also 64.

**आगर्भ॰**—गर्भान्निर्गमात् मर्यादीकृत्य आ॰मं निर्मिता ( a word simply put in out of the fondness for alliteration ) ये निरन्तरा उपकाराः &c. **हृदयेनधारयन्ती**—So that Mál. too might virtually see her. **ते अनुवर्तनीया**—If you are to act according to my wishes, wish to oblige me.

P. 128 **आनन्दमसृणं**—is better taken as an adv. आनन्देन मसृणं ( pleasing, charming ) यथा स्यात्तथा *i. e.* feeling joy as if I were holding him and not with indifference ( न तु ताटस्थ्येन ). **विकासनानि**—विकासयन्तीति; अन added कर्तरि; so सन्तर्पणानि &c. **मोहनानि**—and therefore causing प्रलय ( one of the Sátvika bhávas ). *Fig.* Rûpaka. The first two lines occur in Uttar. (I. 36 ).

P. 129 **वात्सल्य**—Properly affection for children; here used in the sense of kindliness, affection ( रतिसामान्यं ): dissolve वात्सल्येन यो मोहः तेन &c. Trip. explains वात्सल्येन 'मोहश्चित्तस्य शून्यता' इत्युक्तेन व्यभिचारिणा च यत् &c. Fig. यथासंख्य.

P. 130. **मालतीजीवितं**—miserable though it is, and not Mâlati, *i. e.* you do not care to see how Mâl. can live in happiness which she might do by departing from this world.

**वचन॰**—Speeches carefully arranged. **महाबीभत्सारम्भ**—आरम्भ may mean an act, affair; or better still, the beginning of it only, as Mál. wishes to put an end to her existence. **परकीयत्वेनापराद्धं**—Trip. explains as पराधीनत्वेनाप॰; it seems rather to mean—'by having belonged to another.' Inasmuch as she actually came to the temple as a preliminary step towards her marriage with Nandana she might be taken to have accepted the latter as her husband, and so she thinks that Mâdh. might well consider her as परकीया. Herein lay her guilt. The other reading परकीयत्वेनानपराद्धं would mean 'while I am not yet guilty ( towards the cherished lord of my heart ) by belonging to another (which I might do if I live to be married to Nandana ). Jag.'s reading is पराधीनत्वेनानपराद्धम्. This means—I am not guilty since I am in the power of my parents. The reading परोक्षगुणकीर्तनेन (I, who am not guilty towards him by my praising his merits in his absence). does not make very good sense. See the whole question ably discussed in Dr. Bhândarkar's Ed.

**इयमेव प्रकृतिः**—The nature of good fortunes &c., *i. e.* to cause परवत्ता &c. यत्स्तम्भप्रलयवेपथुप्रभृतिसात्त्विकाविर्भावकृतं पारवश्यमित्यर्थः । Trip.

P. 131. **सरले** &c.—The words are so chosen as to appear like Prákrit. See com. न चात्र भाषाश्लेषभ्रान्तिः कार्या । वाच्यभेदाभावाच्छ्लेषत्वानुपपत्तेः । Trip. **साहस॰**—साहसे रागः तम् । **रम्भोरु॰**—रम्भे इव ऊरू यस्याः ( रम्भा + ऊरु + उ ), the ऊ added by 'ऊरूत्तरपदादौपम्ये ।' Pan. VI. 1. 69.

**कामं कुरु**—See the double interpretation given in the com.

**बाष्पोत्पीड**—( उत्पीड् to press upward with force ) a gushing flow ( profusion ) of tears. See *infra p.* 164. l. 8. नयनसलिलोत्पीडरुद्धावकाशां Meg. II. 31; *cf.* पूरोत्पीडे ( an uprush or flow ) तडागस्य; उत्पीड इव धूमस्य; Uttar. III. 29; 9.

**णिरुद्धं**—Jag.'s reading is given in the foot-note. **पक्ष्मल**—Jag reads पक्ष्मलसुकुमारः. पक्ष्मलः स्पर्शः *i. e.* of the body covered with the bristling hair.

P. 132. **दावित**—p. p. p. of दु cau. Trip. reads धूपायित lit. heated, hence distressed. सविशेषं यथा तथा दुःसहः यः प्रारम्भः ( संतापस्य ) तेन दावितः सखीजनः येषु । **चन्द्रातप**—The burning moon-light. See com.

P. 133. **निर्भुग्न**—perfectly rounded. **एकीकृतः** &c.—कर्पूरादिनिषेकः कृत इवेत्यालिङ्गनाक्रियायां निषेकक्रियाध्यवसायात्प्रतीयमानसंतापनिर्वापणनिमित्तक्रियया स्वभावोत्प्रेक्षालंकारः । Trip. *Cf.* with this Uttar. III. 11. where the same idea is more touchingly expressed—आश्चोतनं नु हरिचन्दनपल्लवानां निष्पीडितेन्दुकरकन्दलजो नु सेकः । आतप्तजीवितपुनःपरितर्पणो मे संजीवनौषधिरसो नु हृदि प्रसिक्तः ॥ विनोदित—Dispelled, removed.

P. 134. **संविधानस्य**—The clever arrangement of the events leading to the union of Mâl. and Mâdh. संवि० is also the judicious arrangement of incidents in a play; so here the poet indirectly praises himself also. *Cf.* अस्ति वा कुतश्चित् &c. p. 216.

**वत्सला**—loving or rather kind-hearted ( and so sure to take pity on him one day ). **आबद्ध०**—with the marriage string fastened round it. **प्रणय**—the offering of it ( by you ). Fig. Kávyalinga.

**(हृदयेपि) किं विचारयति**—Will she hesitate ? She will not. What Lav. means is this-Since Mâl. did not oppose Mâdh. when taking possession of her heart, she would not go against him now if he took hold of her hand, having the marriage string on it. She implies that he may take her hand just then. The fastening of a string of white thread soaked in milk, mixed with wool and dyed with saffron and having a piece of turmeric tied to it, round the wrist is one of the ceremonies at a marriage that precede the actual taking of the hand of the bride by the bridegroom; see Ragh. X. 1. Kum. VII. 25.

P. 135. **पुरश्चक्षूरागः**—This is the first stage in the progress of love; *cf.* Śák. कीदृशोऽस्या दृष्टिरागः p. 55. This also indicates the other stages in the growth of love; see com. **जडता**—want of quick action, hesitation, is defined as क्रियास्वपाटवं जाड्यं चिन्तोत्कण्ठाभयादिभिः । **वैदग्ध्यं**—Skill in creating such exquisitely beautiful forms. **विलसतु**—show itself to advantage, bear fruition. Fig. समुच्चय.

**कृष्णचतुर्दशी** &c—Dissolve ०रजन्यां श्मशानसंचारेण निर्वर्तितः विषमः व्यवसायः the arduous or difficult task of येन ( indicating his excessive love for Mâl. ) स चासौ निष्ठापितं completely proved चण्डपाखण्डदोर्दण्डयोः साहसं ( the desperate deed of killing Mal.-showing the great obligation conferred on Mâl. ) येन स च. Here Lav. although appearing to speak on Mâl.'s side cleverly puts her in mind of what Mâdh. had done and suffered for her. Mak. understands this at once.

P. 136. **सदृशस्त्रीयोग०**—*Cf.* for the idea differently expressed Ragh. VII. 14. ( परस्परेणस्पृहणीयशोभं न चेदिदं द्वन्द्वमयोजयिष्यत्। &c. ) **रोदिति**—Because she had a motherly affection for Mâlatî.

**परिणाति**—परिणत्या परिणतौ वा रमणीयाः; परिणाति development, maturity; or end ( and not only in the beginning ).

**प्रसङ्गः**—An occurrence, event; *i. e.* affected by the turn of events Kâm. forgets her dignity and acts in a way she should not do. अतिक्रामति—मर्यादामितिशेषः। यत्सकललोकवन्द्या भगवती मत्प्रणामं कर्तुमिच्छति। अनुचितकर्मणि प्रवर्तते इति भावः।

P. 137. **निर्व्यूढ०**—निर्व्यूढः ( fully proved or vindicated ) सौहृदस्य भरः यया ( having declared her resolve to put an end to her life when about to be married to Nandana or by being ready to marry Mâdhava). **युष्माकमेव**—This is the culminating point in her favour. The fig.s are ( कारण ) समुच्चय and आक्षेप.

**शेवधिः**—The treasure, highest bliss; शे सुखे अवधिः the highest limit of happiness; or शेते अनेन इति शेवं सुखं; व being added to शी ( Unâdi I. 152 ); शेवं धीयतेऽस्मिन्. **धर्मदाराः**—धर्मस्य दाराः धर्मदाराः। तादर्थ्ये षष्ठीसमासः अश्वस्य घास इतिवत्। The fig. is यथासंख्य.

P. 138. **परिणायय**—परिणी properly means to take round; in the marriage ceremony the bridegroom has to take the bride round the sacred fire; hence परिणी means to marry.' So परिणायय means 'get yourself married' ( the lit. sense being lost sight of ). **अस्यां चिन्तायां**—To give thought to this matter; *i. e.* it is not for you to think of what the result will be.

**वाटः**—appears to be used here in the sense of an 'enclosure'; वाटः पथि वृतौ वाटं...इति हैमः।

**फलिनः**—bearing fruit; fr. फल+इन (इनच्). see Jag. **मुग्ध**—Although we have followed Jag. in translating this, मुग्ध should rather be taken with व्याहाराः; मुग्धाः charming, attractive ये विकिरव्याहारास्तद्वन्तः।

प्रेयः—श्रेयः is the reading of Jag. and of five of the Mss. consulted by Dr. Bhândarkar, who thinks that though "in ordinary language it ( श्रेयः ) signifies good whether in this world or the next, Bhavabhûti, his attention being drawn to the distinction made between श्रेयः and प्रेयः in the Kathopanishad, must have used प्रेयः instead. प्रेयः is that which pleases one, *i e.* worldly good, and श्रेयः is eternal good, though not pleasing from a worldly point of view." The passage referred to above is from Kathop. I. 2—अन्यच्छ्रेयोन्यदुतैव प्रेयस्ते उभे नानार्थे पुरुषं सिनीतः । तयोः श्रेय आददानस्य साधु भवति हीयतेऽर्थाद्य उ प्रेयो वृणीते ॥ श्रेयश्च प्रेयश्च मनुष्यमेतस्तौ संपरीत्य विविनक्ति धीरः । श्रेयो हि धीरोऽभिप्रेयसो वृणीते प्रेयो मन्दो योगक्षेमाद्वृणीते ॥ &c. I. 2.

P. 139. कल्याणावतंसा—This refers to Mak.'s marriage. भवति—The reading भवतु should have been preferred as it better expresses the doubt as implied in Mak.'s speech. संदेह एवाऽभवतः–Mak. means that Madh. should not have expressed a doubt after Kâm. had remarked 'कस्त्वमस्यां चिन्तायाम्.' अवशिष्यामहे—We should remain behind, *i. e.* not accompany you. त्वरामहे—*v. l.* We should make haste in this matter ( and go to attend to other arrangements ).

P. 140. कण्टकित—कण्टका अस्य संजाताः असौ. बाहुनाल—बाहुः नाल इव बाहुनालः यस्य. Jag. dissolves this as बाहुरेव नालो यस्य; but this will require करकमलं instead of करं in the 3rd line. Similarly अङ्गुल्यो दलानीव अङ्गुलीदलानि यस्य. द्विरदः &c.—not a happy simile.

## ACT VII.

P. 141. संविधान—carefully carrying out the instructions of. Trip reads भगवत्याः संविधानेन; in this case संविधान means arrangament, plan.

नववधू०—०प्रवेशेन ( हेतुना ) प्रवेशार्थं वा विरचितः &c. तत्र या प्रवृत्तिः तया &c. Trip reads प्रमत्त ( careless, not very particular about their duties ) for प्रवृत्ति which is equally good. अकालः—out of its season; be cause it was not the time of the moon-light festival.

व्यवसितं—undertaking; here the business entrusted to her and Lav., *viz.* to induce Mad. to marry Makaranda and to send them to Káma.'s abode for being married वैलक्ष्य—विलक्षस्य भावः is shame mixed with embarrassment or confusion वैलक्ष्येण स्खलन्त्यक्षराणि यस्य । Jag. reads ०क्षरस्वरः ०स्खलन्त्यक्षराणि यस्मिंस्तादृशः स्वरः यस्य । Read निर्भरसंशुष्कि &c.; रोषानिर्भरेण संशुष्कि ( dried up, checked ) यत्तारुदितं ( loud crying ) तेन प्रस्फुरद्वदनं यस्य । Trip. reads अवरुदितनयनप्रस्फुरद्वदनः which is easier.

**कौमार०—**कौमारे एव बन्धकी ( बध्नाति मनः अत्र; बन्ध् + अक ). **प्रसङ्गेन०—** By this incident, using this as an occasion for.

P. 142. **व्यपदेशेन—**under the pretext ( व्यपदिश्यते अनेन *lit.* that by which the real thing is concealed ); see Jag. **प्रसुप्त०—**प्रसुप्तस्येव लक्षणं यस्य.

P. 143. **अत्याहितं**-Jag. takes this in the sense of 'A transgression ( of the respect due to a husband); its usual meaning of 'a great misfortune' will also do. See p. 82. **वामशीला—**वामं शीलं यस्याः; cross-tempered, surly. **प्रसुप्ता—**fast asleep. **शयनीयोपान्ते—** ०योर्ध्वान्ते *v. l.* at the upper end of the bed. **दुर्मनायते इयं** &c.—is a question, दुर्मना० being used in a slightly different sense—does she get out of temper, get fretted or offended? *Cf.* जामदग्न्यो हि वो मित्रमन्यथा दुर्मनायते । Mah. ch. I.

P. 144. **विदग्धं—**Cleverly, in a manner to win the affection of. **अरोषण—**forbearing, patient रोषण fr. रुष् + अन ( युच् ) added ताच्छील्ये; wrathful. **विप्रतीप—***Lit.* against the current of water; विप्रनिगता आपोऽत्र, fr. विप्रतिं + अप् + अच्; the अ of अप् is changed to ई when preceded by द्वि, अन्तर् or a preposition, by द्व्यन्तरुपसर्गेभ्योऽप ईत् । Pāṇ. VI. 3. 97; hence secondarily 'in a contrary way, against the course of events. **विप्रतीपं न वा** &c.—Hereby Bud. wants to show that she is speaking impartially. **लज्जादोषेण—**Herein she suggests an excuse for Māl.'s conduct so that it is Nandana who is really to blame.

**नववधू०—**नववध्वाः विरुद्धः यः रभसोपक्रमः तस्य स्खलनं ( failure unsuccessfulness ) or स एव स्खलनं ( mistake ) तेन &c. **विच्छर्दित—**properly 'vomited out, ejected; hence entirely given up or abandoned totally destroyed. **अपरिस्थानकं—**नास्ति परिस्थानं यस्य something without ground or support; something deserving condemnation; hence, something unworthy or unbecoming.

P. 145. **कुसुम०—**समानः धर्मो यासां ताः सधर्माणः; कुसुमैः सध० । **सुकुमारोपक्रमाः—**should be gently approached *i. e.* treated, tenderly used. The कामसूत्रकार referred to by Budh is वात्स्यायन and the passage quoted occurs in ch. II of the कन्यासंप्रयुक्तकाधिकरण being the sixth Sûtra, the सद्यः and वि in विद्वेषिण्यः of the text being omitted; after भवन्ति we have तस्मात्सान्नेवोपचरेत् । The two verses सहसा &c. quoted by Jag. are the last two verses of the second chapter.

**लज्जापरा०—**परस्मिन् अधि पराधीनः Loc, Tat. लज्जया पराधीनः लज्जा० । **कुलकुमारी—**कुलपालिका कुमारी ( शाकपार्थिवादिः ) lit. a girl maintaining the honour of her family. **हृदय०—**हृदये शल्यानां निक्षेपाः the planting into of. **संस्मर्यमाण०—**Trip, who translates संभरिज्जन्त by संभ्रियमाण

reads आमरणसंभ्रियमाणदुःसहपरगृहनिवास &c. **अभिजन्मलाभं**—*i. e.* of a daughter in general and not दुःशीला कन्या as Jag. has it.

P. 146. **येन भर्तेष:**—*cf.* भर्ता हि परमं नार्या भूषणं भूषणैर्विना. **अनभिजाता॰**—अनभिजातानि अनभिजातोचितानि अक्षराणि तैरधिक्षेपो यत्र तादृशः य उपालम्भः स यस्मिन् । अनभिजात properly means 'not well born or noble'; hence secondarily what emanates or falls from such a person. **तन्न जानीथ**—is a question. Without न it is an affirmative sentence. **वाचामन्त्रितं**—*i. e.* by Nandana in the words-that harlot of a girl'. Trip. reads कथं वयमसज्जानीमः ।

**तारामैत्रं**—Love or affection produced by the eye ( तारा standing for the eye ), either by the meeting of glances or at sight. Of course it is spontaneous or apparently unaccountable ( owing its origin to impressions received or a connection formed in a previous life ). This seems to be its natural meaning दर्शनमात्रस्नेहः says Trip. Dr. Bhảnd. takes it to mean 'friendship due to the agreement between the stars presiding over the births of two individuals.' But neither Trip. nor the com. of Uttar. understands by तारा stars. In the Uttar. it is said to be otherwise called चक्षूरागः; see Uttar. p. 143. In our note on the passage, however, we have followed Dr. Bhándarkár.

**भर्तुरपक्षाभिनिवेशः**—a comp. सापेक्षत्वेपि गमकत्वात्; अभिनिवेश means firm attachment, strong affection. **अपक्ष**—is one on the opposite side; hence a rival, an opponent; मालत्याः भर्तुरपक्षे अभि॰ Mál.'s strong attachment to her husband's rival **हृदयात्** *i. e.* of Mál. In translating this passage we have connected this with भर्तुः but this way of taking it seems to be better and more natural. Correct the trans. accordingly. Trip reads भर्तुरुपेक्षाभिनिवेशः Mál.'s persistent indifference towards her husband. **निष्कम्पदारुणाः**-निष्कम्पाः *i. e.* fearlessly pursuing their own course; अतएव दारुणाः । **दुरभिषङ्गः**—दुष्टः अभिषङ्गः evil attachment, ill-placed love.

P. 147. **अस्फुटं भणिताः** &c.—*i. e.* I will explain matters; I will make my meaning clear to you. **वा कठोर॰**—**कठोर**—ripened, fully developed. The words may also be separated as वा अकठोर; ॰गर्भस्य इव विभ्रमो येषां ते च ते अवयवाश्च तेषां &c. Drooping limbs are described as adding grace to fair maidens. *Cf.* Śak. III. 8.

**सविभ्रम** &c.—सविभ्रमं यथा तथोल्लसितानि कौतूहलेनोत्फुल्लानि प्रसरन्ति च यानि नयनोत्पलानि तेषां बहलविलासेन मसृणः संचारो यासां ताश्च ता चारवश्च; विलासेन मसृणो यः संचारस्तेन चारव इति वा याः तारकास्तासां विराजमानो विभ्रमो यत्र ।

**नाट्याचार्य** &c.-Trip. reads शृङ्गाराचार्यसर्वागमोपदेश (instruction based on the whole science of love ) &c. **भ्रातुर्दान**—*i. e.* भ्रात्रे मालत्या दानं.

P. 148. उच्छालित-upraised, hence produced. वचनोपन्यास—putting forth, advancing. स्वयंमाहसाहसे—see p. 85. Sl. 1.

P. 149. सखि कतम: &c.-Lav. purposely feigns forgetfulness that Mad.'s thoughts should rest more on Mak. so as to intensify her feeling of love for him.

श्वापदापदेश०—श्वापदस्य अपदेशः (guise) यस्य स चासौ कालश्च. पीवरभुज०—पविर is redundant as स्तम्भ includes the idea of hugeness. दृढ० विकट may also mean 'frightful' (दंष्ट्राभिर्विदारितमत एव विकटं); परि—णाहोस्यास्तीति परिणाहि; ईदृग् वक्षःस्थलं लाञ्छनं यस्य अनएव जरठ०पीडधारिणा इव (which must be supplied). As the इव, however, does not actually occur in the passage, Dr. Bhándarkar adopts the reading ०हारिणा and translates it as 'surpassing a garland of tattered, full-grown Japâ flowers &c.' See his notes p. 61, where this reading is ably defended. ०धारिणा, however, appears to be more natural and original. करुणैकमनसा—करुणा एव एकं तत्र मनो यस्य; करुणा एकं प्रधानं यस्मिन् तादृग्मनो यस्येति वा.

P. 150. वयं—By this she means that she is one with Málatî; whatever good or ill is said of one also belongs to the other. नाम०—Granted that, we acknowledge (नाम अभ्युपगमे). किं वदामि—*i. e.* What is the use of gainsaying your statement. अयं तु &c. —In good season does Lav. fling this retort at Mad.; thereby suggesting that she too was being impulsively led to the same course. कदम्बगोल—refers to her hair standing erect all over the body like a Kadamba tree bristling all over with buds at the first shower of the new clouds (see Supra III. 7).

विशुद्धमुग्धः—&c.—Ironical. You passed a censure on Mál. but how is this that you who are विशुद्ध० and a *Kulakanyaká* have betrayed such emotion?

आत्मानिरपेक्ष०—आत्मनो निर्गतापेक्षा यस्मिन्कर्माणि तद्यथा तथा व्यवस्यतीति तच्छीलस्य. विस्मरित—deprived of its consciousness, शरीर being used for चैतन्यविशिष्ट शरीर; or विस्मरितः शरीरात्संगलित...लोत्पीडो यस्य who was not conscious of the stream of perspiration &c. But there is no beauty in saying-who did not notice the perspiration. Trip. reads विह्वलित which is perhaps better, as we have मोह mentioned immediately after as the next step. भूमि०—आसिलनाया विष्टम्भेन यद्धैर्यं तेन विष्टम्भेन धैर्येण चेति वा धारितः &c मदयन्तिका &c.—०निमित्तमेव निमित्तमात्रं. महामहार्घ०—Trip. reads जीवितः which is better as Mad. can speak with greater propriety of Mak.'s life being extremely valuable at least from her own stand point.

P. 151. व्यवसितं &c.—See Jag. Your body has formed its determination. What she means is this—Although you cannot make up your mind yet openly to declare your love for Mak., your body has done that as shown by its perspiration, the result of inward emotion. Trip.'s reading—अस्वस्थशरीरे किं वाचा दर्शितं शरीरेण मकरन्दसमागमौत्सुक्यम्—makes the sense clear. व्यवसाय often means 'determination, decision.' *Cf.* Bg. II. 41.

**व्यपदेशात्**—व्यपदेश dissimulation; concealment of one's real feelings. See *supra* p. 142.

P. 152. **बुद्धरक्षिता०**—बुद्धरक्षितायाः (माधवे) पक्षपातः तस्मात्तज्जनितो वा प्रत्ययः (confidence) तेन; for this sense of प्रत्यय *cf.* सिद्धादेशप्रत्ययप्रार्थितायाः Rat. I p. 8; आत्मन्यप्रत्ययं चेतः Śak. I. 2. **भृतोद्वृत्त**—भृतं च तदुद्वृत्तं risen to overflowing च; see Jag. **दुर्वार०**—Trip. reads दुर्वारदारुणायासदुःखसंतापदह्यमानचित्त...ताशा. **विजृम्भित** &c.-विजृम्भितश्चासौ अपूर्वश्च अपूर्वं यथा तथेति वा सर्वा० तश्च मदनहुतवहः &c. **प्रत्याशा**- प्रत्याशायाः विमोक्ष एव विमोक्षमात्रं तेन सुलभं यन्मृत्युरेव निर्वाणं (entire disappearance of torment, complete ease) तस्य प्रतिकूलं. **विसंष्ठुला**—unsteady; hence shaky, agitated, disturbed in mind. **जीवलोकपरिवर्त**—जीवलोक the world of the living; hence life in this world; *cf. infra p.* 204, 212. परिवर्त change; a changed condition of life; तदीदृशो जीवलोकस्य परिवर्तः । न शक्तास्मीदृशं जीवलोकपरिवर्तमनुभवितुम् । Uttar. III. p. 79, VII. p. 172.

**मनोरथो०**—मनोरथेन य उन्मादः तेन मोहिता frenzied.

P. 153. **मुहूर्त**—&c.—मुहूर्तं निर्व्यूढः यः विस्मयः तेन विसंष्ठुले उद्वेल्ले च ते विस्तार्यमाणे रक्ते च ये नेत्रपुण्डरीके तयोस्ताण्डवेन उद्भटं (powerfully, intensely) यथा तथा प्ररूढः य मैरेयस्य मदः तेन घूर्णितः यथा स्यात्तथा । **मैरेयः**—a kind of intoxicating wine—शीधुरिक्षुरसे पक्वैरपक्वैरासवो भवेत् । मैरेयं धातकीपुष्पगुडधानाम्बुसंहितम् ॥ Mádhav. Dr. Bhánd. reads मैरेयदर्प (who was under the influence of wine) **निध्यायति** Jag. says चिन्तयति but it also implies the use of the external sense of vision; looks intently, eyes attentively. Better read निध्यायति. निर्वर्णनं तु निध्यानं दर्शनालोकनेक्षणम् । Amara. *Cf.* विद्याधरदारिका तेन राजर्षिणा निध्यातेति कुपितोर्वशी । Vik. IV. p. 91. **कषालित** &c.—कषाया—must rather be taken in the sense of sour, 'astringent' here, to account for the voice being घर्घर (hoarse and स्खलित obstructed, not smoothly proceeding); कलहंसघोषवद् घर्घरा चासौ स्खलिता च या गम्भीरा भारती तया भरितं कर्णयोर्विवरं यस्मिन् कर्मणि तद्यथा तथा ; the same expression (upto घर्घर) occurs in Uttar. (IV. p. 116). **प्रस्फुरत्**-&c.-प्रस्फुरतोः पयोधरयोः उच्छलद् यदुत्तरीयांशुकं तस्याञ्चलस्यावलम्बनमेव परिभवस्तेन (seizing the upper garment of a woman is considered a gross violence) ससंभ्रमं full of agitation च तद् उत्तरङ्गं (उद्गताः तरंगा यस्य lit. ruffled by waves; hence tossed about by emotion, heaving), धमधमायमानं (forcibly beating or trepidating-indicating great bewilderment) च हृदयं यस्याः । धमधमायते—derived fr. धमधमा an onomatopœtic word expressive of the sound of bellows blown very fast, by adding य ( क्यष् ). A final आ ( डाच् ) is added to the latter half of word indicating sound when the word consists of at least two syllables; ( see Pán. V. 4. 57. ) and words ending in आ take the denom. affx. य ( क्यष् ) by लोहितादिडाज्भ्यः क्यष् । by Pán. III. 1. 13.

**विसर्जित**०—विसर्जितं ( left off to get out of his grasp ) अंशुकं यया सा चासौ प्रसृता च. **तत्क्षण** &c.—तत्क्षणं कठोरकमलदण्डवद्दाचरन्तौ ( on account of horripilation ) यौ बाहू तयोः बन्धनेन अपवारितः पयोधरयोरुद्गमः protuberance ( *i. e.* उन्नतपयोधरौ which were laid bare when the garment was thrown off ) यया ताम्. **विघटमान** &c.—विघटमानं displaced अत एव विकलं ( स्रस्तं ) यद् मेखलावलयं तेन संदानिताभ्यां fettered पीवरोरुभ्यां प्रतिषिद्धं विप्रतीपं ( in a direction opposite to him ) गमनं यस्याः । **अत्यादरप्रयत्न** &c.—अत्यादरेण यः प्रयत्नः ( the effort made after a great deal of painstaking or exertion as she could not easily feign anger; or the प्रयत्न may be on his part ) तेन निर्वर्तितः यः ( मुहूर्तं कोपः मुहूर्तकोपः तस्योपरागः ( *cf.* p. 76 ) तेन यद्दुःखं &c; दुःख because she had to put on a semblance of anger. Or उपराग may mean व्यसन a calamity, misfortune ( कोप एवोपरागस्तस्मात् &c.). **स्निग्धपुनरुक्त** &c—स्निग्धस्य ( स्नेहस्य ) पुनरुक्तं (lit. what is said again ) repetition तेन; or स्निग्धस्य पुनरुक्तं यस्मिन् कर्मणि तथा पर्यस्ते लोचने ताभ्यां विभावितः अशेषः चित्तस्य सारः यस्य; who fully knew what my real state of mind was from the casting of my glances which repeatedly indicated my love for him ( my actions to the contrary not-with-standing ). Or पुनरुक्त may mean 'superfluous'; स्निग्धं पुनरुक्तं यस्मिन्कर्माणि with a superfluous expression of love ( which was already known to him ). For the sense *cf.* आशास्यमन्यत्पुनरुक्तभूतं; Ragh. V. 34. The Com. reads निषिद्ध for स्निद्ध which he takes in the sense of निषेध repeated forbidding; see com.

P. 154. **द्विगुण** &c.—द्विगुणौ बाहुदण्डौ तयोः &c.; or द्विगुणं बाहुदण्डयोरावेष्टनं; ०दण्ड indicates the great length and inflexibility of the arms. **प्ररूढ**०—Jag.'s ०नखवत् कठोरं यत्कररुहं ( of Mak. he means ) is not in good taste. प्ररूढ–overgrown with flesh or hardened, as the wounds inflicted by the tiger on Mak.'s bosom were after they were healed. प्ररूढं यत् शार्दूल० क्रमणं ( infliction of the wounds or scratches made by the nails ) तदेव विकटपत्रावली सैव प्रसाधनं ( decoration ) यस्य तादृशि वक्षःस्थले ( his broad chest ) यः निष्ठुरः निवेशः ( his placing me on ) तेन निःसहा ( quite nerveless, overpowered ) ताम् । ओरम्फ a rough scratch; *cf.* Maráthi ओरपणें, ओरखडणें.

**सावेग** &c—आवेगेन सहितं यथा तथा ( in agitation or flurry ) विधुतं ( shaken by me ) यन्मस्तकं तेनाविद्धा ( loosened ) या कबरी तस्यां निहितेन ( *i. e.* by Mak. ) करेण यः परिग्रहः तेन पुञ्जीकृताः ( pressed together;

Dr. Bhándarkear) उन्नामिताः निश्चलाः ये मम मुखावयवाः (*i. e.* the forehead, cheeks, lips &c. ) तेषु स्वच्छन्दविकसने विदग्धं मुखकमलं यस्य । पुञ्जीकृतावयव is not a good expression, although it occurs again in the next line Perhaps the poet meant पुञ्जीकृतैः केशैः उपलक्षिताः ( marked by ) मुखावयवाः । This is an instance of how the poet's fondness for long compounds makes his meaning ambiguous and the construction awkward. **स्वच्छन्दविकसित**—Trip. reads विलसित ( sporting ) which makes the meaning clear. "ओवगिद may also be equivalent to अववल्गितं; अववल्गितं यथा तथा अववल्गितेन वा उन्नामितः *i. e.* her face was raised in a bounding fashion or at once by Mak." Dr. Bhándárkar.

**वामगण्ड**—०निहितः प्रस्फुरन् पुञ्जितः ( here the word is appropriate as the lip is flexible and could be contracted ) यः अधरः तस्मात्समुद्गतः &c. **उद्धर्षित**—horripilated. **उद्भ्रामितशरीरशोभां**—*V. l.* The beauty of whose body was made to whirl round, *i. e.* it appeared to do so owing to the hair standing on end.

P. 155. **उल्लसित०**—&c.—उल्लसिताभ्यामानन्दसाध्वसाभ्यां ( *i. e.* rising in turns ) विषमः यः संभ्रमः तेन यद्वलनं तेन यः मोहः तेन मन्थरे dull भ्रमन्ती च लोचने यस्याः । **स्नेहविभ्रम** &c.—स्नेहविभ्रमाभ्यामुन्मिश्रं. Trip. reads विभ्रमोर्जितं— विभ्रमेण ऊर्जितं ( noble-looking, beautiful ).

**मालतीप्रियसखी**—She means—Being Mál.'s dear friend and her constant companion, she must have noticed such things in the case of Mâl. who was in a similar condition and so she can ask but such questions only. The side meaning is—If you confess this, Lav. will not expose you as she did not Mâlatî. You can freely confess your love for Mak. to us.

P. 156. **निःसंगलग्न** &c.—निर्गतः संगः यस्मिन् कर्माणि तद्यथा तथा ( in a manner not be attracted by any thing else ) लग्ने निश्चले च । Trip. reads निसर्ग ( naturally ) लग्न.

**मन्मथबलात्कारितः**—मन्मथबलात्कारः संजातोस्य; forcibly incited by passion. **कन्दर्पजननी**—(1) The inflamer of his passion; (2) the mother of Pradyumna.

Rukminî was the daughter of Bhishmaka, king of the Vidarbhas ( the modern Berar. Kundinapura was its capital ). Although solicited in marriage by Krishṇa, her brother Rukmî, who was jealous of Krishna and therefore hostile to the match, arranged her marriage with S'iśupâla, king of Chedi. Rukminî, however, who in her heart loved Krishna, sent a letter to him in which she requested him to take her away. Krishna came and assisted by Balarâma carried her off as she proceeded to offer her devotions at a temple. They were hotly pursued but in the battle that ensued, Rukmi was struck to the ground, but his life was spared by Krishna at his sister's intercession.

**का प्रतिपत्ति**—What course will you adopt; how will you act? प्रतिपत्ति is the knowledge and decision of the course of action to be followed or the steps to be taken; *cf.* विषादलुप्तप्रतिपत्ति Ragh. III. 40. Kum. V. 42 & Màl. p. 88; *infra*. p. 182.

P. 157. **दुष्टशार्दूलकवलनात्**—Trip.-मृत्युकवलात्. **कृत्यकर**—According to Dr. Bhând.-possession, property; according to Jag. a prize set apart at a game. In this case the meaning will be-This person is his inasmuch as he won me as a prize at the dangerous game he played with the tiger and saved me.

**स्मरिष्यसि एतद्वचनम्**-Bud. means that she might act differently in Mak.'s presence through bashfulness or under excitement, which she should not do.

**द्वितीयप्रहर०**—द्वितीयप्रहरस्य नाडिकास्तासां विच्छेदः—the termination of the *ghatikâs* making up the second *prahara* or watch. This may also mean the close of each of the *ghatikâs* विच्छेद a division of ) of the second watch; but this does not seem to be intended, as the drum was generally beaten at the end of a Prahara. Trip. reads द्वितीययामविच्छेदः which makes the meaning clear. This shows that it was midinight then.

P. 158. **कथितप्रणय०**—(1) कथितः प्रणयरूपः प्रसादो यस्य. Your favour in the shape of your love for whom has been declared by you; or कथितप्रणय एव प्रसादो यस्य who has received the favour of the declaration of your love. एष तव दासः अस्ति.

**प्रेयान्** &c.—The fig. is कारणसमुच्चय.

P. 159. **ऊर्जितं**—adv. in a noble or glorious manner. **बान्धवधुरा**-बांधवस्य धूः । The yoke ( burden, responsible task ) to be borne by kinsmen. Fig.-may be पर्यायोक्त. **निशीथ०**—निशीथे निःसंचारत्वेन रमणीयता.

**उपरिवलभी०**—may be taken as one word like उपर्यलिन्दक p. 45; having moved through the lofty windows of the top-rooms of mansions. For वलभी see p. 16. **परिणत**—old; परिणतसुराया गन्धसंस्कारः गर्भे यस्य; or परिणतः सुरागन्धः तस्य संस्कारः &c.

P. 160. **मुहुः** &c.—**आमोद**-आमोदः सोऽतिनिर्हारी ( extremely pleasing );—Amara.—मुहुरुपचितोत एव स्फारः कर्पूरवासो यस्य. Fig. अनुमान.

## ACT VIII.

P. 161. **ग्रीष्मदिवसावसान**—&c.—The bath to be taken in the evening. Here although Avalokitâ speaks of the evening bath, it must have been taken at a late hour-probably an hour or two before midnight. For as Mádh. and Màl, together with Avalokitá, are conversing just after having finished their ablution which Mádh. calls प्रत्यग्र ( see further on प्रत्यग्रसायंतनस्नान ), Mad., Lavangiká and others come from Nandana's house, and it is then past midnight as is clear from Bud.'s words ( प्रौढं तमः &c. ) at the end of the seventh Act. And we cannot suppose either the bath or the conversation to have lasted for five or six hours. Again Avalokitâ says that she comes after having saluted Kám. then just returned from Nandana's house. And we know from the prologue to the VIIth Act that when Kám. left Nandana's house the night was pretty well advanced. So we conclude that the bath was taken an hour or two before midnight.

**निशीथस्य**—निशीथ the midnight; नितरां शेरतेऽस्मिन्; fr. शी with नि and aff थ. It is called मन्मथप्रौढ॰ because passion and the desire for enjoyment and revelry are at their height at midnight. मन्मथ उद्दृप्ताहि मन्मथसाध्यानुकूलकरणात् । तत्र समयेसानन्दसाध्वसाः सुरतव्यवसायिन्यो भवन्ति ! इति वात्स्यायनः । इति विबुधरत्नावली ( com. ). The reading निशीथिनीनाथस्य though it appears to be appropriate at first sight, is rejected because the word यौवनश्री goes against it, while it is peculiarly happy in the case of निशीथ. In the following sl. the moon is described as just rising and so it can not be in its Yauvana. Again as shown above it was midnight to which the description belongs.

**दलयति**— &c.—प्राक्प्रकाशः the early light, *i. e.* when the moon was just about to rise or was on the horizon. This is necessary to make it comparable with the परिशुष्यत्प्रौढताली leaf **मन्दमन्दं**—is necessary that the moonlight should be mistaken for the pollen. **माकरन्द॰** *v. l.* will mean—mixed with honey or floral juice, heavy and hence by implication, moving gently. This reading is better as it is more poetical; *cf.* with this Kâli.'s beautiful description of the moonrise when at hand-उदयगूढशशाङ्कमरीचिभिः &c. Vik. III. 6. The reading स्फारस्फारं for मन्द॰ violates the metre. **सान्द्रः**—Thick, moving in a mass. The Ketaka flowers have an abundance of pollen in them. Fig. Utprekshá.

**वामशीलां**—merely means going against ones wishes, obstinate, unyielding; see p. 143. It has not got its usual bad sense here, as in वामा कुलस्याधयः Sâk. IV. 18; or *infra* in IX. 8. **उपावर्तये**—make her turn to me, to act agreeably to my wishes. win her over.

P. 162. **निश्चोतन्ते**—The Atm. is unusual. The poet uses the correct Pada in his Uttar. ( एतास्ता मधुनो धाराः श्चोतन्ति सविषास्त्वयि )

III. 34. **कबरी०**—*i. e.* कबरीजल. **सान्द्र०**—A Bah. ०क्लेदा, instead of the Matub aff. वत्, would have been better for the sake of brevity; the use of. वत् however may be defended; see Jag. **अङ्कपालीं**-पाली ( पालि is more usual; पालयति पाल्यते अनेन अनया वा fr; पाल् + अच् + इ ) means a region; hence अङ्कपाली-large and fleshy lap. **वितर**—give me your lap *i. e.* a seat on it; hence an embrace ( आश्लेषं देहीत्यर्थः ) as shown by the context. Fig.—Samuchchaya.

**निरनुरोधे**—Seeing no inclination on her part to comply with his request, he addresses her thus. निर्गतः अनुरोधः ( regard for, consideration, hence, compliance with ) यस्याः one not yielding to one's wishes, regardless. **निरनुक्रोशे**—*V. l.* without sympathy; pitiless, hard-hearted. See p. 185. l. 9.

**जीवयन्निव**—Śl. occurring in Uttar. also (I. 34. with the reading ससाध्वसभ्रम for समूढसाध्वस ). It is, however, in its proper place here. **समूढ**—grown; *i. e.* excessive ( because Mád.'s remark increased her fear ) **ऐन्दव** &c.—इन्दोः इमे ऐन्दवाः ये मयूखाः तैः चुम्बितः ( kissed, acted upon ) अत एव, तेषां चुम्बितेन वा स्यन्दते असौ स्यन्दनशीलः यः चन्द्रमणिहारस्तस्य इव विभ्रमो यस्य । The arm is compared to a necklace of moon-stones because both are fair, both are to be placed round the neck and both are gracefully covered with drops. Sans. poets conventionally describe moon-stones as oozing when touched by lunar rays. Fig. निदर्शना and व्यतिरेक ( ऐन्दवेत्यादिना सादृश्यमुक्त्वा जीवयन्निवेति विशेषस्योक्तेः Virarághava on Uttar. ).

**संविभाग**—Participation in, joining in.

**दग्धं** &c.—मलयानिल-*cf.* Mál.'s speech at p. 132 ( चन्द्रातपमलयमारुत &c. ). **चन्द्रपादैः**—*cf.* विसृजति हिमगर्भैरग्निमिन्दुर्मयुखैः । Śak. III. 3. **तु**—As to, as regards; *cf.* चन्द्रोपरागं प्रति तु केनापि विप्रलब्धासि Mud. I. **तु**—but. **आमत्त०**—This is put in to explain why his ear was pained. It was pained on account of the note of the cuckoo stirring up his passion. *Cf.* however, Kálidása—एवं गतेपि प्रियेव मे मञ्जुस्वनेति न कोपोस्यां ( परभृतायां ) Vik. IV. Or—The foolish Kokila, thinking that its voice imitates the sweet music of your voice, utters its notes; but they are discordant to my ears; your voice alone, Kinnar-like, can please them. *Cf* स्वरेण तस्याममृतस्रुतेव प्रजल्पितायामभिजातवाचि । अप्यन्यपुष्टा प्रतिकूलशब्दा श्रोतुर्वितन्त्रीरिव ताड्यमाना ॥ Kum. I. 45. The fig. is पर्यायोक्त.

P. 163. **अनिर्वहणशीले**—One not habitually carrying out one's wishes. निर्वहण carrying out or putting into execution one's plans &c.; here Mál.'s desire to request Mádh. to embrace her. **विच्छर्दित**—entirely set aside or given up; see p. p. 144, 150.

**सासूयं**—Because she betrayed her. Or perhaps Ava. attributed to Mál. what she never said but which she would not have the courage to deny in the presence of her lover, and hence her वैदग्ध्यं which Mádh. admires in the next speech. **सर्वतोमुखं**—lit. facing all directions; able to meet every case. It also means 'all-embracing, complete; *cf.* उपपन्ना हि दारेषु प्रभुता सर्वतोमुखी । Śak. V. 26. **वैदग्ध्यं**—विदग्धस्य भावः । विदग्ध—lit. what is well burnt, polished or refined; hence well cultured, skilful.

P. 164. **अनवसितार्थ०**—अनवसितमत एवार्थे मन्थरम् slow to express *i. e.* not expressing the full sense, as it was not finished. **चारुता**—Because the curiosity to hear it was thereby increased.

**बाष्पाम्भसा** &c.—कान्तिरेवामृतं कान्त्यमृतं. Fig. Rûpaka **निवेशिता०**—निवेशितः मयूख एव मृणालदण्डः येन. The lunar ray is the lotus-stalk which is hollow and like a tube and the moon is supposed to drink the nectar by means of it by the process of suction. Fig. A blending of Utpreksha and Rûpaka ( अङ्गाङ्गिभावेन संकरः ).

**उच्छलित**—See Jag; it rather means 'gushing forth'; see p. p. 148; 73 ( उच्छलत् ). **बाष्पोत्पीड**—a swelling up or burst of tears ( see p. 131 ) तेन मन्थरं यथा स्यात्तथा ।

**उदर्कः**—may be derived fr. अर्क् or ऋच् to praise or अर्च् to worship. उदर्क्यते, उदृच्यते, उदर्च्यते वा, and means the final reward, fruit; उदर्कः फलमुत्तरम् । Amara.

P. 165. **वर्धयति**—( more usually वर्धापयति ) Lit. to enrich or cause to prosper; hence to express one's satisfaction or joy at such prosperity, to congratulate one upon. **प्रथमदर्शना०**—दर्शने यः अभिषङ्गः strong emotion or attachment, तस्य साक्षिणी.

**विस्तारिस्तन०**—स्तनौ कुम्भौ इव स्तनकुम्भौ विस्तारिणौ स्तनकुम्भौ कुट्मला इव स्तनकुम्भकुट्मलौ तयोः भरः bulk, size, तस्य उत्संगः the surface तस्मिन्, or विस्तारी यः स्तन—भरः &c. **भर**—fr. भृ to fill + अ ( अच् ), fulness (पूर्णता) bulk, mass, as here and in IX. 24; also excess ( अतिशयः ) as in VI. 17. And hence it has the sense of burden also, as in तस्याः परिस्फुरितगर्भभरालसायाः । Uttar. III. 28. **उत्संग**—Jag. takes this in the sense of क्रोड *i. e.* भुजान्तर ( the space between the arms, bosom ), and has recourse to an unidiomatic Bah. It is better to take it in the sense of 'the surface of'; उत्संग—fr. सञ्ज् with उत् + अ ( घञ् ) added in the sense of आधार or that which supports–hence means the lap; surface, as in दृषदो वासितोत्संगाः Ragh. IV. 74. *Cf.* also त्वय्योत्सङ्गे प्रणयिन इव &c. Meg. I. 66. Or it may simply mean, contact, union.

**पाणिपीडन**—Lit. seizing the hand firmly, so as not to let go the grasp; hence, marrying; *cf.* न प्रमाणीकृतः पाणिः बाल्ये बालेन पीडितः ।

Uttar. VII. 5. **सर्वस्वदायीकृता**—सर्वस्वस्य दायः सर्वस्वदायः न स० असर्व-स्वदायः; असर्व० सर्व० सम्पद्यते तथा कृता given in place of everything.

P. 166. **पदशब्द इव**—Something like a tread of footsteps. **दिष्ट्या वर्धसे**—Lit. you rise by your good luck; you are to be congratulated upon. दिष्टि means good luck, any fortunate occurrence or an auspicious event;—वृद्धि means one's expressing joy at another's good fortune; *cf.* दिष्टिवृद्धिमिव शुश्राव, दिष्टिवृद्धिसंभ्रमो महानभूत् &c. Kád. p. p. 95, 118. Hence दिष्ट्या ( regarded as an indec. ) has come to be used with वृध् in the sense of–to be congratulated upon.

**निर्व्यूढः**—see p. 91. **संभावनाभार**—responsibility of the trust reposed in (the weighty business entrusted to ) her by Kámandakî. संभावना lit. means thinking well about one's ability &c., hence honouring one as by entrusting a business to one. *Cf.* सिध्यन्ति कर्मसु महत्स्वपि यन्नियोज्याः संभावनागुणमवेहि तमीश्वराणाम् Śak. VII. 4. **अभियोगः**—a collision, attack. We have already got the word in the sense of close application to ( p. 18 ), energetic effort &c. I. 34. ( p. 38 ).

P. 167. **अतुल०**—प्रणये लालसः; indicates habit—always delighting in. **साहसे**—in an adventure. *Cf* गजेनेव शैवालकवलग्रास-लालसः करः Kád. **०सस्याहवे**—is another reading; but the context requires साहसे. **क्रणत्**—merely means here rattling against ( the bones of elephants ). **स्फुटत्** &c.—स्फुटन् यः करटः तस्य कोटरात्...... स्थितानामस्थ्नां दलने एकवीरः ( the only one able to do it; pre-eminently fitted to do it ). वीर when compounded with एक should be वीरैक as it ought to take पूर्वनिपात ( precedence ), by Pân. II. 1. 58; but एकवीर which is more often used by poets may be defended by supposing that the operation of the rule above mentioned is not universal-कथमेकवीर इति । पूर्वकालैकेति बाधित्वा परत्वादनेन समासे वीरैक इति हि स्यात् । बहुलग्रहणाद्भविष्यति । Sid. Kau. Fig. अप्रस्तुतप्रशंसा and अनुप्रास.

**विक्रान्तप्लुतं**—Jag. takes this as acc. governed by विलसतः, but against grammar, as विलस् ( to move about dexteriously, to flash about ) is intransitive. It must be taken as an adv. comp.; विक्रान्तानि प्लुतानि यस्मिन्कर्मणि तद्यथा तथा । In a manner full of heroic boundings; moving about dexterously and boldly.

P. 168. **वाक्स्तम्भं**—Because she was deprived of her power of speech by Kapâlakundalá by her mystic power. **सक्रोधहासं**—हास at Mál.'s helplessness as she could not speak.

**कन्याविटः**—The despoiler of a maiden ( कन्यादूषक ) who is to protect you ( a side-meaning of पति; see Jag. ). The speech is, of course, sarcastic. **चिरात्**—and so the vengeance will be terrible. **निकृत्य**—Fr. कृत् 6 conj. to cut, with नि.

P. 169. **संभावित:**—approached by you, found out.

**सावक्षेपा°**—सावक्षेपं यथा तथापविद्धो ( tossed or cast about ) यो विकटौ ऊरुदण्डौ ताभ्यां निष्ठुरं fiercely यथा तथा । **साधिक्षेपं**—treating the danger or enemy with contempt; **दूरनिक्षेपाविद्ध°**—*V. l.* दूरनिक्षेपेण -निक्षेपे वा आविद्धो ( stretched so as to take long strides ) will be a better reading. **सञ्जात°**—सञ्जातो मत्सराधिक्षेपो यस्य ( feeling jealous and insulted ).

P. 170. **पश्चादहं**—Jag. supplies प्रसृता after this. The meaning is I started to look for her but did not see her. See p. 174. **संघट्टदुर्गमात्**—संघट्टेन दुर्गमः तस्मात् that in which passage out was difficult owing to the collision or encounter; hence a hard and close fight. **निर्मलनिरन्तर°**—निर्मलाश्च ते निरन्तरं ( निर्गतमन्तरं यस्मिन्कर्मणि तथा ) उद्गताश्च धौता: &c. **मदलीला** &c.—मदलीलया कलितः ( lit. seized; hence influenced ) कामपालः तस्य विकटभुजदण्डेन आविद्धः यः हलः तस्य हेलया विक्षुभितमत एव उद्वेल्लिततरंगं ( उद्वेल्लिताः तरंगा यस्य ) यत् &c. **कलिन्दतनया**—Daughter of the mountain Kalinda or *Yama, i. e.* Yamuná. *Cf.* आगच्छ यमुने स्नातुमिच्छामीत्याह विह्वलः । तस्य वाचं नदी सा तु मदोक्तामव मन्य वे । नाजगाम ततः क्रुद्धो हलं जग्राह लाङ्गली । गृहीत्वा तां तटे तेन चकर्ष मदविह्वलः ॥ Vis. P. V. 25, 8-10.

Allusion—On one occasion when under the influence of wine Balaráma, wishing to bathe in the Jamuna from which he was at some distance, called upon the river, when elevated with wine, to come to him. His command not being obeyed he plunged his ploughshare into it and dragged the water to him until the river, in a human form, asked his forgiveness and promised good behaviour in future. See Bhâg. P. X. 65; Vis. P. ( quoted above ). This incident is often alluded to by Sans. poets, more than once by Báṇa in his Kád. *cf.* उन्मदहलिहलापकर्षणमयप्रपलायितामिव यमुनां &c. Kád. p. 23; वहसि वपुषि विशदे वसनं जलदाभम् । हलहतिभीतिमिलितयमुनाभम् । Gītagovinda.

**विकट** &c.—विकटं विशृंखलं ( विगता शृंखला restraint यस्मिन्कर्मणि ) च यथा तथा उत्पातितः निर्दयः ( who showed no mercy ) अमन्दः ( moving quickly ) च यः मकरन्दस्तस्य व्यतिकरेण on account of ) यः क्षोभः तेन विकला ये प्रतियोधाः तेषां परिवर्तनेन उद्गतः...वकाशं विशंकलितः (pervading) कलकलः यत्र । **विशंकलित**—spread about, Jag The readings in the foot-note—अवसरत्, विकसत् mean—moving, spreading about. **भीषण** &c.—भीषणः यः भुजः वज्र इव भुजवज्रः तेन जर्जरिताः पञ्जरा (bony frames) येषां ते भीषण...अराः अतएव अवसन्नाः ( drooping, completely enfeebled ) ये सुभटाः तेषां हस्तेभ्यः अवलुप्तानि (snatched away ) विविधानि आयुधानि तेषां निवहेन घातितं कृताघातं ( struck down, wounded ) यद्वशेषं रिपुसैन्यं तेन दत्तः विकटापसारः ( a tumultuous or head long-flight ) तेन रिक्तः यः मार्गः तत्र संचार एव निर्वर्तितं विषमं साहसं येन । This passage is differently read and it is very difficult to see which is the original reading. The Nir, Ed. reads—वज्रखचितपञ्जरपर्यस्तसमरविमुखसुभट.....युधोपरुद्धाशेषारिपुसैन्यविकटापसारव्यतिरिक्तमार्गं०. The reading in Dr. Bhán. Ed. is ०पञ्जरोपसन्न...विविधायुधोपमर्दसमवसारित ( this is preferable to घातित ) सैनिकनिकरं पदातिरिक्तमार्ग० (which, however, should not have been separated from the preceding, since पदातिरिक्तमार्गसंचार is no साहस), &c. Dr. Bhánd. explains उपसन्ना as उपनता उपस्थिता वा 'those who came up to fight him' and quotes तस्मै स विद्वानुपसन्नाय सम्यक्...प्रोवाच तां तत्त्वतो ब्रह्मविद्याम् । Mund. Up. in support of his meaning. In this case the comp. must be taken as ०पञ्जराश्च ते उपसन्नसुभटाश्च तेषां &c The reading अपसरिद (अपसृत) will not do, as it was not possible for Mád., as remarked by Dr. Bhandarkar, to snatch weapons from the hands of the soldiers that had fled away.

P. 171. सौध०—प्रतिहारेण करणेन ( through the door-keeper ) विनयोपन्यासेन ( by sending a conciliatory message ) प्रशमितं विरोधसंकटं येन । The king asked the प्र० to go to Mâdh. and Mak. and to pacify them by using mild words and so got the evil of enmity averted. Dr. Bhánd. reads सौधशिखरान्तरितावतीर्ण &c. and explains- अन्तरित—hidden or placed at a distance from them by his being on the top of the palace. Hence the प्रतिहार was sent to quiet them. सौधशिखरान्तरितः अत एवावतीर्णस्य प्रतीहारस्य प्रतीहारेण वा विनयोपन्यासेन प्रतिक्षामितं ( his reading ) &c. It is difficult to see the propriety of अन्तारित here. We should expect in this case अवतारित instead of अवतीर्ण. उपनीत०—उपनीतौ माध०न्दौ तयोः । प्रस्फुरत्०—प्रस्फुरती मत्सरवैलक्ष्ये एव मषी तया । भूरिवसुनन्दनौ प्रतिबोध्य । Read नन्दनौ for ०नन्दने. नवयौवन०—०नवयौवनं च गुणाश्च तैः &c.

P. 172. प्रेयसः—of my dear friend ( and not प्रीतस्य as Jag. takes it ). निर्व्याज—natural.

दोर्निष्पेष &c.—The cons. is प्राक् वीरान् अनुपत्य दोर्निष्पेषविशीर्णसंचय—०लम् उन्मथ्नतः ततः तत्प्रहरणान्याच्छिद्य विक्रामतः प्रेयसः रन्धाः &c.; दोर्भ्यां यः निष्पेषः (crushing) तेन विशीर्णः यः (अस्थि) संचयस्तेन दलन्ति कंकालानि यथा तथा । उद्वेलत् &c.—उद्वेल्लन्तः ये...खण्डाः तेषां निकरैः आकीर्णस्य । संख्योदधेः—संख्यं the fight एव उदधिः तस्य; the sea in the form of the mass of the fighting soldiers. द्वेधा &c.—As Màdh. dashed forward, the soldiers on either side remained pinned to the ground being paralysed with fear, &c.

अनुशयः--Regret, remorse, melancholy reflection; for a different sense *cf.* VI. 1.

इन्दुमयूख--Probably wine was drunk after being exposed to the moonlight. *Cf.* न च शशिप्रतिमाभरणं मधु । Ragh. IX. 7. भुजार्गल—भुजः अर्गल इव lit. an arm like a bar; huge and muscular. असार-

**विधुरान्**—असारा अत एव विधुराः; असारेण विधुरा वा तान्. **विधुर**—Properly unable to bear a burden, *i. e.* responsibility (विगता धूः कार्यभारो यस्य); hence helpless, pitiable. See p. 181 also. Fig. निदर्शना.

**सस्मितमालती** &c.—सस्मितया मालत्या वलितः यः लोलः कटाक्षः तेन पराहतं caused to be withdrawn. सस्मित—not on hearing of the fight, as Jag. has it, but on hearing from Makar. how Mad.'s secret was tricked out of her and how she was made to elope with Makaranda. For Makar. in the disguise of Mál. had heard the full confession of her love for him made by the unsuspecting Mad. and the detailed description of her love sufferings also. **उल्लसित०**—उल्लसिता ( rising up ) त्रपा तया स्तिमिता दृष्टिर्यस्य। त्रपा because there would be something in Mak.'s description of her love-torment that would make her blush.

P. 173. **आत्मानं विनो०**—The reading in Dr. Bhán.'s ed. is आत्मनः. The word आत्मन्, however, is always used in the sing. and in the Mas. gender; *cf.* गुप्तं ददृशुरात्मानं सर्वाः स्वप्नेषु वामनैः। Ragh. X. 60; आत्मानं बहुमन्यामहे वयम्। Kum. VI. 20. **मम हि** &c—**अनिष्टैकबुद्धेः**—अनिष्टमेव एकं तस्य बुद्धिः तद् बुद्धौ वा यस्य। This was because of his past experience; or because प्रेम पश्यति भयान्यपदेऽपि Kir IX 70. **भृशमयं** &c.—Read बद्धोत्कम्प. This reading which is also Jag.'s reading is adopted in the text in preference to the reading द्रवति हृदयमन्त०; see foot-note. For it is natural that Mád.'s heart should only palpilate forcibly as he has only a suspicion as yet about mishap having ourtaken Mál. The heart is generally described as melting when overpoweringly affected by some strong feeling; *e. g.* by that of love as in द्रवीभूतं प्रेम्णा तव हृदयमस्मिन्क्षण इव। Uttar. III. 13; of pity, see *supra*. V. 28; of fear as in द्रवति हृदयमेतद्भीममुत्प्रेक्ष्य भीमम्। Ven. V. 21. **अन्तर्भ्रंश्यतीवान्तरात्मा** *V. l.*—my internal soul seems to fall off *i. e.* forsake me; or to give way. Fig. समुच्चय.

P. 174. **पश्चादहं** &c.—पश्चाद्द्वावां न तां प्रेक्षावहे। *V. l.* The reading in the text is more in keeping with the context; see p. 170. **किमपि कि०**—Const. यत् यस्मात्कारणात् किमपि &c. तस्मात्परिहासः विरमतु। Jag. takes यत् with परिहास but that is not good. **कलयसि**—If you wish to know or guage ( test ) my love. **अविज्ञाय**—Without knowing the true state of things.

P. 175. **याता भवेत्** &c.—Jag.'s interpretation of this is not satisfactory. The doubts are मालती भगवतीभवनं याता भवेत् किं and जीवितन्युपेष्यति वा ( supposing she did not go to Kám.' dwelling ).

सौदामनी०—For the idea *cf.* भोगा मेघवितानमध्यविलसत्सौदामनीचञ्चलाः ।* Bh. Vair. 36. The word Saudámanî is purposely used to suggest the entrance of Sau. at the beginning of the next Act. See Jag. Fig.—अर्थान्तरन्यास.

## ACT IX.

P. 176. भगवतः—Sau. speaks of the mountain with veneration as being the seat of the attainment of miraculous power by the practice of Yoga and also of मन्त्रसिद्धि. See Jag.

पद्मावती—situated at the confluence of the Párá ( Pârbatî ) and Sindhu ( Sindh ) at a distance of about 25 miles from Narwar in Mâlwa ( see notes p. 14 ), seems to have been a beautiful city from the description given here—adorned with fine palaces and mansions, magnificent temples, city-gates and turrets, &c. The Parbati joins the Sindhu from the left while the river Mohvar or Madhuvar ( probably the Madhumatî of the play ) joins it from the right at some distance further from the junction of the two. The Lavaná ( now called Lun ) is also in the vicinity joining the Sindhu.

संस्तुत &c.—*cf.* संस्तुतनत्तत्प्रियवस्तुदर्शनादुद्दामोयमावेगः । Uttar. III. p. 85. संस्त्यायः—a house; fr. स्त्यै with सम् to be collected I P. A. and aff. अ ( घञ् ). कान्तारः—also *neu.*; a large dreary forest; कस्य सुखस्यान्तः कान्तः, कान्तमृच्छति, fr. ऋ and अ ( अण् ) added कर्मणि. Or कान्ता अरा अस्य; or a pathless region. महारण्ये दुर्गपथे कान्तारः पुंनपुंसकम् । Amara. This passage is variously read ( see Dr. Bhán.'s ed. ). The only variant worth noticing is कान्तारप्रवेशं परिभ्रमतो माधवस्य where ०प्रवेशं must be taken as a *ṇamulanta* ( कान्तारं प्रविश्य ) wandering over the forest having entered it. तथाहमुत्पतिता—She again rises into the sky in search of Mádh. and makes this observation. व्यतिकरः—The mingled or chequered view of.

उत्तुंगसौध &c.—This gives an idea of what the old Indian cities generally used to be. गोपुर—A city-gate ( with a tower on either side ). पुरद्वारं तु गोपुरं Amara. It is derived as गोपायति

---

* So Shakspeare of the happiness of lovers, it is,

"Brief as the lightning in the collid might." And again of the interchange of vows between Romeo and Juliet, it is

" Too like the lightning, which doth cease to be
Ere one can say it lightens."

Wilson.

( पुरं ) fr. गुप्+उर. Or गवां पुरं—Originally so called because the king's cattle were probable kept there in stalls attached to it. अट्ट—a turret, a buttress. उत्तुङ्गसौधानां...पुराणां चाट्टाः तैः आद्री पाटितं पश्चाद्विमुक्तं. Fig.—अपह्नुति based on Utpreksha. The extensive and clear currents of the two rivers are very happily compared here to pieces of the sky detached from the main body by the piercing turrets and so fallen down.

गोगर्भिणी०—गावश्च ताः गर्भिण्यश्चः i. e. गर्भिण्यः गावः cows with calf. The word गो takes पूर्वनिपात i. e. stands first in the comp. ( instead of standing as the second member ) by the Sûtra 'चतुष्पादो गर्भिण्या' Pán. II. 1. 71. i. e. a noun expressive of a quadruped may optionally take पूर्वनि० when compounded with the word गर्भिणी. मालभारि०—see Jag. The final आ of माला is shortened by इष्टकेषिका &c. Pán. VI. 3. 65. (quoted by Jag.). So इष्टकचितं and इषीकतुलम्; ०भारिण्यः अत एव सेव्याः &c. विपिनावलयः—the rows of woods.

P. 177. रसातल—The surface of the earth; usually this means 'पाताल'. यत्रत्य:—यत्र भवः यत्स्थानसम्बद्धो वा; fr. यत्र and त्य (त्यप्) which is added to adverbs of place ending in त्र, and to the indeclinables अमा, इह, क, and those ending in तस्, इहत्य, ततस्त्य &c. by—अव्ययात्त्यप् । Pán. IV 2. 104 and the Vártt. अमेहक्वतसित्रेभ्य एव । अम्बुगर्भ०—अम्बु गर्भे यस्य अत एव गम्भीरः &c. हेरम्ब &c.—हे शिवे रम्बते इति हेरम्बः; fr. रबि शब्दे and aff अ ( पचाद्यच् ); *aluk* comp. by तत्पुरुषे कृति. Pàn. VI. 3. 14. 'हः शंकरे हरौ हंसे' इति नानार्थरत्नमाला. हे उषासि रम्बते इति स्वामी The fig. is Upamâ. तरुण &c.—तरुणाः ( a kind of tree ) च कदम्बाश्च; or तरुणाः ( young ) च ते कदम्बाश्च जम्बवश्च तासां वनैः अवनद्धः ( held or kept confined within ) अन्धकारः येषु एतादृशा गुरवः ( large ) निकुञ्जाः येषु । एतादृक्षु गम्भीरगह्वरेषु उद्गारः ( echo ) यस्याः or गह्वरेषु य उद्गारस्तेनोपलक्षिता गोदावरी तया मुखरिताश्च ताः स्निग्धाश्च ता विशालाश्च मेखलाभुवः येषु तान् । The N. Ed. reads गुरुगिरिनिकुञ्जगुञ्जद्गम्भीरगद्गदोद्गारघोषणगोदावरी &c. दक्षिणारण्यभूधरान्—Jag.'s मलयादीन् is a slip. दक्षिणारण्य is the Dandakáranya and the mountains meant are those about Janasthána in the vicinity of which the Godávarî runs. *Cf.* with this the description in the Uttar. I—अयमविरलानोकहनिवहनिरन्तरस्निग्धनीलपरीसरारण्यपरिणद्धगोदावरीमुखरकन्दरः...गिरिः प्रस्रवणो नाम । p. 27; एते ते कुहरेषु गद्गदनदद्गोदावरीवारयः &c. II. 30.

संभेद—Blending together, i. e. the confluence; *cf.* अन्योन्यसंभिन्नदृशां I. 30. अपौरुषेयप्र०-i. e. the Linga had appeared there spontaneously and was not made and set there being duly consecrated by man.

सुवर्णबिन्दुः—" There is a few miles in the vicinity ( of the junction of Sindhu and Mohwar or Madhuwar,-probably, our Madhumatî ) a place called Sonagir ( Skr. Suvarṇagiri ) in which is probably preserved the name of the god Suvarṇabindu." Dr. Bhândarkar.

**भूतभावन**—Brahmâ is so called in the Uttar.—भगवान्भूतभावन: पद्मयोनि:; II. p. 51. **अखिलवरद्**—Jag. takes this as an epithet of निगम, but it is better to take it separately as an epithet of the god.

P. 178. **संसक्त**—Lit. mixed or mingled, confused; or continuous. **अनोकह**-a tree ; अनसः शकटस्य अकः गतिं हन्तीति.

**दधतीति**—The same occurs in Uttar. (II. 21 ) and Mv. (V. 41). **कुहर**—कुहरं गह्वरे छिद्रे इति रत्नमाला; कुहराणि भजन्ति इति कुहरभाजस्तेषाम्. **गुरूणि**—may also mean 'prolonged'. **अम्बूकृतं**—Properly the sound of the splashing of water; then a sound resembling that, a growl. अम्बुशब्दः उपचारात्तद्वति । अनम्बु अम्बु कृतं अम्बूकृतं Chvi. **स्त्यान**—Magnitude, intensity, depth; भावप्रधानो निर्देशः । **शिशिर०**—विकीर्ण—torn asunder; विशीर्ण *V. l.* is better. **स्त्यायते**—Virarághava in his com. on the Mv. thus comments on this—मूर्तद्रव्ययोग्याया संघानभावभजनक्रियाया अमूर्तेन गुणेन गन्धेन करणवर्णनात्--कर्तरि कर्मव्यतीहारे इत्यात्मनेपदम् । अन्ययोग्यक्रियाया अन्येन करणं हि कर्मव्यतीहारः । अतिशयोक्तिरलंकारः ।

**उद्गतदलं**—implies that the tree could afford good shade. **शिम्बि**—See Jag. **चुम्बितमु०**-*v. l.* शिम्बीनां चुम्बितमेषामस्तीति तादृशानि मुखानि यासां.

**दात्यूहैः स्थितं**—दात्युहाः स्थिताः । **वीरुन्नीड**—Jag. takes नीड in the sense of place of residence ( निवासः ); it may also be taken in its proper sense of ' a nest; वीरुत्सु वीरुत्स्थिता वा नीडास्तत्रस्थाः कपोताः. **अनु**—must be taken separately as a कर्मप्रवनीय in the sense of in return for, with regard to (see Jag.) and *cf.* अनु हुं करुते घनध्वनिं न हि गोमायुरुतानि केसरी । Sis. XVI. 25. **कुकुभाः**—The com. Nányadeva says—कुकुभो ग्रामचटकाकृतिः पक्षिभेदः । यदाह—शरच्चन्द्रिकाकारसितपुच्छो नीलगलः स्याद्ग्रामचटकाकृतिः । कुकुभः कुकुटारावः स्थलजो रक्तवर्णकः ॥ इति ।

P. 179. **प्रविक्षिप्तं**—Violently tossed about by misgivings, disturbed by thoughts. **अन्धतमसं**—अन्धं च तत्तमः; अ is added to तमस् when preceded by अन्धं, सम् and अव. **तस्यां**—with regard to Malatî.

P. 180. **अविज्ञाततत्त्वं**—अविज्ञातं तत्त्वं your true state यस्मिन्कर्मणि तद्यथा तथा । **अद्भुतं**—adv.; in a miraculous way.

**स्वयमागृहीत** &c.—*cf.* समयः स वर्तत इवैष यत्र मां समनन्दयत्सुमुखि गौतमार्पितः । अयमा० as in the text ( Uttar. I. 18 ).

**सरस०**—क्षाम properly, emaciated, thin; hence delicate. Probably the poet had the word क्षामत्व in his mind and wanted to say 'with limbs like withering juicy ( tender ) flowers. **तृणमिव**—See pp. 130, 136. *Cf.* तृणमिव वने शून्ये त्यक्ता Uttar. III. 32. Fig. Sàra.

P. 181. **विकलकरणे**—In which ( the power of ) the senses was overpowered or paralysed; or विकल may mean 'unnerved, drooping'. ०**करुणैः**—*v. l.* means विकलानि out of tune, discordant; or helpless च तानि करुणानि piteous च. We have the same expression in Uttar. II. 28. **मर्मच्छेद**०—मर्मच्छेदस्य इव या व्यथा तया विधुरैः ( overwhelmed with or pitiable on account of ); see *supra* II. 3; VIII. 10. विधुर also means in a pitiable position; *cf.* पुत्रशोकविधुरो धरणीशः; Udár VII. 1. विधुरां ज्वलनातिसर्जनात् Kum. IV. 32. अङ्गानि त्वमनङ्गरागविधुराण्येह्येहि निर्वापय । Rat. III. 11. **स्नेहाकूतं**—an emotional state of the heart full of or brought on by love; स्नेहप्रायं स्नेहजनितं वा आकूतं; आकूत means emotion, a feeling. *Cf.* वयःस्नेहाकूतव्यतिकरघनो यत्र मदनः । Uttar. VI. 35. भावाकूतं Amaru. 4. साकूतं p. 82.

**सावेगं**—Mark how the memory of his beloved intensifies his anguish and causes poignant pain.

**दलति** &c.—This sl recurs *verbatim* in the Uttar., being 31st of the 3rd Act. **गाढोद्वेगं**—accounts for the दलनक्रिया. **द्विधा न तु भिद्यते**—The heart breaks, but is not split up into two parts. Thus there is विरोधाभास here and in the following lines; see Jag. ( यद्दलति तन्न भिद्यते ). It is removed by taking दलति in the metaphorical sense of suffers agonising pain. For the intransitive use *cf.* अपि दलति वज्रस्य हृदयम् । Uttar. I. 28. **विकल**:—Shattered. **कायः**—See Jag. **भस्मसात्**—entirely to ashes. सात् ( साति: ) is added कार्त्स्न्ये *i. e.* in the sense of entirety or tolality; see com. Fig.-There is also विशेषोक्ति in this since the causes are stated and yet the results do not follow. Sl quoted in the S. D. as an instance of खेद ( lassitude ) produced by the workings of the mind ( मनश्चेष्टासमुत्पन्नः श्रमः खेद इति स्मृतः )

**निरवग्रहं**—In a manner unchecked, fiercely; निर्गतः अवग्रहः restraint, check यस्मिन्कर्मणि तद्यथा तथा. निरवग्रहः *v. l.* This is owing to विधातुर्वामत्व; see p. 179. *cf.* अनवग्रहः I. 39.

P. 182. **उन्नाल** &c.—उद्गतानि नालानि येषां तानि उन्नालानि यानि बालकमलानि तेषामाकरः । *Cf.* I. 38. **मांसल**—*Cf.* बहलपरिमलोद्गारसंवलनमसृणमांसल &c. p. 76. **शीकरतुषार**—Jag. takes तुषार in the sense of 'cool'; but it is better to take it in the sense of 'spray, a mist of'; शीकराणां शीकरा एव वा तुषाराः तैः जडः ( अत एव शीतलः by implication ). *Cf.* पृक्तस्तुषारैर्गिरिनिर्झराणां &c. Ragh. II. 13.

**आक्षिपामि**—change the drift of his thoughts, change the subject of his ruminations.

**एतस्मिन्** &c.—Sl. occurring in the Uttar. ( I. 31 ), with the last line read as संदृष्टाः कुवलयिनो भुवो विभागाः to suit the context there.

It is, however, in its proper place there. The poet probably inserted it here, with the necessary change in the fourth line, after he had composed the Uttar. We should reasonably expect Mak. to ask his friend to check the flow of tears rather than to go on weeping and observing the beauty of the lake between the fall of one and the uprise of the next stream of tears. Jag. reads the last line as दृश्यन्तां कुवलयिनो भुवो &c. But this reading, as also Jag.' explanation, are quite out of place here. कुवलयिनः ( looking like, as if, having blue lotuses ) is quite inappropriate after Mak. distinctly tells his friend that the parts of the lake are full of white lotuses.

**मल्लिकाक्ष**—a kind of swan with the beak and legs of a blackish colour. **प्रतिपत्तिशून्यं**—प्रतिपत्त्या शून्यः यथा तथा not knowing what to do; absent mindedly; like one insane. Or प्रतिपत्ति may mean 'apprehension.—without apprehending what is said to him.

P. 183. **सुमनसां**—सुमनस् a kind of Jâti ( Mâlati ); or flowers. **उन्मीलत्** &c.—उन्मीलन्ति कुटजान्येव प्रहासः ( the flowers being white ), स विद्यते एषाम् । **मेघैर्वितानाय्यते**—is an Upamâ.

**जृम्भा**—जृम्भा opening, blooming; *cf.* जृम्भारम्भप्रविततदलोपान्तजालप्रविष्टैः । Ven. II. 8. Dr. Bhând. quotes स्थिनमुपनतजृम्भागर्भबिम्बैः कदम्बैः । Mv. V. 42. **जर्जर**—close pressed. **डिम्ब॰**—डिम्ब: the clusters of the buds; तेषां डम्बेरण घना great, enhanced श्रीः विद्यते एषां तादृशाः कदम्बद्रुमा यासु । **केतक॰**—Jag.'s केतकवृक्षाः is strange. **आविर्गन्ध॰**—आविर्गन्धो येषां तानि आविर्गन्धानि.

P. 184. **दुरालोक॰**—**दुर्** goes with रमणीय; आलोके दुःखेन रमणीयाः and is equivalent in sense to दुरालोकरमणीयत्वाः whose beauty it is painful to look at.

**पौरस्त्य**—पुरो भवः पौरस्त्य; fr. पुरस्+त्य by दक्षिणापश्चात्पुरस्त्यक् । Pân. IV. 2, 28; so दाक्षिणात्य, पाश्चात्य. **स्खलित**—dislodged ( and tossed up ) from their bed. **घर्माम्भो॰**—The first sense given by Jag. is the best; घर्माम्भसो विगमागमौ तयोः &c. His second interpretation may be possible. घर्माम्भसः विगमः आगमः च तयोः व्यतिकरः. As the heat of the sultry season was not yet annihilated, perspiration disappeared when there was a shower and a cool breeze blew but broke out again as the heat increased. In this case, however, the word श्री has no propriety. *Cf.* नववारिधरोदयादहोभिर्भवितव्यं च निरातपार्द्धरम्यैः । Vik. IV. 3.

P. 185. **हेति**—हन्ति अनया अनेन वा ( *m. f.* ) a weapon; a bow. **हरिहेति**—The bow of Indra, rain-bow. **कलह**—Mixed sounds.

निरनुक्रोशा—pitiless; निर्गतः अनुक्रोशः यस्याः । अनुक्रोश fr. क्रुश् with अनु; lamenting along with; showing sympathy; hence pity, compassion.

अपहस्तित—P. p. of the denom. from अपहस्त (अपसारणार्थः हस्तः अपहस्तः) Lit. cast away with the hand, hence cast aside, given up, discarded. मातर्मातर् &c.—Same as Uttar. III. 38. (where the first line, however, begins with हाहा देवि स्फुटति.) सीदन्—distressed, writhing with pain. *Cf.* सीदति मे हृदयं Kād. सीदन्ति मम गात्राणि Bg. I. 28. विष्वक्—(adv.) from all sides, it may also be an adj. (विष्वमञ्चतीति) stupor overpowering all senses; the adv, however, is preferable.

P. 186. बन्धुता—all kinsmen; ता is added in the sense of 'a collection' to ग्राम, जन, बन्धु and सहाय. (हृदयस्य) कौमुदीमहः—the moon-light festival celebrated on the 15th of A's'vin (and not Kártika, as Jag. has it). गात्रेषु—&c.—The fig in this sl. is Rûpaka.

P. 187. धौत—polished राजपट्ट a kind of sapphire or lapis lazuli (as it must be of an azure colour). प्रियावार्ताहरं—This idea is doubtless suggested by Káli.'s Meghadûta.

फलभर॰—This line occurs in Uttar. II. 20. and Mv. V. 40. परिणाह ripening निकुञ्जेषु स्खलनं तेन &c. स्रवन्तीमुत्तरेण—To the north of the river. Words ending in एन govern the Acc. or the Gen.; See Pán. II. 3. 31. and Sid Kau. on it; Gr. § 448 (a). दक्षिणेन ग्रामं ग्रामस्य वा । दक्षिणेन वृक्षवाटिकां Śak. I. उपरि &c.—These two lines are the same as those of Mv. V. 42 (with the readings अपि च for उपरि, and विचटमानप्रौ॰). विघटमानः—विविधं घटमानः (used intransitively) forming into, assuming, different shapes (as acted upon by the wind). उपचित॰—*V. l.* उपचिता घना माला येषां (growing in thick lines) तादृशा ये प्रौढाः तापिच्छाः तद्वन्नीलः ।

कच्चित्सौम्य &c.—This śl. and the mode of addressing a cloud are in the Kálidâsian style. कच्चित्सौम्य is also the beginning of a śl. in Káli.'s Megh. (II. 53). प्रियसहचरी—Lightning is often so spoken of by Sans. poets; *cf.* मा भूदेवं क्षणमपि च ते विद्युता विप्रयोगः । Megh. II. 54. सुभगाः—It is difficult to see the propriety of this word; perhaps we may take the comp. as अविर्भूतमणयाश्च ते सुभगाश्च (fortunate now that they can get water). मुखर *V. l.* would be more appropriate.

साधुसंवाहनाभिः—*Cf.* मन्दं मन्दं नुदति पवनश्चानुकूलो यथा त्वां Megh. I. 10. बिम्बं बिभ्रत् &c.—The line, as it stands, presents some difficulty of meaning. Jag.'s first way is the best. Doubtless the poet meant to say—सुरधनुः तव लक्ष्म शोभां तनोति किम् but then बिभ्रत् hangs loose in the sentence. Perhaps the cons. is सुरपतिधनुः विष्वक् तव लक्ष्म बिभ्रत् तव शोभां &c. Does the rain-bow, every where becoming thy mark, enhance thy beauty ? The reading विष्वग्विष्कक् noticed by Dr. Bhândárkar removes the difficulty—सुरपतिधनुः तव लक्ष्म विष्वक् विष्वक् (wherever thou goest) तव शोभां तनोति किम्. One com. takes बिभ्रत् as Voc. sing. O cloud, bearing &c.

P. 188. प्रतिरव &c —प्रतिरवेण ( *i. e.* of the rumbling of the clouds ) भरिता याः कन्दरास्ताभिरानन्दिता अत एव उत्कण्ठा ये नीलकण्ठाः तेषां कलाः केकाः तासामनुबन्धोस्यास्तीति which was closely followed by the notes of the peacocks, &c.; or प्रतिरवेण भरिताः कन्दरा येन तत् च आनन्दिता०—धि च तेन. आश्वासपादौ &c.—आश्वास्यैवं Megh. II. 52. आशातन्तु &c.—For the idea *cf.* Megh. I. 9—आशाबन्धः कुसुमसदृशं प्रायशो ह्यङ्गनानां सद्यःपाति प्रणयि हृदयं विप्रयोगे रुणद्धि।

P. 189. उन्मादो०—उन्माद एव उपरागः। See Jag.; उपरागस्तु पुंसि स्याद्राहुग्रासेर्कचन्द्रयोः। नवेषु लोध्रप्रसवेषु &c.—*Cf* Megh. II. 44; श्यामास्वङ्गं चकितहरिणीप्रेक्षणे दृष्टिपातं वक्त्रच्छायां शशिनि शिखिनां बर्हभारेषु केशान्। उत्पश्यामि प्रतनुषु नदीवीचिषु भ्रूविलासान् &c; and for a similar idea Ragh. VIII. 59. Fig. विशेषालं.

प्रियजन—&c.—प्रियजनविरहेण य आधिः mental pain or anguish स एव व्याधिः तस्य वेगम्. व्याधि may also be taken in its usual sense of bodily pain or torment. See trans. The fig in this sl is परिकर.

सुलभानुकारः—सुलभः अनुकारः यत्र। निर्माणसंनिवेशः—The arrangement of creation, *i e.* the manner in which created things are presented to view. The poet often uses the word निर्माण in the sense of a created thing. See Jag.; also IX. 50.

P. 190. भवद्भिः—&c.—The address here and in the following Ślokas to the animals of the forest is an obvious imitation of Káli.'s Vik. IV. सर्वाङ्गप्रकृति०—सर्वेषु अङ्गेषु प्रकृतिर० ( प्रकृत्या रमणीया ). कुलवधूः—see कुलकुमारी p. 145. She is कुलवधू ( न तु वारस्त्री ) and hence you should sympathise with me. प्रगल्भ०—*i. e.* just in budding youth. Lit. in an age when the operation of love within is very strong and its external manifestations charming on account of their very imperfectness. *Cf.* for the idea मुग्धत्वस्य च यौवनस्य च सखे मध्ये मधुश्रीः स्थिता। Vik. II. 7.

उच्छिखंड:—शिखिना अम्यते शिखाममति इति वा, शिखा + अम् ( गत्यादिषु ) + the Unâdi aff ड; शकन्ध्वादि ( *i. e.* there is पररूपसन्धि ). गोलाङ्गूल—गोरिव लाङ्गूलं यस्य (having a tail like that of a cow). ध्रुवमनवसर०—न प्रशस्तः ( युक्तः ) अवसरः अनवसरस्तेन ग्रस्तः। Every one, acting under the influence of love, is too much busy with his own affairs to attend to me and so my petition is ill-timed. Fig. अर्थान्तरन्यास.

**कान्तदन्तं॰**—दन्तमालं ( रञ्जिता दन्तमाला यस्य ) *V. l.* is better, as कान्त is not appropriate with the teeth of a monkey. **काम्पिल्लक॰**—गण्डपालि qualifies वक्त्र; प्रसववत् प्रसवेन वा पाटला गण्डपाली यस्य यत्र वा तत्; दन्तमालं, गण्डपालि च अत एव पाका॰कान्ति. The reddened teeth looked like the seeds of the pomegranate while the temple-region and the lips, parted asuder, like its opened rind. Jag. seems to have read ॰पालिः making it an epithet of बलीवदनः; but this is not good. Similarly it will not do to read पालि-ली-पाकारुण॰ as one comp. word; for—If we take पालिपा॰ as one word the comp. will have to be explained as गण्डपालि अतएव पाकारुण &c. But ॰गण्डपालि alone does not bear out the comparison to a ripened pomegranate. The two epithets must be taken together to make the comparison proper. Fig. Nidarśaná.

P. 191. **प्रियतमास्कन्ध॰**—Jag. seems to have read अयं च रोहिणानोकहस्कन्ध॰; *cf.* एष नीपस्कन्धनिषण्णहस्तः नागराजस्तिष्ठति । Vik. IV. p. 103. **स्थिति**—livelihood;-is giving her food. **परिचयप्रागल्भ्यं**—परिचयेन यत्प्रागल्भ्यं तत् unreserved amorons sport on account of familiarity. प्रागल्भ्य=प्रगल्भव्यापार. Fig. Svabhávokti.

**आवर्जित**—drawn together, collected. **ज्यानि**—the state of being old; hence loss, deprivation; fr. ज्या+नि; ग्लाम्लाज्याहाभ्यो निः; so ग्लानि, हानि &c **व्यासंग**—may also mean विगतः आसङ्गः their ( of the bees ) attending to something else. As the bees came there but fonud not the rut, they silently left the elephant. **नूनं**—&c.—The fig. is अनुमान. **स्तम्बेरमः**—स्तम्बे ( a clump of grass or a shrub ) रमते असौ.

P. 192. **प्रत्यग्र**:—प्रत्यग्रं विकसिता ये कदम्बसंघाताः ( bunches of the Kad. flowers ) तेषामिव ॰संघातवद्वा सुरभिः शीतलश्च आमोदः यस्य तादृक् च बहुलं यथा तथा संगलितः यः निष्यन्दः तेन कर्दमितं muddy ( कर्दमोऽस्य संजातः ) च तत्कषायं च ।. शीतलामोदबहलसंवलित *V. l.*—Explain—शीतला ॰मोदेन ( the perfume of the flowers of the Kadambas on the bank ) तेन बहलं यथा तथा संवलितः ( mixed ) यः मांसलः profuse कपोलनिष्यन्दः &c.; or ( 2 ) ॰लामोदवत् संवलितः ( accumulated, collected ) यः &c **कर्दमिततीरं**—*V. l.*—The bank of which was &c. ; or तीर may be a mislection for नीर. Jag's reading is ॰कर्दमितकरटः as an epithet of the elephant ( whose temporal globes were thickly plastered with &c. ); but we have rejected this because when Mâdh. sees the elephant the latter was in the water so that he could not have been कर्दमितकट as the rut must have been washed off. **उद्दलित**—&c and अनवरत &c. may be taken as adv.s or adj.s qualifying सरः ; समुद्दलितानि यानि कमलिनीखण्डानि तेभ्यः प्रकीर्ण. पर्णानां कोमलांकुराणां निकरः यस्मिन्, or यस्मिन्कर्माणि तद्यथा तथा । In translating we have followed the reading प्रकीर्णकेसरमृणाल &c.; see foot-note.

अनवरतं प्रवृत्तं यत्कमनीयं कर्णतालताण्डवं ( the harmonious and regular play *i. e.* flapping of the ears ) तेन प्रचलाः तरङ्गास्तेभ्यो वितता ये नीहारास्तेभ्यो वित्रस्ताः कुररसारसा यस्मिन् or यस्मिन् कर्मणि तथा । ताल is properly the marking of musical intervals by striking together the hands; hence any regular motion as that of the ears here. The use of the word कमनीय shows that the flapping of the ears was regular. The elephant was enjoying the bath and so was moving his ears regularly. For the use of कर्णताल *cf.* Ragh. VII. 39-विस्तारितः कुञ्जरकर्णतालैः &c.

**कान्तानुवृत्ति**०—This expression and the following sl. with the substitution of यद् for न in the last line occur in the Uttar. ( III. 16 ). कान्तायाः अनुवृत्तिः acting in a way pleasing to; gallantry; तत्र चातुर्यम्.

**लीलो**०—लीलया उत्खाताः rooted out, plucked up मृणालकाण्डाः तेषां कवलास्तेषां छेदेषु at the end or termination of, *i. e.* when she finished the eating of The elephant plucked out mouthfuls of lotus stalks and gave them to his mate for eating; and when she finished one morsel he gave her a mouthful of water before he gave her another mouthful of lotus stalks. **पुष्यत्**—developing, blooming. **गण्डूष**०—See Jag.'s remark ( अनेन स्वयं पीत्वा &c. ). Jag. seems to have read पुष्प्यत् blooming. पुष्कर may also mean the tip of the trunk. The water taken ( वासित p. p. p. of वस् cau. ) in the fat tip of the trunk. गण्डूषसंक्रान्ति-*cf.* ददौ रसात्पंकजरेणुगन्धि गजाय गण्डूषजलं करेणुः । Kum. III. 37, where it is the female that humours the male. **कामं**—may be taken with विहितः ( to her heart's content ); Jag. takes it in the sense of युक्तं ( it is proper that ); it may, however, be better taken here in the sense of अकामानुमति *i. e.* when one gives one's consent or expresses one's approval with something to find fault with ( अकामानुमतौ कामम् Amara ); so it means—I grant all this and yet. *Cf.* कामं प्रिया न सुलभा मनस्तु Śak. II. 1. **अनराल**०—न अरालमनरालं नालं यस्य तादृग् नलिनीपत्रमेवातपत्रम् ।

**धिगुच्छ्वसित** &c.—उच्छ्वसितमेव वैशसं cruelty or calamity; lit. the calamity in the shape of life. वैशस properly–destruction or killing; hence also what causes destruction of mental ease, distress, calamity. **धिक्**—generally governs an acc. **त्वदनुभावभावात्**—भाव is any feeling, as of pleasure here; अनुभाव is its external manifestation, as a pleased countenance here; विभाव is the cause of such a feeling, as the sight of beauty. See Introd. p. 2. He means-fie upon that beauty which is enjoyned without your appreciation and enjoyment of it; *i. e.* I will disdain to enjoy beauty without you; see also Jag.'s first way of taking this which is not, however, satisfactory. **रमणीयवस्त्वनुभवान्वृथाभाविनः** *V. l.*—which Jag. thinks is the principal reading. The enjoyments of beautiful objects which are to prove useless ( without you—*i. e.* not enjoyed in your company ). ०वस्त्वनुभवाद्वृथा०—*V. l.* ( see com. ); separate रमणीयवस्तु ( a beautiful object ) धिक्; why ? वृथाभाविनः अनुभवात् since its enjoyment is to prove useless or in vain ( delusive ).

P. 193. **त्वया ( सह )**—तया *V. l.* is bad; Mâd. has been referring to Mak. alone and cannot be expected suddenly to refer to Málatî. **प्रमोद०**—If I seek to experience great joy from any other source it will be simply a mirage. **अपरत्र**—Jag. says युवाभ्यां विना because he reads तया for त्वया. **उन्माद०**—अन्तरित separated from. **व्यञ्जकं**—व्यनक्तीति what manifests; something that awakens or calls up a past impression, an excitant of a feeling. **प्रबुद्धः**—awakened, called up. **सहज**—*i. e.* not brought about by any external means. **जीवितेश्वर**—The lord of my life; *i. e.* my life is in your keeping; if you live I live; see Jag. **जीविताशा०**—जीवितस्याशायां व्यसनं ( persistence in or a persistent or strong desire for life. **परिच्छेद**—final decision or conclusion. See I. 21. p. 34.

**आबद्ध०**—Adv. आबद्धः वेपथुः यस्मिन्कर्मणि तद्यथा तथा; or आबद्धः वेपथुः यस्मिन् adj. qualifying भयं. **विनापि**—Because अतिस्नेहः पापशङ्की as Káli. says; or प्रेम पश्यति भयान्यपदेऽपि । Kir. IX. 70. **गणयता**—Jag. reads गणयतः and connects it with मम; but it cannot be properly so taken as "its position is in the middle of the adjectival subordinate sentence in which अन्वभावि is the verb, while मम belongs to the principal sentence." Dr. Bhándarkar. **तत्सर्वमेकपदे** &c.—Because he had now steeled his heart against the worst that might come to pass.

P. 194. **वरं** Because he could at least enjoy his company being alive. **तथाविधं**—*i. e.* on whose account I always apprehended misfortunes and so had my heart always full of feverish anxiety.

**वज्रकीलं**—वज्रस्य कील इव *i e.* hard to break like; or causing pain like an adamantine nail driven into the heart; or वज्रस्य कीलः यत्र fixed with an adamantine nail and not passing away. *Cf.* मर्मोपघातिभिः प्राणैर्वज्रकीलायितं हृदि ( स्थिरैः *v. l.* ) । Uttar. I. 47. **काष्ठाः शून्याः**—काष्ठाः the quarters; दिशस्तु ककुभः काष्ठा आशाश्च हरितश्च ताः । Amara. *Cf.* शून्यं मन्ये जगत् Uttar. III. 38. **शान्तालोकः**—The world with its light *i. e.* the sun (Mâdh.) gone (set); *cf. supra* निरालोकं लोकं; V. 30. **त्वत्प्रयाणे**—He does not say मरणे; the very idea is horrible to him.

**तत्किं नु खलु** &c.—Mâdh. was yet in a trance which might end in death, and so he wants to die before life had left Mádhava. **अग्रेसरः**—अग्रमग्रेण अग्रे वा सरतीति; Pán. III. 2. 18. अग्रसर is also used; see Ragh. V. 71; IX. 55.

**असितोत्पल॰**—The comparison implies freshness, vigour and glossiness of the body. **अतिदृढ॰**—अतिदृढानि पीडनानि येषु.

P. 195. **उल्लसित॰**—उल्लसितः विस्मयः यासु in which there arose wonder (at the beauty). **निपीतवत्यः**—The idea is peculiar to Sans; नेत्राभ्यां पा means to look at or gaze on intently or longingly, or with eyes rivetted on the object of sight. See Ragh. II. 19. III. 17 &c. Megh I. 16. &c. **नवप्रणय॰**—नवेन प्रणयेन ये विभ्रमाः sportive gestures, dalliance due or springing from fresh or dawning love.

**अचरमे वयसि** &c.—*Cf.* यत्कल्याणं वयसि तरुणे भाजनं तस्य जातः। Uttar.

**आपूर्णश्च** &c.—च यातः च—the two चs indicate the simultaneousness of the two acts. The moment the moon attained fulness she fell into the mouth of Ráhu, &c. **फलेग्रहिः**—see Jag.; formed irregularly; फलेग्रहिरात्मंभरिश्च। Pán. III. 2. 26. The figures of speech in the sl. are समुच्चय and दृष्टान्त. See appendix.

**मालती॰**—स्वयंग्राहेण जीवितेश्वरः स्वयं॰ मालत्याः स्वयंग्राह॰. **॰रन्दानन्द॰**—Better read आनन्दन; मुखचन्द्र may be dissolved as मुखं चन्द्र इव or मुखमेव चन्द्रः; ॰मकरन्दयोः आनन्दनः मुखचन्द्रो यस्य. **अपश्चिमः**—नास्ति पश्चिमो यस्मात् to which there is no other succeeding *i. e.* the last one. It is thus equivalent to पश्चिम; *cf.* अनुत्तम (विदैव द्रव्यमाहुरनुत्तमं,) and अनुत्तर (अनुत्तराणि विलसितानि D. K.). अपश्चिम often occurs in plays अयं पश्चिमः (अपश्चिमः *v. l.*) ते रामस्य शिरसि पादपंकजस्पर्शः Uttar. I. p. 47; तात अम्बायं मे पश्चिमः (or अप॰) प्रणामः; Nág. V. p. 118; see A. dic.

**सहनिवासितया**—सह निवासो ययोस्तौ सहनिवासिनौ तयोः भावः सहनिवासिता. मयैव goes with समं. **बन्धुतया**—बन्धूनां समूहो बन्धुता the collection of relatives; by ग्रामजनबन्धुभ्यस्तल्। Pàn. IV. 2. 43. **निवापसलिलं**—न्युप्यते इति निवापः; fr. वप् with नि and aff. अ (घञ्) added कर्मणि; is an offering made to the Pitris after the सपिण्डीकरण. *Cf.* येभ्यो निवापाञ्जलयः पितॄणां; Ragh. V. 8, Mud. IV. 5 (गुरवे देयो निवापाञ्जलिः). *Cf.* with this sl. मया पीतं पीतं तदनु भवताम्बास्तनयुगं...... निवापाम्भः पूर्वं पिबसि कथमेवं त्वमधुना। Ven. VI. 31.

P. 196. **भगवति आपगे**—Of course he addresses the presiding deity of the river. **प्रियस्य सुहृदो** &c.—*cf.* for a similar idea Nág. IV. 20.

**योगिन्यस्मि**—This she says to inspire confidence in him. **अत्याहितं**—see p. 81. **अनिष्टं व्यवसितः**—Here the root सो is treated as one of the roots (though not mentioned in the list), the p. p. p.s of which are used actively; *e. g.* आकाशमध्यमारूढः सविता, शिवमुपासितः &c. Káli. uses the p. p. p. of the root स्मृ similarly; मधुकर विस्मृतोस्येनां कथं Śak. V. 1. पूर्ववृत्तमन्यसङ्गाद्विस्मृतो भवान् *Ibid.* p. 136. अहो विस्मृतं मे हृदयं Vik. II. p. 43; *cf.* आर्ये दुर्व्यवसितमिदं; Mud. VII. p. 144.

**अनपेक्षितास्मदवस्थः**—What Mâdh. means is that the wind should not have brought him back to consciousness and made him experience the pain of separation again.

P. 197. **भगवन्** &c.—*Cf.* the similar address to the Southern breeze in Vik. II. 20.

**अखिलजन्तु॰**—*Cf.* जगत्प्राणसमीरणाः । Amara. **मातरिश्वन्**—मातरि अन्तरिक्षे श्वयति संचरतीति । This word occurs in the *Veda* and is thus derived by Yâska—मातरिश्वा वायुर्मातर्यन्तरिक्षे श्वसिति मातर्याशु अनिति वा ।

**विकसद्** &c.—विकसन्ति यानि कदम्बानि तेषां निकुरम्बस्तस्य पांसुना । **जीवितं वह**—He means—Do not restore life to my body but bear it, along with the pollen of flowers, to where &c. *Cf.* for a similar request नामानय प्रियमतां मम वा समीपं मां वा नयाशु कलभाषिणि यत्र कान्ता ॥ Vik. IV. 11.

**एते** &c.—( See foot-note ). Cons.—वर्षानिलाः विरहिणः कर्षन्ति । **सून** a flower. **पौर॰**—॰अङ्गनानां व्यालोला अलका वल्लर्य इव ( creeper-like *i. e.* long and flowing ) अलकवल्लर्यः तासु लुटनं तव्द्याजेनोपभुक्तमाननं यैः । **उन्निद्र**—blooming. **व्यूह**—a swarm of उन्निद्राश्च ते कदम्बकुड्मलाश्च तेषां पुटीषु या धूली तस्यां लुटन् यः षट्पदव्यूहस्तस्य व्याहृत्याहरन्तीति हारिणः ।

P. 198. **प्रियतमा॰**—स्तनयोः उन्नाहः स्तनोन्नाहः the lofty region of ( *i. e.* उन्नतस्तनौ ) तत्र दुर्ललिता मूर्तिः यस्याः; or नोन्नाह एव दुर्ललितं यस्यास्तादृशी मूर्तिर्यस्याः having the obstinate desire to lie on; hence which was affectionately worn on. **दुर्ललित**—दुष्टं लालितं यस्य one fondled too much, treated with too much affection. *Cf.* हा मदङ्कदुर्ललित; Ven. IV. p. 86.

**मुग्धेन्द्र** &c.—For comp. see com. अवलोकहेलया ( sport, pleasure ) विशृंखलं ( lit. unrestrained; hence excessive ) यत्कुतूहलं तस्य निह्नवाय *i. e.* as I tried to conceal the agitation of my heart by appearing to weave the wreath. **दुर्न्यस्त**—not only were the flowers not properly put in or arranged but the weaving was also faulty. It is not good to take अपि with लवङ्गिकायाः as Jag. does.

P. 199. **त्वराप्रस्तावः**—त्वरायाः प्रस्तावः । प्रस्तावः fit or proper time for, an occasion for; प्रस्तावः स्यादवसरः Amara; or which calls for, requires. **प्रियाप्रणयिनी**—प्रियायाः प्रणयोऽस्या अस्तीति । **देहोद्दाह॰**—देहोद्दाह एव व्यसनं ( an evil, a calamity ) तेन गुरवः, or better still देहोद्दाहे यद्व्यसनं तेन गुरवः agonising because of their persistence in burning the body. **मन्मथोन्माद॰**—The overbearing pang of love. **प्रगुणं**—प्रकृष्टो गुणो यस्य ( adj. ); यस्मिन् कर्मणि वा ( adv. ). Excellent, very effective. Jag. seems to have read त्वरितं.

P. 200. गाढानुराग०—*i. e.* which indicated strong love. तदा तदा—on various occasions of amorous sports, when they might have transferred it to each other and hence the pl. गतागतानि and not necessarily as Jag. has it; see com. स्नेहाकराणि—the mines *i. e.* abodes of or birth-place of affection as they deepened it more and more every time. Or the manifesters or indicators of; see com.; read स्नेहाकराणि instead of स्नेहकराणि. स्नेहाङ्कानि—*v. l.* The signs or marks of affection. बकुलदाम्नः—स्नेहस्वहस्तस्य *v. l.*—स्वहस्त properly means one's own hand, handwriting; but this meaning will not do here; so it must be taken to mean 'something serving like one's own hand, a true or unmistakable sign of recognition, proof; hence स्नेहस्वहस्त means a true sign or proof of her affection. For a similar use *cf* दयितास्नेहस्वहस्तेन Vik. II. 10 where स्वहस्त means a birch-leaf having a writing committed to it in Urvasîs' own hand. करवाल—a sword ( also करपाल ); करः वालः ( *fr.* वल् वेष्टने ) यस्य, करेण वल्यते वा.

P. 201. रामणीयक०—रामणीयकं ( see I. 21 ) एव गुण: advantage, additional quality, *i. e.* to heighten its beauty तदर्थम्. सुकृतं—that happy combination. अस्तु—should last for the full time. अकाल—Because in autumn the sky is usually quite free from clouds ( and hence शरदिन्दुच० which is very bright ), and any sudden appearance of clouds is untimely. The fig. in this ś'l. is अप्रस्तुतप्रशंसा.

उत्पात०—केतुकवलिता Jag.; उत्पात—any portentous sudden appearance; here that of a comet; ( *cf.* Kum. II. 30 ); धूमलेखा the tail of a comet, whose appearance is sudden and unexpected. Fig. Upamà.

निर्माण—is used here ( as in other places by the poet ) in the sense of–a created form. हि is here अवधारणार्थे ( to be sure; decidedly ). Her very form is so lovely that for its sake ( if not for any other consideration ) she ought certainly to be treated tenderly or with feelings of awe. For आकृतिविशेषेष्वादरः पदं करोति ।

पूतनात्व—For पूतन see p. 102; पूतना fem. a demoness; hence-त्वं cruelty, hard heartedness. शिवतातिः—see p. 124.

P. 202. नैसर्गिकी—निसर्गेण निर्वृत्ता lit. brought about or fixed by nature; natural. These two lines occur in the Uttar. ( see. I. 14. ) न मुसलैः—Jag. reads चरणैः as in the Uttar. ( which is suitable there ) and this reading at first sight appears better as contrasted with मूर्धन्. But the point here is to show the extreme incongruity of the two acts, the idea being—a thing which ought to be treated but gently should not be used with extreme violence.

This is strikingly brought out by the use of मुसल, the blow given by which is instantaneously crushing. Fig. Drshtânta.

**परिपन्थिनी**—परि दोषाख्यानं पन्थयितुं to proclaim शीलमस्याः lit. one given to finding fault with another, hence an enemy.

**गुरुचर्या**—is गुरुसेवा attendance upon and service done to a Guru. This is of primary importance to a religious student. Without Gurubhakti proper success can never be attained in religious practices. *Cf.* यस्य देवे पराभक्तिर्यथा देवे तथा गुरौ । तस्यैते कथिता ह्यर्थाः प्रकाशन्ते महात्मनः ॥ Sve. Up. VI.23; and धर्मार्थौ यत्र न स्यातां शुश्रूषा वापि तद्विधा । तत्र विद्या न वक्तव्या &c. Manu. II. 112. **अभियोग**—close application. See *supra* I. 34. **आक्षेपिणी सिद्धिः**—is the miraculous power obtained by *yoga* to bear one aloft and then through space.

**व्यतिकर इव** &c.—This line occurs in Uttar. (V. 13.) where a similar phenomenon is described as produced by the जृम्भकास्त्र employed by Lava. **कथमिह** &c.—When the darkness ceased and light was restored he found that Màd. was not there. **तामसः वैद्युतश्च**—Jag. understands the व्यतिकर in a metaphorical sense. But Mak.'s words आश्चर्यमाश्चर्यं show that the darkness and the lightning-like flash of light were real. Sau, as she flew into the sky, created these by her miraculous power that Mak. might not at once see what was going to happen.

P. 203. **किमयमर्थो** &c.—See Jag.; Mak. does not know why Sau. should have carried away Mâdh. He has his own misgivings. Is she a friend? Or perhaps Kapâl., wishing to wreak her vengeance on Mâdh. also, might have come in disguise with the Bakula-wreath and managed to carry him away. In this case his worst fears might be realised and the affair might thus prove to be a more serious calamity. This is what Jag. means by कपालकुण्डलानयने &c.

**अस्तोकविस्मयं**—Wonder at the miraculous power displayed by Saud. in creating a mixture of light and darkness. **अपस्मृत**—Sau.'s appearance and the wonderful feat performed by her made Mak. quite forget for a time the past occurrences. अविस्मृत, the reading of the N. Ed., will not do, as it leaves no room for the प्रमोह to be त्रुटित or joy to be संघटित (as the पूर्ववृत्त was not forgotten). **वृतनभय**—on account of the uncertainty that hung over Mádh.'s fate. The rhetorical fig. in this sl. is Kávyalinga.

# ACT X.

P. 204. **प्रतिमुहूर्त०**—प्रतिमुहूर्तं ( मुहूर्ते मुहूर्ते ) विशेषरम्याणि. **चाटूनि**—sweet speeches or lispings.

**अनियत०**—Śl occurring in the Uttar. ( IV. 4. ) where it is addressed by Janaka to Sítá after she was abandoned by Ráma and supposed to be existing no more. अनियत not restricted or fixed being due to any cause ; occurring at random; see. Jag· **विराजत्**—&c.—विराजन्तः कतिपये कोमलदन्ता एव कुड्मलाग्राणि यस्य । **स्मरामि**—I remember with sorrow ( उत्कण्ठापूर्वकं स्मरामि. ). We should have expected the Gen. in this sense. अत्र अनियतरुदितस्मितं स्खलद्समञ्जसमिति विशेषणानुगुण्याद्वदनकमलकमित्यत्र परिणामालंकारः । केवलकमलस्य प्रकृतक्रियान्वयित्वानुपपत्तेः । परिणामक्रियार्थश्चेद्विषयी विषयात्मना । इति लक्षणात् । दन्तकुड्मलाग्रमित्यत्रापि क्रियान्वयविवक्षायां परिणामो रूपकं वा । Virarâghava on Uttar. IV. 4.

**सुप्रसन्न०**--सुप्रसन्नः very bright मुखचन्द्रस्तेन सुन्दरी. **दैवदुर्विनय०**--दैवस्य दुर्विनयः ( a perverse act ) तेन परिणामः ।

P. 205. **उपस्थिता०**--आदावुपस्थितः पश्चादस्तमितः महोत्सवः मालतीलाभरूपः यस्मिन् ।

**अभिनव०**—This is to be taken with लवलीलवङ्गयोः also; Jag.'s dissolution of the comp. in this case as अभिनवौ रागरसौ यत्र will also do in the case of Mâl. and Mâdh. **परिष्वङ्ग**—lit. an embrace, hence union. **लवली**—See Uttar. III. 40; Vik. V. 8. **महावात्या**—वातानां समूहो वात्या । वात + य; पाशादिभ्यो यः । Pán. IV. 2. 49; so पाश्या, तृण्या &c. Fig. Upamá. **उज्जिहान**—pres. p of हा to go with उ.

P. 206. **आलोक**—(1) appearane; (2) light. **स्निग्धा**—(1) Loving; (2) oily. **मलीमस**—मलः अस्यास्तीति fr. मल + ईमस; also इन ( मलिन ); see Pán. V. 2. 114. (1) Darkened, black; (2) gloomy. **प्रगुणीकृतानि**—nourished, caused to be developed; प्रकृष्टो गुणः ( excellence due to proper nourishment ) येषां तथा संपद्यमानानि कृतानि ।

**दन्तपाञ्चालिकेव**—The simile implies that Kâm. did all this with that tenderness of heart with which children fondle and caress their dolls. **विनय**—training, education.

**अकारण०**—अकारणं स्मेरमनएव मनोहरमाननं यस्य । **स्मेर**—See *supra.* 1. 28. *cf.* अनियतरुदितस्मितं above, śl. 2. **गौरसर्षपः**—It was customary to apply the powder of white mustard to the forehead and the top of the head of a new born child to keep off evil influences ( and probably also to prevent the child from catching cold ); *cf.* ०तालुनि विन्यस्तगौरसर्षपोन्मिश्रभूतिलेशः......पुत्रकः &c. Kâd. p. 106. **स्तनंधयः**—स्तनं धयतीति ।

P. 207. जीवितोद्वहनेन—Here we directly get the cause of the निःसहत्व and so this reading is preferable to ०द्वहने. *V. l.*—I am not able to bear my life. Here we have to supply वियोगेन to account for the निःसहत्व. The other reading न समर्थास्मि or असञ्जी-वितोद्वहनसाहसेन (by the fool-hardiness of keeping up my life) is not so good अवधुत्य-धूय—Having shaken *i. e.* thrown myself off.

उत्कण्ठावेगा—Jag.'s explanation of this as—जन्मान्तरेपि &c does not seem to be correct, as such an idea is precluded by the following sl; so this means—the force *i. e.* intensity of anguish (caused by Mal.'s disappearance)

संगमः कर्मणां भेदात् &c.—Here the poet probably follows Bâna–*Cf.* अन्यामेव स्वकर्मफलपरिपाकोपचितामसावशो नीयते भूमिवसाप्यात्मघातिनः केवलमेनसा संयुज्यते। Kád. p. 136. For the idea of the dead meeting in heaven. *cf.*—

> "And father cardinal, I have heard you say
> That we shall see and know our friends in heaven:
> If that be true, I shall see my boy again;"
>
> Shakspeare, King Jhon Act III. Sce. 4.

P. 208. विरमेत०—Because you have Makaranda to look to. एतं जनं—*i. e.* Lav. herself, मधुमतीस्रोतः &c.—मधुमतीस्रोतसा संवानिता (encircled, begirt) अत एव पवित्रा मेखला यस्य. Here the poet treats Madu. as a sacred river. *Cf. supra* मधुमतीसिन्धुसंभेदपावनः; p. 177.

व्यतिकर &c.—The first two lines are the same as at p. 202. Read उपहत for उपहित. Saudaminî's entrance is marked here by the same phenomenon which had appeared at the time of her departure in Act IX. The last two lines are also the same with the necessary changes. संमर्द—a pressing crowd.

P. 209. सुवर्णबिन्दु—*i. e.* that part of the mountain where the Linga of Śiva, called Suvarṇabindu (see p. 77), was situated,

झटिति—&c.—The sudden and wonderful appearance of Mádh. was reassuring to the party and Mad. and Lav. naturally expected to see Mâl also, and hence their remark.

दिष्ट्या &c.—Kâm. and Mak. were just going to express their satisfaction at Mádh.'s sight, and exclaimed दिष्ट्या &c; but before they could finish their speech, they heard the voice of some one announcing how Bhúrivasu, unable to bear the pang of separation from Mâl, was advancing to Suvarṇabindu, resolved upon puttting an end to his existence, and so suddenly broke out into हा कष्टं &c.

**असिपत्र**—may mean the blade of a sword, or a very thin short sword with a broad blade ( असिः पत्रमिव ). ०पत्राणां ०छटायाः ( mass of ) आसारः तयोः &c. Jag. seems here to refer to the असिपत्र tree, which is said to have sharp leaves like sword blades. In the Bhág. P. the seventh hell is mentioned as consisting of an असिपत्रवन ( see Sk. V. 26. 7 ) and a sinner is dragged along the leaves of the असिपत्र tree ( 15 ); see also Ragh. XIV. 48. Jag. probably means—the juice of the leaves of असिपत्र trees which must be sharp and the चन्दन trees. But this does not seem to be intended; *cf.* below अशनिशशधरमयूख &c. The Fig. is अतिशयोक्ति. **अनुकुरुते**—*i. e.* Fate is acting favourably and cruelly at the same time.

**समस्तलोकालोकान्तराल**—The whole space encircled by the mountain Lokáloka. लोकालोक also called चक्रवाल is a belt of mountains that encircles the earth. According to the Pauránic geography it surrounds the outermost of the seven seas, *viz.* the sea of fresh water, which itself encircles Pushkara, the last of the seven continents, and divides the visible world from the region of darkness. It is called लोकालोक because it is lit up on one side and shrouded in darkness on the other, as the sun and the other stars roll within its circle. परेण पुष्करस्याथ आवृत्यावस्थितो महान् । स्वादूदकसमुद्रस्तु स समन्तादवेष्टयत् ॥ स्वादूदकस्य परितः शैलस्तु परिमण्डलः । प्रकाशश्चाप्रकाशश्च लोकालोकः स उच्यते ॥ आलोकस्तत्र चार्वाक् च निरालोकस्ततः परम् । Mat. P. 122. स्वादूदकस्य परतो लोकालोकाचलो महान् । लोकस्य चाप्यलोकस्य मध्ये गिरिरवस्थितः ॥ प्राकार इव संवेष्ट्य लोकान् सर्वान्महामते । लोकालोकाचलो नाम तेनासौ परिकीर्तितः ॥ इति । आवृणोति स तेजांसि सूर्यादीनामपि द्विज । तमनिक्रम्य तेजांसि क्षमन्ते न प्रवर्तितुम् ॥ Padma Puráṇa. *Cf.* प्रकाशश्चाप्रकाशश्च लोकालोक इवाचलः । Ragh. I. 68; लोकालोकविचारि चारणगणैरुद्गीयमानं यशः । Nāg. V. 18. **समस्तलोकान्तराल**—*V. l.* The space between all the worlds. **मङ्गल०**—मङ्गलार्थः प्रदीपः मङ्गलप्रदीपः तथा भूतः ( A comp. सुत्सुपा ) तम् .

**स्यान्न नाम स** :—स्यात्ततोस्तु मा *V. l.* is easy; न स्यादनागमः *V. l.* here the sentence is left incomplete and must be completed by supplying तस्य before and अस्ति after अनागमः. The reading कर्मणां योगात् &c. ( see foot-note ) must be explained as कर्मणां योगात् ( by the operation of Karmans ) यदि सः अपेक्षितः संगमः न स्यान्मास्तु । यतः अनागमः आगमानर्हः.

P 210. **जन्मान्तरादिव**—Here इव indicates an Utpreksha. उपराग इव is an Upamá. **अनर्थ** :—in the shape of Bhûrivasu's impending death. **अन्यथा**—on account of a different cause. **को नाम** &c.—These two lines form the latter part of Uttar. VII. 4, also. **पाकाभिमुखस्य**—here the पाक means destruction of

Mâl. in any way. Fig. Arthântaranyâsa. *Cf.* अथवा भवितव्यानां द्वाराणि भवन्ति सर्वत्र । Śak. I. 15. For an opposite function discharged by fate, *cf.* द्वीपादन्यस्मादपि मध्यादपि जलनिधेर्दिशोप्यन्तात् । आनीय झटिति घटयति विधिरभिमतमभिमुखीभूतः ॥ Rat. I. 6.

**श्रीपर्वतात्** &c.—**तयैव सह**—Jag. is wrong in saying मालत्या सह; it should be तया योगिन्या सह. **अनन्तरं**—अन्तरिता *V. l.*—who disappeared after. Saud., it will be seen, on hearing of the immediate peril in which Bhû. stood, hastened to avert the catastrophe by telling him about Mâl.'s safe arrival there. Mâdh. evidently could not account for her sudden disappearance.

P. 211. **चिरनिरुद्ध०**—चिरनिरुद्धः choked यः निश्वासः तेन निस्फुरं निश्चलम्. **अम्बुनिवह**—The shower was of course caused by Sau. to refresh Mâl. and others.

**वितत०**—Jag. reads विततश्वासा नासा; her nose has the breath flowing through it again. प्रसन्न for प्रणुन्न, however, has no propriety. ०सोत्साहेन प्रणुन्नौ ( heaved up or set in motion ) पयोधरौ यत्र । The fig. in the first three lines is स्वभावोक्ति and in the last Upamâ. The simile is a happy one here; *cf.* Vik. I. 5. (महोत्पलं प्रत्युषसीव पद्मिनी ) 6 and 7.

P. 212. **अग्निचये**—*i. e.* the mass of flames rising up. **गुरु०**—गुरुः संमद्रः joy विस्मयश्च यस्य. **वागमृत** &c.—वागेवामृतं तस्यासारः । Her words were more cooling ( comforting ) than the physical shower as they at once removed their anxiety on account of Bhûrivasu.

**जीव**—Live and so जीवय. एहि *V. l.* is not good. **जीवय** &c.—Because the life of all depended on that of Mâl.

**तुहिन०**—तुहिनसंगवत् or तुहिनसंगेन इव शीतलैः cooling like, or as if by being in the contact of snow ( allaying mental fever ) also. **मनोरथा०**—मनोरथमतिक्रांतं दर्शनं यस्याः lit. whose being seen again was not even to be thought of, was beyond the reach of desire.

P. 213. **कपाल०**—see Jag; तस्माज्जनिता आपद् येन तस्मात् । **निर्बन्ध**—persistent effort, perseverance.

**विजृम्भित**—result, outcome ( also the expansion of the story ). Perhaps here the poet gives his justification for adding the last four Acts.

**पुनरुक्त०**—पुनरुक्तं दारुणं यस्य which repeated its cruelty ( Mâl. being twice in imminent risk of life ) though it was not necessarly for fate to do so, as the first act of cruelty was enough to afflict all For पुनरुक्त see p. 184. Supply अपि after this.

**तत्सर्वं** &c.—Why she exerted herself so much and saved the lives of all-all this is now explained. **भूरिजन** &c.—भूरयो जनाः

भूरिजनास्तेभ्यो जीवितप्रदानं तस्य पुण्यं तस्य भार: (a store) तं धरतीति धारिणी. **हन्त**—expresses joy. **सौहृद**—see *supra* p. 8.

P. 214. **जगतः**—may go with **वन्द्या** or **स्पृहणीयसिद्धिः**. **स्पृहणीयसिद्धिः**—*Siddhi*—such miraculous power acquired by the practice of Yoga as enabled her to produce light and darkness, to cause a shower of rain-water to fall down, &c. **एवंविधैः विलसितैः**—Acts like these—your rescuing Mâl. from the jaws of death and exertions to save the lives of so many other persons &c.. This is an additional reason why she is **वन्द्या**. **अतिबोधिसत्त्वैः**—बोधिसत्त्वान् अतिक्रान्तानि तैः A prep. Tat. comp.; which outdo those of the Bodhisatvas. Bodhisatva* (from बोधि knowledge) is a particular rank in Bhuddhistic Sainthood, attainable by the performance of virtuous and pious acts through a series of births and leading to the attainment of the rank of a supreme Buddha. The performance of benevolent deeds, even at the risk of one's life, is a characteristic of the Bodhisatvas. Hence Kâm.'s remark. **उद्भूत** &c.—उद्भूतानि भूरीणि फलानि तैः शालते तत्। or उद्भूतं grown up च भूरिफलशालि च.

**भगवतीसम्बन्ध**—भगवतीसम्बन्धेन (अस्मासु) पक्षपातिन्या. **भगवती॰**—भगवत्या स्नेहः तस्मान्निर्गतः विशेषः यस्मिन्कर्मणि तद्यथा तथा । **भगवतीनिर्विशेषं** *V. l.* भगवत्या निर्गतः &c. Just like her reverence. **केसरावलीसा॰**—Dissolve अभिज्ञानेन सहितः साभिज्ञानः केसरावल्या साभिज्ञानो हस्तो यस्याः; a comp. like ॰निमित्तसव्यपेक्ष at p. 28. Jag. seems to have read **केसराव**ल्यभिज्ञान॰.

P. 215. **अपि** &c.—चिन्ता thought; *i. e.* one must express a desire and then can the Chintámaṇi grant it. इदं त्व॰—See Jag. The fig. here is व्यतिरेक. For a similar idea comp. Sâk. VII. 30. **प्रत्यस्तव्यसने**—प्रत्यस्तं व्यसनं येन अतएव महीयसि very great, if the reference be to the conflict between him and the town-guards; or प्रत्यस्तानि व्यसनानि (the various calamities that had overtaken him) यस्य. **प्रथमानुराग॰**—प्रथमम् अनुरागेण घटिता । **आशङ्काशल्यं**—The dart in the form of the fear that the king would be highly incensed.

P. 216. **कार्यनिधाने**—The store *i. e.* the prime cause of the successful issue of events. **परिहाससंपूर्णः**—Full of merriment or joy.

---

* A Bodhisatva is one who has knowledge (derived from self-enlightening intellect) for his essence; *i. e.* he is a being who through all his bodily existences is destined in some final existence to become a Buddha. M. W. For other particulars see **M. W.'s** Buddhism, p.p. 98, 180, &c.

**महाद्भुतं प्रकरणम्**-Here although by Prakarṇa the poet apparently means 'an affair, a course of events', he, in his ecstasy of joy, doubtless pronounces his judgment on his own performance, which is a Prakarṇa techuically so colled.

**इतरेतरा॰**—इतरेतरापत्ययोः सम्बन्ध आत्मा यस्य. Here आत्मा may mean स्वरूप, or the essential part. **वस्तुवृत्तं**—Jag. takes these as two words; as one word it means the happening of events ( वस्तुनो वृत्तम् )—Bhū. had not only never signified his wish to bestow Mál. on Mádh., but had actually given her away to Nandana and the marriage had to be brought about clandestinely.

P. 217. **नन्दनोपग्रहात्**—Here उपग्रह may mean 'conciliation, favourableness' ( *cf.* सोपग्रहं Kád. p. p. 118, 202. ) or राहु the malicious planet ( in the shape of Nandana ). We are free from the apprehension of trouble to be expected from Nandana on account of the Mad.-affair. **श्रावकावस्थायां**—श्रावक is used here in the sense of 'a pupil,' in which sense it is used by the Buddha and Jain Bhikshus. It lit. means a devout listener, शृणोतीति श्रावकः fr. श्रु and aff. अक ( ण्वुल् ), and refers to a believer in Buddhism or Jainsism; see Mud. IV. p. p. 99, 100 &c.

**प्रधानप्रकृतिकोपः**—कोप—displeasure. There is some difficulty here as to the meaning to be assigned to प्रधानप्रकृति. According to Amara, प्रकृति is a term generally referring to the constituents of a kingdom, *viz.* स्वाम्यमात्यसुहृत्कोशराष्ट्रदुर्गबलानि च । राज्याङ्गानि प्रकृतयः पौराणां श्रेणयोपि च ॥ See also Kám. N. IV. 1; Manu IX. 294. Here प्रकृति may be taken in its restricted sense of 'a minister' and so it can refer to Nandana who was the king's नर्मसचिव ( a kind of minister ). But as he was not the chief minister, we take प्रधान to mean 'the king' or the chief person in the kingdom, and so this means प्रधानप्रकृत्योः कोपं the displeasure of the king and his minister; if taken in this sense all difficulty vanishes. This seems to be the poet's meaning at least as that was the final object of Kâm., and that was attained, as shown by her words तां याचते नरपतेर्नर्मसुहृन् नन्दनो नृपमुखेन । तत्साक्षात्प्रतिषेधः कोपाय शिवस्त्वयमुपायः ॥ I. 11. and एवं हि प्रतार्यौ नृपनन्दनौ in the next śloka. Dr. Bhândârkar, however, who does not take प्रधान in the sense of 'the king is at some pains to assign a meaning to the words, and wishing to sift the question thoroughly enters into a long discussion of the term प्रकृति. See his notes. He understands by प्रधानप्रकृति Nandana. He quotes Kám. N. VIII. 4.—अमात्यराष्ट्रदुर्गाणि कोशोदण्डश्च पञ्चमः । एताः प्रकृतयस्तज्ज्ञैर्विजिगीषोरुदाहृताः ॥ and thinks that as नन्दन was his नर्मसचिव and so in charge of the अन्तःपुर he was an अमात्य and therefore belonged to the first of the five Prakṛitis mentioned above and was a प्रधानप्रकृति. **कोपः परिहृतः**—According to Kámandaka a king's servant must not offend a नर्मसचिव; *cf.* न नर्मसचिवैः सार्धं किंचिदप्यप्रियं वदेत् । ते हि मर्माण्यभिघ्नन्ति प्रहासेनापि संसदि ॥

**संस्तुतापलापिन्यः—महतां** great by their displomacy; consummate politicians; संस्तुतं ( lit. what is familiar to the mind ) the subject of constant thought, the object in view ) अपलपन्ति ( lit. talk away; conceal ) इति.

**पुण्यैः**—our collective merite; or by your merit. **उपक्रमैः**—plans, schemes or devices. **निष्णातः**—skilfully brought about ( adj. to समा० ); or as Jag. takes it. ( See trans. ).

P. 218. **तथापीदमस्तु**—This is what is technically called the Bharatavákya. See Intro. p. 4.

**सन्तः**—See trans.; सुकृतिनः must not be taken predicatively ( सन्तः सुकृतिनः सन्तु ) as they are not सन्तः if not सुकृतिनः. Or the cons. may be–सुकृतिनः doing pious or righteous deeds सन्तः विध्वस्तपापोदयाः सन्तु । **काले संतत** &c.—As the crops depended in most of the parts of India on timely and copious rain-fall, it is no wonder that a prayer to this effect is found in the Bharatavâkyas of several plays ; *cf.* तत्र भवतु बिडौजाः प्राज्यवृष्टिः प्रजासु; Śak ; वृष्टिं हृष्टशिखण्डिताण्डवकृतो मुञ्चन्तु कालेम्बुदाः । Nâg.; वृष्टिं विधत्तां जगति जलधराली &c. Ven. **घनबन्धु०**—घना या बन्धूनां ( near relatives ) बान्धवानां—( kinsmen ) च &c. गोष्ठी तत्र प्रमोदः यासाम् । This line, with the reading सततं च for घनबद्ध occurs as the last line of the closing stanza of Nâg. **शिवमस्तु** &c.—This śl. is given in the Nir. ed. as the भरतवाक्य; **परहित०**—परेषां हितं तत्र निरताः devoted to ( lit. taking pleasure in ) the good of others. **भूतगणाः**—The communities of men. **दोषाः**—Disturbances, malpractices. This Śl. is found in the Triv. Ed. of the Nâg. as its closing stanza. See our ed.

# मालतीमाधवस्थसुभाषितानि

## 1 SENTENCES.



## ŚLOKAS.

# APPENDIX.

## Figures of Speech mentioned in the Commentary or Notes.*

**अतिशयोक्ति**—or Hyperbole is of four kinds of which one of frequent occurrence is प्रस्तुतस्य यदन्यत्वं–सातिशयोक्तिर्विज्ञेया; *i. e.* when the thing in hand is described as of a different kind ( superior in excellence or beauty ) that is Atis'ayokti.

**अनुप्रास**—or Alliteration is the repetition of similar letters, syllables or sounds.

**अनुमान**—or Inference is defined as अनुमानं तदुक्तं यत्साध्यसाधनयोर्वचः; *i. e.* the ( poetical ) expression of a ( logical ) Reason and a Conclusion.

**अपह्नुति**—प्रकृतं यन्निषिध्यान्यत्साध्यते सा त्वपह्नुतिः—That is Apahnuti in which the matter in hand ( *i. e.* the उपमेय ) is denied or shown to be unreal and another ( *i. e.* the उपमान ) is established as real ( or is superimposed upon it ).

**अप्रस्तुतप्रशंसा**—अप्रस्तुतप्रशंसा सा या सैव प्रस्तुताश्रया-the description of what is not the matter in hand implying the matter in hand. It is of five kinds: कार्ये निमित्ते सामान्ये विशेषे प्रस्तुते सति । तदन्यस्य वचस्तुल्ये तुल्यस्येति च पञ्चधा ॥ *i. e.* when the matter in hand is ( 1 ) an effect, information about which is conveyed by stating the cause; ( 2 ) a cause implied by the statement of the effect; ( 3 ) a general assertion by stating a particular instance; ( 4 ) particular instance by stating a general asseration; and ( 5 ) a similar thing implied by what resembles it.

**अर्थान्तरन्यास**—or Corroboration; ' सामान्यं वा विशेषो वा तदन्येन समर्थ्यते । यत्र सोर्थान्तरन्यासः साधर्म्येणेतरेण वा ॥ Where a general proposition is adduced to support a particular instance, or a particular instance to support a general proposition, either under a resemblance or a contrast, that is *Arthántaranyása.*

**आक्षेप**—( *Cf.* Greek ' Paraleipsis ) निषेधो वक्तुमिष्टस्य यो विशेषाभिधित्सया । वक्ष्यमाणोक्तविषयः स आक्षेपः । That is *A'kshepa* in which something really intended to be said ( *i. e.* the matter in hand ) is apparently suppressed or denied with a view to convey a particular meaning. Vâmana defines this as " उपमानाक्षेपश्चाक्षेपः " which is identical with Mammata's Pratîpa.

---

* The definitions are taken from the K. P. Only the important figures are noticed here.

**उत्प्रेक्षा**—or Poetical Probability: संभावनमथोत्प्रेक्षा प्रकृतस्य समेन यत्। प्रकृतमात्मनः समं करोतीति सममुपमानम्। Apprehending the object under consideration as looking identical with something to which it is compared is what is termed *Utpreksha*. It is of two kinds ( 1 ) expressed or ( 2 ) understood. The expressed is one wherein such words as ध्रुवं, मन्ये &c. are used: the understood is one in which such words are not used. It is again of three kinds, हेतूत्प्रेक्षा, फलोत्प्रेक्षा and वस्तूत्प्रेक्षा or स्वरूपोत्प्रेक्षा.

**उपमा**—or Comparison—साधर्म्यमुपमा भेदे, पूर्णा लुप्ता च साऽग्रिमा। श्रौत्यार्थी च भवेद्वाक्ये समासे तद्धिते तथा॥ The ( striking ) possession of a common property, when there is difference, is *Upamá*.

**उपमान**—means साधारणधर्मत्त्वेन प्रसिद्धः पदार्थः as कमल in the instance कमलमिव मुखं मनोज्ञम्; here मनोज्ञत्व is the साधारणधर्म and कमल is well known to possess this. उपमेय is साधारणधर्मत्त्वेन वर्णनीयः पदार्थः as मुख in the given example. साधर्म्य is explained as समानः धर्मः ययोः ( उपमानोपमेययोः ) तौ सधर्माणौ तयोर्भावः साधर्म्यम्। समान=तुल्य may also mean एक in some cases. भेदे means when the उपमान and उपमेय are two different things and not the same. उपमान or the thing compared to, उपमेय or the thing compared, साधारणधर्म or the common property, and the उपमाप्रतिपादकशब्दः or words conveying the sense of comparison such as यथा, इव, तुल्य, सदृश &c. are the four constituents of उपमा. When all these four are present, the *Upamá* is called पूर्णा or complete, and when one or two or three of these four are dropped the *Upamá* is लुप्ता or Elliptical. The former ( *i. e.* पूर्णा is of two kinds—( 1 ) श्रौती in which such words as यथा इव &c. ( *i. e.* the धर्मवाचक words ) are used; or the aff वत् in the sense of इव by 'तत्र तस्येव' Pán. V. 1. 116. is employed; ( 2 ) and आर्थी in which such words as तुल्य, सदृश &c. ( *i. e.* the धर्मिवाचक words ) are used, or the aff. वत् is used in the sense of तुल्य by 'तेन तुल्यं &c.' Pân. V. 1. 115.

Mammatá mentions in all 25 varieties of *Upamá* but they are not given here as of little use to junior students.

**काव्यलिङ्ग**—or the poetical Reason; काव्यलिङ्गं हेतोर्वाक्यपदार्थता। *Kávyalinga* is the statement of a reason in the form of ( 1 ) a sentence, or ( 2 ) of a word or ( 3 ) words. Or to make the definition simpler वाक्यपदार्थयोः हेतुता—that is काव्य० wherein either a sentence or a word ( or words ) is intended to give a reason for the statement made in the whole sentence. The हेतु according to some must be आर्थ or implied.

**दीपक**—( कारक )—कारकस्य च बह्वीषु क्रियासु सकृद्वृत्तिः दीपकम्॥ When a case-noun occurring once is connected with a plurality of verbs that is ( the second kind of ) दीपक.

**दृष्टान्त**—दृष्टान्तः पुनरेतेषां सर्वेषां प्रतिबिम्बनम् । Illustration by an example is when all these ( *i. e.* the common property, the उपमेय and the उपमान ) are reflectively represented or in which in two different sentences the relation between the उपमेय and a certain property is represented to be the same as that between the उपमान and another property, *i. e.* in which the two do not have a common property but corresponding properties.

**निदर्शना**—निदर्शना । अभवन्वस्तुसंबन्ध उपमापरिकल्पकः ॥ When an ( apparently ) impossible connection of things implies a comparison that is called निदर्शना. निदर्शनं दृष्टान्तकरणं ( citing an instance ) यथाश्रुतमात्रेणासंभवी वस्तुसम्बन्धः ( वस्तुनोर्वाक्यार्थयोः पदार्थयोर्वा सम्बन्धः अन्वयः ) यत्रोपमां कल्पयित्वा पर्यवस्यति सैका निदर्शना । सा च द्विधा अवान्तरवाक्यभेदे तदभेदे च । Pradîpa. 'स्वस्वहेत्वन्वयस्योक्तिः क्रिययैव च साऽपरा'। यत्र क्रिययैव स्वस्य स्वहेतोश्चान्वयो हेतुहेतुमद्भावरूपः ख्याप्यते साऽपरा निदर्शना —where by an action itself is indicated its own connection with its cause ( that of cause and effect ) that is the second kind of *Nidars'aná.*

**परिकर**—विशेषणैर्यत्साकूतैरुक्तिः परिकरस्तु सः । साकूतैः साभिप्रायैः । उक्तिरर्थाद्विशेष्यस्य । That is *Parikara* where there is a description ( of course of the subject ) with attributes which are significant *i. e.* have an implied meaning ( व्यंग्य ). Here विशेषण and विशेष्य are dependent on each other. In *Ka'vyalinga*, कार्यकारणभाव is necessary; so there is no व्यंग्य. But परिकर contains the व्यंग्य which produces the charm. According to Jagannátha, the use of even one significant adjective is sufficient for *Parikara.*

**पर्यायोक्त**—पर्यायोक्तं विना वाच्यवाचकत्वेन यद्वचः । That figure of speech is known as *Paryáyokta* wherein we have the statement of a fact without the relation of वाच्य ( the expressed ) and वाचक ( the expresser ) between that fact and the words which bring it out. This fig. corresponds to ' Periphrasis. '

**भ्रान्तिमान्**—भ्रान्तिमानन्यसंवित्तत्तुल्यदर्शने । When on seeing a thing ( the प्राकरणिक one ) the knowledge of another thing ( the अप्राकरणिक one ) similar to it is attained, that is termed *Bhra'ntima'n.* In other words when the अप्राकरणिक thing is mistaken for the प्राकरणिक, the figure is भ्रान्तिमान् .

**यथासंख्य**—यथासंख्यं क्रमेणैव क्रमिकाणां समन्वयः । That is the connection in the same order, of objects, successively mentioned.

**रूपक** or Metaphor—तद्रूपकमभेदो य उपमानोपमेययोः । The identity of उपमान and the उपमेय is *Rûpaka.* When two things known to be different from each other, still to show their great resemblance, are identified together, the fig. is *Rûpaka*. Hence it is plain that in a *Rúpaka* the उपमेय and the उपमान ( the प्रकृत and the अप्रकृत ) must be mentioned in words.

**विरोध**—विरोधः सोऽविरुद्धेपि विरुद्धत्वेन यद्वचः। When two things are represented as incongruous, when really there is no incongruity between them, that is *Virodha* or Antithesis ( also called विरोधाभास or Semblance of incongruity ).

**विशेष**—विना प्रसिद्धमाधारमाधेयस्य व्यवस्थितिः। When an object is represented as abiding outside its proper abode, it is Vis'esha.

**विषम**—That is *Vishama* in which some unusual or incompatible relation between cause and effect is described.

**व्यतिरेक**—उपमानाद्यदन्यस्य व्यतिरेकः स एव सः। a figure of speech which consists in representing the *Upameya* as superior to the *Upamána* in some particular respect.

**श्लेष**—Pun, *double entendre*, the susceptibility of a word or words to yield two or more meanings.

**सम**—समं योग्यतया योगो यदि संभावितः क्वचित्। The fig. सम occurs when there is an ascertainment of a connection as fit between two things, both ( 1 ) superior or ( 2 ) inferior.

**समुच्चय**—तत्सिद्धिहेतावेकस्मिन्यत्रान्यत्तत्करं भवेत्। समुच्चयोसौ' when one cause of the producing of an effect, is present and yet others are mentioned as producing the same effect, that is *Samuchchaya*.

**सार**—उत्तरोत्तरमुत्कर्षो भवेत्सारः परावधिः। When an excellence goes on rising, until a culminating point is reached, that is Sára or climax.

**ससंदेह**—ससंदेहस्तु भेदोक्तौ तदनुक्तौ च संशयः। When the difference is expressed ( from a poet's point of view ) or not expressed ( there being a close resemblance ) between two objects, that is Doubt or Sandeha.

**स्वभावोक्ति** or Description according to Nature ( also called Játi by some ).—स्वभावोक्तिस्तु डिम्भादेः स्वक्रियारूपवर्णनम्। *Svabhávokti* is the description of the peculiar action or posture ( रूपं वर्णः संस्थानं च ) of an object such as a child and the like. Of course the action &c. must be striking, such as is perceived by the poet alone.

# THE METRES USED IN THE PLAY.

## THEIR DEFINITIONS AND SCHEMES.

1 The quantity of a syllable is determined by its vowel. A syllable with a short vowel is called लघु or light, and one with a long vowel is called गुरु or heavy. But if a light syllable be followed by an *Anuswára* or *Visarga* or by a conjunct consonant the syllable is made heavy. A syllable at the end of a quarter may be short or long according to necessity. सानुस्वारश्च दीर्घश्च विसर्गी च गुरुर्भवेत् ॥ वर्णः संयोगपूर्वश्च तथा पादान्तगोऽपि वा ॥

2 A short syll. is marked as ⏑ , and a long one as—. The following letters are symbols representing different triads ( गणs ):—

य ⏑ – –; र – ⏑ –; त – – ⏑ भ – ⏑ ⏑ ; ज ⏑ – ⏑ ; स ⏑ ⏑ –; म – – – न ⏑ ⏑ ⏑. ग represents a heavy syll. and ल a light one. The following couplet will help the student in remembering the long and short syllables forming each Gana—आदिमध्यावसानेषु यरता यान्ति लाघवम् । भजसा गौरवं यान्ति मनौ तु गुरुलाघवम् ॥

3 The following are the metres occurring in this play, with their definitions and schemes:—

अनुष्टुभ्—or sloka is defined as—पञ्चमं लघु सर्वत्र सप्तमं द्विचतुर्थयोः । गुरु षष्ठं च पादानां शेषेष्वनियमो मतः ॥ In *Anushtubh* the fifth syll. ought to be short and the sixth long in all quarters. The seventh should be short in the second and fourth quarters only. Other syllables are governed by no rule. I. 8, 12, 13; III. 1; V. 12, 21, 33; VI. 11; IX. 41, 51, 52; X. 4, 7, 19, 22.

इन्द्रवज्रा—स्यादिन्द्रवज्रा यदि तौ जगौ गः । Sch. of G. त त ज ग ग. I. 4, 5, 33; III. 4, 11; IV. 5; VI. 1, X 13.

उपेन्द्रवज्रा—उपेन्द्रवज्रा जतजास्ततो गौ । Sch. ज त ज ग ग. I. 10.

उपजाति—अनन्तरोदीरितलक्ष्मभाजौ पादौ यदीजावुपजातयस्ताः । A mixture of इन्द्र. and उपेन्द्र. forms उपजाति III. 3; IX. 27.

रथोद्धता—रान्नराविह रथोद्धता लगौ Sch. र न र ल ग ( 3. 8,* or 4. 7 ) VIII. 3; IX. 21; X. 18.

शालिनी—मात्तौ गौ चेच्छालिनी वेदलोकैः । Sch. of G. म त त, ग ग. ( 4. 7 ) VI. 18; IX. 37.

वियोगिनी—also called सुन्दरी is a particular case of वैतालीय ( which is classed under *Mátrávrittas.* ) विषमे ससजा गुरुः समे सभरा

---

* The numerical figures indicate the cæsura or pause.

लोथ गुरुर्वियोगिनी। This is an *Ardhasamavrita*. See पुष्पि० below. Sch. स स ज ग (odd quarter); स भ र ल ग (even q.) IX. 19.

**अपरवक्त्र**—(a particular kind of *Vaitáli'ya*) अयुजि ननरला गुरुः समे तदपरवक्त्रमिदं नजौ नरौ। Sch. न न ल ग (odd quarter); न ज ज र. (even q). IX. 23.

**औपच्छंदसिक**—is the same as वियोगिनी with a long syll. added at the end; Sch., odd quarters—स, स, ज, ग, ग; even quarters—स, भ, र, य. III. 13.

**द्रुतविलम्बित**—द्रुतविलम्बितमाह नभौ भरौ। Sch. न भ भ र. (4, 8; or 4, 4, 4.). III. 10; IV. 7; VIII. 11; X. 16.

**वंशस्थ**—जतौ तु वंशस्थमुदीरितं जरौ। Sch. of G. ज त ज र. VII. 1; X. 6.

**पुष्पिताग्रा**—अयुजिनयुगरेफतो यकारो युजि च नजौ जरगाश्च पुष्पिताग्रा। Sch. न न र य (odd q.) न ज ज र, ग (even q.) II. 6, 10; III. 15; V. 15; X. 2.

**प्रहर्षिणी**—त्र्याशाभिर्मनजरगाः प्रहर्षिणीयम्। Sch. म न ज र ग (3. 10). I. 37, 38; III. 17; IV. 1; V. 3, 25; IX. 14.

**मञ्जुभाषिणी**—सजसा जगौ च यदि मञ्जुभाषिणी। Sch. स, ज, स, ज, ग, (6-7). I. 39; II. 4; III. 7; V. 8; IX. 9, 43, 48.

**वसन्ततिलका**—उक्ता वसन्ततिलका तभजा जगौ गः। Sch. त, भ, ज, ज, ग, ग. I. 6, 9, 18, 19, 20, 21, 23, 25, 26, 29, 32, 34, 40; II. 8; III. 5; IV. 8; V. 27, 32; VI. 4, 8, 9, 12, 13, 14, 17, 20; VII. 2, 3, 4; VIII. 4, 5, 8, 14; IX. 1, 2, 3, 13, 22, 31, 36, 40, 44, 47, 50, 54; X. 1, 9, 20, 21.

**मालिनी**—ननमयययुतेयं मालिनी भोगिलोकैः। Sch न, न, म, य, य. (8. 7.) I. 22, 24, 27, 28, 41; II. 9; III. 8, 14, 16; IV. 10; V. 1, VI 16; VIII. 1, 12, 13; IX. 5, 6, 24, 28, 53; X. 8.

**पृथ्वी**—जसौ जसयला वसुग्रहयतिश्च पृथ्वी गुरुः। Sch. ज, स, ज, स, य, ल, ग. III. 13; VIII. 7; IX; 35, 38.

**मन्दाक्रान्ता**—मन्दाक्रान्ताजलधिषडगैर्म्भौ नतौ ताद्गुरू चेत्। Sch. म, भ, न, त, त, ग, ग. 4, 6, 7.) I. 3, 15, 35; II. 5; III. 12; IV. 2; V. 20; VI. 2; VII. 5; VIII. 2; IX. 20, 25, 26, 46; X. 5.

**नर्दटक**—यदि भवतो नजौ भजजला गुरुनर्दटकम्। Sch. न, ज, भ, ज, ज, ल, ग, (8. 9). V. 31; IX. 18.

**शिखरिणी**—रसै रुद्रैश्छिन्ना यमनसभला गः शिखरिणी। Sch. य म न स, भ ल ग (6. 11) I. 14, 16, 30, 31; II. 1, 3, 7, 11, 12, 13; III. 9; IV. 3, 4, 6, 9; V. 30, 34; VI. 7, 15; IX. 8, 29, 45.

**हरिणी**—नसमरसला गः षड्वेदैर्हयैर्हरिणी मता। Sch. न, स, म, र, स. ल, ग, (6, 4 7.) I. 17, 36; II. 2; III. 2; V. 5, 26; VI. 6; IX. 10, 11, 12, 42; X. 15.

**शार्दूलविक्रीडित**—सूर्याश्वैर्यदि मः सजौ सततगाः शार्दूलविक्रीडितम्। Sch. म, स, ज, स, त, त, ग. (12, 17). I. 2, 7; V. 2, 7, 9, 10, 11, 13, 14, 18, 19, 22, 24, 28, 29; VI. 3, 5, 19; VIII. 6, 9, 10; IX. 7, 15, 16, 17, 32, 33, 34, 39; X. 23, 24, 25.

**स्रग्धरा**—म्रभ्नैर्यानां त्रयेण त्रिमुनियतियुता स्रग्धरा कीर्तितेयम्। Sch. म, र, भ, न, य, य, य. ( 7. 7. 7 ). I. 1, पद्ममाली &c. ft. note; V. 4, 6, 16, 17; IX, 30.

**दण्डक**—V. 23;-is a metre each quarter or चरण of which has two न gaṇas followed by sixteen र gaṇas thus consisting of 54 letters. It belongs to that species of Dandaka which is known as संग्राम.

**आर्या**—This belongs to the class of metres regulated by the number of *ma'tra's* or syllabic instants. यस्याः पादे प्रथमे द्वादश मात्रास्तथा तृतीयेपि। अष्टादश द्वितीये चतुर्थके पञ्चदश सार्या॥ I. 11; III. 6 VI. 10; IX. 4, 49; X. 3, 10, 11, 12, 14, 17.

---

QUESTIONS FROM THE TEXT SET AT THE

## BOMBAY UNI. EXAMINATIONS.

### 1869 ( B. A. )

I Translate the following into English:—( *a* ) प्रचलितकरिकृत्ति &c. V. 23. ( *b* ) प्रेङ्खद्भूरिमयूर &c. VI. 5. Dissolve the first comp. in ( *a* ) 2 Explain the following, giving the context, and solve the conundrums:—( *a* ) स्नेहश्च निमित्तसव्यपेक्ष इति विप्रतिषिद्धमेतत्। ( *b* ) गुरुबाष्पस्तम्भमन्थरितकण्ठप्रतिलग्नानिश्वासमन्याहृशमेव भगवत्या वचनम्। ( *c* ) तस्यामभिनवो विचित्रः कुसुमेषुव्यापारः। ( *d* ) भगवत्येवंवादिनीत्याख्यायते। ( *e* ) प्रियं खलु युष्माकं मालतीजीवितं न पुनर्मालती। ( *f* ) सखि मदयन्तिके मालती प्रियसख्येवेदृशानि मन्त्रयितुं जानाति। ( *g* ) कं याचे यत्र तत्र ध्रुवमनवसरग्रस्त एवार्थिभावः। ( *h* ) एवंविधैर्विलसितैरतिबोधिसत्त्वैः। Explain the technical terms in the following and give their ordinary senses:—( a ) निसृष्टार्थदूतीकल्पस्तन्त्रयितव्यः। ( 4 ) Is there any Patáká in Mál. Mád.? If so what is it, what is such a minor hero as Makaranda called in connection with such Patáká? Name and define the species of dramatic compositions to which the play you have read belongs, according to Hindu critics. 5 What evidence can you adduce from Mál. Mád. to prove that Bhav. knew of Kálidása and was acquainted with his works? State what ideas or passages in the play bear a very suspicious resemblance to the ideas or passages occurring in any of Káli.'s works. 6 Give the substance of the 6th and 9th Acts of Malatî Mádhava. 7 Translate into English:—परिच्छेदव्यक्तिर्भवति &c. I. 31. अद्यैवेन्दुमयूख &c. VIII. 10. Explain the context of these passages.

## 1874 ( B. A. )

1 Translate, adding an explanation of the stanza in ( *a* ):—( *a* ) यत्सत्यमधुना &c.—लग्ना प्रिया । p. 100. ( *b* ) सावष्टम्भ—स्थिति । V. 22. p. 109. ( *c* ) Dissolve and name the compounds in ( *b* ) (2) Explain the following, giving the context when necessary:—( *a* ) त्वमपि स्वभावेनैव—तासि p. 48. ( *b* ) वाक्प्रतिष्ठानिबन्धनानि—त्मिकैव । p. 89. ( *c* ) अयम०-ते परिष्वंग. p. 195. ( *d* ) सुलभैव बुद्धरक्षिताप्रियसखी भवतः । (*e*) दिष्टया सुहृद्बुद्धया वर्धितोसि मालत्या तदयमवसरः प्रीतिदायस्य । One Ms. reads मालत्याः; which do you prefer and why ? 3 (*a*) What is an Ankávatára ! Give an instance. ( *b* ) How many Rasas are there ? Define and exemplify any one of them from the Mál. Mâd. ( *c* ) Give a sketch of the character of Kámandakî with quotations or references. 4 ( *a* ) Give the meanings of:—( *a* ) अपरिस्थानं; ( *b* ) विधेय०; ( *c* ) तारामैत्रकम्.

## 1875. ( B. A. )

1 ( *a* ) Translate closely:—माधव—अलमनेनायासितेन । ...... मुद्दलितं......ङ्कुरमनवरत......विहरति । भवत्वाभावे । कथमवधीरणा......हा प्रियवयस्य । धिगुच्छ्वसित &c.–त्वदनुभावभावादृते*...जायते । मकरन्द–अये व्यञ्जनात्* –संस्कारः* । p.p. 191–93. (*b*) Explain the expressions marked with*. 2. ( *a* ) Explain, stating the context where necessary—( *a* ) मने। निष्ठाशून्यं.........लिखति च । p. 34 ( *b* ) अप्रास्ताविकी महत्येषा कथा । ( *c* ) न तर्हि प्रागवस्थायाः परिहीयसे । ( *d* ) ओमित्युच्यताममात्यः । ( *e* ) आश्चर्यमुत्पल......मनसा विकारः ॥ Is the reading मनसो or मनसा preferable and why ? ( *b* ) What is the meaning of शेवधि, उपयाचित, इष्ट and पूर्त. How are the last two words ordinarily changed when formed into a compound ? 3 Mention passages in the Mâl. Mád. which seem to have been suggested by the writings of Kâlidâsa. 4 State the Alankáras in the following:—( *a* ) तस्याः सखे—वेधाः p. 26. ( *b* ) स्खलयति...सुभ्रु खेदः । p. 68. ( *c* ) III. 17. ( *d* ) X. 22.

## 1879.

Translate:—क्षिपन्निद्रा...विचरति. How does Jagaddhara take this verse ? Discuss any of the following themes:—( 1 ) The typrography of the play. ( 2 ) An estimate of Jagaddhar's commentary. ( 3 ) The substance of the 7th and 9th Acts. ( 4 ) A comparison between Kálidása and Bhavabhûti.

## 1881.

1 Describe the feelings of Mádh. as depicted in the ninth Act of the play. Translate ( *a* ) V. 31. ( *b* ) IX. 39. ( *c* ) IX. 53. Does this statement occur elsewhere in Bhav. ? If it does, where and with what alterations ? 2 Derive and give the different

senses of:—वास्तव्य, पङ्क्तिपावन, वाचोयुक्ति, तीर्थ, काकतालीय, बीभत्स, अस्तमय. 3 How far has the preternatural agency been resorted to in the development of the plot of the Mâl.? 4 Trans. (*a*) अहो प्रमादः। प्रकृति०—śl. 14 p. 77. (*b*) कुमुदाकरेण...&c. IX 48. 5 Explain according to the context-(*a*) महाभाग सुश्लिष्ट...महार्घताम्। p. 35; (*b*) त्वमपि स्वभावेन...नर्तितासि p. 48. (*c*) साधु—भारः। p. 61. (*d*) अन्य एव -भगवत्याः p. 70. (*e*) अशस्त्रपूतम्-गृह्यतामिदम्। V. 12. (*f*) महानुभाव हृदये—विचारयति। p. 134. 6 State what उपक्षेप, and अङ्कावतार are and give an instance of each from the Mâl, Mâdh. 7 Give the plot of the Mâl. Mâd. (all dramatis personæ and the character of Kámandakî). What observations occur to you in regard to the arrangement of the drama? Are there any parts of the plot which appear to be adaptations from other poets? If there are any, state which.

### 1883.

1 What is meant by the terms आन्वीक्षिकी, उपनिषद् and योग? 2 Are any incidents of Bhavabhúti's having imitated Kâlidása to be found in the play? Note any resemblances, incidents and expressions occurring in the works of Kálidása and the Mál. to support yonr answer. Translate (*a*) माधवः—वर्धतेहि—परागः। p. 161. (*b*) IX. 44. Give the metre of (*b*) and the figure used in (*a*.) 4 Explain the following words and phrases and dissolve the compounds underlined—ऐदम्पर्यम्, कालावबोधः, षडधिकदशनाडीचक्रम्; औद्धत्यमायोजितकामसूत्रम्, पूर्णपात्रवृत्तिः, सांराविणम्, जन्ययात्रा. उच्छ्वसितवैशसम्, अनुभाव, अपश्चिम, अतिबोधिसत्त्वैर्विलसितैः। 5 Explain प्रस्तावना and विष्कंभक and their characteristics. 6 Translate, discussing the readings and briefly giving the context (a) तदनेन नीर्थेन— अभिप्रायः (यत्प्रतिच्छंदकम्—तत्प्रतिच्छंदकम्.) p. 18. (*b*) कोप्यकालो (क इव कालः)--वर्तमानायाः। p. 62. (*c*) सांप्रतं...परित्यक्ष्यामीति (परोक्षगुण०, p. 130. (*d*) न खलु...भवन्ति। p. 36.

### 1886.

Write gram. or explanatory notes on विकलकरुणैः मृत्योः परेण, परिश्मशानं, दरज्वलितम्. Explain fully the words underlined in the following, and freely translate the whole. ममाहि—चैतन्यम् (उपलम्भ, संस्कार, संस्कार, स्मृति). Explain the words and phrases from the Mál.—एतेनाद्य...गमिष्यति p. 45. । अयि विरम निःसहासि जाता। कथं पुनरायुष्मान्...संनिधापितः। अयमवसरः प्रीतिदायस्य। मनोरथनिर्वृत्तसबन्धौ p. 84 कष्टमेतावती...माधवस्य p. 91.। परिणतम्...फलम् p. 91 न खलु महामांसविक्रयादन्यमुपायं पश्यामि। त्रस्तैकहायन...दृष्टि: p. 92. सुवर्णबिन्दुः, दुर्जात, निकुरुम्ब, फलेग्रहि, अपहस्तित, वत्स कृतं साहसेन, तदनेन निर्वर्त्य पक्षद्वारेण साधयामः। तदवश्यम्...विजृम्भितम् p. 119. माधवापकारं...भवामि p. 120.

अनुसंध्यम् , विघस, कङ्काल, स्थपुट, मञ्जीर. 2 Translate :—IX. 27; III 4, V. 10. 3. Give and define the metre of the foll. verse— V. 31. (*b*) To what species of dramatic compositions does the Mál. belong ? In what respects is it similar to a Nátaka ? What are the distinguishing features ? (*c*) In what sense is the word सम्भेद used throughout the play ? Compare it with its etymol. sense. (*d*) Quote the verses in the Mál. which are identical with those occurring in the Uttar. 4. Criticise and give gram. notes on the following forms and case relations. मन्त्रयन्ती, विहस्तीकृत, आत्मनो हृदयस्य प्रभवति, परोक्ष, परार्ध्य, जुगुप्सते, निष्णात, भीतायिता, गुल्फदघ्न, पारेश्मशानं, शिवताति, दुर्मनायते, संदानित, प्रीणयिष्यति, स्तम्बेरम, फलेग्रहि, स्तनंधय.

1886.

1 'There is more passion in the thoughts of *Bhavabhuti* than in those of *Kálidása,* but less fancy. There are few of the elegant similitudes in which the latter is so rich, and there is more that is common-place, and much that is strained and obscure. In none of his dramas does *Bhavabhúti* make any attempt at wit...On the other hand, he expatiates more largely in the description of picturesque scenery and in the representation of human emotion, and is, perhaps entitled to even a higher place than his rival, as a poet. Discuss this remark of Wilson with particular reference to the Mál. Mád , giving quotations from the play to illustrate your answer. 2 Give the context of the following verses:—1 अभिनव...लवलीलवङ्गयोरिव &c. X. 3. 2 प्रेयो मित्रं ...जीवति वा &c VI. 18. 3 प्रियस्य...अनुसंचरः । IX 41. 3 Explain fully:—विहस्तीकृत, आकेकराक्षम्, टुष्टम्, वैचित्य, तटस्थ, पिण्डपातवेला, पूर्णपात्रवृत्ति, वाक्प्रतिष्ठा...तन्त्राणि, अहो नु खलु भोस्तदे...नाम, तारामैत्रकम्, मैरेयदर्प, धमधमायमानहृदया, कूटपाकलः, रणरणकः, इष्टाय कर्मणे, पूर्तायकर्मणे, रमणीयडामरत्वम्, कान्त...धारिणीं करेणुरजनीम्. 4 Translate:–V. 1., 2. 5 Which of the foll. sets of readings do you prefer and why ? (*a*) नैसर्गिकी... अवताडनानि ( चरणैः,-*V. l.* मुसलैः ). (*b*) एवमहं तु सर्वाकार—विधेयीकृतोपि—विषयीकृतोपि. (*c*) सुहृदिव...अनुकूलनाम् ( प्रकटय्य–प्रकटोप्यसुखप्रदः ) पुनरकाण्ड ...रुजम् ( विधिरहो विशिनाष्टि ).

1888.

1 (*a*) State briefly the characteristic incidents that marked the progress of love between Mál. and Mádhav from the time of their first meeting in the garden upto their final union in wedlock What are, in your opinion, the striking points of differece between love and the demeanour of lovers towards each other as depicted by Bh. and depicted by Shakespears and Sir Walter

Scott ? (*b*) Lord Macaulay says of the poetry of Milton that " its effect is produced not so much by what it expresses, as by what it suggests. " Show how this remark applies to the poetry of Bh. ? Illustrate your answer by quotations from or references to the Mál. Mád. 2 Translate :—(*a*) VIII. 10; (*b*) IX. 38; (*c*) II. 13. 3 Explain according to the context :-(*a*) वयमभ्युद्गता...आर्ययानया। (*b*) सुसमाहितः...स्यावसरः। p. 198. (*c*) यस्य प्रसाद...ध्वजेन । (*d*) कवलित...सिक्तः। III. 16. (*e*) व्यतिषजति.. संश्रयन्ते । 4 Discuss the foll readings and state which of them you prefer and why ? (*a*) इयममात्य० ...समादिशति ( अप्रतिहतप्रताज्ञागतिः ) (*b*) कन्यादाने...विमर्शितव्यमेतत् ( अविमर्शितव्यम् ।) (*c*) प्रियमाधवे...करः ( स्वयमागृहीतकमनीयकङ्कणः ).

## 1890.

1 बहिः...भजते ( I. 14 ) taking this as your theme, sketch the part Kâmandakî plays in the Mál. 2. Translate (*a*) I. 37. Do you agree with Jagaddhara, if not give reasons. (*b*) V. 6. ( Third line underlined to be dissolved. ). (*c*) IX. 18. Explain the metre. 3 Explain according, to the context. (*a*) उज्ज्वल... आगतवती। (*b*) प्रभवति...उपन्यस्तम्। p 52. (*c*) वत्स वाक्प्रतिष्ठानि—आयत्तम्। (*d*) महानुभाव...विचारयति । p. 134. (*e*) कथं नाम नव...दुर्मनायिष्यते। p. 144. (*f*) अथ सो...प्रतिपत्तिः । p. 156. 4 Write notes on (1) निसृष्टार्थी दूती, (2) तारामैत्रक, (3) प्रकरण and (4) उपनिषद्। 5 To what class of dramatics compositions does the Mál. belong ? What are the leading features of the class according to writers on Sáhitya ? What special merits does Bhav. himself claim for the composition in the beginning of his work ? Show by references to facts and incidents how each of these merits is seen in the play.

---

1 Translate: (*a*) III. 17; (*b*) I. 41; (*c*) V. 28. 2 What sentiment does the Mál. chiefly develop ? Quote instances. Mention any cases of similarity of thought and expression you may have noticed in the Màl. and other works by the same author ? 3 Explain according to the context. (*a*) अन्यथावस्तु... आर्यायाः। (*b*) एतस्यां तनौ...अभूत्। p. 195. (*c*) श्येनावपात...कवलीकृतासि। (*d*) निष्कम्प...अभिषङ्गादिति । p. 147. (*e*) इयमेव...अभ्युदयानाम् । (*f*) विधि...मदनः। IV. 3. (*g*) दिष्ट्या...प्रजापतेः। p. 40.

## 1902 ( B. A. )

1 Translate into English:—(*a*) यत्सत्यमधुना...सारूप्यतश्चैतन्यम्। p. 100 (*b*) हीमाणहे पेक्खामि विअ...ओसरन्तकलकालं पाइक्कसमूहम्। p. 170 2 Give in Sans. either in Bhavabhûti's or your own words a

bird's eye view of Padmávatî and its surroundings. 3 In what different ways does the egotism of Bhavabhuti show itself in the play? Illustrate your remarks by references.

1903 ( B. A. )

1 Translate:—(*a*) घर्माम्भो &c. I. 37. (*b*) एताश्च चन्दना०. भूधरान् p. 177. 2 Explain the following with reference to the context:—(*a*) सखि लवङ्गिके दिष्टया वर्धसे। ननु भणामि प्रतिबुद्ध एव ते प्रियवदस्यः प्रतिपन्नचेतनो महाभागो मकरन्द इति। (*b*) महाभाग श्लिष्ट...भर्तृदारिका। तद्भवतु विधातुः। p. 31 (*c*) किमपरमतो निर्व्यूढं यत्करार्पणसाहसम्। N. B show the full significance of this by quoting or referring to Ma'latî's own words. (*d*) संप्रति मदयन्तिकासम्बन्धान्नन्दनोपग्रहात्प्रत्यस्तशङ्काः खलु वयम्। 3 Quote ideas from Mál. similar to the following, (*a*) अत्र हि विचार्यमाणे स्वार्थ एव प्राणपरित्यागोयमसह्यशोकवेदनाप्रतीकारत्वादात्मनः। अन्यामिव स्वकर्मफलपरिपाकोपचितामसाववशो नीयते भूमिम्। (*b*) गुर्वपि विरहदुःखमाशाबन्धः साहयति। (*c*) श्यामास्वङ्गं चकितहरिणीप्रेक्षणे दृष्टिपातम्। उत्पश्यामि प्रतनुषु नदीवीचिषु भ्रूविलासान्।

1908.

(1) Translate into English:—( *a* ) अद्याहमन्तनगर एव... गतामेतामभिजातकन्यकामभ्युपपन्नवानस्मि। काम०—( स्वगतम् ) वृत्तेन खलु ...प्रीतिदायस्य। p. 84. ( *b* ) इयमस्ति मालतीप्रथमदर्शनाभि०...माला। प्रेम्णा मद्ग्रथितेति...द्वायीकृता ॥ ६ ॥ p. 165 ( *c* ) कुमुदाकरेण...यूयुजत् ॥ IX. 48. (2) Explain with reference to the context (*a*) कलहंसमकरन्दप्रवेशावसरे तत्सुविहितम्। (*b*) हन्त महतः प्रागनुरागस्योद्भेदः। ( *c* ) हृदयंगमः परिहासः। (*d*) व्यवसितं प्रियसख्याः शरीरेण। ( *e* ) अन्यथा वस्तु वृत्तमन्यथा वचनमार्यायाः। ( 3 ) What religious sets are referred to by Bhavabhûti in Mál.? State their position and estimate their popular influence citing references to the text in support of your remarks. (4) Bhava. claims as some of the merits of Mál. Mádh.—औधत्यमायोजितकामसूत्रं चित्राः कथा वाचि विदग्धता च। What is meant by these? Show accurately where you realise them in the play.

1912.

I Translate into English.—( *a* ) असारं—निरालोकं लोकं...॥ V. 30. ( *b* ) उत्फुल्लार्जुन...।...घर्माम्भोविगमागमव्यतिकरश्रीवाहिणो वासराः ॥ IX. 17 (*c*) Dissolve the compounds in the black type above and name the metres of (*a*) and (*b*). II. Explain clearly, with brief references to the context, the following:—(1) यच्च किल कौशिकी... तदपि साहसाभासम्। p. 57. ( 2 ) नित्यन्यस्त...आत्मानमभ्यागता। V. 2. (3) प्रायेण बान्धव...मेव सौख्यम्। VIII. 14 (4) साधु सखे भूरिवसो साधु। प्रभवति मुपन्यस्तम्। p 52. (5) तदनेन तीर्थेन घटेन तत्प्रातिच्छन्दकमुपोद्घातेन ( उपोद्घाताय )

माधवान्तिकमुपेयाविरयभिप्रायः। (6) सङ्गम...न नाम सः (*v. l.* स्यादनागमः)। Discuss the various readings in (5) and (6) III. Write notes on the following—(1) इष्टाय पूर्ताय च कर्मणेर्धान्; (2) the situation of Padma'vatî; (3) पूर्णपात्रम्; (4) काकतालीयं; (5) नारामैत्रम्; (6) लोकालोक; (7) आमुष्यायण; (8) बोधिसत्व. IV. Bhavabhûti is a master of style and expression and his cleverness in adapting his words to the sentiment is unsurpassed. Illustrate this remark with quotations from the Màl. Màdh. Or–Bring out the salient features of the character of Málatî. Support your answers by references to the text.

---

## Index of important words occuring in the play.

*(The figures refer to pages of this edition.)*

श्रीः ।

# मालतीमाधवम् ।

---

सानन्दं नन्दिहस्ताहतमुरजरवाहूतकौमारबर्हि-
त्रासान्नासाग्ररन्ध्रं विशति फणिपतौ भोगसंकोचभाजि ।
गण्डोड्डीनालिमालामुखरितककुभस्ताण्डवे शूलपाणे-
र्वैनायक्यश्चिरं वो वदनविधुतयः पान्तु चीत्कारवत्यः ॥ १ ॥

---

चञ्चच्चन्द्रिकचन्द्रचारुकुसुमो माद्यज्जटापल्लवो
दृप्यद्दारुणदन्दशूकमणिमांस्तत्पञ्चशाखालयः ।
स्थाणुर्मे फलदो भवत्वतितरां गौरीमुखेन्दुद्रव-
त्पीयूषद्रवदोहदादिव दधद्देवद्रुमत्वं सदा ॥

नत्वा गुरून्गुणगुरूनवलोक्य टीकां
विश्वादिकोषभरतश्रुतिशब्दविद्याम् ।
छन्दांस्यलंकरणमर्थगतिं विचिन्त्य
श्रीमाञ्जगद्धरकृती वितनोति टीकाम् ॥

श्रीकण्ठकण्ठविलुठत्पटुनाटकेऽस्मिन्
टीका मयाल्पमतिनापि वितन्यते यत्
हासाय दुर्जनगणस्य भवेन्न चैत-
दुच्चैः पदं यदभिकाङ्क्षति सर्व एव ॥

---

इह तावदष्टपदां नान्दीं विदधान एव कविरप्रत्यूहमीहितसिद्धिमनुरुध्य प्रचण्डचण्डीपतेरकाण्डताण्डवाडम्बरेण लम्बोदरोत्कीर्तनरूपं मङ्गलं प्रकरणादौ निबध्नाति—**सानन्दमित्यादि** । वैनायक्यो वदनविधुतयश्चिरं वः पान्तु । गजाननाननचालनानि युष्मान्बहुकालं रक्षन्त्वित्यर्थः । इति श्रोतॄन्सामाजिकान्कविराशास्ते । वदनविधूनने कारणमाह—फणिपतौ वासुकिनागे नासाग्ररन्ध्रं नासिकाग्रविवरं सानन्दं विशति सति । नासात्र विनायकस्यैव । त्रस्तस्य झटित्यग्ररन्ध्रप्राप्त्या जीवनप्रत्याशयानन्द इति भावः । अत एव प्रवेशानन्तरमानन्द इति कथं क्रियाविशेषणमिति दोषानवकाशः । अग्ररन्ध्रस्य शीघ्रं प्राप्त्यैवानन्दातिशयात् । यथा भीतस्य शीघ्रं भवनादिप्राप्तौ हर्षः । यद्वा सानन्दं यथा तथा पान्त्विति योज्यम् । यद्वा सानदमित्याहतविशेषणम् । सापेक्षत्वेऽपि गमकत्वात्समासः । क्रियाविशेषणत्वादेव सानन्दमित्यत्र कर्मत्वैकत्वक्लीबत्वानि ।

---

१ भो नर्मने. २ फीत्कार.

इह नासारन्ध्रमिति वक्तव्येऽग्रग्रहणं त्रस्तस्य झटिति प्राप्त्या हर्षसूचनाय । यद्वा रन्ध्रप्रवेशोऽग्रप्रवेशस्यार्थसिद्धस्यापि शब्देन कीर्तनादुक्तिपोष एवायमलंकारः । यदाह दण्डी--'उक्तिपोषः । क्वचिदाक्षेपलब्धस्य साक्षाच्छब्देन कीर्तनात् ॥' इति । कीदृशे फणिपतौ । भोगः फणा कायो वा तस्य संकोचोऽविकाशस्तं भजतीति भोगसंकोचभाक् । तस्मिन् । विवरानुसरणे भोगिभोगसंकोच इति जातिनियमः । तदनेन महाकायस्य नासाग्रप्रवेशयोग्यतोक्ता । प्रवेशे हेतुमाह--शूलपाणेः शिवस्य ताण्डवे नृत्ये सति नन्दी गणभेदस्तस्य हस्तेनाहतस्य ताडितस्य मुरजस्य मर्दलस्य रवेण शब्देनाहूतो यः कौमारबर्ही कार्तिकेयमयूरस्तस्य त्रासाद्भयात् । अत्र नन्दिहस्ताहतत्वेन मुरजस्य गभीरताररवशालिता दर्शिता । मयूरस्य भुजंगभोजित्वेन त्रासकत्वम् । विधुतयः कीदृश्यः । गण्ड उड्डीनाभिरूर्ध्वं गताभिरलिमालाभिर्भ्रमरपङ्क्तिभिर्मुखरिताः शब्दीकृताः ककुभो दिशो याभिस्ताः । तथा चीत्कारो भीतकरिणां त्रासध्वनिस्तत्सहिताः । विनायकस्य गजाननत्वात् । इह साहित्यमात्रं मत्वर्थः । तथा च भयान्मुखे विधूननचीत्कारौ युगपद्वृत्ताविति भावः । जातिरलंकारः । विधुतेरचेतनत्वेऽपि देवतानुभावादेव रक्षणकर्तृत्वम् । अत एव त्रस्तस्यापि तत्कर्तृत्वम् । इह गम्भीरमुरजरवश्रुतिकृष्टमयूरभयेन फणिनां विवरानुसरणं जलदकालचिह्नम् । अत एव जलदकालमनुभाव्यैवैतत्प्रकरणवृत्तान्त इति ध्वनितम् । तथा च वक्ष्यति--'धारासिक्तवसुंधरासुरभयः' इत्यादि । मुरजघातेन वाद्यम्, अलिमालया दिशां मुखरीकरणेन गीतम्, वदनविधूननेन नृत्यं च सूचयता तौर्यत्रिकमुक्तम् । चीत्कारेण नृत्यतः प्रव्यक्तपाठोऽपि सूचितः । 'कुमारः क्रौञ्चदारणः' इत्यमरः । कुमारस्येदं कौमारम् । 'तस्येदम्' इत्यण् । 'मयूरो बर्हिणो बर्ही नीलकण्ठो भुजङ्गभुक् । इत्यमरः । 'नासा नाशा तु नासिका' इति शब्दभेदः । 'भोगः सुखे स्त्र्यादिरतावहेश्च फणकाययोः' । इति विश्वः । उड्डीन इति उत्पूर्वाड्डीङ्धातोः क्तः । 'ओदितश्च' इति चकारान्नत्वम् । 'प्रडीनोड्डीनसंडीनान्येताः खगगतिक्रियाः' । इत्यमरः । 'दिशस्तु ककुभः काष्ठाः' इति च । 'ताण्डवं नटनं नाट्यं लास्यं नृत्यं च नर्तनम्' । इति च । 'विनायको विघ्नराजद्वैमातुरगणाधिपाः' । इति च । विनायकस्येदं वैनायक्यम् । तस्येदमित्यण् । 'टिड्ढाणञ्--इति ङीप् । विधुतिरिति विपूर्वाद्धुञः स्त्रियां क्तिन् ॥ १ ॥ नाटकादौ प्रवृत्तिः प्रेक्षावतां सप्रयोजना । यदाह भरतः--'न तज्ज्ञानं न तच्छिल्पं न सा विद्या न ताः कलाः । नासौ नयो न तत्कर्म नाटके यन्न दृश्यते ॥' नाटके विघ्नविघातायादौ नान्दी कार्या । यदाह भरतः--'यद्यप्यङ्गानि भूयांसि पूर्वरङ्गस्य नाटके । तथाप्यवश्यं कर्तव्या नान्दी विघ्नप्रशान्तये ॥' नान्दीलक्षणं च भरते--'देवद्विजनृपादीनामाशीर्वचनपूर्विका । नान्दी कार्या बुधैर्यत्नान्नमस्कारेण संयुता ॥ गङ्गा नागपतिः सोमः स्वधानन्दो जयाशिषः । एभिर्नामपदैः कार्या नान्दी कविभिरङ्किता ॥ प्रशस्तपदविन्यासा चन्द्रसंकीर्तनान्विता । आशीर्वादपरा नान्दी योज्येयं मङ्गलान्विता ॥ काचिद्द्वादशपदा नान्दी

अपि च ।

चूडापीडकपालसंकुलगलन्मन्दाकिनीवारयो
विद्युत्प्रायललाटलोचनपुटज्योतिर्विमिश्रत्विषः ।
पान्तु त्वामकठोरकेतकशिखासंदिग्धमुग्धेन्दवो
भूतेशस्य भुजङ्गवल्लिवलयस्रङ्नद्धजूटा जटाः ॥ २ ॥

काचिदष्टपदा स्मृता । सूत्रधारः पठेदेनां मध्यमं स्वरमास्थितः ॥ चन्द्रसंकीर्तनं यत्र तदधीनो रसोत्तमः । प्रीते चन्द्रमसि स्फीता रसश्रीरिति भात्वि (ल्लु) किः ' ॥ तत्र केचन पदं विभक्त्यन्तमास्थिषत । केचित्त्विदं पद्यस्य भागमूचिरे । तादिह द्वितीयपक्षनिक्षेपेण पद्यद्वयेनाष्टपदा नान्दीति । बहुविघ्नशङ्कया तन्नाशाय पुनर्मङ्गलमाचरन्नष्टपदां नान्दीं निर्वाहयति—**चूडापीडेत्यादि** । भूतेशस्य हरस्य जटास्त्वां सभाप्रधानं पान्तु । कीदृश्यः । चूडायां शिखायां य आपीडस्तिर्यङ्नद्धमाला तस्याः कपालैः शुष्कशिरोऽस्थिपिण्डैः संकुलं व्याप्तमत एव गलन्मन्दाकिनीवारि गङ्गाजलं यासु ताः । माला चेह कपालानामेव । यद्वा येषां कपालानि तेषामन्यैर्जङ्घाजान्वाद्यस्थिभिराभरणार्थं तिर्यङ्माला । तत्संबद्धानि कपालानीत्यर्थः । तथा विद्युत्प्रायं विद्युन्निभं यल्ललाटलोचनपुटं ललाटस्थनेत्रसंपुटं तत्तेजसा विमिश्रा मिलिता त्विट् प्रभा यासां ताः । अत्र पुटस्थस्य समस्तनेत्रभागस्य तेजोमयता पुटपदेनोक्ता । तथाकठोरया कोमलया संपूर्णया वा केतकशिखया केतकीकुसुमाग्रेण संदिग्धः संशयितो मुग्धो रम्यो बालो वेन्दुर्यासु ताः । हरशिरसि किं केतकशिखेयमित्यनौचिती । तदयं संशयोऽप्यनौचित्यमूलक एवेति भावः । तथा भुजङ्गाः सर्पा एव वल्लयो लतास्ता एव वलया मण्डलाकारेण स्थिताः स्रजः पुष्पमालास्ताभिर्नद्धो बद्धो जूटो जूलको निबद्धस्रज ऊर्ध्वभागो यासु ताः । तदनेन जटाजूटस्यानवरतस्नानकपिशस्यापि भुजङ्गनद्धतया तिरोहितरूपत्वेनातिश्यामत्वेन मेघोदयमत एव सर्पविहरणसूचनम्, गङ्गाजलगलनेन वर्षणम्, कपालमालया बलाकावलिम्, ललाटनेत्र-

१ शिखिज्वाला. २ केतक. ३ चूडा. ५ अतःपरमिदं श्लोकद्वयं पठ्यते कैश्चित् ।

अपि च ।

दन्तश्रेणिषु संगलत्कलकलव्यावर्तनव्याकुला
नासालोचनकर्णकुञ्जकुहरेषूद्गद्गद्ध्वानिनः ।
गण्डग्रन्थ्यभिघातशीर्णकणिकाश्चूडास्रवन्त्यूर्मयः
शंभोस्त्र्यक्षकपालकंदरपरिस्पन्दोल्बणाः पान्तु वः ॥

अन्यच्च ।

पक्ष्मालीपिङ्गलिम्नः कण इव तडितां यस्य कृत्स्नः समूहो
यस्मिन्ब्रह्माण्डमीषद्विघटितमुकुले कालयज्वा जुहाव ।
अर्चिर्निष्टप्तचूडाशशिगलितसुधासाङ्गं [ शात्-१ ] कारिकोणं
तार्तीयीकं पुरारेस्तदवतु मदनप्लोषणं लोचनं वः ॥

( नान्यन्ते )

**सूत्रधारः**—अलं[1]मतिविस्तरेण । ( पुरं[2]तोऽवलोक्य । ) अये उदितभूयिष्ठ एषं[3] भगवाँ[4]नशेषभुवनद्वीपदीपस्तपनः । तदु[5]पतिष्ठे । ( प्रणम्य । )

---

त्विषा विद्युदुद्द्योतम्, शिशुशशिना च केतकशिखावत्त्वं दर्शयता मदनमदोद्दीपनमुदिरमेदुरघनसमयसूचनेन शृङ्गाररसशालिताप्यस्य प्रकरणस्य कटाक्षिता । अचेतनाया जटाया रक्षकत्वं देवतानुभावादवधेयम् । वल्लिवलयस्रगित्यत्र रूपकनामालंकारः । यत्र मिथोऽपेक्षा तत्र अपि चेति प्रयुज्यत इति व्युत्पत्तिः ॥ २ ॥ **नान्यन्त इति** ॥ उक्तलक्षणं नाटकाद्यं पद्यं नान्दी । आशीर्योगादिना नन्दयतीति नन्दः । पचाद्यच् । नन्द एव नान्दः । प्रज्ञादित्वादण्प्रत्ययः । 'टिड्ढाणञ्' इति ङीप् । नान्दी । सूत्रधारलक्षणं च भरते–'नाट्यस्य यदनुष्ठानं तत्सूत्रं स्यात्सबीजकम् । रङ्गदैवतपूजाकृत्सूत्रधार उदीरितः ॥' इति । ननु नान्यन्ते सूत्रधार इत्यसंगतम् । नहि नान्दीपाठानन्तरं सूत्रधारो रङ्गभूमिं प्रविशति । किंतु प्रविश्य पठति । न वान्येनैव पठनीया । सूत्रधारपठनीयत्वेनैव नान्द्या उक्तत्वात् । 'सूत्रधारः पठेन्नान्दीं मध्यमं स्वरमास्थितः' । इति वचनात् । उच्यते । नान्दीं पठित्वा सूत्रधारः प्रविशति पठति वा । नान्यन्ते सूत्रधारस्यैव श्रुतत्वेनेयमपि तेनैव पठनीया । प्रथमं सूत्रधारः प्रविशतीति नोक्तम् । मङ्गलार्थं देवतानमस्कारादेरेव विधानात् । यद्वा नान्दी तावद्रङ्गप्रवेशानन्तरं सूत्रधारेणैव पठनीया । नान्यन्ते सूत्रधार इति सूत्रधारसाम्यात्स्थापके प्रयोगः । यदाह भरतः—नान्दीं प्रयुज्य निष्क्रामेत्सूत्रधारः सहानुगः । स्थापकः प्रविशेत्पश्चात्सूत्रधारगुणाकृतिः ॥ पूर्वरङ्गं विधायादौ सूत्रधारे विनिर्गते । प्रविश्य तद्वदपरः काव्यमास्थापयेन्नटः' ॥ अत एव केचिन्नान्यन्ते स्थापक इत्येवं पठन्ति । ननु प्रस्तावनायाः पूर्वं बहूनि नाट्याङ्गानि सन्ति तानि किमिति नोक्तानि । यदाह भरतः–' रङ्गप्रसादमधुरैः श्लोकैः काव्यार्थसूचकैः । ऋतुं कंचिदुपादाय भारतीं वृत्तिमाश्रयेत् ॥ भेदैः प्ररोचनायुक्तैर्वीथिप्रहसनामुखैः । सूत्रधारो नटीं ब्रूते मारिषं वा विदूषकम् ॥ स्वकार्यं प्रस्तुताक्षेपि चित्रोक्त्या यत्तदामुखम् ॥' अत एवाह—**अलमिति** । अयमाशयः—पूर्वोक्तान्यङ्गानि न भवन्ति किंतु परिषदोऽभिमुखीकरणानि । सा चेत्स्वयमेव कृतावधाना नवनाटकविलोकनोत्का च तदन्यत्प्रयुज्यमानमपि रसभङ्गाय परं भवतीति कृतं तत्प्रणयनेन । अन्यथा सभाया रसविच्छेदो भवेदिति निष्फलनेति । अये इति निपातो व्यासङ्गादिनानाकलितस्याकलनेन संभ्रमवाचकः । अकस्मात्सूर्योदयाकलनात् । ' ततः श्लोकं पठेदेकं गम्भीरस्वरसंयुतम् । देवस्तोत्रं पुरस्कृत्य यस्य पूजा प्रवर्तते ॥ ' इति भरतमतमनुसृत्य माङ्गलिकतया रङ्गद्वारपाठ्यं श्लोकमुत्थापयति—**उदितेति** । उदितं भूयिष्ठं बहु यस्य सः । अस्य बहुतरभाग उदितः । किंचिदेवोदयायावशिष्यत इति भावः । अत्र ' नेक्षेतादित्यमुद्यन्तम्' इति निषेधादुदितभूयिष्ठ इत्युक्तम् । भगं ज्ञानादिसंपत्तिस्तद्वान् भ-

---

१ अलमलम्. २ पुरो०, प्राचीम०. ३ स, एव. ४ नम्बरमणिः; दीपः—दीपकः. ५ तम०, तदेनमु०.

कल्याणानां त्वमसि महसां भाजनं विश्वमूर्ते
धुर्यां लक्ष्मीमथ मयि भृशं धेहि देव प्रसीद ।
यद्यत्पापं प्रतिजहि जगन्नाथ नम्रस्य तन्मे
भद्रं भद्रं वितर भगवन्भूयसे मङ्गलाय ॥ ३ ॥

( नेपथ्याभिमुखमवलोक्य ) मारिष सुविहितानि रङ्गमङ्गलानि संनिपतितश्च भगवतः कालप्रियनाथस्य यात्राप्रसङ्गेन नानादिगन्तवास्तव्यो महाजनसमाजः । आदिष्टश्चास्मि विद्वज्जनपरिषदा यथा केनचिदपूर्वप्रकरणेन वयं विनोदयितव्या इति । तत्किमित्युदासते भरताः ।

---

गवानित्यर्थः । उपतिष्ठे । श्लोकेनेति शेषः । तदेवाह—**कल्याणानामित्यादि** । भो विश्वमूर्ते सर्वमयदेव । दीव्यतीति देवो द्युतिमांस्तादृश हे । कल्याणानां महसां माङ्गलिकानां तेजसां त्वं भाजनं पात्रमसि । अतः प्रसीद प्रसन्नो भव । मयि मद्विषये धुर्यां नृत्यधुरंधरां लक्ष्मीं संपत्तिमपि भृशमतिशयेन धेह्यारोपय । अथशब्दः समुच्चयार्थः । धेहीति स्थाने देहीति पाठे ददस्वेत्यर्थः । तथा हे जगन्नाथ भुवनपते यद्यत्पापमारब्धविरुद्धं नम्रस्य मेऽस्ति तत्प्रतिजहि नाशय । यद्यदिति वीप्सया कायिकवाचिकमानसिकरूपं पापत्रयमुक्तम् । वीप्सा तु न तच्छब्दे कृता । वीप्सितस्यैव तच्छब्देन परामर्शात्तथैव व्युत्पत्तेः । क्वचिद्यत्पद इव तत्पदेऽपि वीप्सा । यथा ' यां यां प्रियां प्रैक्षत ' इत्यादौ । भद्रमदोषं भद्रमभीष्टं वितर देहि । यद्वा । भद्रं भद्रमतिशयेनाभीष्टं देहीत्यर्थः । किमर्थम् । मङ्गलाथाशंसनीयकर्मार्थम् । तादर्थ्ये चतुर्थी । मङ्गलाय मङ्गलं कर्तुमिति वा । कीदृशाय । भूयसे प्रचुराय । तदिह हरिहरादीनपास्य भानोरुपस्थानेन प्रकरणनायकस्य ब्राह्मण्यं सूचितम् । अत एव देहीति ब्राह्मणोचिता प्रार्थना । सर्वक्षुद्रसत्त्वक्षयहेतोः प्रभातस्यादरेण प्रकरणकथाबीजसूचनमपि । तथाहि यद्यदिति वीप्सया शार्दूलाघोरघण्टविमर्दसूचनम् । पापप्रतिघातानन्तरं च भद्रं भद्रमिति वीप्सया स्वस्य मालतीलाभेन मकरन्दस्य च मदयन्तिकालभेनेष्टसिद्धिः सूचिता । भूयो मङ्गलपदेन कपालकुण्डलापकृतमालतीलाभो विद्यालाभादिकं च सूचितम् ॥ ३ ॥ **नेपथ्येति** । नेपथ्यं रङ्गभूमिः । 'नेपथ्यं रङ्गभूमौ स्यात् ' इति विश्वः । ' मान्यो भावेति वक्तव्यः किंचिन्न्यूनस्तु मारिषः ।' इत्यमरः । मारिष एव मर्षणान्मार्षः । सूत्रधारोक्तनिर्वाहसहिष्णुरित्यर्थः । सुविहितानि भक्तिश्रद्धाकृतानि । रङ्गो नृत्यं तदर्थं मङ्गलानि लोकपालपूजादीनि । 'रङ्गो नृत्ये रणक्षितौ' इति विश्वः । संनिपतितः सर्वत आगत्यैकत्र मिलितः । कालप्रियनाथस्य तद्देशदेव-

---

१ त्वमिह महसामीशिषे त्वं विधत्से. २ पुण्याम्. ३ इह. ४ समूहः; जनः । तत्किमित्युदासते भरताः । आदिष्टोऽस्मि विद्वत्परिषदा यथा—अद्य त्वयाऽपूर्ववस्तुप्रयोगेण वयं विनोदयितव्या इति । तत्परिषदं निर्दिष्टगुणप्रबन्धेनोपतिष्ठावः ।

( प्रविश्य )

**पारिपार्श्विकः**—भाव परिषन्निर्दिष्टगुणं प्रबन्धं नावगच्छामः ।

**सूत्रधारः**—मारिष कतमे ते गुणास्तत्र यानुदाहरन्त्यार्यविदग्धमिश्रा भगवन्तो भूमिदेवाश्च ।

**नटः**—

**भूम्ना रसानां गहनाः प्रयोगाः सौहार्दहृद्यानि विचेष्टितानि ।**
**औद्धत्यमायोजितकामसूत्रं चित्राः कथा वाचि विदग्धता च ॥४॥**

---

भेदस्य । यात्राप्रसङ्गेनेति नृत्यकालसूचनम् । ' इदं ध्वजमहः श्रीमन्महेन्द्रस्य प्रवर्तते । इत्यभिधानात् । वास्तव्यो वासी । महाजनसमाजो विद्वद्गोष्ठी । उदासत उदासीना भवन्ति । भरता नटाः ॥ पारिपार्श्विकलक्षणं भरते—' सूत्रधारस्य पार्श्वे यः प्रवचन्कुरुतेऽर्थनाम् । काव्यार्थसूचनालापं स भवेत्पारिपार्श्विकः ॥ ' इति । भाव मान्यनट । परिषदा प्रेक्षकेण निर्दिष्टो गुणो यत्र तं प्रबन्धं प्रकरणम् । प्रेक्षकस्तु—' यस्तुष्टे तुष्टिमायाति शोके शोकमुपैति च । क्रुद्धः क्रुद्धे भये भीतः स नाट्ये प्रेक्षकः स्मृतः ॥ ' इति भरतोक्तः । पूजावाक्यगर्भं प्रश्नमाह—**कतम इति** । ' गोत्रं नाम च बध्नीयात्पूजावाक्यं च सर्वतः । ' इति भरतः । कतमे । कियन्त इत्यर्थः । आर्याः सुकुलादिसंपन्नाः । यदाह भरतः—' कुलं शीलं दया दानं धर्मः सत्यं कृतज्ञता । अद्रोह इति येष्वेतत्तानार्यान्संप्रचक्षते ॥ ' विदग्धाश्चतुःषष्टिकलावेदिनः । मिश्रा वेदान्तवेदिनः । भगवन्तः स्मृतिधराः । यदाह—' देवाश्च लिङ्गिनश्चैव नानास्मृतिधराश्च ये । भगवानिति ते वाच्याः पुरुषाः स्त्रिय एव च ॥ ' इति । यद्वा । आराद्याता दूरं गताः ग्राम्यत्वादिदोषेभ्य इत्यार्याः । विदग्धाः काव्यरमवशमनसः । मिश्राः पूज्याः । पूज्ये मिश्रपदं नित्यं बहुवचनान्तम् । ' मरीचिमिश्रैर्दक्षेण ' इति विष्णुपुराणात् । भगवन्तो ज्ञानादिसंपन्ना भूमिदेवा ब्राह्मणाः । इह तत्रोद्घातकरूपा प्रस्तावना । यदाह भरतः—' सुप्रतीतं विस्मृतं वा यत्र कार्यं प्रकाश्यते । तदुद्घातकमित्याहुः प्रश्नोत्तरमनोहरम् ॥ ' इति ॥ प्रबन्धे गुणानाह—**भूम्नेति** । यत्र प्रबन्धे रसानां शृङ्गारादीनां भूम्ना प्राचुर्येण गहना गम्भीराः सहृदयमात्रग्राह्याः प्रयोगाः सन्ति । एतेनास्य रसमयत्वमुक्तम् । यत्र प्रबन्धे विचेष्टितानि मालतीमाधवादेः परस्परव्यापाराः सौहार्देन प्रेम्णा हृद्यानि । मनोज्ञानि । यत्रौद्धत्यं नायकनायिकासखीभृत्यादिगुणमाहात्म्यमस्ति । कीदृशम् । आयोजितं विहितं कामसूत्रमनङ्गप्रयोगो यत्र तत् । यद्वा । औद्धत्यं निजोत्कर्षपुरःसरमन्यावज्ञाविष्करणम् । तच्चायोजितस्य समन्तात्कार्याभिमुखीकृतस्य कामस्य मन्मथेच्छायाः सूत्रं सूचकम् । सूत्रं संभोगः पटारम्भकस्तन्तुर्वा । अनेनात्र का-

---

**नटः**—( प्रविश्य । ) भाव कतमे ते गुणा यानुदाहरन्त्यार्यमिश्रा भगवन्तो भूमिदेवाः । **सूत्रधारः**—भूम्ना इ० । **नटः**—भाव कस्मिन्प्रकरणे । **सूत्र**—( विचिन्त्य ) स्मृतम् । अस्ति दक्षिणापथे०—इ. पाठान्तरम्. २ नाधि०. ३ अनुवर्तन्ते; आर्या विद्वद्विदग्ध.

**सूत्रधारः**—स्मृतं तर्हि ।

**नटः**—भाव किमिव ।

**सूत्रधारः**—अस्ति दक्षिणापथे विदर्भेषु पद्मपुरं नाम नगरम् । तत्र केचित्तैत्तिरीयिणः काश्यपाश्चरणगुरवः पङ्क्तिपावनाः पञ्चाग्नयो धृतव्रताः सोमपीथिनो उदुम्बरनामानो ब्रह्मवादिनः प्रतिवसन्ति

**ते श्रोत्रियास्तत्त्वविनिश्चयाय भूरि श्रुतं शाश्वतमाद्रियन्ते ।**
**इष्टाय पूर्ताय च कर्मणेऽर्थान्दारानपत्याय तपोऽर्थमायुः ॥ ५ ॥**

---

मोद्दीपकत्यौद्धत्यं गुणाय । स्वाभाविकस्य तस्य भूषणत्वमिति दर्शितम् । यत्र चित्राश्चर्यजनिका कथा । कल्पितकथत्वात् रसमयत्वाच्चाश्चर्यम् । वाचि वचने विदग्धता परिपाको निर्दोषत्वं वक्रता च यत्र । एतेनान्यनाटकादस्याधिकगुणवत्त्वमुक्तम् । तं प्रबन्धं नर्तितुमादिशन्ति । मिश्रा इति शेषः ॥ ४ ॥ **नटः**—किमिव । किं स्मृतमित्यर्थः । अधुना 'रुणद्धि रोदसी चास्य यावत्कीर्तिरनश्वरी । तावत्किलायमध्यास्ते सुकृतं वैबुधं पदम् ॥' इति निजनामादिकथनफलमनुरुध्य तदाचरते—**अस्तीत्यादि** । दक्षिणदेशस्य शृङ्गाररसवशतया तद्देशजत्वेन स्वस्य तदुभयरसवर्णनशक्तिरुक्ता । विदर्भेष्वित्यनेन वैदर्भीरीतिपरिचयचातुरी दर्शिता । पद्मनगरं पद्मावती नाम प्रसिद्धौ । न तु नामपदमभिधानार्थम् । तदा प्रकृत्यादित्वात्तृतीया स्यादित्यवधयेम् । तैत्तिरीयिणः । तैत्तिरीयकनामशाखाविशेषपाठिन इत्यर्थः । काश्यपाः काश्यपगोत्राः । चरणगुरव इति चरणशब्दः शाखाविशेषाध्ययनपरैकतापन्नजनसङ्घवाची । तत्र समूहे ते गुरवः क्रियां कृत्वा वेदाध्यापयितारः । 'स गुरुर्यः क्रियां कृत्वा वेदमस्मै प्रयच्छति ।' इति स्मृतेः । यद्वा चरणैः कलापादिभिर्गुरवो महान्तः । पङ्क्तिपावनाः पङ्क्तौ भोजनादिगोष्ठ्यां पावना अग्रभोजिनः पवित्रा वेत्यर्थः । यद्वा 'यजुषां पारगो यस्तु साम्नां यश्चापि पारगः । अथर्वशिरसोऽध्येता ब्राह्मणः पङ्क्तिपावनः ॥' इति लक्षिताः । पञ्चाग्नयो दक्षिणाग्निगार्हपत्याहवनीयसभ्यावसथ्यरूपाग्निपञ्चकोपासकाः । धृतव्रताश्चान्द्रायणादिव्रतयोगिनः । सोमपीथिनः सोमो लताविशेषो हुतशेषो वा तत्पायिनः । अनेन सोमयागयाजित्वमुक्तम् । डम्बरनामानो डम्बरमुत्कर्षसूचकं कुलनाम येषां ते । यद्वा डम्बरं प्रसिद्धं नाम येषां ते । 'प्रसिद्धौ डम्बरं विदुः' इति विश्वः । ब्रह्मवादिनः । वेदज्ञा इत्यर्थः ॥ **त इत्यादि** । कथितरूपाः श्रोत्रियाश्छन्दोऽध्येतारः । जन्मादिसंपन्ना ब्राह्मणा वा । भूरि प्रचुरम् । शाश्वतं सार्वकालिकम् । श्रुतमध्ययनमाद्रियन्ते श्रद्दधति । यद्वा शाश्वतं नित्यागमं वेदाख्यमाद्रियन्ते । कीदृशम् । भूरि श्रुतं बहुभ्यो बहुधा बहुभिः सहाभ्यस्तम् । किमर्थम् । धर्मस्य कर्तव्याकर्तव्यरूपस्य विनिश्चयाय निर्णयाय । वैदिककर्मणि निर्णयादेव प्र-

---

१ क इव. २ नगरं. ३ तैत्तिरीया. ४ पीतिनः थिनो, ब्राह्मणाः. ५ डम्बर०, औदु०. ६ वसन्ति स्म. ७ विनिर्णयाय.

तदा[1]मुष्यायणस्य तत्रभवतः सुगृहीतनाम्नो भट्टगोपालस्य पौत्रः पवित्र[2]कीर्तेर्नीलकण्ठस्यात्म[3]संभवो भट्टश्रीकण्ठपदलाञ्छनो [4]भवभूतिर्नाम जातूकर्णीपुत्रः कविर्निसर्गसौ[5]हृदेन भरतेषु स्वकृतिमेवं[6]प्रायगुणभूयसीमस्माक[7]मर्पितवान् । यत्र[8] खल्वियं वाचोयुक्तिः ।

**ये नाम केचिदिह नः प्रथयन्त्यवज्ञां**
**जानन्ति ते किमपि तान्प्रति नैष यत्नः ।**
**उत्पत्स्य[9]तेऽस्ति मम कोऽपि समानधर्मा**
**कालो ह्ययं निरवधिर्विपुला च पृथ्वी ॥ ६ ॥**

---

वृत्तेरिति भावः । 'श्रोत्रियश्छन्दोऽधीते' इति पाणिनिसूत्रम् । 'जन्मना ब्राह्मणो ज्ञेयः संस्कारैर्द्विज उच्यते । विद्यया याति विप्रत्वं त्रिभिः श्रोत्रिय उच्यते ॥' इति स्मृतिः । शाश्वतमित्यत्र कालाठ्ञं बाधित्वा शाश्वते प्रतिषेध इति भाष्यवचनादण् । तथा तेऽर्थान्धनान्याद्रियन्ते । इष्टाय कर्मणे यागादिकार्यार्थम् । पूर्ताय कर्मणे खातादिकार्यार्थम् । यागादीनां धनसाध्यतया तेषां तदादरो न तु भोगायेति भावः । दारान्पत्नीराद्रियन्ते । अपत्याय संतत्यर्थं न तु कामायेत्यर्थः । त आयुर्जीवतमाद्रियन्ते । तपोर्थं तपश्चरणार्थं न तु व्यसनार्थम् । क्लेशबहुलं धर्म्यं कर्म तपः । तदनेन तेषां सर्वगुणवत्वं दर्शितम् । 'भूयिष्ठं भूयश्च भूरि च' इत्यमरः । 'अथ क्रतुकर्मेष्टं पूर्तं खातादिकर्मणि' । 'पुंभूम्नि दाराः' इति च । विनिश्चयायेत्यादौ तादर्थ्ये चतुर्थी ॥५॥ अत्र कुले जात आमुष्यायणः । तत्रभवतः पूज्यस्य । सुगृहीतं शोभनोच्चारणं वलिकर्णादिवन्मङ्गल्यं नाम यस्य । भट्टश्चतुःशाखाभिज्ञः । पवित्रा पुण्या कीर्तिर्यस्य । तस्यात्मसंभवः पुत्रः । श्रीः सरस्वती कण्ठे यस्य स श्रीकण्ठः । तद्वाचकं पदं लाञ्छनं चिह्नं यस्य सः । नाम्ना श्रीकण्ठः । प्रसिद्ध्या भवभूतिरित्यर्थः 'श्रीर्वेशरचनाशोभाभारतीसरलद्रुषु' । इति मेदिनीकरः । जतुकर्णगोत्रप्रसूत' जातूकर्णी तस्याः पुत्रः । निसर्गसौहृदेन साहजिकसौहार्देन । ननु 'हृद्भगसिन्ध्वन्ते पूर्वपदस्य च' इत्युभयवृद्ध्या सौहार्दमिति स्यात् । उच्यते । हृदित्यादौ प्रतिपदोक्तस्य ग्रहणात् 'हृदयस्य हृल्लेख–' इति हृदादेशस्यादिवृद्धिः । यद्वा 'संज्ञापूर्वको विधिरनित्यः' इति वचनादुभयपदवृद्धेरनित्यत्वम् । यद्वा 'सुहृद्दुर्हृदौ मित्रामित्रयोः' इति निपातस्य सुहृच्छब्दस्यावयवो हृच्छब्दस्तदन्तोत्तरपदवृद्धिर्भवति । एवंप्रायगुणभूयसीं 'भूम्ना रसानाम्' इत्यादिप्रायैर्गुणैरुपचितामर्पितवान्प्रयोगतोऽर्थतश्च संक्रमितवान् । खलु प्रसिद्धौ वाक्यभूषायां वा । वाचोयुक्तिर्वचनरचनम् । 'वाग्दिक्पश्यद्भ्यो युक्तिदण्डहरेषु' इति षष्ठ्यलुक् । संप्रति स्वकौशलबलेन सगर्वमाह—**ये नामेत्यादि** । इह तावत्त्रिविधाः पुरुषाः । केचिदज्ञा एव । केचिदद्वैतमतमग्नमनसः काव्यरसविरसाः । इतरे सहृदयहृदयामोदिकाव्यभव्यरसभररसिकाः । तत्राद्या-

---

१ तत्रा २ कीर्तिः. ३आत्मजः. ४ पदवाक्यप्रमाणज्ञः भव०, भवभूतिनामा. ५सौहार्देन, —देन वर्तमानः. ६ एवंगुण. ७ अस्माकं हस्ते. ८ तत्र तस्य कवेः. ९ स्यते च.

अपि च ।

**यद्वेदाध्ययनं तथोपनिषदां सांख्यस्य योगस्य च ।**
**ज्ञानं तत्कथनेन किं नहि ततः कश्चिद्गुणो नाटके ।**
**यत्प्रौढित्वमुदारता च वचसां यच्चार्थतो गौरवं**
**तच्चेदस्ति ततस्तदेव गमकं पाण्डित्यवैदग्ध्ययोः ॥ ७ ॥**

---

न्प्रत्याह—ये केचिदज्ञा नोऽस्माकमिह प्रबन्धेऽवज्ञामवधीरणं प्रथयन्ति ख्यापयन्ति । नाम संभावनायाम् । संभाव्यत इव न तु वास्तवमित्यर्थः । ते किमपि किंचिदल्पं जानन्ति । तान्प्रति तांल्लक्षीकृत्य मम नैष यत्नः । न हि बधिरे गीयते । यद्वा किंशब्द आक्षेपे । ते किं जानन्ति । किंतु न जानन्तीत्यर्थः । द्वितीयान्प्रत्याह—ये नाम निश्चये वैषयिकसुखविमुखा मुमुक्षव इहावधीरणामाचरन्ति ते किमपि वाङ्मनसागोचरं परं ब्रह्म जानन्ति । ते नमस्यास्तान्प्रति मम नैष यत्नः । न हि सम्राजमधिकृत्य कौपीनं सृज्यत इति भावः । अन्त्यान्प्रत्याह मम समानधर्मा तुल्यगुणः कोऽपि जन उत्पत्स्यते जन्मास्यत्यस्ति विद्यते वा । तं प्रत्येष यत्न इति भावः । इहाल्पज्ञत्वेन साधर्म्यमनौद्धत्याय । बहुज्ञत्वेन साधर्म्यं कदर्यदुर्जनविवर्जनायेत्युभयत्र विवक्षा । अथेदानीमनुत्पन्नस्य कथमुत्पादोऽत्रानुपलब्धस्य वा कथमुपलम्भ इत्युभययोग्यतामाह—यतः कालोऽयं निरवधिर्विगतावसानः । विपुला महती च पृथ्वी भूमिः । तथा च तस्येदानीमनुत्पन्नस्य कालान्तर उत्पाद इहानुपलब्धस्य देशान्तर उपलम्भश्च स्यादिति भावः । इह प्रथमार्धे बहुत्वेन प्रयोगो द्वितीयार्धे एकत्वेन प्रयोगश्च न दोषः । भिन्नवाक्यार्थत्वात् । एकवाक्यार्थत्वे तादृक्प्रयोगस्यायोग्यतया दोषत्वात् । तथैव व्युत्पत्तेरित्यवधेयम् । यद्वा अवज्ञाप्रथावसरेऽहंकारेणात्मनो गौरवाद्बहुत्वं निजसमतावसरे शान्त्यात्मन्येकत्वम् । यद्वा जात्यभिप्रायमेकवचनम् ॥ ६ ॥ अधुना निजगुणगरिमोपदर्शनेन निजग्रन्थे विदग्धादरमाह—**यद्वेदेत्यादि** । यत्र खल्वियं वाचोयुक्तिरित्यत्राप्यनुषज्यते । अद्वैतप्रतिपादको वेदभाग उपनिषत्तज्ज्ञानम् । योगः पातञ्जलशास्त्रम् । तयोरध्ययनज्ञानयोः कथनेन किम् । अपि तु न किमपीत्यर्थः । यतस्ततो वेदाध्ययनादेर्नाटके कश्चिद्गुणो नास्ति । तेषां नाटकेऽनुपयोगात् । तत इति ल्यब्लोपे पञ्चमी । तान्प्राप्य नाटके न कश्चिद्गुण इत्यर्थः । वयं सर्वमेव विद्मः अनङ्गतया पुनस्तदत्र न निबद्धमिति भावः । तर्ह्यत्र कवेर्वेदादिज्ञानज्ञापनं किमर्थमत आह—यदिति । वचसां यत्प्रौढत्वं वाक्यार्थे पदं पदार्थे वाक्यं तत्कृतिः । यथा न दैवीयं किं तु मानुषीत्यर्थे निमेषवती ।

---

१ अस्मात्प्राक्—तद्गुच्यन्तां तत्प्रख्यापनाय सर्वे कुशीलवा यथा—स्वसंगीतकप्रयोगे वार्णिकापरिग्रहे च त्वर्यतामिति । कविवर्णनां प्रति तेनैवमुक्तम् ।

**गुणैः सतां न मम को गुणः प्रख्यापितो भवेत् ।**
**यथार्थनाम्ना भगवान्यस्य ज्ञाननिधिर्गुरुः ॥**

अतो यदस्माकमर्पितं प्रियसुहृदा तत्रभवता भवभूतिनाम्ना प्रकरणं स्वकृतिर्मालतीमाधवं नाम तदेव तत्रभवतः कालप्रियनाथस्य पुरतः प्रयोगेण प्रख्यापयितुमुद्यताः । तत्सर्वे कुशीलवाः संगीतप्रयोगेण मत्समीहितसंपादनाय प्रवर्तन्ताम् ।

**नटः**—( स्मृत्वा ) एवं क्रियते युष्मदादेशः । किं तु या यस्य युज्यते भूमिका तां खलु तथैव भावेन सर्वे वर्ग्याः पाठिताः । सौगतजरत्परिव्राजिकायास्तु कामन्दक्याः प्रथमां भूमिकां भाव एवाधीते तदन्तेवासिन्यास्त्वहमवलोकितायाः ।

**सूत्रधारः**—ततः किम् ।

---

चन्द्रवदित्यर्थे ' नयनसमुत्थं ज्योतिरत्रेः ' इति । यदाह दण्डी—' पदार्थे वाक्यवचनं वाक्यार्थे च पदाभिधा । प्रौढिर्व्याससमासौ च साभिप्रायत्वमस्य च ॥' इति । यच्च वचसामुदारता विकटत्वं यस्मिन्सति पदानि जनो नृत्यन्तीवेति मन्यते । यद्वा उदारतालंकारादिदोषशून्यत्वम् । यद्वा उदारता गुणभेदः । यदाह दण्डी—' उत्कर्षवान्गुणः कश्चिदुक्ते यस्मिन्प्रतीयते । तदुदाराश्रयं तेन सनाथा काव्यपद्धतिः ॥ ' इति । यच्चार्थतो गौरवमनर्घार्थता । यद्वा स्वल्पं वचनमर्थसार्थप्रसरसमर्थमित्यर्थः । तद्यदि नाटकेऽस्ति ततस्तदेव पाण्डित्यवैदग्ध्ययोर्गमकं बोधकम् । पण्डितो वेदाध्ययनादिकुशलस्तस्य भावः पाण्डित्यम् । वैदग्ध्यं रसादियोगिप्रबन्धनकौशलम् । अनेन ग्रन्थे सर्वगुणवत्त्वमुक्तम् । तत्कर्तृत्वेनात्मनः सर्वपथीनमतिमत्त्वमप्युक्तम् । नाटक इति । ननु नाटक इत्युक्तम् । अस्य प्रकरणत्वात् । प्रकरणनाटकयोर्भेदात् । मैवम् । नट नृत्ताविल्यस्य घञि स्वार्थे कनि नाटकमिति । तथा च नाटके नाट्य इत्यर्थात् ॥ ७ ॥ भूमिका व्याजप्रवेशः । यदाह भरतः—' अन्यरूपैर्यदन्यस्य प्रवेशः स तु भूमिका ' । इति । वर्गे भवा वर्ग्याः । नटमेलकस्था इत्यर्थः । सौगतस्य बौद्धस्य । जरत्परिव्राजिका वृद्धा भिक्षुकी । एतादृशी दौत्ये प्रशस्ता । यदाह भरतः—' विधवेक्षणिका दासी भिक्षुकी शिल्पकारिका । प्रविश्य चाशु विश्वासं दूतीकार्यं च विन्दति ॥ ' इति वृद्धत्वं चास्या रूपशून्यत्वसर्ववदस्यत्वप्रगल्भत्वसूचकम् । यदाह—' लज्जितं नार्थवन्तं वा रूपिणं वा तथातुरम् । दूतं वाप्यथ वा दूतीं न तु कुर्यात्कथंचन ।॥ ' अन्तेवासिनी निकटशिष्या । अहं भूमिकामधीय इत्यन्वयः ॥ **ततः किमिति ।** एतावदुक्त्वा किमिति विरतोऽसीत्यर्थः । प्रकरणलक्षणं भरते—' आत्मशक्त्या कवेर्यत्र कथां नायकमेव च । औत्पत्तिकं प्रकुरुते तद्धि प्रकरणं विदुः ॥ ' इदं च शुद्धम् । यदाह भरतः—' द्विधा प्रकरणं तत्तु शुद्धं संकीर्णमेव च । कुलस्त्रीर-

---

१ दात्रभ०, भवता काश्यपेन भत्र० ब्राह्मणेन. २ तदेतदेव. ३ नाथस्य सकलजगदेकचक्षुषो विश्वात्मनः सूर्यस्य पुरतो यथाप्रयो० अहमुद्यतः. ४ संगीतकः प्रयोगेण भूमिकाकरणेन च. ५ स्मृत्वा सहर्षम्. ६ स एषः. ७ प्रव्राजि०. ८ पथमभू०.

**नटः**—ततः प्रकरणनायकस्य मालतीवल्लभस्य माधवस्य वर्णिका[1]-परिग्रहः कथम् ।

---

चितं शुद्धं संकीर्णं वेश्यया कृतम् ॥' अत्र नाटके यादृशो नियमस्तादृशः । नायक लक्षणं भरते—' नेता विनीतो मधुरस्त्यागी दक्षः प्रियंवदः । रक्तलोकः शुचिर्वाग्मी रूढवंशः स्थिरो युवा ॥ धृत्युत्साहस्मृतिप्रज्ञाकलामानसमन्वितः । शूरो दृश्यश्च तेजस्वी शास्त्रचक्षुश्च धार्मिकः ॥ विनयः शीलसंपत्तिर्मधुरः प्रियदर्शनः । त्यागः सर्वस्वदानं स्याद्दक्षः क्षिप्रकरो मतः ॥ प्रियंवदोऽनुत्कटवाक्स्नेहो लोकरञ्जकः । मितप्रस्तुतवाग्वाङ्मी नित्यकर्मरतः शुचिः ॥ ख्यातवंशो रूढवंशः षोडशात्रिंशको युवा । वाङ्मनःकर्मभिर्यश्च न चलः स स्थिरो मतः ॥ धृतिः सर्वेषु या प्रीतिरुत्साहोऽग्लानिरेव च । स्मृतिः कालान्तरज्ञानं प्रज्ञा तीक्ष्णमतिर्मता ॥ कलाश्चात्र चतुःषष्टिर्मानश्चित्तसमुन्नतिः । शूरः संग्रामनिपुणो रूपवान्दृश्य उच्यते ॥ अतिप्रतापस्तेजस्वी शास्त्रचक्षुस्त्रयीपरः । आत्मवत्सर्वभूतानि यः पश्यति स धार्मिकः ॥' इति । ननु मालतीवल्लभत्वं माधवस्य न योग्यं माधवेन वसन्तेन समं वर्षाकालीनाया मालत्या जातेः संबन्धाभावात् । मैवम् । अपूर्वमेव हि पदार्थसार्थं योगिनीप्रभावात्संपन्नमासाद्य सहृदयहृदयचमत्कारकारिणीं वैदग्धीमेव कविरयमुत्प्रेक्षितवानित्यदोषः । माधव इति नाम्ना शृङ्गारमयतोक्ता । वसन्तस्य शृङ्गारमयत्वात् । शृङ्गारमयत्वेन विष्णुदैवतत्वमपि कटाक्षितम् । यदाह भरतः—'शृङ्गारो विष्णुदैवतः' इति । अत एव श्यामत्वमपि वक्ष्यति कुवलयदलश्यामोऽयमित्यादिना । 'श्यामो भवेत्तु शृङ्गारः' इत्यपि भरतः । अयममात्यत्वाद्धीरोदात्तो नायकः । यदाह भरतः—'सेनापतिरमात्यश्च धीरोदात्तौ प्रकीर्तितौ' । इति । मालती नायिका । तल्लक्षणं भरते—'स्वान्यसाधारणस्त्रीति तद्गुणा नायिका त्रिधा । स्वकीया तत्र वक्तव्या मुग्धा मध्या प्रगल्भिका ॥ शीलार्जवादिसंयुक्ताऽकुटिला च पतिव्रता । लज्जावती चापलस्था निपुणा च प्रियंवदा ॥ साधारणस्त्री गणिका कलाप्रागल्भ्यधौर्त्ययुक् । रूपकेषु च रक्तैव कर्तव्या प्रहसं विना । अन्यस्त्री द्विविधा प्रोक्ता कन्यकोढा तथा परा । रसे प्रधाने कर्तव्या नान्योढा नाट्यवेदिभिः ॥ कन्यानुरागमिच्छातः कुर्यादङ्गाङ्गिसंश्रयम् ॥' इति । अन्यदपि प्रसङ्गादुच्यते । तथा हि—'नाटके वृत्तयः प्रोक्ताश्चतस्रो नाट्यवेदिभिः । भारती कैशिकी चैव सात्त्वत्यारभटी तथा ॥' तत्र शृङ्गारे कामकलावच्छिन्नो व्यापारः कैशिकी ॥ 'विशोका सात्त्वती सत्त्वशौर्यत्यागार्जवादिभिः । मायेन्द्रजालसंग्रामक्रोधोद्भ्रांतादिचेष्टितैः । भवेदारभटी नाम नाट्ये तिस्रस्तु वृत्तयः ॥ भारती शब्दवृत्तिः स्याद्रसे रौद्रे च युज्यते । शृङ्गारे कैशिकी वीरे सात्त्वत्यारभटी पुनः ॥ एवमङ्गानि कार्याणि प्रधानस्याविरोधतः । आदौ विष्कम्भकं कुर्यादङ्कं वा कार्ययुक्तितः ॥ अपेक्षितं परित्यज्य नीरसं वस्तुविस्तरम् । यदा संदर्शयेच्छेषं कुर्याद्विष्कम्भकं तदा । यदा तु सरसं वस्तु मूलादेव प्रवर्तते । आदावेव तदाङ्कः स्यादामुखाक्षेपसंश्रयः ॥

---

१ काञ्चुः.

**सूत्रधारः**—कलहंसमकरन्दप्रवेशावसरे तत्सुविहितम् ।

**नटः**—तेन हि तत्प्रयोगादेवात्रभवतः सामाजिकानुपास्महे ।

**सूत्रधारः**—बाढम् । एषोऽस्मि कामन्दकी संवृत्तः ।

**नटः**—अहमप्यवलोकिता । ( इति परिक्रम्य निष्क्रान्तौ । )

**प्रस्तावना ।**

( ततः परिवृत्य रक्तपट्टिकानेपथ्ये कामन्दक्यवलोकिते प्रविशतः । )

**कामन्दकी**—वत्से अवलोकिते ।

**अवलोकिता**—आज्ञापयतु भगवती ( आणवेदु भअवदी । )

---

प्रत्यक्षनेतृचरितो बिन्दुव्याप्तिपुरःसरः । अङ्को नानाप्रकारार्थसंविधानरसाश्रयः ॥ अनुभावविभावाभ्यां स्थायिना व्यभिचारिभिः । गृहीतमुक्तैः कर्तव्यमङ्गिनः परिपोषणम् ॥ न चातिरसतो वस्तु दूरविच्छिन्नतां नयेत् । रसं वा न तिरोदध्याद्वस्त्वलंकारलक्षणैः ॥ एको रसोऽङ्गीकर्तव्यो वीरः शृङ्गार एव वा । अङ्गमन्ये रसाः सर्वे कुर्यान्निर्वहणेऽद्भुतम् ॥ शृङ्गारहास्यकरुणरौद्रवीरभयानकाः । बीभत्सोद्भुत इत्येवमष्टौ नाट्ये रसाः स्मृताः ॥ यद्यपि 'अविकारस्थितिः शान्तः शान्तस्तु नवमो रसः' । इत्यस्ति तथापि स न सर्वसंमतो न वा नाट्यविषयश्चेति न पृथगुक्तः । स्थायिभावाभावात्तस्य नाट्यविषयता न संभवतीति दिक् । नायिका च माल्त्युदात्तनिभृता । कुलस्त्रीत्वात् । यदाह भरतः—'उदात्तनिभृता चैव भवेत्तु कुलजाङ्गना । इति । वर्णिका मषी ॥ बाढं दृढम् । कामन्दकी संवृत्तः कामन्दकीरूपः । एतेन सूत्रेणैव काव्यार्थसूचनं कार्यमिति मतमनुमत्य कामन्दकीसूचनमपि सूत्रसूचनमेव वृत्तमिति दर्शितम् । यद्वा अग्रे मकरन्देन मालतीरूपं कर्तव्यमिति पुंसः स्त्रीत्वापत्यात्र सूचितम् । कामन्दकीं नीतिग्रन्थभेदस्तं वेत्तीति कामन्दकी । 'तदधीते' इत्यण् ङीप् च । अनया नामव्युत्पत्त्या नीतिवेदितावोधनेन प्रकृतसिद्धिहेतुतोक्ता ॥ तदन्तेवासिनी अवलोकिता दृष्टिरेति कार्यसिद्धिदृष्टेरपि कार्यसिद्धिहेतुतोक्ता तदुत्तेजनिकेति । निष्क्रान्तौ । सूत्रधारनटाविति शेषः ॥ **प्रस्तावनेति** । निवृत्तेति शेषः एतल्लक्षणं भरते—'नटी विदूषको वापि पारिपार्श्विक एव वा । सूत्रधारेण सहिताः संलापं यत्र कुर्वते ॥ आमुखं नाम तस्यैव सैव प्रस्तावना मता ॥' इति । परिवृत्य पुनरागत्य । रक्तपट्टिका लोहितपट्टिका नेपथ्यमलंकारो ययोस्ते ॥ अधुना कामन्दकी समस्तप्र-

---

१ हंसक. २ तदेहि; तत्प्रसिद्धप्रयोगादेव तर्हि; तत्प्रतिबद्धप्रबन्धप्रयो०, तत्प्रबन्धप्रयो०. ३ प्रविश्य रक्तपटेन कृतनेपथ्या कामन्दक्य० च; रक्तपटिककृतनेपथ्ये उभे. ०पटिकानेपथ्ये उपविष्टे प्रविशतः.

**काम०**—अपि नाम तयोः कल्याणिनोर्भूरिवसुदेवरातापत्ययोर्मालती-माधवयोरभिमतः पाणिग्रहः स्यात् । ( वामाक्षिस्पन्दनं सूचयित्वा सहर्षम् । )

**विवृण्वतेव कल्याणमान्तरज्ञेन चक्षुषा ।**
**स्फुरता वामकेनापि दाक्षिण्यमवलम्ब्यते ॥ ८ ॥**

**अव०**—महान्खल्वेष भगवत्याश्चित्तविक्षेपः । आश्चर्यमाश्चर्यं यदिदानीं चीरचीवरपरिच्छदां पिण्डपातमात्रप्राणयात्रां भगवतीमीदृश आयासेऽमात्यभूरिवसुर्नियोजयति । तत्र चोत्खण्डितसंसारावग्रह आत्मा युष्माभिरपि नियुज्यते । ( महन्तो क्खु एसो भअवदीए चित्तविक्खेवो । अच्चरिअं अच्चरिअं जं दाणिं चीरचीवरपरिच्छदं पिण्डपादेमत्तपाणअत्तं भअवदिं ईरिसे आआसे अमच्चभूरिवसू णिओएदि । तहिं अ उक्खण्डिदसंसारावग्गहो तुह्मेहिं वि अप्पा णिउज्जीअदि । )

---

करणोपयुक्तमुपक्षेपमाह—**अपीत्यादि** । यदाह—' काव्यार्थस्य समुत्पत्तिरुपक्षेपः स्मृतो बुधैः । ' इह तु मालतीमाधवयोर्विवाहनिर्वाहः काव्यार्थः । **अपि नामेति** । नाम सम्भावनायाम् । तेन भवेदपीत्यर्थः । निश्चये वा नाम । तेन निश्चितमेव भवेदित्यर्थः । कल्याणिनोरित्यनेनाशंसनीयकुशलतयानुग्राह्यत्वमुक्तम् । भूरिवसुर्मालतीपिता । महाधनिककन्याया आवश्यकी वराकाङ्क्षेति नामतात्पर्यम् । देवरातो माधवपिता । देववद्राति दत्ते । ' रा दाने कर्तरि क्तः । देवरातः । तथा च जनो दातरि विवाह्यत इति महाधनिकवद्वदान्यत्वप्रभुत्वादियोगिनोऽनुरूप एव प्रायः पुत्र इति वरे कन्याकाङ्क्षासूचनं नामानुनयेन । एवं च योग्ययोर्योग्य एव सम्बन्ध इति भावः । पाणिग्रहो विवाहः । **विवृण्वतेति** । अपिरवधारणे । तेन वामकेनैव वामेनैव चक्षुषा दाक्षिण्यमवलम्ब्यते । कीदृशेन स्फुरता स्पन्दवतात एव कल्याणं विवृण्वता सूचयता । स्त्रीणां वामाङ्गस्फुरणस्य शुभसूचकत्वात् । आन्तरज्ञेनेव मदीयचित्तवृत्तिज्ञेनेव । इवोत्प्रेक्षायाम् । ' उत्प्रेक्षा व्यज्यन्ते शब्दैरिवशब्दोऽपि तादृशः । ' इति दण्डी । अथवापिर्विरोधे । वामेनापि प्रतिकूलेनापि दाक्षिण्यमानुकूल्यमवलम्ब्यत इति विरुद्धमिदम् । वामक इति स्वार्थे कन् ॥ ८ ॥ **अवलोकिता** । अत्र खलु निश्चये । चित्तविक्षेपोऽसद्विषयाभिनिवेशः । चीरेण वस्त्रखण्डेन । चीवरं सौगतपरिव्राजकवासस्तदेव परिच्छदः परिकरो यस्यास्ताम् । पिण्डपातो नाम बौद्धानां भिक्षाभ्रमणेन भोजनम् । तन्मात्रेण प्राणयात्रा जीवनं यस्यास्ताम् । ईदृशे विवाहकार्ये । इह पुरन्ध्रीणामेवाधिकारो न तु भवादृशीनामिति भावः । उत्खण्डित उन्मूलितः संसाररूपोऽवग्रहो मोक्षप्रतिबन्धो यत्र

---

१अभिमतं पाणिग्रहमङ्गलम्. २ ०स्पन्दं, मृग०, अभिनीय ३ चीवरमेन. ४ पाणउत्तिं ( प्राणवृत्तिं ). ५ ईरिसेसु आरामेसु. ६ तास्सिं

**काम०**—वत्से मा मैवं ब्रूहि ।

**यन्मां विधेयविषये सभवान्नियुङ्क्ते**
**स्नेहस्य तत्फलमसौ प्रणयस्य सारः ।**
**प्राणैस्तपोभिरथ वाभिमतं मदीयैः**
**कृत्यं घटेत सुहृदो यदि तत्कृतं स्यात् ॥ ९ ॥**

अयि किं व वेत्सि यदेकत्र नो विद्यापरिग्रहाय नानादिगन्तवासिनां साहचर्यमासीत् । तदैव चास्मत्सौदामिनीसमक्षमनयोर्भूरिवसुदेवरातयोर्वृत्तेयं प्रतिज्ञाऽवश्यमावाभ्यामपत्यसम्बन्धः कर्तव्य इति । तदिदानीं विदर्भराजमन्त्रिणा सता देवरातेन माधवं पुत्रमान्वीक्षिकीश्रवणाय कुण्डिनपुरादिमां पद्मावतीं प्रहिण्वता सुविहितम् ।

**अपत्यसम्बन्धविधिप्रतिज्ञा प्रियस्य नीता सुहृदः स्मृतिं च ।**
**अलोकसामान्यगुणस्तनूजः प्ररोचनार्थं प्रकटीकृतश्च ॥ १० ॥**

---

सः । यद्वा उन्मूलितः संसाररूपोऽपकृष्टो ग्रहो यत्र सः । **कामन्दकी** । मा मेति वीप्सात्यन्तनिषेधे । **यन्मामित्यादि** । सभवान्पूज्यो भूरिवसुर्यन्मां विधेयविषये नियोज्यगोचरे नियुङ्क्ते नियोजयति तत्स्नेहस्य प्रीतेः फलम् । स ह्यस्माकं प्रेमपात्रमिति भावः । असौ नियोगः प्रणयस्य प्रश्रयस्य सार उत्कर्षो निर्यासो वा । यदि मदीयैः प्राणैरथवा मदीयैस्तपोभिः सुहृदो मित्रस्याभिमतं वाञ्छितं कृत्यं कार्यं घटेत तदा तत्कार्यं कृतं स्यात् । मत्प्राणादिभिरपि भवेदित्यर्थः । यद्वा सुहृदोऽभिमतमिदं यदि घटेत निष्पद्येत तदा मदीयैः प्राणैस्तपोभिर्वा तत्कृत्यं कृतं स्यात् । अघटने तु सर्वमिदं व्यर्थमित्यर्थः । एतेनावश्यकर्तव्यतोक्ता । 'प्रणयः प्रेम्णि विश्वासे याच्ञाप्रश्रययोरपि ।' इति विश्वः ॥ ९ ॥ भूरिवसोः स्वीकारबीजमेवंविधप्रश्रयोपपत्तिं चाह—**किं नेत्यादि** । न इति बहुवचनेन स्वभूरिवसुदेवरातानामुपादानम् । **अस्मदिति** । अस्माकं सौदामिन्याश्च प्रत्यक्षमित्यर्थः । अपत्यसम्बन्धो विवाहः । सौदामिनीसमक्षमित्यनेन तस्या देवरातबन्धुतया नवमाङ्के माधवप्राणत्राणकारणत्वमस्या नाम च सूचितम् । युक्तं चेदम् । 'नासूचितं विशेत्पात्रम्' इति भरतः । एवमन्यत्रापि सूचितस्यैव प्रवेशः । आन्वीक्षिकी न्यायशास्त्रम् । तत्र तर्कच्छलादिनिष्टङ्कनेन तदभ्यासान्माधवस्य चोरिकाविवाहे कौशलमुक्तम् । श्रवणं पाठः । कुण्डिनपुरं विदर्भनृपराजधानी । प्रहिण्वता प्रस्थापयता । सुविहितं शोभनं कृतम् । **अपत्येत्यादि** । देवरातेन पुत्रं प्रहिण्वतापत्यसम्बन्धविधिप्रतिज्ञा विवाहप्रतिज्ञा प्रियस्य सुहृदः प्रीतिमित्रस्य भूरिवसोः । सुहृदः शोभनचित्तस्य वा । स्मृतिं स्मरणं

---

१ यदेकत्र नो...वासिनोः साह०. २स्मदन्तेवासिनी सौ०. ३ राजस्य. ४ हितं विहितम् । अस्मात्परं-कृतः । ५ अनन्य.

**अव०**—ततः किमिति मालतीममात्यो माधवस्यात्मना न प्रतिपादयति येन चोरिकाविवाहे भगवतीं त्वरयति । ( तदो किंत्ति मालदिं अमच्चो माहवस्स अप्पणा ण प्पडिवादेदि जेण चोरिआविवाहे भअवदिं तुवरावेदि । )

**काम०**—

**तां याचते नरपतेर्नर्मसुहृन्नन्दनो नृपमुखेन ।**
**तत्साक्षात्प्रतिषेधः[1] कोपाय शिवस्त्वयमुपायः ॥ ११ ॥**

**अव०**—आश्चर्यमाश्चर्यम् । न खल्वमात्यो माधवस्य नामापि जानातीति निरपेक्षतया लक्ष्यते । ( अच्चरिअं अच्चरिअं । ण क्खु अमच्चो माहवस्स णाम वि जाणादित्ति णिरवेक्खदाए[2] लक्खीअदि ।

**काम०**—वत्से संवरणं हि तत् ।

**विशेषतस्तु बालत्वात्तयोर्विवृतभावयोः ।**
**तेन माधवमालत्योः कार्यः स्वमतिनिह्नवः ॥ १२ ॥**

अपि च ।

**अनुरागप्रवादस्तु वत्सयोः सार्वलौकिकः ।**
**श्रेयो[3] ह्यस्माकमेवं हि प्रतार्यौ राजनन्दनौ ॥ १३ ॥**

---

नीता प्रापिता । अलोकसामान्यगुणो लोकविलक्षणगुणः पुत्रः प्ररोचनार्थं प्रवृत्तिपाटवार्थं स्फुटीकृतश्च । प्ररोचनस्यैव सर्वकार्यसिद्ध्यङ्गत्वात्तत्करणम् ॥ १० ॥ **अवलोकिता** । अत्रामात्यो भूरिवसुः माधवस्य कृत इति शेषः । प्रतिपादयति ददाति । चोरिकया विवाहस्य धर्मशास्त्रे निषेधादिति भावः । **तामित्यादि** । नन्दननामा राज्ञोऽन्तःपुरसचिवो नृपद्वारा तां याचते । तत्र साक्षान्निषेधः कोपाय राज्ञः । अयं तु मद्द्वारा संयोजनात्मक उपायः शिवः । परिणामसुरस इत्यर्थः । आर्या छन्दः । 'स्यान्नर्मसचिवः सोऽयं कुपितस्त्रीप्रसाधकः ।' नन्दयतीति नन्दनः । एतेनानन्दजनकत्वादन्तःपुरसचिवता युक्तेति नामतात्पर्यम् ॥ ११ ॥ **कामन्दकी** । संवरणं सङ्गोपनम् । **विशेषत इत्यादि** । तेन भूरिवसुना तयोर्वत्सयोर्विशेषेण स्वमतिनिह्नवः कार्यो निजज्ञानगोपनं कर्तव्यम् । बालत्वाच्छिशुत्वेन प्रकाशिताभिप्राययोः यथा तावपि प्रकृतं न जानीतस्तथा कृतं तेनेति भावः । युक्तं चादः । 'नादेशे नाकाले नापरिपक्वेन्द्रिये न गुणहीने । कथयति हि कथां स्वगतां न तथास्य कथा भवति वन्ध्या ॥' इति नीतेः ॥ १२ ॥ **अनुरागेत्यादि** । तयोरनुरागप्रवादः सर्वलोकविदितः सन्नस्माकं श्रेयः श्रेयोलम्भी । 'श्रेयान्' इति वा पाठः । यत एवं सति राजा नन्दन-

---

१ प्रतिबन्धः २ पेक्खं. ३ श्रेयोऽप्यस्माकं.

पश्य ।

बहिः सर्वाकारप्रगुणरमणीयं व्यवहर-
न्पराभ्यूहस्थानान्यपि तनुतराणि स्थगयति ।
जनं विद्वानेकः सकलमतिसंधाय कपटै-
स्तटस्थः स्वानर्थान्घटयति च मौनं च भजते ॥ १४ ॥

अव०—मयापि युष्मद्वचनात्तेन तेन वचनोपन्यासेन भूरिवसुमन्दिरासन्नराजमार्गेण माधवः संचार्यते । ( मए वि तुह्मवअणादो तेण तेण वअणोवण्णासेण भूरिवसुमन्दिरासण्णराअमग्गेण माहवो संचारीअदि । )

काम०—कथितमेव नो मालतीधात्रेय्या लवङ्गिकया ।

भूयो भूयः सविधनगरीरथ्यया पर्यटन्तं
दृष्ट्वा दृष्ट्वा भवनवलभीतुङ्गवातायनस्था ।
साक्षात्कामं नवमिव रतिर्मालती माधवं य-
द्गाढोत्कण्ठा लुलितलुलितैरङ्गकैस्ताम्यतीति ॥ १५ ॥

---

श्लोभौ वञ्चनीयौ तयोरन्योन्यानुरागादेव परिणयो वृत्तो न मया कारित इति वक्तव्यमेवेति भावः । सार्वलौकिक इत्यत्र सर्वलोकाद्ठञ् । अन्योन्यानुरागेण गान्धर्वविवाहोऽपि सूचितः ॥ १३ ॥ बहिरित्यादि । विद्वान्सुबुद्धिरेकः श्रेष्ठो द्वितीयो वा सकलं जनं कपटैरति(भि)सन्धाय वञ्चयित्वा स्वानर्थान्स्वप्रयोजनानि सम्पादयति । मौनमभाषणं भजते च । विधिनिषेधपरं वचो न वदतीत्यर्थः । अत एव तटस्थ उदासीन इवानभिव्यक्तव्यापार इत्यर्थः । कथम् । सर्वाकारेणेङ्गितादिना स्वभावसुन्दरं यथा भवति तथा बहिः प्रगटं व्यवहरन्नतिसूक्ष्माण्यपि पराभ्यूहस्थानानि परस्य तर्कस्थानानि स्थगयति पिदधाति । अपिर्भिन्नक्रमः 'अतिसन्धिर्वञ्चनार्थः' इति धातुसंग्रहः । 'केवलश्रेष्ठयोरेकः' इति धरणिः ॥ १४ ॥ अवलोकिता । अत्रोपन्यासो व्याजेन कार्योद्भेदः । राजमार्गेणेत्यनेन सर्वसाधारण्यान्माधवस्यानौद्धत्यमद्वितीयवेषता च सूचिता । सञ्चारणं च तद्दर्शनेन मालत्या अनुरागायेति भावः । अत्र कामन्दक्यावलोकितायामेवमनुक्तत्वात्कथं तव वचनादिति घटत इति न देश्यम् । प्राणैस्तपोभिरित्यादिना तदभिधानात् । कामन्दकी । धात्रेय्युपमातृसुता । एतेन बाल्यात्प्रभृति सकलचेष्टावेदित्वं ध्वनितम् । तथा च लवङ्गिका मालतीगतं यत्कथयति तत्प्रमाणमेवेत्येवकारव्यङ्ग्यम् । अनेनास्याः सखीत्वमप्युक्तम् । यदाह भरतः—'कारुर्दासी च धात्रेयी प्रतिवेश्या च शिल्पिका । बाला प्रव्रजिता चेति नायिकानां सखीजनः ॥' इति । न इति बहुवचनेनात्मनि लवङ्गिकाहृदयजागरूकबहुमानेन वञ्चकतानिरासः सूचितः । भूय इत्यादि । मालत्यङ्गकैस्ताम्यति खिद्यत इति कथितमेव लवङ्गिकयेत्यन्वयः । अङ्गकैरित्यत्रा-

---

१ प्रवण. २ अभिसं. ३ सन्नतर. ४ ललित.

**अव०—बाढम्** । तयाप्यात्मनो विनोदनिमित्तं माधवप्रतिच्छन्दकमालिखितं तल्लवङ्गिकया मन्दारिकाया हस्तेऽद्य निहितं तावत् ।
( बाढम् । ताँए वि अत्तणो विणोदणिमित्तं माहवपडिच्छन्दअं ओलिहिअं तं लवङ्गिआए मन्दारिआए हत्थे णिहिदं दाव । )

---

ल्पार्थे कन् । अल्पता मृदुत्वेन । वहुवचनात्सर्वाङ्गमुक्तम् । तथा च मृदुभिः सर्वाङ्गैरित्यर्थः । कीदृशैः । तं माधवं दृष्ट्वा दृष्ट्वा पुनः पुनरवलोक्य । गाढोत्कण्ठया दृढाकाङ्क्षया लुलितलुलितैरतिम्लानकान्तिभिः । 'ललितलुलितैः' इति पाठे पूर्वं ललितै रम्यैरधुना लुलितैर्म्लानैरित्यर्थः । कीदृशम् । सविधनगरीरथ्यया मालतीगृहनिकटराजमार्गेण भूयो भूयः पुनः पुनः पर्यटन्तं गच्छन्तम् । इह राजमार्गोपन्यासेन माधवस्य निःशङ्कः सञ्चारो मालत्याश्च तद्दर्शनेन परवितर्काभावः सूचितः । गमने पौनःपुन्येन दर्शनं प्रति दार्ढ्यमुक्तम् । दर्शने च पौनःपुन्येन तस्या उत्कण्ठातिशय उक्तः । यद्वा प्रथमवीप्सया दर्शनं दृष्ट्वानुवृत्त्या प्रथमं रम्यवस्तुचमत्कारेण तत उद्भिद्यमानानुरागनवाङ्कुरेण नेत्रप्रीतिर्युज्यते । द्वितीयवीप्सया सहचरीभिरप्यज्ञाता नयनप्रीतिरुक्ता । नगरीपदेन रथ्याया अनेककौतुकाधारतोक्ता । तथा चेतस्ततोऽनेककौतुकदर्शनतरलि ( न निर ) तत्वेन माधवस्य सम्यग्दर्शनसम्पादकनिकटार्थकसविधपदनिगर्व उक्तः । क्त्वाप्रत्ययेन चानन्तरभाविविह्वलताया विषयान्तरसञ्चारेणापि व्यवधानस्यापादनादत्यन्तानुरागोद्रेकः सूचितः । कथमन्तःपुरस्था सा ददर्शेत्यत आह—भवनेति । भवनस्य प्रासादादेर्या वलभ्युपरिकुटी तस्याः तुङ्गमुच्चं यद्वातायनं गवाक्षस्तत्रस्था । तुङ्गतया यथाकाङ्क्षं दर्शनमुक्तम् । वातायनेत्यनेन वातस्यायनं गमनं यत्रेति व्युत्पत्त्या घर्मादितापवती गभीरसमीरपरिशीलनार्थं यातीति प्ररोहेण निरर्गलमस्या गमनं तत्रेति सूचितम् । यद्यपि 'सौधोपरिकुटीं वलभीं विदुः' इति भवनपदमत्र गतार्थं तथाप्युक्तिपोषालङ्कारद्योतनार्थं भवनपदम् । यद्वा भवनरूपा वलभी मालतीवसतिः सौधोपरिकुटीत्यर्थः । एतेनास्या निजगृहाद्वलभीगमनं किमर्थमित्यन्याशङ्कापरिहारो निरर्गलं च तद्दर्शनं भवतीति ध्वनितम् । यथा रतिः कामकान्ता नवं दाहानन्तरमुत्पन्नं साक्षात्प्रत्यक्षं कामं दृष्ट्वाङ्गैस्ताम्यति तथेत्यर्थः । मालती रतिर्माधवश्च काम इति तयोर्बहललोकसङ्कुलेऽपि पथि रागसागरोऽन्योन्यं बबन्ध इति भावः । यद्वा कामोऽनङ्गतयाप्रत्यक्षो वृद्धश्च । अत्रोत्प्रेक्षा विशिष्टस्यैव । साक्षात्प्रत्यक्षं नवं काममिवेत्यर्थः । ताम्यतीत्यनेनोद्वेग उक्तः । यदाह भरतः—'चिन्तानिःश्वासखेदेन हृद्दाहाभिनयेन च । श्लथाङ्गोपाङ्गचेष्टाभिरुद्वेगाभिनयो भवेत् ॥' इति ॥ १५ ॥ 'रथ्याप्रतोली विशिखा' इत्यमरः । वातायनं गवाक्षोथ इति च । साक्षात्प्रत्यक्षतुल्ययोरिति धरणिः । **अवलोकिता** । बाढमतितरामनुरक्ता मालतीत्यर्थः । विनोदः क्रीडा हर्षो वा । प्रतिच्छन्दकं प्रति-

---

१ जदो ताए, ताए उव्वेअ ( उद्वेग ) विणोअणं. २ अभि. ३ णिक्खित्तं ( निक्षिप्तम् ).

**काम०**—( विचिन्त्य ) सुविहितं लवङ्गिकया यतो माधवानुचरः कलहंसकस्तां विहारदासीं मन्दारिकां कामयते । तदनेन तीर्थेन घटेत तत्प्रतिच्छन्दकमुपोद्घाताय माधवान्तिकमुपेयादित्यभिप्रायः ।

**अव०**—माधवोऽपि कौतूहलमुत्पाद्य मया प्रवृत्तमदनमहोत्सवं मकरन्दोद्यानमद्य प्रभातेऽनुप्रेषितः । तत्र किल मालती गमिष्यति । ततोऽन्योन्यदर्शनं भवत्विति । ( माहवो वि कोदूहलं उप्पादिअ मए पउत्तमअणमहूसवं मअरन्दुज्जाणं अज्ज पभादे अणुप्पेसिदो । तत्थ किल मालदी गमिस्सदि तदो अण्णोण्णदंसणं होदु त्ति । )

**काम०**—साधु वत्से साधु । अनेन मत्प्रियाभियोगेन स्मारयसि मे पूर्वशिष्यां सौदामिनीम् ।

**अव०**—भगवति सा सौदामिन्यधुना समासादिताश्चर्यमन्त्रसिद्धिप्रभावा श्रीपर्वते कापालिकव्रतं धारयति । ( भअवदि सा सोदामिणी अहुणा समासादिदअच्चरिअमन्तसिद्धिप्पहावा सिरीपव्वदे कावालिअव्वदं धारेदि । )

**काम०**—कुतः पुनरियं वार्ता ।

**अव०**—अस्त्यत्र नगर्यां महाश्मशानप्रदेशे कराला नाम चामुण्डा । ( अत्थि एत्थ णअरीए महामसाणप्पदेसे करालो णाम चामुण्डा । )

---

रूपकम् । तावत्पदेन मन्दारिकाहस्तनिधानस्य प्रकृतकार्योपक्रमः सूचितः । अत एव कामन्दक्या सुविहितमित्युक्तम् । **कामन्दकी** । विहारः सौगतप्रव्राजिकानामालयः । तत्र व्यापृता दासी विहारदासी । एतेन प्रकरणबाह्यत्वमुक्तम् । यदाह दण्डी–'शकारः कुट्टिनी दासी धर्मशास्त्रबहिष्कृताः । विटचेष्टादयो नित्यं बाह्याः प्रकरणे मताः ॥ तीर्थेन द्वारा उपायेन वा । 'तीर्थमुपायद्वारमन्त्रिषु' इति विश्वः । उपोद्घातेन प्रसङ्गेन । अभिप्रायस्तावदिति वादिन्यास्तवेति शेषः ॥ **अवलोकिता** । 'कौतुकं तु कुतूहलम्' इत्यमरः । मदनमहोत्सवेन वसन्तकालः सूचितः । तस्य च वैवाहिकत्वम् । यदाह-'शरत्सङ्ग्रामविषये विवाहे ज्येष्ठमाधवौ । इति । किल प्रसिद्धौ । इति हेतौ । अनुप्रेषणे तत्र किलेत्यादेर्हेतुत्वम् । अन्योन्यदर्शनेनोभयानुरागे विवाहनिर्वाहः ॥ प्रिये प्रीतिविषये कार्येभियोग आसङ्गः । अत्र कपालव्रतं महाव्रतम् । कुत इत्यादिना श्मशानाङ्कसूचनम् ॥

---

१ ०हंसो नाम. २ तीर्थेन ततः घटते. ३ उपोद्घातेन ( टी ). ४ मअणज्जाणं (मबनो०). ५ करालो.

**काम०**—अस्ति यां किल विविधजीवोपहारप्रियेति साहसिकानां प्रवादः ।

**अव०**—तत्र खलु श्रीपर्वतादागतस्य रात्रिविहारिणो नातिदूरारण्यवासिनः साधकस्य मुण्डधारिणोऽघोरघण्टनामधेयस्यान्तेवासिनी महाप्रभावा कपालकुण्डला नामानुसन्ध्यं समागच्छति । तत इयं प्रवृत्तिः ।
( तहिं क्खु सिरीपव्वदादो आअदस्स रत्तिविहारिणो णादिदूरारण्णवासिणो साहअस्स मुण्डधारिणो अघोरघण्टणामहेअस्स अन्देवासिणी महाप्पहावा कवालकुण्डला णाम अणुसंज्झं समाअच्छदि । तदो इअं पउत्ती । )

**काम०**—सर्वं सौदामिन्यां सम्भाव्यते ।

**अव०**—अलं तावदेतेन । भगवति सोऽपि सहचरो माधवस्य बालमित्रं मकरन्दो नन्दनस्य भगिनीं मदयन्तिकां यदि समुद्वहति तदपि माधवस्य द्वितीयं प्रियं कृतं भवति । ( अलं दाव एदिणा । भअवदि सो वि सहअरो माहवस्स बालमित्तं मअरन्दो णन्दणस्स वहिणिं मदअन्तिअं जइ समुव्वहदि तं वि माहवस्स दुदीअं पिअं किदं होदि । )

**काम०**—नियुक्तैव तत्र मया तत्प्रियसखी बुद्धरक्षिता ।

**अव०**—सु विहितं भगवत्या । ( सु विहिदं भअवदीए । )

**काम०**—( विचिन्त्य ) तदुत्तिष्ठ । माधवप्रवृत्तिमुपलभ्य मालतीमेव पश्यावः ।

---

**कामन्दकी** । किल प्रसिद्धौ । विविधा नानारूपा जीवा मानुषादय उपहारा बलयः प्रिया यस्याः सा । अनेन मालत्युपहारः सूचितः । आत्मनिरपेक्षं कर्म साहसं तेन वर्तन्ते ते साहसिकाः । प्रवादः प्रसिद्धिः । इह प्रियेत्यस्यानन्तरमिति पदं देयमन्यथा पूर्वापरानन्वयात् । तथा च प्रियेत्यनेनाकारेण साहसिकानां प्रवाद इत्यर्थः । अत एव वाक्यार्थकर्मादावितेरध्याहारः ॥ **अवलोकिता** । इह खलु प्रसिद्धौ । तस्याश्चामुण्डाया नातिदूरेणात्यासन्ने वस्तुं शीलं यस्य तस्य । एतेन देवकुलस्य लोकसङ्कुलतया किंचिद्विप्रकृष्टं साधकसंस्थानमुक्तम् । साधकस्य योगिनः । मुण्डधारिणः कापालिकस्य । **अघोरघण्टेति** । 'कापालिकास्तु घण्टान्तनामानः समुदाहृताः ।' इति भरतः । अघोरोऽविमृष्यकारीति नामव्युत्पत्तिः । अनुसन्ध्यं सन्ध्यायाम् । प्रवृत्तिर्वार्ता । सर्वमघोरघण्टनाशनमाधवरक्षणादिकम् । अत्रैतेन कापालिकादेः कथनेनालं निष्फलमधुनानुपयोगात् ॥ **अवलोकिता** । बालमिति भावप्रधानम् । तेन बाल्यान्मित्रमित्यर्थः । समुद्वहति विवहति ॥ **कामन्दकी** । बुद्धरक्षितेत्यनेन भिक्षुकीत्वं सूचितम् । अत एव दौत्ये नियुक्ता ॥ **कामन्दकी** । उत्तिष्ठेत्यत्रोर्ध्वकर्मत्वान्न तङ् ॥

---

१ सा. २ साधकानां. ३ इदो नादिदूरमसाणवा०. ४ मुण्डमालाधा०. ५ महानुभावा. ६ गअेर समा०. ७ सर्वं हि. ८ पास्स ( पार्श्व० ).

( उभे उत्तिष्ठतः । )

**काम०**—( विचिन्त्य । ) अत्युदारप्रकृतिर्मालती । तन्निपुणं निसृष्टार्थदूतीकल्पः सूत्रयितव्यः । सर्वथा

शरज्ज्योत्स्ना कान्तं कुमुदमिव तं नन्दयतु सा
सुजातं कल्याणी भवतु कृतकृत्यः स च युवा ।
वरीयानन्योन्यप्रगुणगुणनिर्माणनिपुणो
विधातुर्व्यापारः फलतु च मनोज्ञश्च भवतु ॥ १६ ॥

( इति निष्क्रान्ते । )

**विष्कम्भकः ।**

---

( ततः प्रविशति गृहीतचित्रफलकोपकरणः कलहंसः । )

**कलहंसः**—कुत्रेदानीं तुलितमकरध्वजावलेपरूपविभ्रमावाक्षिप्तमालतीहृदयमाहात्म्यं नाथमाधवं प्रेक्षिष्ये । ( परिक्रम्य ) परिश्रान्तोऽस्मि ।

---

**कामन्दकी** । अत्युदात्ता गभीरा प्रतिपन्नार्थसंवादिनी प्रकृतिर्यस्याः सा तथा । निसृष्टार्थेति । नायिकाया नायकस्य वा मनोरथं ज्ञात्वा स्वमत्या कार्यं साधयति सा निसृष्टार्था दूती तस्याः कल्पो व्यापारः प्रस्तावनीय इत्यर्थः । दूती च त्रिविधा । यदाह—'निसृष्टार्था मितार्था च तथा शासनहारिका । सामर्थ्योत्पादिताहीना दूती तु त्रिविधा मता ॥' इति । **शरदित्यादि** । सा मालती तं माधवं नन्दयतु प्रीणातु । यथा शरच्चन्द्रिका कुमुदं नन्दयति । तथा चन्द्रिकाकुमुदयोर्नित्यं प्रीतिस्तथा तयोरप्यस्त्विति भावः । कीदृशम् । कान्तं रम्यम् । सुजातं शोभनजन्मानम् । शोभनता च गुणवत्त्वेन । यद्वा कान्तमन्यस्त्रीभोगचिह्नशून्यम् । यदाह भरतः—'अन्यस्त्रीभोगसम्भूतं चिह्नं यस्य न विद्यते । देहे वाप्यधरे वापि स कान्त इति कीर्तितः ॥' सा कीदृशी । कल्याणी । निरवद्या । स च युवा कल्याणीं विवाहकल्याणयोगी संस्तां प्राप्य कृतकृत्यः कृतार्थो भवतु । युवेत्यनेन कन्यायां मदनमदोद्दीपकतायोगित्वमुक्तम् । एवं सति विधातुः प्रयत्नः सफलो भवतु मनोहरश्च भूपनन्दनाविरोधेन सर्वोवर्जकोऽस्त्वित्यर्थः । कीदृशः । अन्योन्यं कामिनोः प्रगुणा अनुरूपा ये गुणास्तेषां निर्माणे कुशलोऽत एव वरीयाञ्श्रेष्ठो गरीयान्गुरुर्वा । यद्वा अन्योन्यं प्रगुणा उत्कृष्टा ये गुणास्तेषां निर्माणे कुशलः ॥ १६ ॥ निष्क्रान्ते कामन्दक्यवलोकिते । **विष्कम्भक इति** । 'कुतोऽपि स्वेच्छया प्राप्तः सम्बन्धेनोभयोरपि । विष्कम्भकः स विज्ञेयो यस्तु काव्यार्थसूचकः ॥ विष्कम्भस्तु द्विधा सोऽयं शुद्धः सङ्कीर्ण एव च । शुद्धो मध्यमपात्रेण सङ्कीर्णो मध्यमाधमैः ॥' इति भरतः ॥ उपकरणमुपढौकनम् ॥ **कलहंसः** ।

---

१ इत्यु. २ मालती नाम. ३ तन्त्रायितव्यः. ४ गरीयान्. ५ मिश्रवि०. ६ चित्रोपकरणः, गृहीतचित्रफलकः, चित्रफलकहस्तः.

यावदस्मिन्नुद्याने मुहूर्तं विश्रम्य मकरन्दनन्दनं नाथमाधवं प्रेक्षिष्ये । ( कहिं दाणिं तुलिदमअरद्धवलेअरूवविब्भमावक्खित्तमालदीहिअअमाहप्पं णाहमाहवं पेक्खिस्सं । परिस्सन्तो ह्मि । जाव इमस्सिं उज्जाणे मुहुत्तं विस्समिअ मअरंदणन्दणं णाहमाहवं पेक्खिस्सं । ) ( इति प्रविश्योपविशति । )—

( ततः प्रविशति मकरन्दः । )

**मकरन्दः**—कथितमवलोकितया मदनोद्यानं गतो माधव इति । भवतु । तत्रैव गच्छामि । ( परिक्रम्यावलोक्य च । ) दिष्ट्यायं वयस्य इत एवाभिवर्तते । ( निरूप्य । ) अस्य तु

**गमनमलसं शून्या दृष्टिः शरीरमसौष्ठवं**
**श्वसितमधिकं किं न्वेतत्स्यात्किमन्यदितोऽथ वा ।**
**भ्रमति भुवने कन्दर्पाज्ञा विकारि च यौवनं**
**ललितमधुरास्ते ते भावाः क्षिपन्ति च धीरताम् ॥ १७ ॥**

---

अत्र तुलितो मकरध्वजस्य कामस्यावलेपो गर्वो येन रूपविभ्रमेण सौन्दर्यविलासेन तेनावक्षिप्तं तिरस्कृतं मालतीहृदयस्य माहात्म्यं गाम्भीर्यं येन तम् । 'अवलेपः स्मृतो गर्वः' इति शाश्वतः । मकरन्दस्य नन्दनं हर्षकम् । कलहंसो राजहंसः । स च शरदि विराजमानोऽपि योगिनीप्रभावाद्वसन्ते मिलित इति नामाभिप्रायः ॥ **मकरन्दः** । दिष्ट्येत्यव्ययं हर्षे । माधवस्य वसन्तस्य मकरन्दः पुष्परसः सहचरो युज्यत एव । इत एवात्रैव । इह शृङ्गारो द्विविधः । यदाह भरतः 'सम्भोगो विप्रलम्भश्च शृङ्गारो द्विविधो मतः' । सम्भोगोऽपि विप्रलम्भपूर्वक एव स्वदते यदाह—'न विना विप्रलम्भेन सम्भोगः पुष्टिमर्हति । कषायिते हि वस्त्रादौ भूयान्रागोऽभिजायते ॥ स च दशारम्भः । यदाह भरतः—'अप्राप्तरतिभोगस्य नवस्त्रीरागजन्मनः । दश स्थानानि कामस्य काममन्तर्विसर्पतः ॥ अभिलाषोऽत्र प्रथमे द्वितीये चिन्तनं तथा । अनुस्मृतिस्तृतीये च चतुर्थे गुणकीर्तनम् ॥ उद्वेगः पञ्चमे ज्ञेयो विलापः षष्ठ उच्यते । उन्मादः सप्तमे प्रोक्तो भवेद्व्याधिस्तथाष्टमे । नवमे जडता प्रोक्ता दशमे मरणं भवेत् ॥ इति । तदिहानुस्मृत्यवस्थो माधवो मकरन्देन कथ्यते—**गमनमिति** । अस्य गमनमलसं मन्दं न तु शरीरम् । हस्तादेराकुञ्चनप्रसारणात् । अन्तरान्तरा विलम्बस्यात्यन्तासक्तिवशाज्जायमानत्वाच्च । इदमनुस्मृतिचिह्नम् । यदाह—' मुहुर्मुहुर्निःश्वसितैरधोमुखविचिन्तनैः । प्रद्वेषादन्यकार्याणां कथितानुस्मृतिर्यथा ॥' तथा यतो मामपि न पश्यति ततोऽन्तःकरणं क्वापि लग्नम् । तथा च चिन्तासन्ततिपरतया ध्यानावधानेन शून्या बाह्यार्थाग्राहिणी दृष्टिरस्य । यदाह—' शून्या दृष्टिः स्मृता चिन्तासंमोहप्रणया-

---

१ ० रद्धरूआवलेअवि. २ इह. ३ सहअरं (सहचरं). ४ णाहं. ५ किं न्वे. ६ न्यदतो. ७ नेने.

( ततः प्रविशति यथानिर्दिष्टो माधवः[1] । )

**माधवः—**( स्वगतम् )

**तामिन्दुसुन्दरमुखीं सुचिरं विभाव्य**
**चेतः कथं कथमपि व्यपवर्तते मे ।**
**लज्जां विजित्य विनयं विनिवार्य धैर्य-**
**मुन्मथ्य मन्थरविवेकमकाण्ड एव ॥ १८ ॥**

---

दिषु ' शून्यदृष्टिलक्षणमप्याह—' निश्चला समतारा च ध्यानाद्ग्राह्यमगृह्णती । तथा समपुटोपेता शून्या दृष्टिरुदाहृता ॥ ' तथा मनस्तापवतो ग्लानिः । सा च क्षीणकपोलतादिनोन्नीयते । अत उक्तं शरीरमसौष्ठवं विकलम् । इष्टजनालाभभावनार्थमाह—श्वसितमधिकम् । एतत्किं नु स्यात् । एतदलसगमनत्वादिकं रोगजं कामकृतं वेति वितर्क इत्यर्थः । रोगलिङ्गाभावादनङ्गलिङ्गसङ्गाच्च निश्चयमाह—किमन्यदिति । अथवा पक्षान्तरे । इतः कामात्किमन्यत् । नान्यदित्यर्थः । किंशब्दो निषेधे । अत्र पांशुक्रीडनात्प्रभृत्यनुभूतमाधवशरीरे तत्तद्विकारदर्शनात्तर्कविद्याविदो मकरन्दस्य परिच्छेदो युज्यत एवेति । निश्चयलिङ्गमाह—भुवने कंदर्पाज्ञा भ्रमति सर्वे जनमास्कन्दति । विकर्तुं शीलमस्येति विकारि । पूर्वदशात्यागेन दशान्तरयोगो विकारस्तद्योगि यौवनम् । अयं तु युवेत्यर्थः । अत्र भ्रमतिपदेनानवच्छिन्नक्रियता तद्द्वारा सर्वकालता भुवनपदेन सर्वदेशता आज्ञापदेन युक्तिजिज्ञासां विना स्वीकारः विकारिपदेन माधवाङ्गीकारिता च ध्वनिता । ललिताः सुन्दरा मधुराः परिभाव्यमानास्ते ते प्रसिद्धा भावा रमणीवदनविभ्रमादया धीरतां धैर्यं क्षिपन्त्यपनयन्ति । तदनेन कामकृतमेतदुन्नीयत इति भावः । प्रकृतिमधुराः ' इत्यपि पाठः । तत्र प्रकृत्या स्वभावत एव मधुरा मनोहराः ॥ १७ ॥ माधवप्रवेश इह द्विपदिकया । यदाह—' शोकविभ्रमयुक्ते तु व्याधिचिन्तासमाश्रिते । श्रुतवार्तादिवैरूप्ये योज्या द्विपदिका बुधैः ॥' इति । **स्वगतमिति** । ' यत्तु श्राव्यं न सर्वस्य स्वगतं तदिहोच्यते । ' इति भरतः ॥ अनुस्मृतिमाह—**तामित्यादि** । तां नायिकामचिरमधुनैव विचिन्त्य मम चेतः । कर्तृ । कथं कथमपि महता कष्टेन व्यपवर्तते व्यावर्तते नागच्छति वा । तस्यां लग्नं तामेव धावतीत्यर्थः । किं कृत्वा । बालत्वेन कुलीनत्वेन च या लज्जा तामकाण्ड एवाप्रस्ताव एव विजित्य । रभसकाल एव हि लज्जाद्यभावप्रस्ताव इति भावः । विनयं मनोमलक्षालनोपदेशं दूरीकृत्य । महानायकतया साहजिकं धीरत्वमुन्मूल्य । कीदृशम् । मन्थरो मन्दो विवेक इतिकर्तव्यता यत्र तत् । क्रियाविशेषणं वा । कीदृशीम् । इन्दोश्चन्द्रात्सुन्दरं मुखं यस्यास्ताम् । वैयधिकरण्येऽपि गमकत्वात्समासः । इह तामित्यनुस्मृतिः इन्दुसुन्दरेति गुणकीर्तनम् वि-

---

१ निर्दिष्टरूपः; प्रविशति माधवः.

आश्चर्यम्।

> यद्विस्मयस्तिमितमस्तमितान्यभाव-
> मानन्दमन्दममृतप्लवनादिवाभूत्।
> तत्संनिधौ तदधुना हृदयं मदीय-
> मङ्गारचुम्बितमिव व्यथमानमास्ते ॥ १९ ॥

**मकरन्दः**—( उपसृत्य ) सखे माधव इत इतः।

**माधवः**—( परिक्रम्य ) कथं प्रियवयस्यो मम मकरन्दः।

**मकरन्दः**—सखे माधव ललाटंतपस्तपति तपनस्तदस्मिन्नुद्याने मुहूर्तमुपविशावः।

**माधवः**—यदभिरुचितं वयस्याय। ( उभौ परिक्रामतः। )

**कलहंसः**—( दृष्ट्वा ) कथं मकरन्दसहचर इदमेव बालबकुलोद्यानमलंकरोति नाथमाधवः। तद्दर्शयाम्यस्य मदनवेदनाखिद्यमानमालतीलोचनसुखावहमात्मनः प्रतिच्छन्दकम्। अथवा मुहूर्तं विश्रामसौख्यं

---

भाव्येति चक्षुःप्रीतिः कथमपीत्युद्वेगः लज्जां विजित्येत्युन्माद: मन्थरविवेकमिति जडतेत्यनेकावस्थोक्ता ॥ १८ ॥ **यदित्यादि**। तत्संनिधौ यन्मदीयं हृदयं विस्मयेनाद्भुतरसेन स्तिमितं निश्चलम्। एतेन स्तम्भ उक्तः। अत एवास्तमितो नाशं प्रापितोऽन्यो भावो विस्मयातिरिक्तो धर्मो यत्र तत्। अनेन जडतोक्ता। यदाह—'इष्टं वानिष्टं वा सुखदुःखे वा न वेत्ति यो मोहात्। तूष्णीकः परवशगः स भवति जडसंज्ञकः पुरुषः ॥' आनन्देन निरन्तरसुखेन मन्दं मन्थरं चाभूत्। अमृतप्लवनादिव सुधासेकादिव। अथ च योगाभ्यासेन कुण्डलिन्याचरणेनामृतसेकादिवेत्यर्थः। तत्रापि परमानन्दसंदोहो भवत्येव। एतेनाद्भुतनायिकादर्शनजातभावभरमन्थरता दर्शिता। तद्धृदयमधुना तद्वियोगेऽङ्गारचुम्बितमिवाङ्गारावसृष्टमिव व्यथमानं पीडायुक्तमास्त इत्याश्चर्यम्। न च प्रियासङ्गे सुखं तद्वियोगे दुःखमिति दृष्टचरमेव तत्कथमाश्चर्यमिति वाच्यम्। अननुभूतरसस्य तस्य शिशुत्वेन किमिदं यदकाण्ड एव व्यथेति तत्संभवात् ॥ १९ ॥ **मकरन्दः**। इत इतः। इहागच्छेत्यर्थः। आद्यादित्वात्तसिः। एतेन माधवस्य बाह्यार्थाग्रहान्मित्रादर्शनं सूचितम् ॥ **मकरन्दः**। ललाटं तपति ललाटंतपः। 'असूर्यललाटयोः' इति खश्प्रत्ययः। खित्त्वान्मुम्। माधवीयमन्मथोन्मादमपह्नोतुकामस्येदं वचनम् ॥ **माधवः**। वयस्यायेति 'रुच्यर्थानां प्रीयमाणः' इति संप्रदानता। **कलहंसः**। अत्र मकरन्देन पुष्परसेन सहचरो माधवो वसन्तो बालबकुलमलंकरोतीति ध्वनिरप्युन्मिषति। मुहूर्तं चेत्यत्र सुस्थिते चित्ते वक्तुं युक्तमिति भावः ॥

---

१ सान्द्र. २ आसीत्. ३ घर्मांशुः, इयं च ते शरीरावस्था ( इत्यधिकं क्वचित् ). ४ यथा प्रियवयस्याय रोचते. ५ इत्युभावुपविशतः।

तावदनुभवतु । ( कधं मअरन्दसहअरो इदं ज्जेव्व बालवउलुज्जाणं अलंकरोदि णाह-माहवो । ता दंसेमि से मअणवेअणाक्खिवज्जमाणमालदीलोअणसुहावहं अत्तणो पडिच्छन्दअं । अहवा मुहुत्तं विस्सामसोक्खं दाव अणुहोदु । )

मक०—तदस्यैव तावदुच्छ्वसितकुसुमकेसरकषायशीतलामोदवासितोद्यानस्य काञ्चनारपादपस्याधस्तादुपविशावः ।

( उभौ तथा कुरुतः )

मक०—वयस्य माधव अद्य किल सकलनगराङ्गनाजनप्रवर्तिमहोत्सवाभिरामकामदेवोद्यानयात्राप्रतिनिवृत्तमन्यादृशं भवन्तमवधारयामि । अपि नाम मनागवतीर्णोऽसि रतिरमणबाणगोचरम् ।

( माधवः सलज्जमधोमुखस्तिष्ठति )

मक०—( विहस्य । ) तत्किमवनतमुग्धमुखपुण्डरीकः स्थितोऽसि । पश्य ।

अन्येषु जन्तुषु रजस्तमसावृतेषु
विश्वस्य धातरि समः परमेश्वरे च ।
सोऽयं प्रसिद्धविभवः खलु चित्तजन्मा
मा लज्जया तव कथंचिदपह्नुतिर्भूत् ॥ १० ॥

---

**मकरन्दः** । उत्फुल्लपुष्पाणां ये केसराः किञ्जल्कास्तैः कषायो लोहितः शीतलश्च य आमोदस्तेन वासितं सुगन्धीकृतमुद्यानं येन तस्य । 'कषायः सुरभौ लोहितेऽन्यवत् ।' इति मेदिनीकरः । कषायादिसम्बन्धेन सौरभस्यातिगभीरतोक्ता । आमुद्यतेऽनेनेत्यामोद इति । कषायादिसम्पदे काञ्चनारेत्युक्तम् ॥ प्रवर्तितः कृतः । अभिरामेति यात्रान्वयि । इह मकरन्दवचनेन नर्मरूपः प्रतिमुखसन्धिरुक्तः । यदाह 'शृङ्गारार्थे त्रपाकारि वाक्यं गोष्ठीषु नर्म तत् ।' इति । अपिः समुच्चये । नाम सम्भावनायाम् । इदं सम्भाव्येतापीत्यर्थः । मनागल्पम् । रतिरमणः कामः । **मकरन्दः** । मुग्धं किंकर्तव्यताशून्यम् । पुण्डरीकं सितपद्मम् । विरहधूसरत्वेन मुखस्य पुण्डरीकसाम्यम् । तस्य लज्जयाऽकथनमाशङ्क्याह—**अन्येष्वित्यादि** । माधव तवापह्नुतिर्लज्जया कथंचिदपि मा भूत् । लज्जयापह्नवं मा कृथाः । एवमप्रतीकारः स्यादिति भावः । खलु यतः सोऽयं चित्तजन्मा कामः प्रख्यातपौरुषः । चित्तोन्माथविषय इति भावः । कीदृशः । विश्वस्य धातरि जगत्स्रष्टरि

---

१ एतन्नास्ति क्वचित् २ काञ्चनपाद०. ३ अद्यैव तावत्. ४मदनो०. ५दृशमिव. ६ गोचरनाम ७ अवनम्र. ८ च यः, बहिः. ९ अपि. १० किल.

**माधवः**—वयस्य किं न कथयामि श्रूयताम् । गतोऽहमवलोकिताजनितकौतुकः कामदेवायतनम् । तत्र चेतस्ततः परिक्रम्यावलोक्य च परिश्रमादुल्लसितमदिरामोदमधुरपरिमलाकृष्टसकलामिलदलिपटलसंकुलाकुलितमुकुलावलीमनोहराभरणरमणीयस्याङ्गनभुवो बालबकुलस्यालवालपरिसरे स्थितः । तस्य च यदृच्छया निरन्तरनिपतितानि विकसितानि कुसुमान्यादाय विदग्धरचनामनोहरां स्रजमभिनिर्मातुमारब्धवानस्मि । अनन्तरं च संचारिणीव देवस्य मकरकेतनस्य जगद्विजयवैजयन्तिका निर्गत्य गर्भभवनादुज्ज्वलविदग्धमुग्धनेपथ्यविरचनाविभावितकुमारीभावा महानुभावप्रकृतिरत्युदारपरिजना कापि तत एवागतवती ।

---

हरेऽन्येषु जन्तुषु मानुषादिषु च रजस्तमोगुणप्रधानेषु समस्तुल्यव्यापारः । यद्वा अन्येषु मानुषादिषु रजस्तमसावृतेषु च तिर्यग्योनिषु विश्वस्य धातरि ब्रह्माणि परमेश्वरे हरे च सम इति भिन्नमेव योज्यम् । अतो लज्जां त्यक्त्वा कथयेति भावः ॥ २० ॥ **माधवः** । परिश्रमात्स्थित इत्यन्वयः । परिश्रमात्स्थितोऽहं न तु साकाङ्क्षत्वादिति भावः । मदिरामोदवन्मनोहरो यः परिमलः शुभगन्धः । 'स्याच्छुभगन्धे परिमलः' इति विश्वः । मिलन्मिलितम् । संकुलेन व्याप्ताकुलिता या बकुलमुकुलावली विकासाभिमुखकलिकाराजिः सैव मनोहरमाभरणं तेन रमणीयस्य । यद्वा मदिरामोदेन मधुर इति समासः । तेन मदिरामोदस्य बकुलपुष्पोद्गमं प्रति दोहदत्वमाह । अङ्गनभुवोऽङ्गनस्थस्य । अनेन निकटवर्तिनः सेकादिना मनोज्ञता दर्शिता । इहाङ्गनपदेऽनुविधायकाभावाण्णत्वश्रुतिरयुक्ता पृषोदरादित्वाण्णत्वमित्यपि वचोऽमूलकमेव । प्रत्युत ' अङ्गनं प्राङ्गणे जाले कामिन्यामङ्गना मता । ' इति विश्वादिकोषात्तवर्गपञ्चमोपात्तमङ्गनं केवलमिति शब्दप्रकाशाच्च नान्तत्वमेवेत्यवधेयम् । आलवालं खल इति ख्यातम् 'स्यादालवालमावालमम्भसां यत्र धारणम्' । इत्यमरः । **विदग्धेति** । मालानिर्माणं कामशास्त्रवैदग्ध्यद्योतनाय । उक्तं च मालाग्रथनविकल्पा इत्यादिनेति भावः । अतिसुकुमारतया कामिनोर्मनोहरतया सुगन्धितया सुन्दरतया चान्यपुष्पाणि त्यक्त्वा बकुलपुष्पैर्मालाग्रथनमिह । अत एव दमयन्तीस्वयंवरादावपि बकुलमालासममधूकमालापरिग्रहः । संचारिणी गमनशीला मकरकेतोः कामस्य वैजयन्तिका पताका । गर्भभवनान्मध्यावासादुज्ज्वलया निर्मलयाग्राम्यया च शिशुप्रसाधनविरचनयोन्नीतः कुमारीभावः कुमारीत्वं यस्याः । कुमारीत्वेनावगुण्ठनपटाद्यभावात्तदुन्नयनमिति भावः । महानुभावप्रकृतिरतिप्रभावस्वभावा । अत्युदारो महान्दक्षिणो वा । 'उदारो महति दक्षिणे'

---

१ कौतूहलः. २ बकुलमु०. ३ निरन्तरविक०, विकसितनिर०. ४ आदायादाय कुसु०. ५ विदग्धवि० वनया स्रज. ६ मकरकेतोः. ७ मुग्धबाल.

सा रामणीयकनिधेरधिदेवता वा
सौन्दर्यसारसमुदायनिकेतनं वा ।
तस्याः सखे नियतमिन्दुसुधामृणाल-
ज्योत्स्नादि कारणमभून्मदनश्च वेधाः ॥ २१ ॥

अथ सा प्रणयिनीभिरनुचरीभिरविरलकुसुमसंचयावचयलीलादोहदिनीभिरभ्यर्थ्यमाना तमेव बकुलपादपोद्देशमागतवती । तस्याश्च कस्मिन्नपि महाभागधेयजन्मनि बहुदिवसोपचीयमानमिव मन्मथव्यथाविकारमुपलक्षितवानास्मि । यतोस्याः

इति शाश्वतः । परिजनदाक्षिण्यं सान्निध्यानयनेन ज्ञेयम् । तत एव तत्रैव ॥ तद्गुणकीर्तनमाह—**सेत्यादि** सा स्त्री रामणीयकस्य मनोहरताया निधेराधारस्याधिदेवताधिष्ठात्री देवता । यद्वा रामणीयकमेव निधिस्तस्याधिष्ठात्री रक्षिका देवता । सौन्दर्यसारसमुदायस्य कान्तिनिर्यासपूरस्य निकेतनं गृहं वा । निकेतनस्याजहल्लिङ्गतया सामानाधिकरण्यम् । मनोहरत्वं कान्तिमत्त्वं च तत्रैव दृष्टमिति भावः । वा समुच्चये । यद्वा वा विकल्पे । तत्र निर्णेतुं न शक्यत इति विकल्पार्थः । यद्वा वेवार्थे । रामणीयकनिधेर्देवतेवेत्यर्थः । 'वा स्याद्विकल्पोपमयोरिवार्थेऽपि समुच्चये ।' इति विश्वः । यद्वा रामणीयकं रूपादिसम्पत्तिस्तन्निधेरधिदेवता । अनेन शोभोक्ता । यदाह—'रूपयौवनलावण्यैरुपभोगोपबृंहितैः । अलङ्करणमङ्गानां शोभेति परिकीर्तिता ॥' सौन्दर्येत्यादिना कान्तिरुक्ता । यदाह—'शोभैव कुसुमास्त्रेण पूरिता कान्तिरुच्यते ।' अतोऽनयोर्भेदः । अत्यन्तविलक्षणां तामालोक्योत्प्रेक्षते । नियतं नूनं तस्याः कारणं समवायिकारणमिन्दुसुधामृणालज्योत्स्नादिकमभूत् । चन्द्रो मुखस्य सुधाधरस्य मृणालं भुजयोः ज्योत्स्ना लावण्यादीनामिति भावः । आदिपदेन पद्मे पादयोः किसलयौ चरणयोरिति ग्राह्यम् । सर्वोपमाद्रव्यघटितेयमिति भावः । एवं मदन एवास्या वेधाः स्रष्टाभूत् । चकारोऽवधारणे । वेदजडस्य पुराणस्य ब्रह्मणो नात्र निर्माणकौशलमिति भावः । अत्र कामस्य स्रष्टृत्वेनाश्रुतत्वात्कथमिति न देश्यम् । अस्या मोहनीत्वेन मोहनपटुकामजन्यत्वोत्प्रेक्षणात् । अदृष्टचरत्वस्योत्प्रेक्षायामनुकूलत्वात् । असदारोपणस्योत्प्रेक्षात्वात् । नियतपदमुत्प्रेक्षाव्यञ्जकम् । 'नूनमित्येवमादिभिः' इति वचनात् ॥ २१ ॥ प्रणयिनी स्निग्धा । अनुचरी दासी । सञ्चयः समूहः । अवचयस्त्रोटनम् । दोहदोऽभिलाषः । सहर्षमाह—**तमेवेति** । स्योद्देशमाह—**कस्मिन्नपीति** । 'भागधेयं भाग्यम्' इत्यमरः । इहानुमानरूपो गर्भसन्धिः कस्मिंश्चिदित्यनेनोक्तः । यदाह—व्याप्येन व्यापकज्ञानमनुमानमुदीरितम् । इति ॥ विकारचिह्नमाह—

१ कला. २ अनवरत. ३ कुतूहलिनीभिः, अभिलाषिणीभिः. ४ बालबकुल. ५ कस्मिंश्चिदपि. ६ उपलब्धवा.

परिमृदितमृणालीम्लानमङ्गं प्रवृत्तिः
  कथमपि परिवारप्रार्थनाभिः क्रियासु ।
कलयति च हिमांशोर्निष्कलङ्कस्य लक्ष्मी-
  मभिनवकरिदन्तच्छेदपाण्डुः कपोलः ॥ २२ ॥

सा पुनर्मम प्रथमदर्शनात्[1][2]प्रभृत्यमृतवर्तिरिव चक्षुषो[3]र्निरतिशय[4]मानन्द-मुत्पादयन्त्ययस्कान्तमणिशलाकेव लोहधातुमन्तःकरणमाकृष्टवती[5] सर्वथा । किं बहुना ।

सन्तापसन्ततिमहाव्यसनाय तस्या-
  मासक्तमेतदनपेक्षितहेतु चेतः ।
प्रायः शुभं च विदधात्यशुभं च जन्तोः
  सर्वंकषा भगवती भवितव्यतैव ॥ २३ ॥

---

**परिमृदितेति** । यथास्या अङ्गं परिमृदिता मर्दनविषयीकृता या मृणाली बिसलता तद्वन्म्लानम् । क्रियासु ताम्बूलभक्षणादिषु परिजनयाचनाभिरस्याः कथमपि प्रवृत्तिः । इह मृणालीपदेन तनुता म्लान्या निद्राच्छेदः कथमपीत्यादिना विषयनिवृत्तिः कथिता । तनुत्वम्लानत्वमान्द्यैर्ग्लानिरुक्ता । यदाह–'ग्लानौ तनुत्ववैवर्ण्यमन्दतादिनिदर्शनम् ।' ननु तनुत्वादिना व्यभिचारिणा कथं कामविकारोन्नयनमत आह–कलयतीति । तस्याः कपोलो हिमांशोः शोभां कलयति । अनेन पाण्डुता दर्शिता । कीदृशः । नूतनदन्ति-दन्तखण्डगौरः । छिद्यत इति च्छेदः खण्डः । इहाभिनवपदेन सपुलकत्वं ध्वनितम् । तथा च कपोलपाण्डुत्वसपुलकत्वादिना कामविकारव्याप्तेन तदुन्नयनमिति भावः । विरहे पाण्डुतापि । यदाह–'अङ्गस्यासौष्ठवं तापः पाण्डुता कृशता रतिः ।' ॥२२॥ वर्तिर्नेत्राञ्जनलेखा । अयस्कान्तो लोहाकर्षको मणिः । लोहधातुर्लोहरूपं द्रव्यम् । अन्तःकरणं मनः । ममान्तःकरणं कृष्टवतीत्यर्थः । किं बहुनेत्यनेन सखेदनिःश्वाससूचनम् । **सन्तापेत्यादि** । ममैतच्चेतस्तस्यां विषय आसक्तं समन्तान्नम्रमस्तीत्यर्थः । सन्तापपरंपरैव महाव्यसनं तदर्थम् । तादर्थ्ये चतुर्थी । सन्ततिपदेन मालतीलाभमन्तरेण यावज्जीवमविच्छेदस्तदलाभे प्राणहानिश्चोक्ता । कीदृशम् । अनपेक्षितनिमित्तम् । एतेन विषयालाभेऽप्यस्य स्वाभाविकी प्रीतिरुक्ता । यदाह–'अभ्यासादभिमानाच्च तथा संप्रत्ययादपि । विषयेभ्यश्च तत्त्वज्ञा विदुः प्रीतिं चतुर्विधाम् ।' अनेन निजमुच्छृङ्खलत्वमपि निरस्तम् । अत एवाह–प्राय इति । बाहुल्येन भगवती भवितव्यतावश्यंभावि प्राक्तनकर्म जीवानां शुभमशुभं च विदधाति । अत एव सर्वंकषा सर्वहरा । तथा च ममावश्यकं दुःखं त्वं तु यथोचितं कुर्या इति भावः । आसक्तेत्याङ्पूर्वात् षञ्ज् समवाये क्तः ।

---

१ कान्तः. २ दर्शनक्षणात्. ३ नयनयोः. ४ शयानन्दं, निरन्तरमा°. ५ उपसंहृतवती.

**मकरन्दः**—वयस्य माधव स्नेहश्च निमित्तसव्यपेक्षश्चेति विप्रतिषिद्धमेतत् । पश्य ।

**व्यतिषजति पदार्थानान्तरः कोऽपि हेतु-**
**र्न खलु बहिरुपाधीन्प्रीतयः संश्रयन्ते ।**
**विकसति हि पतङ्गस्योदये पुण्डरीकं**
**द्रवति च हिमरश्मावुद्गते चन्द्रकान्तः ॥ २४ ॥**

ततस्ततः ।

**माधवः**—ततश्च तत्र

**सभ्रूविलासमथ सोऽयमितीरयित्वा**
**सप्रत्यभिज्ञमिव मामवलोक्य तस्याः ।**
**अन्योन्यभावचतुरेण सखीजनेन**
**मुक्तास्तदा स्मितसुधामधुराः कटाक्षाः ॥ २५ ॥**

---

सर्वंकषेति खच्प्रत्यये खिलान्मुम् ॥ २३ ॥ **मकरन्दः** । माधवोक्तप्रीतेरनिमित्तकत्वमुपपादयति—**स्नेह इति** । निमित्तमिह द्वयं बाह्यमाभ्यन्तरं च । तदिह बाह्यहेत्वपेक्षः स्नेहोऽस्थिर एव । निमित्तनिवृत्तौ तन्निवृत्तेरावश्यकत्वात् । अत आन्तरनिमित्तापेक्षैव स्नेहस्येति भावः । विप्रतिषिद्धं विरुद्धम् । बाह्यनिमित्तापेक्षया विरोध इति भावः । स्वोक्ते युक्तिमाह—**व्यतिषजतीत्यादि** । आन्तरो हेतुः कोऽप्यनिर्वचनीयः पदार्थान्नरनारीप्रभृतीन्व्यतिषजति विशेषतो मेलयति । यतः प्रीतयो बहिरुपाधीन्बाह्यहेतून्सौन्दर्यादीन्न संश्रयन्ते प्रकर्षेणावलम्बन्ते । अत्र कोऽपीत्यनेन जन्मान्तरानुभवजनितसंस्कारताध्वनिः । न खल्वित्यनेन दृष्टश्रुतानुमितसकलैहिकोपाधिनिषेधात्तथावसायः । अत एव विशेषप्रकर्षद्योतकाभ्यामुपसर्गाभ्यामासङ्गस्य जीवितावधित्वमुक्तम् । उक्तं द्रढयति—यतः पतङ्गस्य सूर्यस्योदये पुण्डरीकं विकसति । चन्द्र उद्गत उदिते सति चन्द्रकान्तो द्रवति क्षरति च । तथा च तीक्ष्णकरोदये कोमलकमलदलविकासादमृतकरोदये पाषाणदारणाच्च सहजसिद्ध एव हेतुः । इह किं बाह्यं कारणं दृश्यते । तद्वत्प्रकृतेऽपि स्वाभाविक एव स्नेह इति भावः । पुण्डरीकपदमिह पद्ममात्रपरम् । अर्थान्तरन्यासोऽयम् ॥ २४ ॥ ततस्तत इति कथोपक्रमरीतिः ॥ **माधवः** । तत्र स्थाने । **सभ्रूविलासमित्यादि** । अथ तस्याः सखीजनेन तदा सोऽयमित्युक्त्वा सप्रत्यभिज्ञमिव पूर्वदृष्टमिव मामवलोक्य सभ्रूविलासं सभ्रूभङ्गं यथा तथा कटाक्षाः क्षिप्ताः । एतेन कटाक्षाणां पूर्वदृष्टप्रत्यभिज्ञाकारार्पणत्वमुक्तम् । कीदृशेन । अन्योन्याशयविज्ञेन । अनेन नायिकाव्युत्पत्त्यतिशय उक्तः । कीदृशाः स्मितमीषद्धसितमेवामृतं तेन मनोज्ञाः । 'ईषत्प्रफुल्लितैर्गण्डैः

---

१ वुद्गते. २ इतीव नाम. ३ न्यमेत्र.

**मकरन्दः**—( स्वगतम् ) कथं प्रत्यभिज्ञापि नाम ।

**माधवः**—अथ ताः सलीलमुत्तालकरकमलतालिकातरलवलयावलीकमुत्रस्तमत्तकलहंसविभ्रमाभिरामचरणसंचरणझणझणायमानमञ्जुमञ्जीररसितानुविद्धमेखलाकलापकलकिङ्किणीरणत्कारमुखरं परिवृत्य ' भर्तृदारिके दिष्ट्या वर्धामहे । यदत्रैव कोऽपि कस्यापि तिष्ठति ' इति मामङ्गुलीदलविलासेनाख्यातवत्यः ।

**मकरन्दः**—( स्वगतम् )। हन्त महतः प्रागनुरागस्योद्भेदः ।

---

कटाक्षैः सौष्ठवान्वितैः । अदृष्टदन्तकुसुमैरुत्तमानां स्मितं मतम् ॥ ' इति भरतः । स्वस्यादृष्टचरत्वेन संभावनायामिहेवशब्दः । अवलोक्येति । ललिता दृष्टिरियम् । यदाह—'मधुराकुञ्चितारा च सभ्रूक्षेपा च सस्मिता । समन्मथविकारा च दृष्टिः सा ललिता मता ॥ ' इह तु हर्षादियमुचिता यदाह—' धृतौ हर्षे च ललिता ' । भ्रूविलासेत्यनेन मोट्टायितमपि कटाक्षितम् ॥ २५ ॥ **मकरन्दः** । प्रत्यभिज्ञैकस्य तत्तेदन्तावैशिष्ट्यम् । अस्या एवाकारः सोऽयमिति । नाम संभावनायाम् । अदृष्टचरत्वेन माधवप्रत्यभिज्ञाया असम्भवादिति भावः । तामेव स्फोटयति—**अथेति** । अनन्तरं ताः सख्यो हे भर्तृदारिके स्वामिपुत्रि हर्षेण वयं वर्धामहे यतोऽत्रैव स्थाने कस्यापि कोऽपि तिष्ठतीत्युक्त्वा मामङ्गुलीखण्डलीलया कथितवत्यः । किं कृत्वा । सलीलं सविलासचेष्टितं यथा तथा प्रतिनिवृत्य । 'स्त्रीणां विलासचेष्टितं लीला' इति भरतः । उत्तालमुद्भटम् । विभ्रमो विलासो विशिष्टभ्रमणं वा । मञ्जुर्मनोज्ञः । मञ्जीरो नूपुरः । रसितानुविद्धः शब्दानुगतः । मेखलायाः कलापो गुच्छः । यद्वा मेखला च कलापश्च तयोः किङ्किणी क्षुद्रघण्टिका ॥ ' मेखला च कलापश्च भवेच्छ्रोणिविभूषणम् । एकयष्टिर्भवेत्काञ्ची मेखला त्वष्टयष्टिका ॥ रशना षोडश ज्ञेया कलापः पञ्चविंशतिः ॥ ' इति भरतः । इदं सर्वं निवर्तनक्रियाविशेषणम् । गतिरियं विकला । यदाह—' आवेगे चैव हर्षे च कार्ये च त्वरयान्विते । एतेषु च गतिं प्राज्ञो विकलां संप्रयोजयेत् ॥ ' इति । ' राजा भट्टारको देवस्तत्सुता भर्तृदारिका ' । राजपदमीश्वरमात्रपरम् । तेनामात्यकन्यापि भर्तृदारिकेत्युच्यत इत्यवधेयम् । कोऽपि कस्यापीत्यनेनानुद्भटोद्भावनेन तासां चातुर्यमुक्तम् । अत एव कस्यापीति सामान्यनिर्देशात्क्लीबत्वम् । अन्यथा स्त्रीलिङ्गनिर्देशः स्यात् । कोऽपीति पुंलिङ्गनिर्देशस्तु स्पष्टार्थः । अन्यथा किमपीति निर्देशे पुष्पादिप्रतिपत्त्या संशयः स्यादिति भावः । अङ्गुलीदलपदेन सविलासाख्यानमुक्तं सङ्गुसमाख्यानं वा ध्वनितम् । इदमाख्यानं नर्मवाक्यम् । यदाह—' सहास्यवचनप्रायं नर्मेच्छन्ति मनीषिणः ' ॥

---

१ रणरणायमान. २ प्रतिनिवृत्य. ३ वर्धसे. ४ कस्या अपि वल्लभः. ५ दर्शितवत्यः. ६ महतः खलु. ७ प्रथमानु०. ।यानु०.

**कलहंसः**—( आकर्ण्य ) कथं सरसरमणीयानुबन्धिनी स्त्रीजनकथा ।
( [१]कथं सरसरमणिज्जाणुबन्धिणी इत्थीअणकहा । )

**मकरन्दः**—ततस्ततः ।

**माधवः**—

अत्रान्तरे किमपि वाग्विभवातिवृत्त-
वैचित्र्यमुल्लसितविभ्रममुत्पलाक्ष्याः ।
तद्भूरिसात्त्विकविकारमपास्तधैर्य-
माचार्यकं विजयि मान्मथमाविरासीत् ॥ २६ ॥

ततश्च ।

स्तिमितविकसितानामुल्लसद्भ्रूलतानां
मसृणमुकुलितानां प्रान्तविस्तारभाजाम् ।
प्रतिनयननिपाते किंचिदाकुञ्चितानां
विविधमहमभूवं पात्रमालोकितानाम् ॥ २७ ॥

---

**मकरन्दः** । हन्त हर्षे । उद्भेदः प्रकाशः ॥ **कलहंसः** । अनुबन्धिनी प्रतीयमाना ॥ **अत्रान्तर इत्यादि** । सखीनां दर्शनावसर एव पद्माक्ष्याः संबन्धि तन्मान्मथं कामजमाचार्यकमुपदेशकर्माविरासीत्प्रकटीभूतम् । कीदृशम् । किमप्यनिर्वचनीयमत एव वाग्विभवाद्वचनप्रपञ्चादतिवृत्तमतिशयितं वैचित्र्यं यस्य तत् । उल्लसित उत्थितो विभ्रमो भावभेदो यत्र तत् । 'यच्चित्तवृत्तेरनवस्थितत्वं शृङ्गारजो विभ्रम उच्यतेऽसौ । भेदात्रयस्तस्य महानुबन्धकार्कश्यसंज्ञाः कथिता विदग्धैः ॥' इति भरतः । भूरि प्रचुरः सात्त्विकविकारो यत्र तत् । सत्त्वं मानसं किमपि तेन निर्वृत्तः सात्त्विको भावः । यदाह—'सत्त्वोत्कटे मनसि ये प्रभवन्ति भावास्ते सात्त्विका निगदिताः कविभिः पुराणैः ।' तेच—'स्वेदः स्तम्भोऽथ रोमाञ्चः स्वरभङ्गोऽथ वेपथुः । वैवर्ण्यमश्रु प्रलय इत्यष्टौ सात्त्विका मताः॥' इति । अपास्तं क्षिप्तं धीरत्वं येन तत् । महाभिजनत्वाद्यनपेक्षत्वादिति भावः । विजयि सर्वत्राप्रतिहतम् । कुमार्यां अपि शिशुत्वाद्विजय इति भावः । उत्पलाक्ष्या इत्यनेन बहुविधे नेत्रविकारे प्रीतिगो हाव इहोक्तः । यदाह—'भ्रूनेत्रादिविकाराद्यः शृङ्गाराकारसूचकः। स्थायिभावः स्थितो हाव ईर्ष्यातः प्रीतिगोऽपि च ॥' इह श्लोके विलास उक्तः । यदाह—' दयिताक्लोकनादौ विशेषोऽङ्गक्रियासु यः । शृङ्गारचेष्टसहितो विलासः समुदीरितः ॥ २६ ॥ सम्प्रति 'हेला हावत्समुत्थिता' इति भरतानुसारेण हावानन्तरं हेलामाह—**स्तिमितेत्यादि** । 'नारीणां प्रियसम्भोगलज्जासाध्वसकौतुकैः । स्वभावाविष्कृतो वेगो हेलेति परिकीर्तितः ॥' इति भरतः । श्लोकार्थस्तु तस्या आलोकितानां सहसा दर्शनानां पात्रं योग्योऽहमभूवं वृत्तोऽस्मि । 'सहसा दर्शनं यत्स्यात्तदालोकितमुच्यते ।' इति भरतः । कीदृशानाम् । मदीयरूपानिरूपणाश्चर्येण । स्तिमितानि निश्चलानि हर्षेण विकसितानि प्रफुल्लानि च तेषाम् । दृष्टिरियमद्भुता ।

---

१ एतासां ( अनयाः ). २ वाग्निवृत्तिं–वर्ती. ३ आयताक्ष्याः ४ मनसि. ५ प्रीति.

तैश्च[1] ।

> अलसवलितमुग्धस्निग्धनिष्पन्दमन्दै-[2][3]
> रविकविकसदन्तर्विस्मयस्मेरतारैः ।
> हृदयमशरणं मे पक्ष्मलाक्ष्याः कटाक्षै-
> रपहृतमपविद्धं[4] पीतमुन्मूलितं च[5] ॥ २८ ॥

---

यदाह—' समाकुञ्चितपक्ष्माग्रा विस्मयोद्धततारका । सौम्या विकसितान्ता च दृष्टिः स्यादद्भुताभिधा ॥ ' यद्वा स्तिमितं मन्दं यथा तथा विकसितानां प्रकाशितानां प्रथमं नायकदर्शनेन शनैः शनैः प्रसारणमिति भावः । अनेनोत्तरोत्तरदर्शनाभिलाषः सूचितः । उल्लसन्ती चपला भ्रूर्लतेव येषु तेषां । दीर्घत्वेन भ्रूलतयो रूपकम् । अनेन कान्तादृष्टिरुक्ता । यदाह—' हर्षप्रसादजनिता कान्तात्यर्थं समन्मथा । सभ्रूक्षेपकटाक्षा च शृङ्गारे दृष्टिरिष्यते ॥ ' मसृणानि चिक्कणानि लज्जया मुकुलितानि च तेषाम् । दृष्टिरियं मुकुलिता—' मुग्धा निमीलितान्ता च मुकुला दृष्टिरिष्यते । ' इति भरतः । यद्वा सुखभावनया मसृणं मन्दं यथा भवति तथा मुकुलितानाम् । एतेन दर्शनजनितानन्दसंपत्पर्यवसानं सूचितम् । पुनः पुनर्दर्शनकाङ्क्षया तिर्यगायतत्वेन प्रान्ते निकटे च विस्तारवताम् । शङ्किता दृष्टिरियम् । यदाह—' किंचिच्चलस्थिरा किंचिन्नमिता तिर्यगायता । गूढा चकिततारा च शङ्किता दृष्टिरुच्यते ॥ ' अनेन कटाक्षपर्यवसानमुक्तम् । प्रतीपदिगायतमन्नेत्रपाते सति लज्जया दर्शनोत्सुकतया च किंचिदाकुञ्चितानां मुद्रितानाम् । आकुञ्चितेयं दृष्टिः । यदाह—' अनाकुञ्चितपक्ष्माग्रा पुटैराकुञ्चितैस्तथा । सन्निकुञ्चिततारा च कुञ्चिता दृष्टिरुच्यते ॥ ' न च ' कुञ्चिता सूचिता नष्टदुष्प्रेक्षाक्षिव्यथासु या ' । इति भरते नियमादिह कुञ्चितदृष्टिकथनमयुक्तमिति वाच्यम् । लज्जया माधवे दुष्प्रेक्षत्वसंभवात् । पात्रं कीदृशम् । विविधं नानाप्रकारम् । स्तिमितदृष्टिप्रयोगेऽपि मयापि तथैव दृष्टिप्रयोगः कृत इत्यर्थः । ' योग्यभाजनयोः पात्रम् ' इत्यमरः । अभूवमिति भुवो लुङि सिचि रूपम् ॥ २७ ॥ **अलसेत्यादि** । पक्ष्मलाक्ष्याः प्रशस्तपक्ष्मयुक्तायास्तैरवलोकितैः कटाक्षतामापन्नैर्मम हृदयमपहृतं स्ववशीकृतम् । इह रक्षकबाहुल्येन गमनत्वरया शङ्कया वावलोकितानामेव कटाक्षत्वमुक्तम् । कटाक्षस्तिर्यग्विलोकनात्मकः । कर्णाभ्यर्णसंचारितारकः सर्वानङ्गरङ्गजनक इति भावः । तथा निश्चलत्वेनापविद्धं मथितम् । मथ्यमानतया द्रवरूपत्वेन पीतम् । अत एवोन्मूलितम् । तदा किमपि मया न ज्ञातमित्यर्थः । अत एवाशरणं रक्षकशून्यं जातम् । ततो

---

१ ततः. २ चलित. ३ निष्यन्द. ४ अपि. ५ अस्यानन्तरमिदं पद्यं पुस्तकान्तरे—

> तद्वक्त्रं नयने च ते स्मितसुधासिक्तं च तद्वाचिकं
> सा वेणी स भुजक्रमोतिसरलो लीलालसा सा गतिः ।
> तन्वी सेति च सेति सेति सततं तद्ध्यानबद्धात्मनो
> नो निन्दा न रतिर्न चापि विरतिः शून्यं मनो वर्तते ॥

एवमहं तु तस्याः सर्वाकारहृदयङ्गमायाः संभाव्यमानस्नेहरसेनाभिसंधिना[1] विधेयीकृतो[2]ऽपि पारिप्लवत्वमात्मनोऽपनिह्नोतुकामः[3] प्राक्प्रस्तुतस्य बकुलदाम्नो[4] यथाकथञ्चिदवशेषं[5] ग्रथितवानेव । ततो मिलितवेत्रशस्त्र-

यथार्हं कुर्विति भावः । कीदृशैः । लज्जयालसैर्मन्दैः कौतुकेन वलितैश्चलितैः । अथ मुकुलनेन मुग्धैः रम्यैः । प्रीत्या स्निग्धैः । रूपदर्शनाद्भुतचिन्ताभ्यां निष्पन्दैरनिमेषैः पुनः कोऽयं द्रष्टव्य इति विषादान्मन्दैरित्यर्थः । इयं विषादिनी दृष्टिः । यदाह— 'विषादविस्तीर्णपुटा पर्यस्तान्तानिमेषिणी । किञ्चिन्निष्टब्धतारा च नार्या दृष्टिर्विषादिनी॥' यद्वा अलसं मन्दं यथा तथा वलितैः । इयं निर्विकारा दृष्टिः । यदाह–'ललिता कुञ्चिता या च या च धीरावलोकिनी । निर्विकारा दृगिष्टा सा साध्व्येवाकारगुप्तिषु ॥' तथा प्रथमदर्शनापेक्षयाधुना विशेषदर्शनादधिकं विकसतान्तर्विस्मयेन स्मेरा मुग्धा तरा येषां तैः । इयं दृष्टिः स्निग्धा । यदाह—'किंचित्सहासेव सविस्मयेन सभ्रूसमुत्क्षेपकटाक्षयुक्ता । स्निग्धा निकामं प्रमदैकनिष्ठा शृङ्गारजा दृष्टिरिह प्रदिष्टा ॥ यद्वा कटाक्षैर्मम हृदयमपहृतमित्यनेन प्रीतिरुक्ता । अन्यस्यापि चक्षुःप्रीतिहेतोर्मनोहरत्वं भवत्येव । अपविद्धमित्यनेन चित्तासङ्ग उक्तः । अपव्यधेरत्यन्तासङ्गवाचित्वादिति भावः । पीतमात्मायत्ततां नीतम् । अनेन संकल्प उक्तः । मानसव्यापारस्यात्मवशत्वादिति भावः । उन्मूलितमित्यनेन विषयनिवृत्तिः सूचिता । अशरणमित्यनेन चित्तापहरणादिनिवारकाभाव उक्तः । नायिकाया निरवद्यरूपता च सूचिता । अलसेत्यनेन निद्रोद्भेदः वलित इत्यनेन त्रपानाशः मुग्धत्वेन मधुरता स्निग्धत्वेन साभिलाषत्वम्, अभिलषणीयस्य स्नेहविषयत्वान्निष्पन्दतया निकोचवैमुख्यं मंदत्वेन सहर्षत्वम् अधिकेत्यादिनान्तर्विकासिनी स्मेरतारा चेत्युक्तम् । एवं चालसवलितैरपहृतम् । योऽपि हि चौरादिः किंचिदपहरति स मन्दं मन्दं वलत इति भावः । मुग्धैः सहजरूपदर्शनातिमोहवद्भिः स्निग्धैर्मद्विषयस्नेहसूचकचेष्टावद्भिरपविद्धं क्षिप्तम् । पराभूतमिति यावत् । 'विद्धक्षिप्तेरिताः समाः' इत्यमरः । अनेन चेतसोऽनायत्तिर्दर्शिता । ननु चित्तावक्षेपनिवारकं तदनुध्यानादिकं किमिति न कृतमत आह—निष्पन्दैर्विमुखैर्मदेकविश्रान्तैश्च पीतं तदितरानुसंधानशून्यं कृतम् । तथा च नान्यविषयपरिशीलनकथेति भावः । अधिकेत्यादिनोन्मूलितम् । अनेन मनोनिग्रहाभावो मित्रोपदेशानवसरश्च सूचितः । इह पूर्वश्लोकेन नार्थपौनरुक्त्यम् । आलोकितावस्थाकटाक्षावस्थयोर्भेदात् । नायकस्य रसाक्षिप्तचित्तत्वाद्वा ॥ २८ ॥ **एवमिति**–तथाविधभावदर्शनेन हृदयङ्गमत्वम् । संभाव्यते । अपदेऽपि प्रेम्णोऽनिष्टाशङ्कित्वादिति भावः । अभिसंधिरभिप्रायः । यथाकथञ्चिदिति । चेतसस्तदपहृतत्वादिति भावः । वर्षवराः क्लीबास्तत्प्रायास्तत्प्रधानाः ।

१ मांनिधिना. २ विषयीकृतः. ३ अपह्नोतु. ४ बकुलपुष्प ५ कथं कथंचित्.

पाणिर्वर्षवरप्रायपुरुषपरिवारा गजवधूमारुह्य नगरगामिनं मार्गमिन्दुवदनालंकृतवती । तदा च

यान्त्या मुहुर्वलितकन्धरमाननं त-
दावृत्तवृन्तशतपत्रनिभं वहन्त्या ।
दिग्धोऽमृतेन च विषेण च पक्ष्मलाक्ष्या
गाढं निखात इव मे हृदये कटाक्षः ॥ २९ ॥

ततः प्रभृति

परिच्छेदातीतः सकलवचनानामविषयः
पुनर्जन्मन्यस्मिन्ननुभवपथं यो न गतवान् ।
विवेकप्रध्वंसादुपचितमहामोहगहनो
विकारः कोऽप्यन्तर्जडयति च तापं च कुरुते ॥ ३० ॥

अपि च ।

---

यद्वा ' विनीताः सर्वसत्त्वाश्च क्लीबाश्चैव स्वभावतः । जात्या न दोषिणश्चैव ते वै वर्षवरा मताः ॥ ' इति परिभाषिता वर्षवराः । हस्तिनीसमारोहणादिना महावंशजत्वेन मालत्या उत्तमस्त्रीत्वं सूचितम् । यद्वा हस्तिनीसमारोहणेनात्युच्चयानतया दूरदर्शित्वं सूचितम् । तत्रापि मन्थरगतिसूचनाय हस्तिनीग्रहणम् । हस्तिजातावपि स्त्रिया मन्थरगतिमत्त्वात् । एतदुभयं चिरं माधवालोकनायेति भावः । **यान्त्येत्यादि** । तया पक्ष्मलाक्ष्या यान्त्या मम हृदये गाढं यथा तथा कटाक्षो निखात इव दत्त इव । तदा तदवलोकनं मम हृदये लग्नमिवेत्यर्थः । निखात इत्यनेन कटाक्षस्य दुःसहत्वमुक्तम् । कीदृश्या । तदाननं वहन्त्या । कीदृशम् । मुहुर्वलिता वक्रिता कन्धरा ग्रीवा यत्र तत् । क्षणं क्षणं व्यावर्तमानम् । पश्यन्त्येत्यर्थः । आवृत्तवृन्तमावर्जितनालं यच्छतपत्रं पद्मं ततो निरतिशया भा दीप्तिर्यस्य तत् । तन्निभं तत्तुल्यमिति वा । वृन्तादारभ्यावर्तनेन पद्मविवर्तनासिद्धिः । कीदृशः । प्रथममानन्दहेतुतयामृतेन दिग्ध उपचितः पश्चाद्दर्शनानन्दविच्छेदाद्विषेण दिग्धः ॥२९॥ ततः प्रभृति तस्मादारभ्य । **परिच्छेदेत्यादि** । विकारः कामजो भावोऽन्तर्जडयति मोहयति तापं च कुरुते व्यथयति । यदा तत्प्राप्तिचिन्ता तदा जडतेतरकार्याप्रतिपत्तिः यदा च तद्व्यतिरेकचिन्ता तदा ताप इति कालभेदेन जाड्यतापयोर्न विरोधः । तदुभयजनकवस्तुनोऽभावमाशङ्क्याह—कोऽपि विशिष्यानिर्वचनीयः परिच्छेदमियत्तामतीतोऽतिक्रान्तो निर्वक्तुमशक्यश्च । यः पुनरस्मिञ्जन्मन्यनुभवपथं न गतवानत एव परिच्छेत्तुं निर्वक्तुं चाशक्य इति भावः । साम्प्रतं तदनुभवेन तद्द्वयं किमिति न क्रियत इत्याशङ्क्याह—विवेकप्रध्वंसात्प्रशस्तज्ञानाभावादुपचितमहामोहेन गहनः संकटः । तदानीं विवेकाभाव इति भावः । अनेन जडता

---

१ वेत्रधर व०. २ परिवृता, परिवारा. ३ करेणुकां. ४ नगरमार्गम्. ५ करणानां. ६ पदे. ७ मन्दयति च. ८ तनुते.

परिच्छेदव्यक्तिर्न भवति पुरःस्थेपि विषये
भवत्यभ्यस्तेऽपि स्मरणमतथाभावविरसम् ।
न सन्तापच्छेदो हिमसरसि वा चन्द्रमसि वा
मनो निष्ठाशून्यं भ्रमति च किमप्यालिखति च ॥३१॥

कलहंसः—दृढं खल्वेष कयाप्यपहृतः । अपि नाम मालत्येव सा भवेत् । ( दिढं क्खु एसो कए वि अवहरिदो । अवि णाम मालदी एव्व सा भवे । )

मकरन्दः—( स्वगतम् । ) अहो अभिष्वङ्गः । तत्किं निषेधयामि सुहृदम्[3] । अथवा ।

मा मूमुहत्खलु भवन्तमनन्यजन्मा
मा ते मलीमसविकारघना मतिर्भूत् ।
इत्यादि नन्विह निरर्थकमेव यस्मा-
त्कामश्च जृम्भितगुणो नवयौवनं च ॥ ३२ ॥

( प्रकाशम् ।[4] ) अपि वयस्येन[5] विदिते तदन्वयनामनी ।

---

दर्शिता ॥ ३० ॥ **परिच्छेदव्यक्तिरित्यादि** सन्निकृष्टेऽपि घटादौ परिच्छेदव्यक्तिर्निर्णयाभिव्यक्तिर्न भवति । घटादिकमपि निर्णेतुं न शक्नोमीत्यर्थः । अनेन बाह्येन्द्रियाणां विषयव्यावृत्तिरुक्ता । अभ्यस्तेऽपि वारंवारमनुभूतेऽपि स्मरणमतथाभावेन खण्डस्फुटिततया विरसं वैरस्यवत् । एतेन मनसोऽपटुत्वमुक्तम् । इयमनुस्मृत्यवस्था । विषयनिवृत्त्या सन्तापः शीतलसेवनादपि नापैतीत्याह–हिमसरसि शीतलसरोवरे चन्द्रमस्यमृतकरकिरणे वा मे न सन्तापहानिः । चन्द्रमःपदं लक्षणया स्वकिरणमाह । इयमुद्वेगावस्था । यदाह—' आसने शयने वापि न तिष्ठति न तुष्यति । औत्सुक्यं च भवेन्नित्यमुद्वेगस्थान एव च ॥ ' निष्ठाशून्यं धैर्यरहितं मनो भ्रमति च स्वल्पत्वात् । किमपि मनोरथमालिखत्यालिङ्गति । अनेनोन्मादावस्थोक्ता ॥ ३१ ॥ **कलहंसः** । अपहृतो वशीकृतः । अपिः संभावनायाम् । नाम प्राकाश्ये ॥ **स्वगतमिति** । ' यत्तु श्राव्यं न सर्वस्य स्वगतं तदिहोच्यते । ' इति भरतः । अभिष्वङ्ग आसक्तिरूपो मनःपराभवः । ' आक्रोशशापाभिभवेष्वभिषङ्गपदं विदुः । ' इति शाश्वतः ॥ **मा मूमुहादिति** । अनन्यजन्मा कामः खल्वत्यर्थं मा मूमुहत् । न चित्तविभ्रमसहितमजीजनत् । एवं च ते मतिर्मलीमसविकारेण कामजेन घना निबिडा मा भूदित्यादि निषेधवाक्यमिहानर्थकमेव । ननुपदमनन्वये । यतः कामो जृम्भितो वलयितो गुणो ज्या यस्य सः । जृम्भितगुण उपचितव्यापारो वा कामः । नवयौवनं च जृम्भितगुणम् । प्रकाशितरूपादिकमस्तीत्यर्थः । अतस्तत्पराधीनोऽयं न निषेद्धुं शक्य इत्यर्थः ॥ ३२ ॥ **प्रकाशमिति** ' यत्तु सर्वजनश्राव्यं प्रकाशं तदिहेष्यते ।

---

१ अथवा. २ ष्वङ्गः, मुहानभि. ३ प्रियसु. ४ यस्मिन्. ५ वयस्य अपि.

**माधवः**—सखे श्रूयताम्। अथ तस्याः करेणुकारोहणसमय एव महतः सखीकदम्बकादन्यतमा वारयोषिद्विलम्ब्य बालबकुलकुसुमावचयक्रमेण नेदीयसी भूत्वा प्रणम्य कुसुमापीडव्याजेन मामेवमुक्तवती—'महाभाग सुश्लिष्टगुणतया रमणीय एष वः सुमनसां संनिवेशः। कुतूहलिनी च नो भर्तृदारिकास्मिन्वर्तते। तस्या अभिनवो विचित्रः कुसुमेषु-व्यापारः तद्भवतु कृतार्थता वैदग्ध्यस्य फलतु निर्माणरमणीयता विधातुः ममासादयतु सरस एष भर्तृदारिकायाः कण्ठावलम्बनमहार्घताम्' इति।

**मकरन्दः**—अहो वैदग्ध्यम्।

---

इति भरतः। अन्वयो वंशः॥ **माधवः**। करेणुका हस्तिनी। अन्यतमान्या। स्वार्थे तमप्। यद्वा एकपर्यायोऽयमव्युत्पन्न एवान्यतमशब्दः। वारयोषिद्गणिका। तस्या ईदृक्त्वादुपादानमिह। विलम्ब्यैकाकिनी भूत्वा। नेदीयसी निकटस्था च भूत्वा। उभयत्र पुष्पत्रोटनक्रमेणेति योज्यम्। कुसुमापीडव्याजेन पुष्पदामच्छलेन। अभ्यर्थनाभङ्गभयेन छलेन मामाहेति भावः। अथ च कुसुमेनापीडयति कुसुमापीडः कामः। तद्व्याजेन मां प्रणम्येत्यर्थः। महाभाग महाभाग्य। 'भागो भाग्यार्धयोरपि' इति विश्वः। सुश्लिष्टगुणतया सुलग्नसूत्रत्वेन। संनिवेशो रचनाभेदः। कुतूहलिनी पुष्पदाम्नि कौतुकवती। भर्तृदारिकेत्यनेन कन्यात्वाद्दर्शनौत्सुक्यमुक्तम्। यद्वा भरतेन कन्याया विस्रम्भपात्रत्वस्वीकारादिह कन्यात्वेन तत्सूचनम्। अभिनवो लोकोत्तरो विचित्रो बहुप्रकारः। कुसुमेषु पुष्पेषु व्यापारो रचनाप्रबन्धः। एतेन माल्यग्रथनकुशलाद्भुतकौशलकुतूहलिनी सेत्युक्तम्। वैदग्ध्यस्य ग्रथनचातुर्यस्य। कृतार्थता कृतप्रयोजनता। विदग्धप्रेयसीयं प्रशंसयेति भावः। फलतु सफलोस्तु। विदग्धजनाय दानात्। सरस एवाम्लान एव स्रक्संनिवेशः। महार्घतां बहुमूल्यताम्। पक्षे वो युष्माकं संनिवेशः संयोगः परस्परानुरूपादिना रमणीयः क्रीडार्होऽर्हणीय एव। इह व इति 'युष्मदो गुरावेकेषाम्' इति गौरवे बहुवचनम्। कुतूहलिनी द्यूतसमाजे साकाङ्क्षा। अभिनवोऽभूतपूर्वः तदेकासक्तत्वात्। विचित्रः साधुः। विविधविकारकारित्वेनाश्चर्यजनको वा। कुसुमेषोः कामस्य व्यापारो मोहनम्। वैदग्ध्यस्य सकलकलाभिज्ञतायाः सार्थकत्वम्। विदग्धप्रीतिजनकत्वात्। निर्माणरमणीयता घटनसौन्दर्यम्। फलतु अनुरूपजनसंसर्गात्। नो चेदिदं सर्वं व्यर्थमिति भावः। रसः शृङ्गारोऽनुरागो वा। कण्ठावलम्बनमालिङ्गनम्। महार्घता दुर्लभत्वम्। तदिह श्लिष्टपदेन नायकव्युत्पत्तिमभिप्रायं च ज्ञात्वा दूतीव्यापारः प्रसरतीति ध्वनितम्॥ **मकरन्दः**। वैदग्ध्यं श्लिष्टपदप्रयोगादिति भावः।

---

१ धिगे. २ ततः ज्ञास्कि वर्नते। ३ तस्या माभि. कुसुमेषुव्या. ३ स्त्रीक, कदम्बाम. ४ मभिहित.

**माधवः**—तया च मदनुयुक्तया समाख्यातम्—इयममात्यभूरिवसोः प्रसूतिर्मालती नामाहं च भर्तृदारिकायाः प्रसादभूमिर्धात्रेयिका लवङ्गिका नामेति ।

**कलहंसः**—( सहर्षम् । ) किं नाम मालतीति । दिष्ट्या विलसितं खलु भगवता देवेन कुसुमायुधेन । जित[2]मस्माभिः । ( किं णाम मालदित्ति । दिट्ठिआ विलसिदं क्खु भअवदा देवेण कुसुमाउहेण । जिदं अह्मेहिं ।)

**मकरन्दः**—( स्वगतम् ) अमात्यभूरिवसोरात्मजेत्यपर्याप्तिर्बहुमानस्य । अपि च मालती मालतीति मोदते भगवती कामन्दकी । तां च । राजानन्दनाय प्रार्थयते[4] इति किंवदन्ती श्रूयते ।

**माधवः**—तया चाहमनुरुध्यमानस्तां बकुलमालामात्मनः कण्ठादवतार्य दत्तवान् । असौ पुनरभिनिविष्टया दृशा मालतीमुखावलोकनविहस्ततया विषमविरचितैकभागां तामेव बहुमन्यमाना महानयं प्रसाद इति गृहीतवती । अनन्तरं च यात्राभङ्गप्रचलितस्य महतः पौरजनस्य संकुलेन विघटितायां तस्यामागतोऽस्मि ।

**मकरन्दः**—वयस्य मालत्या अपि स्नेहदर्शनात्सुश्लिष्टमेतत् । योपि हि कपोलपाण्डुतादिभिश्चिह्नसूचितः प्राक्प्रवृद्धस्तस्याः कामाभिष्वङ्गः सोऽपि त्वन्निबन्धन इति व्यक्तमेवैतत् । एतत्तु न ज्ञायते क्व दृष्टपूर्वस्तया वयस्य इति । न खलु तादृश्यो महाभागधेया[11]ः कुमार्योन्यत्रासक्तचेतसो भूत्वापरत्र चक्षूरागि[12]ण्यो भवन्ति । अपि च ।

---

**माधवः** । अनुयुक्तया पृष्टया । प्रसूतिरपत्यम् । प्रसादभूमिर्विश्वासस्थानं तस्याः । तव च प्रसादभूमिरनुकम्पापात्रं मालादानात् । **कलहंसः** । अत्र विलसितं विजृम्भितम् । अनयोरन्योन्यानुरागादिति भावः । **मकरन्दः** । बहुमानस्य गौरवस्यापर्याप्तिरनवधिकत्वम् । अनभियोज्यत्वरक्षत्वादियोगादिति भावः । **माधवः** । अनुरुध्यमानो मद्युयाच्यमानः असौलवङ्गिका । अभिनिविष्टयातियत्नान्निवेशितया । विहस्ततया व्याकुलतया । **महानयं प्रसाद इति** । यतो न वस्तुनि प्रेम किंतु गुणेष्विति भावः । **मकरन्दः** । सुश्लिष्टं निश्चितम् । दृष्टपूर्वः पूर्वं दृष्टः । तादृश्यो महाकुलजाः । चक्षूरागानुरागयोरेकविषयत्वं भरतमतम् । अन्यदप्यनु-

---

१ एकापत्यरत्नं. २ तज्जित०.३ च किल. ४ याचते. ५ चानुबध्य०,अभ्यर्थ्य०.६ प्रतिगृ. ७ पौरनैगम, पौराङ्गना. ८ चिह्नः. ९ प्रागनुरागः. १० भिषक्कः. ११ धेयजन्मानः । १२ चानुरागिण्यः.

**अन्योन्यसंभिन्नदृशां सखीनां**
**तस्यास्त्वयि प्रागनुरागचिह्नम् ।**
**कस्यापि कोऽपीति निवेदितं च**
**धात्रेयिकायाश्चतुरं वचश्च ॥ ३३ ॥**

**कलहंसः**—( उपसृत्य । ) इदं च । (एदं अ । ) ( इति चित्रफलकं दर्शयति । )

( उभौ पश्यतः । )

**मकरन्दः**—कलहंसक केनैतन्माधवस्य प्रतिच्छंदकमभिलिखितम् ।

**कलहंसः**—येनैवास्य हृदयमपहृतम् । ( जेण जेव्व से हिअअं अवहरिदं । )

**मकरन्दः**—अपि मालत्या ।

**कलहंसः**—अथ किम् । ( अह इं । )

**माधवः**—वयस्य मकरन्द प्रसन्नप्रायस्ते वितर्कः ।

**मकरन्दः**—कलहंसक कुतोऽस्याधिगमः ।

**कलहंसः**—मया तावन्मन्दारिकाहस्तात् । तयापि लवङ्गिकासकाशात् । ( मेए दाव मन्दारिआहत्थादो ताए वि लवङ्गिआसआसादो । )

**मकरन्दः**—अथ किमाह मन्दारिका माधवालेख्यप्रयोजनं मालत्याः ।

**कलहंसः**—उत्कण्ठाविनोद इति । ( उक्कण्ठाविणोदो त्ति । )

**मकरन्दः**—वयस्य माधव सर्वथा समाश्वसिहि ।

---

रागचिह्नमाह—**अन्योन्येत्यादि** । त्वयि तस्याः प्रागनुरागचिह्नं व्यक्तमेवास्ति । कथम् । सखीनामन्योन्यसंगतदृशां कस्यपि कोऽपीति निवेदनमेकम् । कथमन्यथा सखीजनस्त्वां वीक्ष्य कटाक्षयति तां कथं वा सखीजनो वदत्येवमिति भावः । अपरं लवङ्गिकाया व्युत्पन्नं वचनम् । कथमन्यथा कुतूहलिनीत्यादि वदतीयमिति भावः । ' संगते दारिते भिन्नः ' इति विश्वः ॥ ३३ ॥ **कलहंसः** । अत्र येन जनेनापहृतम् । यन्निबन्धनोऽस्य कामविकार इति भावः ॥ **मकरन्दः** । मालत्या लिखितमित्यर्थः ॥ **कलहंसः** । अथ किं स्वीकारे ॥ **माधवः** । वितर्क ऊहः । **मकरन्दः** । अधिगमः प्राप्तिः ॥ **कलहंसः** । उत्कण्ठाविनोद इति । माधवानुरक्ता मालती तमननुप्राप्तवती चित्रलिखितालोकनेनापि रमत इति भावः ॥

---

१ कोऽप्येष इतीहितं. २ अस्मात्परम्—माधवः–किं चान्यत् । मकरन्दः–धात्रे० इति केचित्. ३ एदं चित्तम्. ४ अपि नाम. ५ मह ( मम ).

या कौमुदी नयनयोर्भवतः सुजन्मा
तस्या भवानपि मनोरथबन्धबन्धुः।
तत्संगमं प्रति सखे न हि संशयोऽस्ति
यस्मिन्विधिश्च मदनश्च कृताभियोगः[1] ॥ ३४ ॥

द्रष्टव्यस्वरूपा च भवतो[2] विकारहेतुस्तदत्रैवालिख्यतां मालती।

**माधवः**—यदभिरुचितं वयस्याय। तदुपनय चित्रफलकं चित्रवर्तिकाश्च[3]। (मकरन्द उपनयति।)

**माधवः**—(लिखन्।) सखे मकरन्द

वारं वारं तिरयति दृशोरुद्गमं[4] बाष्पपूर-
स्तत्संकल्पोपहितजडिम स्तम्भमभ्येति गात्रम्।
सद्यः स्विद्यन्नयमविरतोत्कम्पलोलाङ्गुलीकः
पाणिर्लेखाविधिषु नितरां वर्तते किं करोमि ॥ ३५ ॥

---

**येत्यादि**। हे सखे तत्संगमं प्रति नैव संशयोऽस्ति। भवतो नयनयोर्या कौमदी ज्योत्स्ना आनन्दकारित्वात्। तस्या मनोरथबन्धुरभिलाषनिबन्धनाय प्रियः शोभनजन्मा भवानपि। ननु परस्परानुरागेऽपि विधिकामवैमुख्यान्न सिद्धिरत आह—यस्मिन्संगमे विधिमदनौ कृतप्रयत्नौ। चक्षुःप्रीत्या काम एतद्देशानयनाद्विधिः कृताभियोग इत्यर्थः। अभियोगाच्च कन्यालाभः। यदाह—'अभियोगाद्धि कन्याया लाभो निश्चित एव च।' इति ॥ ३४ ॥ चित्रेण माधवचित्तानुरागमुद्दीपयति—**द्रष्टव्येति**। **माधवः**। वयस्यायेत्यत्र 'रुच्यर्थानां प्रीयमाणः' इति संप्रदानता। अधुना मनःसङ्गे हर्षात्सात्त्विकभावमाह **वारं वारमित्यादि**। अयं मम पाणिर्लेखाविधिषु चित्रनिर्माणेषु नितरामत्यर्थं वर्तत एव न तु लिखति। अत्र किं करोमि। यथा तथा लिखामीत्यर्थः। 'नतराम्' इति पाठे नैव वर्तत इत्यर्थः। यतो बाष्पपूरस्तदनुध्यानादानन्दाश्रुप्रवाहो वारंवारं दृशोरुद्गमं प्रचारं तिरयति छादयति। तस्याः संकल्पेन चिन्तनेनोपहितो जडिमा सर्वकार्याप्रतिपत्तिर्यस्य तद्गात्रं शरीरं स्तम्भं निश्चलत्वमभ्येति। 'हर्षभयरोगविस्मयविषादमददोषसंभवः स्तम्भः।' इति भरतः। कीदृशः। सद्यो लिखनोपक्रमकाल एव स्विद्यन्नार्द्रीभवन्। अविरतोत्कम्पेनाधिकचलनेन लोलाङ्गुली यत्र सः। अङ्गुल्या लिखनहेतुतया तच्चापल्यादलिखनं सूचितम्। तदिहाश्रुस्तम्भस्वेदकम्पा उक्ताः। रोमाञ्चादिकं च नोक्तम्। तेषां लिखनाप्रतिकूलत्वात्। सर्वमिदं सात्त्विकं हर्षात्। यदाह—'क्रोधभयहर्षलज्जादुःखश्रमरोगतापपीडाभ्यः। व्यायामसाध्वसादेः स्वेदः स्यात्पीडनेनापि॥ शीतभयहर्षरोषस्पर्शजरारोगजः कम्पः॥' इति ॥ ३५ ॥ अधुना मालती चित्रं

---

१ योगो. २ तत्रभवतः. ३ वर्ति. ४ दृशावुद्गतः.

तथापि व्यवसितोऽस्मि। (चिरादालिख्य दर्शयति।)

**मकरन्दः**—(चित्रं निर्वर्ण्य।) उपपन्नस्तावदत्रभवतोऽभिष्वङ्गः। (सकौतुकम्।) कथमचिरेणैव निर्माय लिखितः श्लोकः। (वाचयति)

**जगति जयिनस्ते ते भावा नवेन्दुकलादयः**
**प्रकृतिमधुराः सन्त्येवान्ये मनो मदयन्ति ये।**
**मम तु यदियं याता लोके विलोचनचन्द्रिका**
**नयनविषयं जन्मन्येकः स एव महोत्सवः॥ ३६॥**

(प्रविश्य सत्वरं)

**मन्दारिका**—कलहंसक पदानुसारेणोपलब्धोऽसि। (माधवमक-

द्रक्ष्यतीति सानुरागोपालम्भं श्लोकं लिखति—**जगतीत्यादि**। ते ते नवेन्दुकलादयो भावाः पदार्था जयिनो मदजनने सर्वत्राप्रतिहताः स्वभावतो मनोज्ञा अन्ये सन्त्येव ये मनो मदयन्ति। मम पुनर्न मदहेतवः प्रत्युत दाहहेतव एवेति भावः। अत्र जयिन इत्यनेन कालविशेषे देशविशेषे च जयशालिन आनन्दसंदोहदा इत्युक्तम्। भाव्यन्ते भावनामर्हन्ति सुन्दरतयेति भावाः। मालतीभिन्नाः सहृदयहृदयाह्लादकाः। ते त इति वीप्सया चन्द्रादयो देवादयश्च प्रसिद्धा एवेति दर्शितम्। सर्वनाम्ना च ये यत्र चेतःप्रतिष्ठास्ते तत्र गृह्यन्त इति ध्वनितम्। तुशब्देनान्येषां तथात्वं तत्संप्रतिपत्तिद्वारेत्युक्तम्। कस्तर्हि मदहेतुरत आह—मम पुनरियं चित्रलिखिता मालती नयनयोर्ज्योत्स्ना यन्नेत्रगोचरं प्राप्ता स एवैकोऽत्र जन्मनि महोत्सवः। अत्र किं पुनः संभोगादिकमित्यनुरागः। स एव महोत्सवः। अनुरागो भवतु मा वा भूदित्युपालम्भः। एतेनात्यन्तानुरागो मालत्यां दर्शितः। एकपदेनान्येषामाविर्भावेऽपि नानन्दकत्वम्। अत एव स एवेत्यनेन तल्लोपः। जन्मनीति सामान्यनिर्देशेन समस्तजन्मनि मालतीतुल्या नास्तीति व्यज्यते। वाचिकोऽयं रसः। यदाह—'रसानुरूपैरालापैः श्लोकैर्वाक्यैः पदैस्तथा। नानालंकारसंयुक्तैर्वाचिको रस उच्यते॥' इति। इह प्रकृतिमधुरत्वेऽपि मालत्या एव मदजननाद्व्यतिरेकालंकारः। प्रियाख्यानात्प्रियोऽलंकारः। विलोचनचन्द्रिकेति रूपकम्। न चात्र नवेन्दुकला प्रतिपच्चन्द्रकला सा च न मदहेतुरिति वाच्यम्। यतो नूयत इति नवः। प्रशस्तेन्दुरित्यर्थः। यद्वा नवं नूतनमिन्दुकलादिकं चेति द्वन्द्वः। यद्वा नवः सागरादुत्थितमात्रः। पूर्ण एवेत्यर्थः॥ ३६॥ **प्रविश्येति**। यत्र पटीक्षेपेण प्रवेशस्तत्र प्रविश्येत्युक्तिः। अनुसारोऽनुसरणम्। एतेऽपि ये चित्रफलके लिखिताः। इह गौरवादेकत्वे बहु-

१ अवहितः. २ विलोक्य. ३ जाता. ४ मनोरथ. ५ पटाक्षेपेण. ६ कलहंस कलहंस चोर चोर.

रन्दौ विलोक्य सलज्जम् । ) कथमेतावपि महानुभावाविहैव । ( उपसृत्य । ) प्रणमामि । ( कलहंसअ पआणुसारेण उवलद्धोसि । कधं एदे वि महाणुहावा इह जेव्व । ) ( पणमामि । )

उभौ—मन्दारिके इत आस्यताम् ।

मन्दा०—( उपविश्य । ) कलहंसक उपनय मे चित्रफलकम् । ( कलहंसअ उवणेहि मे चित्तफलअं )

कल०—गृहाणैतत् । ( गेह्ण एदं । )

मन्दा०—( विलोक्य । ) कलहंसक केन किंनिमित्तं वात्र मालत्यालिखिता । ( कलहंसअ केण किंणिमित्तं वा एत्थ मालदी आलिहिदा । )

कलहंसः—य एव यन्निमित्तं मालत्या । ( जो जेव्व जंणिमित्तं मालदीए । )

मन्दा०—( सहर्षम् । ) दिष्ट्या दर्शितफलमिदानीं विज्ञानं प्रजापतेः । ( दिट्ठिआ दंसिदफलं दाणिं विण्णाणं पआवईणो । )

मक०—मन्दारिके यदत्र वस्तुन्येष ते वल्लभः कथयति अपि तत्तथा ।

मन्दा०—महाभाग अथ किम् । ( महाभाअ अध इं । )

मक०—क्व पुनर्मालती माधवं प्राग्दृष्टवती ।

मन्दा०—लवङ्गिका भणति वातायनगतेति । ( लवङ्गिआ भणादि वादाअणगदत्ति । )

मक०—वयस्य नन्वमात्यभवनासन्नरथ्ययैव बहुशः संचरावहे । तदुपपन्नमेतत् ।

मन्दा०—अनुमन्येतां मां महानुभावौ । यावदेतद्भगवतो देवस्य

---

वचनम् । द्वित्वे वा बहुवचनम् ॥ मालत्या अभिलिखित इति शेषः । तथा च मालत्या विनोदाय माधवो लिखितस्तेनापि सा तदर्थं लिखितेत्यर्थः । **मन्दारिका** । अत्र विज्ञानं शिल्पिकौशलम् । अनुरूपानुरागादनयोरिति भावः । अवितथं सत्यम् । **तत्तथेति** । एवमेतन्मालत्यैव माधवप्रतिच्छन्दकं लिखितमित्यर्थः । वातायनगता दृष्टव-

---

१ दृष्ट्वा. २ एत्थ ( अत्र ). ३ आगम्यताम्. ४ गृहीत्वा वि०, निरूप. ५ केन उण ( पुनः ). ६ सह० स्वगतं. ७ वइणा ८ सखि मन्दा०. ९ अप्यवितथं तत्. १० तत्तहा. ११ महाभागौ.

मदनस्य सुचरितं प्रियसख्यै लवङ्गिकायै निवेदयामि। (अणुमण्णन्तु मं महा-णुभाआ। जाव एदं भअवदो देवस्स मअणस्स सुचरिदं पिअसहीए लवङ्गिआए णिवेदेमि।)

**मक०**—प्राप्तावसरमेतद्भवत्याः।

(मन्दारिका चित्रफलकं गृहीत्वा निष्क्रान्ता।)

**मकरन्दः**—वयस्य खरतरकिरणोयं भगवान्सहस्रदीधितिरलंकरोति मध्यमह्नस्तदेहि संस्त्यायमेव गच्छावः। (इत्युत्थाय परिक्रामतः।)

**माधवः**—एवं हि मन्ये।

**घर्माम्भोविसरविवर्तनैरिदानीं**
**मुग्धाक्ष्याः परिजनवारसुन्दरीणाम्।**
**तत्प्रातर्विहितविचित्रपत्ररेखा-**
**वैदग्ध्यं जहति कपोलकुङ्कुमानि॥ ३७॥**

अपि च।

**उन्मीलन्मुकुलकरालकुन्दकोश-**
**प्रश्च्योतद्घनमकरन्दगन्धबन्धो।**
**तामीषत्प्रचलविलोचनां नताङ्गी-**
**मालिङ्गन्पवन मम स्पृशाङ्गमङ्गम्॥ ३८॥**

---

तीत्यर्थः। लवङ्गिकाया द्वारा माधवानुरागो मालत्यामस्त्वित्यर्थः॥ **मकरन्दः**। संस्त्यायो गृहम्। 'संस्त्यायः संनिवेशे च संघातेऽपि च दृश्यते।' इति मेदिनीकरः॥ **घर्मेत्यादि**। मालत्याः परिजनवारसुन्दरीणां कपोलकुङ्कुमानि प्रातर्विरचितविचित्रपत्रावलीवैदग्ध्यं यत्तदधुना मध्याह्ने जहति त्यजन्ति। कैः घर्माम्भसो विसरस्य समूहस्य विवर्तनैर्विविधजलकणैः करणैः। अनेन नायिकायाः सुकुमारतया निःसहत्वमुक्तम्। मालत्याः कन्यात्वेन पत्रावल्यभावात्परिजनेत्युक्तम्। माङ्गल्यतया प्रातरेव कुङ्कुमेन पत्रावलीलिखनम्। अत एव वसन्तकालस्य शीतत्वात्कुङ्कुमेन भूषाकरणमिति मतमपास्तम्। 'धारासिक्तवसुंधरासुरभयः' इत्यभिधानाद्वर्षाकालप्रस्तावात्। 'समूहनिवहव्यूहसंदोहविसरव्रजाः।' इत्यमरः। इहोन्मादावस्था। अत एवात्र तत्संबद्धा कथा यदाह—'तत्संबद्धां कथां युङ्क्ते सर्वावस्थागतामिह।' इति॥ ३७॥ **उन्मीलदिति**। हे पवन उन्मीलन्मुकुलेन विकचकोरकेण करालाद्विषमात्कुन्दगुच्छात्क्षरन्निबिडमकरन्दश्च गन्धश्च तयोर्बन्धो। मकरन्दस्य यो गन्धस्तद्बन्धो तत्सह-

---

१ अणुमण्णन्तु मडाभाओ: महाभाआ. २ णिवेदिस्सामि. ३ भाण्डम्. ४ मध्यान्हो वर्तते। तदेहि. ५ ०रीभिः. ६ कुण्डलानि. ७ गुच्छ, कोषात्. ८ प्रच्यो०. ९ ललित, प्रचलितलो०.

**मकरन्दः**—( स्वगतम् । )

> **अभिहन्ति हन्त कथमेष माधवं**
> **सुकुमारकायमनवग्रहः[1] स्मरः ।**
> **अचिरेण वैकृतविवर्त[2]दारुणः**
> **कलभं कठोर इव कूटपाकलः[3] ॥ ३९ ॥**

तदत्र[4] भगवती कामन्दका नः शरणम् ।

**माधवः**—( स्वगतम्[5] । ) आश्चर्यम् ।

> **पश्यामि तामित इतः पुरतश्च पश्चा-**
> **दन्तर्बहिः[6] परित एव विवर्तमानाम् ।**
> **उद्बुद्धमुग्धकनकाब्जनिभं वहन्ती-**
> **मासक्त[7]तिर्यगपवर्तित[8]दृष्टि वक्त्रम् ॥ ४० ॥**

---

चरेति वा । ईदृशोऽपि त्वं मे न सुखाय किंतु तापायातस्तां मालतीमिपदालिङ्गन्ममाङ्गमङ्गं प्रत्यङ्गं स्पृश । अमृतमयतदङ्गसङ्गशीतस्त्वं मम तापशान्तये भविष्यसीति भावः । यद्वा तदीयतापशान्तिर्भवत्वित्यनुरागात्तामालिङ्गन्नित्युक्तम् । तां कीदृशीम् । प्रचलनेत्रां विरहे पवनस्य दुःसहत्वेन भयादितस्ततः क्षिप्तनेत्राम् । अत एव नम्रीभवदङ्गां च । इह विषमकुन्दकोशसंचरणेन गतिप्रतिबन्धान्मान्द्यं मकरन्दसङ्गाच्छैत्यं गन्धबन्धुतया सौगन्ध्यं च वायोरुक्तम् । ईषदालिङ्गन्नित्यनेन सुरभिपदेनाभिघातनिःसहत्वं मालत्या-मुक्तम् । ‘ करालो दन्तुरे तुङ्गे ’ इत्यमरः ॥ ३८ ॥ माधवस्यानङ्गदुःसहत्वमाह **अभिहन्तीत्यादि** । एष स्मरोऽनवग्रहः प्रतिरोधशून्यः कोमलकायं माधवं कथमचिरेणैवाभिहन्ति । हन्तानुकम्पायाम् । ‘ हन्त हर्षेऽनुकम्पायाम् ’ इत्यमरः । कीदृशः । विकृतस्य भावो वैकृतं तस्य विवर्तोऽन्यथावस्थानं तेन दारुणो दुःखदः । यथा कलभं करिबालकं मृदुकायं कठोरो दुःसहः कूटपाकलो हस्तिवातज्वरः अचिरेण हन्ति तथेत्यर्थः । सोऽप्यनवग्रहोऽप्रतिकरणीयो विकृतिविवर्तदारुणश्च भवति । ‘ गजं वातज्वरो हन्ति तथा वै कूटपाकलः । ’ इति वैद्यके ॥ ३९ ॥ **मक-रन्दः** । इदं स्वगतम् । स्वयमनध्यवसायादाह—**तदत्रेति** । अत एव भगवती ज्ञानसंपन्नेह शरणं रक्षिका । द्वितीयाङ्कावतारोऽयम् । यदाह–‘ अङ्कावसाने यत्रैव भाविनोऽङ्कस्य सूच्यते । वस्तुबीजमुपोद्घातैः सोऽङ्कावतार इष्यते ॥ ’ इदानीमु-न्मादावस्थोद्भावनाबलात्तन्मयत्वमाह—**पश्यामीत्यादि** । तामेकामेव विवर्त-मानां प्रपञ्चरूपां परितः सर्वत्र पश्यामीत्याश्चर्यम् । विवर्तमानत्वमेवाह । इत इत उभयपार्श्वे । पुरतोऽग्रे । पश्चात्पृष्ठे । अन्तर्मनसि । बहिस्त्वग्भागे । अनेन तदा-वेशात्सर्वत्र तन्मयत्वमुक्तम । यदाह–‘ यो येन भावनाविष्टः सुखदेनेतरेण वा । स

---

१ ग्रहस्मरः. २ विवर्ण. ३ पालकः. ४ अत्रभवती. ५ आत्म०. ६ बहिश्च परितश्च. ७ मासङ्ग,-ङ्गि. ८ वर्जित.

( प्रकाशम् ) वयस्य मम हि संप्रति

**प्रसरति परिमाथी कोऽप्ययं देहदाह-**
**स्तिरयति करणानां ग्राहकत्वं प्रमोहः ।**
**रणरणकविवृद्धिं बिभ्रदांवर्तमान**
**ज्वलति हृदयमन्तस्तन्मयत्वं च धत्ते ॥ ४१ ॥**

( इति निष्क्रान्ताः सर्वे । )

**इति बकुलवीथी नाम प्रथमोऽङ्कः ।**

---

तदाहितसंस्कारः सर्वं पश्यति तन्मयम् ॥ ' परित इत्यत्र ' पर्यभिभ्यां च ' इति तसिः । कीदृशीम् । वक्त्रं वहन्तीम् । उद्बद्धं विकसितं मुग्धं कान्तं यत्सुवर्णपद्मं ततो निरतिशया भा दीप्तिर्यस्य तत् । तन्निभं तत्तुल्यमिति वा । एतेन गौरीत्वमुक्तम् । आसक्तेन मय्यासक्त्या तिर्यगपवर्तिता दृष्टिर्यस्य तत् । यथा यान्त्या तयाहं दृष्टस्तथैव तां पश्यामीति भावः ॥ ४० ॥ अधुना सर्वाकारेण पीडामाह—**प्रसरतीत्यादि** । वयस्य पश्य । संप्रति मम कोऽप्यनिर्वचनीयस्वरूपो देहदाहः प्रसरति व्याप्नोति । अत एव परिमाथी सर्वतो मथनशीलः । करणानामिन्द्रियाणामर्थग्राहकत्वं मे प्रमोहस्तिरयति पिदधाति । सर्वेन्द्रियसंमोहो ममेत्यर्थः । मम गात्रं शरीरम् । कर्तृ । रणरणकस्य वियोगतरोर्वृद्धिमुपचयं बिभ्रदावर्तिं भ्राम्यदस्ति । यद्वा रणरणकः कामस्तस्य विवृद्धिमधिकाधिकदशागामित्वम् ' मारो रणरणः कामो विषयः ' इत्युत्पलिनी । तथा मम हृदयम् । कर्तृ । अन्तर्दहति । ज्वलतीत्यर्थः । तन्मयत्वं मालतीमयत्वं च धत्ते । ईदृशी मम दशा सद्य एव विपत्तिमादधाति । तदत्र यथावत्त्वमाचरेति भावः । अत्रावर्तीति व्याधिः । ज्वलतीत्युद्वेगः । तन्मयत्वमित्युन्मादः । हृदयस्य तु तन्मयत्वधारणेन दुःसहदशायामपि जीवनाशा दर्शिता । ' करणं क्षेत्रगात्रेन्द्रियेष्वपि ' इत्यमरः ॥ ४१ ॥ **निष्क्रान्ता इति** । बीजार्थं युक्तं कृत्वा निष्क्रमो भवति । यदाह—' बीजार्थं युक्तियुक्तं च कृत्वा कार्यं यथारसम् । निष्क्रमं तत्र कुर्वीत सर्वेषां रङ्गवर्तिनाम् ॥ ' इति ॥ **बकुलवीथीति** । 'नानारससमायुक्ता सन्धिद्वयविभूषिता । अर्थप्रकृतिभिः पूर्णा स्यादेकाङ्का तु वीथिका ॥ त्रिभिः पात्रैः प्रयोज्येयमुत्तमाधममध्यमैः । कर्तव्या नायिका चात्र शृङ्गारद्वयसंयुता ' ॥ इति भरतः ॥

प्रासूत यं रत्नधरो गुणाढ्यो गुणाढ्यरूपा दमयन्तिका च ।
जगद्धरं तत्कृतटिप्पणेऽङ्को गतोऽयमाद्यो रसराजराजी ॥

**इति प्रथमोऽङ्कः ।**

---

१ प्रमोदः. २ बिभ्रदावर्ति गात्रम्. ३ इति मालतीमाधवे ब०, श्रीमन्मालतीमाधवनाम्नि नाटके ।

# द्वितीयोऽङ्कः।

( ततः प्रविशतश्चेट्यौ । )

**प्रथमा**—हला संगीतशालापरिसरेऽवलोकिताद्वितीया त्वं किं मन्त्रयन्त्यासीः । ( हला संगीदसालापरिसरे अवलोइदादुदीआ तुमं किं मन्तअन्ती आसी । )

**द्वितीया**—सखि तेन किल माधवप्रियवयस्येन मकरन्देन सकल एव मदनोद्यानवृत्तान्तो भगवत्यै निवेदितः । ( सहि तेण किल माहवप्पिअवअस्सेण मअरन्देण सअलो ज्जेव्व मअणुज्जाणवुत्तन्तो भअवदीए णिवेदिदो । )

**प्रथमा**—ततः किम् । ( तदो किं । )

**द्वितीया**—ततो भर्तृदारिकां द्रष्टुकामया भगवत्या प्रवृत्तिनिमित्तमवलोकितानुप्रेषिता । मयापि तस्यै कथितं यथा लवङ्गिकाद्वितीया विविक्ते भर्तृदारिका वर्तत इति । ( तदो भट्टिदारिअं दट्ठुकामाए भअवदीए पउत्तिणिमित्तं अवलोइदा अणुप्पेसिदा । मए वि ताए कधिदं जधा लवङ्गिआदुदीआ विवित्ते भट्टिदारिआ वट्टदि त्ति । )

**प्रथमा**—हला लवङ्गिका खलु केसरकुसुमान्यवचिनोमीति मदनोद्यानादेव नागता तत् किं सांप्रतं संप्राप्ता । ( हला[1] लवङ्गिआ क्खु केसरकुसुमाइं अवइणुम्मि त्ति मअणुज्जाणादो ज्जेव्व णागदा ता किं संपदं संपत्ता । )

---

अधुना वकुलमालादानाय लवङ्गिका गता तां प्रतीक्षमाणा मालती सौधारूढा तन्मार्गं पश्यति मकरन्दश्च 'कामन्दकी नः शरणम्' इत्युक्त्वा तां तत्कथनाय गतः इति स्थिते चेट्योः प्रवेशः । चेटीभाषा सौरसेनी । यदाह—'नायिकायां च चेट्यां च सौरसेनी प्रयुज्यते' । न च 'नाटकप्रकरणयोरङ्काः कार्याः प्रत्यक्षनायकाः । इति भरतादिह माधवप्रवेशाभावात्कथमङ्कावतार इति देश्यम् । मालत्या नायकत्वेन तत्सत्त्वात् । यदाह—'गुरुः पुरोहितोऽमात्यो नायको नायिकापि च । सार्थवाह इति प्रोक्ताः षडेते नायका बुधैः ॥' इति ॥ **प्रथमा** । अत्र हला सखि । परिसरे निकटे ॥ **द्वितीया** । अत्र वृत्तान्तो वार्ता ॥ **द्वितीया** । भर्तृदारिका मालती । प्रवृत्तिर्वार्ता । विविक्तं विजनम् । इह मकरन्दाज्ज्ञातमाधवावस्थया कामन्दक्या प्रकृतसिद्धयेऽवसरज्ञानार्थं मालतीवार्तां ज्ञातुं प्रहितावलोकितेति भावः ॥ **प्रथमा** । अत्र केसरो वकुलः । अवचिनोमि त्रोटयामि । इति

---

१ सहि. २ भअवदी कामन्दई किं वि. ३ सहि. ४ गआ मअणुज्जाणं किं संपदं णिउत्ता.

**द्वितीया**—अथ किम् । तां खलु परीवर्तमानामेव हस्ते गृहीत्वा प्रतिषिद्धपरिजना भर्तृदारिकोपर्यलिन्दकं समारूढा । ( अध इं । तं खु परावट्टन्तीं जेव्व हत्थे गेह्णिअ पडिसिद्धपरिअणा भट्टिदारिआ उअरिअलिन्दअं समारूढा । )

**प्रथमा**—नूनं तस्य महानुभावस्य संकथयात्मानं विनोदयति । ( णूणं तस्स महाणुहावस्स संकधाए अत्ताणं विणोदेदि ।

**द्वितीया**—( निःश्वस्य । ) कुतस्तस्या आश्वासः । एतेनाद्य सविशेषदर्शनेनातिभूमिं खलु तस्या अभिनिवेशो गमिष्यति । अन्यच्च । कल्य एव नन्दनस्य कारणान्महाराजो भर्तृदारिकां प्रार्थयमानोऽमात्येन विज्ञप्तः । ( कुदो से आस्सासो । एदिणा अज्ज सविसेसदंसणेण अदिभूमिं क्खु ताए अहिणिवेसो गमिस्सदि । अण्णं अ । कल्लि एव्व णन्दणस्य कारणादो महाराओ भट्टिदारिअं पत्थअन्तो अमच्चेण विण्णत्तो । )

**प्रथमा**—किमिति । ( किं त्ति । )

**द्वितीया**—प्रभवति निजस्य कन्यकाजनस्य महाराज इति । तज्जात आमरणं खलु मालत्या हृदयशल्यं माधवानुराग इति तर्कयामि । ( पहवदि णिअस्स कण्णआजणस्स महाराओ त्ति । तां जादो आमरणं खु मालदीए हिअअसल्लं माहवाणुराओ त्ति तक्केमि । )

**प्रथमा**—अपि नाम भगवत्यत्र किमपि भगवतीत्वं दर्शयिष्यति । ( अवि णाम भअवदी एत्थ किं वि भअवदित्तणं दंसइस्सदि । )

**द्वितीया**—अयि असंबद्धमनोरथे एहि । ( अइ असंबद्धमणोरहे एहि । )

---

हेतौ । **द्वितीया** । अत्र परापतन्ती सत्वरमागच्छन्ती । कृतकार्यत्वेन सत्वरमागमनं भृत्यधर्मः । उपर्यलिन्दकम् । बाह्यपटशालाया उपरीत्यर्थः ॥ **द्वितीया** । अत्रातिभूमिमुत्कर्षम् । अभिनिवेश आसक्तिः । कल्यं प्रातः । ' कल्लि ' इति पाठे कल्लिशब्दो देशी पूर्वदिनवाचकः । अत एव ' कल्लि पल्लीनिवासिनः ' इति ॥ **प्रथमा** । किं विज्ञप्तमित्यर्थः ॥ **द्वितीया** । इदमभूताहरणं वाक्यम् । यदाह—' अभूताहरणं तत्स्याद्यद्वाक्यं कपटाश्रयम् ' ॥ वाक्यतत्त्वमज्ञात्वाह । अत्र दुःखदत्वे शल्यमिव शल्यम् । अजहल्लिङ्गम् ॥ **प्रथमा** । अत्रापि नाम संभावनायाम् । भगवतीत्वं ज्ञानादिवैभवम् । निष्क्रान्ते

---

१ परापतन्तीं ( टी. ). २ अपरि०. ३ एतन्नास्ति क्वचित् । ४ अदो आमरणं जादो.

[ इति परिक्रम्य निष्क्रान्ते । ]

**प्रवेशकः ।**

( ततः प्रविशत्युपविष्टा सोत्कण्ठा मालती लवङ्गिका च । )

**मालती**—हुं सखि ततस्ततः । ( हुं सहि तदो तदो । )

**लवङ्गिका**—ततस्तेन महानुभावेनोपनीता म इयं बकुलमाला । ( इति मालामर्पयति । ) ( तदो तेण महाणुभावेण उवणीदा मे इअं बउलमाला । )

**माल०**—( गृहीत्वा सहर्षं निर्वर्ण्य । ) सखि एकपार्श्वविषमप्रतिबद्धा खल्वेषा विरचना । ( सहि एक्कपासविसमपडिबद्धा क्खु एसा विरअणा । )

**लव०**—अत्र तावदरमणीयत्वे त्वमेवापराद्धासि । ( एत्थ दाव अरमणिअत्तणे तुमं जेव्व अवरद्धासि । )

**माल०**—कथमिव । ( कहं विअ । )

**लव०**—येन स दूर्वाश्यामलाङ्गस्तथा विहस्तीकृतः । ( जेण सो दुव्वासामलङ्गो तह विहत्थीकिदो । )

**मालती**—प्रियसखि लवङ्गिके सर्वथाश्वासनशीलासि । ( पिअसहि लवङ्गिए सव्वहा आसासणसीलासि । )

---

चेष्टौ । **प्रवेशक इति** । वक्तव्यस्य च बहुत्वाद्रसभङ्गप्रसङ्गेनान्योक्त्या प्रवेशकः । यदाह—'यस्तु प्रयोगबाहुल्यादङ्केऽर्थो न समाप्यते । बहुवृत्तान्तोऽल्पकथैः स विधेयः प्रवेशकैः ॥ अङ्कानामन्तरालेषु संक्षिप्तार्थप्रयोजनैः । भृत्यवर्गे कथाबद्धो विज्ञेयोऽयं प्रवेशकः ॥' **मालती** । हुं प्रश्ने । लवङ्गिकाकथितबकुलमालाप्रार्थनापर्यन्तश्रुतवार्तया माल्त्याग्रिमवार्ताकर्णनोत्कया पृच्छयत इत्यर्थः । विरहोत्कण्ठितेयम् । यदाह—'अनेककार्यसंयुक्तो यस्या नागच्छति प्रियः । तदनागमदुःखार्ता विरहोत्कण्ठिता तु सा ॥ प्रियकथापरत्वे मोट्टायितभावोऽयम् । यदाह—'श्रुत्वा कथां प्रियजनस्य सखीमुखेभ्यः कर्णोदरस्थितचलत्तनुतर्जनीकम् । यत्साङ्गभङ्गमिह जृम्भितमङ्गनानां मोट्टायितं तदुदितं कविभिः पुराणैः ॥' **मालती** । प्रतिबद्धा घटिता ॥ **मालती** । मालती माधवचेष्टाकर्णनाकाङ्क्ष्याजानतीवाह—**कथमिव** । कथं ममापराध इत्यर्थः ॥ **लवङ्गिका** । अत्र दूर्वेत्यादिना शृङ्गारित्वे तात्पर्यमुक्तम् । तथानिर्वचनीयप्रकारेण । विहस्तो

---

१ इअं. २ अवरज्झसि ( अपराध्यासि ). ३ मुद्ध (मुग्ध) दुव्वा.

**लव०**—सखि कात्राश्वासनशीलता । ननु भणामि सोऽपि प्रियसख्या मन्दमारुतोद्वेल्लत्प्रफुल्लपण्डरीकविभ्रमाभ्यां प्रथमारब्धबकुलावलीविरचनापदेशसंयमितबलात्कारविस्तृताभ्यां लोचनाभ्यां विजृम्भमाणविस्मयस्तिमितदीर्घपर्यन्तपरिवर्तनाविलासताण्डवितभ्रूलताविडम्बितानङ्गशारङ्गविभ्रमविदग्धमवलोकयन्प्रत्यक्षीकृत एव । ( सहि का एत्थ आसासणसीलदा । णं भणामि । सो वि पिअसहीए मन्दमारुदुव्वेल्लन्तपफुल्लपुण्डरीअविब्भमेहिं पढमारद्धवउलावलीविरअणावदेससंजमिदबलामोडिअवित्थरन्तेहिं लोअणेहिं विअम्भमाणविम्हअत्थिमिददीहपेरन्तपरिअत्तणाविलासतण्डविदभूलदाविडम्बिदाणङ्गसारङ्गविब्भमविअड्ढं अवलोअअन्तो पच्चक्खीकिदो ज्जेव्व । )

**मालती**—( लवङ्गिकां परिष्वज्य । ) आम् । प्रियसखि किं तावत्तस्य महानुभावस्य स्वाभाविका एव ते मुहूर्तसंनिधायिनो जनस्य विप्रलम्भयितृका विलासा आहोस्विद्यथा प्रियसखी संभावयति । ( आम् । पिअसहि किं दाव तस्स महाणुभावस्स साहाविआ ज्जेव्व ते मुहुत्तसंणिधाइणो जणस्स विप्पलम्भइत्तआ विलासा आदु जहा पिअसही संभावेदि । )

---

व्याकुलः । **लवङ्गिका** । **सोपीति** । अत्र स त्वयापि विलोचनाभ्यां पश्यन् प्रत्यक्षीकृतो दृष्ट एवेत्यन्वयः । अपिर्भिन्नक्रमः । उद्वेल्लत्कम्पमानम् । विभ्रमो विशिष्टा भ्रान्तिः सोऽयमित्याकारा । सादृश्यं वा विभ्रमः । माधवस्य पुण्डरीकाक्षत्वात् । विरचनापदेशेन घटनव्याजेन यः संयमोऽन्यादर्शनं तं प्रापिताभ्यां बलामोड्या बलात्कारेण विस्तरं गच्छद्भ्याम् । बलामोडिर्बलात्कारे देशी । यद्यप्यवलोकयन्नित्यनेन लोचनाभ्यामिति प्राप्तं तथापि विशिष्टलोचनप्रतिपादनार्थं तदुक्तम् । विजृम्भमाणो वर्धमानः । स्तिमितः स्निग्धः । दीर्घपर्यन्तमातिदीर्घम् । परिवर्तना पुनःपुनर्गमनं तत्र विलासो विशिष्टदृष्टिव्यापारस्तेन ताण्डवितया नर्तितया भ्रूलतया विडम्बितः समीकृतोऽनङ्गशारङ्गविभ्रमः कामधनुर्विलासस्ततो विदग्धमिति क्रियाविशेषणम् । 'गमनासनपाणिपादचेष्टा सविशेषं नयनभ्रुवां च कर्म । दयितोपगमे यदप्रयत्नात् क्रियते नूनमयं विलास उक्तः ॥' इति भरतः । शारङ्गरङ्गत इति प्रयोगाच्छारङ्गेति भिन्नो रेफः ॥ 'शारङ्गं धनुषि स्मृतम्' इति शाश्वतः । ततस्त्वदवलोकनविकलता मालारम्यत्वे हेतुरिति तात्पर्यमिह ॥ **मालती** । आमिति तदुक्तस्वीकारे । 'अम्मो' इति पाठे अम्मो हर्षे वितर्के वा । विप्रलम्भितो विप्रलम्भं

---

१ मारुअप्पआलिअ ( प्रचलित ). २ संअमण ( संयमन ). ३ विलासुल्लसिअ ( सोल्लसित ). ४ लदाविभाविदानङ्गसंरम्भवि०. ५ हेतुआ ( हेतुकाः ), विप्रलम्भितकाः ( टी० ).

**लव०**—( विहस्य सासूयमिव । ) त्वमपि स्वभावेनैव तस्मिन्नवसरेऽसंगीतकं नर्तितासि । ( तुमं वि सहावेण जेव्व तस्सिं अवसरे असंगीदअं णत्तिदासि । )

**मालती**—( सलज्जं विहस्य । ) हुं ततस्ततः । ( हुं तदो तदो । )

**लव०**—ततः प्रतिनिवर्तमानयात्राजनसंकुलेनान्तरिते तस्मिन्मन्दारिकाया गृहमुपगतास्मि । तस्याः खलु चित्रफलकं प्रभाते हस्तीकृतमासीत् । ( तदो पडिणिउत्तमाणजत्ताजणसंकुलेण अन्तरिदे तस्सिं मन्दारिआए घरं उवगदह्मि । ताए क्खु चित्तफलअं पभादे हत्थीकिदं आसी । )

**मालती**—किंनिमित्तम् । ( किंणिमित्तम् । )

**लव०**—तां खलु माधवानुचरः कलहंसको नाम कामयते । सा तस्य दर्शयिष्यतीति । ततः प्रियनिवेदिका मन्दारिका संवृत्ता । ( तं क्खु माहवाणुअरो कलहंसओ णाम कामेदि । सा तस्स दंसइस्सदित्ति । तदो पिअणिवेदिआ मन्दारिआ संउत्ता । )

**मालती**—( स्वगतम् ) नूनं तेनापि कलहंसकेन तत्प्रतिच्छन्दकमात्मनः प्रभोर्दर्शितं भविष्यति । ( प्रकाशम् । ) सखि किमिदानीं ते प्रियम् । ( णूणं देण वि कलहंसएण [3]तं पडिच्छन्दअं अत्तणो [4]पहुस्स दंसिदं भविस्सदि । ) ( सहि किं दाणिं दे पिअं । )

**लव०**—एतत्खलु संतापितस्य संतापकारिणो दुर्लभमनोरथावेशदुःसहायासदह्यमानचित्तस्य क्षणमात्रनिर्वापकं तव प्रतिच्छन्दकम् । ( इति चित्रं[5] दर्शयति । ) ( एदं क्खु संदाविदस्स[6] संदावआरिणो दुल्लहमणोरहावेसदुसहाआसदज्झन्तचित्तस्स खणमेत्तणिव्वाव[7]अं तुह पडिच्छन्दअं । )

---

प्रापितः । तारकादित्वादितच् ततः स्वार्थे कः । आदुशब्दोऽत्राहोस्विद्वाचकः । शीलस्य बहुकालपरिचेयतया मुहूर्तमात्रसंनिधाने विप्रलम्भचिन्ता । किमिदं नयनविकारादिस्वाभाविकमानुरागिकं वेति ज्ञातुं न शक्यत इति भावः । ' विप्पलम्भइत्तका: ' इति पाठे विप्रलम्भचिन्तका इति ज्ञेयम् ॥ **लवङ्गिका** । अत्र मन्मथेनेति शेषः । असंगीतकं निभृतनृत्यं यथा तथा नृत्यं कारितासीत्यर्थः । सासूयं परद्वेषसहितम् । **मालती** । हुमिति प्रणयकोपे ॥ **लवङ्गिका** । अत्र कामयत इच्छति । **लवङ्गिका** । अत्र दुर्लभायां त्वयि मनोरथाभिनिवेशस्तेन यो दुःसहायासस्तेन दह्यमाने चित्ते क्षणमात्र-

---

१ एतन्नास्ति क्वचित्. २ स्वगतं सानन्दम्. ३ एदं. ४ णाहस्य, पहुणः. ५ चित्रफलकं. ६ ०दस्स तुह. ७ व्वावइत्तकं ( यितृकं ).

**मालती**—(सहर्ष निर्वर्ण्य।) अहो इदानीमपि हृदयस्य मेऽनासङ्गो येनैवमप्याश्वासनं विप्रलम्भ इति संभावयामि। कथमक्षराण्यपि। (इति वाचयति। 'जगति जयिनः' इत्यादि (१।३६) पूर्वोक्तं पठित्वा सानन्दम्।) महाभाग सदृशं खलु ते निर्माणस्य वचनं मधुरतया लक्ष्यते। दर्शनं पुनस्तत्कालमनोहरं परिणामदीर्घसंतापदारुणम्। धन्याः खलु ताः कन्यका यास्त्वां न प्रेक्षन्ते। प्रेक्ष्य वात्मनो हृदयस्य प्रभवन्ति। (इति रोदिति।) (अह्मो दाणिं वि हिअअस्स मे अणासङ्गो जेण एदं वि आसासणं विप्पलम्भोत्ति संभावेमि। कधं अक्खराइं पि। महाभाअ सरिसं क्खु दे णिम्माणस्स वअणं महुरदाए। दंसणं उण तक्कालमणोहरं परिणामदीहसंदावदारुणं। धण्णाओ क्खु ताओ अम्मकाओ जाओ तुमं ण पेक्खन्दि। पेक्खिअ वा अत्तणो हिअअस्स पहवन्दि।)

**लव०**—सखि किमेवमपि ते नास्त्याश्वासः। (सहि किं एवं वि दे णत्थि आसासो।)

**मालती**—कथमिव। (कधं विअ।)

**लव०**—यस्य कारणादुत्खण्डितबन्धनमिव कङ्केल्लिपल्लवं क्लाम्यन्नवमालिकाकुसुमनिःसहा परिखिद्यसे सोऽपि ज्ञापितो भगवता मन्मथेन संतापस्य दुःसहत्वमिति। (जस्स कारणादो उक्खण्डिअबन्धणं विअ कङ्केल्लिपल्लवं किलम्मन्तणोमालिआकुसुमणीसहा परिक्खिज्जसि सो वि जाणाविदो भअवदा मम्महेण संदावस्स दूसहत्तणं त्ति।)

---

निर्वापकमिति॥ **मालती**। अत्रानासङ्गोऽनाश्वासः। लवङ्गिका स्वयं लिखित्वा माधवलिखितत्वेन बोधयतीति भावः। **सदृशमिति**। मधुरतया निर्माणस्य सदृशं वचनमित्यर्थः॥ तवाकृतिर्मधुरा यथा तथा वचोऽपि मधुरमित्यर्थः। यस्येदृशं वचस्तस्य कथमेवं दर्शनमित्युपालम्भपूर्विका पृच्छा। यदाह—'यत्र भावनयोपेतमात्मानमथवा परम्। पृच्छन्निवाभिधत्तेऽर्थं सा पृच्छेत्यभिधीयते॥' नाट्यधर्मत्वेन परोक्षस्यापि प्रत्यक्षीकरणम्। यदाह-परोक्षेऽपि च वक्तव्यो नार्यो प्रत्यक्षवत्प्रियः'॥ अम्मकाशब्दः स्त्रियां कन्यायां वा देशी॥ **लवङ्गिका**। अत्रोत्खण्डितं छिन्नम्। बन्धनं वृन्तशाखासंयोगः। कङ्केल्लिरशोकः।

---

१ सहर्षं चिरं चित्रं, संहर्षोच्छ्वासं. २ अण।सासो. ३ संभाविअदि (संभाव्यते). ४ लक्खीअदि (लक्ष्यते) इत्य०. ५ ०हारि. ६ इत्थिआओ. ७ एतन्नास्ति पुस्तकान्तरे. ८ सहि कधं. ९ तुमं उक्ख० णं कङ्के-त्तं विअ हिअअं धारेन्दी ०णीसहा कुसुमाउहेण पडिहिज्जासि (परिहीयसे)

**मालती**—कुशलमिदानीं तस्य महानुभावस्य भवतु। मम पुनः दुर्लभ आश्वासः। (सास्रम्) विशेषतोद्य प्रियसखि (कुसलं दाणिं तस्स महाणुभावस्स होदु। मह उण दुल्लहो आसासो। विसेसदो अज्ज पिअसहि)— (संस्कृतमाश्रित्य।)

> **मनोरागस्तीव्रं विषमिव विसर्पत्यविरतं**
> **प्रमाथी निर्धूमो ज्वलति विधुतः पावक इव।**
> **हिनस्ति प्रत्यङ्गं ज्वर इव गरीयानित इतो**
> **न मां त्रातुं तातः प्रभवति न चाम्बा न भवती ॥ १॥**

**लव०**—एवमेव प्रत्यक्षसौख्यदायिनः परोक्षदुःखदुःसहाः सज्जनसमागमा भवन्ति। अपि च। यस्य वातायनान्तरमुहूर्तदर्शनेनापि सविशेषसमिद्धहुतवहायमानपूर्णचन्द्रोदया निष्करुणकामव्यापारसंश—

निःसहाक्षमा। परिखिद्यसे परिहीयसे। एतेन कामावस्था तनुतोक्ता॥ **मालती**। अस्रं नेत्रजलम्। **संस्कृतमिति**। आसन्नमरणतया प्रकृतिविपर्ययद्योतनाय स्त्रियाः संस्कृताश्रयणम्। यद्वा मरणसमये प्राकृतस्मरणस्य हीनयोनिजन्मफलकत्वेन बोधनात्तत्काले स्त्रियाः संस्कृताश्रयणम्। यद्वा वैदग्ध्यद्योतनाय तत्। यदाह—संस्कृतभाषावाचः प्रायो नाट्ये खलु स्त्रियाः श्लाघ्याः। क्वचिदपि विदग्धतायाः प्रबोधनार्थं प्रशस्यन्ते॥ **मनोराग इत्यादि**। प्रियसखि मामद्य त्रातुं न तातः प्रभवति न वा माता न वा त्वम्। कुतः। मनोराग आधिरविरतं प्रमाथी क्षोभकारी यथा तीव्रं विषं तथा विसर्पति व्याप्नोति। यथा धातुत्वगादिषु विषं व्याप्नोति तथाङ्गानि म उद्वेग इत्यर्थः। यद्वा सविशेषदर्शनाच्चित्तानुराग इच्छाभेदस्तीव्रं यथा तथा मनो विसर्पति व्याप्नोति दाहकारित्वाद्विषमिव। तथा विधुतः संधुक्षितोऽग्निर्यथा ज्वलति विधूननान्निर्धूमं यथा तथा स एव रागो ज्वलति ज्वालामालाकुलीभवति। इत इतः सर्वत्र प्रत्यङ्गं हिनस्ति पीडयति गरीयाञ्ज्वर इव। तं त्यक्त्वा ममाधिस्त्वया समाधातुं न शक्यत इति भावः। यद्वा तातस्त्रातुं न शक्नोति। नन्दननिरासेन माधवाय मददानात्। अम्बापि न तथा। तथानुवर्तमानस्य तातस्यानिषेधात्। लवङ्गिकायाश्च तयोः समशीर्षिकया गणनं स्वाच्छन्द्येन स्वमतप्रकाशनाय॥ १॥ **लवङ्गिका**। अत्र भणितव्यं युज्यत एवेत्यर्थः। यस्याव्यक्तं दर्शनं चन्द्रस्याग्नित्वं जीवितसंशयं च कुरुते तस्य व्यक्तं दर्शनं त्वदुपन्यस्तप्रकारं तापं कुरुत इति किमत्र चित्रम्। चन्द्रेऽग्नित्वेन ज्ञानान्निद्राच्छेद उक्तः। सुकुमारायामस्यामतिपीडाकारित्वेन निष्करुणत्वम्। व्यापारो दशावस्थः। किमत्र क-

१ सखि कु०. २ महापहावस्स. ३ मनोरोगस्तीव्रो...विसर्पन्. ४ निर्धूमं. ५ बलीयान्. ६ समृद्ध.

यितजीविता ते शरीरावस्था तस्यैव संप्राप्तसविशेषदर्शना भूत्वाद्य संतप्यसीति किमत्र भणितव्यम् । तत्प्रियसखि श्लाघनीयं दुर्लभमनोरथफलं जीवलोकस्य यद्गुरुकानुरागसदृशो महानुभाववल्लभसमागम इत्येतावज्जानीमः । ( एव्वं[1] जेव्वं पच्चक्खसोक्खदाइणो परोक्खदुक्खदूसहा[2] सज्जणसमाअमा होन्दि । अवि अ । जस्स वादाअणन्दरमुहुत्तदंसणेण[3] वि सविसेससामिद्धहुदवहाअन्तपुण्णिमाचन्दोदआ[4] णिक्करुणकामव्वावारसंसइदजीविदा दे सरीरावत्था तस्स जेव्व संपत्तसविसेसदंसणा[5] भविअ अज्ज संतप्पसि त्ति किं एत्थ भणिदव्वं । ता[6] पिअसहि सलाहणिज्जं दुल्लहमणोरहफलं जीअलोअस्स जं[7] गुरुआणुराअसरिसो महाणुभाअवल्लहसमाअमो त्ति एत्तिअं जाणीमो ।

**मालती**—सखि दयितमालतीजीविते साहसोपन्यासिनि अपेहि । ( सास्रम् । ) अथ वा अहमेव वारंवारं विलोकयन्ती दुःखव्यवस्थापितधीरत्वावष्टम्भेनात्मनो दूरविगलितलज्जेन दुर्विनयलघ्वी अत्रापराद्ध्यामि । तथापि प्रियसखि । ( सहि दइदमालदीजीविदे साहसोवण्णासिणि अवेहि । अह वा अहं जेव्व वारंवारं विलोअअन्ती दुक्खव्ववत्थाविदधीरत्तणावट्ठम्भेण[8] अत्तणो हिअएण दूरविअलिदलज्जेण[9] दुव्विणअलहुआ[10] एत्थ अवरद्धम्मि । तहावि पिअसहि । ) ( भूयः संस्कृतमाश्रित्य । )

> ज्वलतु गगने रात्रौ रात्रावखण्डकलः शशी
> दहतु मदनः किं वा मृत्योः परेण विधास्यति ।
> मम तु दयितः श्लाघ्यस्तातो जनन्यमलान्वया
> कुलममलिनं न त्वेवायं जनो न च जीवितम् ॥ २ ॥

---

तव्यमित्यत आह—**तादिति** । तथा च गुरुतरानुरागस्यैतत्फलं यत्सखीद्वारा वल्लभसमागमः कारयितव्य इति भावः ॥ **मालती** । अत्र दयितं प्रियम् । महाकुलकलङ्कशङ्कया साहसम् । अत एव रोदनम् । तथा च त्वमपेह्यपगच्छ । प्रियभाषिणीं त्वां किमधिक्षिपामि यदहमेवात्र वाच्येत्याह—**अथवेति** । अत्र क्षणं क्षणमालोकनाकुलत्वाद्दुःखव्यवस्थापितं यद्धीरत्वं तस्यावष्टम्भोऽविद्यमान एवैतदारोपस्तेनेत्यर्थः । लघ्वी लघुतां गता । अहमत्रापराध्यामीति येन तवैतादृशसाहसोपन्यास इति भावः । तथापि प्रियसखि । अधुना साहसाकरणं हृदि निधाय सनिर्वेदमाह—**ज्वलत्वित्यादि** । प्रतिरात्रं पूर्णश्चन्द्रो ज्वलतु तापयतु तथापि न साहसं करोमीति भावः । गगन इत्यनेनाप्राप्यत्वादनुपागमनीयतोक्ता । तर्हि कामस्त्वां

---

१ एदं. २ दूसहाआसकारिणो. ३ मुहुत्तमत्त. ४ सुसामि० पुण्णचं०. ५ संपदं ( सांप्रतं ). ६ दंसणादो अज्ज. ७ ता एत्थ. ८ जं...सरिसं. ९ पलाअन्तपडिट्ठाविद ( पलायमानप्रतिष्ठापित ). १० दूरविज्जम्भमाणदुव्विणअलहुएण ( दूरविजृम्भमाणदुर्नयलघुकेन ); दूरं विलीअन्तलज्जत्तेण ( विलीयमानलज्जात्वेन ).

लव०—( स्वगतम् । ) अत्रेदानीं क उपायः । ( एत्थ दाणिं को उवाओ । )

( अथ नेपथ्यार्धप्रविष्टा )

प्रतीहारी—एषा भगवती कामन्दकी । ( एसा भअवदी कामन्दई । )

उभे—किं भगवती । ( किं भअवदी । )

प्रती०—भर्तृदारिकां द्रष्टुकामागता ( भट्टिदारिअं दट्ठुकामा आअदा । )

उभे—ततः किं विलम्ब्यते । ( तदो किं विलम्बीअदि । )

( प्रतीहारी निष्क्रान्ता । मालती चित्रं[1] प्रच्छादयति । )

लव०—( स्वगतम् । ) सुसमीहितं खलु जातम् । ( सुसमीहिदं[2] क्खु जादम् । )

( ततः प्रविशति कामन्दक्यवलोकिता च । )

काम०—साधु सखे भूरिवसो साधु । प्रभवति निजस्य कन्यका-जनस्य महाराज[3] इत्युभयलोकाविरुद्धं वचनमुपन्यस्तम्[4] । अपि च । अद्य मन्मथोद्यानवृत्तान्तेन भगवतो विधेरप्यनुकूलतामवगच्छामि । बकुला-

---

पीडयिष्यतीत्यत आह । मदनो दहतु । मृत्योर्मरणात्परं स किं करिष्यति । मरणे सति दुःखस्यापि त्यागादिष्टमेव तदिति भावः । परेणेति । 'प्रकृत्यादिभ्य उपसंख्यानम् ।' इति तृतीया । इदं नायिकायाः सत्त्वजधैर्यम् । यदाह—'चापलेनानुपहतं चित्तं धैर्यमुदीरितम् ।' ननु दुःखहानाय माधवानुसरणमेव वरमत आह–मम पुनस्तातः पिता दयित इष्टः । कीदृशः । श्लाघ्यः सर्वश्लाघाविषयः । अमलवंशा मातेष्टा । निर्मलं कुलं चेष्टम् । अयं हृदिस्थो जनो माधवो नैवेष्टः । साहसक्रियायेति शेषः । तर्हि कथं जीवनमत आह–न च जीवितमिष्टम् । अत्र जीवितद्वेषादुद्वेगावस्था । यदाह--'प्रद्वेषः प्राणितव्ये यः स उद्वेगः स्मृतो बुधैः ।' इति ॥ २ ॥ **लवङ्गिका** । उद्वेगनाशोपायं चिन्तयन्ती लवङ्गिकाह--अत्रेदानीं क उपायः ॥ **प्रतीहारी** । एषा भगवती कामन्दकी । मालतीजीवनोपाय इति भावः । प्रतीहारीत्यनेन संबन्धघटनं सूचितम् । यदाह--'संधिविग्रहसंबन्धनानाचारसमन्वितम् । निवेदयन्ति याः कार्यं प्रतीहार्यस्तु ता मताः ॥' प्रतीहारीत्यत्र बहुलवचनान्मनुष्येऽपि दीर्घः । **उभयोर्वाक्ये** । किमर्थमागतेत्यर्थः । अत एवाग्रिमवाक्ये तद्व्यापारकथनम् । **लवङ्गिका** । सुसमीहितं खलु जातम् । इदानीं यत्कामन्दक्यागमनमिति भावः । **कामन्दकी** । उभयेति । इहलोकाविरुद्धं साक्षादप्रतिषेधेन राजकोपाजननात् ।

---

१ चित्रफलकम्. २ सुसमाहिदं. ३ देवः. ४ उत्तरम्.

वलीचित्रफलकव्यतिकरसंविधानकौतुकमद्भुतं प्रमोदमुल्लासयति । इतरेतरानुरागो हि दारकर्मणि परार्ध्यं मङ्गलम् । गीतश्चायमर्थोऽङ्गिरसा यस्यां मनश्चक्षुषोरनुबन्धस्तस्यामृद्धिरिति ।

अव—एषा मालती । (एसा मालती ।)

काम०—(निर्वर्ण्य ।)

निकामं क्षामाङ्गी सरसकदलीगर्भसुभगा
कलाशेषा मूर्तिः शशिन इव नेत्रोत्सवकरी ।
अवस्थामापन्ना मदनदहनोद्दाहविधुरा-
मियं नः कल्याणी रमयति मनः कम्पयति च ॥ ३ ॥

अपि च ।

परिपाण्डुपांसुलकपोलमाननं
दधती मनोहरतरत्वमागता ।
रमणीयजन्मनि जने परिभ्रम-
ल्ललितो विधिर्विजयते हि मान्मथः ॥ ४ ॥

नियतमनया संकल्पनिर्मितः प्रियसमागमोनुभूयते । तथा ह्यस्याः

नीवीबन्धोच्छ्वसनमधरस्पन्दनं दोर्विषादः
स्वेदश्चक्षुर्मसृणमधुराकेकरस्निग्धमुग्धम् ।
गात्रस्तम्भः स्तनमुकुलयोरुत्प्रबन्धः प्रकम्पो
गण्डाभोगे पुलकपटलं मूर्च्छना चेतना च ॥ ५ ॥

---

परलोकाविरोधस्त्वात्मीयस्य कुमारीजनस्य प्रभुर्न परस्येति साधारणोक्त्यासत्यानुदीरणादित्यर्थः । व्यतिकरो मिलनं तद्रूपं संविधानम् । दारकर्मणि परिणये । परार्ध्यं श्रेष्ठम् । अनुबन्धो रतिः । ऋद्धिरुपचयः ॥ **निकाममित्यादि** । इयं कल्याण्यस्माकं मनो रमयति । कुतः । अत्यर्थं क्षीणाङ्गी । सरस आर्द्रः । अपर्युषित इति यावत् । कदल्या गर्भो मज्जा तद्वद्रम्या क्षीणत्वपाण्डुत्वाभ्याम् । इह गर्भपदेनातिपाण्डुत्वं चोक्तम् । कलाशेषा शशिनो मूर्तिरिव द्वितीयाचन्द्रलेखेव । अत एव प्रस्तुतकार्यसंपादकत्वेन रमयति । उद्दाहेनोत्कटदाहेन विह्वलां दशामापन्ना सती मनः कम्पयति । अतिपीडनादनिष्टशङ्कित्वादिति भावः । इह तनुताख्या कामदशा सूचिता ॥ ३ ॥ **परीत्यादि** । पांसुलं रूक्षम् । पाण्डुरूक्षकपोलवदनापीयं रम्या । यतो मनोज्ञजन्मनि जने वल्लकायस्य विकारो यादृशस्तादृश ईप्सितः सन्विजयी भवति ॥ ४ ॥ संकल्पो मनोव्यापारः । **नीवीत्यादि** । जघनवस्त्रब-

---

१ करस्तु कमप्यद्भुतनर्म. २ विवाहक०. ३ निबन्धः; अनुराग; ऋद्धिः—सिद्धिः. ४ दृष्ट्वा नि०, विलोक्य. ५ नोन्माद, नोद्दाम. ६ परिस्फुरन्. ७अथ वा निय०. ८ मितप्रिय. ९ खेदः. १० मुकुलाकेकर. ११ नारम्. १२ कलशयोः.

( इत्युपसर्पति । )

( लवङ्गिका मालतीं चालयति । उभे उत्तिष्ठतः )

**मालती**—भगवति वन्दे । ( भवअदि वन्दामि । )

**काम०**—महाभोगे समीहितफलभाजनं भूयाः ।

**लव०**—सुविहितमासनम् । अत्रोपविशतु भगवती । ( सुविहिदं आसणं । एत्थ उवविसदु भअवदी । )

( सर्वा उपविशन्ति )

**मालती**—कुशलं भगवत्याः । ( कुशलं भअवदीए । )

**काम०**—( निःश्वस्य । ) कुशलमिव ।

**लव०**—( स्वगतम् । ) प्रस्तावना खल्वेषा कपटनाटकस्य ।

---

न्धनं नीवी । तस्या बन्धस्य ग्रन्थेरुच्छ्वसनं शिथिलता । वासःश्लथतानुरागादपि । यदाह—'स्वेदोत्कम्पथुस्तम्भाः श्लथता जघनच्छदे । आविर्भवति नारीणामनुरागवशात्मनाम् ॥' अधरस्पन्दनमधरकम्पनम् । एतत्तु स्फुरितचुम्बने । यदाह—'रदने विशान्तमोष्ठं ग्रहीतुं या समिच्छति । निजोष्ठः कम्पते यच्च स्फुरितं चुम्बनं मतम् ॥' दोर्विषादो बाह्वोर्निःसहत्वमालिङ्गनसौख्यात् । स्वेद आयासात् । मसृणं कोमलम् । मधुरं ललितम् । संकल्पलब्धस्य दुरालोकत्वादाकेकरम् । शृङ्गारात्स्निग्धम् । सुखभावनया मुग्धम् । चक्षुः—संकल्पमात्रलब्धतया प्रियेऽसूयायोगाज्जिह्मा दृष्टिः । जिह्मा दृष्टिरसूयायाम् । यदाह—'ललिताकुञ्चितपुटा शनैस्तिर्यग्विसर्पिणी । निगूढागूढतारा च जिह्मा दृष्टिरुदाहृता ॥' लब्धे सति धृतिहर्षाभ्यां ललितम् । तल्लक्षणं तूक्तमेव । आकेकरा घनालोके विच्छेदे प्रोषितेषु च । आकुञ्चितपुटापाङ्गसंगतार्धनिमेषिणी ॥ मुहुर्व्यावृत्ततारा च दृष्टिराकेकरा मता ॥' 'दोर्दोषा भुजा भुजः' इति शब्दभेदः । गात्रस्तम्भः शरीरनिश्चलता । अतिहर्षात् । यदाह—'अतिहर्षभयरोषरागेभ्यः स्तम्भसंभवः ॥' मुकुलाकारत्वात्स्तनावेव मुकुलौ । तयोरप्रबन्धो विच्छेदरहितः कम्पः । प्रियस्य गाढालिङ्गनात् । गण्डाभोगे गण्डमण्डले पुलकपटलं रोमाञ्चसंघः । प्रियचुम्बनसंकल्पात् । आत्यन्तिकत्वार्थे पटलग्रहणम् । मूर्च्छना मोहः । निरतिशयानन्दयोगात् । यदाह—'स्रस्तता वपुषि मीलनं दृशोर्मूर्च्छना च रतिलाभलक्षणम्' । रतिविलाससंकल्पेनान्तरा चेतना च ॥ ५ ॥ **मालती** । बौद्धानां प्रव्रजितं प्रति वन्दामीति नतिसंप्रदायः । यद्वा वन्दामि वन्द इति सामान्यत एव ॥ **कामन्दकी** । मालतीचित्तविनोदाय स्वस्य च तद्विषयावष्टम्भदर्शनायाह—भाजनमिति । **लवङ्गिका** । कपटमेव नाटकम् । अत्र

---

१ चालयित्वा. २ काम०–( निःश्वस्य ). ३ वत्से; महाभागधेयजन्मनायाः फलस्य. ४ अभिमतफल०; ०फलस्य भा०. ५ भअवदि एदं पवित्तं आसणम्.

( प्रकाशम् । ) गुरुकबाष्पस्तम्भमन्थरितकण्ठप्रतिलग्ननिःश्वासमन्यादृशमेवाद्य भगवत्या वचनम् । तत्किमिदानीमुद्वेगकारणं भविष्यति । ( पत्थावणा क्खु एसा कवडणाडअस्स । ) ( गुरुअबाह्त्थम्भमन्थरिदकण्ठपडिलग्गणीसासं अण्णारिसं जेव्व अज्ज भअवदीए वअणम् । ता किं दाणीं उव्वेअकारणं भविस्सदि । )

**काम०**—नन्वयमेव चीरचीवरविरुद्धः परिचयः ।

**लव०**—कथमिव । ( कधं विअ । )

**काम०**—अयि त्वमपि किं न जानासि ।

**इदमिह मदनस्य जैत्रमस्त्रं सहजविलासनिबन्धनं शरीरम् ।**
**अनुचितवरसंप्रदानशोच्यं विफलगुणातिशयं भविष्यतीति ॥ ६ ॥**

( मालती वैचित्त्यं नाटयति । )

**लव०**—अस्त्येतन्नरेन्द्रवचनानुरोधिनामात्येन नन्दनस्य प्रतिपन्ना मालतीति सकलो जनोऽमात्यं जुगुप्सते । ( अत्थि एदं णरेन्दवअणाणुरोहिणा अमच्चेण णन्दणस्स पडिवण्णा मालदित्ति सअलो जणो अमच्चं जुगुच्छेदि । )

**मालती**—( स्वगतम् । ) कथमुपहारीकृतास्मि राज्ञस्तातेन । ( कधं उवहारीकिदह्मि राइणो तादेण । )

**काम०**—आश्चर्यम् ।

---

बाष्पं नेत्रजलम् । स्तम्भः प्रतिबन्धः । मन्थरितो मन्दीकृतः । तादृशकण्ठे प्रतिलग्नो निःश्वासो यत्र तत् ॥ **कामन्दकी** । परिचयो मालत्यभिष्वङ्गः । उद्वेगकारणमिति शेषः । **इदमित्यादि** । मालत्या इदं शरीरं विफलगुणातिशयं भविष्यतीति त्वं किं न वेत्सि । अनुचितजामातृसंबन्धशोचनावहम् । यतः । **इह** जगति यत्कामस्य जैत्रं जयनशीलमस्त्रं सहजविलासस्य निबन्धनं कारणं च । एतेनैव सहजविलासा जायन्त इत्यर्थः । 'वरो जामातरि श्रेष्ठे' इति विश्वः ॥ ६ ॥ वैचित्यं विमनस्कत्वम् । नाटयति करोति ॥ **लवङ्गिका** । पितृनिन्दैव पूर्वश्लोकार्थ इति द्योतयति लवङ्गिका । अत्र जुगुप्सते निन्दति । **मालती** । अत्रानुपहरणीयाप्युपहारीकृतेत्यनेन च्व्यर्थेन पितुर्गुणानभिज्ञत्वं सूचितम् । उपहारश्च मरणशरणच्छागादिः क्रियत इति मरणतुल्यतास्य दर्शिता । इह पश्चात्तापनामा नाट्यालंकारः । यदाह–' अनुतापातिरेकस्तु पश्चात्ताप उदाहृतः ' ॥ इति । बाल्यात्प्रे-

---

१ बाहम्भर. २ णिग्गमं. ३ विअ. ४ अयि किं, जा०–जानीषे. ५ संप्रयोग. ६ वैचित्र्यं. ७ रोहेण.

गुणापेक्षाशून्यं कथमिदमुपक्रान्तमथ वा
कुतोऽपत्यस्नेहः कुटिलनयनिष्णातमनसाम् ।
इदं त्वैदंपर्यं यदुत नृपतेर्नर्मसचिवः
सुतादानान्मित्रं भवतु स हि नो नन्दन इति ॥ ७ ॥

मालती—( स्वगतम् । ) राजाराधनं खलु तातस्य गुरुकं न पुनर्मालती । ( राआराहणं क्खु तादस्स गुरुअं ण उण मालदी । )

लव०—एवं यथा भगवत्याज्ञप्तम् । अन्यथा तस्मिन्वरे दुर्दर्शनेऽतिक्रान्तयौवने किमिति न विचारितममात्येन । ( एव्वं जधा भअवदीए आणत्तं । अण्णधा तस्सिं वरे दुद्दंसणे अदिक्कन्दजोव्वणे किं ति ण विआरिदं अमच्चेण । )

मालती—( स्वगतम् । ) हा हतास्मि समुपस्थितानर्थवज्रपतना मन्दभागिनी । ( हा हदह्मि समुँपत्थिदाणत्थवज्जपडणा मन्दभाइणी । )

लव०—तद्भगवति प्रसीद परित्रायस्वास्माज्जीवितमरणात्प्रियसखीम् । तवाप्येषा दुहितैव । ( ता भअवदी पसीद परित्ताहि इमादो जीविदमरॅणादो पिअसहिं । तुह वि एसा दुहिदा जेव्व । )

काम०—अयि सरले किमत्र मया भगवत्या शक्यम् । प्रभवति

---

ह्यच तातस्य गुणानभिज्ञत्वं मालती न जानातीत्याशयेनाह—**गुणेत्यादि** । इदं कार्यं गुणनिरपेक्षममात्येन कथमारब्धम् । रूपादिमति पुरजने सति तद्रहितनन्दनाय मालतीदानं कथमुपक्रान्तमिति भावः । अत एवाश्चर्यम् । अथ वा पक्षान्तरे । कुटिलनये परवञ्चननीतौ कुशलचित्तानां कुतोऽपत्यस्नेहः । नैवेत्यर्थः । स्नेहस्य निरुपाध्युपकारेच्छारूपस्य नृपानुरञ्जनादावुपाधावभावादित्यर्थः । इदं यदुपक्रान्तं तदैदंपर्यमिदंपरम् । एतदभिप्रायकमिति यावत् । चतुर्वर्णादित्वादिदंपरशब्दे ष्यञ् । उत निश्चये वितर्के वा । यन्नृपतेर्नर्मसचिवो नन्दनः कन्यादानादस्माकं मित्रमनपकारी भवत्वित्येवमुपक्रान्तम् । निष्णात इत्यत्र 'निनदीभ्यां स्नातेः कौशले इति षत्वम् । 'उत निश्चयवितर्कयोः' इति धरणिः । कामोपचरणं नर्म । यदाह—'उपचारः स्त्रीपुंसयोर्मनोजन्मनिबन्धनः । स एवात्र परिज्ञेयो नर्मसंज्ञः प्रयोक्तृभिः ॥' इति भरतः ॥ ७ ॥ **लवङ्गिका** । इतीति दुर्दर्शनादिकम् ॥ **लवङ्गिका** । अत्र जीवितमपि निष्फलत्वदुःखबहुलत्वाभ्यां मरणकल्पं जीवितमरणम् ॥ **कामन्दकी** । उक्तप्रबन्धेन मालतीनैराश्यं विधायाह—**अयीति** । भगवत्येति 'कृत्यानां कर्तरि

---

१ स हि मे; स भवान्. २ बहुमदं. ३ जहा भअवदी आणवेदि तं तह एव्व । ४ समुत्थि०. ५ जीवन्द, जीवण.

प्रायः कुमारीणां जनयिता दैवं च । यच्च किल कौशिकी शकुन्तला दुष्यन्तमप्सरा उ[1]र्वशी पुरूरवसं चकम इत्याख्यानविद आचक्षते वासवदत्ता च संजयाय राज्ञे पित्रा दत्तमात्मानमुदयनाय प्रायच्छदित्यादि तदपि साहसाभो[2]समित्यनुपदे[3]ष्टव्य एवायमर्थः । सर्वथा

**राज्ञः प्रियाय सुहृदे सचिवाय का[4]र्या-**<br>
**हत्वात्मजां भवतु निर्वृतिमानमात्यः ।**<br>
**दुर्दर्शनेन घटतामियमप्यनेन**<br>
**धूमग्रहेण विमला शशिनः कलेव ॥ ८ ॥**

**मालती**—( सास्रं स्वगतम् । ) हा तात त्वमपि मम नामैवमिति सर्वथा जितं भोगतृष्णया । ( हा ताद तुमं वि मम णाम एव्वं त्ति सव्वधा जिदं भोगतिण्हाए । )

**अव०**—चिरायितं भगवत्या । ननु भणाम्यस्वस्थशरीरो महाभागो माधव इति । ( चिराइदं भअवदीए । णं भणामि अस्सत्थ[5]सैरीरो महाभाओ माहवोत्ति । )

**काम०**—इदं गम्यते । वत्से अनुजानीहि माम् ।

**लव०**—( जनान्तिकम् ) सखि मालति सांप्रतं भगवत्याः सकाशात्तस्य महानुभावस्योद्गमं जानीमः । ( सहि मालदि संपदं भअ[6]वदीए सआसादो तस्स महाँणुभावस्स उग्गमं जाणीमो । )

---

वा ' इति तृतीया न तु षष्ठी । अशक्यमित्यकारप्रश्लेषसंभवात् । गान्धर्वविवाहे कन्यावरौ प्रभवत इति प्रायःपदतात्पर्यम् । जनयितेति । न राजेति भावः । माधवविवाहे भूरिवसुरेव सानुग्रहः । अत एव सरल इत्युक्तम् । किल प्रसिद्धौ । कौशिकी कुशिकवंशजा । चकमे कामयते स्म । आख्यानं पुरावृत्तम् । इहाख्याननामा नाट्यालंकारः ॥ यदाह—' आख्यानं तु तदुद्दिष्टं यत्पुरावृत्तकीर्तनम् ॥ ' इति । निदर्शननामा नाट्यालंकारोऽपि । यदाह–' कथनादन्यचेष्टानां साध्यसिद्धिर्निदर्शनम् ॥ इति । कल्पपदेनोपदेष्टव्यत्वसूचनम् ॥ अधुना साहसेऽपि प्रवृत्त्यर्थं मालत्यनुशयाय पितुर्वरस्य च दोषमाह–**राज्ञ इति** । कार्यादाराधनादेर्न त्वदृष्टार्थमित्यर्थः । अनेन सचिवेन । वार्धक्यात्कौरूप्याच्च दुर्दर्शनेन । धूमग्रहेण राहुणोत्पातधूमग्रहेण वा । पीडाकारित्वाद्दुर्दर्शनेन वा । ग्रहणं ग्रहः ॥ ८ ॥ **मालती** । मालती जातानुशयाह–एवं निःस्पृह इत्यर्थः । भोगेति । स्वभोगाय । त्वमेवं करोषीत्यर्थः । **अवलोकिता** । अत्र चिरायितं बहुकालमागतम् । इतीति । अतः शीघ्रं गम्यतामिति भावः ॥

---

१ एतन्नास्ति क्वचित्. २ साहसकल्पम्. ३ ०देष्टव्यमेव. ४ भार्याम्. ५ चिन्तो. ६ ०वदीस०. ७ महाभाअस्स.

**माल०**—( अपवार्य ) सखि अस्ति मे कौतूहलम् । ( सहि अत्थि मे कोदूहल्लम् । )

**लव०**—( प्रकाशम् ) क एष माधवो नाम यस्य भगवती स्नेहगुरुकमात्मानं धारयति । ( [1]को एसो माहवो णाम जस्सि[2] भअवदी[3] सिणेहगुरुअं अत्ताणं धारेदि । )

**काम०**—अप्रास्ताविकी महत्येषा कथा ।

**लव०**—तथाप्याचष्टां भगवती । प्रसादं करोतु । ( तधा वि आचक्खदु[4] भअवदी । प्रसादं करेदु । )

**काम०** —श्रूयताम् । अस्ति विदर्भाधिपतेरमात्यः[5] समग्रधुर्यपुरुषप्रकाण्डचक्रचूडामणिर्देवरातो[6] नाम यमशेषभुवनमहनीयपुण्यमहिमानमात्मनः सतीर्थ्य[7] पितैव ते जानाति योऽसौ यादृशश्चेति । अपि च ।

> **व्यतिकरितदिगन्ताः श्वेतमानैर्यशोभिः**
> **सुकृतविलसितानां स्थानमूर्जस्वलानाम् ॥**
> **अकलित[8]महिमानः केतनं मङ्गलानां**
> **कथमपि[9] भुवनेऽस्मिंस्तादृशाः संभवन्ति ॥ ९ ॥**

---

**लवङ्गिका** । जनान्तिकमिति । ' उक्तस्याश्रवणं कार्यात्पार्श्वस्थैः स्याज्जनान्तिकम् ।' इति भरतः । लवङ्गिका मालतीं साकाङ्क्षयति । उद्गममुत्पत्तिम् ॥ **मालती** । अस्ति मे कुतूहलम् । तत्पृच्छेत्यर्थः । **लवङ्गिका** । अत्र यस्य कृत इति शेषः ॥ **कामन्दकी** । सकृत्रिमावहित्थमाह—अप्रास्ताविकीति । अयमाशयः—माधवगुणस्तुतावुपाधिमाशङ्क्य मालत्या अनादरे मम तटस्थता न घटेत ॥ **लवङ्गिका** । अतः सानुबन्धं पृच्छत्विति सानुबन्धमियमप्याहेति ॥ **कामन्दकी** । समग्रः संपूर्णः । धुरि कार्यभारे साधुर्धुर्यो मन्त्री । प्रकाण्डं प्रशस्तम् । चूडामणिरिव चूडामणिः श्लाघ्यः सर्वमन्त्रिप्रधानमित्यर्थः । महनीयं पूज्यम् । पुण्यं प्रशस्तम् । यद्वा महनीयौ पुण्यमहिमानौ यस्य तम् । सतीर्थ्य एकगुरुः । समानं तीर्थमुपाध्यायो यस्य । ' समानतीर्थे वासी ' इति यप्रत्ययः । **व्यतिकरितेत्यादि** । इह जगति कथमपि शापादिना तादृशाः स्वर्गिणः संभवन्ति । कीदृशाः । यशोभिर्व्याप्तदिक्स्वरूपाः । श्वेतमानैरिति वर्तमाननिर्देशेन तेषामभिनवयशोयोगित्वमुक्तम् । बलवतां पुण्यविपाकानां त एव स्थानम् । त एव महासुकृतिन इत्यर्थः । यद्वा पुण्यविलासानां बलवतां च त एव स्थानम् । तथा च पुण्यवन्तो बलवन्तश्च त एवेत्यर्थः । अत एवाधिकमहत्त्वाः । मङ्गलानामर्थसिद्धीनां केतनं निवासः ।

---

१ जनान्तिकम्. २ भअवदि को. ३ जस्सिं. ४ वदी एव्वं. ५ आअक्खिअ (आख्याय.) ६ ०भराजस्व, विदर्भाधिपस्य नरपतेः. ७ समग्र-स्त-पुरुष०. ८ सातीर्थ्यात्. ९ अगणित. १० कथमिव.

**माल०**—( जनान्तिकम् । ) सखि तं खलु भगवतीगृहीतनामधेयं सर्वदा तातः स्मरति । ( सहि तं क्खु भअवदीगहीदणामहेअं सव्वदा[3] तादो सुमेरेदि । )

**लव०**—सखि समं किल विद्याधिगमः कृत इति तत्कालवेदिनो जना मन्त्रयन्ते । ( सहि समं किल[4] विज्जाहिगमो किदो त्ति तक्कालवेदिणो जणा मन्तअन्दि । )

**काम०**—

> तत उदयगिरेरिवैक[5] एव
> स्फुरितगुणद्युतिसुन्दरः कलावान् ।
> इह जगति महोत्सवस्य हेतु-
> र्नयनवतामुदियाय बालचन्द्रः ॥ १० ॥

**लव०**—( जनान्तिकम्[6] । ) सखि अपि नाम माधवो भवेत् । ( अवि णाम माहवो हवे । )

**काम०**—

> असौ विद्याधारः[7] शिशुरपि विनिर्गत्य भवना-
> दिहायातः संप्रत्यविकलशरच्चन्द्रमधुरः[8] ।
> यदालोकस्थाने भवति पुरमुन्मादतरलैः
> कटाक्षैर्नारीणां कुवलयितवातायनमिव ॥ ११ ॥

---

' केतनं तु ध्वजे कार्ये निमन्त्रणनिवासयोः । ' इति विश्वः ॥ ९ ॥ **मालती** । अत्र नामाग्रहणं श्वशुरत्वेनाङ्गीकारात् । ' गुरोर्नाम न गृह्णीयात् ' इति स्मृतेः । तं देवरातम् ॥ **लवङ्गिका** । अत्र समं तुल्यं यथा तथा पाठः कृतो देवरातभूरिवसुभ्याम् । मन्त्रयन्ते कर्णाकर्णिकया वदन्ति । **कामन्दकी** । प्रकृतसिध्यर्थं पितृगुणानुक्त्वा नायकगुणानाह—**तत इत्यादि** । ततो देवरातादेक एव बालश्चन्द्र उदियाय । एको बालो जात इत्यर्थः । यद्वा बालश्चन्द्र इव बालचन्द्रः । एकापत्यतया स्नेहाधिक्यसूचनार्थमेकग्रहणम् । धरायामेकाधिपत्यकथनाय वा । कीदृशः । स्फुरिता व्यक्तीकृता गुणानां शीलादीनां या द्युतिरौज्ज्वल्यं तया सुन्दरः । यद्वा स्फुरितगुणद्युतिश्चासौ सुन्दरश्चेति । कलावांश्चतुःषष्टिकलायुक्तः । ' नायके वर्णयेद्दूती कलावत्त्वं च रम्यताम् । ' इति भरतः । नयनवतां चक्षुष्मतां महोत्सवस्य कारणम् । नेत्रप्रीतिजनकत्वात् । यथोदयगिरेरेको बालचन्द्रोऽभिनवशश्युदेति । सोऽपि स्फुरितगुणोन्मीलन्नैर्मल्यादिका या द्युतिः प्रभा तया सुन्दरः कान्तः कलावान्नेत्रानन्दहेतुश्च भवति ॥ १० ॥ बालत्वादितस्तदागमनमाशङ्क्याह—**असावित्यादि** । असौ शिशुरपि बालोऽपि संप्रतीहागतः । अस्तीति

---

१ अपवार्य. २ भअवदीए ३ सव्वहा [ सर्वथा ]. ४ किल भअवदीए गुरुसआसादो विज्जा०...वेदिणो मन्तअन्ति. ५ एव. ६ अपवार्य. ७ शाली, ८ वदनः.

अत्र बालसुहृदा मकरन्देन सह विद्यामान्वीक्षिकीमधिगच्छति । एष माधवो नाम ।

**मालती**—( सानन्दं जनान्तिकम् । ) सखि श्रुतं त्वया । (सहि सुदं तुए ।)

**लव०**—( जनान्तिकम् । ) सखि कुतो वा महोदधिं वर्जयित्वा पारिजातस्योद्गमः । ( सहि कुदो वा महोदहिं वज्जिअ पारिजाअस्स उग्गमो । )

[ नेपथ्ये शङ्खध्वनिः ]

**काम०**—अहो कालातिपातः । संप्रति हि

**क्षिपन्निद्रामुद्रां मदनकलहच्छेदसुलभा-**
**मवाप्तोत्कण्ठानां विहगमिथुनानां प्रथमतः ।**
**दधानः सौधानामलघुषु निकुञ्जेषु घनता-**
**मसौ संध्याशङ्खध्वनिरनिभृतः खे विचरति ॥ १२ ॥**

---

शेषः । कीदृशः । विद्याधारः । त्रयीतदङ्गविद्यावित् । बालः पञ्चदशवर्षवयस्कः । 'बालो वाप्यूनषोडशः' इति वचनात् । भवनाद्विनिर्गत्य बहिर्भूय । अनेन पथिकत्वमप्यास्तम् । यौवनमाह–अविकलः पूर्णो यः शारदशशी तस्मान्मनोज्ञः । तद्वद्वा मनोज्ञः । यद्दृष्टिविषये पुरं नारीणां कटाक्षैः संजातनीलनलिनगवाक्षमिव भवति । कुवलयितमित्यत्र तारकादित्वादितच् । कीदृशैः । उन्मादतरलैः कामावेशचपलैः । यदायं रथ्यया याति तदोन्मादान्विता युवत्यो वातायनैरेनं पश्यन्ति । तत्तु तन्नयनैः संजातकुवलयमिव लक्ष्यत इत्याशयः । अनेन विद्यावत्त्वनूतनत्वरम्यत्वादिकमुक्तम् ॥ ११ ॥ विद्यामित्यनेन विद्यावशेनायात इत्यनौद्धत्यं संबन्धार्थदेवरातप्रस्थापनगोपनं च कृतम् ॥ **मालती** । सखि श्रुतं त्वया । एतेनाभिलाषं दर्शयति ॥ **लवङ्गिका** । लवङ्गिकैतद् द्रढयति । अनेन महाकुलीनत्वं न तु कामन्दक्याः कल्पनेति दर्शितम् । **कामन्दकी** । कालातिपातः कालक्षेपः ॥ **क्षिपन्नित्यादि** । संप्रति गगनेऽयं संध्याशङ्खध्वनिः संध्याकालसूचकः शङ्खशब्दो विचरति श्रूयते । किं कुर्वन् । विहगमिथुनानां चक्रद्वन्द्वानां प्रत्यासन्नविरहात्सोत्कण्ठानाम् । निद्रैव मुद्रा । संभाषणप्रतिरोधात् । तां प्रथमतः क्षिपन्हरन् । कीदृशीम् । मदनकलहः सुरतं तस्य च्छेदोऽवसानं तेन सुलभाम् । यद्वा मदनकलहश्छिद्यतेऽनेनेति घञ् । 'पुंसि संज्ञायाम्' इति वा घः । मदनकलहच्छेदो रतं ततः सुलभाम् । सुरतश्रमजनितामित्यर्थः । संप्रति धवलगृहाणां महत्सु गह्वरप्रदेशेषु प्रतिध्वनितो घनतां दधानः । अत एवानिभृतः प्रौढः सन्विचरति । यद्वा प्रथमतः खे विचरति तदनु दिवा केलिकलहच्छेदात्सौधसमीपतरुनिवासकलविङ्कमि-

---

१ तद्; अत्रैव. २ अधीते. ३ सहि लवङ्गिए; कहं महाउलप्पसूदो महाणाओत्ति. ४ वेला. ५ उपात्तो०, त्तोत्कम्पानां. ६ अनिभृतः.

तदुत्तिष्ठामः । ( इत्युत्तिष्ठति । )

**माल०**—( अपवार्य । ) कथमुपहारीकृतास्मि राज्ञस्तातेन । राजाराधनं खलु तातस्य गुरुकं न पुनर्मालती । ( सास्रम् । ) हा तात त्वमपि नाम ममैवमिति सर्वथा जितं भोगतृष्णया । ( सानन्दम् । ) कथं महाकुलप्रभवोपि स महाभागः । सुष्ठु भणितं प्रियसख्या कुतो वा महोदधिं वर्जयित्वा पारिजातस्योद्गम इति । अपि नाम तं पुनरपि प्रेक्षिष्ये । ( कधं उवहारीकिदह्मि राइणो तादेण । राआराहणं क्खु तादस्स गुरुअं ण उण मालदी । हा ताद तुमं वि णाम मम एव्वं ति सव्वधा जिदं भोअतिह्णाए । कधं महाउलप्पभओ सो महाभाओ । सुट्ठु भणिदं पिअसहीए कुदो वा महोअहिं वज्जिअ पारिजादस्स उग्गमो त्ति । अवि णाम तं उणो वि पेक्खिस्सं । )

**लव०**—अवलोकिते इत इतः । एतेन सोपानेनावतरावः । ( अवलोइदे इदो इदो । एदिणा सोवाणेण ओदरह्म । )

**काम०**—( अपवार्य । ) साधु संप्रति मया तटस्थयैव मालतीं प्रति निसृष्टार्थदूतीकृत्यस्य लघूकृतो भारः । तथा हि

**वरेऽन्यस्मिन्द्वेषः पितरि विचिकित्सा च जनिता**
**पुरावृत्तोद्गारैरपि च कथिता कार्यपदवी ।**
**स्तुतं तन्माहात्म्यं यदभिजनतो यच्च गुणतः**
**प्रसङ्गाद्वत्सस्येत्यथ खलु विधेयः परिचयः ॥ १३ ॥**

( इति परिक्रम्य निष्क्रान्ताः सर्वे । )

**इति धवलगृहो नाम द्वितीयोऽङ्कः ।**

---

धुनानां निद्रामुद्रां क्षिपन्विचरति । ते हि प्रबलशङ्खध्वनिनिबोधिताः कलकलं कुर्वन्तीति भावः ॥ १२ ॥ **मालती** । अपवार्य निभृतम् । ‘ निगूढभावसंयुक्तमपवारितकं भवेत् । ’ इति भरतः । अधुना मन प्रतिष्ठासाहसवाञ्छया ब्रूते—**लवङ्गिका** । ‘ संजननेन ’ इति पाठे संजननं सोपानमेव । **कामन्दकी** । तटस्थतया घटितत्वेन साधुत्वम् । **निसृष्टार्थेति** । ‘ स्त्रीपुंसयोराशयमादधाना स्वयं च कार्यं प्रतिपादयन्ती । सृष्टार्थिका सा परदारयोगे दूती नियोज्या बहुधा सुधीभिः ॥ इति भरतः । मालतीं प्रतीत्यनेन मदयन्तिकां प्रति विद्यत एवेति प्रकृते निष्पन्नं स्वव्यापारमाह—**वर इत्यादि** । अन्यस्मिन्वरे नन्दने द्वेषः कारितः । पितरि निन्दा जनिता । पुरावृत्तोद्गारैः शकुन्तलादीनां पितृनिरपे-

---

१ वत्से सुखं स्थीयताम्. २ सहि कधं. ३ °पसूदो, वोप्पसो. ४ सुभ°. ५ संजवणेण ६ अवलोकिते साधु. ७ °वृत्तस्य, र्थदूत्यस्य. ८ कुतः. ९ माहाभाग्यं. १० विधिवि°.

# तृतीयोऽङ्कः ।

( ततः प्रविशति बुद्धरक्षिता । )

**बुद्धरक्षिता**—( परिक्रम्य । आकाशे । ) अवलोकिते अपि जानासि क्व भगवतीति । ( अवलोइदे अवि जाणासि कहिं भअवदित्ति ।

**अवलोकिता**—( प्रविश्य[1] ) बुद्धरक्षिते किं प्रमुग्धासि । कोऽपि कालो भगवत्याः पिण्डपातवेलां वर्जयित्वा मालतीमनुवर्तमानायाः । ( बुद्धरक्खिदे किं पमुद्धासि । को वि[2] कालो भअवदीए पिण्डपादवेलं[3] वज्जिअ मालदीं अणुवट्टमाणाए । )

**बुद्ध०**—हुं । त्वं पुनः कुत्र प्रस्थितासि । ( हुं । तुमं उण कहिं पत्थिदासि । )

**अव०**—अहं खलु भगवत्या माधवसकाशमनुप्रेषिता । संदिष्टं च तस्य शंकरगृहासंबद्धं कुसुमाकरं नामोद्यानं गत्वा कुब्जकनिकुञ्जपर्यन्तरक्ताशोकगहने तिष्ठेति । गतश्च तत्र माधवः । ( अहं क्खु भअवदीए माहवसआसं अणुप्पेसिदा । संदिट्ठं अ तस्स[4] संकरघरसंबद्धं[5] कुसुमाअरं णाम उज्जाणं गदुअ कुब्जअणिउञ्जपेरन्तरत्तासोअगहणे[6] चिट्ठेत्ति । गदो अ तत्थ माहवो । )

---

क्षात्मदानकथनैः कार्यपरिपाटी कथिता । माहात्म्यं महत्त्वं तस्य स्तुतं यत्कुलाद्यच्च गुणात्तदपि । इति हेतोः । अनन्तरं वत्सस्य परिचयः समागमो विधातुः कर्तव्यः । एतेनाङ्कावतारोऽपि सूचितः । प्रसङ्गाद्व्याजादन्यापदेशादिति सर्वत्र योज्यम् ॥१३॥ **धवलगृह इति**। धवलगृहोपलक्षित इत्यर्थः ॥

असूत यं रत्नधरोऽनवद्योऽनवद्यरूपा दमयन्तिका च ।
जगद्धरं तत्कृतटिप्पणेऽङ्कोऽगमद्द्वितीयो रससराशिवासः ॥

## इति द्वितीयोऽङ्कः ।

---

परिचयस्यान्योन्यदर्शनालापादिरूपसमागमात्मकतया तदारम्भस्य प्रतिज्ञातत्वेन तन्निर्वाहिकाया मदयन्तिकायाः सूचनाय तत्संबन्धाद्बुद्धरक्षिताप्रवेशः । यद्वा नियुक्तैव मया बुद्धरक्षितेत्यनेन प्रथमाङ्के द्वितीये च मालतीं प्रति लघूकृतो भार इत्यनेन सूचितो बुद्धरक्षितायाः प्रवेशः ॥ **अवलोकिता** । अत्र प्रमुग्धा प्रस्मृता । पिण्डपातः सौगतान्नम् । कोऽप्यकालो निषिद्धकालः । तथा चैव सदैव मालतीसमीपे भगवती वर्तत इत्यर्थः ॥ **बुद्धरक्षिता** । हुमनुमतौ स्मरणे वा । **अवलोकिता** । अत्र कुब्जकं 'कूओं' इति ख्यातस्तरुविटपः । कुब्जकव्याप्तरक्ताशोकवनस्य दुःसंचारत्वाद्विजनत्वं सूचितम् । पर्यन्तो मध्यम् । 'काननं गहनं वनम्' इत्य-

---

१ प्रविश्य अव०; उपसृत्य. २ को विअ (क इव)., ३ पारणवेलं विसज्जिअ (विसृत्य). ४ तस्स जधा. ५ संकरउरसंबन्धि कुसुमाअरुज्जाणं. ६ कुब्जणि०.

**बुद्ध०**—किमिति तत्र माधवोनुप्रेषितः । ( [1]किं ति तत्थ माहवो अणुप्पेसिदो । )

**अव०**—अद्य कृष्णचतुर्दशीति भगवत्या समं मालती शंकरगृहं गमिष्याति । तत एवं किल सौभाग्यं वर्धेत इति देवताराधननिमित्तं स्वहस्तकुसुमावचयमुद्दिश्य लवङ्गिकाद्वितीयां मालतीं भगवत्येव कुसुमाकरोद्यानमानेष्यति । ततोऽन्योन्यदर्शनं भवत्विति । त्वं पुनः क्व प्रस्थिता । ( अज्ज किसणचउद्दसित्ति भअवदीए समं मालदी संकर[3]घरं गमिस्सदि । तदो एव्वं किल सोहग्गं वड्ढदि त्ति देवदाराहणणिमित्तं सहत्थकुसुमावअअं उद्दिसिअ लवङ्गिआदुदीअं मालदिं भवअदी जेव्व कुसुमाअरुज्जाणं आणइस्सदि । तदो अण्णोण्णदंसणं होदु[5] त्ति । तुमं उण कहिं पत्थिदा )

**बुद्ध०**—अहं खलु शंकरगृहमेव प्रस्थितया प्रियसख्या मदयन्तिकयामन्त्रिता । अतो भगवत्याः पादवन्दनं कृत्वा तत्रैव गच्छामि । ( अहं क्खु संकरघरं जेव्व पत्थिदाए पिअसहीए मदआन्तिआए आमान्तिदा । अदो भअवदीए पादवन्दणं कदुअ तहिं जेव्व गच्छामि )

**अव०**—त्वं खलु भगवत्या यस्मिन्प्रयोजने नियुक्ता तत्र को वृत्तान्तः । ( तुमं क्खु भअवदीए जस्सिं पओअणे निउत्ता तत्थ को वुत्तन्तो । )

**बुद्ध०**—मया खलु भगवत्याः समादेशेन तासु तासु विस्रम्भकथास्वीदृशस्तादृश इति मकरन्दस्योपरि प्रियसख्या मदयन्तिकाया दूरमारोपितः परोक्षानुरागः । एष च तस्या मनोरथोऽपि नाम तं प्रेक्ष इति । ( मए क्खु भअवदीए समादेसेण तासु तासु विस्सम्भकधासु ईरिसो तारिसो त्ति मअरन्दस्स उवरि पिअसहीए मदआन्तिआए दूरं[6] आरोविदो परोक्खाणुराओ । एसो अ से मणोरहो अवि णाम तं पेक्खामि त्ति । )

---

मरः ॥ **अवलोकिता** । अत्र किलालीके सौभाग्यवृद्धिप्रयोजनस्य व्याजत्वात् । **एवमिति** । स्वहस्तत्रोटितपुष्पैर्देवताः पूजयेत्यर्थः । **आनेष्यतीति** । मालतीमाधवयोरतर्कितदर्शनेन विजने तयोरनुरागो वर्धतामिति भगवत्या आशय इति भावः ॥ **बुद्धरक्षिता** । अत्रामन्त्रिताहूता । गच्छामि । मदयन्तिकास्थानमिति शेषः । **अवलोकिता** । मकरन्दमदयन्तिकापरिणये किं वृत्तमिति भावः । **बुद्धरक्षिता** । अत्र विस्रम्भो विश्वासः । ईदृशस्तादृश इति मकरन्दगुणप्रकाश-

---

१ अवलोइदे किं. २ जणणीए. ३ संकरउरं. ४ हाविस्सदि. ५ तदा. ६ तहा दूरं. ७ मणो० .

**अव०**—साधु बुद्धरक्षिते साधु (साहु बुद्धरक्खिदे साहु[1]।)

**बु॰**—एहि गच्छावः। (ऐहि गच्छह्म।)

(इति निष्क्रान्ते[2]।)

**(प्रवेशकः।)**

---

(ततः प्रविशति कामन्दकी।)

**कामन्दकी**—

**तथा विनयनम्रापि मया मालत्युपायतः।**
**नीता कतिपयाहेन[3] सखीविस्रम्भसेव्यताम् ॥ १ ॥**

संप्रति हि।

**व्रजति विरहे वैचित्त्यं[4] नः प्रसीदति संनिधौ**
**रहसि रमते प्रीत्या वाचं ददात्यनुवर्तते[5]।**
**गमनसमये कण्ठे लग्ना निरुध्य[6] निरुध्य मां**
**सपदि शपथैः प्रत्यावृत्तिं प्रणम्य च याचते ॥ २ ॥**

इदं च तत्र साधीयः प्रत्याशानिबन्धनम्[8]।

**शाकुन्तलादीनितिहासवादा-**
**न्प्रस्तावितानन्यपरैर्वचोभिः।**
**श्रुत्वा मदुत्सङ्गनिवेशिताङ्गी**
**चिराय चिन्तास्तिमितत्वमेति ॥ ३ ॥**

---

नमित्यर्थः। तस्या मदयन्तिकायाः। तं मकरन्दम् ॥ **अवलोकिता**। त्वया भगवतीभारो लघूकृत इति भावः ॥ **तथेत्यादि**। तथा तेन प्रकारेण विनयनम्रानुद्धताकारतया नम्रा मालती कतिपयदिनैरुपायाच्छकुन्तलादिकथया मया सख्यानिव विश्वासबुद्धिप्रवर्तनेन सेव्यतां शालीनत्वादिपरिहारं नीता। अत्रापिशब्द एवार्थे। यद्वा अविनयनम्रापीत्यकारप्रश्लेषः। कतिपयाहोभिरित्यत्राह्नो जातिपरतया न समासान्तविधिः ॥ १ ॥ सखीचिह्नं दर्शयति—**व्रजतीत्यादि**। संप्रति यताऽस्माकं विरहे दौर्मनस्यं गच्छति नः संनिधौ प्रसन्ना भवति। विजने रमते। मया सहेति शेषः। प्रीत्या दायं सोल्लुण्ठनमुत्तरं ददाति। यद्वा दायं कर्पूरादिदेयं ददाति। गमनसमये मामनुवर्ततेऽनुगच्छति। ततः कण्ठे लग्ना सती पुनःपुनर्निरुध्य मां शपथैः प्रणम्य तत्क्षणमेव प्रत्यावृत्तिं पुनरागमनं याचते च। सख्योऽप्येवं कुर्वन्ति। अतः सखीत्वं गता सा मे मनोगतं करिष्यतीति भावः। 'देये दाने च दायः स्याद्दायः सोल्लुण्ठभाषणे। इति मेदिनीकरः ॥ २ ॥ साधीयः साधु। निबन्धनं कारणम्। **शाकुन्तलादीनित्यादि**। इयं शाकुन्तलादीनितिहासवादान्पुरावृत्तान्यन्यपरैर्वचोभिरन्यकथाप्रसङ्गेन प्रस्तावयति। शकुन्तलादिभिः पितृनि-

---

१ साहु। एहि गच्छह्म. २ परिक्रम्य नि. ३ कतिपयाहोभिः. ४ वैचित्त्यम्. ५ वदति. ६ दायं. ७ निरुध्य च मां बलात्. ८ प्रीत्याशा.

तदद्य माधवसमक्षमुत्तरमुपक्रमिष्ये । (नेपथ्याभिमुखमवलोक्य ।) वत्से इत इतः ।

(ततः प्रविशति मालती लवङ्गिका च ।)

**मालती**—(स्वगतम् ।) कथमुपहारीकृतास्मि (कधं उवहारी किदम्हि) इत्यादि पूर्वोक्तं पठति ।

**लवङ्गिका**—सखि एष खलु मधुरमधुरसार्द्रार्द्रमञ्जरीकवलनकेलिकलकोकिलकुलकोलाहलाकुलितसहकारशिखरोड्डीनचटुलचञ्चरीकनिकरव्यतिकरोद्दलितदलकरालचम्पकाधिवासमनोहरो मरालमांसलजघनपरिणाहोद्वहनमन्थरोरुभरविसंष्ठुलस्खलितचरणसंचारमसृणगमनोऽपनीतस्वेदशीकरसुधाबिन्दूयमानमुग्धमुखचन्द्रचन्दनायमानशीतलस्पर्शस्त्वां परिष्वजति कुसुमाकरोद्यानमारुतस्तदेहि प्रविशावः । (सहि एसो क्खु महुरमहुरसोल्लोल्लमञ्जरीकवलणकेलिकलकोइलउलकोलाहलाउलिदसहआरसिहरुड्डीणचडुलचञ्चरीअणिअरव्वइअरुद्दलिददलकरालचम्पआहिवासमणोहरो मरालमंसलजहणपरिणाहुव्वहणमन्थरोरुभरविसंठुलक्खलिदचलणसंचारमसिणगमणोवणीदसेअसीअरसुहाबिन्दुईज्जन्तमुद्धमुहचन्दचन्दणाअमाणसीअलफंसो तुमं परिस्सअदि कुसुमाअरुज्जाणमारुदो ताँ एहि पविसह्म ।)

(परिक्रम्य प्रविशतः ।)

---

रपेक्षमेवात्मा दत्त इति भगवति किं सत्यमिति मां पृच्छतीति भावः । अत्रान्यपदेनाखेटकाश्रमवर्णनशुश्रूषादेः साक्षादुद्देश्यत्वं साहसकरणं चाशयस्थमिति सूचितम् । एवमिति श्रुत्वा चेतोधृतनायकानुस्मरणान्मदीयक्रोडे निवेशितशरीरा भवति । ततः किमेवं करोमीति चिन्तास्तिमितत्वं निश्चलत्वं चिरकालमेति । चिन्तेत्युपलक्षणम् । निःश्वासादिनापि लक्षिता भवतीत्यर्थः । यद्वा मदिति पञ्चमी । मत्सकाशाच्छ्रुत्वैवं करोतीत्यर्थः ॥ ३ ॥ समक्षं प्रत्यक्षम् । उत्तरमनन्तरकृत्यम् ॥ इत आगच्छेति शेषः ॥ **लवङ्गिका** । अत्रैव खलु कुसुमाकरोद्यानमारुतस्त्वां परिष्वजतीति संबन्धः । कीदृशः अतिमधुरमधुरसेनात्यार्द्राया मञ्जर्याः कवलने भक्षणे केलिः क्रीडा तया कलमव्यक्तध्वानं यत्कोकिलकुलं तस्य कोलाहलेनाकुलितादतिसुरभिचूतशिखरादुड्डीनश्चटुलो मनोज्ञो यो भ्रमरसमूहस्तस्य संपर्केण विकसितपुटस्यात एव करालस्य दन्तुरस्य चम्पकस्याधिवासेन गन्धेन मनोहरः । एतेन शैत्यसौगन्ध्ये दर्शिते । सहकारमञ्जरीणां कोकिलाकुलत्वं भ्रमरस्य तत्त्यागे हेतुः । मरालो हस्ती हंसो वा । तस्येव मांसलजघनपरिणाहोद्वहनेन मन्थरावलसौ यावूरू । त्वदीयाविति भावः । तयोर्गौरवेण विसंष्ठुलं विषमं यथा तथा स्खलितस्य चरणस्य संचारेण मसृणं मन्दं

---

१ श्यामः. २ महुरसाद्द. ३ कवल केलि. ४ मरालजहण. ५ संचलणोवणीद. ६ बिन्दुज्जलमुद्ध. ७ तासहि इदो परिक्कमामो.

(ततः प्रविशति माधवः।)

**माधवः**—(सहर्षम्।) हन्त परागता भगवती। इयं हि मम

**आविर्भवन्ती प्रथमं प्रियायाः सोच्छ्वासमन्तःकरणं करोति।**
**संतापदग्धस्य शिखण्डियूनो वृष्टेः पुरस्तादचिरप्रभेव ॥ ४ ॥**

(दृष्ट्वा) अये लवङ्गिकाद्वितीया मालत्यपि।

**आश्चर्यमुत्पलदृशो वदनामलेन्दु-**
**सांनिध्यतो मम मुहुर्जडिमानमेत्य।**
**जात्येन चन्द्रमणिनेव महीधरस्य**
**संधार्यते द्रवमयो मनसा विकारः ॥ ५ ॥**

---

यद्गमनं तेनोपनीतेन स्वेदशीकरेणामृतबिन्दुसंदृशे मुग्धमुखचन्द्रे। अर्थात्तव। चन्दनायमानः शीतलः स्पर्शो यस्य सः। अनेन मान्द्यं शैत्यमपि ध्वनितम्। 'सहकारोऽतिसौरभः' इत्यमरः। 'चञ्चरीकोऽलिगीतयोः' इति धरणिः। 'करालो दन्तुरे' इत्यमरः। 'मरालो हंसगजयोर्मरालो विस्तृते शुभे।' इति विश्वः। तेन मरालस्य विस्तृतस्य शुभस्येति वा योज्यम्। 'मसृणं चिक्कणं समम्' इत्यमरः॥ **माधवः**। हन्त हर्षे। परागतायाता॥ **आविरित्यादि**। इयं भगवती प्रियायाः पुरस्तादाविर्भवन्ती प्रथमं मम चित्तं सविकासं करोति। कीदृशस्य। संतापदग्धस्य कामाग्निदग्धस्य। यथा विद्युद्वृष्टेः पुरस्तादाविर्भवन्ती मयूरतरुणस्य चित्तं सोच्छ्वासं करोति। निदाघतप्तस्य युवग्रहणमुन्मादहेतुद्योतनाय। प्रियाया इत्यत्र 'षष्ठ्यतसर्थप्रत्ययेन' इति षष्ठी। अत एव प्रियायाः प्रथममिति न योजना। प्रथमपदयोगेषष्ठ्यभावात्। अनेन प्रियाप्यागमिष्यतीति सूचितम्॥ ४॥ मालतीत्यत्रापिशब्दो गौरवे। निपातानामनेकार्थत्वात्। **आश्चर्यमित्यादि**। अस्याः पद्माक्ष्या मुखनिर्मलचन्द्रसंनिधौ वारंवारं जडिमानं सर्वकार्याप्रतिपत्तिरूपं प्राप्य जाड्येन जडिम्ना करणेन मम मनसा विकारः स्वरूपान्यथाभावः संधार्यते। कीदृशः। द्रवमय इव द्रवमयः। हृदयद्रवीकरणात्स्वेदादिमत्त्वाच्च। अन्यस्याः समागमाद् द्रवमयो विकारोऽस्यास्तु सान्निध्यादेवेति कर्मातिशयदर्शनादाश्चर्यम्। यदाह भरतः—'कर्मातिशयनिर्वृत्तो भवेद्विस्मयसंभवः। सिद्धिस्थानेष्वसौ साध्यः प्रहर्षपुलकादिभिः॥' यथामलेन्दुसंनिधौ जडिमानं शैत्यमासाद्य शैत्येनैव चन्द्रकान्तेन शैलस्य द्रवमयो विकारो द्रवत्वं संधार्यते। अत्र महीधरसादृश्येन माधवस्य धीरत्वादिगुणावष्टम्भसंभार उक्तः। 'जात्येन' इति पाठे जात्येन जातिमता। उत्कृष्टेनेति यावत्। चन्द्रकान्तेनेत्यस्य परं विशेषणं द्रष्टव्यम्। यद्वा। मनोविशेषणमपि। जात्ये-

---

१ निदाघसंतप्तशि०. २ दिष्ट्या. ३ पुनर. ४ जाड्येन. ५ संचा०. ६ श्रुषमयो. ७ मनसः

संप्रति रमणीयतरा मालती ।

**ज्वलयति मनोभवाग्निं मदयति हृदयं कृतार्थयति चक्षुः ।**
**परिमृदितचम्पकावलिविलासललितालसैरङ्गैः ॥ ६ ॥**

**मालती**—सखि अस्मिन्कुब्जकनिकुञ्जे कुसुमान्यवचिनुवः ।
( सहि इमस्सिं कुज्जअणिउञ्जे कुसुमाइं अवचिणुह्म । )

**माधवः**—

**प्रथमप्रियावचनसंश्रवस्फुर-**
**त्पुलकेन संप्रति मया विडम्ब्यते ।**
**घनराजिनूतनपयःसमुक्षण-**
**क्षणबद्धकुड्मलकदम्बडम्बरः ॥ ७ ॥**

**लव०**—सखि एवं कुर्वः । ( सहि एव्वं करेह्म । )

( पुष्पावचयं नाटयतः । )

**माधवः**—अपरिमेयाश्चर्यमाचार्यकं भगवत्याः ।

**मालती**—सखि इतोऽप्यन्यस्मिन्नवचिनुवः । ( सहि इदो वि अण्णस्सिं अवचिणुह्म । )

---

नाभिजनवतापि । अत्रापिरध्याहार्यः । अत एवाश्चर्यम् ॥ ५ ॥ **संप्रतीति** । पुरा कामवेगस्याङ्कुरावस्थया रमणीया । अधुना तु तस्य पल्लवितत्वेन रमणीयतरा ॥ इदमेव स्फोटयति-**ज्वलयतीत्यादि** । संप्रति मालत्यङ्गैः कामाग्निमुद्दीपयति । चित्तं सोन्मादं करोति । नेत्रं कृतप्रयोजनं विधत्ते । ममेति शेषः । **कीदृशैः** । परिमृदितचम्पकमालावद्विलासैर्ललितैश्च अलसैर्मन्दैर्लज्जया निभृतत्वेनेति भावः । 'यानस्थानासनादीनां नेत्रवक्त्रादिकर्मणाम् । उपयातविशेषो यः स विलासो मतो बुधैः ॥ इति भरतः । 'हस्तपादाङ्गविन्यासभ्रूनेत्रोष्ठप्रयोजितम् । सुकुमारविधानेन ललितं तन्निगद्यते ॥' इति भरतः । यद्वा । परिमृदितचम्पकमालाविलासानि म्लानानि । ललितानीतस्ततः क्षिप्तानि । अलसानि मन्दानि । ततस्त्रिपदकर्मधारयः । ललधातुश्चाञ्चल्यार्थेऽपि धातोरनेकार्थत्वात् । 'लुलितालसैः' इति पाठे लुलितानीतस्ततः क्षिप्तानीत्यर्थः ॥ ६ ॥ **प्रथमेत्यादि** । संप्रति मया मेघमालानवजलसेचनेन क्षणबद्धकलिकनीपस्य डम्बरः साम्यं प्रपञ्चो वावलम्ब्यते । कीदृशेन । प्रथमप्रियावचनसंश्रवणाद्व्यक्तरोमाञ्चेन । संस्तवेति पाठे संस्तवः परिचयः । तदनेन दृष्टान्तेन सर्वाङ्गीणं पुलकं तस्य च स्थैर्यमुक्तम् । 'घनजीमूतमुदिर' इत्यमरः ॥ ७ ॥ **माधवः अपरिमेयेत्यादि** । पुष्पत्रोटनकाले मालतीस्तनमुकुलादिदर्शनादानन्दसंदोहेन माधवस्य संतोषप्रकाश इति

---

१ कुब्ज. २ प्रथमं. ३ अवलम्ब्यते. ४ समुच्छ्वसत्. ५ प्रति० ६ अवरस्सिं०.

**कामन्दकी**—( मालतीं परिष्वज्य । ) अयि विरम विरम । निःसहासि जाता । तथाहि ।

स्खलयति वचनं ते संश्रयत्यङ्गमङ्गं
जनयति मुखचन्द्रोद्भासिनः स्वेदबिन्दून् ।
मुकुलयति च नेत्रे सर्वथा सुभ्रु खेद-
स्त्वयि विलसति तुल्यं वल्लभालोकनेन ॥ ८ ॥

( मालती लज्जां नाटयति । )

**लव०**—शोभनं भगवत्याज्ञप्तम् । ( सोहणं भअवदीए आणत्तं । )

**माधवः**—हृदयंगमः परिहासः ।

**काम०**—तदास्यताम् । किंचिदाख्येयमाख्यातुकामास्मि ।

( सर्वा उपविशन्ति । )

**काम०**—( मालत्याश्चुबुकमुन्नमय्य । ) शृणु चित्रमिदं सुभगे ।

**मालती**—अवहितास्मि । ( अवहिदह्मि । )

**काम०**—अस्ति तावदेकदा प्रसङ्गतः कथित एव मया माधवाभिधानः कुमारो यस्त्वामिव मामकीनस्य मनसो द्वितीयं निबन्धनम् ।

**लव०**—स्मरामः । ( सुमरामो । )

---

भावः ॥ अज्ञातमाधवसंनिधानां मालतीं श्रमोपन्यासव्याजेन कामन्दकी श्लिष्टनर्मवचनमाह—**अयीत्यादि** । निःसहा परिश्रान्तासि त्वमतो विरम त्यज खेदमिति शेषः । यद्वा विरम पुष्पावचयात् । उपविशेति भावः । पक्षे निःसहा कामाद् ग्लाना त्वं जातासि ततो विशेषेण रमस्व । आशंसायां लोट् ॥ **स्खलयतीत्यादि** । हे सुभ्रु शोभनभ्रूयुते वल्लभालोकनेन समं यथा तथा त्वयि खेदो विलसति स्वव्यापारं कुरुते । यथा वल्लभालोकनं तथा खेद इति भावः । पक्षे वल्लभेनावलोकनं खेदश्च । अत एव सर्वथेति तुल्यत्वम् । तदेवाह—खेदो वचनं तव स्खलयति । प्रत्यङ्गं संश्रयत्याश्रयति । 'स्रंसयति' इति पाठे शिथिलयति । आस्यशशिनो निःसरत्स्वेदकणाञ्जनयति । नयनद्वयं मुकुलयति च । 'रतान्ते च श्रमे चैव सुखसम्भोगभावने । गन्धे स्पर्शे च हर्षे च मुकुला दृष्टिरिष्यते ॥' इति भरतः । वल्लभालोकनेऽप्येवं भवति । इह वल्लभालोकनं त्वयि वर्तत इति भावः ॥ ८ ॥ **लवङ्गिका** । विरम्यतामित्याशयः ॥ **कामन्दकी** । चिबुकमधरतलावयवमुन्नमय्योत्तोल्य । सुभग इत्यनेन माधवचित्ताकर्षणेन त्वमेव सौभाग्यवतीति ध्वनितम् । **कामन्दकी** । कुमार इत्यनेन विस्मय उक्तः । निब-

---

१ यतः. २ संश्र०. ३ ल्लासि०. ४ लज्जते. ५ विचित्रम्. ६ प्रसङ्गात्.

**काम०**—स खलु मैदनोद्यानयात्रादिवसात्प्रभृति दुर्मनायमानः परवानिव शरीरोपतापेन। तथा हि।

यदिन्द्रावानन्दं प्रणयिनि जने वा न भजते
व्यनक्त्यन्तस्तापं तदयमतिधीरोऽपि विषमम्।
प्रियङ्गुश्यामाङ्गप्रकृतिरपि चापाण्डुमधुरं
वपुः क्षामं क्षामं वहति रमणीयश्च भवति॥ ९॥

**लव०**—एतदपि तस्मिन्नवसरे भगवतीं त्वरयन्त्यावलोकितयोदीरितमासीदस्वस्थशरीरो माधव इति। (ऐदं वि तस्सिं अवसरे भअवदिं तुवराअन्तीए अवलोइदाए उदीरिदं आसि अस्सत्थशरीरो माहवो त्ति।)

**काम०**—यावदशृणवं मालत्येवास्य मन्मथोन्मादहेतुरिति। ममापि स एव निश्चयः। कुतः।

अनुभवं वदनेन्दुरुपागमन्नियतमेष यदस्य महात्मनः।
क्षुभितमुत्कलिकातरलं मनः पय इव स्तिमितस्य महोदधेः॥ १०॥

**माधवः**—अहो उपन्याससंशुद्धिः। अहो महत्त्वारोपणे यत्नः। अथ वा।

शास्त्रेषु निष्ठा सहजश्च बोधः
प्रागल्भ्यमभ्यस्तगुणा च वाणी।
कालानुबोधः प्रतिभानवत्व-
मेते गुणाः कामदुघाः क्रियासु॥ ११॥

---

न्धनमालम्बनम्। **कामन्दकी**। परवानस्वतन्त्रः॥ **यदित्यादि**। शरीरोपतापेनायं परवानिव। यद्यस्माच्चन्द्रे प्रणयिनि जने वानन्दं प्रीतिं न भजते न लभते। तत्तथार्थे। तथापि धैर्ययुक्तोऽप्ययं दुःसहमन्तस्तापं प्रकाशयति। फलिनीश्यामशरीरस्वभावोऽप्यापाण्डुमधुरमीषत्पाण्डु मनोहरमतिक्षीणं वपुर्वहति च यथा यथा तथा तथा। रम्यश्च भवति। अपिर्विस्मये। चकारः समुच्चये। अपि चेति समस्त एव समुच्चये वा। तदिह रागावस्थायां यथोचितं विधेहीत्याशयः। 'प्रियङ्गुः फलिनी' इत्यमरः॥ ९॥ **कामन्दकी**। यावदवधारणे। मालत्येव हेतुरित्येवाशृणवमित्यर्थः। अशृणवमश्रौषम्॥ **अनुभवमित्यादि**। अयं वदनेन्दुरस्य महात्मनो निश्चितमेवानुभवमुपागमदुपागतः। यत्कारणादस्य स्तिमितस्य स्थिरस्य मनो विचलितम्। तदेवं ममापि स एव निश्चयः। किंभूतम्। उत्कण्ठाचपलम्। यथा स्तिमितस्य निश्चलस्य महात्मनोऽगाधस्य समुद्रस्य चन्द्रानुभवात्कल्लोलचपलं जलं क्षुभ्यति। 'कथितोत्कलिकोत्कण्ठाहेलासलिलवीचिषु।' इति मेदिनीकरः॥ १०॥ **माधवः**। शुद्धिरक्लिष्टता॥ दूतीगुणानाह—**शास्त्रेष्वित्यादि**। निष्ठेदमित्थ-

---

१ मन्मथो०. २ च मनोज्ञश्च. ३ एवं. ४ जह अस्स०. ५ यावदहं. ६ एष. ७ बुद्धिः. ८ अहो मम च. ९ कालानुरोधः. १० कामदुहः.

**काम०**—[1]अतस्तेन जीवितादुद्विजमानेन दुष्करमपि न किंचिन्न क्रियते । [2]असौ हि

> **धत्ते चक्षुर्मुकुलिनि रणत्कोकिले बालचूते**
> **मार्गे गात्रं क्षिपति बकुलामोदगर्भस्य वायोः ।**
> **दा[3]हप्रेम्णा सरसबिसिनीपत्रमात्रान्तराय-**
> **स्ताम्यन्मूर्तिः श्रयति बहुशो मृत्यवे चन्द्रपादान् ॥ १२ ॥**

**माधवः**—अन्य एवाक्षुण्णः कथाप्रकारो भगवत्याः ।

**मालती**—( स्वगतम् ) अतिदुष्करं करोति । ([5]अदिदुक्करं करेदि । )

---

मेवेति निर्णयः । तत्र सहजो बोधो नैसर्गिकं ज्ञानम् । ज्ञाने सति प्रागल्भ्यं वावदूकता । अभ्यस्ता गुणा श्लेषादयो यत्र तादृशी वाणी । यद्वा अभ्यस्तमभ्यासस्तदनुगुणा वाणी च । कालावबोधः समयज्ञानम् । प्रतिभानमनुरूपं तात्कालिकस्मरणं तद्योगित्वम् । एते गुणाः सर्वकर्मसु प्रकरणाद् दूतीकृत्येषु वा कामदुहोऽभिलषितप्रदाः । तत्र शास्त्रनिष्ठया पटुत्वं प्रागल्भ्येन धाष्ट्य प्रतिभानवत्त्वेनेङ्गितज्ञत्वं दूतीगुण उक्तम् । यदाह–' पटुता धृष्टता चेतीङ्गितज्ञत्वं प्रतारणम् । देशकालज्ञता चैव दूतीकृत्ये गुणा मताः॥ ' कामदुह इत्यत्र सत्स्वित्यादिना क्विप् ॥ ११ ॥ **कामन्दकी** । जीवितादुद्विजमानेनेति ' प्रद्वेषः प्राणितव्येषु ' इति भरतानुसरणम् । न क्रियत इति पाठे नः शिरश्चालने ॥ दुष्करमेवाह—**धत्त इत्यादि** । तेन दुष्करं क्रियते । यस्मादयं नवाम्रे कलिकायुक्ते ध्वनत्कोकिले मृत्यवे मरणाय नेत्रं धत्ते । बकुलगन्धबन्धोर्वातस्य वर्त्मनि शरीरं क्षिपति स्थापयति । अत्र मार्गपदेनानागतेन वायुना येन पथा समागन्तव्यं तत्सूचितम् । बकुलामोदपदेन स्वकार्यक्षमता गर्भपदेन बाह्यान्तरभावनादृढतोक्ता । दावप्रेम्णा वनवह्निप्रीत्या चन्द्रकिरणान् वारंवारं श्रयति । एतेन चन्द्ररश्मीनां दाहकत्वमुक्तम् । अत्र प्रेमपदेन नायिकानुरागस्य च विरोधिविमर्शशून्यत्वं तृतीयया चाङ्गसंगहेतुत्वं च ध्वनितम् । कीदृक्षः । सरसपद्मिनीपत्रमात्रान्तरितो ग्लायमानकायः । सर्वत्र मृत्यव इति योज्यम् । तथा च मरणाय कृतोयम इति भावः । यदा अन्तरायो मरणे विघ्नः । तत्र पद्मिनीपत्रहेतुत्वम् । तदिह चन्द्रपादादीनां कामोद्दीपकतयानर्थहेतुत्वेन विप्रलम्भस्योत्कर्षः सूचितः । किं च मनोविकार इन्द्रियजन्य इत्यनेनेन्द्रियाणां शान्तिः कृता । नवचूतदर्शनेन नेत्रस्य । चूतैरानद्धत्वमुकुलितत्वाभ्यामातिदुःखदत्वम् । कोकिलरवाकर्णनेन श्रोत्रस्य । बकुलगन्धसंबन्धेन घ्राणस्य । वायुचन्द्रकरयोः स्पर्शेन त्वच इति ॥ १२ **माधवः** । अक्षुण्णोऽन्याननुभूतः कथाप्रकारः कथनक्रमः ॥ **मालती** । बालचूतदर्शनादेरतिपीडाकरत्वेन माल-

---

१ यतः. २ तथा हि. ३ दाव. ४ ग्रोत्तरीयः. ५ एवं...करेदि सो.

**काम०**—तदेवं प्रकृत्या सुकुमारः कुमारः कदाचिदप्यन्यत्रापरिक्लिष्टपूर्वस्तपस्वी । यतोधुना शक्यमनेन मरणमप्यनुभवितुम् ।

**मालती**—( जनान्तिकम् ) सखि आत्मनः कारणात्तस्य सर्वलोकालंकारभूतस्य किमप्याशङ्कमानया भगवत्या भीतायितास्मि । तत्किमिदानीमत्र प्रतिपत्स्ये । ( सहि अत्तणो कारणादा तस्स सव्वलोआलंकारभूदस्स किं वि आसकन्तीएँ भगवदीए भीदाविदह्मि । ता किं दाणिं एत्थ पडिवज्जिस्सं । )

**माधवः**—दिष्ट्या अनुकम्पितोऽस्मि भगवत्या ।

**लव०**—भगवत्येवंवादिनीत्याख्यायते । अस्माकमपि भर्तृदारिका भवनासन्नरथ्यामुखमुहूर्तमण्डनस्य तस्यैव बहुशोऽनुभूतदर्शना भूत्वा रविकिरणाश्लिष्टमुग्धकमलिनीकन्दसुन्दरावयवशोभाविभावितानङ्गवेदनाधिकतररमणीयापि परिजनं दुनोति । नाभिनन्दति केलिकलाः । केवलं कमलायमानकान्तहस्तपर्यस्तगण्डमण्डला दिवसं गमयति । अपि च विकासितारविन्दमकरन्दनिःस्यन्दसुन्दरेण दरदलितकुन्दमाकन्दमधुबिन्दुसंदोहवाहिना भवनोद्यानपर्यन्तमारुतेनोत्ताम्यति । ( भअवदी एव्वंवादिणि त्ति आचक्खीअदि । अह्माणं वि भट्टिदारिआ

---

त्यापि ज्ञानादेवमुक्तमिति भावः । **कामन्दकी** । अन्यत्रेत्यादिना त्वय्येव प्रथममनुरक्तोऽयमिति दर्शितम् । तपस्व्यनुकम्प्यः । ' तपस्वी तापसे चानुकम्प्ये च' इति विश्वः । अनेन वैदेशिकोऽयं वराक इति मयैतदुच्यते न कारणादित्युक्तम् । शक्यमिति । तथा च त्वमनुरागिणी भवेत्यर्थः ॥ **मालती** । अत्रात्मनो मम । किमपीत्यमङ्गलतयावचनीयं मरणमित्यर्थः । भीतायितेत्यत्राचारे क्यङ् । **किमिति** । तज्जीवनाय ममापि तत्रानुराग इति वक्तुमुचितमपि कुमारीत्वेनानुक्तमतस्त्वं वदेति भावः । कामन्दकीं प्रति । जनान्तिकमिदम् । माधवश्च गुप्तः । स श्रुत्वाह—दिष्टयेत्यादि ॥ **लवङ्गिका** । अत्र एवंवादिनीत्यत्र कामावस्था गुरुजने लज्जया वक्तुमनर्हापि मालतीनिमित्तमाधवावस्थाश्रवणात्सापि तन्निमित्ता कथ्यत इति भावः । अस्माकं भर्तृदारिका परिजनं दुनोतीत्यन्वयः । आश्लिष्टं स्पृष्टम् । मुग्धो बालः । कन्दं बिसम् । बालकमलिनीमूलं मृदुतरं रविकरस्पर्शान्म्लानं च भवति । तदनेन दृष्टान्तेन निःसहत्वतनुत्वे अवयवानामुक्ते । तद्दशायामपि सौन्दर्यद्योतनाय सुन्दरपदम् । अधिकतररमणीयापीत्यनेन कामालिङ्गितकायस्य कान्तिप्रकर्ष उक्तः । अत एवापिर्विस्मये । अतिकान्तस्य सुखजनकत्वनैयत्येन दुःखजनकत्वे चित्रात् । दुःखप्रकारमाह—नाभीत्यादि ।

---

१ मच (मर्त्य). २ आसंकमाणा भूदाविदह्मि अ न आणामि किं पडिवज्जिस्सं–स्सदि–नि

भवणासण्णरच्छामुहमुहुत्तमण्डणस्स तस्स उज्जेव्व बहुसो अणुभूददंसणा भविअ रविकिरणासिलिद्धमुद्धकमलिनीकन्दसुन्दरावअवसोहाविभाविदाणङ्गवअणाधिअदररमीणआ वि परिअण दुम्मेदि । णाहिणन्दइ केलिकलाओ । केवलं कमलाअन्तकन्तहत्थपल्हत्थगण्डमण्डला दिअसं गमेदि । अवि अ विअसिदारविन्दमअरन्दणीसन्दसुन्दरेण दरदलिदकुन्दमाअन्दमहुबिन्दुसंदोहवाहिणा भवणुज्जाणपेरन्तमारुदेण उत्तम्मदि ।)

यच्च तस्मिन्यात्रादिवसे निजमहोत्सवाभ्युदयदर्शनप्रतिपन्नरूपस्य भगवतः कामस्येव कामकाननालंकारकारिणस्तस्य विविधविभ्रमाभिराममनुरूपानुरागानुबन्धमहार्घीकृतयौवनारम्भमन्योन्यदृष्टिविनिपातवञ्चनावसरखिद्यमानचित्तत्वरमाणकौतूहलं समुल्लसितसाध्वसस्तम्भमन्थरावयवप्रतिलग्नस्वेदपुलकोत्कम्पसुन्दरमानन्दितसखीजनं प्रियसख्या परस्परावलोकनसुखं समासादितं ततः प्रभृति सविशेषदुःसहायासविजृम्भमाणोद्दामदेहदाहदारुणं दशापरिणाममनुभवन्ती मुहूर्तमात्रसंप्राप्तपूर्णचन्द्रोदयेव बालकमलिनी प्रम्लायति । (जं अ तस्सिं जत्तादिअहे णिअमहूसवाब्भुदअदंसणपडिवण्णरूवस्स भअवदो कामस्सं विअ कामकाणणालंक्कारआरिणो तस्सं विविहविब्भमाहिरामं अणुरूआणुराआणुबन्ध-

अत्र यत इत्यध्याहार्यम् । केलिः क्रीडा । कलाश्चतुःषष्टिः। यद्वा । केलीनां कलांशमात्रम् । कथं तर्हि दिनानि गमयतीत्याह केवलमित्यादि । कमलायमानं प्रसारितम् । इदं भरतानुमतम् । यदाह—'अप्राप्ते च प्रिये कार्यः स्त्रीभिर्गण्डान्वितः करः ।' पर्यस्तं क्षिप्तम् । निःस्यन्दः क्षरणम् । 'ईषदर्थे दराव्ययम्' इत्यमरः । दलितं विकसितम् । माकन्दश्चूतः । पुष्पपरमत्र । 'माकन्दः सहकारेऽस्त्री' इति मेदिनी । एतेन वायोस्त्रैगुण्यमुक्तम् । यच्चेति । यच्च प्रियसख्या यात्रादिने तस्य दर्शनसुखं समासादितं तत आरभ्य सा कमलिनीव प्रम्लायतीत्यन्वयः । प्रतिपन्नरूपस्य कृतदेहपरिग्रहस्य । कामस्यानङ्गत्वात्पुरातनत्वाच्च । महोत्सवदर्शनार्थमिदमुक्तमिति भावः । अद्भुतप्रतिपन्नरूपस्येत्याहिताग्न्यादिः । विविधविलासैरभिरामम् । यद्वा विविधभ्रमणमभिरामोऽभिरतिर्यत्र तत् । वञ्चना दर्शनाभावः । त्वरमाणं शीघ्रमुपजायमानम् । कथं पश्यामीति कुतुकं तयोश्चित्तेऽभवदित्याशयः। आनन्दितसखीजनं कामसंपत्त्येति भावः। विजृम्भमाणो वर्धमानः ।

१ संदसणा. २ अदा (करा). ३ वइउर (व्यतिकर.). ४ दूणेदि (दूनयति). ५ कलाकीलाओ (क्रीडाः). ६ मिलाअन्त (म्लायमान), किमिलाअन्त. ७ दिअहो (दिवसान्). ८ अण्णं अ जदो प्पहुदि. ९ दंसणत्थं. १० मम्महस्स (मन्मथस्य). ११ तस्स माहवस्स. १२ विब्भमाणुराआणु०.

महग्घीकिदजोव्वणारम्भं अण्णोण्णदिट्ठिविणिवाअवञ्चणावसरखिज्जन्ताचित्तुवरन्तकोदूहलं समुल्लसिदसद्धसत्थम्भमन्थरावअवपडिलग्गसेदपुलअउक्कम्पसुन्दरं आणन्दिदसहीअणं पिअसहीए परप्परावलोअणसुहं समासादिदं तदो पहुदि सविसेसदूसहआसविअम्भमाणुद्दामदेहदाहदारुणं दसापरिणामं अणुहोन्ती मुहुत्तमेत्तसंपत्तपुण्णचन्दोदआ विअ बालकमलिणी पम्मलाअदि )

तथापि च मुहूर्तमात्रहृदयविनिहितनिर्मीयमाणवल्लभसमागमा निर्भरसलिलासारसिच्यमानेव मेदिनी शीतलायत इति जानामि । येन प्रस्फुरत्कान्तदशनच्छदोच्छलद्दन्तमौक्तिकपङ्क्तिकान्तिसविशेषशोभितं निरन्तरोल्लसितपुलकपक्ष्मलकान्तकपालघूर्णमानसंततानन्दबाष्पस्तबकमीषद्विकसितनिष्पन्दमन्दतारोत्तानमसृणमुकुलायमाननेत्रनीलोत्पलमाविरलोद्भिन्नस्वेदजलबिन्दुसुन्दरललाटपट्टनवचन्द्रलेखामनोहरं मुग्धमुखपुण्डरीकमुद्वहन्ती विदग्धसहचरीचित्तसंशायितकौमारभावा भवति । ( तहा वि अ मुहुत्तमेत्तहिअअविणिहिदणिम्माअन्तवल्लहसमाअमा णिब्भरसलिलासारसिच्चमाणा विअ मेदिणी सीअलाअदि त्ति जाणामि । जेण पप्फुरन्तकन्तद-

हान् । दारुणो भयंकरः । मरणशङ्कयेति भावः । दशा कामावस्था । यथा क्षणमात्रप्राप्तचन्द्रोदया कमलिनी म्लायति तथेयमपि प्राप्तपूर्णचन्द्रोदया म्लायति । चन्द्रकरमपि सोढुमक्षमेति भावः । यद्वा यथा प्राप्तचन्द्रोदया पद्मिनी म्लायति तथा प्राप्तदर्शनसुखेयं म्लायतीत्यर्थः । ननु चन्द्रेण विरोधात्पद्मिन्या म्लानिर्युक्ता । अस्यास्तु माधवानुरागात्तद्दर्शने कथं म्लानिरिति । मैवम् । यथा शीतस्पर्शत्वेन चन्द्रः क्षणं पद्मिनीं सुखयति तथा माधवो मालतीमिति विवक्षितत्वात् । यद्वा मुहूर्तपदेनेह प्रथमचन्द्रोदय उक्तः । एवं चाभिनवोदितं चन्द्रं रक्ततया सूर्याभं दृष्ट्वा भ्रांत्या मुहूर्तं पद्मिनी तिष्ठत्यथ प्रम्लायति तथेयमपीत्यर्थः ॥ तथापि चेत्यत्रापिचेति भिन्नक्रमः । तथा शीतलायत इत्यपि जानामि चेति संबन्धः । निर्मायं मायारहितं सत्यमित्यर्थः । समागमेति भावनाबलादिति भावः । मेदिनी ग्रीष्मावसानकालीनेत्यर्थः । समागममेव द्रढयति । **येनेति** । येन हृदिस्थकान्तसंगमेनैवं सा भवति तेन विदग्धसहचरीचित्तसंशयितकौमारभावा भवति । वैदग्ध्ययुक्ततया सहचरीसंघेनैवं संशय्यते यन्मत्परोक्षेऽपि प्रियसंगतेयम् । कथमन्यथैतादृक् संस्थानमस्या इति भावः । दशनच्छदमधरम् । उच्छलन् प्रकाशमानः । अधरस्फुरणं भावनार्पितप्रियतमचुम्बनात् । 'मुक्तिका मौक्तिकं मुक्ता' इति शब्दभेदः । **निरन्तरेति** । संकल्पकृतवल्लभसमागमोद्भूतसात्त्विकभावेनेत्याशयः । घूर्णमानं लसमानम् । यद्यपि रोमाञ्चः सर्वाङ्गीण एव भवति तथापि रागातिशयद्योतनाय

१ कोदूहलुल्लसिद. २ पुलअकम्पाणन्दिअ. ३ णुद्दामदारुणद०. ४ पप्फुरिदरदणच्छउच्छलन्त.

सणच्छदुच्छलन्तदन्तमोत्तिअ[1]पन्तिकन्तिसविसेससोहिदं णिरन्तरुल्लसिदपुलअपह्मलकन्त-कवोलघोलन्तसंतदाणन्दबाहत्थवअं ईसिविअसिअणिप्फन्दमन्द[2]तारुत्ताणमसिणमुउला-अन्तणेत्तणीलुप्पलं अविरलुब्भिण्णसेअजलबिन्दुसुन्दरलला[3]टपट्टणवचन्दलेहामणोहरं मुद्धमु-हपुण्डरीअं उव्वहन्ती विअक्कसहअरीचित्तसंसइदकोमारभावा भोदि। )

किं चोद्दामशिशिरशशिमयूखनिकुरम्बचुम्बितप्रवृत्तनिःस्यन्दचन्द्रमणि-हारधारिणी प्रचुरकर्पूरसविशेषशिशिरचन्दनरसच्छटासारनिकरदन्तुरित-बालकदलीपत्रसंवाहनादिव्यापारत्वरमाणसहचरीसार्थविरचितोपनीतकमलि-नीदलजलार्द्राशयनीय उन्निद्रा[4] रजनीर्गमयति। ( किं अ उद्दा[5]मसिसिरससि-मउहणिउरुम्बचुम्बिदपउत्तणिस्सन्दचन्दमणिहारधारिणी पउरकप्पूरसविसेससिसिरचन्दण-रसच्छडासारणिअरदन्तुरिदबालकदलीवत्त[6]संवाहणादिव्वावारतुवरन्तसहअरीसत्थविरइदो-वणीदकमलिणीदलजलद्दा[7]सअणीए उण्णिद्दा र[8]अणीओ गमेदि। )

कथमप्युपलब्धनिद्रासुखा स्वेदप्रसृतपादपल्लवोद्भ्रान्तपिण्डालक्तक-

---

कपालपुलक एव वर्ण्यते कविसंप्रदायेनेत्यवधेयम्। मन्दतारं किञ्चिच्चलत्तारकम्। उत्तानमूर्ध्वविस्तृतम्। भावनोपनीतप्रिये लज्जादिदृक्षाभ्यामीषद्विकासितत्वम्। नि-ष्पन्दता मौग्ध्यात्। मन्दतारता नखदशनक्षतभावनया प्रियं प्रति सासूयत्वात्। उत्तानत्वं मुखदिदृक्षया। मसृणत्वं स्नेहभावनया। मुकुलत्वं रतावसानभावनया। यदाह–'निश्चलत्वं तदा यातो मुकुलत्वं च लोचने।' उद्भिन्नमुद्भूतम्। **स्वेदेति**। रतिश्रमादयं स्वेदः। तदनेन प्रबन्धेन तृप्तिरुक्ता। यदाह—'रोमाञ्चो वेपथुः स्वेदो लुलिते च विलोचने। मज्जन्त्या इव देहेषु आश्लेषरतृप्तिलक्षणम्॥' तदिह यदीयं वल्लभसमागमं न जानाति तदा कथमधरस्पन्दादिमती स्यात्। कुमारस्य भावः कौमारं शैशवं तस्य भावोऽभिप्रायः कटाक्षविक्षेपादिः संशयितो यस्याः सा। निशाचेष्टामाह–**किं चेति**। निकुरम्बः समूहः। चुम्बितेन चुम्बनेन प्रवृत्तनिःस्यन्दः संजातक्षरणः। छटा 'च्छट' इति यस्याः प्रसिद्धिः। दन्तुरितं विषमीकृतम्। संवाहनमर्पणम्। विरचितोपनीतं विरचनेनाङ्कदत्तम्। अस्मिन् पदे पूरः समूहः पूरणं वा। सविशेषपदेन शीतलकर्पूरसंस्पर्शादतिशीतलत्वमुक्तम्। कदलीपत्रस्य बाल-त्वेन शैत्यसौकुमार्ये उक्ते। कमलिनीदलमेव जलार्द्रार्द्रवस्त्रं तच्छय्यायाम्। 'आर्द्र-वस्त्रं जलार्द्रा स्यात्' इति हारावली। औन्निद्र्येणोन्निद्रतया। आत्मनः सखीनां चेति शेषः। एतेन निद्राच्छेदोद्वेगावुक्तौ॥ [ **कथमपीति**। ] निद्रैव सुखं निद्रासु-खम्। उद्वेगादिदुःखमयजागराविपर्ययरूपत्वादिदम्। निद्रेयं चिन्तावशात्। यदाह—

---

१ मुत्तिआवलिकन्ति. २ मन्थर. ३ णिडालचन्द; णिड्डिलवट्टेंदु. ४ औन्निद्र्येण इति ज०-संमतः पाठः। ५ उद्दामससि. ६ पत्तसअणा पादसंवा. ७ जलद्दतालउन्ता. ८ एव्व रअणिं.

रसा थरथरायमानपीवरोरुमूलविसंवादितनीवीबन्धनोत्क्षु[1]भ्यद्धृदयान्तरोत्तरङ्ग-निःश्वासवशविषमोच्छ्वसत्पक्ष्मलपयोधरोपरिनिहितवेपमानभुजलतावेष्टबन्धना झटिति प्रतिबोधवेलाविसर्जितोद्विग्नदृष्टिविनिपातविज्ञातशून्यशयनीयसंजात-मोहमीलल्लोचना ससंभ्रमसखीजनप्रयत्नप्रतिपन्नमूर्च्छाविच्छेदसमयसंगलि-तदीर्घनिःश्वासशेषजीविता किंकर्तव्यतामूढतया प्रथमप्रार्थितनिजजीविताव-सानं दुर्वारदैवदुर्विलसितोपालम्भमात्रव्यापारमस्मादृशं जनं करोति । ( कथं वि उवलद्धणिद्दासुहा सेदपज्झ[2]रिदपादपल्लवुव्वन्तपिण्डालत्तअरसा थरथराअन्तपीवरोरुमूल[3]-विसंवदिदणीविबन्धणा उक्खुब्भन्ताहिअअन्तरुत्तरङ्गणीसा[4]सवसविसमुच्छसन्तपह्मलपओ-हरोवरिणिहिद[5]वेवन्तभुअलदावेढ[6]बन्धणा झत्ति पडिबोधवेलाविसज्जिदुव्विण्णदिट्ठिविणिवाद-विण्ण[7]ादसुण्णसअणिज्जसंजादमोहमीलन्तलोअणा ससंभमसहीअणपअत्तपडिवण्णमुच्छावि-च्छेअसमअसंगलिददीहणीसा[8]ससेसजीविदा किंकादव्व[9]दामूढदाए पढमपत्थिदणिअजीवि-दावसाणं दुव्वारदेव्वदुव्विलसिदोवालम्भमेत्तव्वावारं अह्मारिसं जणं करेदि । )

तत्प्रेक्षतां भगवत्येषु तावल्लावण्यभूयिष्ठनिर्माणपरिपेलवेष्वङ्गेषु दारुण-विजृम्भितस्य कियच्चिरं कुशलावसानता मन्मथस्य भविष्यति ।

---

'दौर्बल्यालस्यचिन्ताद्यैर्निद्रा स्यात्कथयापि च ।' इति । वल्लभसमागमसंकल्पजस्वेदेन प्रस्रुतश्चरणपल्लवेनोद्वान्तः पिण्डीभूतालक्तकरसो यस्याः सा । अलक्तकच्छलेनानुरागमि-वोद्गमतीति भावः । अतिघनत्वार्थं पिण्डपदम् । थरथरायमानं कम्पमानम् । पीवरं महत् । वशं संसक्तम् । विसंवदितं स्खलितम् । प्रियस्योर्वाक्रमणभावनया प्रकम्पः । तदाकर्षणभावनया नीवीस्खलनम् । उत्खण्ड्यमानमुच्छलत् । उत्तरङ्गो यातायातवान् । विषमं यथा तथोच्छ्वसन् । पक्ष्मलः सरोमाञ्चः । वेष्टनं वेष्टः । इह हृदयोत्खण्डनादिकं प्रियसंभोगव्यायामभावनया । उपरिवर्तिप्रियस्य भुजलताबन्धनमालिङ्गनभावनया । प्रियप्राप्त्या प्रबुद्धा । प्रबोधश्च स्पर्शादिना भवति । मोहेति । शून्यशय्यादिदर्शनान्मूर्छि-तेत्यर्थः । ससंभ्रमः सादरः सावेगो वा । संगलितो निःसृतः । अनेन युगपन्नासापुट-निःसरणमाह । मूर्च्छाविच्छेदे तथैव श्वासप्रवृत्तेः । **जीवितेति** । मोहे सखीजनसेका-दिना मूर्च्छापगमे दीर्घनिःश्वासेन जीवतीत्यवधार्यत इत्यर्थः । **किंकर्तव्येति** । जीविता सती किं करोमीति न वेत्तीत्यर्थः । **प्रथमेति** । वयमेव प्रथमं म्रियामह इत्यर्थः । स्वयमन-ध्यवसायाल्लवङ्गिका कामन्दकीं पृच्छति-**तस्मात्प्रेक्षतां भगवतीति** । पेलवं कोम-

---

१ उत्खण्ड्य-ल्य-मान ( टी० ) २ पक्खालिद. ३ मुल-पास वश. ४ णिस्सासविसम-समुसन्तपुलकपह्मल. ५ विक्खित्त. ६ वेट्ठण. ७ विण्णाण ( विज्ञान ). ८ णीसासजणिदजी-विदास:. ९ ०दव्वमूढ. १० सहीजणं.

कथं चेमानि रमणकेलिकलहकोपोपरागपल्लवितकेरलीकपोलकोमलोद्वेल्लोद्भिमल्चन्द्रचन्द्रिकोद्दामदलिततिमिरावरणानि विभावरीमुखानि । इमे चोल्लसितदुग्धसिन्धुपूरधवलोज्ज्वलज्योत्स्नाजलप्रक्षालितगगनाङ्गनाः परिमलितपाटलाबकुलनिर्मथनबहलपरिमलोद्गारसंवलनमसृणमांसलमलयमारुतोद्धूमायितदशादिङ्मुखा वसन्तरजनीपरिणाहा अनर्थकारिणो भविष्यन्ति प्रियसख्या इति । ( ता पेक्खदु भअवदी इमेसु दाव लावण्णभूइट्ठणिम्माणपरिपेलवेसु[1] अङ्गेसु दारुणविअम्भिदस्स किअच्चिरं कुसलावसाणदा मम्महस्स भविस्सदि । कधं अ इमाइं रमणकेलिकलहकोवोवराअ[2]पल्लविदकेरलीकपोलकोमलुव्वेल्लन्त[3]विमलचन्दचन्दिओ[4]द्दामदलिदतिमिरावरणाइं विभावरीमुहाइं । इमे अ उल्लसिददुद्धसिन्धु[5]पूरधवलुज्जलजोण्हाजलपक्खालिदगअणङ्गणा[6] पारिमलिदपाडलावउ[7]लणिम्महणबहल[8]परिमलुग्गार[9]संवलणमसिणमसलम[10]मलअमारुदुद्धूमाविददहदिसामुहा वसन्तरअणीपरिणाहा[11] अणत्थआरिणो भविस्सन्ति पिअसहीए त्ति । )

**काम०**—लवङ्गिके

> यदि तद्विषयोनुरागबन्धः
> स्फुटमेतद्धि फलं गुणज्ञतायाः ।
> इति नन्दितमप्यवस्थयास्या
> हृदयं दारुणया विदीर्यते[12] मे ॥ १३ ॥

---

लम् । दारुणत्वं देहदाहादिकारित्वात् । इमानि विभावरीमुखानि प्रियसख्याः कथमेवं भविष्यन्तीत्यन्वयः । उपरागो लौहित्यम् । पल्लवितः पल्लवाकारीकृतः । केरली केरलदेशस्त्री । तस्या अतिगौरत्वेन लौहित्यार्थं ग्रहणम् । उद्वेल्लन्पतन् । उद्दामदलितमतिदारितम् । इह दृष्टकेरलीकपोलसाम्येनोदितचन्द्रेण तिमिरावरणनाशे रात्रेरुपक्रमः कथितस्ततश्चन्द्रस्य दुःसहता मालत्या ध्वनिता । परिमलितं कृतम् । निर्मन्थनं मर्दनम् । उद्गार उद्गमः । संवलनं मिश्रीभावः । मसृणं मन्दम् । मांसलः पुष्टः । धूमायितं धूमेनेवाकुलीकृतम् । परिणाह आभोगः ॥ **कामन्दकी** । एवं श्रुत्वा कामन्दकी तटस्थेवाह—**यदीत्यादि** । यदि तद्विषयोऽनुरागस्तदा गुणज्ञतायाः प्रव्यक्तमेतद्विशिष्टं फलम् । तदा सैव गुणं जानातीत्यर्थः । एतद्भाति पाठ एतद्गुणज्ञतायाः फलमेवेत्यर्थः । हिरवधारणे । इति नन्दितमानन्दं प्रापितमपि मे हृदयमस्या अवस्थया विदार्यते । एतदवस्थतया मरणमप्यस्याः सं-

---

१ पेसलेसु. २ कोवराअ ३ व्वेल्लन्तविमल. ४ विमलचन्दिआ. ५ धारा. ६ नहोक्कणा. ७ मुडल ( मुकुल ). ८ बहुल. ९ लुप्पीडसंकलन. १० मसलाअन्त ( मांसलायमान ). ११ परिणामा. १२ विदार्यते.

**माधवः**—स्थान[1] एव हृल्लासो[2] भगवत्याः ।

**काम०**—अहो प्रमादः ।

**प्रकृतिललितमेतत्सौकुमार्यैकसारं**
**वपुरयमपि सत्यं दारुणः पञ्चबाणः ।**
**चलितमलयवातोद्धूतचूतप्रसूनः**
**कथमयमपि कालश्चारुचन्द्रावतंसः ॥ १४ ॥**

**लव०**—अन्यच्च ज्ञातं भवतु भगवत्या । एतन्माधवप्रतिच्छन्दकसनाथं चित्रफलकम् । ( मालत्याः स्तनांशुकमपनीय दर्शयति । ) एषापि तस्यैव स्वहस्तविरचितेति कण्ठावलम्बिता बकुलमाला जीवनं प्रियसख्या इति । ( अण्णं अ जाणिदं होदु भअवदीए । एदं माहवप्पडिच्छन्दअसणाहं चित्तफलअं । एसा वि तस्स ज्जेव्व सहत्थविरइदत्ति कण्ठावलम्बिदा बउलमाला जीविणं पिअसहीए[6] त्ति ।

**माधवः**—( सस्पृहं )

**जितमिह भुवने त्वया यदस्याः**
**सखि बकुलावलि वल्लभासि जाता ।**
**परिणतबिसकाण्डपाण्डुमुग्ध-**
**स्तनपरिणाहविलासवैजयन्ती ॥ १५ ॥**

---

भाव्यत इति भावः ॥ १३ ॥ **माधवः** । स्थाने युक्तम् । स्थानेशब्दोऽत्र योग्यवाची । हल्लासो हृदयशोषः **कामन्दकी** । प्रकृतीत्यादि । अस्या वपुरिदं स्वभावसुन्दरं सौकुमार्यमेवैकः सारः स्थिरांशो यत्र तत् । एतत्सत्यं निश्चितम् । अयमेव कामचरितानुभावात्कामोऽप्ययं निर्दयः । अदोऽपि सत्यम् । पञ्चबाण इत्यनेनैकबाणापेक्षया दुःसहत्वमुक्तम् । अयमपि कालश्चलन्मलयानिलकम्पितचूतपुष्पश्चारुचन्द्रभूषणश्च । कथमिति शिरश्चालने । हिमादेरपगमाच्चारुचन्द्रत्वम् । तदीदृशेऽनर्थहेतौ कथमियं जीविष्यतीत्यहो प्रमादः । अत्र नाथपदेन चित्रगतस्यापि माधवस्य मालतीनाथत्वं ध्वनितम् ॥ १४ ॥ **लवङ्गिका** । विरचितेति हेतोः । जीवितफलकत्वाज्जीवितम् । कार्यकारणयोरभेदात् । **माधवः** । स्तनांशुकापनयनेन व्यक्तस्तनदर्शनात्सस्पृहम् । **जितमित्यादि** । सखि बकुलमाले त्वयेह भुवने जितम् । प्रौढमृणालदण्डपाण्डुमनोहरस्तनविलासपताकेवास्या मालत्या वल्लभा जातासि । मालतीवल्लभत्वात्सखीत्युक्तम् । हृदयधारणेन वल्लभेत्युक्तम् । तथा च मालत्यालिङ्गनं तव

---

१ अहो स्थाने. २ हृदयोद्वेगः, अभ्युल्लासः. ३ ०मार्यस्य. ४ प्रसृतिः. ५ जीवितं, संजी०. ६ इति बकुलमालामपनीय दर्शयति इत्यधिकं क्वचित्. ७ दण्डकाण्डपाण्डुस्त०. ८ विशाल.

( नेपथ्ये कलकलः । सर्वे आकर्णयन्ति । पुनर्नेपथ्ये । )

रे रे शंकरगृहाधिवासिनो जानपदा एष खलु यौवनारम्भगर्वसंभृतदुर्विषहामर्षरोषव्यतिकरबलात्कारविघटितोद्घाटितलोहपञ्जरनिबद्धशृङ्खलानिरोधप्रतिभङ्गसंकलितनिजलीलावि[1]लासोद्वेल्लद्बहलोत्तुङ्गलाङ्गूलविकटवैजयन्तिका[2]डम्बरोद्दामशरीरसंनिवेशो मठादपक्रम्य तत्क्षणसतृष्णकवलितानेकदेहावयमध्यनिष्ठुरास्थिखण्डटंकारकटकटायमानकरपत्रकठिनदंष्ट्राकरालमुखकन्दरः प्रचण्डवज्रनिर्घातदारुणचपेटामोटनपा[3]तितानेकनरतुरङ्गजाङ्गलोद्गारभरितगलगुहागर्भगम्भीरघर्घरोराल्लिगलपूरणशब्दसंदर्भप्रतिरवाभोगभीषितनष्टनिष्ठापिताशेषजननिवहः कठोरनखरकर्पराक्रमणनिर्दयदारितजन्तुगात्रावयवप्रवृत्तरक्तकर्दमितगतिपथो दुष्टशार्दूलः कुपितकृतान्तलीलायितं करोति। तत्परिरक्षत यथाशक्ति प्रियसख्या मदयन्तिकाया जीवितमिति। (रे रे सं[4]कर-

---

संपन्नं न ममेति भावः ॥ १५ ॥ कलकलः कोलाहलः । **पुनर्नेपथ्य इति** । अत्रैष व्याघ्रः क्रूद्धयमविलासं कुरुते । सर्वं भक्षयतीत्यर्थः । मठाच्छात्रादिगृहान्निर्गत्य । कीदृशः । यौवनारम्भेण प्रवृद्धौ यो दुःसहावक्षान्तिक्रोधौ तयोर्मिलनेन यो बलात्कारस्तेन विघटितं त्यक्तबन्धीकृतमुद्घाटितं मोटितं च यल्लोहपञ्जरं तत्र च प्रतिबद्धभृङ्खलानिरोधप्रतिभङ्गो विपरीतभङ्गस्तेन संकलिता मिलिता या निजलीला तद्विलासपर्यन्त उद्वेल्लन्कम्पमानोत एवोच्छलन्नूर्ध्वं गच्छन्यो बहलतुङ्गलाङ्गूलः स्थूलोच्छ्रितलाङ्गूलस्तस्य विस्तीर्णवैजयन्तिकासदृशप्रपञ्चेनोड्डामर उत्कटकठोरक्रियः शरीरसंनिवेशो यस्य सः। परगुणासहिष्णुतामर्षः । रोषः क्रोध एव । यद्वा स्थिरः क्रोध एवामर्षः । यदाह–'क्रोधः कृतापराधेषु स्थिरोऽमर्ष इति स्थितः । प्रतिकूलेषु तैक्ष्ण्यस्य प्रबोधः क्रोध उच्यते ॥' यद्वा अमर्षोऽक्षान्तिः । तत्क्षणं सतृष्णं कवलिता येऽनेकप्राणिशरीरावयवास्तेषां मध्ये कठोराणि यान्यस्थीनि तेषां खण्डे खण्डने यष्टङ्कारो ध्वनिभेदस्तेन कटकटायमानाः करपत्रवत्कठिना या दंष्ट्रास्ताभिः करालो भीषणो मुखकंदर आस्यकुहरं यस्य सः । टङ्कारेण दुर्भेद्यत्वमुक्तम् । दुर्भेद्यप्रवृत्तौ दन्तानां कटाकटाशब्दकरणं स्वभावः । विस्तीर्णत्वात्कन्दर इव कन्दरः । प्रचण्डवज्रप्रहारदारुणो यश्चपेटः पाणितलप्रहारस्तेन यदामोटनं चूर्णनं तेन कवलिता आस्वादिता येऽनेकनरास्तुरङ्गाश्च तेषां जाङ्गलं मांसं तस्योद्गारेण प्रपूरणेन भरितो यो गलगुहागर्भस्तत्र गम्भीरो घर्घरो दीर्घमधुरो य उरल्लिर्गलगर्जितं तेन यो गल्लपूरणशब्दस्तस्य संदर्भेण समूहेन प्रतिरवाभोगः प्रतिशब्दविस्तारस्तेन भीषितो भयं नीतो नष्टो विद्राणो निष्ठापितो निष्ठापर्यन्तं लम्भितोऽशेषजननिवहो येन सः । कठोरनखकर्पराक्रमणेन निर्दयं दारितं यज्ज-

---

१ विलासपर्यन्तोद्वेलदुच्छलद्बह० (टी.). २ कावलम्बितडम्बरोड्डामर ( टी.). ३ कवलित. ४ ०पुरवासिजाण०.

धराधिवासिणो जाणवदा एसो क्खु जोव्वणारम्भ[1]गव्वसंभारिददुव्विसहामारिसरोसवइअरब- लामेडिअविहडिदुग्घाडिदलोहपञ्जर[2]णिबद्धसिङ्खलाणिरोहपडिभङ्गसंकलिदाणिअलीलाविला- सुव्वेल्लि[3]न्तबहलुत्तुङ्गलङ्गुलीवअडवजअन्तिआडम्बरद्दाम[4]सरीरसंणिवेसो मठादो अवक्कमिअ तक्खणसतिक्खवलिदाणेअदेहिदेहावअवमज्झणिग्गत्थिखण्डटंकारकडकडाअन्तकरवत्तकठि- णदाढाकरालमुहकन्दरो प[5]अण्डवज्जानिग्घाददारुणचवेडामोडणप्प[6]ाडिदाणेअणरतुरङ्गजङ्गलु- ग्गारभारिदगलगुहागब्भगम्भीरघग्घरोरल्लिगल्लूरणसद्दसंदब्भपडिरवाँ[7]भोअभीसाविदणट्ठणि- द्दा[8]विदासेसजणणिवहो कठोरणहरकप्परक्कमणनिद्दअदारिदजन्तुगत्तावअवप्पउत्तरत्तकद्दमि-[9] अगइवहो दुट्ठसद्दूलो कुविअकअन्तलीलाइदं करेदि । ता पडिरक्खध जधासत्ति[10] पिअसहीए मदअन्तिआए जीविदं ति ।

(प्रविश्य[11] संभ्रान्ता)

**बुद्धरक्षिता**—परित्रायध्वं परित्रायध्वम् । एषा नः प्रियसख्य- मात्यनन्दनस्य भगिनी मदयन्तिकैतेन दुष्टशार्दूलेन विनिहतविद्राविताशेषपरिजनाभिभूयते । (परित्ताअध परित्ताअध । एसा णो पिअसही अमच्चणन्दणस्स बहिणिआ एदिणा दुट्ठसद्दूलेण विणिहदविद्दाविदासेसपरिअणा अभिभवीअदि ।)

**मालती**—लवङ्गिके अहो महान्प्रमादः । (लवङ्गिए[12] अहो महन्तो पमादो ।)

**माधवः**—(ससंभ्रममुत्थाय ।) बुद्धरक्षिते क्वासौ ।

**मालती**—(माधवं दृष्ट्वा सहर्षसाध्वसमात्मगतम् ।) अहो एषोऽपीहस्थ एव । (अम्महे एसो वि इहत्थो[13] एव्व ।)

**माधवः**—(स्वगतम् ।) हन्त पुण्यवानस्मि यदहमतर्कितोपनतदर्शनोल्लसित[14]लोचनयानया

---

न्तुशरीरं ततः प्रवृत्तरक्तेन संजातरुधिरेण कर्दमीकृतो गतिपथो गमनवाटो येन सः । कर्पर इव कर्परः । निम्नत्वात् । 'उरल्लिर्गलगर्जितम्' इति रत्नकोशः । **माधवः** । मदयन्तिकापरिरक्षणत्वरयाह—**क्वासाविति** । **मालती** । अम्महे सभयहर्षे आश्चर्ये वा । एषोऽपीहस्थ एव । अत्रापिर्विस्मये । यस्यावस्था भगवत्योक्ता

---

१ रम्भभरिद. २ पञ्जरपडिलग्गसंगलिअणिअलो (प्रतिलग्नसंगलितनिगडो). ३ सुव्वेल्लवल्लह (सोद्वेल्लवल्लभ). ४ ०अन्तिआविसमडामरुद्दा०; डम्बरुद्दाम. ५ विअडविइंभणुद्दाम (विकटविजृम्भणोद्दाम). ६ मोडिअपरिमिलिद (मोटितपरिमिलित). ७ परिपूरिअणहोअलो (परिपूरितनभस्तलो) णिद्दाणिव्विसिदण०;णट्ठ०. ८ विद्दाविदा (विद्राविता). ९ दलिआकट्ठ (दलिताकृष्ट). १० जधासत्ति अत्तणो (आत्मनः) जीविदं त्ति. ११ प्रविश्य बु०—सत्रासम्. १२ सहि लव०. १३ एत्थ. १४ ०ल्लसिनयानया.

अविरलमिव दाम्ना पौण्डरीकेण नद्धः[1]
स्नपित इव च दुग्धस्रोतसा[2] निर्भरेण[3]।
कवलित इव कृत्स्नश्चक्षुषा स्फारितेन
प्रसभममृतमेघेनेव[4] सान्द्रेण सिक्तः ॥ १६ ॥

**बुद्ध०**—महाभाग एष खलूद्यानबाह्यरथ्यामुखे । ( महाभाअ एसो क्खु उज्जाणबाहिअरत्थामुहे । )

( माधवः साटोपं परिक्रामति । )

**काम०**—वत्स अप्रमत्तो भुत्वा विक्रमस्व ।

**मालती**—( जनान्तिकम् । ) लवङ्गिके हा धिक् हा धिक् संशयः खलु जातः । ( लवङ्गिए हद्धी हद्धी संसओ क्खु जादो । )

( सर्वास्त्वरितं परिक्रामन्ति[5]। )

---

यन्निमित्ता वा ममेयमवस्था स एष इति भावः । स्वच्छन्दप्रियालोकनतुष्टस्य माधवस्योक्तिः-**हन्तेत्यादि । अविरलमित्यादि**-अयं श्लोको गद्यादिः । हन्त हर्षे । अचिन्तितोपस्थितदर्शनानन्दितलोचनयानया चक्षुषा पौण्डरीकेणेव दाम्ना स्रजाविरलं घनं यथा तथाहं नद्धो बद्धः । आवृत इति यावत् । कान्तालोचनेन सात्त्विकभावाविर्भावात्स्वीयस्तम्भं ज्ञात्वा नद्ध इत्युत्प्रेक्षितम् । अत्राविरलपदेन पौनःपुन्यं पुण्डरीकपदेन श्वेतभागविभावनं च ध्वनितम् । दुग्धस्रोतसा दुग्धाम्भःप्रवाहेण निर्भरेण निरतिशयेन संसक्तेन वा स्नपित इवाप्लुत इवाहम् । तथाविधावलोकनजातरोमाञ्चतया स्नपितत्वेनोत्प्रेक्षितम् । अत्र निर्भरपदेन परिचयपर्यवसानतोक्ता । एवं च द्वाभ्यां नेत्रनैर्मल्यमुक्तम् । कृत्स्नो निःशेषोऽहं स्फारितेन विस्तारितेन चक्षुषा कवलित इव पीत इव । स्फारितत्वेन कवलनयोग्यतोक्ता । कवलने बाह्यसंवेदनाभावात्प्रणय उत्प्रेक्षितः । सान्द्रेण निबिडेन सुधामयजलधरेण प्रसभं बलात्सिक्त इवाहम् । आनन्दातिशयशालितयामृतसिक्तत्वेनोत्प्रेक्षा । तदिह माधवस्य परमनिर्वृतिसौख्यमुक्तम् । तत्र च प्रथमपदेन तारकातरलता, द्वितीयेन गोलकचाञ्चल्यम्, तृतीयेन पुटविस्तारो विलासश्च, चतुर्थेन चैतत्त्रयसंपत्तौ पुण्यवत्तोपपादनम् । तत्रापि मेघपदेन संतापशान्तिः, अमृतपदेन स्तम्भसंभावना, प्रसभपदेन तत्संगतिरेव विपत्प्रतीकार इति सूचितम् । सेचनपदेन तस्मिन्दरालोकनेऽसम्पूर्णता, सान्द्रपदेन तत्कालिकसकलक्लेशविलयः सूचितः । स्रोतसां निर्झरेणेति पाठे निर्झरेण प्रवाहेणेत्यर्थः ॥१६॥ **बुद्धरक्षिता** । [ महाभागेति ] कासाविति प्रश्नस्योत्तरमिदम् । **माधवः** । साटोपं सावेगम् । **कामन्दकी** । अप्रमत्तं सावधानम् । क्रियावि-

---

१ बद्धः. २ स्रोतसां. ३ निर्झरेण, निर्घनेन. ४ वर्षणेव. ५ माधवमनुगच्छन्ति.

**माधवः**—( अग्रे दृष्ट्वा सबीभत्सम् । ) अहह ।

**संसक्तत्रुटितविवर्तितान्त्रजाल-**
**व्याकीर्णस्फुरदपवृत्त[2]रुण्डखण्डः ।**
**कीलालव्यतिकरगुल्फदघ्नपङ्कः**
**प्राचण्ड्यं [3]वहति नखायुधस्य मार्गः ॥ १७ ॥**

अहो प्रमादः ।

**वयं बत विदू[4]रतः क्रमगता पशोः कन्यका**

**सर्वाः**—हा मदयन्तिके । ( हा मदअन्तिए । )

**काम०माधवौ**—( [5]सहर्षाकूतम् । )

**कथं तदव[6]पातितादधिगतायुधः पूरुषा[7]त् ।**
**कुतोऽपि मकरन्द एत्य सहसैव मध्ये स्थितः**

**इतराः**—साधु महाभाग साधु । ( साहु महाभाअ साहु । )

**काम०माधवौ**—( सभयम् )

**दृढं च पशुना हतः**

---

शेषणमिदम् ॥ **माधवः** । रुधिरादिकं वीक्ष्य सबीभत्सं सघृणम् । अहह विस्मये खेदे घृणायां च । **संसक्तेत्यादि** । नखायुधस्य व्याघ्रस्य मार्गः प्राचण्ड्यं रौद्रत्वं वहति । कीदृशः । संसक्तः संलग्नस्त्रुटितश्छिन्नो विवर्तितः खण्डखण्डीकृतोऽन्त्रजालमन्त्रसमूहस्तेन व्याकीर्णं व्याप्तं सद्योहतत्वात्स्फुरत्किंचिच्चलदपवृत्तमधोमुखं रुण्डखण्डं कवन्धरूपं शकलं यत्र सः । उरुबुकेति पाठ उरु महद् बुकमग्रमांसम् । कीलालव्यतिकरेण रक्तसंघेन गुल्फदघ्नो गुल्फपरिणामः पङ्कः कर्दमो यत्र । अत एव बीभत्सयोगितत्वम् । 'कबन्धे रुण्डमस्त्रियाम्' इत्यमरः । कीलालं रुधिरे तोये' इति मेदिनीकरः । प्रमाणे दघ्नच् । 'पङ्कः पापे च कर्दमे' इति विश्वः ॥ १७ ॥ **वयमिति** । वयमित्यादिना दंष्ट्रायुधपर्यन्तेन पृथ्वीच्छन्दसा श्लोकः । स वाचनिकः । वयं तस्य व्याघ्रस्यातिदूरतः । पशोः क्रमगता क्रमणं प्राप्ता । कन्यका मदयन्तिका । कथं मकरन्दः कुतोऽपि स्थानादेत्यागत्य शीघ्रं मध्ये व्याघ्रमदयन्तिकयोः स्थितः । तेन व्याघ्रेणावपातिताद् गृहीतात्पूरुषाद् गृहीतखड्गः सन् । अत आकाङ्क्षितलाभः । अत एव सहर्षाकूतमित्युक्तम् । 'पुरुषाः पूरुषा अपि' इत्यमरः । पूरुषशब्दश्छन्दस्येव युज्यत इत्यदेश्यम् । 'पूर्वपूरुषतपांसि जयन्ति' इत्यादिनैषददर्शनाद्भाषायामपि तत्प्रयोगात् । मकरन्दः पशुना दृढं निहतो

---

१ निव. २ तुण्ड, मुण्ड. ३ वदति. ४ रगाः. ५ सहर्षम्. ६ दभि०. ७ संभ्रमात्. ८ परशुना.

**इतरा:**—अत्याहितम् अत्याहितम् । ( अच्चाहिदं अच्चाहिदं । )

**काम० माधवौ:**—( सहर्षम् । ) प्रमथितश्च दंष्ट्रायुधः ॥ १८ ॥

**इतरा:**—( सानन्दम् । ) दिष्ट्या प्रतिहतं दुर्जातम् । ( दिट्ठिआ पडिहदं दुज्जादं । )

**काम०**—( सानन्दम् । ) कथं व्यालनखरप्रहारानिःसृतरक्तनिवहः क्षितितलनिषक्तखड्गलतावष्टम्भनिश्चलः संभ्रान्तमदयन्तिकावलम्बितस्ताम्यतीव वत्सो मे मकरन्दः ।

**इतरा:**—हा धिक् हा धिक् गाढप्रहारतया क्लाम्यति महाभागः । ( हद्धी हद्धी गाढप्पहारदाए किलम्मदि महाभाओ । )

**माधवः**—कथं प्रमुग्ध एव । ( कामन्दकीं प्रति । ) भगवति परित्रायस्व माम् ।

**काम०**—अतिकातरोऽसि वत्स । तदेहि तावत् । पश्यामः ।

( इति परिक्रम्य निष्क्रान्ताः सर्वे । )

**इति शार्दूलविद्रावणो नाम तृतीयोऽङ्कः ।**

---

दृढमाहतस्ताडितो वा । रक्तदर्शनेन सभयम् । अत्याहितं महाभयम् । 'अत्याहितं महाभीतिः' इत्यमरः । का० **माधवौ** । व्याघ्रभयत्राणोपकारितया व्यवस्थितमदयन्तिकासंबन्धात्सहर्षत्वम् । दंष्ट्रायुधो व्याघ्रः । प्रमथितो निहतः । अमुनेत्यर्थात् ॥ १८ ॥ **इतरा** । दुष्टमुपक्रान्तं दुर्जातम् ॥ **काम०** । 'व्याघ्रे चौरे च व्यालः' इति शाश्वतः । स मकरन्दः क्षितितलनिषक्तखड्गलतावष्टम्भेन निश्चलः । इह मकरन्दक्षतेन रुजारूपः संधिप्रवेश उक्तः । यदाह—'रुजा प्रोक्ता प्रहारव्यथा' इति । अवष्टम्भनमवष्टम्भः । संभ्रान्ता विमुग्धा । प्रमुग्धो मोहं गतः ॥ **काम०** । पश्याम इति दर्शनात्समाश्वास इति भावः ॥

प्रासूत यं रत्नधरोऽतिमान्योऽतिमान्यरूपा दमयन्तिकापि ।
जगद्धरं तत्कृतटिप्पणेऽङ्कोऽगमत्तृतीयो रसराजिरम्यः ॥

**इति तृतीयोऽङ्कः ।**

---

१ व्यमुरसौ कृतश्चामुना. २ अस्मात्प्राक्-प्रियं प्रियं नः संवृत्तम् । इति टी० ३ विषक्त. ४ निषण्णः. ५ भागो मकरन्दः. ६ परि० परित्रायस्व. ७ नन्वेहि पश्य.वत्स्तावत्.

# चतुर्थोऽङ्कः ।

( ततः प्रविशतो मदयन्तिकालवङ्गिकाभ्यामवलम्बितौ प्रमुग्धौ माधवमकरन्दौ संभ्रान्ता कामन्दकी मालती बुद्धरक्षिता च । )

**मद०**—प्रसीद भगवति परित्रायस्व परित्रायस्व मदयन्तिकानिमित्तं संशयितजीवितं विपन्नजनानुकम्पिनं महाभागम् । ( पसीद भअवदि परित्ताहि परित्ताहि मदअन्तिआणिमित्तं संसइदजीविदं विवण्णजणाणुकम्पिणं महाभाअं । )

**इतराः**—हा धिक् हा धिक् । किमिदानीमस्माभिरत्र प्रेक्षितव्यम् । ( हद्धी हद्धी । किं दाणिं अह्मेहिं एत्थ पेक्खिदव्वं । )

**काम०**—( उभौ कमण्डलूदकेन सिक्त्वा । ) ननु भवत्यः पटाञ्चलेन वत्सौ वीजयन्तु ।

( मालत्यादयस्तथा कुर्वन्ति । )

**मकरन्दः**—( समाश्वस्यावलोक्य च । ) वयस्य अतिकातरोऽसि । किमेतत् । ननु स्वस्थ एवास्मि ।

**मद०**—( सहर्षम् । ) अहो प्रतिबुद्धमिदानीं मकरन्दपूर्णचन्द्रेण । ( अह्महे पडिबुद्धं दाणिं मअरन्दपुण्णचन्देण । )

**मालती**—( माधवस्य ललाटे हस्तं दत्वा । ) महाभाग दिष्टचा वर्धसे । ननु भणामि प्रतिबुद्ध एव ते प्रियवयस्यः प्रतिपन्नचेतनो महाभागो मकरन्द इति । ( महाभाअ दिट्ठिआ वड्ढसि । णं भणामि पडिबुद्धो ज्जेव दे पिअवअस्सो पडिवण्णचेअणो महाभाओ मअरन्दो त्ति । )

**माधवः**—( समाश्वस्य । ) वयस्य साहसिक एह्येहि । ( इत्यालिङ्गति । )

**काम०**—( उभौ शिरस्याघ्राय । ) दिष्टचा जीवितवत्सास्मि ।

**इतराः**—प्रियं प्रियं नः संवृत्तम् । ( पिअं पिअं णो संउत्तं । )

( सर्वा हर्षं नाटयन्ति । )

**बुद्ध०**—( जनान्तिकम् । ) हला मदयन्तिके एष एव सः । ( हला मदअन्तिए एसो ज्जेव्व सो । )

---

**तत इति** । संभ्रान्ता व्याकुला ॥ **मद०** । अत्रापन्नमापद्गतम् ॥ अम्महे हर्षे आश्चर्ये वा ॥ **मालती** । वर्धस इत्यनेन वर्धापनं याचनोक्तिप्रकारः **काम०** । शिरस्याघ्राणमायुर्वर्धनायेति वृद्धाः । **बुद्ध०** । हलेति सखीसंबोधनम्

---

१ मालनी. २ संभ्रान्ताश्च. ३ णिमित्तसं०. ४ विपण्णानु०. ५ पुण्णिमा. ६ सखि लवङ्गिके. ७ आश्वस्य. ८ जीवद्वत्सा.

**मद०**—सखि ज्ञातमेव मया यथैष माधवोऽयमपि स जन इति। (सहि जाणीदं ज्जेव्व मए जह एसो माहवो[1] अअं वि सो जणो त्ति।

**बुद्ध०**—अपि सत्यवादिन्यहम्। (अवि सच्चवादिणी अहं।)

**मद०**—न खल्वन्यादृशेषु युष्मादृश्यः पक्षपातिन्यो भवन्ति। (माधवमवलोक्य।) सखि मालत्या अपि रमणीयोऽस्मिन्महानुभावेऽनुराग-प्रवादः। (पुनर्मकरन्दमेव सस्पृहमवलोकयति।) (ण क्खु अण्णारिसेसु तुह्मारिसीओ[2] पक्खवादिणीओ होन्ति। सहि मालदीए वि रमणीज्जो[3] इमस्सिं महाणुहावे अणुराअप्पवादो।)

**काम०**—(स्वगतम्।) रमणीयोर्जितं हि मदयन्तिकामकरन्दयो-र्दैवादद्य दर्शनम्[4]। (प्रकाशम्।) वत्स मकरन्द कथं पुनरायुष्मान-स्मिन्नवसरे मदयन्तिकाजीवितपरित्राणहेतुर्[5]भगवता दैवेन संनिधापितः।

**मक०**—अद्याहमन्तर्नगर[6] एव कांचिद्वार्तामुपश्रुत्य माधवस्य चि-त्तोद्वेगमधिकमाशङ्कमानस्त्वरितमवलोकितानिवेदितकुसुमाकरोद्यानवृत्तान्तः परापतन्नेव शार्दूलावस्कन्दगोचरगतामेतां[7]मभिजातकन्यकामभ्युपपन्नवानस्मि।

(मालतीमाधवौ विमृशतः।)

**काम०**—(स्वगतम्।) वृत्तेन[8] खलु मालतीप्रदानेन भवितव्यम्। (प्रकाशम्।) वत्स माधव दिष्ट्या सुहृद्बुद्ध्या वर्धितोऽसि मालत्या। तदयमवसरः प्रीतिदायस्य।

---

मकरन्दनामाग्रहणेन स्वामित्वमभिप्रैति। **मदयन्तिका**। संभावनायामपिशब्दः। न हि पक्षपातिन्यस्त्वादृश्यो मन्दं भद्रं वदन्तीति भावः। **काम०**। अक्लेशोपन-तत्वेन रमणीयम्। शार्दूलनाशेनोपकारपूर्वकमुत्पन्नत्वादूर्जितं सातिशयम्। 'आयु-ष्मानिति वृद्धेन वाच्यो बालः शुभाशयः'॥ इति भरतः। **मक०**। उद्यान-वृत्तान्तो मालतीप्रत्यक्षमुत्तरोपक्रमः। परापतन्नागच्छन्। अवस्कन्दोऽतिक्रमः। गोचरमित्यजहल्लिङ्गतयान्वयः। अभिजाता कुलीना। तथा चाभिजात्येन मदुपकारं ज्ञास्यतीति भावः। आभिजात्येन ज्ञानं च तथाविधाकारादिना। कन्यकेत्यत्रानुकम्पायां कन्। अभ्युपपत्तिः प्राप्तिः। विमृशतः। परस्परक्लेशका-

---

१ एस पिओ जणो; एस महाभाओ माह० अअं. २ अह्मा०. ३ ०णिज्जो एव्व. ४ संदर्श ५ हेतोः. ६ नगरे. ७ इमाम्. ८ वृत्तान्तेन.

**माधवः**—भगवति ईयं हि

**यद्व्यालव्रणितसुहृत्प्रमोहमुग्धं**
**सौजन्यात्विहितवती गतव्यथं माम् ।**
**तत्कामं प्रभवति पूर्णपात्रवृत्त्या**
**स्वीकर्तुं मम हृदयं च जीवितं च ॥ १ ॥**

**लव०**—प्रतीष्टः खलु नः प्रियसख्यायं प्रसादः । (पडिच्छिदो क्खु णो पिअसहीए अअं पसादो ।)

**मदयन्तिका**—(स्वगतम् ।) जानाति महानुभावोऽयं जनोऽवसरे गुरुकरमणीयं मन्त्रयितुम् । (जाणादि महाणुहावो अअं जणो अवसरे गुरुअरमणिज्जं मन्तिदुं ।)

**मालती**—(स्वगतम्) किं नाम मकरन्देनोद्वेगकारणं श्रुतं भविष्यति । (किं णाम मअरन्देण उव्वेअकालणं सुदं भविस्सदि ।)

**माधवः**—वयस्य का पुनर्ममाधिकोद्वेगहेतुर्वार्ता ।

(प्रविश्य)

**पुरुषः**—वत्से मदयन्तिके भ्राता ते ज्यायानमात्यनन्दनः समादिशति । अद्य परमेश्वरेणास्मद्भवनमागत्य भूरिवसोरुपरि परं विश्वासमस्मासु च प्रसादमाविष्कुर्वता स्वयमेव प्रतिपादिता मालती । तदेहि संभावयावः प्रमोदमिति ।

**मक०**—वयस्य इयं सा वार्ता ।

---

भावः ॥ प्रीतिदायस्य वर्धापकदानस्य ॥ **यदित्यादि** । व्याघ्रखण्डितसुहृत्प्रमोहेन संतप्तं मां सौजन्येन विगतक्लेशं कृतवती ततोऽत्यर्थं मम हृदयं जीवितं च पूर्णपात्रवृत्त्या वर्धापकेन स्वीकर्तुमियं प्रभवति । त्वं च प्रभवसीत्यर्थः । तदायत्ते मे हृदयजीविते इति भावः । यद्वा चोरिकाविवाहसंपादनेन हृदयहारिता नोचेज्जीवितहारितेत्यर्थः । 'वर्धापकं यदानन्दादलङ्कारादिकं पुनः । आकृष्य गृह्यते पूर्णपात्रं पूर्णानकं च तत् ॥' इति हारावली । 'पूर्णपात्रं वर्धापकेऽपि च' इति मेदिनीकरोऽपि ॥ १ ॥ **मदयन्तिका** । गुरुकरमणीयं श्रोत्रसुखम् । **माधवः** । मकरन्देन कांचिद्वार्तामुपश्रुत्येति यदुक्तमेतच्छङ्कमानः पृच्छति—वयस्येति । **पुरुषः** । ज्यायाञ्ज्येष्ठः । परमेश्वरो

---

१ इयं मालती. २ कारुण्यात्. ३ भगवति. ४ महाभाअधेओ; णुहावो जणो. ५ गुरुअ इति नास्ति क्वचित्. ६ उद्वेगवार्ता. ७ प्रसादम्.

( मालतीमाधवौ वैवर्ण्यं नाटयतः । )

**मद०**—( सहर्षं मालतीमाश्लिष्य । ) सखि मालति त्वं खल्वेकनगरनिवासेन सहपांसुक्रीडनात्प्रभृति मे प्रियसख्यासीर्भगिनिका च । सांप्रतं पुनर्गृहस्य मण्डनं जातासि । ( सहि मालदि तुमं क्खु एक्कणअरणिवासेण सहपंसुकीलणादो पहुदि मे पिअसही आसी वहिणिआ अ । संपदं उणं घरस्स मण्डणं जादासि । )

**काम०**—वत्से मदयन्तिके दिष्ट्या वर्धसे भ्रातुर्मालतीलाभेन ।

**मद०**—युष्माकमाशिषां प्रभावेण । सखि लवङ्गिके फलिता नो मनोरथा युष्माकं लाभेन । ( तुह्माणं आसिसाणं पहावेण । सहि लवङ्गिए फलिदा णो मणोरहा तुह्माणं लाहेण । )

**लव०**—सखि किमस्माकमप्येतन्मन्त्रायितव्यम् । ( सहि किं अह्माणं वि एदं मन्तिदव्वम् । )

**मद०**—सखि बुद्धरक्षिते इदानीं विवाहमहोत्सवं संभावयावः । ( सहि बुद्धरक्खिदे दाणिं विवाहमहोसवं संभावेह्म )

**बुद्ध०**—सखि एहि गच्छावः । ( सहि एहि गच्छह्म । ) ( इत्युत्तिष्ठतः । )

**लव०**—( जनान्तिकम् । ) भगवति यथैते हृदयभरितोद्वृत्तविस्मयानन्दसुन्दरा आन्दोलायमानधीरत्वमनोहराः पर्यस्यन्ति मदयन्तिकामकरन्दयोर्दलितनीलोत्पलदामसदृक्षाः कटाक्षविक्षेपास्तथा तर्क-

---

राजा । विश्वासमभेदम् । संभावयामः कारयामः । उत्सवपूर्वको हर्षः प्रमोदः । **मदयन्तिका** । मद्भ्रातृवधूर्भविष्यसीति भावः । **कामन्दकी** । नोशब्दोऽस्माकमित्यर्थे निषेधे च तुल्यरूप इति निषेधोऽप्यत्र स्फुरति । अत एव सोत्कण्ठमाह—भ्रातुरित्यादि । **मदय०** उभयत्रोत्तरमाह । युष्माकमिति । भरिआ इति पाठे भृताः पूर्णा इत्यर्थः । **लवङ्गिका** । अयमभिसंधिः । यूयं राज्ञः प्रणयिनो वयं सेवकाः । अतो युष्मत्संबन्धेन वयं पूर्णमनोरथा इति वचनमात्रम् । वस्तुतस्तु त्वत्संबन्ध एवास्माकं न भवितेति । माधवविवाहस्यावश्यकत्वात् । यद्वा यदेतत्त्वया मन्त्रितमस्माकं मनोरथाः पूर्णा युष्माकं लाभेनेति वयमेव तद्वदामः । तेन त्वं मकरन्देन परिणेतव्येति मनोरथा अस्माकमेव पूर्णा भविष्यन्तीति गूढमुक्तम् । व्यक्तं तु युष्माकं राजमित्राणां लाभेन राजसेवका वयमेव पूर्णमनोरथा इति भावः । यद्वा एतत्कामन्दक्याख्यं मन्त्रिरूपं द्रव्यमस्माकमप्यत्र विषये वर्तते तेन प्रतिहतमेतत् । **लवङ्गिका** । अत्र भरमितो भरितः । शकन्ध्वादित्वात्पररूपम् । यद्वा भरणं भरः । भरः संजातोऽस्य । तारकादित्वादितच् । व्यवस्थितविभाषया वेट्प्राप्तेः । अत एव वासवदत्तादौ भरितेति प्रयोगः । हृदये भरितौ पूर्णावुद्वृत्ता-

---

१ आलिङ्ग्य. २ उण अह्माणं ( अस्माकं ). ३ पसादेण. ४ भरिआ. ५ अत्थि. ६ एहि दाव महोसवं. ७ परिवर्तन्ते.

यामि मनोरथनिर्वृत्तसमागमावेताविति । ( भअवदि जहा[1] एदे हिअअभरिदु-व्विसविम्हआणन्दसुन्दरा[2] आन्दोलाअन्तधीरत्तणमहोहरा पल्लत्थन्ति मदअन्तिआमअ-रन्दाणं दलिदकन्दो[3]ट्टदामसरिच्छा कडक्खविक्खेवा तहा तक्केमि मणोरहणिव्वुत्तस-[4]माअमा एदे त्ति । )

**काम०**—( विहस्य । ) नन्विमौ विलोकनेन मा[5]नसं मुहुर्मुहुर्मो[6]हनम-नुभवतः । तथा हि

> **ईषत्तिर्यग्व[7]लनविषमं कूणि[8]तप्रान्तमेत-**
> **त्प्रेमोद्भेदस्तिमितलु[9]लितं किंचिदा[10]कुञ्चितभ्रु ।**
> **अन्तर्मोदानुभवमसृणं स्तं[11]भनिष्कम्पपक्ष्म**
> **व्यक्तं शंसत्यचिरमनयोर्दृष्टमाकेकराक्षम् ॥ १ ॥**

---

वमान्तौ विस्मयानन्दौ ताभ्यां सुन्दराः । व्याघ्रनिपाताद्धृदयनिहितो विस्मयः । इष्टदर्शनादानन्दः । आन्दोलितं परित्यक्तं यद्धीरत्वं तेन मनोहराः । दलितं विकसि-तम् । कन्दोट्टं नीलोत्पलम् । सदृक्षास्तुल्याः । कान्तादृष्टिरियम् । **कामन्दकी** । मोहनं सुरतम् । अत एव कामशास्त्रम्–' मोहनं नारभेत्तावद्यावन्नोत्कण्ठिता प्रिया ' । इति । **ईषदित्यादि** । एतदनयोर्दृष्टं दर्शनं व्यक्तं शंसति । यदेतौ मानसं मोहन-मनुभवत इत्यन्वयः । दृष्टं कीदृशम् । ईषन्मनाक्तिर्यग्वलितेन विषमं मन्दम् । अनेन संकल्पसंगतानङ्गस्य पराभ्यूहशङ्कितेयं दृगित्युक्तम् । यदाह—' शङ्कायां शङ्किता ज्ञेया ' इति । कुञ्चितप्रान्तमाकुञ्चितापाङ्गम् । मदयन्तिकाया जडत्वान्मकरन्दस्यान्यद-र्शनसासूयत्वाज्जिह्मा दृष्टिः । यदाह—' जिह्मा दृष्टिरसूयायां जडतालस्ययोस्तथा ' । इति । दृष्टिद्वयेन सुरतप्रागवस्थोक्ता । प्रेम्ण उद्भेदादतिपरिपाकात्स्तिमितं स्थिरं लुलित-मर्धमुकुलितं च । अर्धमुकुलितेयं दृक् । यदाह—' अङ्गादिष्वर्धमुकुला गन्धस्पर्शसुखा-दिषु । अर्धव्याकोषपक्ष्माग्रा ग्रस्तार्धमुकुलैः पुटैः ॥ स्मृतार्धमुकुला दृष्टिः किंचिन्मी-लिततारका ' ॥ अनेन रताभोग उक्तः । नखदशनक्षतादिशङ्कया मानं सूचयति । किंचिदाकुञ्चिते अनमिते भ्रुवौ यत्र तत् । एकस्या एव भ्रुव उत्क्षेपणं कुञ्चनमिह । यदाह–' एकस्या एव उत्क्षेपो भ्रुवः कुञ्चनमुच्यते ' । कोपे चास्य प्रयोगः । यदाह– ' कोपे वितर्के हेलायां लीलादौ सहजे तथा । दर्शने ग्रहणे चैव भ्रुवमेकां समुत्क्षिपेत् ॥ मानस्याल्पत्वसूचनार्थमाङ्प्रयोगः । रतावसानमाह—हृदये हर्षानुभवेन मसृणं स्निग्धं मन्दं वा । रतान्ते लज्जामाह–स्तम्भं लज्जान्विततया पतितार्धपुटत्वात् । कथं पुनः संभोगो भावीति चिन्तया निष्कम्पम् । शून्यतया निष्कम्पं वा । तादृशं पक्ष्म

---

१ भरिउव्वमन्त ( भरितोद्वमत् ). २ सुन्दरं, ०रघोलाविदधीरपेरन्त ( घूर्णितधीरपर्यन्त ). ३ ०न्दोट्ठमंसलच्छविआ दिट्ठिसंभेआ तह मण्णे. ४ सम्बन्धा. ५ परस्परं मा०. ६ मानंस मोह०. ७ बलित. ८ कुञ्चित. ९ ललितं. १० आचित. ११ त्रस्त.

**पुरुषः**—वत्से मदयन्तिके इत इतः ।

**मद०**—(अपवार्य ।) सखि बुद्धरक्षिते अपि पुनरपि द्रक्ष्यते एष जीवितप्रदायी पुण्डरीकलोचनः । (सहि बुद्धरक्खिदे अवि पुणोपि दीसइ एसो जीविदप्पदाई पुण्डरीअलोअणो ।)

**बुद्ध०**—यदि दैवमनुकूलं भविष्यति । (जइ देव्वं अणुऊलं भविस्सदि । (इति पुरुषेण सह निष्क्रान्ते ।)

**माधवः**—(अपवार्य ।)

**चिरादाशातन्तुस्त्रुटतु बिसिनीसूत्रभिदुरो**
**महानाधिर्व्याधिर्निरवधिरिदानीं प्रसरतु ।**
**प्रतिष्ठामव्याजं व्रजतु मयि पारिप्लवधुरा**
**विधिः स्वास्थ्यं धत्तां भवतु कृतकृत्यश्च मदनः ॥ ३ ॥**

अथ वा

**समानप्रेमाणं जनमसुलभं प्रार्थितवतो**
**विधौ वामारम्भे मम समुचितैषा परिणतिः ।**
**तथाप्यस्मिन्दानश्रवणसमयेऽस्याः प्रविगल-**
**त्प्रभं प्रातश्चन्द्रद्युति वदनमन्तर्दहति माम् ॥ ४ ॥**

---

यत्र । तद्विच्छेदमाह—आकेकरमाक्षि यत्र तत् । 'आकेकरा त्वरालोके विच्छेदे प्रेषितेषु च ।' इत्याद्युक्तम् । तदिहाकेकरलक्षण आकुञ्चितेत्यादि प्रथमपदेनोक्तम् । द्वितीयेन मुहुर्व्यावृत्ततारेत्युक्तम् । तृतीयेन हर्षितार्धेत्याद्युक्तम् ॥ २ ॥ **मदयन्तिका** । अपि नाम संभावनायाम् । अव्ययसमुदायत्वात् । **माधवः** । करुणावस्थामाह—चिरादित्यादि । चिरशङ्कितः आशातन्तुर्मालतीप्राप्त्याशारूपहृदयावलम्बनं संप्रति भिद्यताम् । बिसिनीसूत्रवद्भिदुरो भेदनस्वभावो यतः । भिदेः कर्मकर्तरीति कुरच् । संभूय त्रुटितत्वेन मृणालतन्तुसाम्यम् । नैराश्यान्मरणमाह—आधिर्मनोव्यथा तद्रूपो व्याधिरनवच्छिन्नोऽत एव महान् । व्याप्नोतु । इह महत्त्वनिरवधित्वाभ्यां मरणमाह । आशाच्छेदानन्तरं च मरणमुचितमेव । यदाह—'सर्वैः कृतैः प्रतीकारैर्यदा नास्ति समागमः । कामाग्निना समाप्तस्य जायते मरणं ततः ॥' स्त्रीहेतुमरणादधीरत्वमाशङ्क्यानुशोत्तरमाह । पारिप्लवधुरा चपलकक्षा [अव्याजं] सत्यं [प्रतिष्ठां] स्थितिं मयि बध्नातु । अभीष्टलाभेन विधिर्निराकुलो भवतु । मालतीं विना दुःसहवेदनादायी मनोभूः कृतकृत्यो भवतु । मरणादधिकं किं कर्तव्यमस्येत्यर्थः । एतदुपालम्भगर्भं वच उद्वेगात् । यदाह—'हृद्दाहचिन्तानिःश्वासग्लानिखेदप्रजागरैः । रोदनैर्मन्दभणितैर्दैवोपालम्भनेन च ॥' इति ॥ ३ ॥ **समानेत्यादि** । वामारम्भे प्रतिकूले विधौ ममैषा परिणतिः पूर्वोक्ता युक्तैव । की-

---

१ एतन्नास्ति क्वचित्. २ द्रक्ष्यते. ३ अविणाम. ४ आधिर्व्या०. ५ व्याजा. ६ स्थैर्यम्. ७ समुदिता. ८ पारि०.

**कामन्दकी**—( स्वगतम् । ) एवमतिदुर्मनायमानः पीडयति मां वत्सो माधवो वत्सा मालती च दुष्करं निराशा प्राणिति । ( प्रकाशम्[2] । ) वत्स माधव पृच्छामि तावदायुष्मन्तम् । अपि[1] भवानमंस्त यथा भूरिवसुरेव मालतीमस्मभ्यं दास्यतीति ।

**माधवः**—( सलज्जम् । ) नहि नहि ।

**काम०**—न तर्हि प्रागवस्थायाः परिहीयसे[3] ।

**मक०**—भगवति दत्तपूर्वेत्याशङ्क्यते[4] ।

**काम०**—जानामि तां खलु वार्ताम् । इदं तावत्[5]प्रसिद्धमेव यथा नन्दनाय मालतीं प्रार्थयमानं भूरिवसुर्नृपतिर्मुक्तवान्[6]प्रभवति निजस्य कन्यकाजनस्य महाराज इति ।

**मकरन्दः**—अस्त्येतत् ।

**कामन्दकी**—अद्य च राज्ञा स्वयमेव दत्ता मालतीति पुरुषेणा[7]वेदितम् । तद्वत्स वाक्प्रतिष्ठानि[8] देहिनां व्यवहारतन्त्राणि । वाचि पुण्यापुण्यहेतवो व्यवस्थिताः[9] । सर्वं च वचनानामायत्तम् । सा च भूरिवसोर्वागनृतात्मिकैव । न खलु महाराजस्य मालती निजा कन्यका । कन्यकाप्रदाने[10] च नृपतयः प्रमाणमिति नैवंविधो धर्माचारसमयः । तस्मादविमर्शितव्यमेतत्[11] । कथं च वत्स मामनवधानां मन्यसे । पश्य ।

---

दृशस्य । तुल्यप्रीतिं दुष्प्रापं जनं याचितवतः । वामे हि विधौ सुलभमपि न लभ्यते किं पुनरसुलभमिति भावः । दृष्टकारणस्यानुपलम्भाद्विधेर्वामत्वम् । असुलभत्वं परतन्त्रत्वात् । यद्यपि युक्तेऽर्थे खेदो नास्ति तथाप्यस्या मालत्यास्तादृशं मुखं मामन्तर्दहति । एतन्मुखं वीक्ष्य मनस्तापो मे भवतीति भावः । अस्मिन्दानश्रवणसमये नन्दनाय मालती दातव्येति श्रुत्वा खेदात्कान्तिशून्यत्वम् । अत एव प्रातश्चन्द्रकान्ति क्वापि विगतकान्ति भवति । अथ च प्रातश्चन्द्रोपमया रागध्वनेर्विधिं प्रति मालतीकोपोऽपि सूचितः ॥ ४ ॥ **कामन्दकी** । दुष्करं यथा तथा प्राणिति जीवति । अमंस्त मन्यते स्म । प्रागवस्था मालतीप्राप्तिलक्षणा । तद्दानस्याज्ञानादिति भावः । दत्तपूर्वा पूर्वं दत्ता । सुप्सुपेति समासः । इदं च तापहेतुः । **वागिति** । वाचि सर्वं प्रतिष्ठितमिति भावः । अनृतात्मिकासत्या । धर्माचारसमयो धार्मिकसिद्धान्तः ।

---

१ एतद्-अपि भवानित्यस्य प्राक् क्वचित्. २ अथ किं. ३ भूरिवसुः परिहीयते. ४ अदत्तपूर्वा. ५ नु. ६ एवमुक्त०. ७ संप्रत्येव पुरु०. ८ निबन्धनानि, ९ व्यवस्थाः सर्वेषां जनानामायतन्त इति. १० कन्यादाने. ११ मेवैतत्.

मा वां सपत्नेष्वपि नाम तद्भू-
त्पापं यदस्यां त्वयि वा विशङ्क्यम् ।
तत्सर्वथा संगमनाय यत्नः
प्राणव्ययेनापि मया विधेयः ॥ ५ ॥

मक०—सुष्ठु युज्यमानमादिश्यते युष्माभिः । अपि च ।

दया वा स्नेहो वा भगवति निजेऽस्मिञ्शिशुजने
भवत्याः संसाराद्विरतमपि चित्तं द्रवयति ।
अतश्च प्रव्रज्यासुलभसमयाचारविमुखः
प्रसक्तस्ते यत्नः प्रभवति पुनर्दैवमपरम् ॥ ६ ॥

( नेपथ्ये । )

भगवति कामन्दकि एषा भट्टिनी विज्ञापयति मालतीं गृहीत्वा त्वरितमागच्छेति । ( भअवइ कामन्दइ एसा भट्टिणी विण्णावेदि जधा मालदिं घेत्तूण तुरिदं आअच्छेत्ति । )

कामन्दकी—वत्से उत्तिष्ठ ।

( सर्वे उत्तिष्ठन्ति । )

( मालतीमाधवौ सकरुणानुरागमन्योन्यमवलोकयतः । )

---

'समयाः शपथाचारकालसिद्धान्तसंविदः' । इति विश्वः । निजावधानमाह—**मा वेति**। अस्यां मालत्यां त्वयि च यत्पापं विवाहानिर्वाहे मरणरूपं शङ्कनीयं विप्रयोगजन्यदुःखादि वा तच्छत्रुष्वपि । नाम प्राकाश्ये । मा वाभून्नैव भविष्यति । वाशब्द एवार्थे । स्वकर्तव्यमाह—तदिति । तस्माद्युवयोः संबन्धाय सवप्रकारेण जीवत्यागेनापि मया प्रयत्नः कार्यः । यदि बुद्धिकौशलेन न सिद्धिस्तदा प्राणव्ययेनापि साध्यमित्यपेः स्वरसः। मरणादेरमङ्गलतया पापपदेनोपन्यासः। शत्रुष्वपि माभूदिति लोकोक्तिच्छायालङ्कारः॥५॥ **दयेत्यादि** । हे भगवति अस्मिन् शिशुजने बालजने माधवे मालत्यां च दया करुणा स्नेहो ममता च संसाराद्विरक्तमपि भगवत्याश्चित्तं द्रवयत्यार्द्रीकरोति । भवत्या इति दयान्वयि चित्तान्वयि च काकाक्षिगोलकवत् । वाशब्दौ चार्थे । अत एव चित्तद्रवणात् । व्रतग्रहणपूर्वकसर्वैषणानिवृत्तिः प्रव्रज्या । तस्यां सुलभः अवश्यंभावी समयाचारोऽनुष्ठानविशेषो ध्यानादिविषयस्तत्र विमुखो निरुद्धो यत्नस्ते प्रसक्तोऽविच्छिन्नः सन् प्रभवति । च एवार्थे । कार्यासिद्धिरदृष्टविलम्बात् । तत्र न भवत्या दोष इत्याह । अपरं पुनर्दैवं प्रभवति । ईश्वरस्त्रीषु राज्ञीपदोपचारेण भट्टिनीत्युक्तम् । भरतोऽप्याह–' राजस्त्रियस्तु संभाष्याः सर्वाः परिजनेन तु । भट्टिनी स्वामिनी-

---

१ वां. २ सर्व सुष्ठु. ३ ततश्च. ४ समयस्तुलभा०. ५ भर्त्री वि० यथा ( जधा ). ६ घेऊण. ७ आअच्छदु. ८ उत्तिष्ठोत्तिष्ठ.

**माधवः**—( स्वगतम् । ) कष्टमेतावती हि लोकयात्रा मालत्या समं माधवस्य । अहो नु खलु भोः—

> **सुहृदिव प्रकटय्य सुखप्रदः**
> **प्रथममेकरसामनुकूलताम् ।**
> **पुनरकाण्डविवर्तनदारुणः**
> **प्रविशिनष्टि विधिर्मनसो रुजम् ॥ ७ ॥**

**मालती**—( अपवार्य[1] । ) महाभाग लोचनानन्द एतावद्दृष्टोऽसि । ( महाभाअ[3] लोअणाणन्द[4] एत्तिअं दिट्ठोसि । )

**लव०**—हा धिक् हा धिक् । शरीरसंशयमेव नः प्रियसख्यारोपितामात्येन । ( हद्धी हद्धी । सरीरसंसअं ज्जेव्व णो पिअसही आरोविदा अमच्चेण । )

**मालती**—( स्वगतम् । ) परिणतमिदानीं मे जीविततृष्णायाः फलम् । निर्व्यूढं च निष्करुणतया तातस्यापि कापालिकत्वम् । परिनिष्ठितो दुष्टदैवस्य दारुणसमारम्भसदृशः परिणामः । तत्कमिहोपालभे मन्दभागिनी कं वाशरणा शरणं प्रतिपद्ये । ( परिणदं दाणिं मे जीवितितिह्लाए फलम् । णिव्वूढं अ णिक्करुणदाए तादस्स वि कावालिअत्तणं । परिणिट्ठिदो[5] दुट्ठदेवस्स[6] दारुणसमारम्भसरिसो परिणामो । ता कं एत्थ उवालभामि मन्दभाइणी । कं वा असरणा सरणं परिवज्जामि । )

**लव०**—सखि इत इतः । ( सहि इदो इदो । ) ( इति कामन्दक्या सह निष्क्रान्ते । )

---

त्येवं नाट्ये प्राहुर्विचक्षणाः' ॥ ६ ॥ **माधवः** । लोकयात्रा दर्शनादिकम् । अहो नु खलु भो इत्यव्ययसमुदायो निर्वेदे । **सुहृदित्यादि** । एकत्रैव रसो रतिर्यस्यास्ताम् । यद्वा । एक एव रसः शृङ्गारो यस्यां ताम् । निरन्तरां वानुकूलतामानुकूल्यं प्रथमं प्रकाश्य सुखप्रदो विधिः पुनर्मनसो रुजं पीडां प्रविशिनष्टयतिशयितां करोति । कीदृशः । अकाण्डादकस्माद्विवर्तनेनान्यथाभावेन विरुद्धवर्तनेन वा दारुणो दुःखदायी । सुहृदिव । यथा मित्रमानुकूल्यमुत्पाद्य सुखप्रदं सदकाण्ड एव विरुद्धाचरणान्मनःपीडां करोति तथेत्यर्थः ॥ ७ ॥ **मालती** । पुनर्दर्शनं न भवितेति भावः । अत एवैतावदित्यनेन करुणा । नयनानन्देत्यनेनानुरागः । **मालती** । अत्र पुरा विरहदशायां माधवप्रतिच्छन्दकादिदर्शनाद्धारितस्य जीवितस्य पर्यवसानं वृत्तमिति परिणतपदस्यार्थः । कापालिकत्वं नृशंसता । अघोरघण्टस्य सूचनमप्येतत् । **माधवः** । जन्मसाफल्यं माल-

---

१ प्रदाम्. २ ( स्वगतम् ). ३ महाणुभाअ. ४ ॰णन्दकर. ५ पडिट्ठिदो. ( प्रतिष्ठितः ). ६ देव्वहदअस्स.

**माधवः**—( स्वगतम् । ) नूनमाश्वासनमात्रमेतन्माधवस्य सहजस्नेहकातरा करोति भगवती । ( सोद्वेगम् । ) हन्त सर्वथा संशयितजन्मसाफल्यः संवृत्तोऽस्मि । तत्किमिदानीं कर्तव्यम् । ( विचिन्त्य । ) न खलु महामांसविक्रयाद[1]न्यमुपायं पश्यामि । ( प्रकाशम् । ) वयस्य मकरन्द अपि भवानुत्कण्ठते मदयन्तिकायाः[2] ।

**मक०**—अथ किम् ।

**तन्मे मनः क्षिपति यत्सरस[3]प्रहार-**
**मालोक्य मामगणितस्खलदुत्तरीया ।**
**त्रस्तैकहायनकुरङ्गविलोलदृष्टि-**
**राश्लिष्टवत्यमृतसंवलितैरिवाङ्गैः[4] ॥ ८ ॥**

**माधवः**—सुलभैव[5] बुद्धरक्षिताप्रियसखी भवतः । अपि च ।

**प्रमथ्य क्रव्यादं मरणसमये रक्षितवतः**
**परिष्वङ्गं लब्ध्वा तव कथमिवान्यत्र रमताम् ।**
**तथा च व्यापारः कमलनयनाया[6] नयनयो-**
**स्त्वयि व्यक्तस्नेहस्तिमितरमणीयश्चिरमभूत् ॥ ९ ॥**

---

तीप्राप्त्या । महामांसेति भाव्यङ्कसूचनम् । वीरहस्तान्मांसं गृहीत्वा वीरायाभिमतवरदानमिति श्मशानसिद्धयोगिनीमतम् । यद्वा उभयथा मरणमुपस्थितम् । महामांसविक्रये मालतीलाभोऽपि शङ्क्यत इति तत्करणम् । मांसविक्रयस्य मकरन्दसांनिध्यावश्यकत्वान्मकरन्दं मदयन्तिकां प्रत्युत्कण्ठयति—वयस्येति । मदयन्तिकायाः कृत इति शेषः । यद्वा अधीगर्थेति कर्मणि षष्ठी । **मकरन्दः** । अथ किं स्वीकारे । **तन्म इत्यादि** । तन्मम चित्तं हरति यदेतादृशैरङ्गैर्मामालिङ्गितवती । सरसः सरक्तः प्रहारो यत्र तादृशं मामवलोक्य । अत एव त्वरयागणितं स्खलत् प्रभ्रश्यदुत्तरीयं स्तनावरणवासो यस्याः सा । एतेन निरन्तरस्तनस्पर्शः सूचितः । अत एवानन्दसंदोहदायित्वादमृतसिक्तैरिव । भयवत्त्वेन त्रस्तैकवर्षीयहरिणस्येव चञ्चला दृष्टिर्यस्याः सा । 'वर्षोऽब्दो हायनोऽस्त्री स्यात्' इत्यमरः ॥ ८ ॥ **माधवः** । त्रासेन त्वदालिङ्गनं न तु स्नेहादिति शङ्कापनोदाय दूतीसुलभतयानुरागमेवाह—सुलभेति । **प्रमथ्येत्यादि** । सा तवालिङ्गनं प्राप्यान्यत्र कथं रमताम् । अपि तु नैव । इवशब्दोऽनवक्लृप्तौ । कुलीनैकमालिङ्ग्य नान्यत्र रमत इति भावः । कीदृशस्य । क्रव्यमाममांसमत्तीति क्रव्याद्व्याघ्रः । तं विनाश्य मरणकाले तां

---

१ अन्यदुपायान्तरम्. २ ०कायाम्. ३ सहसाप०. ४ रपाङ्गैः ५ न दुर्लभा. ६ वदनायाः.

मक[1]०—तदुत्तिष्ठ । पारा[2]सिन्धुसंभेदमवगाह्य नगरीमेव प्रविशावः ।

( उत्थाय परिक्रामतः । )

मा[3]धवः—अयमसौ महानद्योर्व्यतिकरः[4] । य एषः

जलनिबिडितवस्त्रव्यक्तनिम्नोन्नताभिः
परिगततटभूमिः स्नान[5]मात्रोत्थिताभिः ।
रुचिरकनककुम्भश्रीमदाभोगतुङ्ग-
स्तनविनिहितहस्तस्वस्तिकाभिर्वधूभिः ॥ १० ॥

( इति निष्क्रान्ताः सर्वे । )

इति शार्दूलविभ्रमो नाम चतुर्थोऽङ्कः ।

---

रक्षितवतः । एतेन कृतोपकारितोक्ता । अतोऽपि नान्यत्र रमते । पद्माक्ष्याश्चक्षुषोस्तथा तेन प्रकारेण त्वयि व्यापारश्च व्यक्तः स्नेहास्तितमितो मन्दोऽत एव रमणीयश्चिरमभूत् । रागेण तया साभिलाषमालोकितोऽसीति भावः । एतेनानुराग उक्तः । यदाहानुरागप्रकरणे—' तुष्यत्यस्य कथाभिस्तु सस्नेहं च निरीक्षते ' ॥ ' क्रव्यमामिषमुद्धासम् ' इति हारावली ॥ ९ ॥ पारा च सिन्धुश्च ते नद्यौ तयोः संभेदः संगमः । अवगाह्य विलोड्य । स्नात्वेति यावत् । क्लमशान्तिहेतुतया महामांसादानहेतुतया च स्नानम् । व्यतिकरः संगमः । **जलेत्यादि** । वधूभिर्नारीभिः सेविततटदेशः । कीदृशीभिः । जलेन निबिडितमङ्गलग्नं यद्वासस्तेन व्यक्तौ निम्नोन्नतौ जघनादिस्तनाद्यौ यासाम् । अत एव स्नानमात्रोत्थिताभिः । मात्रपदेन स्नानार्द्रवस्त्रापरित्यागः सूचितः । अत एव चाह्लादहेतुतया स्नानमपि । तौ दृष्ट्वा तासां लज्जामाह—मनोज्ञस्वर्णघटशोभावानाभोगः परिपूर्णता ययोरुच्चकुचयोस्तयोर्विनिहितौ दत्तौ हस्तावेव स्वस्तिकौ याभिस्ताभिः । हस्ताभ्यां स्वस्तिकोऽन्योन्यवामदक्षिणविन्यासः । यदाह—' मणिबन्धनविन्यस्तावरालौ स्त्रीप्रयोजितौ । उत्तानौ वामपार्श्वस्थौ स्वस्तिकः परिकीर्तितः ॥ ' अरालश्चैवम्—' आद्या धनुर्लताकारा कुञ्चितोऽङ्गुष्ठकस्तथा । शेषा भिन्नोर्ध्ववलिता अरालेऽङ्गुलयः करे ॥ ' कनकेत्यादिना तासां गौरीत्वमुक्तम् । मङ्गलकलशानामिवैषां दर्शनेनेष्टसिद्धिरपि सूचिता ॥ १० ॥

असूत यं रत्नधरो द्विजेशो द्विजेशकन्या दमयन्तिकापि ।
जगद्धरं तत्कृतटिप्पणेऽङ्कोऽगमच्चतुर्थो रससाशिवासः ॥

इति चतुर्थोऽङ्कः ।

---

१ एतन्नास्ति क्वचित्. २ वरदा. ३ मक०. ४ संभेदः. ५ स्नात.

# पञ्चमोऽङ्कः ।

( ततः प्रविशत्याकाशयानेन भीषणोज्ज्वलवेशा कपालकुण्डला । )

**कपालकुण्डला—**

> षडधिकदशनाडीचक्रमध्यास्थितात्मा
> हृदि विनिहितरूपः सिद्धिदस्तद्विदां यः ।
> अविचलितमनोभिः साधकैर्मृग्यमाणः
> स जयति परिणद्धः शक्तिभिः शक्तिनाथः ॥ १ ॥

---

**तत इति** । संप्रति प्रमथ्य क्रव्यादमित्यनेनाघोरघण्टकपालकुण्डलाप्रवेशे सूचिते महामांसविक्रयप्रतिज्ञया च माधवस्य श्मशानप्रवेशे सत्यङ्कावतारः । आकाशयानेन प्रवेशो योगसिद्धिसूचनाय । भीषणा भयंकरी । उज्ज्वलवेशा विशुद्धशरीरा । एतदपि योगिनीत्वादेव । **षडधिकेत्यादि** । स शक्तिनाथः शिवो जयति जययुक्तो भवति । कालसामान्ये भवत्विति वक्तव्ये भाष्यकारवचनात् कालत्रितयेऽपि वा लट् । श्मशाननाथस्य जयेन श्मशानसाधनसिद्धिः सूचिता । कीदृशः । अविचलितं निःस्पन्दीभूतम् । विषयान्तरव्यावृत्तमिति यावत् । मनो येषां तैः साधकैर्मृग्यमाणोऽन्विष्यमाणः । अनेन ध्यानानुष्ठानमुक्तम् । यदाह—'रूपवर्णप्रमाणाढ्यं परिकल्प्य सुबुद्धिना । तथा ध्यायेत देवेशं यथा चित्तं स्थिरं भवेत्' ॥ चित्तस्थैर्यं तु निर्विषयतयैव । यदाह—'मन एव मनुष्याणां कारणं बन्धमोक्षयोः । बन्धस्य विषयासङ्गि मुक्तेर्निर्विषयं मनः ॥' तथा च निराकारोऽप्ययं सहसैव न साक्षात्कारविषयो भवतीति न योग्यानुपलम्भमात्रेण निरस्य इत्यपि कटाक्षितम् । शक्तिभिर्ब्राह्मीमाहेश्वरीकौमारीवैष्णवीवाराहीमाहेन्द्रीचामुण्डाचण्डिकाख्याभिरष्टाभिः परितो नद्धो वेष्टितो भैरवमूर्तित्वात् । यद्वा शक्तिभिर्ज्ञानेच्छाप्रयत्नात्मिकाभिः परिणद्ध उपचितः । अत एव शक्तीनामणिमादीनां नाथः प्रभुः । अत एव जयति सर्वोत्कृष्टो वर्तते । कीदृशः । षट्सु कर्णनाभिहृत्कण्ठतालुभ्रूमध्यवर्तिषु शिवशक्तिसंघट्टस्थानेषु नाडीसंघट्टेषु हृदाद्यधिष्ठितप्राणविशेषचलनयोगाच्चक्रेष्विव मध्येऽधिकं प्रधानं यद्दशनाडीचक्रमिडापिङ्गलासुषुम्णागान्धारीहस्तिजिह्वापूषारुणालम्बुषाकुहूशङ्खिन्याख्या दश नाड्यो हृद्गतैकोत्तरशतसंख्यासु तिर्यगूर्ध्वाधोगतनाडीषु प्रधानतमास्तासां चक्रं तस्य मध्ये पद्ममध्यवर्तिसूक्ष्माकाशदेशे प्राणाद्याधारे स्थित आत्मा कूटस्थो नित्यो यस्य स तथा । तत्र प्रमाणम्—'आशिरःश्रवणं देहं यद्यपि व्याप्य तिष्ठति । तथाप्यस्य परं स्थानं हृत्पङ्कजसमुद्गकम् ॥' इति । स्थितिरपि तस्य तत्र परमात्मतत्त्वाविर्भाव एव । यद्वा । षड्भिरधिका दशनाड्यः षोडशसंख्यास्तासां चक्रं तत्र मध्ये स्थितश्चासावात्मा चात्मस्वरूपः । तदुक्तम्—'सर्वं शिवमयं मतम्' इति । यद्वा षडधिकं यद्दशनाडीचक्रम् । मतभेदे-

---

१ -ज्ज्वला.

इयमहमिदानीम् ।

> नित्यं न्यस्तषडङ्गचक्रनिहितं हृत्पद्ममध्योदितं
> पश्यन्ती शिवरूपिणं लयवशादात्मानमभ्यागता ।
> नाडीनामुदयक्रमेण जगतः पञ्चामृताकर्षणा-
> दप्राप्तोत्पतनश्रमा विघटयन्त्यग्रे नभोऽम्भोमुचः ॥ १ ॥

नैते पक्षाः । हृदि हृत्पद्मे विनिहितरूपो ध्यानमूर्तिः सन्यस्तद्विदां शिवसाक्षात्कारवतां सिद्धिदोऽणिमाद्यैश्वर्यप्रदः । अत्र मानम्—'ईश्वरः सर्वभूतानां हृद्देशेऽर्जुन तिष्ठति ॥ सकलं चिन्तयेत्तस्मात्सिद्ध्यर्थं सततं शिवम् ॥ ध्यानेन तत्परं गच्छेत्सनैश्वर्यगुणाष्टकम् । महिमा लघिमाणुत्वं प्राकाम्यं वशितेशिता । प्राप्तिः कामावसायित्वं शम्भोरैश्वर्यमष्टधा' ॥ मृग्यमाणोऽप्ययं केनापि ज्ञायते न तु सर्वेण यदाह—'यततामपि सिद्धानां कश्चिन्मां वेत्ति तत्त्वतः ।' इति । यद्वा तद्विदां ताः सिद्धीरुपायदेशकालप्रमाणेतिकर्तव्यताभिर्ये विदन्ति तेषां सिद्धिदोऽभिलषितसिद्धिद इत्यर्थः ॥ १ ॥ आत्मनि योगसिद्धिमाह—**नित्यमित्यादि** । इयमहमिदानीमभ्यागताभीष्टस्थानाभिमुखमागता श्रीपर्वतादित्याक्षेपात् । कीदृशी । शिवस्वरूपमात्मानं पश्यन्ती । लयवशाच्चित्तैकाग्रतया । अनेन सर्वेषां तत्प्रकाशोऽपास्तः । कीदृशम् । नित्यमविनाशिनम् । न्यस्तानि देहे मन्त्रन्यासेनार्पितानि यानि षडङ्गानि हृदयशिरःशिखानेत्रकवचास्त्राणि तेषां चक्रे समूहे निहितमारोपितं मन्त्रन्यासेन । यदाह—'षडङ्गमेतत्कथितं सर्वसिद्धिप्रदायकम् । न्यसेद्वै भक्तियुक्तात्मा साधको ज्ञानचिन्तकः ॥ त्रिकालमेककालं वा शरीरे विन्यसेद्बुधः ।' अनेनाङ्गावरणमुक्तम् । नित्यन्यस्तेति पाठे नित्यं प्रत्यहं न्यस्तानीत्यर्थः । हृत्पद्ममध्ये हृत्कमलकर्णिकायां ध्यानाभ्यासात्सूर्यवदुदितम् । यदाह—'पद्मसंकाशसंस्थानं हृदयं तत्र दृश्यते । सूक्ष्मो हि पुरुषो ज्ञेयः परमात्मा हृदि स्थितः ॥ अभ्यासात्पश्यते सूर्यं परमात्मानमात्मना' । नाडीनां पूर्वोक्तानामिडापिङ्गलादीनामुदयक्रमेण वायुपूरणपरिपाट्या जगतः शरीरस्य पञ्चभूतात्मकस्य पञ्चामृतानां पृथिव्यप्तेजोवाय्वाकाशानां योगर्द्धिबलाद् आकर्षस्तस्मादप्राप्तोऽलब्ध उत्पतनेनाकाशयानेन श्रमो यया सा । यद्वा अमृतमिवामृतं देहस्थितिहेतुत्वात् । तत् पुनर्बिन्दुस्थानात् कुण्डलिनीस्रावणेन स्रवद्रसविशेषो रसनाधःस्थितरन्ध्रस्रवद्रसविशेषो वा । स हि व्यापकत्वेन पञ्चशब्दवाच्यः । तदाकर्षणात् । यद्वा जगतः शरीरस्य पञ्च यान्यमृतानि शिवशक्त्यात्मकानि रूपरसगन्धस्पर्शशब्दलक्षणानि नित्यानि स्थूलमहाभूतमामात्रा परिपोषकाणि । योगिनीनां तेषामुपयोगात्तदाकर्षणेन सामर्थ्यादिकं योगिनीनामिति भावः । न च लयवशत्वेन निष्क्रियतयोत्पतनं न संभवतीति वाच्यम् । लयस्यान्यत्रापि सामर्थ्यात् । यदाह—'मनोऽप्यन्यत्र निक्षिप्तं चक्षुरन्यत्र पातितम् । तथापि योगिनां योगो ह्यविच्छिन्नः प्रकीर्तितः ॥' उत्पतनादिमाहात्म्यादेवाग्रेभुवः पुरोवर्तिनो मेघान् विघटयन्ती द्विधा

१ नित्यन्य०. २ अग्रेभवो.

अपि च ।

उल्लोलस्खलितकपालकण्ठमालासंघट्टक्कणितकरालकिंकिणीकः ।
पर्याप्तं मयि रमणीयडामरत्वं संधत्ते गगनतलप्रयाणवेगः ॥ ३ ॥

तथा हि ।

विष्वग्वृत्तिर्जटानां प्रचलति निबिडग्रन्थिबद्धोऽपि भारः
संस्कारक्काणदीर्घं पटु रटति कृतावृत्तिखट्वाङ्गघण्टा ।
ऊर्ध्वं धूनोति वायुर्विवृतशवशिरःश्रेणिकुञ्जेषु गुञ्ज-
न्नुत्तालः किंकिणीनामनवरतरणत्कारहेतुः पताका[३]ः ॥ ४ ॥

कुर्वती । अग्रे नभ इति पाठ आकाशमेघानग्रे विघटयन्तीत्यर्थः । न च नभःपदवैयर्थ्यम् । वनपर्वतादावपि मेघसद्भावेन तद्विघटन आकाशगामित्वोत्कर्षाप्रतिपादनात् । यद्वा । अग्रे नभो नभसि मेघान् विघटयन्ती । अग्रेशब्दो विभक्तिप्रतिरूपको निपातः । तस्य विभक्त्यर्थेऽव्ययीभावः । अनेन श्लोकद्वयेन शान्तो रस उक्तः । अत्र भरतोऽपि 'शान्तस्तु नवमो रसः' इत्याह । स च विषयवैरस्यादुपजायते । यदाह । 'शान्तो विषयवैरस्याद्रसः संजायते पुनः ।' इति ॥ २ ॥ कपालकुण्डलायाः पूर्वोक्तभीषणोज्ज्वलत्वमुपपादयति–**उल्लोलेति** । गगनतलगमनवेगो मयि सकलं रमणीयडामरत्वं रमणीयत्वं मनोहरत्वं डामरत्वं भीषणत्वमुद्भटत्वं वा केलिसंरम्भनिर्भरत्वं वा संधत्ते समर्थं कुरुते । 'डामरोड्डामरौ भीमे केलिसंरम्भनिर्भरे' । इति रत्नकोशः । वेगबलादुल्लोलेन यातायातेन स्खलिता या कपालानां कण्ठवर्तिनी माला तस्याः संघट्टक्कणितेनान्योन्यकपालसंघृष्टिध्वनिना कराला मूका क्षुद्रघण्टिका यत्र सः । कपालमालोच्चध्वनिना तद्ध्वनेरश्रवणान्मूकत्वमिव मूकत्वम् । यद्वा तथाविधक्कणितेन कराला दन्तुरा । विषमेति यावत् । किङ्किणी यत्र सः । कुलयोगिनीनां किङ्किण्यादिध्वनिना सानन्दत्वम् । यदाह–'समुद्रघोषसंभारकिङ्किणीघण्टिकास्वनैः । सदानन्दो भवेद्योगी न निद्रा न क्षुधा तृषा ॥' इति ॥ ३ ॥ तदेवाह–**विष्वगिति** । जटानां भारः समूहो निबिडं दृढं यथा तथा ग्रन्थिबद्धोऽपि विष्वग्वृत्तिः सर्वतोव्यापी सन् प्रचलति । गगनगमनवेगादित्यर्थात् । विष्वक्शब्दो नानार्थः सुषमादिषु पठ्यते तेन षत्वम् । कृतावृत्तिः कृतगतागता कृतमण्डलभ्रमणा खट्वाङ्गसहिता घण्टा संस्कारेण संतानेन यः क्काणो ध्वननं तेन दीर्घं पटु रमणीयं च यथा तथा रटति शब्दायते । एतेन डामरत्वमुक्तम् । खट्वाङ्गं वाद्यभेदः । वायुरूर्ध्वं पताका धूनोति कम्पयति । धूञ् कम्पने । दीर्घान्तः स्वरतीत्यादिसूत्रे न्यासकारेणोक्तः । कीदृशः । विवृतानि यानि निर्मांसतया शवशिरांसि तेषां श्रेणयः पङ्क्तयस्तासां यानि कुञ्जानि गहनाः प्रदेशास्तेषु गुञ्जन्ध्वनन् । अत एवोत्ताल उद्भटध्वानः क्षुद्रघण्टिकानामजस्ररणत्कृति-

१ उद्वृत्त; उद्भिन्न. २ नद्धो. ३ पताकाम्.

(परिक्रम्यावलोक्य च गन्धमाघ्राय ।) इदं तावत्पुराणनिम्बतैलाक्तपरिभृज्यमानरसोनगन्धिभिश्चिताधूमैः पुरस्ताद्विभावितस्य महतः श्मशानवाटस्य नेदीयः करालायतनं यत्र पर्यवसितमन्त्रसाधनस्यास्मद्गुरोरघोरघण्टस्याज्ञया सविशेषमद्य पूजासंभारो मया संनिधापनीयः । कथितं च मे गुरुणा—वत्से कपालकुण्डले अद्य भगवत्याः करालायाः प्रागुपयाचितं स्त्रीरत्नमुपहर्तव्यं तदत्रैव नगरे विदितमास्ते इति । तद्विचिनोमि । (सकौतुकमग्रेऽवलोक्य ।) तत्कोऽयमतिगम्भीरमधुराकृतिरुत्तम्भितकुटिलकुन्तलः कृपाणपाणिः श्मशानवाटमवतरति । य एष

कुवलयदलश्यामोऽप्यङ्गं दधत्परिपाण्डुरं
ललितचरणन्यासः श्रीमान्मृगाङ्कनिभाननः ।
हरति विनयं वामो यस्य प्रकाशितसाहसः
प्रविगलदसृक्पङ्कः पाणिर्ललज्जरजाकुलः ॥ ५ ॥

---

हेतुश्च । अनेन रमणीयत्वमुक्तम् । ' निक्वाणो निक्वणः क्वाणः क्वणः क्वणनमित्यपि । ' इत्यमरः । यद्वा पटुरटनेन रमणीयत्वं पताकाकम्पनेन डामरत्वमत्रोक्तम् ॥ ४ ॥ **इदं तावदिति** । पुराणेत्यादिना चिताधूमानां स्वभावाख्यानम् । अक्तं म्रक्षितम् । परिभर्जनं वह्निमध्यनिक्षेपपाकः । अम्लरसेनैकेनोनं पञ्चरसं रसोनम् । लसून इति ख्यातम् । वव्यते वेष्ट्यतेऽनेनेति वाटः । हलश्चेति घञ् । ' पन्था वाटः पथो माथः ' इति भागुरिः । नेदीयो निकटम् । पर्यवसितं समाप्तं विनष्टं च । मन्त्रसाधनं पुरश्चरणजपादि । संभारः समूहः । उपयाचितं मनीषितार्थं स्वीकृतम् । ' यद्दीयते तु देवेभ्यो मनोराज्यस्य सिद्धये । उपयाचितकं तत्तु दोहदं संप्रचक्षते ॥ ' इति हारावली । **स्त्रीरत्नमिति** । 'जातौ जातौ यदुत्कृष्टं तद्धि रत्नं प्रचक्षते' । इति विश्वः । विदितमुपलब्धम् । विचितमिति पाठेऽन्विष्टम् । **गम्भीरेत्यादि** । ' विकाराः सहजा यस्य हर्षक्रोधभयादिषु । भावेषु नोपलभ्यन्ते तद्गाम्भीर्यमुदाहृतम् ॥ ' इति । अभ्यासात्करणानां तु श्लिष्टत्वमुपजायते । महत्स्वपि विकारेषु तन्माधुर्यमुदाहृतम् ॥ ' इति भरतः । उत्तम्भितो जूटाकारेण बद्धः कुटिलो वक्रः कुन्तलः केशो यस्य सः । एतेन रौद्ररसवत्तोक्ता । **कुवलयेत्यादि** । य एष स्वभावान्नीलनलिनपत्रवच्छ्यामोऽपि विप्रलम्भात्सर्वतः पाण्डुरमङ्गं दधत् । ललितो रमणीयो विकटो भीषणो न्यासो देहन्यासो यस्य सः । ललितत्वं स्वभावात् । विकटत्वं रौद्रात् । यद्वा न्यासः करचरणादिचालनम् । श्रीमानतिरम्यः । मृगाङ्कभिरतिशया भा यत्र तादृशमाननं यस्य । अत एव हेयत्वार्थं मृगाङ्कपदेनोपन्यासः । **यस्य वामः** पाणिर्विनयं हरत्यपनयति । अत्र हेतुमाह । प्रविगलदसृक्पङ्कः स्रवद्रुधिरकर्दमः ।

---

१ रसोनकरस. २ अधस्तात्. ३ हि. ४ अद्य मया. ५ विचितं. ६ कुन्तलभारः. ७ धूसरम्. ८ विकट.

(निरूप्य।) अये स एष कामन्दकीसुहृत्पुत्रो महामांसस्य पणायिता माधवः। तत्किमनेन। भवतु समीहितं संपादयामि। विगलितप्रायः पश्चिमसंध्यासमयः। तथा हि। संप्रति

व्योम्नस्तापिच्छगुच्छावलिभिरिव तमोवल्लरीभिर्व्रियन्ते
पर्यन्ताः प्रान्तवृत्त्या पयसि वसुमती नूतने मज्जतीव।
वात्यासंवेगविष्वग्विततवलयितस्फीतधूम्याप्रकाशं
प्रारम्भेऽपि त्रियामा तरुणयति निजं नीलिमानं वनेषु॥ ६॥

(परिक्रम्य निष्क्रान्ता।)

विष्कम्भकः।

---

(ततः प्रविशति यथानिर्दिष्टो माधवः।)

**माधवः**—(साशंसम्।)

प्रेमार्द्राः प्रणयस्पृशः परिचयादुद्गाढरागोदया-
स्तास्ता मुग्धदृशो निसर्गमधुराश्चेष्टा भवेयुर्मयि।
यास्वन्तःकरणस्य बाह्यकरणव्यापाररोधी क्षणा-
दाशंसापरिकल्पितास्वपि भवत्यानन्दसान्द्रो लयः॥ ७॥

---

ललज्वलं नरजाङ्गलं महामांसं यत्र सः। नहि विनीतो रक्तं महामांसं च धारयति। अत्र पूर्वार्धेन ललितत्वमुत्तरार्धेन विकटत्वमुक्तम्। अत एव व्यक्तसाहसः। महामांसधारित्वेन वीरबीभत्सरसावुक्तौ। यदाह—'उत्साहाध्यवसायाद्विस्मयहर्षाच्च मोहाच्च। विविधाद्बन्धविशेषाद्वीररसो नाम संभवति॥ अनभिमतदर्शनेन च गन्धरसस्पर्शशब्ददोषैश्च। उत्तेजनैश्च बहुभिर्बीभत्सरसः समुद्भवति॥' दधदित्यत्र नाभ्यस्ताच्छतुरिति नुमो निषेधः। 'जाङ्गलं निर्जनस्थाने त्रिलिङ्ग्यां पिशितेऽस्त्रियाम्' इति मेदिनीकरः॥ ५॥ पणायिता विक्रेता। विगलितप्रायो भ्रष्टप्रायः॥ **व्योम्न इत्यादि**। गगनस्योपान्ता ध्वान्तलताभिर्व्याप्यन्ते। तमालपुष्पस्तबकपङ्क्तिभिरिव। एवं च पृथिव्युपान्तभागेन नूतने जले मज्जतीव। उत्प्रेक्षेयम्। त्रियामा रात्रिः। प्रारम्भे प्रदोषमात्रेऽपि नीलत्वं निजं वनेषु तरुणयति। कीदृशम्। वातानां समूहो वात्या तस्याः संवेगेन विवर्तनेन विष्वक् चतुर्दिशं वितता विस्तारिता वलयिता वलयाकारा स्फीता गभीरा या धूम्या धूमसमूहो नीहारो वा तत्सदृशम्। एवं चान्धकारोपगमाद्गतप्राया संध्येत्यर्थः। 'धूम्या धूमसमूहेऽपि नीहारपि निगद्यते।' इति धरणिः॥ ६॥ साशंसं सप्रार्थनम्। **प्रेमेत्यादि**। मुग्धदृशो मालत्यास्तास्ता अनुभूताश्चेष्टाः संभोगे चुम्बनादयो मयि पुनर्भूयासुः। 'चेष्टाविशेषाः संभोगे चुम्बनालिङ्गनादयः।' इति

---

१ यथासमी०. २ प्रायश्च. ३ भ्रियन्ते. ४ संगेन. ५ विलसित. ६ शुद्धवि. ७ विषय. ८ आशंका. ९ सान्द्रोदयः

किं च ।

अतिमुक्तमन्मथितकेसरावली-
सतताधिवाससुभगार्पितस्तनम् ।
अपि कर्णजाहविनिवेशिताननं
प्रियया तदङ्कपरिवर्तमाप्नुयाम् ॥ ८ ॥

अथ वा दूरे तावदेतत् । इदमेव प्रार्थये ।

संभूयेव सुखानि चेतसि परं भूमानमातन्वते
यत्रालोकपथावतारिणि रतिं प्रस्तौति नेत्रोत्सवः ।
यद्बालेन्दुकलोच्चयादवचितैः सारैरिवोत्पादितं
तत्पश्येयमनङ्गमङ्गलगृहं भूयोऽपि तस्या मुखम् ॥ ९ ॥

---

कण्ठाभरणम् । कीदृश्यः । प्रथमं प्रेम्णा संभोगप्रीत्यार्द्रा इव तापशान्तिहेतुरोमाञ्चादिजनकत्वात् । ततो विश्वासमुपेत्य चित्तप्रसादस्पृशः । ततः परिचयात्सुखास्वादभेदादुद्भटरागोद्रेकाः । निसर्गमधुराः सहजमनोज्ञाः । यास्वाशंसोपनीतास्वपि क्षणान्निरतिशयसुखघनो लयो लीनता भवति । तासु चेष्टासु मनो लीयत इत्यर्थः । कीदृशः । अन्तःकरणस्य मनसो बाह्येन्द्रियव्यापारावरोधनशीलः । मालतीमयत्वेन मन्मनो बाह्यविषये न व्याप्रियत इत्यर्थः । अत एवानेकशङ्कातङ्कसंकुलेऽपि तत्र स्थाने माधवस्य न साध्वसादिकमपीति भावः । यद्वा तास्ताश्चेष्टा बकुलवीथ्यादिषु यास्तया कृतास्तास्ता मयि भवेयुः । तासामेव दुर्लभत्वादाशंसनीयता ॥ ७ ॥ प्रथमप्रीतिहेतुत्वादालिङ्गनमाशास्ते--**अतिमुक्तेत्यादि** । प्रियया सह तदङ्कपरिवृत्तिमप्यहमाप्नुयाम् । तत्तस्या अङ्के क्रोडे सर्वतोभावेन वर्तनम् । हृदयालिङ्गनमित्यर्थः । अपिर्भिन्नक्रमः । यद्वा तदङ्के परिवर्तनमूर्ध्वाधःक्रमेण पुरुषायितमाप्नुयाम् । कीदृशः । प्रियया कर्णजाहे कर्णमूले विनिवेशितमाननं यत्र । ममापि सः । प्रथमपक्षे कर्णमूलेऽर्पितमाननं येन सः । 'तस्य पाकमूले पील्वादिकर्णादिभ्यः कुणब्जाहचौ' इति मूले जाहच्प्रत्ययः । अतिक्रान्ता मुक्ता यया सातिमुक्ता । मुक्ताहारमपास्य तदर्पणादतिक्रमः । यद्वा अतिमुक्तातिविरला मालत्यवलोकनव्यासङ्गात् । एतादृशी या मन्मथिता केसरावली तस्याः सतताधिवासेन सुभगः सुरभिरर्पितः स्तनो यत्रेति क्रियाविशेषणम् । अविमुक्तेति पाठो न मनोहरः । अवियुक्तत्वादेव सतताधिवासस्य लब्धत्वात्सततग्रहणस्य व्यर्थत्वात् ॥ ८ ॥ **संभूयेत्यादि** । तस्यास्तन्मुखं पुनरपि पश्येयमित्येतदेव प्रार्थये । अङ्कप्राप्तेर्दुर्लभत्वादिति भावः । कीदृशम् । कामस्य मङ्गलार्थं गृहम् । तत्र कामो हृष्टो वसतीत्यर्थः । यद्वा कामस्य मङ्गलघटितं हिरण्यघटितं गृहम् । 'कल्याणं मङ्गलं विद्यात्काञ्चनं च तदक्षमम् ।' इति विश्वः । यद्वा अनङ्गस्य मङ्गलानामुपचयहेतूनां सौकुमार्यादीनां गृहम् । अत एवोत्प्रेक्षते । बा-

---

१ कमप्र०, मुन्मथित. २ कण्ठ. ३ ननः. ४ वङ्क. ५ परिवृत्तिं. ६ मेव तावत्. ७ कलोदयात्; दुपचितैः. ८ वासादितं.

यत्सत्यमधुना[1] तत्संदर्शनेनातिस्वल्पोऽपि न विशेषः । मम हि संप्रति सातिशयप्राक्तनोपलम्भसंभावितात्म[2]जन्मनः संस्कारस्यानवरतप्रबोधात्[3]प्रतायमानस्तद्विसदृश[4]प्रत्ययान्तरैरतिरस्कृतप्रवाहैः[5] प्रियतमास्मृतिप्रत्ययोत्पत्तिसंतानस्तन्मयमिव करोति[6] अन्तर्वृत्तिसारूप्यतश्चैतन्यम् । तथा हि ।

**लीनेव प्रतिबिम्बितेव लिखितेवोत्कीर्णरूपेव च**
**प्रत्युप्तेव च वज्रलेप[7]घटितेवान्तर्निखातेव च ।**

---

ल्चन्द्रकलोदयाद्बृंहितैः सारैरुत्पादितमिति । अत्रोदयादिति भावेन द्रव्याभिधानान्नवेन्दुकलाया अवचिताः सारास्तैरुत्पादितामिवेत्यर्थः । सकलजनानन्दिनवेन्दुकलातोऽप्यधिकमनोहरमिति भावः । यद्वा ल्यब्लोपे पञ्चमी । तेन बालेन्दुकलोदयं प्राप्यावचितैरित्यर्थः । यद्वा बालेन्दुकलोदयात्प्रतिपच्चन्द्रकलोदयादारभ्यावचितैः पूर्णिमापर्यन्तमित्यर्थात् । आरभ्येत्यस्य लाभः पञ्चमीत एव । तथा च पूर्णेन्दुना मुखसाम्यं लभ्यते । क्वचित्कलोच्चयादिति पाठः । तत्रोच्चयात्समूहादित्यर्थः । यत्र मुखे संमुखीभूते सुखानि । कर्तृणि । मिलित्वेव परं भूमानं बाहुल्यं विस्तारयन्ति चित्ते । अनेनान्तःप्रीतिरुक्ता । इवशब्द उत्प्रेक्षायाम् । एवपाठे विस्मय एवशब्दः । बहिःप्रीतिमाह--नेत्रोत्सवोऽलब्धलाभाभिमानोऽनुरागं प्रस्तौति स्रवति । रतेर्द्वेवमयोत्वात् । समाधिरलङ्कारः ॥ ९ ॥ मानसमौत्सुक्यातिशयमाह—**मम हीति** । मामकीनः प्रियास्मरणरूपज्ञानोत्पत्तेः संतानः परिणातिसमूहः स्मृतिरूप एव मम चैतन्यमात्मतत्त्वं तन्मयमिव करोति मालतीमयं करोतीत्यर्थः । कीदृशः । प्रतायमानो दीर्घीभवन् । अत्र हेतुः संस्कारस्य भावनाया अतिशयितप्रबोधादुद्रेकात् । कीदृशस्य संस्कारस्य । सातिशयात्सादरास्फुटाकाराद्वा बकुलवीथ्यां पूर्वकालानुभवाल्लब्धजन्मनः । प्रतायमानत्वमेवोपपादयति--तद्विसदृशैर्मालतीविलक्षणविषयैर्ज्ञानान्तरैरतिरस्कृतप्रवृत्तिः । तथा चान्तरा विषयान्तरास्फुरणान्न प्रवाहतिरस्कार इति भावः । नन्वात्मतत्त्वस्य पुष्करपलाशवन्निर्लेपतया कथं मालतीमयत्वमत आह—अन्तरिति । अन्तःपदमिह बुद्धितत्त्वपरम् । तथा च बुद्धितत्त्वस्य या प्रवृत्तिः सहजसिद्धो व्यापारः सा यत आत्मतत्त्वे भेदाग्रहात्प्रतिभासते तस्मात् । सांख्यदर्शने बुद्धेर्भोक्तृत्वात् । यद्वा अन्तर्वृत्तिरिति भावप्रधानम् । तथा चान्तर्वृत्तित्वमन्तरवस्थानरूपं सादृश्यमात्मबुद्ध्योस्तस्मात् । स्वोक्तमेव दर्शयति—**लीनेवेत्यादि** । सा प्रियास्माकं चेतसि लग्ना संबद्धा । संबद्धत्वे यथासंभवं प्रकारानाह--लीनेव निह्नुतेव । यत्र यस्य संबद्धस्य न प्रत्यक्षोपलम्भस्तत्र तल्लीनमित्युच्यते । यथा पयसि लीनं लवणम् । सर्वत्रात्र लग्नत्वस्य प्रकारभेदे-

---

१ अधुना संदर्शनं नेति स्वल्पोऽपि विशेषः. २ संभावितात्मनः. ३ प्रबोधनात्; प्रता०-प्रतीय०. ४ विसदृशैः. ५ प्रभावः. ६ करोति वृत्ति०. ७ लेख.

सा नश्चेतसि कीलितेव विशिखैश्चेतोभुवः पञ्चभि-
श्चिन्तासंततितन्तुजालनिबिडस्यूतेव लग्ना प्रिया ॥ १० ॥

नोपमाभेदः पूर्वपूर्वापरितोषाद्वा । तथा हि । लीनत्वस्याप्रतिभासात्स्पष्टप्रतिभासार्थमाह—प्रतिबिम्बितेव । यत्र स्वच्छद्रव्याभिहतं चक्षुः परिवृत्य द्रव्यान्तरं गृह्णाति तत्तत्र प्रतिबिम्बितमित्युच्यते । यथा स्फटिके रक्तपुष्पम् । प्रतिच्छायाया वस्त्वन्तरसंसर्गाधीनत्वेनासाहजिकत्वात्साहजिकत्वोपवर्णनायाह—लिखितेव । यत्प्रशिथिलावयवसंयोगाश्रयेण द्रव्येण घनद्रव्योपरि संस्थानविशेषवन्निर्मीयते तत्तत्र लिखितमित्युच्यते । यथा पत्रे लिपिः । लिखितस्य जलाद्युपनिपातविनाशितया न चिरस्थायित्वमतस्तदर्थमाह—उत्कीर्णरूपेव । यद्यत्र निबिडद्रव्ये तादृशेन किंचिदवयवविभागः क्रियते तत्तत्रोत्कीर्णम् । यथा टङ्कादिना शिलादि । अस्याप्येकभागवृत्तितया सर्ववृत्तित्वार्थमाह—प्रत्युप्तेव । प्रत्युप्तमर्धरोपितम् । यद्यत्र द्रव्यान्तरसंसर्गि तत्तत्र प्रत्युप्तम् । यथाङ्गुलीयके मण्यादि । अस्यापि शक्योद्धारत्वान्निबिडसंबन्धायाह—वज्रलेपघटितेव । यद्यत्र किंचिद्घनद्रव्याभिघातजन्यकर्मजन्यसंयोगविभागानाश्रयि तत्तत्र वज्रलेपघटितम् । यथा हीरकादि । तथापि लेपस्य बहिर्वृत्तित्वादन्तःसंसर्गार्थमाह—अन्तर्निखातेव । यद्यत्र संबद्धमूर्ध्वाधःसंयोगादिना धृतं नोपलभ्यते तत्तत्र निखातमुच्यते । यथा भूमौ मूलकादि । निखातत्वं सर्वरोपणमुप्तत्वमर्धरोपणमित्यनयोर्भेदः निखातस्यापि निर्बन्धातिशयेन शक्योद्धारतया विवेकादिदुःशक्यत्वार्थमाह—कामस्य पञ्चभिः शरैः कीलितेव । कीलितस्य प्रतिकीलनोद्धार्थतयाशक्योन्मूलनायाह-चिन्तापरम्परासूत्रसमूहेन गाढं यथा स्यात्तथा स्यूतेव सीवनं प्रापितेव । जालनिबिडसीवनेनानुच्छेदनीयत्वमुक्तम् । इहोपधेयाभेदेऽप्युपाधिभेदादपौनरुक्त्यमित्यवधेयम् । एकमेव हि वस्तु तत्तदुपाधिवैशिष्ट्यात्[illegible]भिन्नबुद्धिविषयो यथा दण्डिकुण्डलित्वादि । यद्वा नोऽस्माकं चेतसि सा लग्ना दृढं संबद्धा । दृढसंबद्ध एव लग्नपदार्थः । 'शरो लग्नः' इत्यादौ तथादर्शनात् । दृढसंबद्ध एव नानाप्रकारेण स्थिरीक्रियते । कामबाणपञ्चकेन कीलितेव । चिन्ताप्रवाहरूपतन्तुसंतत्या स्यूतेव । ननु द्वयमप्यदो न युक्तम् । तया सहान्तरस्य चैतन्यस्य संबन्धाभावात् । अतो विषयविषयिणोस्तदात्मरूप एव संबन्ध इति योगाचारमतमनेनोक्तम् । प्रतिबिम्बितेवेति सांख्यमतोपदर्शनम् । लिखितेवेति सौत्रान्तिकमतोपदर्शनम् । तत्र हि ज्ञानेन स्वीयाकारार्पणं विषये क्रियत इति तत्तदाकारस्याभिव्यक्तिः । शिलादौ तुरगादिवदिति लिखनसाम्यम् । उत्कीर्णरूपेवेति विषयाकारेण चैतन्यपरिणाम इहोत्कीर्णरूपता । अतस्त्रिदण्डिमतम् । प्रत्युप्तेवेति पूर्वरूपतिरोधानादन्यरूपाविर्भावेन सुवर्णरचितभाजनादाविव तत्तद्विषयाकारतया ज्ञानविपरिणाम इति पातञ्जलमतम् । वज्रलेपघटितेवेति नैयायिकमतम् । तदीयमात्ररूपो हि स्वभावभेदः प्रकाशस्य विषयविषयिभावः । अयं च यावद्वस्तुस्थिरतया वज्रलेपघटनातो न भिद्यते । अन्तर्नि-

( नेपथ्ये कलकलः । )

**माधवः**—( आकर्ण्य । ) अहो संप्रति प्रगल्भमानकौणपनिकायस्य महती श्मशानवाटस्य रौद्रता । अस्मिन् हि

**पर्यन्तप्रतिरोधिमेदुरचयैस्त्यानं चिताज्योतिषा-**
**मौज्ज्वल्यं परभागतः प्रकटयत्याभोगभीमं तमः ।**
**संसक्ताकुलकेलयः किलकिलाकोलाहलैः संमदा-**
**दुत्तालाः कटपूतनाप्रभृतयः सांराविणं कुर्वते ॥ ११ ॥**

---

खातेवेति विज्ञानवादिमतोपदर्शनम् । अत्र हि विज्ञानस्यान्तर्निखनननाम्ना बाह्यवस्तुस्थितिरिति । इहापि तथा । एते च विषयविषयिभावविकल्पास्तच्चिन्ताप्रकारत्वान्माधवस्य चित्ते विपरिवर्तन्ते । एवं च चेतसा सह संबन्धः । पश्चात्कीलनेन वा सीवनेन वा गाढसंबद्धतां गता भवति लग्ना । ततश्च तद्दर्शनं महापुरुषानुभूतं तस्येति किमत्र चित्रमिति भावः । अत्र पञ्चभिरित्यनेन युगपत्कामबाणविषयत्वमात्मनो निवेदयता दुःसहदशाशालित्वं सूचितम् । चेतोभुव इत्यनेन तत्प्रभवस्य तस्य मर्मज्ञता ध्वानिता । 'यथाशक्ति यथायुक्ति यथागति यथामति । यथाधीति यथानीति विवेचितमिदं मया ॥' ॥१०॥

**माधवः** । कौणपनिकायो राक्षससमूहः । रौद्रता भीषणत्वम् । **पर्यन्तेत्यादि** । तमः कर्तृ । चिताज्योतिषामौज्ज्वल्यं परभागतो गुणोत्कर्षाधानात्प्रकटयति व्यक्तीकरोति । तमसि संनिहिते सति तेजसां कान्त्युत्कर्षः स्फुट एवेति भावः । कीदृशं तमः आभोगात्परिपूर्णतया भीमम् । चितालोकमण्डलस्य पर्यन्तं निकटदेशे प्रतिरोधनशीलं मेदुरं स्निग्धं चयेन संघेन स्त्यानं घनम् । यद्वा । पर्यन्ते यः प्रतिरोधोऽन्धकारस्य प्रसरणनिवारणं तेन मेदुरो मांसलो यश्चयस्तेन घनमित्यर्थः । कटाः शवाः पूतनाः श्मशानवासिनो राक्षसास्तत्प्रभृतयोन्येऽपि तत्रत्याः शृगालादयः किलकिलारूपारावैः सांराविणं परस्पराह्वानं कुर्वते । संमदाद्धर्षात् । उत्ताला उद्भटाश्चञ्चला वा । तालादुद्गताः । सुप्सुपेति समासः । तेनान्योन्यहस्ततालवन्त इति वा । संसक्ता मिलिता आकुलास्त्वरायुक्ताः केलयः क्रीडा येषां ते । यद्वा संसक्तत्वेनाकुल केलिर्येषां ते । संसक्त इति भावप्रधानम् । यद्वा संसक्ता कुलेन स्वयूथेन केलिर्येषां ते त्रिपदबहुव्रीहावुत्तरपदत्वाभावान्न पुंवद्भावः । 'सान्द्रे स्निग्धे च मेदुरः' इत्यमरः । किलकिलेत्यव्यक्तशब्दः । अविभावितविशेषः शब्दसमूहः कोलाहलः । संपूर्वाद्रौतेरभिविधौ भाव इनुण् । तदन्तात्स्वार्थेऽण् । आदिवृद्धिः । शवानां शब्दकरणं वेतालाधिष्ठानात् । रौद्ररस इह । तल्लक्षणं तु भरते- 'इति रौद्रो रसो दृष्टो रौद्रैरेवाङ्गचेष्टितैः । शस्त्रप्रहारभूयिष्ठभयकम्पाक्रियात्मकः ॥' इति

---

१ वर्धमानं; संप्रतीतस्ततः प्रवर्तमान-निकरस्य. २ प्रतिरोध. ३ वन. ४ रोचिषाम्. ५ उत्तानाः.

भवत्वाघोषयामि तावत् । ( उच्चैः ) भो भोः श्मशाननिकेतनाः कटपूतनाः ।

अशस्त्रपूतमव्याजं पुरुषाङ्गोपकल्पितम् ।
विक्रीयते महामांसं गृह्यतां गृह्यतामिदम् ॥ १२ ॥

( पुनर्नेपथ्ये कलकलः । )

**माधवः**—कथमाघोषणानन्तरमेव सर्वतः समुच्चलदुत्तालवेतालमुक्त-तुमुलाव्यक्तकलकलाकुलः प्रचलित इवाविर्भवद्भूतसंकटः श्मशानवाटः । आश्चर्यम् ।

कर्णाभ्यर्णविदीर्णसृक्कविकटव्यादानदीप्ताग्निभि-
र्दंष्ट्राकोटिविसङ्कटैरित इतो धावद्भिराकीर्यते ।
विद्युत्पुञ्जनिकाशकेशनयनभ्रूश्मश्रुजालैर्नभो
लक्ष्यालक्ष्यविशुष्कदीर्घवपुषामुल्कामुखानां मुखैः ॥ १३ ॥

---

भो भो इत्यभिमुखीकरणरूपे संबोधने । निकेतनं गृहम् । **अशस्त्रेत्यादि** । अशस्त्रपूतं संमुखपतितस्य स्वर्गिणो मांसं शस्त्रपूतमतस्तेषामग्राह्यम् । इदमिति न तादृशमिदम् । यद्वा अशस्त्रपूतं शस्त्रेणाच्छिन्नम् । धातूनामनेकार्थत्वात् । शस्त्रहतमांसस्य रणे सुलभतया तेषामस्पृहात इदमतादृशमिति भावः । अव्याजं निष्कपटम् । यद्वा 'इष्टसिद्धिं पणीकृत्य साहसाद्युपार्जितम् । अशस्त्रपूतं निर्व्याजमेतन्मांसं विदुर्बुधाः ॥ इति परिभाषितमेव । 'स्त्रियश्चतुष्पदे श्रेष्ठाः पुरुषा द्विपदे तथा ।' इति वचनात्प्राशस्त्यार्थमाह—पुरुषस्याङ्गादानीयोपकल्पितम् । विक्रीयत इष्टसिद्धिमूल्येनेत्यर्थात् । विक्रयस्य मूल्यसापेक्षत्वात् । यद्वा विक्रीयते दीयते धातोरनेकार्थत्वात् ॥१२॥ 'उच्चैर्घुष्टं तु घोषणा' इत्यमरः । वेतालः श्मशानदेवताकिङ्करः । तुमुलं रणसंकुले' इत्यमरः । तेषामन्योन्यस्पर्धया रणे संकुलत्वम् । आविर्भावितार्थत्वेनाव्यक्तत्वम् । प्रचलित उच्चावचः । संकटो व्याप्तः । **कर्णेत्यादि** । उल्का ज्वाला मुखे येषां ते उल्कामुखाः शृगालभेदाः । तेषां मुखैर्नभ आकीर्यते व्याप्यते । यद्वा उल्कामुखा एव एतन्नामप्रसिद्धा रणवासिणो जन्तुभेदाः । कीदृशैः । कर्णसमीपविदीर्णसृक्कभ्यां करालं यद्व्यादानमास्यविकाशस्तेन दीप्तोऽग्निर्येषु । ऊर्ध्वाधःस्थितदंष्ट्राणां कोटिभिरग्रैर्विसङ्कटैः संकुलैर्विकरालैर्वा । सर्वतो धावद्भिः । विद्युत्पुञ्जतुल्यानि केशनयनभ्रूश्मश्रूजालानि यत्र तैः । पिङ्गलत्वात्केशादीनां विद्युत्तुल्यता । अत एवोल्कामुखः शृगालान्यो जन्तुभेद इति पक्षः साधीयान् । उल्काप्रकाशाल्लक्ष्याण्यन्यदालक्ष्याणि दुर्बलानि दीर्घाणि वपूंषि येषां तेषाम् । एतेन दुर्बलत्वमुक्तम् । 'प्रान्तावोष्ठस्य सृक्कणी' इत्यमरः । केशेत्यादौ पूर्वनिपातविधेरनित्यत्वाद्भ्रूशब्दमपहाय केशशब्दस्य पूर्वनिपातः । लक्ष्यशब्दोऽपि यकारवान् । कर्मणि घञि तद्रहित इत्यवधेयम् । अद्भुतरसोऽयम् ॥ १३ ॥

---

१ तदुच्चैराघोषयामि । भोः. २ निर्व्याजं. ३ तामिति. ४ आभाषणा-आघोषा. ५ उत्ताल-तुमुलव्यक्त; वेतालकुलमुक्त. ६ रापूर्यते. ७ विकाश

अपि च ।

एतत्पूतनचक्रमक्रमकृतग्रासार्धमुक्तैर्वृका-
नुत्पुष्णत्परितो नृमांसविघसैराघर्घरं क्रन्दतः ।
खर्जूरद्रुमदघ्नजङ्घमसितत्वङ्नद्धविष्वक्तत-
स्नायुग्रन्थिघनास्थिपञ्जरजरत्कङ्कालमालोक्यते ॥ १४ ॥

( समन्तादवलोक्य विहस्य च । ) अहो प्रकारः पिशाचानाम् । एते हि ।

ततपृथुरसनोग्रमास्यगर्तं
दधति विदार्य विवर्णदीर्घदेहाः ।
ललदजगरघोरकोटराणां
द्युतिमिह दग्धपुराणरोहिणानाम् ॥ १५ ॥

---

**अपि चेति** । अपिर्जुगुप्सायाम् । च समुच्चये । गर्हामाह—**एतदित्यादि** । एतत्पूतनचक्रं श्मशानप्रेतसमूह आलोक्यते । किं कुर्वत् । अत्याकुलतयाक्रमेण युगपत्कृतो यो ग्रासस्ततोऽर्धं भूमौ पतितमर्धं चर्वणेन मुख एव स्थितम् । तत्र भूमिपतितैरर्धमुक्तैर्मनुष्यमांसविघसैरुच्छिष्टैः सर्वत्र वृकान्कोकानारण्यकुक्कुरादीनुत्पुष्णत्पुष्टान्कुर्वत् । अक्रमत्वं प्रतिपक्षशङ्कया । अभिलाषातिशयाद्वा । कीदृशान् । अहमहमिकया मांसग्रहणादीषद्घर्घरमव्यक्तशब्दं यथा स्यादेवं रुदतः । एतत्तु कुक्कुरेषु स्फुटमेव । कीदृशं पूतनचक्रम् । खर्जूरद्रुमदघ्ना तत्प्रमाणा जङ्घा यस्य तत् । एतेन जङ्घानां ग्रन्थियोगित्वकर्कशत्वनीरसत्वलोमशत्वानि दर्शितानि । असिता श्यामा या त्वक् चर्म तया नद्धाः सर्वतो विस्तीर्णा याः स्नायवो 'नहरु' इति ख्यातास्ताभिर्ग्रन्थिषु संधिभागेषु घनानि दृढान्यस्थीनि पञ्जराणि येषां तादृशा जरन्तो जीर्णाः कंकाला मांसादिशून्यास्थिभागा यस्य तत् । वृकपदं शृगालाद्युपलक्षणपरम् । 'कोक ईहामृगो वृकः' इत्यमरः । यद्वा 'शालावृकाः कपिक्रोष्टृश्वानः' इति नानार्थेऽमरदर्शनादेतस्यैवैकशब्दः वृकशब्दः । तेन भीमभीमसेनादिवदस्यापि तावदर्थप्रतिपादकतेत्यवधेयम् । यद्वा वृको 'घोघ' इति ख्यातः 'विघसो भोजनशेषेऽपि' इत्यमरः । 'स्याच्छरीरास्थ्नि कङ्कालः' इत्यमरः ॥१४॥

**विहस्येति** । अतिसात्त्विकेऽपि मयि भीषणत्वममी पूतनाः कुर्वन्तीत्यसंबद्धक्रियया हासः । यदाह—'असंबद्धैस्तु हासः स्यादाम्रेपथ्याक्रियादिभिः ।' इति । प्रकारो वैलक्षण्यम् । **ततेत्यादि** । एते पूर्वोक्तादन्ये पिशाचा विस्तृतदीर्घजिह्वाभीषणमुखविवरं विदार्य व्यादाय दग्धपुराणरोहिणानामिव द्युतिं दधति धारयन्ति । दग्धत्वेन श्यामत्वं पुराणत्वेन जीर्णत्वं दर्शितम् । रोहिणो 'रोहण' इति ख्यातस्तरुः । 'घोघराति' इति ख्यातो वा । रोहितोऽपि स एव । अत एव 'रोहितः प्लीहनाशकः' इत्यमरोऽपि । रोहणानामिति पाठे रोहन्तीति रोहणास्तरवस्तेषामित्यर्थः । ललता चलताजगरेण सर्पेण भीषणच्छिद्राणाम् । 'निष्कुहः कोटरं वा ना' इत्यमरः । तदिह कोटरेणाजगरमज ।

---

२ नुत्फुल्लत्. २ आवर्दरम्. ३ ततः. ४ पृथुचल–तर, ५ रशनाग्रम्. ६ विवृत्य. ६ विशीर्णशुष्क. ७ चलद. ८ इव.

( परिक्रम्यावलोक्य च । ) हन्त बीभत्समेवाग्रे वर्तते ।

उत्कृत्योत्कृत्य कृत्तिं प्रथममथ पृथूच्छो[3]फभूयांसि मांसा-
न्यंसस्फिक्पृष्ठपिण्डा[4]द्यवयवसुलभान्युग्रपूती[5]नि जग्ध्वा ।
आत्तस्नाय्वन्त्रनेत्रः प्रकटितदशनः प्रेतरङ्कः करङ्का-
दङ्कस्थादस्थिसंस्थं स्थपुटगतमपि क्रव्यमव्यग्रमत्ति ॥ १६ ॥

अपि च ।

निष्टापस्विद्यदस्थ्नः क्वथनपरिणमन्मेदसः प्रेतकाया-
न्कृष्ट्वा संसक्तधूमानपि कुणपभुजो भूयसीभ्यश्चिताभ्यः ।
उत्पक्वस्रंसिमांसं प्रचलदुभयतः संधिनिर्मुक्तमारा[11]-
देते निष्कुष्य[12] जङ्घानलकमुदयिनीर्मज्जधाराः पिबन्ति ॥ १७ ॥

---

गरेण रसना रोहिणेन पिशाच उपमीयन्ते । भयानको रसः । यदाह—' विकृतरवसत्त्वदर्शनसंत्रासारण्यशून्यगृहगमनात् । गुरुनृपयोरपराधात्कृतश्च भयानको ज्ञेयः ॥ ' ॥ १५ ॥ बीभत्सं घृणाकरम् । **उत्कृत्येत्यादि** । अयं प्रेतरङ्कः प्रेतरूपो रङ्कः क्षुधाभिशुष्यच्छरीरोऽव्यग्रमनाकुलं यथा तथा क्रव्यं मांसमत्ति खादति । किं कृत्वा । प्रथममादौ कृत्तिं चर्म निर्भिद्य निर्भिन्नीकृत्य पश्चादुत्कृत्य छित्त्वा । उत्कृत्येति पाठे चर्मकोषाकर्षणमुत्कर्तनं तत्पुनः पुनः कृत्वेत्यर्थः । अथानन्तरं पृथुना महतोच्छोफेन भूयांसि बहूनि मांसानि जग्ध्वा भक्षयित्वा । कीदृशानि । अंसयोः स्कन्धयोः स्फिचोः कटिमांसपिण्डयोः पृष्ठे कायपश्चाद्भागे पिण्डयोर्जङ्घापाश्चात्यभागयोरादिपदा कक्षामूलाद्यवयवेषु सुलभानि । उच्छूनत्वात्तेषाम् । उग्रपूतीन्यूत्कटगन्धानि । पृथूत्सेधेति पाठे पृथुनोत्सेधेन कायेन बहुतां गतानीत्यर्थः । यद्वा उत्सेधेनोन्नत्या भूयांसीत्यर्थः । ' उत्सेधः काय उन्नतिः ' इत्यमरः । कीदृशो रङ्कः । आर्तस्वरावान् । पर्यस्तमितस्ततः क्षिप्तं नेत्रं येन सः । एतदुभयं रङ्केषु प्रसिद्धमेव । ' अन्तःपर्यस्तनेत्र इति पाठेऽन्तर्मध्ये स्थितनेत्रः । रङ्कत्वेन कोटराक्षत्वादित्यर्थः । ' आत्तस्नाय्वन्त्रनेत्रः ' इति पाठ आत्तानि गृहीतानि स्नाय्वन्त्रनेत्राणि येन सः । अत एवान्त्राद्युत्पाटनाय प्रकटितदन्तः । दौर्बल्यप्रकर्षणात्प्रकटितदशनत्वम् । अङ्कस्थात्क्रोडीकृतात्करङ्कात् कपालादाकृष्येत्याक्षेपात् । अन्यथापादानानुपपत्तिः । कीदृशं क्रव्यम् । अस्थिषु यत्संतिष्ठति तत् । स्थपुटगतमपि निम्नोन्नतविषयस्थानगतमपीत्यर्थः । अत एव रङ्कः । ' स्त्रियौ स्फिचौ कटिप्रोथौ ' इत्यमरः । ' पिण्डः खण्डेऽङ्गभेदे स्यात् ' इति मेदिनीकरः । ' करङ्को मस्तकेऽपि स्यात् ' इति धरणिः । अयं बीभत्सो रसः ॥ १६ ॥ **निष्टापेत्यादि** । एतेऽपि कुणपभुजः शवभक्षकाः पिशाचाः बह्वीभ्यश्चिताभ्यः प्रेतकायानाकृष्य तेषामेव जङ्घानलकं जङ्घाप्रधानमस्थि निष्कुष्य विगतमांसावरणं कृत्वा मज्जधाराः पिबन्ति । मज्जास्थिमध्यस्थितस्नेहः । कीदृशीः

---

१ अतिबीभत्समग्रतो. २ निर्भिद्यो० ( टी० ). ३ त्सेध. ४ पीठा. ५ गन्धीनि. ६ आर्तः पर्यस्तनेत्रः, अन्तःपर्य. ७ दस्रः. ८ परिगलन्. ९ धूमात. १० प्रचलम्. ११ सारा‌द्, माद्राथ. १२ निष्कृष्य, निश्चूष्य.

(विहस्य ।) अहो प्रादोषिकः प्रमोदः पिशाचाङ्गनानाम्[1] । तथा हि ।

अन्त्रैः कल्पितमङ्गलप्रतिसराः स्त्रीहस्तरक्तोत्पल-
व्यक्तोत्तंसभृतः पिनह्य सहसा[2] हृत्पुण्डरीकस्रजः[3] ।
एताः शोणितपङ्ककुङ्कुमजुषः संभूय कान्तैः पिब-
न्त्यस्थिस्नेहसुराः[4] कपालचषकैः प्रीताः पिशाचाङ्गनाः ॥१८॥

आराद्दूरत एवोदयिनीलम्बमानाः । द्रवमयत्वात् । यद्वा आरात्समीपे पिबन्तीति योजना । 'आराद्दूरसमीपयोः' इति विश्वः । चिताभूयस्त्वेनातिभीषणतोक्ता । कीदृशान् । निष्टापेनेषत्तापेन स्त्रियन्त्यसृञ्जि येषाम् । 'पद्दन्नो—' इत्यादिसूत्रेणासृक्शब्दस्यासन्नादेशेऽप्येपे रूपम् । अस्र इति पाठो न युक्तः । तृतीयादावस्थीत्यादिनानङ्विधानात् । यद्वा प्रेतकायादिति पञ्चम्यन्तः पाठः । अतोऽस्र इति पञ्चम्यामनङि रूपम् । चिताभ्य इति ल्यब्लोपे पञ्चमी । निसस्तपताविस्यनभ्यावृत्तौ षत्वम् । क्रथनेन पाकक्रमेणाङ्गेषु परिणमज्जीर्यन्मेदो येषां तान्संसृष्टधूमानपि । कीदृशं जङ्घानलकम् । उत्पक्वमुच्छूनं कृत्वा पक्वमत एव स्रंसनशीलं मांसं यस्मात् । यद्वा उत्पक्वेनोद्गतपाकेन स्रंसि मांसं यस्मात् । उत्पक्व इति भावे क्तः । प्रचलन्तः शिथिलीभवन्त उभयतो जानूरुपर्वणो गुल्फाश्च ये सन्धयोऽस्यां परस्परमिलनस्थानानि तैर्निर्मुक्तम् । प्रचलमिति पाठ उभयतः पार्श्वाभ्यां प्रचलम् । अत एव सन्धिपरिमुक्तमित्यर्थः । 'कुणपः शवमस्त्रियाम्' इत्यमरः । नलकं 'नरहड'. इति ख्यातम् । 'संरी' इति ख्यातं वा । बीभत्स एवात्र रसः ॥ १७ ॥ अहो इति बीभत्सशृङ्गारदर्शनेनाश्चर्यम् । प्रादोषिको रात्रिप्रारम्भजः । शृङ्गारबीभत्सयोः परस्परविरोधेऽपि संस्थानसाम्यात्संभेदाभास इह । प्रसाधनाच्चात्र शृङ्गारः । यदाह—'ऋतुमाल्यालङ्कारैः प्रियजनगान्धर्वकाव्यसेवाभिः । उपवनगमनविहारैः शृङ्गाररसोऽपि संभवति ॥' अत एवायं श्लोकः कण्ठाभरणेऽपि रससंकराभास उदाहृत इति । **अन्त्रैरित्यादि** । एताः पिशाचस्त्रियः कान्तैः संभूय मिलित्वा कपालचषकैरस्थिस्नेहसुरा मज्जमयानि पिबन्ति । कीदृश्यः । अन्त्रै रचितो मङ्गलार्थं प्रतिसरो हस्तसूत्रमूर्णामयं याभिस्ताः । अवैधव्याचिह्नं मङ्गलप्रतिसरो भवति । यद्वा प्रतिसरः कङ्कणम् । तदप्यवैधव्याविहतया मङ्गलम् । 'कङ्कणे करसूत्रे च भवेत्प्रतिसरोऽस्त्रियाम्' । इति मेदिनीकरः । स्त्रीहस्त एव रक्तपद्मं तेन व्यक्तमुत्तंसं कर्णभूषणं बिभ्रति याः । सहसा शीघ्रं हृत्पद्ममालाः पिनह्य परिधाय । हृत्पद्मस्य श्वेततया पुण्डरीकपदेनोपन्यासः । यदाह—'द्वादशाङ्गुलसंपूर्णे श्वेते हृदयपङ्कजे ।' इति । मालाया मनोहरतयान्या मा गृह्णात्विति परिधाने शीघ्रता । अत एव प्रीताः । रक्तकर्दमकुङ्कुमवत्यः । अत्र पिबन्त्यस्थीत्यादौ यतिभङ्गशङ्का न

१ पिशाचानाम्. २ रत्नो. ३ शिरसो-सा, शिरसां. ४ हृत्पुण्डरीके. ५ सुराम्.

( परिक्रम्य । पुनः अशस्त्रपूतमित्यादि पठित्वा । ) कथं नाम प्रशान्त-भीषणविभीषिकाप्रकारैर्झटित्यपक्रान्तं पिशाचैः । अहो निःसत्त्वता पिशाचानाम् । ( परिक्रम्य दृष्ट्वा सनिर्वेदम् । ) विचितश्चैष समन्ताच्छ्मशानवाटः । तथा हि खल्वियं पुरत एव

गुञ्जत्कुञ्जकुटीरकौशिकघटाघूत्कारसंवेलित-
क्रन्दत्फेरवचण्डडात्कृतिभृतप्राग्भारभीमैस्तटैः ।
अन्तःशीर्णकरङ्ककर्करपयःसंरोधकूलंकष-
स्रोतोनिर्गमघोरघर्घररवा पारेश्मशानं सरित् ॥ १९ ॥

( नेपथ्ये । )

हा तात निष्करुण एष इदानीं ते नरेन्द्रचित्ताराधनोपकरणं

---

कार्यो । संधिकृतपदविच्छेदे तस्यादोषत्वात् । 'रेवां द्रक्ष्यस्युपलविषमाम्' इत्यादौ तथा दर्शनात् । 'चषकं पानपात्रं स्यात्' इति हारावली । इह बीभत्समिश्रः शृङ्गाररसः ॥ १८ ॥ झटिति शीघ्रम् । विभीषिका परभयदायिनी रौद्ररूपता । तस्याः प्रकारा भेदाः । अपक्रान्तं प्रपलाय्य गतम् । निःसत्त्वा इत्यनेनात्मप्रौढिर्दर्शिता । महामांसविक्रयादपि नेष्टलाभ इति निर्वेदः । विचितो व्याप्तः । तमोव्याप्तत्वेन कथं विचितत्वज्ञानमित्यत आह—इयमिति । **गुञ्जदित्यादि** । इयं सरित्पुरत एवास्ति । पारेश्मशानं श्मशानपारदेशे 'पारे मध्ये षष्ठ्या वा' इति समासः । कुञ्ज एव कुटीरोऽल्पा कुटी तत्र या कौशिकघटा पेचकसमूहः । गुञ्जन्तीनां कुञ्जकुटीरकौशिकघटानां घूत्काररूपं संवल्गितं ध्वानितम् । क्रन्दच्छृगालानां डात्कृतिर्डात्कारः शब्दविशेषः । अनयोर्द्वन्द्वः । ताभ्यां भृतः पूरितो यः प्राग्भारोऽग्रतटं तेन भीषणस्तटैर्लक्षिता । लक्षणे तृतीया । अन्तरभ्यन्तरे । शीर्णास्त्रुटिता ये करङ्काः कपालानि तेषां कर्करो भग्नावयवः 'काकर' इति प्रसिद्धो वा कर्करो यत्र । अत एव तरतां संतरणशीलानां संरोध्यवरोधकः कूलङ्कषः कूलविदारको यः स्रोतोनिर्गमस्तेन घोरो घर्घरोऽव्यक्तरूपो रवः शब्दो यत्र सा । तरःसंरोधीति पाठे तरसा वेगेन संरोधि गमनविरोधि । कर्करेण दृढेन तरसा संरोधीत्यर्थः । 'अल्पा कुटी कुटीरः स्यात्' इत्यमरः । घटाशब्दः समूहमात्रवचनोऽपि करिघटादौ त्वात्यन्तिकस्तस्य प्रयोग इत्यवधेयम् । घूत्कारडात्कृती अनुकरणशब्दौ । क्वचित् फात्कृतीति पाठः । तत्रापि फात्कृतिरनुकरणशब्द एव । 'फेरुफेरवजम्बुकाः' इत्यमरः । 'तटः प्राग्भार इत्यपि' इत्यमरः । 'कर्करो भग्नभागेऽपि दृढेऽपि खण्डितेऽपि च ।' इति धरणिः । तदिह करङ्ककर्करसंकुलनदीप्रवाहस्तीरं पातयति घर्घररवं च कुरुत इति स्फुटमेव ॥ १९ ॥ **नेपथ्ये** । हा तात इत्यत्र

---

१ द्रागतिप्र०, नामानिभीषण. २ विकारैः. ३ निःसत्त्वाः सर्वे. ४ एष सर्वः. ५ संवेल्लित, संवर्गित; संवर्धित. ६ धात्कृति. ७ कीर्ण. ८ कर्पर. ९ तरःसं०, तरस्सं० ( टी० ).

जनो विपद्यते । ( हा ताद णिक्करुण एसो दाणिं दे णरेन्दचित्ताराहणोवअरणं जणो विपज्जइ । )

**माधवः**—( साकूतमाकर्ण्य । )

**नादस्तावद्विकलकुररीकूजितस्निग्धतार-**
**श्चित्ताकर्षी परिचित इव श्रोत्रसंवादमेति ।**
**अन्तर्भिन्नं भ्रमति हृदयं विह्वलत्यङ्गमङ्गं**
**देहस्तम्भः स्खलयति गतिं कः प्रकारः किमेतत् ॥ २० ॥**
**करालायतनाच्चायमुच्चरन्करुणो ध्वनिः**
**विभाव्यते ननु स्थानमनिष्टानां तदीदृशाम् ॥ २१ ॥**

भवतु पश्यामि । ( इति परिक्रामति । )

( ततः प्रविशतो देवतार्चनव्यग्रौ कपालकुण्डलाघोरघण्टौ कृतवध्यचिह्ना मालती च । )

**मालती**—हा तात निष्करुण एष इदानीं ते नरेन्द्रचित्ताराध-

---

हायोगेऽपि न द्वितीया । हाशब्दस्य शोकवाचिन उपग्रहात् । तस्य च संबोधने प्रथमाप्रयोगात् । तदन्यार्थस्य योगे द्वितीयेति न्यासः । अङ्कमुखे स्त्रीरत्नापहारस्य सूचितत्वान्नेपथ्ये भणनमिदम् । **नाद इत्यादि** । अयं तावन्नादः श्रोत्रयोः संवादं पूर्वोपलम्भाकारतामेति । कीदृशः । विकला त्रस्ता या कुररी ' हापूती ' इति प्रसिद्धा पक्षिवधूस्तस्याः कूजितवत्स्निग्धः स्नेहलस्तार उच्चश्च । त्रासान्मालत्यास्तारो नादः । अत एव चित्ताकर्षी प्रियत्वाच्चित्तानुकर्षकः परिचित इव पूर्वमुपलब्ध इव । अत एव श्रोत्रसंवादितास्य । परिचयश्च शङ्करगृहे वृत्तः । यदि श्रोत्रसंवादमेति कथं तर्हिविकार इत्यत आह । अन्तर्भिन्नं द्विधाभूतं संशयाक्रान्तं हृदयं भ्रमति दोलायते । उभयत आकर्षात् । अत्र मालतीगमनासंभवात्संवादस्य च स्फुटत्वात् । यद्वा अन्तर्भिन्नं विद्धममसंभवेनेत्यर्थात् । तथा बन्धुगतानिष्टशङ्काकलङ्कात्प्रत्यङ्गं विह्वलति । करादीनि कम्पन्त इत्यर्थः । तस्याः कथमिहावस्थानमिति भयाद्देहस्तम्भः । यदाह–' हर्षव्याधित्रासरोषाद्यैः स्तम्भः संभवति । चिन्तास्तिमितत्वाद्गतिश्च स्खलति ' । कथमकस्मादेव ममेदं वृत्तमिति विमर्शमाह–'कोऽयं प्रकारः किंनिमित्तं स्नेहमाविष्करोति । किमेतत् । सैवेयं किमन्यद्वा तत्तुल्यमित्यर्थः । संबाधमिति पाठे कर्णपीडां करोतीत्यर्थः । नादश्रुत्या मोहात् ॥ २० ॥ **करालेत्यादि** । अयमुत्थितकरुणरसो ध्वनिः कथं वा संभाव्यत इत्यन्वयः । उच्चरन्नुत्तिष्ठन् । वितर्कसंप्रधारणमाह—**नन्विति** । ननु संभावनायाम् । ईदृशां संभाव्यमानजातीयानामनिष्टानां जनवधानामिदं करालायतनं स्थानमिति संभाव्यते ॥ २१ ॥ वध्यचिह्नं न्यस्तालक्तकेत्यादि ।

---

1 वावज्जइ. २ गात्र०, देहोत्कम्पः. ३ करुणध्व. ४ ईदृशाम्. ५ देवार्च०; र्चना०.

नोपकरणं जनो विपद्यते । हा अम्ब स्नेहमयहृदये हतासि दैवदुर्विलसितेन । हा मालतीमयजीविते मम कल्याणसाधनैकमुक्तसकलव्यापारे भगवति चिरस्य ज्ञापितासि दुःखं स्नेहेन । हा प्रियसखि लवङ्गिके स्वप्नावसरमात्रदर्शनाहं ते संवृत्ता । ( हा ताद णिक्करुण ऐसो दाणिं दे णरेन्दचित्ताराहणोवअरणं जणो विपज्जइ । हा अम्ब सिणेहमअहिअए हदासि देव्वदुव्विलसिदेन । हा मालदीमअजीविदे मह कल्लाणसाहणेक्कमुक्कसअलव्वावारे भअवदि चिरस्स जाणाविदासि दुक्खं सिणेहेण । हा पिअसहि लवङ्गिए सिविणअवसरमेत्तदंसणा अहं दे संवुत्ता । )

**माधवः**—हन्त सैवेयं हरिणेक्षणा । संप्रति निरस्त एव संदेहः । तदपि नामैनां जीवन्तीं संभावये । ( त्वरितं परिक्रामति । )

**कापालिकौ**—देवि चामुण्डे नमस्ते नमस्ते ।

**सावष्टम्भनिशुम्भसंभ्रम[11]नमद्भूगोलनिष्पीडन-**
**न्यञ्चत्कर्परकूर्मकम्पविगलद्ब्रह्माण्डखण्डस्थिति ।**
**पातालप्रतिमल्लगल्लविवरप्रक्षिप्तसप्तार्णवं**
**वन्दे नन्दितनीलकण्ठपरिषद्व्यक्त[12]र्द्धि वः क्रीडितम् ॥ २२ ॥**

[13]अपि च ।

**प्रचलितकरिकृत्तिपर्यन्तचञ्चन्नखाघातभिन्नेन्दुनिःस्यन्दमानामृतश्च्योतजीवत्कपालावलीमुक्तचण्डाट्टहासत्रसद्भूरिभूतप्रवृत्तस्तुति**

---

**मालती** । अत्र भगवति कामन्दकि इति शेषः । चिरस्य बहुकालम् । एकशुभस्थाने । एकमुखमिति पाठ एकमुखमेकवाक्यतापन्नम् । **माधवः** । हन्तेति निश्चयलाभे । **कापालिकौ** । **सावष्टम्भेत्यादि** । देवि युष्माकं क्रीडितं नृत्यं वन्दे । कीदृशम् । साटोपो यो निशुम्भो निर्दययन्त्रणं करणभेदस्ततः संभ्रमादानमतो भूगोलस्यावनिचक्रस्य निष्पीडनेन न्यञ्चदधोगच्छत् कर्परं पृष्ठास्थि यस्य कूर्मस्य तस्य कम्पेनाकचालनेन विगलन्ती भ्रस्यन्ती ब्रह्माण्डखण्डस्य स्थितिर्यत्र तत्तथा । अनेन भूकम्प उक्तः । तथा च नम्रीभूतभूगोले त्वर्णवानामुत्सेकात्पातालतुल्यगल्लविवरे प्रक्षिप्ताः सप्तार्णवा यत्र तत् । नन्दितभैरवसभं च प्रकटविभवम् । 'उत्क्षिप्ता तु भवेत्पार्ष्णिर्निशुम्भोऽयं निगद्यते । अङ्गुल्योग्राञ्चिताः सर्वाः पादाग्रतलसंचरे ॥ ' इति भरतः । 'कटाहे च कपालेऽपि पृष्ठास्थनि च कर्परः । ' इति शाश्वतः । नाट्येश्वरीवर्णनमिदम् ॥ २२ ॥ दण्डकमाह—**प्रचलितेत्यादि** । देवि युष्माकं ताण्डवमुद्धतं नृत्यमस्माकमभीष्टया अशुभनाशाय तुष्ट्या

---

१ मातः. २ दुव्वारदेव्व. ३ णेक्कसुह (शुभ). ४ मदिरे०. ५ हन्त संप्रति०. ६ एव मे. ७ तदहमपि ८ संभावयेयमिति. ९ झटिति. १० चामुण्डे भगवति. ११ निर्भर. १२ व्यक्तं तव. १३ अघोर०.

श्वसदसितभुजङ्गभोगाङ्गदग्रन्थिनिष्पीडनस्फारफुल्लत्फणापीठ-
निर्यद्विषज्योतिरुज्जृम्भणोड्डामरव्यस्तविस्तारिदोःखण्डपर्या-
सितक्ष्माधरम् ।

ज्वलदनलपिशङ्गनेत्रच्छटासौटभीमोत्तमाङ्गभ्रमिप्रस्तुतालातचक्र-
क्रियास्यूतदिग्भागमुत्तुङ्गखट्वाङ्गकोटिध्वजोद्धूतिविक्षिप्ततारागणं
प्रमुदितकटपूतनोत्तालवेतालतालस्फुटत्कर्णसंभ्रान्तगौरीघना-
श्लेषहृष्यन्मनस्त्र्यम्बकानन्दि वस्ताण्डवं देवि भूयादभीष्ट्यै च
हृष्ट्यै च नः ॥ २३ ॥ ( इत्यभिनयतः । )

---

आनन्दाय च भूयात् । अरिष्ट्या इति पाठे रिष्टिरशुभं तदभावोऽरिष्टिस्तस्यै । अनेन भाव्यनिष्टार्थसूचकदण्डोऽप्युक्तः । यदाह—'आकस्मिकसंबद्धं समर्थमिव यद्भवेत् । वाचामन्ते स दण्डः स्याद्भाव्यनिष्टार्थसूचकः ॥' 'रिष्टिः खड्गे नाशुभे स्त्री' इति मेदिनीकरः । अरिष्टे तु शुभाशुभे' इत्यमरः । यद्वा 'ऋकारो देवमाता स्यात्' इति कोशादृशब्दात्संबुद्धौ गुणे च हे अः देवमातः इष्ट्या अभीष्ट्यै भूयादित्यर्थः । कीदृशम् । प्रचलितगजासुरचर्मपर्यन्तेषूत्रमतां नखानामाघातैर्भिन्नात्स्फुटिताद्देवीमस्तकस्थचन्द्रात्क्षरदमृतस्य श्च्योतेनाप्लवेन जीवन्तीभिः कपालावलिभिर्मुण्डमालाभिर्मुक्तैश्चण्डाट्टहासैरत्युग्रहसनैस्त्रसतां बहुभूतगणानां प्रवृत्ता स्तुतिर्यत्र । यद्वा भूतगणैः प्रवृत्ता प्रवर्तिता स्तुतिर्यत्र तत् । अन्तर्भावितण्यर्थः । यद्वा प्रचलितः करिचर्मरूपोऽवधिर्यत्र तत् । पश्चात्कर्मधारयः । तथा ताण्डवाडम्बरायासेन श्वसतां श्यामसर्पाणां कायैर्ये केयूराकारग्रन्थयस्तेषु निष्पीडनेनोत्फाल उद्गतमुखविकासस्तरलो वा फुल्लन्विस्तारिताङ्गचयः फणापीठः । विस्तारितया पीठेन रूपकम् । ततो निर्गतविषाग्नेरुज्जृम्भणेनाधिक्येनोड्डामरः केलिसंवस्तुरसातिशयो भयंकरो वा विषमो वा व्यस्त इतस्ततोगामी विस्तारी दीर्घो यो दोःखण्डः समूहस्तेन पर्यासितः क्षिप्तः पर्वतो यत्र तत् । देव्या अनेकबाहुशालितया दोःखण्ड इत्युक्तम् । 'अब्जादिकदम्बे खण्डमस्त्रियाम्' इत्यमरः । तथा ज्वलतानलेन पिङ्गलं यन्नेत्रं ललाटलोचनं तस्य च्छटा ज्वालानिर्गमप्रसरस्तस्य साटेन विस्तारेण भीमं यदुत्तमाङ्गं शिरस्तस्य भ्रमिर्मण्डलाकारेण भ्रमणं तया प्रस्तुता प्रारब्धालातचक्रक्रिया वह्निप्रज्वलितार्धकाष्ठविशेषकर्म तया स्यूता इवैकत्र प्रतिबद्धा इव दिग्भागा यत्र तत् । तथातिमहाखट्वाङ्गाग्रध्वजोत्कम्पाद्विक्षिप्त इतस्ततस्ताराप्रणो यत्र तत् । तथा हृष्टकटपूतनोद्भटवेतालानां तालेन कलकलेन स्फुटत्कर्णात एव संभ्रान्ता त्रसन्ती सत्वरा वा गौरी तस्या निबिडालिङ्गनेन हृष्यच्चित्तं त्र्यम्बकं शिवमत्यर्थमानन्दयति इति । आभीक्ष्ण्ये णिनिः । 'साटो निकुञ्जे विस्तारे' इति विश्वः । 'शृङ्गमग्रे-

---

१ व्रितोत्फाल, नोत्फुल्ल. २ व्यक्त, विस्तार. ३ च्छन्न, मार, सार; पिशङ्गरिङ्खज्जटाजूट-भीमो०. ४ शृङ्गध्व०. ५ वरिष्ट्यै.

**माधवः**—( विलोक्य । ) हा धिक् प्रमादः ।

'न्यस्तालक्तकरक्तमाल्यवसना पाखण्डचण्डालयोः
पापारम्भवतोर्मृगीव वृकयोर्भीरुर्गता गोचरम् ।
सेयं भूरिवसोर्वसोरिव सुता मृत्योर्मुखे वर्तते
हा धिक्कष्टमनिष्टमस्तकरुणः कोऽयं विधेः प्रक्रमः ॥ २४ ॥

**कपालकुण्डला**—

तं भद्रे स्मर दयितोऽत्र यस्तवाभू-
द्‌ध त्वां त्वरयति दारुणः कृतान्तः ।

**मालती**—हा दयित माधव परलोकगतोऽपि युष्माभिः स्मर्तव्योऽयं जनः । न खलु स उपरतो यस्य वल्लभो जनः स्मरति । ( हा दइअ माहव परलोअगदो वि सुमरिदव्वो तुह्मेहिं अअं जणो । ण हु सो उवरदो जस्स वल्लहो जणो सुमरेदि । )

---

ऽपि कीर्तितम्' इति शाश्वतः ॥ २३ ॥ **माधवः** । धिक् प्रमाद इत्यत्र वर्तत इति क्रियाध्याहारः । तत उपपदविभक्तेः कारकविभक्तिर्बलीयसीति धिग्योगे द्वितीयां बाधित्वा प्रथमेत्यवधेयम् । **न्यस्तेत्यादि** । सेयं भूरिवसोः सुता यस्याः कृते मयैवं दुःखमनुभूयते पाखण्डचण्डाल्योर्गोचरं संमुखं गता । पाखण्डेषु चण्डालोऽसौ । तद्दर्शनाविरुद्धक्रियाकारित्वात् । यदाह—'न भुञ्जीतार्कपत्रेषु स्त्रीबालं नैव घातयेत्' । यद्वा । पाखण्डौ च तौ चण्डालौ च । निषिद्धक्रियत्वात् । यदाह—'अवध्यास्तु सदाख्याताः सर्वयोनिगताः स्त्रियः ।' चण्डालत्वादेव पापारम्भवतोर्मारणप्रवृत्तयोः । न्यस्ते अलक्तकरक्ते माल्यवसने यस्यां सा । एतद्वध्यचिह्नम् । यथा मृगी वृकयोः संमुखं गता तथेयं भीरुः । मृगीत्यनेन भयचलनेत्रतोक्ता । वसोर्देवताभेदस्य । एतेनास्य सुखित्वमुक्तम् । मृत्योर्यमस्य मुखे वर्तते । अत एव हाशब्दः परिदेविते स्त्रीरत्नमपि वध्यत इति । निन्दायां धिगिति । विषादे कष्टम् । कोपेऽनिष्टम् । अस्ता नष्टा करुणा दया यत्र । एतादृशो विधेरारम्भः कोऽयम् । निन्दितोऽयम् । कीदृग्वा । 'किं वितर्के परिप्रश्ने क्षेपे निन्दाप्रकारयोः ।' इति विश्वः । करुणोऽयं रसः । 'इष्टवधदर्शनाद्वा करुणरसो नाम संभवति ।' इति भरतः । 'चण्डालोऽपि च चाण्डालः' इति शब्दभेदः । पुष्पपुष्पस्रजौ माल्यम्' इत्यमरः ॥ २४ ॥ **तं भद्र इत्यादि** । प्रहर्षिणीच्छन्दसा श्लोकार्धम् । चामुण्डे भगवतीत्याद्यग्रिमार्धम् । हे भद्रे यस्तव दयितो वल्लभत्वेनेष्टस्तं स्मर । गुरुत्वात्स्मरणमस्य । यदाह—'पतिरेको गुरुः स्त्रीणाम्' इति । यद्वा मदुपहरणीयत्वेन स इह जन्मनि ते वल्लभो न भूत एव । अतो जन्मान्तरेऽपि तल्लाभाय तं स्मर । यदाह—'यं यं वापि स्मरन्भावं त्यजत्यन्ते कलेवरम् । तं तमेवैति कौन्तेय सदा तद्भावभावितः ॥' इति । कृतान्तो यमः । **मालती** ।

---

१ पाषण्ड–खण्डि. २ कयोः. ३ मरिष्ट. ४ त्वं. ५ णाह; दइअणाह.

**कपाल०**—हन्त माधवानुरक्तेयं तपस्विनी ।

**अघोरघण्टः**—( शस्त्रमुद्यम्य । ) यदस्तु तदस्तु व्यापादयामि ।

**चामुण्डे भगवति मन्त्रसाधनादा-**
**वुद्दिष्टामुपनिहितां भजस्व पूजाम् ॥ २५ ॥**

( इति हन्तुमुपक्रान्तः । )

**माधवः**—( सहसोपसृत्य प्रकोष्ठे मालतीं विक्षिप्य । ) आः दुरात्मन् अपेहि । प्रतिहतोऽसि कापालिकापसद ।

**मालती**—( सहर्षावलोक्य । ) परित्रायतां परित्रायतां महाभागः । ( परित्ताअदु परित्ताअदु महाभाओ । ) ( इति माधवमालिङ्गति । )

**माधवः**—महाभागे न भेतव्यं न भेतव्यम् ।

**मरणसमये त्यक्त्वा शङ्कां प्रलापनिरर्गलं**
**प्रकटितनिजस्नेहः सोऽयं सखा पुर एव ते ।**
**सुतनु विसृजोत्कम्पं संप्रत्यसाविह पाप्मनः**
**फलमनुभवत्युग्रं पापः प्रतीपविपाकिनः ॥ २६ ॥**

---

स्मरणफलमाह—यस्येत्यत्राधीगर्थेति कर्मणि षष्ठी । यस्य गुणमिति वा । अन्तकाले माधवस्मरणं मुक्तिहेतुरिति कटाक्षितम् । **कपालकुण्डला** । हन्त खेदे । कामन्दकीमित्रपुत्रत्वान्ममापि माधवस्तादृश एव । तदनुरक्ता चेयं कथं वध्येति खेद इति भावः । अत एव तपस्विन्यनुकम्प्या । **अघोरघण्टः** । उद्दिष्टां वाचा प्रतिज्ञाताम् । उपनिहितामुपढौकिताम् ॥ २५ ॥ **माधवः** । कफोणेरधोभागो मणिबन्धपर्यन्तः प्रकोष्ठः । विक्षिप्यापसार्य । खड्गहस्तत्वेन बाहुमध्येऽपसारणं जातिः । प्रतिहतो निराकृतः । अपसद निन्दित । **मरणेत्यादि** । सोऽयं तव मित्रं पुरत एव वर्तत इत्याक्षेपात् । यो वकुलवीथ्यादिषु सानुरागदर्शनप्रसभया त्वया स्वीकृतः । मरणसमय इत्यनेनानुराग उक्तः । यदाह—'साहसानुरक्तं हि स्त्रियो भजन्ते' इति । तत्र मुक्ताशङ्को निर्भयः । पाखण्डादिति भावः । अत एव प्रतानेन निरर्गलोऽनभिभाव्यः । प्रलापेति पाठे हा नाथ माधवेत्यादिमालतीप्रलापेन निरर्गल उच्छृङ्खल इत्यर्थः । त्यक्त्वा शङ्कामिति पाठे शङ्का भयं लज्जादिकं वा त्यक्त्वा । प्रतापनिराकुलो वा प्रतापनिरङ्कुशो वेत्यर्थः । यद्वा शङ्कां त्यक्त्वा यं प्रति त्वया प्रकटितो निजस्नेहः सोऽयमित्यर्थः । यद्वा अयं कीदृशः । प्रकाशितात्मस्नेहः । मरणसमये रक्षणादिति भावः । हे सुतनु अत उद्गतं कम्पं त्यज । असौ पापः संप्रत्येव पाप्मनो निषिद्धाचरणस्य फलं मरणरूपमुग्रं तीव्रमनुभविष्यति । संप्रतीत्य-

---

१ वराकी. २ शक्ति०. ३ एतन्नास्ति क्वचित्. ४ नार्थम्. ५ खड्गं प्रकोष्ठेन वि०; मालतीं गृहीत्वा वि० खड्गं. ६ माधवम०, विलोक्य. ७ भाओ माहवो. ८ मुक्ताशंकः (टी०). ९ र्गलः. १० वा पुनः

**अघोर०**—आः क एष पापोऽस्माकमन्तरायः संवृत्तः ।

**कपाल०**—भगवन् स एवास्याः स्नेहभूमिः कामन्दकीसुहृत्पुत्रो महामांसस्य पणायिता माधवः ।

**माधवः**—( सास्रम् । ) महाभागे किमेतत् ।

**मालती**—( चिरादाश्वस्य । ) महाभाग अहमपि न जानामि । एतावत्पुनर्जानामि । उपर्यलिन्दकं प्रसुप्तेह प्रबुद्धास्मि । यूयं पुनः क्व ।
( महाभाअ अहं[1] वि ण जाणामि । एत्तिअं उणं जाणामि । उवरिअलिन्दअं पसुत्ता इह पबुद्धह्मि । तुह्मे उण कहिं )

**माधवः**—( सलज्जम् । )

**त्वत्पाणिपङ्कजपरिग्रहधन्यजन्मा**
**भूयासमित्यभिनिवेशकदर्थ्यमानः ।**
**भ्राम्यन्नृमांसपणनाय परेतभूमा-**
**वाकर्ण्य भीरु रुदितानि तवागतोऽस्मि ॥ २७ ॥**

**मालती**—(स्वगतम्[3]।) कथं मम कारणादेवात्मनिरपेक्षः परिक्रामति ।
( कधं मम कालणादो एव्व[4] अप्पणिरपेक्खो परिक्कामदि । )

---

नेन प्रकृतोपयुक्तं निजाप्तत्वं पौरुषं च ध्वनितम् । कीदृशस्य । प्रतीपो विपरीतो विपाको विरुद्धपरिणतिर्यत्र तस्य । अनुभवतीत्यत्र वर्तमानसामीप्ये वर्तमानवद्वेति भविष्यति लट् । शृङ्गारवीरसंभेदोऽत्र ॥ २६ ॥ **अघोरघण्टः** । अन्तरायो विघ्नः । **कपालकुण्डला** । भूमिः स्थानम् । **मालती** । त्रासातिशयाच्चिरान्निःश्वासः । अत्रोपरि सौधोपरि आलिन्दे । 'ओट्ठ' इति प्रसिद्धे । **यूयमिति** । अहमबला सुप्ता चान्येनानीता यूयं धीराधीरा विबुद्धा अपीदानीमिह किमर्थमागता इत्यर्थः । **त्वदित्यादि** । हे भीरु महामांसविक्रयाय श्मशाने भ्रमंस्तव क्रन्दितान्याकर्ण्यागतोऽस्मि । महामांसविक्रयफलमाह—त्वदिति । त्वद्विवाहेन धन्यजन्मा पुण्यजन्माहं भवामीत्यभिनिवेशेनातियत्नेनावेशेन वा कदर्थ्यमानः पीड्यमानः । अतस्त्वां विना न मे जीवनमिति संभाव्यमानफलतया मांसविक्रये प्रवृत्तोऽस्मीति भावः । त्वत्पादपङ्कजेति पाठे प्रेयसीचरणग्रहणस्य मान एव कर्तव्यतया मानप्रसादनमेवोत्तरोत्तरं चरितेत्याशंसितवान् । अत एव सलज्जमित्युक्तमिति भावः । 'धन्यः पुण्य इति स्मृतः इति विश्वः । कुत्सितोऽर्थः कदर्थः । भीरु इत्यनेन रोदनोपपत्तिरुक्ता । तदिह त्वन्निमित्तमहं साहसी त्वं पुनः कीदृशीति न जाने इति तात्पर्यम् ॥ २७ ॥ **मालती** । अत एव हर्षविस्मयवशादाह मालती—**कथमित्यादि** । परिभ्रमणमितस्ततो गमनम् । आत्मनिरपेक्षः श्मशानभ्रमणेन ।

---

१ अहं न किंवि. २ जेव्व. ३ अपवार्य. ४ एव्वं एदे... ०पेक्खं—खा परिब्भमन्दि; एवमेते आ० पेक्षं- क्ष्य परिभ्रमन्ति.

माधवः—अहो नु खलु भोः तदेतत्काकतालीयं नाम । संप्रति हि

राहोश्चन्द्रकलामिवाननचरीं दैवात्समासाद्य मे
दस्योरस्य[1] कृपाणपातविषयां[2]माच्छिन्दतः प्रेयसीम् ।
आतङ्काद्विकलं द्रुतं करुणया विक्षोभितं विस्मया-
त्क्रोधेन ज्वलितं मुदा विकसितं चेतः कथं वर्तताम्[3] ॥ १८ ॥

अघोर०—रे रे ब्राह्मणडिम्भ

व्याघ्राघ्रात[4]मृगीकृपाकुलमृगन्यायेन हिंसारुचेः
पापं[5] प्राण्युपहारकेतनजुषः प्राप्तोऽसि मे गोचरम् ।
सोऽहं प्राग्भवतैव भूतजननीमृप्णोमि खड्गाहति-
च्छिन्न[6]स्कन्धकबन्धरन्ध्ररुधिरप्राग्भारनिःस्यन्दिना ॥ १९ ॥

---

**माधवः** । विस्मयेऽह्रो नु खलु भोः । काकतालीयमचिन्तितोपनतम् । यथा काकागमनतालपतनयोरेकदा संभवो दैवाधीनस्तथेदमपीत्यर्थः । **राहोरित्यादि** । दैवाद्विधिवशादासाद्य प्राप्य । अर्थात्प्रियाम् । अस्य दस्योश्चौरस्य खड्गपातविषयात्प्रेयसीमाकर्षतो मम चेतः कथं वर्तताम् । नवनवरसोदयात्तन्न जान इत्यर्थः । कामिव । राहोराननचरीमिन्दुकलामिव । कृपाणपातविषयामिति पाठे खड्गपतनस्य विषय आश्रयो यत्र तामेतादृशीं प्रेयसीं प्राप्य कथं मम चेतो वर्ततामिति योजना । यद्वा अस्य कीदृशस्य । आच्छिन्दतो द्विधाकर्तुमुद्यतस्य । प्रियामित्यर्थात् । ततो जीवनाभाव एवास्या इति भावः । चोरिकयापहरणेन दस्युत्वम् । तदिह प्रथमार्धेन हेतुरुक्तः । द्वितीयेन फलमाह—आतङ्काच्चित्तचमत्काराद्विकलं न त्वस्य निसर्गसात्त्विकस्य भयमिति यद्यपि तथापि प्रियप्राप्त्या जीवनसव्यपेक्षतया भयमुक्तिमेव । पूर्वं तु जीवननिरपेक्षतया निर्भयत्वमित्यातङ्को भयमेव । राहोरित्युपमानं भयहेतुः । चन्द्रकलोपमया जगन्नेत्रोत्सवकरीयं व्यसनमुपगतेति करुणया द्रवीभूतम् । दैवादासाद्येति विस्मयाद्विचलितम् । दस्योरित्यनेन मालतीमयं हन्तुमुद्यतश्चौर इति कोपेन दीप्तम् । आच्छिन्दतः प्रेयसीमिति प्रियाजीवननिर्वाहेण हर्षेण प्रसन्नम् ॥ १८ ॥ **अघोरघण्टः** । ब्राह्मणेति सिद्ध्यनुगुणशुचित्वार्थं यज्ञोपवीतधारणात् । डिम्भो बालकः । ब्राह्मणकपालभोजिनो मम ब्राह्मणवधेऽपि न दोष इत्युक्तमनेनेत्यपि भावः ॥ **व्याघ्रेत्यादि** । हे पाप मालत्युपहारकृत्यपरस्य मे गोचरं समीपं यत्प्राप्तोऽसि । अत एव विघ्नकारितया पापेति । कीदृशस्य मे । व्याघ्रगृहीतहरिणीकृपयाकुलो यो मृगस्तन्न्यायेन मृगीमनुसरन्व्याघ्रसंनिधौ पतन्मृगस्तस्य वध्यो भवत्येवं हिंसारुचेः । एनां न रक्षसि त्वं तु म्रियस इति भा-

---

१ धीरस्य. २ विषयाम्. ३ वर्तते. ४ घ्राण. ५ पापः. ६ व्यस्त.

माधवः—दुरात्मन्पाखण्डचण्डाल

असारं संसारं परिमुषितरत्नं त्रिभुवनं
निरालोकं लोकं मरणशरणं बान्धवजनम् ।
अदर्पं कंदर्पं जननयननिर्माणमफलं
जगज्जीर्णारण्यं कथमसि विधातुं व्यवसितः ॥ ३० ॥

वमाश्रित्य । पाठान्तरं हिंसारुचे इति संबोधनं वा । सोऽहं भवतैव प्रागग्रे भूतजननीं जगन्मातरं चण्डिकामृध्नोमि प्रीणयामि । ऋधु वृद्धाविति स्वादिरपीति धातुप्रदीपः । कीदृशेन खड्गहत्या व्यस्तस्कन्धश्छिन्नग्रीवः । अत एव कबन्धस्तस्य रन्ध्राद्रुधिरप्राग्भारं श्चोतनं समूहं वा निःस्यन्दितुं शीलं यस्य तेन । रुचेरिति पञ्चम्यन्तपाठे रुचेर्हेतोर्मे गोचरं प्राप्तोऽसीत्यर्थः । पापस्थाने प्रायःपाठे समस्तमेव पदम् । 'केतनं कृत्ये केतावुपनिमन्त्रणे' इत्यमरः । 'गोचरस्तु समीपे स्यात्' इति धरणिः । यत एव च्छिन्नग्रीवोऽत एव कबन्ध इति हेतुहेतुमद्भावेनोक्तिपोष एव । वीररसोऽयम् ॥ २९ ॥ मारणेऽपराधमाह–**असारमित्यादि** । हे पाखण्ड जगदसारं सारशून्यं विधातुं कर्तुं कथं व्यवसितः कृतप्रारम्भोऽसि । 'अशक्यानि दुरन्तानि समव्ययफलानि च । असत्यानि च कार्याणि नारभेत विचक्षणः ॥' इति न श्रुतं त्वया । तथा च संसारसारभूतेयमेव । अनया विनासार एव स इति । यदाह—'सारं तु महिलारत्नं संसार इति निश्चयः ।' इति । 'जातौ जातौ यदुत्कृष्टं तद्धि रत्नं प्रचक्षते ।' इति । तत्सर्वमाकृष्येयं निर्मिता अतो रत्नमियम् । मनोहरत्वदीप्तिमत्त्वतरलत्वादिनेयं वा रत्नम् । अत एव तदभावात्प्रमुषितरत्नं त्रिभुवनं कर्तुं व्यवसितोऽसि । तदेतत्सर्वविषयं चौर्यं दुरन्तमिति भावः । इयमतिकान्त्या जगदुद्योतयतीत्यालोकभूता । एतदभावान्निरालोकं तमःप्रविष्टं लोकं जनं कर्तुं व्यवसितोऽसि । अत एवोत्कृष्टं प्रति लोकोक्तिस्तेन विनान्धकारस्तत्सत्त्व उद्योत इति । बान्धवजनानामेतत्सखीनामियं जीवनहेतुः । अत एतन्नाशान्मरणशरणं सखीजनं विधातुं व्यवसितोऽसि । अन्यस्त्रीनाशे तत्सख्यो दुःखिताः । एतन्नाशे तु म्रियन्त एवेति भावः । अत्रासारं संसारमित्यादिना नायिकागतरामणीयकातिशयवर्णनमुपक्रम्य मरणशरणमित्यादिस्नेहविषयताप्रतिपादनान्नैकवाक्यतयैकरसनिर्वाह इत्यदेस्यम् । मात्रादिबन्धुव्यतिरिक्तोदासीनबान्धवसंग्रहपराज्जनशब्दात्स्वस्यैव माधवस्तथा विपत्तिं सूचयतीत्यदोषात् । तदीयनानागुणचिन्तनादेव मरणशरणता ममेत्यारब्धनिर्वाहाच्च । कन्दर्पश्चैतया मोहनास्त्रेण दर्पं करोति एतदभावाददर्पं कन्दर्पम् । जननयनस्यैतद्दर्शनमेव फलम् । अत एतन्नाशात्तदफलम् । जगदनयालंकृतमेव । एतदभावाज्जीर्णारण्यतुल्यं तदिति । अत्र प्रियाप्रशंसया शृङ्गारो बन्धुमरणात्करुणः पाखण्डाक्षेपाद्वीरः कथमित्यद्भुत इति नाना

१ आः दुरा०; पाषण्ड. २ विषसितः.

अपि च । रे पाप

**प्रणयिसखीसलीलपरिहासरसाधिगतै-**
**र्ललितशिरीषपुष्पहननैरपि ताम्यति यत् ।**
**वपुषि वधाय तत्र तव शस्त्रमुपक्षिपतः**
**पततु शिरस्यकाण्डयमदण्ड इवैष भुजः ॥ ३१ ॥**

**अघोर०**—आः दुरात्मन् प्रहर प्रहर । नन्वयं न भवसि ।

**मालती०**—प्रसीद नाथ साहसिक । दारुणः खल्वयं हताशः । तत्परित्रायस्व माम् । निवर्त्यतामस्मादनर्थसंशयात् । (पसीद णाह साहसिअ । दारुणो क्खु अअं हदासो । तो परित्तासु मं । णिअत्तीअदु इमादो अणत्थसंसआदो । )

**कपाल०**—भगवन् अप्रमत्तो भूत्वा दुरात्मानं व्यापादय ।

**माधवाघोरघण्टौ**—( मालतीकपालकुण्डले प्रति । ) अयि भीरु

**धैर्यं निधेहि हृदये हत एष पापः**
**किं वा कदाचिदपि केनचिदन्वभावि ।**
**सारङ्गसंगरविधाविभकुम्भकूट-**
**कुट्टाकपाणिकुलिशस्य हरेः प्रमादः ॥ ३२ ॥**

---

रसाः ॥ ३० ॥ पुनरपि दोषमुद्भाव्य दण्डं चिकीर्षुराह—**प्रणयीत्यादि** । हे पाप तव शिरस्येष भुज आकस्मिकयमदण्ड इव पततु । आकस्मिकत्वेनाप्रतिक्रियत्वमुक्तम् । कीदृशस्य । तत्र वपुषि वधाय शस्त्रमुत्तोलयतः । अत्र भुजपदेन बाहुव्यापारमात्रेणैव हन्तव्योऽसीति शौर्यातिशय उक्तः । यद्वपुः सुकुमारशिरीषपुष्पाघातैरपि ताम्यति खिद्यति । कीदृशैः सप्रश्रयसखीसविलासपरिहासरसप्राप्तैः । अत्रापि शृङ्गारवीरकारुण्यसंभेदः ॥ ३१ ॥ **मालती** । अत्र त्वज्जीवने मम जीवनमपि सफलम् । अन्यथा तु मरणमेव वरमिति भावः । **कपालकुण्डला** । मालतीव कपालकुण्डलापि स्वनाथमाह—**भगवन्निति** । अवष्टम्भार्थमप्रमत्त इति । द्वयोर्भयं ज्ञात्वोभावाहतुः—**धैर्यमित्यादि** । हे भीरु त्वं हृदये धैर्यं कुरु । एष पापो हतः । अस्य वधे कुतः संशय इति वृथा भयं त इति भावः । अत्र युक्तिमाह—सारङ्गेण मृगेण सह युद्धविधाने हरेः सिंहस्य प्रमादोऽनवधानता किं वा केनचित्कदाप्यनुभूतः । कीदृशस्य । इभकुम्भरूपं यत्कूटमुच्चप्रदेशस्तत्कुट्टनशीलं हस्त एव वज्रं यस्य । यद्वा हरेरिन्द्रस्य हस्तिना सह

---

१ प्रणय. २ एतन्नास्ति क्वचित्. ३ पडिणि० ( प्रतिनिवर्त्यतां–टी० ). ४ अत्थ०. ५ विक्रमस्व. ६ संहति, सूदन.

( नेपथ्ये कलकलः । सर्वे आकर्णयन्ति । पुनर्नेपथ्ये । )

भो भो मालत्यन्वेषिणः[1] सैनिकाः[2] इयममात्यभूरिवसुमाश्वासयन्त्य-प्रतिहतप्रज्ञा[3]गतिर्भगवती कामन्दकी वः समादिशति[4] । पर्यवष्टभ्यता-मेतत्करालायतनम् ।

**नाघोरघण्टादन्य[6]स्य कर्मैतद्दारुणा[7]द्भुतम् ।**
**न करालोपहाराच्च फलमन्यद्विभाव्यते ।**

**कपाल०**—भगवन्[8] पर्यवष्टब्धाः स्मः ।

**अघोरघण्टः**—संप्रति विशेषतः पौरुषस्यावसरः ।

**मालती**—हा तात हा भगवति । ( हा ताद हा भअवदि । )

**माधवः**—भवतु बान्धवसमाजसुस्थितां मालतीं विधाय तत्समक्षमेनं[10] व्यापादयामि । ( मालतीमन्यतः प्रेरयन्परिक्रामति । )

**माधवाघो०**—( अन्योन्यमुद्दिश्य । ) आः पाप

---

युद्धे नास्ति प्रमादः । कीदृशस्य । हस्तिकुम्भवत्पीवरश्रृङ्गकुट्टाकं पाणिस्थकुलिशं यस्य । कुम्भकूटपाणिकुलिशपदे शाकपार्थिवादिः । 'सारङ्गः पुंसि हरिणे चातके च मतङ्गजे ।' इति मेदिनीकरः । वीरो रस इह ॥ ३२ ॥ मालतीगृहकथाकथनायाह—**भो भो इति** । अप्रतिहतेति सत्यवचनेत्यर्थः । एतेनाघोरघण्टकृतो मालत्यपहार इति कामन्दकीवचनं सत्यम् । मालतीमाधवयोश्च विवाहः सत्य इति षष्ठाङ्कावतार इति सूचितम् । पर्यवष्टम्भनं सर्वतो वेष्टनम् । **नेत्यादि** । एतत्कर्म मालत्यपहरणात्मकं भीषणं सिंहकौशलहरणात् । अद्भुतं बहुरक्षकरक्षिताया अपि हरणात् ॥ ३३ ॥ **कपालकुण्डला** । त्रीत्वाद्भयेन पलायनेच्छुराह—**भगवन्निति** । **अघोरघण्टः** । संग्रामादपसरणस्याधर्महेतुतया सात्विकतया चाह—**संप्रतीति** । पौरुषं पुरुषस्य व्यापारस्तेजो वा । 'पौरुषं पुरुषस्योक्तं भावे कर्मणि तेजसि ।' इति विश्वः । **मालती** । मालती तत्रावेगातिशयादाह–हा तात हा भगवति इति । **माधवः** । मालतीरक्षार्थं कापालिको मया हत इत्यमात्यो जानात्वित्याशयेन मालतीं च कातरां वीक्ष्याह—**भवत्विति** । बान्धवेत्यादिना भाविकार्योपयोग उक्तः। अन्यतः कापालिकादन्यदेशं स्वसंमुखमिति यावत् ।

---

१ त्यन्वेषणतत्पराः. २ पुरुषाः. ३ चक्षुः, हतप्रतिज्ञा. ४ समाज्ञापयति. ५ तनं द्रुतम् । इति श्लोकार्धम्. ६ दन्यस्मात्. ७ दारुणादभूत्; भीषणा०. ८ कपालकुण्डलाप्रणयिनो नाघोरघण्टादन्यतश्चैतत्कर्म भीषणाद्भुतम् । इति पा. १० एनं दुरात्मानम्. ११ कापालिकं चान्यतः. १२ रे रे.

**कठोरास्थिग्रन्थिव्यतिकररणत्कारमुखरः**
**खरस्नायुच्छेदक्षणविहितवेगव्युपरमः।**
**निरातङ्कः पङ्केष्विव पिशितपिण्डेषु विलस-**
**न्नसिर्गात्रं गात्रं सपदि लवशस्ते विकिरतु ॥ ३४ ॥**

( इति निष्क्रान्ताः सर्वे । )

**इति श्मशानवर्णनं नाम पञ्चमोऽङ्कः ।**

---

माधवाघोरघण्टौ द्वावप्येकश्लोकेन प्रहारव्यापारमाहतुः—**कठोरेत्यादि** । हे पाप ममासिः खड्गस्तव प्रत्यङ्गं लवशः खण्डं खण्डं सपदीदानीमेव विक्षिपतु । कर्दमेष्विव मांसपिण्डेषु निरातङ्को यथारुचि विचरन्सन् । कीदृशः । कठिनास्थिग्रन्थिघटनेन यो रणत्कारोव्यक्तध्वनिस्तेन मुखरः सशब्दः । कठिनस्नायुच्छेदेषु मुहूर्ते कृतवेगोपरमश्च ॥ ३४॥

कतीह पञ्चमाङ्कके स्फुरन्ति नोद्गता रसाः ।
मदीयबुद्धिरल्पिका क्क वेद तानशेषतः ॥
प्रासोष्ट यं रत्नधरोऽतिभव्योऽतिभव्यरूपा दमयन्तिकापि ।
जगद्धरं तत्कृतटिप्पणेऽङ्कोऽगमन्मनोहारिणि पञ्चमोऽयम् ॥

**इति पंचमोऽङ्कः ।**

---

१ ञ-घ-णात्का. २ व्युपशमः, वेग-खेद. ३ खण्डेषु निपतन्.

## षष्ठोऽङ्कः ।

( ततः प्रविशति कपालकुण्डला । )

**कपाल०**—आः दुरात्मन् मालतीनिमित्तं व्यापादितास्मद्गुरो माधवहतक अहं त्वया तस्मिन्नवसरे निर्दयं निघ्नत्यपि स्त्रीत्यवज्ञाता । ( सक्रोधम् । ) तदवश्यमनुभविष्यसि कपालकुण्डलाकोपस्य विजृम्भितम् ।

शान्तिः कुतस्तस्य भुजङ्गशत्रोर्यस्मिन्नमुक्तानुशया सदैव ।
जागर्ति दंशाय निशातदंष्ट्राकोटिर्विषोद्गारगुरुर्भुजङ्गी ॥ १ ॥

( नेपथ्ये । )

भो राजानश्चरमवयसामाज्ञया संचरध्वं
कर्तव्येषु श्रवणसुभगं भूमिदेवाः पठन्तु ।
चित्रं नानावचननिवहैश्चेष्टयतां मङ्गलेभ्यः
प्रत्यासन्नस्त्वरयतितरां जन्ययात्राप्रवेशः ॥ २ ॥

---

संप्रति पूर्वाङ्कवृत्तगुरुवधवर्तमानाङ्कभाविमालतीविवाहभविष्यदङ्कमालतीहरणा-न्याह—**तत इत्यादि** । आः पीडायां कोपे च । ' आस्तु स्यात्कोपपीडयोः ' इत्यमरः । स्त्रीनिमित्तं कापालिकवधेन पापेति । इहानुभविष्यसीत्यनेन क्रमरूपो गर्भसंधिरुक्तः । यदाह-' भाविनोऽर्थस्य यज्ज्ञानं क्रमः स परिकीर्तितः । दुरात्मन् कामोपहतात्मन् । विजृम्भितं मालत्यपहरणेनेति भावः । तदेवाह— **शान्तिरित्यादि** । तस्य भुजङ्गशत्रोः सर्पहिंसकस्य गरुडस्य वा कुतः शान्तिर्निर्वृतिरुपशमो वा । अपि तु नैव । यस्मिन्नत्यक्तकोपा तिग्मदन्ताग्रा विषोद्गारेण दुःसहा सर्पी सदैव दंशाय जागर्ति । एवकारेण मुहूर्तमात्रमपि न स्वस्थेत्याशयः । अनुशयो गाढरोषः । गरुडपक्षे तादृशी दंशार्थे जागर्ति । तस्यातिबलत्वान्न तत्करोतीति युक्तमेव ॥ ॥ **नेपथ्ये** । अधुना विवाहमङ्गलकृत्यं दर्शयति—**भो राजान इत्यादि** । जन्या वरस्य स्निग्धास्तेषां यात्रायाः प्रवेशो वधूगृहप्राप्तिः प्रत्यासन्नः समीपवर्त्यत एवात्यर्थं त्वरयति । ततो भो राजानः क्षत्रियाः विवाहकृत्येषु चरमवयसां वृद्धानामाज्ञया संचरध्वं प्रवर्तध्वम् । विवाहारम्भे वृद्धोपदिष्टमेव कर्मकारैः क्रियते । इह तु प्रभुतातिशयान्नृपा एव कर्मकारा इति दर्शितम् । भूमिदेवा ब्राह्मणाः कर्णमनोहरं यथा तथा पठन्तु । वैवाहिकमङ्गलवेदानित्यर्थात् । यद्वा यद्वेदस्वरूपं श्रवणसुभगं मङ्गलत्वात्तत्पठन्त्वित्यर्थः । पुरन्ध्रीर्लक्ष्यीकृत्याह—नानारचनानां मङ्गलादीनां समूहैः करणैश्चित्रमद्भुतं यथा तथा चेष्टयताम् । भावे तङ् । यद्वा चित्रं

---

१ आः पाप. २ विनिपातिता. ३ फलम्. ४ निबद्धा. ५ हे. ६ रचन; वचनविहितैश्चेष्टतां.

यावच्च संबन्धिनो न परापतन्ति तावद्वत्सया मालत्या नगरदेवतागृहमविघ्नमङ्गलाय गन्तव्यमित्यादिशन्ति भगवतीनिदेशवर्तिनोमात्यदाराः। अन्यच्च यथा गृहीतसविशेषमण्डनः प्रतीक्ष्यतामानुयात्रिको जनः।

**कपाल०**---भवतु। इतो मालतीविवाहपरिकर्मसत्वरप्रतीहारजनशतसंकुलात्प्रदेशादपक्रम्य माधवापकारं प्रत्यभिनिविष्टा भवामि।

(इति निष्क्रान्ता।)

**इति विष्कम्भकः।**

---

[ततः प्रविशति कलहंसकः।]

**कल०**---आज्ञप्तोऽस्मि नगरदेवतागर्भगृहस्थितेन समकरन्देन नाथमाधवेन यथा जानीहि तावद्यात्राभिमुखं प्रवृत्ता मालती न वेति। तद्यावदेनमानन्दयिष्यामि। (आणत्तोह्मि णअरदेव्वदागब्भघरट्ठिदेण समअरन्देण णाहमाहवेण जहा जाणीहि दाव जत्तोहिमुहं प्पउत्ता मालदी ण वेत्ति। ता जाव णं आणन्दइस्सं।)

(ततः प्रविशतः माधवमकरन्दौ।)

---

नानाकर्म। केचिन्मङ्गलगीतं केचिद्वाद्यं केचिन्नृत्यं कुर्वन्त्वित्यर्थः। मङ्गलेभ्यो मङ्गलं कर्तुम्। क्रियार्थोपपदस्येति चतुर्थी। तादर्थ्ये वा। संचरध्वमिति 'समस्तृतीयायुक्तात्' इति तङ्। 'वरस्निग्धेऽपि जन्यः स्यात्।' इति मेदिनीकरः। एतेन चोरिकाविवाहमङ्गलमपि ध्वनिनोक्तम् ॥ २ ॥ संबन्धिनो वरस्य भ्रात्रादयः। पित्रादीनां नन्दने वृद्धेऽसम्भवादिति। परापतन्त्यायान्ति। अविघ्नेति माधवविवाहायेति भावः। नन्दनविवाहस्य विघ्नवत्त्वात्। निदेश आज्ञा। अमात्यो भूरिवसुः। दाराः स्त्रियः। अनुयात्रानुगमनं तत्र नियुक्त आनुयात्रिको मालत्यनुगामी। **कपालकुण्डला**। कामन्दकीनामश्रवणभीता निष्क्रमणार्थमाह---**भवत्विति**। परिकर्मेतिकर्तव्यता। **अपक्रम्येति**। अमङ्गलवेशतयान्येनापि संभावितनिःसारणायत इति भावः। माधवापकारमित्यनेनाष्टमाङ्कं सूचयन्ती विघ्नमुद्योतयति। अभिनिविष्टा बद्धकक्षा ॥ 'भो राजानः' इत्यादौ श्लेषेण चोरिकाविवाहस्याप्यभिधानाज्जन्यपदेन माधवपरिजनतया कलहंसस्यापि वचनात्तत्प्रवेशमाह---**प्रविश्येति**।

---

१ गम्यताम्. २ दिशति भगवती कामन्दकी. ३ एतन्नास्ति क्वचित्. ४ सहस्रसं०. ५ दस्मात्प्रदे०. ६ कलहंसः-(प्रविश्य). ७ वट्टिणा. ८ मअरन्दसणाहेण माह०. ९ इदो०.

माधवः—

मालत्याः प्रथमावलोकदिवसादारभ्य विस्तारिणो
भूयःस्नेहविचेष्टितैर्मृगदृशो नीतस्य कोटिं पराम् ।
अद्यान्तः खलु सर्वथास्य मदनायासप्रबन्धस्य मे
कल्याणं विदधातु वा भगवतीनीतिर्विपर्येतु वा ॥ ३ ॥

मक०—वयस्य कथं भगवत्याः सुमेधसो नीतिर्विपर्येष्यति ।

कल०—( उपसृत्य । ) नाथ दिष्ट्या वर्धसे । प्रवृत्ता खलु यात्राभिमुखं मालती । ( णाह दिट्ठिआ वड्ढसि । पउत्ता क्खु जत्ताहिमुहं मालदी । )

माधवः—अपि नाम सत्यम् ।

मक०—सखे किमश्रद्दधानः पृच्छसि । न केवलं प्रवृत्ता प्रत्यासन्ना च वर्तते । तथा हि ।

अस्माकमेकपद एव मरुद्विकीर्ण-
जीमूतजालरसितानुकृतिर्निनादः ।
गम्भीरमङ्गलमृदङ्गसहस्रजन्मा
शब्दान्तरग्रहणशक्तिमपाकरोति ॥ ४ ॥

---

गर्भगृहवर्तित्वेन माधवस्य गुप्तत्वम् । **माधवः** । राजविरुद्धचौरिकाविवाहस्य दुष्करतया कामन्दकीप्रतिज्ञासत्यत्वेन च संदेहवानाह—**मालत्या इत्यादि** । ममास्य विप्रलम्भजक्लेशस्य सर्वथोभयप्रकारेण निश्चितमद्यान्तः समाप्तिः । कीदृशस्य । मृगदृशो मालत्याः प्रचुरप्रेम्णा यानि विचेष्टितानि तैः परां कोटिं प्रकर्षकाष्ठां प्रापितस्य । आद्यदर्शनदिनादारभ्य विस्तारं गतैः । तत्र प्रथमे बकुलवीथिचेष्टाभिर्द्वितीये माधवचित्रावलोकनादिना तृतीये स्वप्नोपभोगवर्णनादिना चतुर्थे मोहनाशककरस्पर्शादिना पञ्चमे भयकम्पिताङ्गालिङ्गनादिना विस्तार इति भावः । पर्यवसानमाह—भगवतीनीतिः कामन्दकीनिसृष्टार्थदूतीकल्पः कल्याणं शुभं मालतीविवाहलक्षणं वा करोतु विपर्यये तु विफला वा भवतु । तथा च विवाहे सति शृङ्गारसंभोगलाभेन कामायासशान्तिः विपर्यये मरणादिति भावः ॥ ३ ॥ **मकरन्दः** । सुमेधसः सुबुद्धेः । विपर्येष्यति विपर्ययमेष्यति ॥ **कलहंसकः** । अत्र यात्रा गमनम् । तस्य मुखमारम्भम् ॥ **माधवः** । तद्वाक्यस्याश्वासपरत्वं तर्कयन्नाह—**अपीति** । अपि नामेति संभावनायाम् ॥ **अस्माकमित्यादि** । वातविस्तारिमेघसमूहशब्दिततुल्यो गम्भीरमङ्गलार्थमुरजसहस्रजन्मा शब्द एकपद

---

१ लोकनदिनादा. २ सस्य मे सर्वतः. ३ सुमेधायाः; सा मेधाशक्तिः. ४ णाह माहव. ५ इहोमुहं. ६ सत्यमेतद्. ७ वधान इव. ८ पदमेव. ९ निनदा. १० श्रवण.

तदेहि । जालमार्गेण पश्यामः । ( तथा कुर्वन्ति । )

**कलहंसकः**—नाथ प्रेक्षस्व प्रेक्षस्व । इमे तावदुत्पतितराजहंसविभ्रमाभिरामचामरसमीरणोद्वेल्लकदलिकावलीतरङ्गितोत्तानगगनाङ्गनसरोवरनिरन्तरोद्दण्डपुण्डरीकविभ्रमं वहन्तो धवलातपत्रनिवहा दृश्यन्ते । इमाः सविलासकर्वलिततताम्बूलैर्वीटिकापूरितकपोलमण्डलाभोगव्यतिकरस्खलितमधुरमङ्गलोद्गीतबद्धकोलाहलैर्विविधरत्नालंकारकिरणावलीविडम्बितमहेन्द्रचापविच्छेदविच्छुरितनभःस्थलैर्वारसुन्दरीकदम्बैरध्यासिता उत्क्वणत्कनककिंकिणीजालझणझणझंकारिण्यः करिण्यः । ( णाह पेक्ख पेक्ख । इमे दाव उप्पडिअराअहंसविब्भमाहिरामचामरसमीरणोव्वेल्लकदलिआवलीतरङ्गिदुत्ताणगअणङ्गणसरोवरणिरन्तरुद्दण्डपुण्डरीअविब्भमं वहन्तो धवलादवत्तणिवहा दीसन्ति । इमाओ सविलासकवलिदतम्बूलवीडिआपूरिदकवोलमण्डलाभोअव्वइअरक्खलिदमहुरमङ्गलुग्गीअबद्धकोलाहलेहिं विविहरअणालंकारकिरणावलीविडम्बिदमहिन्दचावविच्छेअविच्छुरिदणहत्थलेहिं वारसुन्दरीकदम्बेहिं अज्झासिआ ओक्कणन्तकणअकिंकिणीजालझणझणझंकारिणीओ करिणीओ । ) ( माधवमकरन्दौ सकौतुकं पश्यतः । )

**मकरन्दः**—स्पृहणीयाः खल्वमात्यभूरिवसोर्विभूतयः । तथा हि ।

**प्रेङ्खन्दूरिमयूखमेचकचयैरुन्मेषिचाषच्छद-**
**च्छायासंवलितैर्विवर्तिभिरिव प्रान्तेषु पर्यावृताः ।**

---

एकस्मिन्क्षणेऽस्माकं शब्दान्तरग्रहणसामर्थ्यं निराकरोति । वाद्यरवेणान्यशब्दो न श्रूयत इत्यर्थः । सहस्रग्रहणमनेकोपलक्षणम् । सहस्रपत्रवत् ॥ ४ ॥ **कलहंसकः** । माधवोत्साहार्थमाह—**नाथेति** । अत्र उत्पतित उड्डीनः विभ्रमो विलासो विशिष्टभ्रमणं वा । अभिरामस्तुल्यः । उद्वेल्लन्कम्पमानः । कदलिका पताका । तरङ्गितं तरङ्गयुक्तम् । उत्तानमगभीरम् । गगनमेव सरः । उद्दण्डमुद्गतदण्डम् । आतपत्रं छत्रम् । मङ्गलातपत्रमिति पाठे विवाहे शुक्लच्छत्रस्य प्रशस्ततया मङ्गलपदेन श्वेतत्वमुक्तम् । एताः करिण्यश्च दृश्यन्त इत्यन्वयः । चकारोऽत्राध्याहर्तव्यः । चर्वितं भक्षितम् । व्यतिकरः संघट्टः । स्खलितं भङ्गिमत् । मङ्गलोद्गीतं मङ्गलरूपमुच्चैर्गानम् । विडम्बितं सदृशीकृतम् । विच्छेदः खण्डः । विच्छुरितं व्याप्तम् । झणझणारूपो झङ्कारशब्दः । **प्रेङ्खदित्यादि** । तरणिकिरणसंपर्कादूर्ध्वमुखैर्मणिदीप्तिसङ्घैर्विवर्तिभिरितस्ततो गतैः प्रान्तेषु निकटेषु पर्यावृता

---

१ चर्वितता०(टी.). २ लावलिपू०. ३ स[illegible]णि०. ४ मङ्गलध०. ५ चापखण्ड. ६ किंकिणीझण०; जालरणिअ. ७ सकौतुकौ. ८ सस्पृहमिद्दत्य०. ९ रमणीयाः.

व्यंक्ताखण्डलकार्मुका इव भवन्त्युच्चित्रचीनांशुक-
प्रस्तारस्थगिता इवोन्मुखमणिज्योतिर्वितानैर्दिशः ॥ ५ ॥

**कलहंसकः**—कथं ससंभ्रमानेकप्रतिहारमण्डलावर्जितोज्ज्वलकनककलधौतपत्रविचित्रवेत्रलतापरीक्षिप्तरेखारचितमण्डलो दूरत एव संस्थितः परिजनः । एषा च बहलसिन्दूरनिकरसंध्यारागोपरक्तमुखघूर्णत्कान्तनक्षत्रमालाभरणधारिणीं करेणुरजनीमलंकुर्वतीत एव कौतूहलोन्मुखसमस्तलोकदृश्यमानमनोहरा पाण्डुरपरिक्षामदेहशोभा प्रथमचन्द्रलेखाविभ्रमं वहन्ती किंचिदन्तरं प्रसृता मालती । ( कधं ससंभमाणेअपडिहारमण्डलावज्जिदुज्जलकणअकलधौअवेंत्तविचित्तवेत्तलदापरिक्खित्तरेहारइदमण्डलो दूरदो ज्जेव्व से संठिदो परिअणो । एसा अ बहलसिन्दूरणिभरसंज्झाराओवरत्त-

---

व्याप्ता इव दिशो व्यक्तेन्द्रचापा इव भवन्ति । कीदृशैः । प्रेङ्खन्त इतस्ततश्चलन्तो भूरीणां सुवर्णानां मयूखाः किरणा यत्र तादृशो मेचकः स्निग्धश्चयो येषु तैः । मयूरमेचकनिभैरिति पाठे प्रेङ्खन्नृत्यन्यो बहुमयूरस्तस्य मेचकाच्चन्द्रकान्निरतिशया भा येषां तैः । 'मेचकश्चन्द्रके स्निग्धे श्यामलेऽपि च दृश्यते ।' इति विश्वः । 'भूरि क्लीबं सुवर्णे च प्राज्ये स्याद्वाच्यलिङ्गकम् ।' इति मेदिनीकरः । उन्मेष्युड्डीनो यश्चाषः पक्षिभेदस्तस्य च्छदच्छायया पक्षकान्त्या संवलितैरिव मिलितैः । कीदृश्यः । उद्गतचित्रस्य चीनदेशभववस्त्रस्य प्रस्तारेण शय्यया प्रसारेण वा च्छन्ना इव । 'प्रस्तारस्तनितं शय्या' इति हारावली । मणय इहाभरणस्थरत्नानि ॥ ५ ॥ **कलहंसकः** । अत्रावर्जिता तिर्यक्त्यक्ता । कनकं हिरण्यम् । कलधौतं रजतम् । 'कलधौतं हेमरौप्ययोः' इति विश्वः । पङ्केन लेपेन । वेत्रलता वेत्रदण्डिका । परिक्षिप्ता रचिता । (रचित)**मण्डल** इति । अस्मान्मण्डलात्केनापि न बहिर्गन्तव्यमिति भावः । दूरत एव माल्त्या इत्यर्थात् । पृथुसिन्दूरपूर एव सन्ध्यारागस्तेनोपरक्ता किञ्चिदारक्ता चटुला चपला घूर्णती लम्बमाना या नक्षत्रमाला सप्तविंशतिमौक्तिकमाला हस्तिप्रसाधनभेदो वा सैवाभरणं तद्धारिणीम् । रात्रिपक्षे नक्षत्रमाला तारकामाला । करेणुर्हस्तिनी सैव रात्रिस्ताम् । दृश्यमाना चासौ मनोहरा चेति समासः । पाण्डुरा धूसरा परिक्षामातिकृशाङ्गदीप्तिर्यस्याः सा । एतेन चन्द्रकलासाम्यमुक्तम् । दृश्यमानेत्यनेनान्येषां दर्शनमात्रं तव परमुपभोगो माल्त्या इति सूचितम् । पाण्डुरेत्यादिना माल्त्यामान्तर उद्वेग उक्तः । किञ्चिदन्तरं कियद्दूरम् । प्रसृता गता । कलधौतटङ्कपत्रेति पाठे टङ्कपत्रं पट्टिकेत्यर्थः ।

---

१ त्यक्ता. २ रक्तचटुलघू.(टी.). ३ पङ्क—पत्त-लिप्त. ४ दूरसंठिदो.

मुंह[1]घोलन्तकन्तणक्खत्तमालाभरणधारिणिं करेणुरआणिं अलंकरन्ती इदो ज्जव्वे कोदूहलुम्मुंह[2]समत्थलोअदिस्सन्तमणुहरा पण्डुरपरिक्खामदेहसोहा[3] पढम[4]चन्दलेहाविब्भमं वहन्दी[5] किंचि[6] अन्तरं पसरिदा मालदी ।)

**मकरन्दः**—वयस्य पश्य पश्य ।

> **इयमवयवैः पाण्डुक्षामैर[7]लंकृतमण्डना[8]**
> **कलितकुसुमा[9] बालेवान्तर्लता परिशोषिणी ।**
> **वहति च वरारोहा रम्यां[10] विवाहमहोत्सव-**
> **श्रियमुदयिनीमुद्गाढां[11] च व्यनक्ति मनोरुजम् ॥ ६ ॥**

कथं निषादिता गजवधूः ।

**माधवः**—( सानन्दम् । ) कथमवतीर्य भगवतीलवङ्गिकाभ्यां समन्वितः प्रवृत्तैव ।

( ततः प्रविशति कामन्दकी मालती लवङ्गिका च । )

**कामन्दकी**—( सहर्षमपवार्य । )

> **विधाता भद्रं नो वितरतु मनोज्ञाय विधये**
> **विधेयासुर्देवाः परमरमणीयां परिणतिम् ।**
> **कृतार्था[12] भूयासं प्रियसुहृदपत्योपयमने[13]**
> **प्रयत्नः[14] कृत्स्नोऽयं फलतु शिवतातिश्च[15] भवतु ॥ ७ ॥**

---

**इयमित्यादि** । इयं वरारोहा प्रशस्तश्रोणिका विवाहमहोत्सवसंपत्तिं प्रकृष्टां रम्यां च वहति । सहजरमणीयत्वात् । उद्गाढां प्रबलां चित्तपीडां च प्रकाशयति । कीदृशी । पाण्डुक्षामैरङ्गैरलङ्कृतभूषणा । अतिरम्यतयामीभिरेव भूषणान्यलंक्रियन्त इति भावः । अन्तरभ्यन्तरे परिशोषिणी । अत एवाङ्गानां पाण्डुक्षामत्वम् । कलितं परिहितं कुसुमं यया सा । बाला षोडशवर्षवयस्का । अवयवैरित्यनेन सर्वाङ्गीणं पाण्डुत्वायुक्तम् । लतेव । यथा लता नवा वसन्तादिप्रभावात्सुपुष्पापि कुतश्चिद्वैकृतादन्तःपरिशोषं वहति तथेयमपीत्यर्थः । निषादिता उपवेशिता । अवतारणार्थमिदम् ॥ ६ ॥ **कामन्दकी** । सहर्षमित्यभीष्टसंपादनादिति भावः । **विधातेत्यादि** । नोऽस्माकं मनोज्ञाय हृदिस्थाय विधये व्यापाराय प्रकृतविवाहाय भद्रं कुशलमविघ्नं विधाता ददातु । विधय इत्यत्र तादर्थ्ये चतुर्थी । क्रियार्थोपपदस्येति वा । वृत्तेऽपि कार्ये राजविरोधादनिष्टमाशंक्याह—परमरमणीयामविरोधिनीं परिणतिमुत्तरविशुद्धिं देवाः कुर्वन्तु । स्वस्यापि फलमाह—अहं कृतकृत्या भूयासम् । यतो मालतीमाधवयोर्विवाहे समस्तोऽयं प्रयत्नः फलतु । उत्तरकालशुद्ध्या फलदायी भवत्वित्यर्थः । परिणतिशुद्ध्या शिवदायी भवतु । कल्याणकरोऽस्त्वित्यर्थः ।

---

१ मुहमहुर. २ हलुप्फुल्लमुह. ३ सोहाविभाविदाणङ्गवेअणा. ४ पढमुग्गअचन्द. ५ हसन्ती. ६ किंपि ( किमपि ). ७ क्रान्तैः. ८ मण्डला. ९ सुमनत्रातेवा; मा जातेवा०. १० रम्या. ११ मुद्धतां. १२ कृतार्थी. १३ त्योपयमनः; हृदि यत्नैराभिमतः. १४ प्रयासः. १५ शिवदायी.

**मालती**—( स्वगतम् । ) केन पुनरुपायेन सांप्रतं मरणनिर्वाणस्यान्तरं संभावयिष्ये । मरणमपि मन्दभागधेयानामभिमतमिति दुर्लभं भवति । ( केण उण उवाएण संपदं मरणणिव्वाणस्स अन्दरं संभावइस्सं । मरणं वि मन्दभाअधेआणं अहिमदं त्ति दुल्लहं होदि । )

**लवङ्गिका**—( स्वगतम् ) अतिक्लामिता खलु प्रियसख्येतेनानुकूलविप्रलम्भेन । ( अदिकिलम्मिदा क्खु पिअसही एदिणा अणुऊलविप्पलम्भेण । )

( प्रविश्य पेटालकहस्ता )

**प्रतीहारी**—भगवति अमात्यो भणाति एतेन नरेन्द्रानुप्रेषितेन विवाहनेपथ्येन देवतापुरतोऽलंकर्तव्या मालतीति । ( भअवदि अमच्चो भणादि एदिणा णरिन्दाणुप्पेसिदेण विवाहणेवत्थेण देवदापुरदो अलंकरिदव्वा मालदि त्ति । )

**कामन्दकी**—युक्तमाहामात्यः । माङ्गलिकं हि तत्स्थानम् । अतो दर्शय ।

**प्रती०**—एतत्तावद्धवलपट्टांशुकचोलकमेतच्चोत्तरीयरक्तवर्णांशुकम् । इमे च सर्वाङ्गिका आभरणसंयोगाः । अयं च मौक्तिका-

---

शिवतातिश्च भवत्विति पाठे शिवतातिः शिवकरः । सर्वदेवात्तातिल्नियनुवर्तमाने 'शिवशमरिष्टस्य करे' इति तातिल् । अत्र मरणमेव सर्वदुःखनाशकतया निर्वाणं मोक्षस्तस्यान्तरमवसरः । यद्वा मरणमेव निर्वाणं निर्वृतिः सुखम् । 'निर्वाणं निर्वृतौ मोक्षे' इति विश्वः । 'अन्तरमवसराध्यात्मसदृशेषु' इति मेदिनीकरः ॥ ७ ॥ **मालती** । संभावयिष्ये सम्यक् प्राप्स्यामि । भू प्राप्तावित्यस्यात्मनेपदिनो रूपम् । सांप्रतमित्यनेन माधवालाभान्नन्दनलाभविलम्बनाच्चेति दर्शितम् । मन्दभाग्यतया माधवप्राप्तिवन्मरणमपि न स्यादिति भावः । **लवङ्गिका** । अत्र क्लामिता क्लमं श्रमं प्रापिता । अनुकूलेन माधवेन सह विप्रलम्भो विरहस्तेन । यद्वा अनुकूलो नन्दनस्तस्य विप्रलम्भेन वञ्चनया । **प्रतीहारी** । पेटकं मञ्जूषा । 'पेटकं पुस्तकादीनां मञ्जूषायां कदम्बके ।' इति मेदिनीकरः । पेटकग्रहणं तु नन्दनप्रसाधनार्थम् । अत्र नेपथ्यं प्रसाधनम् । **कामन्दकी** । **युक्तमिति** । एतत्प्रसाधनेन मकरन्दमलंकृत्य मदयन्तिकां विवाहयिष्यामीति भावः । माङ्गलिकं मङ्गलहेतुः । **प्रतीहारी** । अत्र धवलं यत्पट्टं सूत्रमयमंशुकं तेन निर्मितश्चोलकः कूर्पासकः ।

---

१ मे मन्दभाअधेआए अहिमदं अदिदु०. २ अदिकीलालिआ ( अतिक्लेशिता ); किलामिदा. ३ पेटालक, भूषणपटलक. ४ अमच्चो भअवदिं विण्णवेदि. ५ देवदाए.

हारः । एतच्चन्दनम् । एष सितकुसुमापीड इति । (एदं दाव धवलपट्टंसुअ-चोलिअं एदं अ उत्तरीअरत्तवण्णंसुअं । इमे अ सव्वङ्गिआ आहरणसंजोआ अअं अ मोत्तिआहारो । एदं चन्दणं । एसो सिदकुसुमापीडो त्ति । )

**काम०**—( अपवार्य । ) रमणीयं हि वत्सं मकरन्दमवलोकयिष्यति मदयन्तिका ( प्रकाशम् । गृहीत्वा । ) भवत्वेवमित्युच्यताममात्यः ।

**प्रती०**—तथा । ( तहा । ) ( इति निष्क्रान्ता । )

**काम०**—लवङ्गिके प्रविश त्वमभ्यन्तरं वत्सया मालत्या सह ।

**लव०**—अथ भगवती पुनः क्व । ( अध भअवदी उण कहिं । )

**काम०**—अहमपि तावद्विविक्तेऽलंकरणरत्नानां प्राशस्त्यं शास्त्रतः परीक्षिष्ये । इति निष्क्रान्ता । )

**मालती**—( स्वगतम् ) लवङ्गिकामात्रपरिवारास्मि संवृत्ता । ( लवङ्गिकामेत्तपरिवाराह्मि संउत्ता । )

**लव०**—एतद्देवतामन्दिरद्वारम् । तत्प्रविशावः । ( एदं देवतामन्दिर-दुवारं । पविसह्मं । )

( इति प्रविशतः । )

**मक०**—वयस्य इतस्तावत्स्तम्भापवारितौ तिष्ठावः । ( तथा कुरुतः । )

**लव०**—सखि अयमङ्गरागः । इमाः कुसुममालाः । ( सहि अअं अङ्गराओ । इमाओ कुसुममालाओ । )

**मालती**—ततः किम् । ( तदो किं । )

---

'चोलः कूर्पासकोऽस्त्रियाम्' इत्यमरः । उत्तरीयरूपं रक्तांशुकं सिन्दूरीवस्त्रम् । 'आपीडः शेखरोऽस्त्रियाम्' इति मेदिनीकरः । भवतीति संबोधनम् । **कामन्दकी** । गुरुसमक्षं मालत्यनुरागानुभवो माधवस्य न स्यादत उक्तम्—प्रविश त्वमिति । **कामन्दकी** । विविक्ते विजने । **मालती** । हृद्गतमरणावकाशप्राप्त्या सानन्दोक्तिरियम् । बाह्यसंवेदनाभावान्मालती न पश्यतीति भावः । **मकरन्दः** । अपवारितं व्यवहितम् ॥ **लवङ्गिका** । अत्राङ्गरागः कुङ्कुमादिः । **मालती** । तत्प्रयोजनमपश्यन्तीवाह—ततः किं मयानेन कर्तव्यमित्यर्थः ।

---

१ जुअलं. २ रीअं; रत्तंसुअं. ३ इमे. ४ सिदेति नास्ति क्वचित्. ५ जनः. ६ भवत्वोमि. ७ आत्मगतम्. ८ वारा वाव. ९ अस्मात्परं ( प्रकाशं ) एदं देवता० इ०. १० ता ( तत् ) पविसदु पिअसही. ११ इतः स्तम्भान्तरितौ पश्यावः ।

**लव०**—सखि अस्मिन्पाणिग्रहणमङ्गलारम्भे कल्याणसंपत्तिनिमित्तं देवताः पूजयेत्यम्बयानुप्रेषितासि । ( सहि इमस्सिं पाणिग्गहणमङ्गलारम्भे कल्लाण-संवत्तिणिमित्तं देवदाओ पूजेहि त्ति अम्बाए अणुप्पेसिदासि । )

**मालती**—किमिदानीं दारुणसमारम्भदैवदुर्विलासपरिणामदुःखनिर्दग्ध-मानसां पुनः पुनर्मर्मच्छेददुःसहं मां मन्दभागिनीं दुनोषि । ( किं दाणि दारुणसमारम्भदेव्वदुव्विलसपरिणामदुक्खणिद्दह्ममाणसं पुणो पुणो मम्मच्छेददूसहं मं मन्दभाइणीं दूमावेसि । )

**लवङ्गिका**—अथ किमसि वक्तुकामा । ( अह किंसि वत्तुकामा । )

**मालती**—यदिदानीं दुर्लभाभिनिवेशमनोरथविसंवेदद्भागधेयो जनो मन्त्रयते । ( जं दाणिं दुल्लहाहिणिवेसमणोरहाविसंवदन्तभाअधेओ जणो मन्तेदि । )

**मकरन्दः**—सखे श्रुतम् ।

**माधवः**—श्रुतमसंतोषश्च हृदयस्य ।

**मालती**—( लवङ्गिकां परिष्वज्य । ) परमार्थभगिनि प्रियसखि लवङ्गिके एषेदानीं ते प्रियसख्यनाथा मरणे वर्तमानागर्भनिर्गम-निरन्तरोपकारोपरूढविस्रम्भसदृशं परिष्वज्य त्वां प्रार्थयते । यदि तेऽहमनुवर्तनीया ततो मां हृदयेन धारयन्ती समग्रसौभाग्यलक्ष्मी-

---

**लवङ्गिका** । अत्र पाणिग्रहणेति सामान्योक्त्या माधवनन्दनयोर्विवाहश्लेषेण नर्मस्फोटोऽयं भावः । यदाह—' श्लेषेणोक्तिस्तु भावानां नर्मस्फोट इतीरितः । **मालती** । अत्र दुर्विलासपरिणामः प्रियत्यागाप्रियप्राप्तिलक्षणः । दुःसहमिति क्रिया-विशेषणम् । अनया श्लिष्टं मद्वचो न ज्ञातमत इयमेवं वदत्वित्यत आह ( लव० अथ किमित्यादि ) **मालती** । अत्राभिनिवेशिना मनोरथेन विसंवादं प्रतिकूलं भाग्यं यस्य सः । **मकरन्दः** । माधवे दुर्लभां वाञ्छां मत्वाह—सखे श्रुतमिति । **माधवः** : श्लिष्टे वचस्यनिष्टाशङ्कितमाह—असन्तोष इति । **मालती** । अत्र परमार्थेत्यादिना विश्वासपात्रत्वमुक्तम् । विरूढ उपचितः । सदृशं यथा तथा परिष्वज्येत्यन्वयः । अनुवर्तनीयोपकर्तव्या । समग्रसौभाग्य-पदेनारविन्दस्पर्धिनी शोभोक्ता । यदाह—' उत्तमैर्गुणिभिः स्पर्धा या

---

१ ग्गहणारम्भे. २ देवदा. ३ निव्वेद. ४ अइ. ५ विसंवाद ( टी. ). ६ किं. ७ श्रूयताम्. ८ मस्तु. ९ कारविरूढ.

परिग्रहैकमङ्गलं श्रीमाधवस्य मुखारविन्दमानन्दमसृणमवलोकयिष्यसि । ( परमत्थबहिणि पिअसहि लवङ्गिए एसा दाणि दे पिअसही अणाहा मरणे वट्टमाणा आगब्भणिग्गमणिरन्तरोवआरोवरूढविस्सम्भसरिसं परिस्सज्जिअ तुमं पत्थेदि । जइ दे अहं अणुवट्टणीआ तदो मं हिअएण धारअन्ती समग्गसोहग्गलच्छीपरिग्गहेकमङ्गलं माहवसिरिणो मुहारविन्दं आणन्दमसिणं अवलोअइस्ससि ) ( इति रोदिति । )

**माधवः**—वयस्य मकरन्द

**म्लानस्य जीवकुसुमस्य विकासनानि**
**संतर्पणानि सकलेन्द्रियमोहनानि ।**
**आनन्दनानि हृदयैकरसायनानि**
**दिष्ट्या मयाप्यधिगतानि वचोमृतानि ॥ ८ ॥**

**मालती**—यथा तस्य जीवितप्रदायिनो जनस्यावसितेति मां श्रुत्वा संतप्यमानस्य तत्तथाविधं शरीररत्नं न परिहीयते यथा च लोकान्त-रगतामपि मामुद्दिश्य स जनः स्मरणसंकथामात्रपरिशेषां कालान्त-

---

सा शोभा प्रकीर्तिता । ' मां हृदये धारयन्तीत्यनेन परंपरया ममापि दर्शनं स्यादित्युक्तम् । माधवश्रिय इत्यत्र प्राकृते पूर्वनिपातानियमाच्छ्रीमाधवस्येत्यर्थः । आनन्दमसृणत्वेन स्निग्धा दृष्टिरुक्ता । **म्लानस्येत्यादि** । वचांस्येवामृतानि मयापि दिष्ट्या निर्णीतानि । त्वया श्रुतमित्यादिना निर्णीतानि मया त्वधुनेत्यपिपदार्थः । अमृततुल्यत्वमाह—म्लानस्य प्रत्याशाभङ्गज्ञानेन संकोचितस्य जीवपुष्पस्य प्रकाशनानि । अमृतेऽपि सर्वप्रकाशकतया म्लानपुष्पप्रकाशकत्वम् । संतर्पणानि तृप्तिकरणानि । अमृतेऽप्येवम् । संतर्पणे सति बाह्येन्द्रियतर्पकाणि । अमृतेऽप्येवम् । आनन्दनान्यन्तर्मोदकानि । आय्यत आनीयतेनेनेत्यायनम् । रसस्यायनं रसायनम् । वचसां चित्तोल्लासकत्वेन नवत्वजननादि वा मृतस्य जरादिनाशकत्वेन नवत्वजननादिदमिति भावः । यद्वा अमृतपदेन जलमोक्षपीयूषाण्युच्यन्ते । तत्राद्यपदेन जलसाम्यम् । मोक्षसाम्यार्थपदत्रयम् । मोक्षे हि सम्यक्तृप्तिविषये निराकाङ्क्षतैव । इन्द्रियमोहोऽपि विषयग्रहाभावात् । 'आनन्दं ब्रह्मणो रूपं तच्च मोक्षे प्रतिष्ठितम् ।' इति श्रुतेरानन्दमयता मोक्षे । यद्वा आद्यपदाभ्यां जलसाम्यमितरपदाभ्यां मोक्षसाम्यम् । पीयूषसाम्यार्थं शेषपदम् । अमृतं मोक्षपीयूषसलिलेषु घृतेऽपि च ।' इति धरणिः ॥ ८ ॥ **मालती** । अत्रावसिता

---

१ णिग्गमणिम्मिद. २ अब्भत्थेदि. ३ माहवस्स सिरिमुहा०. ४ पलोएहि ( प्रलोकय ). ५ परलोक०.

रेपि लोकयात्रां न शिथिलयति तथा कुरुष्व । एवमेव प्रियसख्याः प्रसादान्मालती कृतार्था भवति । ( जहा तस्य जीविदप्पदाइणो जणस्स अवसिदत्ति मं सुणिअ संदप्पमाणस्स तं तहाविहं सरीररअणं ण परिहीअदि जहा अ लोअन्दरगदं वि मं उद्दिसिअ सो जणो सुमरणसंकधामेत्तपरिसेसं कालन्दरे वि लोअजत्तं ण सिढिलेदि तहा करेसु । एवं जेव्व पिअसहीए पसादादो मालदी किदत्था भोदि । )

**मकरन्दः**—हन्त अतिकरुणं प्रस्तुतम् ।

**माधवः**—

**नैराश्यकातरधियो हरिणेक्षणायाः**
**श्रुत्वा निकामकरुणं च मनोहरं च ।**
**वात्सल्यमोहपरिदेवितमुद्वहामि**
**चिन्ताविषादविपदं च महोत्सवं च ॥ ९ ॥**

**लवङ्गिका**—अयि प्रतिहतमिदानीं तेऽमङ्गलम् । नातोऽप्यधिकतरं श्रोष्यामि । ( अइ पडिहदं दाणिं दे अमङ्गलं णे अदो वि अधिअदरं सुणिस्सं । )

---

मृता । तथाविधमनिर्वचनीयम् । न परिहीयते न नश्यति तथा करिष्यसीत्यन्वयः । लोकयात्रा गार्हस्थ्यम् । सपत्नीकत्वं वा । माधवाप्तिप्रत्याशानाशादेवमेवेत्यवधारणम् । **मकरन्दः** । हन्तानुकम्पायाम् । **करुणमिति** । आलस्यादिसमुत्थो निरपेक्षभावः करुणः । औत्सुक्यचिन्तासमुत्थः सापेक्षभावो विप्रलम्भ इत्यनयोर्भेदः । अत एव निरपेक्षपदोपलक्षितनैराश्यमाह माधवः—**नैराश्येत्यादि** । नैराश्येन प्रत्याशानाशेन कातरा विसंष्ठुला धीर्यस्या हरिणनेत्रायाः । वात्सल्यं प्रियविश्लेषे प्राणत्यागेच्छा । मोहो भ्रमः सप्रत्याशत्वेऽपि नैराश्याभिमानः । ताभ्यां यत्परिदेवितं विलपनं वृत्तवर्तमानभाव्यार्थचिन्तनमतिकरुणं मनोज्ञं च श्रुत्वा चिन्तया यो विषादस्तेन विपत्तिमुद्वहामि । चिन्ताविषादरूपां वा विपत्तिं महोत्सवं चोद्वहामि । चकारो मिथोविरुद्धरसयोजने । इह हेतुफलभावेनान्वयः । तथा हि नैराश्यकातरबुद्धित्वाद्वात्सल्यम् । ततः परिदेवनम् । तच्छ्रुत्वा मनोविषादः । तथा हरिणेक्षणत्वेनापहृतचित्तस्य ममालाभान्मनोज्ञपरिदेवितं श्रुत्वा महोत्सवः । 'स पुनः क्रन्दनैर्मोहैः प्रलापैः परिदेवनैः । देहायासाभिघातैश्च करुणाभिनयो भवेत् ॥' इति भरतः ॥ ९ ॥ **लवङ्गिका** । अत्रामङ्गलप्रतिघातो विवा-

---

१ कालन्तरेण. २ एव्वं दे पिअसही मालदी सकामा होइ. ३ वर्तते. ४ वसान, वसाद. ५ इदो वि अवरं णं.

**मालती**—सखि प्रियं खलु युष्माकं मालतीजीवितं न पुनर्मालती । ( सहि पिअं क्खु तुह्माणं मालदीजीविदं ण उण मालदी । )

**लवङ्गिका**—सखि किमेवं भणितं भवति । ( सहि किं एँब्वं भणिदं भोदि । )

**मालती**—( आत्मानं निर्दिश्य[1] । ) येन प्रत्याशानिबन्धनैर्वचनसंविधानैर्जीवयित्वेमं महाबीभत्सारम्भमनुभावितास्मि । सांप्रतं पुनर्मनोरथो मे एष एव यत्तस्य देवस्य परकीयत्वेनापराद्धमात्मानं परित्यक्ष्यामीति । तदस्मिन्प्रयोजने प्रियसखी मेऽपरिपन्थिनी भवतु । ( जेण पच्चासाणिबन्धणेहिं वअणसंविहाणेहिं जीआविअ इमं महाबीभच्छारम्भं अनुभाविदाह्मि । सपदं उणं मणोरहो मे एसो ज्जेव्व जं तस्स देवस्स परकेरअत्तणेण अवरद्धं अत्ताणं परिच्चइस्सं त्ति । ता इमस्सिं पओअणे पिअसही मे अपरिपन्थिणी होदु । ) ( इति पादयोः पतति । )

**मकरन्दः**—सैषा परमा सीमा स्नेहस्य ।

( लवङ्गिका माधवं संज्ञया समाह्वयति । )

**मकरन्दः**—वयस्य उपसृत्य लवङ्गिकास्थाने तिष्ठ ।

**माधवः**—परवानस्मि साध्वसेन ।

**मकरन्दः**—इयमेव नेदीयसां प्रकृतिरभ्युदयानाम् ।

( माधवः स्वैरं लवङ्गिकास्थाने तिष्ठति । )

**मालती**—सखि कुर्वनुकूलतया प्रसादम् । ( सहि करेहि अणुऊलदाए पसादं । )

हार्दिति वाह्यम् । माधवसन्निधानादित्यान्तरम् । **मालती** । बाह्यार्थमाकलय्याह—अत्र तच्छरीरावच्छिन्नात्मा मालती । जीवनं त्वदृष्टविशेषकारितदेहात्मसंयोग इति जीवनमालत्योर्भेदः । जीवनस्य सुखहेतुतया प्रियत्वं तच्चेह दुःखसंततिजनकमतस्त्याज्यमेव भवतीति भावः । **मालती** । अत्रान्यजनेत्यत्रान्यपदेन माधवाभिधानम् । नन्दनापेक्षयान्यत्वात् । दुर्लभत्वेन परकीयत्वारोपाद्वा । बीभत्समिह नन्दनविवाहार्थमङ्गलस्यानिष्टस्य दर्शनात् । अनपराद्धमितीपदर्थे नञ् । आनन्दनविवाहपर्यन्तस्थायित्वे महापराधो यतः । अन्यस्य संभोगादेरभावादेष एवेत्युक्तम् । अपरिपन्थिन्यविरोधिनी । एतदात्मत्यागरूपम् । संज्ञया संकेतेन ॥ **माधवः** । परवानायत्तः । साध्वसेन जडतया । **मकरन्दः** । अत्यभीष्टलाभादियम् । नेदीयसां निकटानाम् ॥ स्वैरं शनैः । **मालती** । अत्र मर्तुं स्वीकुर्वित्यर्थः ॥

१ ति. २ उद्दिश्य. ३ अन्यजनप्र० (टी.). ४ पराधीनत्वेनानप० ५ उण मे. ६ महाभाअस्स- ७ परोक्खगुणसंकित्तणेण. ८ अण१०. ९ परिच्चइअ णिव्वुदा हुविस्सं ( परित्यज्य निर्वृता भविष्यामि ). १० वयस्य पर०. ११ स्वैरमुपसृत्य. १२ नार्ये.

**माधवः—**

**सरले साहसरागं परिहर रम्भोरु मुञ्च संरम्भम्।**
**विरसं विरहायासं सोढुं तव चित्तमसहं मे ॥ १० ॥**

**मालती—**सखि अलङ्घनीय एव ते मालतीप्रणामः। (सहि अलङ्घणीओ ज्जेव्व दे मालदीप्पणामो।)

**माधवः—**(सहर्षम्।)

**किं वा भणामि विच्छेददारुणायासकारिणि।**
**कामं कुरु वरारोहे देहि मे परिरम्भणम् ॥ ११ ॥**

**मालती—**(सहर्षम्।) कथमनुगृहीतास्मि। (उत्थाय) इयमालिङ्गामि। दर्शनं पुनः प्रियसख्या बाष्पोत्पीडेन निरुद्धं न लभ्यते। (आलिङ्ग्य सानन्दम्।) सखि कठोरकमलगर्भपक्ष्मलोऽन्यादृश एव तेऽद्य निर्वापयति मां शरीरस्पर्शः। (सास्रम्।) किं च मौलिविनिवेशिताञ्जलिर्मम वचनेन विज्ञापय तं जनं न मया मन्दभाग्यया विकसत्पुण्डरी-

---

माधवस्य संस्कृतभाषया लवङ्गिकाभ्रमो न स्यादिति भाषासमावेशेनाह—**सरल इत्यादि**। साहस आत्मनिरपेक्षकार्ये रागमनुरागं परिहर। रम्भोरु कदलीसमोरुदेशे हे संरम्भं मरणे त्वरां त्यज। जीवन्त्यां प्रत्याशापि स्यादिति भावः) विरसं रसशून्यं तव विश्लेषदुःखं सोढुं मे चित्तमक्षमं यतः। अतोऽयं वल्लभस्त्वयि दत्तोऽतस्त्यज मरणाभिनिवेशमिति लवाङ्गिकाभिप्रायः। अत एव सरले अङ्ग ऋजुप्रकृतिके वा। माधवपक्षे सरले अजानति हे तव विरहायासं सोढुं मे चित्तमसहमतस्तव समीपमागतोऽस्मि तन्मरणं त्यज इतरत्सममेव। तदिह संस्कृतप्राकृतयोः साम्यात्प्राकृतसमकम् ॥ १० ॥ **किं वेत्यादि**। किं वा भणामि। त्वदारम्भनिषेधं न करोमीत्यर्थः। हे विरहदुःसहकष्टकारिणि सुश्रोणि काममभीष्टं कुरु। यद्येवं तदा ममालिङ्गनं देहीति लवङ्गिकापक्षे। माधवपक्षे तु किंवा भणामि किं वक्तव्येन। कामं कामव्यापारं कुरु। अतः परिरम्भणं देहि। 'आरोहः श्रोणिकाययोः' इति धरणिः। श्लोकद्वयमिदं सौरसेन्या। यदाह—स्पष्टार्थं लक्षणं प्रोक्तं सौरसेन्याः प्रपञ्चतः। लक्षणं त्वेकमेवास्याः संस्कृताद्यदनूनता' ॥ ११ ॥ **मालती** अत्र उत्पीडः प्रबलीभूय निर्गमः। उत्पीडः समूहो वा। अपश्चिमं चरमम्। प्रियस्पर्शाह्लादात्सहर्षम्। कठोरमरालगर्भो बीजकोशः। पक्ष्मलो रोमाञ्चयोगात्। समाधिना सुकुमारः। अन्यादृश एवानुभूतसखीस्पर्शविधर्मा श्मशानानुभूतस्पर्शतुल्यः। निर्वापयति तापं शमयति। तथा तादृशः स्पर्शः शङ्काविषयोऽप्यत्र नेति निर्वेदात्साश्रुता। अत्र विकसन्ति शतं पत्राणि यस्य तत्। अन्यथेदं व्यर्थं स्यात्। मण्डलपदं संपूर्णत्वार्थम्।

---

१ विरसा. २. वोढुम्. ३ एषः. ४ त्वां. ५ कारिणि. ६ पीडनेन निरुद्धं प्रियसख्या अपश्चिमं न (टी०). ७ पक्ष्मलसुकुमारः (टी०,). ८ विज्ञापयिष्यामि (टी०). ९ यथा न.

कलक्ष्मीविलासहारिणो मुखचन्द्रमण्डलस्य ते स्वच्छन्ददर्शनेन संभावितश्चिरं लोचनमहोत्सवः। मुधामनोरथैश्चाविरतविजृम्भमाणदुर्वारोद्वेगव्यातिकरोद्वर्तमानबन्धनं धारितं हृदयम्। गमिताश्च वारंवारं सविशेषदुःसहारम्भदावितसखीजनाः शरीरसंतापाः। कथमप्यतिवाहिता च चन्द्रातपमलयमारुतप्रमुखाऽनर्थपरम्परा। सांप्रतं पुनर्निराशास्मि संवृत्तेति। त्वयापि प्रियसखि सर्वदा स्मर्तव्यास्मि। एषा च श्रीमाधवस्वहस्तनिर्माणमनोहरा बकुलमाला मालतीनिर्विशेषं प्रियसख्या द्रष्टव्या सर्वदा हृदये धारणीया।

(इति स्वकंठादपनीय माधवस्य हृदि बकुलमालां विन्यस्यन्ती सहसापसृत्य साध्वसोत्कम्पं नाटयति।)

(कधं अणुगहीदह्मि। इअं आलिङ्गामि। दंसणं उण पिअसहीए बाहु(ह)[1]पीडेणं[2] णिरुद्धं ण लब्भीअदि। सहि कठोरकमलगब्भपह्मलो[3] अण्णारिसो ज्जेव्व दे अज्ज णिव्वावेदि मं सरीरप्फंसो। किं अ। मौलिविनिवेसिदञ्जली मह वअणेण विण्णवेहि तं जणं जह ण मए मन्दभाइणीए विअसन्तपुण्डरीअलच्छीविलासहारिणो[5] मुहचन्दमण्डलस्स[6] दे सच्छन्ददंसणेण संभाविदो चिरं लोअणमहोसवो[7]। मुधामणोरहेहिं अ अविरआविअम्भमाणदुव्वारुव्वेअवइअरुव्वत्तमाणबंधणं धारिअं हिअअं। गमिआ अ वारंवारं सविसेसदूसहारम्भदूमाविदसहीअणा[8] सरीरसंदावा। कधं वि अदिवाहिदा अ चन्दादपमलअमारुदप्पमुहा अणद्धपरम्परा। संपदं उण णिरासह्मि संउत्तेति। तुए वि पिअसहि सव्वदा सुमरीदव्वह्मि। एसा अ माहवसिरीसहत्थणिम्माणमणुहरा वउलमाला मालदीणिव्विसेसं पिअसहीए दट्ठव्वा सव्वदा हिअए[10] धारणिज्जा त्ति।)

---

चिरमित्यनेन स्वाधीनभर्तृकात्वमुक्तम्। सुरतादिरसैर्यस्या बद्धः पार्श्वगतः प्रियः। सामोदगुणसंप्राप्ता भवेत्स्वाधीनभर्तृका॥' निवेद्य दुःखं सुखी भवेदिति पूर्वानुभूतदुःखं निवेदयति—**अविरतेत्यादि**। उद्वर्तमानमुन्मूलितं बन्धनं स्थैर्यं यस्य तत्। बन्धनं स्वस्थानावस्थानं तस्योद्वर्तनमुन्मूलनारम्भ इति पाठान्तरव्याख्या। गमिताश्चेत्यादिना व्याध्यवस्थोक्ता। अतिवाहितातिक्रान्ता। चन्द्रातप इति तापकारित्वादातपः। एतेषामनर्थत्वमाह भरतः—'संभोगे ये सुखं कुर्युस्ते दुःखं विरहे भृशम्।' इति। स्मर्तव्येत्यनेन करुणव्यभिचारिभावं स्मरणमाह। यदाह व्यभिचारिणोऽस्य— 'निर्वेदो ग्लानिमरणव्याधिदैन्यभ्रमादयः।' नैराश्याच्च मरणोदयः। यदाह— 'सर्वैरेतैः प्रतीकारैर्यदि नास्ति समागमः। कामाग्निना प्रदीप्ताया जायते मरणं

---

१ दुन्मुच्य. २ पीडणेण. ३ पच्चक्खं, णिरुद्धं पिअसहीए अपच्छिमं. ४ कमलपह्मलो, ०पह्मलसुउमारो ५ सदपत्त; सदपत्तपुण्ड०. ६ संपुण्णचन्दमण्डलाहिरामस्स मुहस्स. ७ महोसवो लोअणाणं. ८ दूसहाआस, ०रम्भदूमणाइअ (दुर्मनायित—टी०). ९ पराओ. १० हिअएण.

**माधवः**—( अपवार्य । ) हन्त ।

**एकीकृतस्त्वचि निषिक्त[1] इवावपीड्य**
**निर्भुग्न[2]पीनकुचकुड्मलयानया मे ।**
**कर्पूरहारहरिचन्दनचन्द्रकान्त-**
**निःस्यन्दशैवलमृणालहिमादिवर्गः ॥ १२ ॥**

**मालती**—( स्वगतम् । ) अहो लवङ्गिकया मालती विप्रलब्धा । ( [3]अहो लवङ्गिआए मालदी विप्पलद्धा । )

**माधवः**—अयि स्वचित्तवेदनामात्रवेदिनि[4] परव्यथानभिज्ञे इयमुपालभ्यसे ।

**उद्दामदेहपरिदाहमहाज्वराणि**
**संकल्पसंगमविनोदित[6]वेदनानि ।**
**त्वत्स्नेहसंविदवलम्बितजीवितानि**
**किं वा मयापि न दिनान्यतिवाहितानि ॥ १३ ॥**

**लव०**—सखि उपालम्भनीयैवोपालब्धासि । ( सहि उवालम्भणिज्जेव्वँ उवालद्धासि । )

---

ततः' ॥ विप्रलम्भकरुणानन्तरं स्थायिनः शृङ्गारस्योपक्रममाह—**एषा चेति** । साध्वसं भयम् । **माधवः** । हन्त हर्षे । **एकीकृत इत्यादि** । अनया मालत्या कर्पूरादिवर्ग एकीकृतः सन्नालिङ्ग्य मे त्वचि निषिक्त इव । स्पर्शस्य त्वगिन्द्रियग्राह्यतया त्वचीत्युक्तम् । निर्भिन्नौ निरन्तरावलग्नौ पीनौ स्तनकुड्मलौ यस्यास्तया । हरिचन्दनं चन्दनविशेषः । निःस्यन्देन द्रव्याभिधानम् । 'कृदभिहितो भावो द्रव्यवत्प्रकाशते ।' इति न्यायात् । निःस्यन्दीति पाठे निःस्यन्दिनः सरसाः शैवालादय इत्यर्थः । अनेन प्रशान्तो मे कामजस्ताप इत्युक्तम् । बहूपमेयम् ॥ १२ ॥ आत्मानुरागप्रकाशनायानुभूतवेदनामाह—**अयीति** । **उद्दामेत्यादि** । एतादृशानि दिनानि मयापि किं वा नातिक्रान्तानि । अपि त्वतिक्रान्तान्येव । किं वेति संभावनायाम् । यद्वा किं निषेधे वैवार्थे । कीदृशानि । उद्दाम उद्भटो देहदाह एव महाज्वरो येषु । एतेनोद्वेग उक्तः । संकल्पसंगमेनापनीता व्यथा येषु । अनेनोन्माद उक्तः । यदाह—'बाहू प्रसार्य गमनं संकल्पाकल्पिते प्रिये । निवृत्तिः सहसान्यस्मिन्नुन्मादे हि प्रजायते ॥' यद्वा । संकल्पसंगमेनान्यस्त्रीद्वेषः सूचितस्तेन च निःसपत्नीकत्वं कन्योहरणबीजमाह । यदाह—'आसक्तिं वा दर्शयेत्सुखमनुपहतमेकपत्नीकत्वे त्वा वर्णयेत्' । इति । त्वदीयस्नेहज्ञानेनावलम्बितं जीवितं येषु । त्वत्स्नेहाज्ञाने मम मरणमेव स्यादित्याशयः । 'उपलब्धिश्चित्संवित्' इत्यमरः ॥१३॥ **लवङ्गिका** ।

---

१ विषक्त. २ निर्भिन्न. ३ अह्महे. ४ निवे०. ५ व्यसना. ६ विनोदन, निवेदित. ७ ०णिज्जं.

**कल०**—अहो सरसरमणीयता संविधानस्य । ( अहो सरसरमणीअदा संविहाणस्स । )

**मक०**—महाभागे एवमेतत् ।

> त्वं वत्सलेति कथमप्यवलम्बितात्मा
> सत्यं जनोऽयमियतो दिवसाननैषीत् ।
> आबद्धकंकणकरप्रणयप्रसाद-
> मासाद्य नन्दतु चिराय फलन्तु कामाः ॥ १४ ॥

**लव०**—महानुभाव हृदयेऽप्यप्रतिहतस्वयंग्राहसाहसोऽयं जनः किमिदानीं कंकणाभरणं करं विचारयति । ( महाणुहाव हिअए वि अप्पडिहदसअंगाहसाहसो अअं जणो दाणिं किं कंकणाभरणं करं विआरेदि । )

**मालती**—हा धिक् । कन्यकाजनविरुद्धं किमप्येषोपन्यस्यति । ( हद्धि । कण्णआजणविरुद्धं किं वि एसा उवण्णस्सदि । )

( प्रविश्य । )

**कामन्दकी**—पुत्रि कातरे किमेतत् ।

( मालती कम्पमाना कामन्दकीमालिङ्गति । )

**काम०**—( तस्याश्चिबुकमुन्नमय्य । ) वत्से ।

---

अर्हऽनीयर् । **कलहंसकः** । अत्र सरसत्वेन शृङ्गारादित्वेन रम्यता । यदाह—' शृङ्गारकरुणावेव रसेष्वादौ प्रकीर्तितौ ' । संविधानं नायिकासंघट्टनप्रकारः । **त्वमित्यादि** । त्वं वत्सला सस्नेहेति हेतोरयं जनो माधवो विधृतजीवितः सन्सत्यमियद्दिनानि कथमप्यनैषीन्नीतवान् । अत आबद्धकङ्कणो धृतविवाहसूत्रो धृतविभूषणो वा यः करस्तस्य प्रणयो विवाहकाले ग्रहणं तद्रूपं प्रसादं प्राप्य नन्दतु । बहुकालमभीष्टाः संभोगादयः फलन्तु । ' कङ्कणं भूषणे सूत्रे ' इति विश्वः ॥ १४ ॥ **लवङ्गिका** । अत्राप्रतिहतः परिगृहीतः । अयं जनो मालती । स्वयमेवास्याः करं गृहाणेत्याशयः । **मालती** । अत्र अम्मका कुलकन्यका । विरुद्धमिति कुलकन्यकाविवाहा दैवार्षब्राह्मा एव शुभा दृश्यन्त इति भावः । **कामन्दकी** । स्वयंग्राहविवाहं कर्तुमनर्हमिति मन्यमानां मालतीमाह—**पुत्रीति** । अत्र गौरादित्वान्ङीषित्यवधेयम् । कातरे विह्वले ॥ **मालती** । करग्रहभयेन तदङ्गस्पर्शेन माधवस्य दर्शनहर्षेण च मालत्याः कम्पः । यदाह—' शीतभयहर्षरोपस्पर्शजरासंभवः कम्पः ' । नर्मस्फोटोऽयम् । यदाह—' नर्मस्फोटस्तु भावानां देहस्थानां प्रकाशनम् ' । **कामन्दकी** । चिबुकमुन्नमय्यौष्ठाधःप्रदेशमुत्तोल्य । ' अधः स्याच्चिबुकम् ' इत्यमरः ।

---

१ वदिय. २ आलब्ध. २ महाणुभाअ. ३ दाणिं करग्गहणे. ४ हा हद्धि ( इत्यस्मि ). ५. अम्मका ( टी० ).

पुरश्चक्षूरागस्तदनु मनसोऽनन्यपरता
तनुग्लानिर्यस्य त्वयि समभवद्यत्र च तव ।
युवा सोऽयं प्रेयानिह सुवदने मुञ्च जडतां
विधातुर्वैदग्ध्यं विलसतु सकामोऽस्तु मदनः ॥ १५ ॥

लव०—भगवति कृष्णचतुर्दशीरजनीश्मशानसंचारनिर्वर्तितविषमव्यवसायनिष्ठापितचण्डपाखण्डप्रचण्डदोर्दण्डसाहसः साहसिकः खल्वेषः । अतः प्रियसख्युत्कम्पिता । ( भअवदि किसणचउद्दसीरअणिमसाणसंचारणिव्वत्तिदविसमव्ववसाअणिट्ठाविदचण्डपाखण्डपअण्डदोद्दण्डसाहसो साहसिओ क्खु एसो । अदो पिअसही उक्कम्पिदा । )

मक०—( स्वगतम् । ) साधु लवङ्गिके साधु । अवसरे खल्वनुरागोपकारयोर्गरीयसोरुपन्यासः ।

मालती—हा तात हा अम्ब । ( हा ताद हा अम्ब । )

काम०—वत्स माधव ।

---

पुरावृत्तं सङ्कलय्याह—**पुर इत्यादि** । प्रथमं नेत्रप्रीतिरथ मनसस्तद्गतत्वं शरीरग्लानिश्च त्वद्विषये यस्याभूद्यद्विषये तवाप्येतादृशा अभूवन् । हे सुमुखि सोऽयं युवा प्रेयान् प्रियतमः । अतो जडतां कार्याप्रतिपत्तिं त्यज गान्धर्वविवाहपरा भवेत्याशयः । तेन विधातुः प्रयत्नो विलसतु । कामः पूर्णेच्छो भवतु । आत्मव्यापारस्त्वनौद्धत्याय नोक्तः । इह चक्षूरागादिकं कामावस्था । यदाह—'चक्षुःप्रीतिर्मनःसंगः संकल्पोत्पत्तिरेव च । निद्राच्छेदस्तनुत्वं च व्यावृत्तिर्विषयान्तरात् ॥ लज्जाप्रणाश उन्मादो मूर्च्छा मरणमेव च ' इति । मनसोऽनन्यपरतया मनःसंगसंकल्पोत्पत्ती उक्ते । ग्लानिरित्यनेन निद्राच्छेदादयो मूर्च्छान्ता उक्ताः । तेषां ग्लानिहेतुत्वात् । अत्र च पुरस्तदन्वित्यादिना हेतुफलभावः सूचितः । युवत्वप्रियत्वे प्रवृत्तिहेतू उक्ते । प्रियश्च 'यो विप्रियं न कुरुते न चायुक्तं प्रभाषते । तथार्जवसमाचारः स प्रियः परिकीर्तितः॥ इति भरतोक्तः । तत्रापि प्रकर्षे ईयसुन् । जडता प्रियदर्शनात् ॥ १५ ॥ **लवङ्गिका** । अत्र कृष्णरजनी कृष्णपक्षचतुर्दशीरात्रिः । विषमव्यवसायो महामांसविक्रयः । निष्ठापितो निहतः । पाखण्डोऽघोरघण्टः । साहसं स्त्रीवधरूपम् । साहसिकाद्धि भयं भवत्येव । तथा च प्राणदानेन माधवक्रीतमात्मानं कथं न समर्पयसीति भावः । **मालती** । साहसविवाहारम्भाद्दुर्जनभयात्पित्रादिवियोगशङ्कनाच्च खेदे हाशब्दः ।

---

१ ग्लानि. २ संचरण. ३ णिव्वूढ. ४ णिव्व।पिअ ( निर्वापित—टी. ). ५ **काम०**—लवङ्गिके स्थाने खल्वनुरागो०. ६ ( स्वगतम् ) हा. ७ एतन्नास्ति पुस्तकान्तरे ।

**माधवः**—आज्ञापय ।

**काम०**—इयमशे[1]षसामन्तमस्तकोत्तंसपरागरञ्जितचरणाङ्गुलेरमात्यभूरिवसोरेके[2]मपत्यरत्नं मालती भगवता सदृशसंयोगरसिकेन वेधसा मन्मथेन मया च तुभ्यं दीयते । ( इति रोदिति[3] । )

**मक०**—फलितं नै[4]स्तर्हि भगवतीपादप्रसादेन ।

**माधवः**—तत्किं[5]मिति बाष्पायितं भगवत्या ।

**काम०**—( चीवरा[6]ञ्चलेन नेत्रे प्रमृज्य । ) विज्ञा[7]पयामि कल्याणिनिम ।

**माधवः**—नन्वा[8]ज्ञापय ।

**काम०**—

**परिणतिरमणीयाः प्रीतयस्त्वद्विधाना-**
**म[9]हमपि तव मान्या हेतुभिस्तैश्च तैश्च ।**
**तदिह सुवदनायां तात मत्तः परस्ता[10]-**
**त्परिचयकरु[11]णायां सर्वथा मा विरंसीः ॥ १६ ॥**

( इति नन्तुं[12]मिच्छति । )

**माधवः**—( वारयन् । ) अहो वात्सल्यादतिक्रामति प्रसङ्गः ।

**मक०**—भगवति

---

**कामन्दकी** । 'उत्तंसः कर्णपूरे च शेखरे च प्रकीर्तितः ।' इति विश्वः । **अङ्गुलि**पदेन चरणाग्रे प्रणामादश्लृष्यतोक्ता । अन्योन्यदर्शनेन धात्रा । प्रीतिजननात्कामेन । चौरिकाविवाहान्मयेत्याशयः । **माधवः** । बाष्पायितमुद्गतबाष्पं वृत्तम् । मातृवत्स्नेहेनेदमुपपन्नम् । **परिणतीत्यादि** । त्वद्विधानां कुलादिमतां प्रीतयः परिपाकरम्या भवन्ति । अधुनावश्यत्वेन परिणतिपदम् । तैस्तैर्हेतुभिः पितृबन्धुत्वोपदेशकत्वादिभिरहं तव मान्या । हेतूनां बहुत्वेन वीप्सा । तत इह मालत्यां मत्तः परस्तान्मत्परोक्षे परिचयरूपकरुणायां मा विरंसीर्मा विरतो भविष्यसि । करुणाया इति पाठे 'जुगुप्साविरामप्रमादार्थानामुपसंख्यानम् ।' इति पञ्चमी । **तातेति** । सर्वं ततं व्याप्तमनेनेति तात व्यापक हे । यद्वा तातो विधेयः । 'तातो विधेये जनके' इति विश्वः । विरंसीरित्यत्र माङि लुङिति भविष्यति लुङ् । वात्सल्यात्प्रपन्नानुकम्पातः । अतिक्रमोऽन्यथात्वम् । अत्र माला नाम नाट्यालङ्कारकथनम् । यदाह—'माला

---

१ अशेषभुवन. २ एकापत्यं. ३ बाष्पं विसृजति. ४ हि. ५ किमित्यतिबाष्पायितमाननं भगवत्याः. ६ चीरा०, परिमृज्य. ७ वत्स किमपि कल्याणिनं वक्तुकामास्मि । **मा०**—तत्किम् । का०—विज्ञापयामि । ८ आज्ञापय. ९ वय. १० परस्मात्. ११ णायाः. १२ पादयोः पतितुम्

श्लाघ्यान्वयेति नयनोत्सवकारिणीति
निर्व्यूढसौहृदभरेति गुणोज्ज्वलेति ।
एकैकमेव हि वशीकरणं गरीयो
युष्माकमेवमियमित्यथ किं ब्रवीमि ॥ १७ ॥

**कामन्दकी**—वत्स माधव ।

**माधवः**—आज्ञापय[2] ।

**काम०**—वत्से मालति ।

**मालती**[3]—आज्ञापयतु भगवती । ( आणवेदु भअवदी । )

**काम०**—

प्रेयो मित्रं बन्धुता वा समग्रा
सर्वे कामाः शेवधि[4]र्जीवितं वा ।
स्त्रीणां भर्ता धर्मदाराश्च पुंसा-
मित्यन्योन्यं वत्सयोर्ज्ञातमस्तु ॥ १८ ॥

**मक०**—अथ किम् ।

**लव०**—भगवती यथाज्ञापयति । ( भअवदी जधा आणवेदि । )

---

बहूनां हेतूनां निर्देशः साध्यसिद्धये ।' इति ॥ १६ ॥ **श्लाघ्यान्वयेत्यादि** । उज्ज्वलकुला । चक्षुःप्रीतिजननी रूपवती । उपचितसौहार्दातिशयानुरक्ता । गुणोज्ज्वला शीलादिमती । एतत्सर्वं वशीकरणमस्त्येव गुरुतरम् । एवं सति युष्माकमियमिति हेतोरनन्तरं किं ब्रवीमि । अतः परं न वाच्यमस्तीत्यर्थः । इतिकारचतुष्टयं स्वरूपोपदर्शनाय । तथा च त्वदभ्यर्थना सहजसिद्धैवेति भावः । इह प्रसिद्धिनामा नाट्यालङ्कारः । यदाह—'वर्णने वस्तुनो यत्तु गुणस्योत्कीर्तनं भवेत् । प्रसिद्धिरिह सा ज्ञेया नाटके कथिता बुधैः ॥' इति ॥ १७ ॥ **प्रेय इत्यादि** । वत्सयोर्मालतीमाधवयोरन्योन्यमेतद्विदितमस्तु यत्स्त्रीणां भर्ता प्रेयः प्रियतमं वस्तु मित्रं सुहृद् बन्धुता बन्धुसमूहः सर्वे ईप्सिताः समग्रा मिलिताः शेवधिर्निधिर्जीवनं च । पुरुषाणां धर्मदाराः पाणिगृहीताः प्रेय इत्यादि । बन्धुतेत्यत्र 'ग्रामजनबन्धुसहायेभ्यस्तल् ।' इति समूहे तल् । 'निधिर्ना शेवधिः' इत्यमरः । अनेन गान्धर्वविवाहो दर्शितः । स चानुरागमूलत्वाच्छ्रेष्ठः । यदाह—'अनुरागात्मकत्वेन गान्धर्वः श्रेष्ठतां गतः' । इति ॥ १८ ॥ **मकरन्दः** । जवनिका पिधानपटः ।

---

१ रम. २ अस्मात्परं—**काम०**–स्वीक्रियतामियम् । **मा०**–स्वीकरोमि । **का०**–वत्स माधव वत्से मालति । **मा०**–आज्ञापय । इत्य०. ३ लव०. ४ संपत्ती. ५ जह तुम्हे आणवेत्थ.

**काम०**—वत्स मकरन्द त्वमनेनैव वैवाहिकेन मालतीनेपथ्येन प्रसाधितः परिणाययात्मानम् । ( इति पेटलकमर्पयति )

**मक०**—यथाज्ञापयति भगवती । यावदितश्चित्रजवनिकामन्तर्धाय नेपथ्यं धारयामि । ( तथा करोति । )

**माधवः**—भगवति सुलभबह्वनर्थमतिसंकटमिदं वयस्यस्य ।

**काम०**—आः कस्त्वमस्यां चिन्तायाम् ।

**माधवः**—एवं भगवत्येव जानाति ।

**मक०**—( प्रविश्य विहसन् । ) वयस्य मालत्यस्मि ।

( सर्वे सविस्मयं सकौतुकं पश्यन्ति । )

**माधवः**—( मकरन्दं परिष्वज्य सोपहासम् ) भगवति कृतपुण्य एव नन्दनो यः प्रियामीदृशीं कामयिष्यते ।

**काम**—वत्सौ मालतीमाधवौ इतो निर्गत्य वृक्षगहनेन गम्यतामुद्वाहमङ्गलार्थमस्माद्विहारिकायाः पश्चादुद्यानवाटः । सुविहितं च तत्र वैवाहिकं द्रव्यजातमवलोकितया । भूयश्च

**गाढोत्कण्ठकठोरकेरलवधूगण्डावपाण्डुच्छदै-**
**स्ताम्बूलीपटलैः पिनद्धफलिनव्यानम्रपूगद्रुमाः ।**
**कंक्कालीफलजग्धिमुग्धविकिरव्याहारिणस्तद्भुवो**
**भागाः प्रेङ्खितमातुलुङ्गवृतयः प्रेयो विधास्यन्ति वाम् ॥ १९ ॥**

---

तत्रान्तर्धानम् । स्त्रीणामग्रे स्त्रीवेषादिकरणेनौचित्यात् । **मकरन्दः** । मालत्यस्मि संवृत्त इत्यनेन वैमूढकनामा भाव उक्तः । यदाह 'वैमूढकं तु लास्यं स्यात्पुंसः स्त्रीवेषधारणम्' । इति । **माधवः** । कामयिष्यत इत्यनेन पराङ्कावतारः कृतः । **कामन्दकी** अनुपलम्भार्थमाह—वृक्षगहनेनेति । गहनेन वनेन विषमेण वा । 'गहनं विषमे त्रिषु' इति विश्वः । उद्वाहमङ्गलं विवाहार्थं कर्म । **गाढेत्यादि** । तद्भुवो भागा उद्यानवाटिकायाः प्रदेशा वां युवयोः श्रेयः शृङ्गारादिकं विधास्यन्ति । शृङ्गारस्योपवनविहरणजन्यत्वात् । यदाह—'उपवनगमनविहारैः शृ-

---

१ नेपथ्येनापवारितः प्रवर्तस्व परिणयायात्मनः. २ यदाज्ञापयसि. ३ सुलभमपि. ४ संकटमेतद्व०. ५ मालतीवेषधारी म०. ६ गाढं म०. ७ एतन्नास्ति क्वचित् ८ यतः प्रियवयस्यमीदृशं मनसा मुहूर्तमपि. ९ र्थम् । अस्ति तत्र दीर्घिकायाः. १० संनिहितम्; च तत्र-तत्रैव-११ ण्डाच्छ. १२ फलित. १३ कंकोली. १४ जग्ध. १५ मातुलि—ल-ङ्ग.

गत्वा च तत्रैव मकरन्दमदयन्तिकागमनं यावत्स्थातव्यम् ।

**माधवः**—( सहर्षम् । ) कल्याणान्तरावतंसा हि कल्याणसंपदुपरिष्टाद्भवति ।

**कल०**—दिष्ट्या एवमपि नो भविष्यति । (दिट्ठिआ एव्वं वि णो भविस्सदि।)

**मक०**—कथं संदेह एवात्र भवतः ।

**लव०**—श्रुतं प्रियसख्या । ( सुदं पिअसहीए । )

**काम०**—वत्स मकरन्द भद्रे लवङ्गिके इतः प्रतिष्ठामहे ।

**मालती**—सखि त्वयापि गन्तव्यम् । (सहि तुए वि गन्दव्वं । )

**लव०**—( विहस्य । ) सांप्रतं खलु वयमत्रावशिष्यामहे । ( संपदं क्खु अह्मे एत्थ उवराम । )

---

ङ्गाररसः समुद्भवति ।' कीदृशाः । ताम्बूली पर्णलता तासां समूहैः पिनद्धा वेष्टिता फलिनाः फलयुक्ता अत एवानताः क्रमुकवृक्षा येषु ते । सापेक्षत्वेऽपि गमकत्वात्समासः । कीदृशैः । गाढोत्कण्ठा यस्याः सा च कठोरा तृतीययौवनवयाः केरलदेशवधूस्तस्याः कपोलवदवपाण्डुरीषद्धूसरश्छदः पत्रं येषां तैः । 'रतिसंभोगे दक्षा प्रतिपक्षासूयिका गुणाढ्या च । अनिभृतगर्वितचेष्टा सा विज्ञेया तृतीया तु' ॥ इति भरतः । अत एवोत्कण्ठाधिक्यम् । केरलदेशजत्वेन गौरत्वमुक्तम् । अतः पीतसंबन्धाच्छ्वेत ईषत्पाण्डुरत्वम् । यदाह-'सितपीतसमायोगादीषत्पाण्डुरिति स्मृतः ।' पिनद्धेति 'वष्टि भागुरिरल्लोपम्' इत्यल्लोपे रूपम् । फलिन इति फलबर्हाभ्यामिनज्मत्वर्थीयः । तथा कक्कोलीफलस्य जग्ध्या भक्षणेन मुग्धा प्रीता ये विकिराः पक्षिविशेषास्तेषां व्याहार उक्तिर्येषु ते । 'कक्कोली बदरी कोली' इत्यनेकार्थः । भूमिं नखैर्विलिख्य ये चरन्ति ते विकिराः । 'नगौकोवाजिविकिरविविष्किरपतत्रयः ।' इत्यमरः । अदो जग्धिः । 'व्याहार उक्तिर्लपितम्' इत्यमरः । तथा प्रोङ्खिता वातेन चलिता मातुलुङ्गवृतिर्वेष्टनं येषु ते । तथा चैवंविधनानागुणवनगमनेन मनोरथसिद्धिस्ते भविष्यतीति भावः । मातुलुङ्गश्छोलङ्गवृक्षः । 'रुचको मातुलुङ्गकः' इत्यमरः ॥ १९ ॥ **माधवः** । कल्याणान्तरावतंसा मकरन्दविवाहकल्याणभूषणा माधवविवाहसंपत्तिः । कलहंसकवाक्ये दिष्ट्येत्यादि । मकरन्दविवाहेनाप्यस्माकं प्रमोदः स्यादित्यर्थः । **कामन्दकी** । संभोगार्थं विजनकरणाय कर्तव्यमकरन्दविप्रलम्भार्थं च सर्वेषां निष्क्रमणमाह—**वत्स इत्यादि** । **मालती** । सखि त्वयापि गन्तव्यम् । एकाकिन्या मयात्र कथं स्थातव्यमिति भावः । **लवङ्गिका** । सांप्रतं

---

१ मद०न्दयोर्यावदागमनम्. २ कल्याणावतंसा. ३ भवतु. ४ इदं वि पिअं णो. ५ माध०. ६ तुए. ७ वत्से. ८ इत इतः. ९ तुव-अवस-रामो.

( इति निष्क्रान्ताः कामन्दकीलवङ्गिकामकरन्दाः । )

**माधवः—अयमहमिदानीम्**

**आमूलकण्टाकितकोमलबाहुनाल-**
**मार्द्राङ्गुलीदलमनङ्गनिदाघतप्तः ।**
**अस्याः करेण करमाकलयामि कान्त-**
**मारक्तपङ्कजमिव द्विरदः सरस्याः ॥ २० ॥**

( इति निष्क्रान्ताः सर्वे । )

**इति चौरिकाविवाहो नाम षष्ठोऽङ्कः ।**

---

खलु वयमत्रावशिष्यामहे । यूयं सर्वे एव स्वार्थं चलिता इत्यर्थः । **आमूलेत्यादि ।** अस्या रम्यं हस्तं हस्तेन गृह्णामि । यथा सरस्या ईषद्रक्तपद्मं मनोज्ञं हस्ती करेण स्थूलहस्तेन गृह्णाति तथेत्यर्थः । कोमलाङ्ग्याः कर ईषद्रक्त एवेति साम्यम् । कीदृशम् । आमूलं कक्षादेशपर्यन्तं कण्टकितो रोमाञ्चितः । कोमलो बाहुरेव नालं यस्य तम् । 'कण्टकः क्षुद्रशत्रौ च रोमाञ्चेऽपि च दृश्यते ।' इति विश्वः । आर्द्राङ्गुल्य एव दलानि पत्राणि यस्य तम् । रोमाञ्चितत्वार्द्रत्वे सात्विकभावात् । अहं कीदृशः । अनङ्ग एव ग्रीष्मस्तेन तप्तः । तथा च कामतापप्रशान्त्यर्थं करग्रहणमित्यर्थः । पद्मस्याभ्युद्गततया तस्य कण्टकितकोमलनालत्वमार्द्रपत्रत्वं च भवति । गजोऽपि ग्रीष्मतप्तः । पद्मपक्ष आमूलं कन्दपर्यन्तम् । तदनेनानन्तरकर्तव्यताध्यवसायस्य धैर्यमुक्तम् ॥ २० ॥

सूते स्म यं रत्नधरः पवित्रः पवित्ररूपा दमयन्तिकापि ।
जगद्धरं तत्कृतटिप्पणेऽङ्कः षष्ठोऽगमद्भव्यरसाधिवासः ॥

**इति षष्ठोऽङ्कः ।**

---

१ मालत्युपहारः, ०स्वयंवरः.

## सप्तमोऽङ्कः ।

( ततः प्रविशति बुद्धरक्षिता । )

**बुद्धरक्षिता**—अम्महे सुश्लिष्टमालतीनेपथ्यलक्ष्मीविप्रलब्धनन्दनकृतकरग्रहोऽमात्यभूरिवसुमन्दिरे भगवतीवचनसंविधानैः क्षेमेण गोपायितो मकरन्दः । अद्य [1]वयमपि नन्दनावासमुपगताः । ततो भगवती नन्दनमापृच्छ्य गता निजावसथम् । अयं च नववधूगृहप्रवेशविरचिताकालकौमुदीमहोत्सवप्रवृत्तिपर्याकुलाशेषपरिजनः प्रदोषोऽनुकूलयिष्यत्यद्य नो व्यवसितम् । सांप्रतं त्वरमाणकामः कामिनीं कामयितुं बहुशः सपादवन्दनमभ्यर्थ्य पुनरपि बलात्कारेणाभिद्रवन्मकरन्देन निष्ठुरं प्रतिहतो जामाता । [2]ततः स खल्वधिकवैलक्ष्यस्खलदक्षरो रोषनिर्भरदुःखितो मदप्रस्फुरन्नयनो न मे सांप्रतं त्वया कौमारबन्धक्या प्रयोजनमिति सशपथं प्रतिज्ञां कृत्वा वासभवनान्निर्गतः । तस्मादनेन प्रसङ्गेन

---

अधुना मालतीरूपधारिणा मकरन्देन कथं नन्दनविप्रलम्भो मदयन्तिकाहरणं च कृतं भवेदिति प्रबन्धाभिधानाय नियुक्तैव तत्र मयेत्यादिना प्रथमाङ्कसूचितबुद्धरक्षिताप्रवेशः ॥ **बुद्धरक्षिता** । अत्र माधवविवाहनिर्वाहाद्धर्षाश्चर्येऽम्महेशब्दः । सुश्लिष्टत्वं मकरन्दस्य गौरत्वाश्मश्रुलत्वादिना मालतीसाम्यात् । भगवतीति—भगवत्यैवालंकृत्य प्रहित इत्यर्थः । क्षेमेण कुशलेन । एतत्तु केनाप्यनुपलम्भात् । गोपायितो गुप्तीकृतः । आपृच्छ्य संवादं कृत्वा । तत्र नन्दनगृहं गच्छामीति तद्भवाननुमन्यतामिति संवादः । आपृच्छिः संवादार्थ इति शाब्दिकाः । अत एव ' आपृच्छस्व प्रियसखममुम् ' इति मेघदूतादौ टीकाकृता तथैव विवृतमित्यवधेयम् । आवसथं गृहम् । कौमुद्याश्विनपूर्णिमाव्रतम् । यद्वा कार्तिक्यां चन्द्रमण्डलपूजा कौमुदीव्रतम् । तदुभयं च ग्रीष्मे प्रवृत्तमित्यकालकौमुदीत्युक्तम् । यद्वा जननयनानन्दकत्वेन कौमुदीव कौमुदीति रूपकम् । कौमुदी चन्द्रज्योत्स्ना यथाकालसंभवा संध्याकालीना वर्षर्तुभवा च जनानन्दाय तथेयमपीत्यर्थः । अः केशवस्तस्य कालो वर्षाकालः संध्याकालश्च । ' प्रदोषो रजनीमुखम् ' इत्यमरः । व्यवसितं मदयन्तिकाविवाहरूपम् । अन्यकार्यव्यापृते जने तदप्रत्यूहं निर्वहेदिति भावः । त्वरमाणेति विलम्बासहकामावेश इत्यर्थः । तिरस्काराद्वैलक्ष्येण स्खलन्नक्षरैः सह स्वरो यस्य सः । रोषेण निर्भरं व्याप्तम् । खुलुङ्कितमिति पाठे खुलुङ्कितं मौनम् । खुलुङ्कितमाहुर्मुखसंकोचं च काव्यविदः । इत्याभिधानात् । कौमारबन्धकी वेश्या । माधवानुरक्तत्वात् । तदत्र नन्दनस्य विवाहदिन एव बलादभिद्रवणेनाधार्मिकत्वं कामशास्त्राविज्ञत्वं

---

१ च वयमिमं नन्दनावसथमु० ( टी. ). २ स चाधिकतरवैलक्ष्यस्खलदक्षरस्वरो रोषनिर्भरः संज्ञाष्किनारुदितप्रस्फुरद्वदनः ( टी. ).

मदयन्तिकामानीय मकरन्देन सह संयोजयिष्यामि । ( अम्महे सुसिलिट्ठमालदीणेवत्थलच्छीविप्पलद्धनन्दनकिदकरग्गहो अमच्चभूरिवसुमन्दिरे भअवदीवअणसंविहाणेण खेमेण गोवाइदो मअरन्दो । अज्ज अह्मे वि णन्दणावासं उवगदा । तदो भअवदी नन्दणं आपुच्छिअ गदौ णिआवसहं । अंअं अ णववहूघरप्पवेसविरइदाकालकोमुदीमहूसवप्पैउत्तिपज्जाउलासेसपरिअणो पदोसो अणुऊलइस्सइ अज्ज णो व्ववसिदं । संपदं तुवरन्तकामो कामिणीं कामेदुं बहुसो सपादवन्दणं अब्भत्थिअ पुणो वि बलामोडिअ अभिद्दवन्तो मअरन्देण निट्ठुरं पडिहदो जामादा । तदो सो क्खु अधिअवेल्लक्खखलन्तअक्खरो रोसणिब्भरदुक्खिदो मदपप्फुरन्तणअणो ण मे संपदं तुए कौमारबन्धईए पओअणं त्ति ससवहं पइण्णं काउण वासभवणादोणिग्गदो । ता एदेण पसङ्गेण मदअन्तिअं आणीअ मअरन्देण सह संजोजइस्सं । ) ( इति निष्क्रान्ता । )

### प्रवेशकः ।

( ततः प्रविशति शय्यागतो मालतीवेशो मकरन्दो लवङ्गिका च । )

**मकरन्दः**—लवङ्गिके अपि नाम बुद्धरक्षितासंक्रान्ता भगवतीनीतिर्विजेष्यते ।

**लव०**—कः संदेहोत्र महानुभावस्य । किं बहुना । यथैष मञ्जीरशब्दः श्रूयते तथा जानामि तेन व्यपदेशेनानीता बुद्धरक्षितया मदयन्तिकेति । तदुत्तरीयापवारितः प्रसुप्तलक्षणास्तिष्ठ । ( को संदेहो एत्थ महाणुभाअस्स । किं बहुणा । जहा एसो मञ्जीरसद्दो सुणीअदि तहा जाणामि तेण ववदेसेण आणीदा बुद्धरक्खिदाए मदअन्तिआ त्ति । त पसुत्तलक्खणो चिट्ठ । )

---

च दर्शितम् । यदाह—' सुकुमाराः पुरुषाणामाराध्या योषितः सदा । अनिच्छया प्रवृत्तश्चेच्छृङ्गारं नाशयेद्रसम् ' । बन्धकीति परुषवाक्येन दुराचारत्वमप्यस्य । यदाह—' ताडनं बन्धनं वा यो न विमृश्य समाचरेत् । ब्रूते परुषवाक्यं च दुराचारः स उच्यते ॥ ' प्रसङ्गेन संविधानकेन । एतेन सूचनात्प्रवेशः । **शय्यागत इति** । सुप्तस्य प्रवेशो भरतनिषिद्ध इति शय्यागत इत्युक्तम् । **मकरन्दः** । भगवतीनीतेरव्यभिचारित्वे ऽप्याश्रयभेदात्तदाशङ्क्याह-अपीति संभावनायाम् । अव्यभिचारित्वमेवाह । लवङ्गिकावाक्ये । कः संदेहोऽत्रमहानुभावस्य । मदयन्तिकापरिणयोऽवश्यं भावीति भावः । अत्र किंबहुना भणितेनेत्यर्थः । मञ्जीरो नूपुरम् । व्यपदेशेन मालतीप्रबोधच्छले-

---

१ णन्दणकर. २ भअवदीए संविहाणेन. ३ गदा आवसहं. ४ अण्णं. ५ प्पमत्त. ६ क्खु, अ, तुव. ७ पडणं. ८ वेलक्खरोसक्ख. ९ सरोस; ओरुइदणअणपप्फुरन्तवअणो ( अवरुदितनयनप्रस्फुरद्वदनः ). १० इमाए. ११ वड्डुईए ( वर्धक्या ). १२ महाभाअस्स. १३ एतन्नास्ति क्वचित् १४ सुत्त.

( मकरन्दस्तथा करोति । )

( ततः प्रविशति मदयन्तिका बुद्धरक्षिता च । )

**मद०**—सखि सत्यमेव परिकोपितो मम भ्राता मालत्या । ( सहि सच्चं जेव्व परिकोविदो मे भादा मालदीए । )

**बुद्ध०**—अथ किम् । ( अध इं । )

**मद०**—अहो अत्याहितम् । तदेहि वामशीलां मालतीं निर्भर्त्सयावः । ( अहो अच्चाहिदं । ता एहि वामसीलं मालदीं णिब्भच्छेह्म । ) ( इति परिक्रामतः । )

**बुद्ध०**—इदं वासभवनद्वारम् । ( इदं वासभवणंदुवारं । ) ( उभे प्रविशतः । )

**मद०**—सखि लवङ्गिके ज्ञायते प्रसुप्ता ते प्रियसखीति । ( सहि लवङ्गिए जाणीअदि पसुत्ता दे पिअसही त्ति । )

**लव०**—सखि एहि मैनां प्रतिबोधय । एषा हि चिरं दुर्मनायमानेदानी-मेवेषन्मन्युमुज्झित्वा प्रसुप्तेति । अतः शनैरिहैव शयनीयोपान्त उपविश । ( सहि एहि मा णं पडिबोधेहि । एसा हि चिरं दुम्मणाअन्दी दाणिं जेव्व ईस मेण्णुं उज्झिअ पसुत्तेत्ति । अदो सणिअं इध जेव्व सअणुंपन्ते उवविस । )

**मद०**—( तथा कृत्वा । ) सखि दुर्मनायत इयं वामशीला । ( सहि दुम्मणाअदि इंअं वामसीला । )

---

न । उत्तरीयेति उपरिवासःपिहिताङ्ग इत्यर्थः । इह नर्मगर्भो कैशिकीवृत्तिः । यदाह– ‘ कार्यकारणतो यत्र नायको गोपयेत्तनुम् । नर्मगर्भः स कथितो नाट्यवेदिभिरुत्तमः ॥ ’ **मदयन्तिका** । अत्रात्याहितमतिक्रमः । **निर्भर्त्सयाव इति** । त्रिरात्रं नायकं ज्ञात्वा वाचा हीनं तु कन्यका । पश्यन्ती स्तम्भवच्छन्नं निर्विद्येत ततः परम् ’ ॥ इति भरतानुरोधेन कन्याविस्रम्भपरे मे भ्रातरि व्यर्थमियं रुष्टेति निर्भर्त्सनमस्या इति भावः । बुद्धरक्षितावाक्ये—एतद्वासभवनद्वारम् । तत्प्रविशेति शेषः । **लवङ्गिका** । अत्र कथमस्माद्दुराचारात्स्थास्यामीति चिन्तया दौर्मनस्यान्निद्रा । यदाह—‘ आलस्यदौर्मनस्यक्लेशश्रमचिन्तनस्वभावेभ्यः । रात्रौ जागरणादपि निद्रा मनुजे दिवापि संभवति ’ ॥ तथा च दुःखहानाय निद्रयापि क्षणं नय-

---

१ ०भवणं. २ जदो एसा. ३ मण्णे पसुत्तेति. ४ सअणद्धम्भि ( शयनार्धे ); ०णुद्धन्ते (शयनोर्ध्वान्ते ). ५ कहं इअं.

लव०—कथं नाम नववधूविस्रम्भणोपायज्ञातारं मनोहरं विदग्ध-मधुरभाषिणं सस्नेहमरोषणं च ते भ्रातरं भर्तारं समासाद्य दुर्मनायिष्यते मे प्रियसखी। ( कहं णाम णववहूविस्सम्भणोवाअजाणुअं लडहं विअड्ढमहुरभासिणं ससिणेहं अ दे भादरं भत्तारं समासादिअ दुम्मणाइस्सदि मे पिअसही। )

मद०—बुद्धरक्षिते पश्य विप्रतीपं वयमप्युपालभ्यामहे। ( बुद्धरक्खिदे पेक्ख विप्पदीअं अह्मे वि उवालम्भीआमो। )

बुद्ध०—विप्रतीपं न वा विप्रतीपम्। ( विप्पदीअं ण वा विप्पदीअं। )

मद०—कथमिव। ( कधं विअ। )

बुद्ध०—यत्तावच्चरणपतितोपि भर्ता न बहुमानितोऽत्र लज्जादोषेणैष जन उपालम्भनीयः। यदपि प्रियसखि नववधूविरुद्धरभसोपक्रमस्खलन-वैलक्ष्यविच्छर्दितमहानुभावत्वस्य भ्रातुस्ते वाचागतं किमप्यपरिस्थानं तेन

---

...तव्यमित्याशयः। **लवङ्गिका**। अत्र विस्रम्भणं विश्वासमुत्पाद्य वशीकरणम्। लडहं मनोहरम्। विदग्धं कलाभिज्ञम्। नववधूविस्रम्भणोपायस्ताम्बूलादिदानम्। यदाह—'बाला ताम्बूलमालाफलरसमुरसाहारसंमानहार्या' इत्यादिकः सुप्रसिद्ध एव। प्रकृते तूपालम्भपरत्वादिपरीतार्थकत्वमिति भावः। **मदयन्तिका**। विप्रतीपं विपरीतम्। पादपतितनन्दनाननुवर्तनान्मालत्येवोपालभ्या तदकरणाद्विपरीतत्वमिति भावः। पादपतनेऽनुवृत्तौ भरतः—'व्रीडायुक्तापि या योषिदतिरुष्टापि या भवेत्। पादे पतन्तं पुरुषमनुवर्तेत सर्वदा॥' **बुद्धरक्षितावाक्ये**। विप्रतीपं न वा विप्रतीपम्। तच्चित्तानुवर्तनेन स्वीकृतयुक्त्या निराकरणेन न वैपरीत्यमिति भावः। **बुद्धरक्षिता**। स्वाभिप्रायं गोपयितुं साधारणोक्त्या स्ववचो वदति—अत्रेयमिति वक्तव्ये जन इत्यभिधानं मालतीमकरन्दसाधारण्यार्थम्। नववध्वा लज्जयातिक्रमेण दोषः। यदाह—'नवपरिणीता योषियत्नादपनीय साध्वसं सद्यः। विविधविनोदकथाभिर्विश्वासं नीयते सरसैः॥' रभसोपक्रमः सहसा प्रवृत्तिः स च विरुद्धः। यदाह—'सहसा वाप्युपक्रान्ता कन्याचित्तमविन्दता। साध्वसं त्रासमुद्वेगं सद्यो द्वेषं च विन्दति॥ सा प्रीतियोगमप्राप्य तेनोद्वेगेन दुःखिता। पुरुषद्वेषिणी वा स्याद्विद्विष्टा वा ततोऽन्यगा॥' स्खलनमुपक्रान्तानिर्वाहः। विच्छर्दितं विशीर्णम्। अपरिस्थानकमपरिस्थितिः। अधैर्यमिति यावत्। यूयमुपालभ्या इति मदयन्तिकां प्रति वचनम्। भ्रातृपक्षप्रवेशात्। अह्मे इति पाठे बुद्धरक्षिता मदयन्तिकया सह

---

१ विअद्धं. २ सही ण दुम्मणा०. ३ पश्य पश्य...वयमेव [टी०]. ४ विप्पदीपं उवालद्धं ह्म ( उपालब्धाः स्मः। ).

यूयमिति । किंच । ( संस्कृतमाश्रित्य । ) 'कुसुम[1]सधर्माणो हि योषितः सुकुमारोपक्रमाः। तास्त्वे[2]नधिगतविश्वासैः प्रसभमुपक्रम्यमाणाः सद्यः संप्रयोगविद्वेषिण्यो भवन्ति । ' एवं किल कामसूत्रकारा आमनन्ति । ( जं दाव चलणपडिदो वि भत्ता ण बहुमाणिदो एत्थ लज्जादोसेण एसो जणो उवालम्भणिज्जो । जं वि पिअसहि [3]णेवबहूविरुद्ध[4]रहसोपक्कमक्खलणवेलक्खविच्छडिदमहाणुहावत्तणस्स भादुणो दे वाआगअं किं वि अपरि[5]ट्ठाणं ते[6]णं तुह्मोत्ति। एवं किल कामसुत्तआरा आमणन्ति। )

**लव०**—( सास्रम् । ) गृहे गृहे पुरुषाः कुलकन्यकाः समुद्वहन्ति । न खलु कोऽपि लज्जापराधीनमनपराद्धं मुग्धसुकुमारस्वभावं कुलकुमारीजनं प्रभवामीति वाचानलेन प्रज्वालयति । एते खलु ते हृदयशल्यनिक्षेपा आमरणं संस्मर्यमाणदुःसहाः पतिगृहनिवासवैराग्यकारिणो महापरिभवा येषां कृते स्त्रीजन्मलाभं जुगुप्सन्ते बान्धवाः । ( घरे घरे पुरुसा कुलक[7]ण्णकाओ समुव्वहन्दि । ण क्खु को वि लज्जा[8]पराधीणं अणवरद्धं मुद्धलडहसहावं कुलकुमारीअणं पहवामि त्ति वाआणलेण पज्जालेदि । एदे क्खु दे हिअअसल्लणिक्खेवा आमरणं संभरिज्जन्तदूसहा पदिघरणिवासवेरग्गकारिणो महापरिहवा जाणं किदे इत्थिआजम्मलाहं जुगुच्छन्ति बान्धवा । )

**मद०**—बुद्धरक्षिते अति[9]दूना प्रियसखी लवङ्गिका । अतिमहान्कोऽपि मे भ्रात्रा वाचापराधोस्याः कृतः । ( [10]बुद्धरक्खिदे अदिदूम्मिदा पिअसही लवङ्गिआ । अतिमहान्तो को वि मे भादुणा वाआवराहो से किदो । )

**बुद्ध०**—अथ किम् । श्रुतमस्माभिर्यथा न मम त्वया सांप्रतं कौमारबन्धक्या प्रयोजनमिति । ( अध इं । सुदं अ[11]ह्मेहिं जधा ण मम तुए संपदं कोमारबन्धईए पओअणं त्ति । )

---

स्वाभेदं मन्यमाना वयमित्याह । शिल्पकारित्वात्संस्कृताश्रयणम् ॥ यदाह—' दिव्याया गणिकायाश्च शिल्पकार्यास्तथैव च । विदग्धायाः स्त्रिया भाषां संस्कृतेनापि योजयेत् ॥ ' यद्वा कामसूत्रानुकरणात्संस्कृतभाषा । सधर्माणस्तुल्याः । उपक्रम आरम्भः । प्रसभं हठात् । संप्रयोगः सुरतम् । किल प्रसिद्धौ । कामसूत्रकारा मन्त्रयन्ते । **लवङ्गिका** । अत्र निक्षेप आरोपणम् । जुगुप्सन्ते निन्दन्ति । दुःशीला कन्या मा जायतामिति भावः । **मदयन्तिका** ।

---

१ सम. २ ताश्चा. ३ अहिणव. ४ साहसो. ५ अप्पडिट्ठाणं ( अप्रतिष्ठानं ). ६ तेण जाणीआदि किआवराहा उवालम्भणिज्जा अम्हेत्ति. ७ अणकाओ; उव्वहन्ति. ८ लज्जापसाहणं ( प्रसाधनं ). ९ अत्युपतापिता. १० अइ सहि बु०. ११ ज्जेव्व अह्मेहिं ण मे संपदं इमाए कोमारवहूइए पओअणं त्ति ससपहं पइण्णं काऊण वासभवणादो णिग्गदो.

**मद०**—( कर्णौ पिधाय । ) अहो अतिक्रमः । अहो प्रमादः । सखि लवङ्गिके असमर्थास्मि ते मुखमपि सांप्रतं दर्शयितुम् । तथापि प्रभवामीति किमपि मन्त्रयिष्ये । ( अहो अदिक्कमो । अहो पमादो । सहि लवङ्गिए असमत्थह्मि दे मुहंपि संपदं दंसिदुं तधा वि पहवामि त्ति किं वि मन्तइस्सं । )

**लव०**—स्वाधीनस्तेऽयं जनः । ( साहीणो दे अअं जणो । )

**मद०**—तिष्ठत्वेव मम भ्रातुर्दुःशीलतापरिस्थानं च । युष्माभिरपीदृशोपि सांप्रतं यथाचित्तमनुवर्तनीयो येन भर्तैष इति । अन्यच्च यूयमस्यानभिजाताक्षराधिक्षेपोपालम्भदूषणस्य यन्मूलं तन्न जानीथ । ( चिट्ठदु ज्जेव्व मह भादुणो दुःसीलदा अवरिट्ठाणं अ । तुह्मेहिं वि ईदिसो वि संपदं जधाचित्तं अणुवट्टणीओ जेण भत्ता एसो त्ति । अण्णं अ तुह्मे इमस्स अणहिजादक्खराहिक्खेवोवालम्भदूसणस्स जं मूलं तं ण जाणह । )

**लव०**—कथं वाचामीन्त्रितमपि नाम न जानीमः । ( कधं वाआमन्दिदं वि णाम ण जाणीमो । )

**मद०**—यदिदानीं तस्मिन्महानुभावे माधवे किमपि किल मालत्यास्तारामैत्रकमासीत्तत्र सर्वलोकस्यातिभूमिं गतः प्रवादः । तत्खल्वेतद्विजृम्भते । तत्प्रियसखि यथैष भर्तुरपक्षाभिनिवेशो निरवशेषं हृदयादुद्ध्रियते तथा कुरुत । अन्यथा महादोष इति ज्ञातं भवतु । निष्कम्पदारुणाः कन्यका दुर्न्वन्ति हृदयं मनुष्याणामीदृशाद्दुरभिष-

---

कथमन्यथात्युद्विग्नेयमिति भावः । **मदयन्तिका** । अत्र प्रभवामीति वरभगिन्यपि त्वयि प्रणयवशादाश्वासवत्यहमिति भावः । **लवङ्गिका** । अत्र यथेच्छसि तथा ब्रूहीत्यर्थः । **मदयन्तिका** । अत्रेदृशोऽपि दुःशीलोऽपि । यथाचित्तं चित्तानतिक्रमेण । **भर्तेति** । 'कोऽपि देवः कुलस्त्रीणां पतिरेव पतन्नपि ।' इतिवचनात् स्त्रीषु भर्ता प्रभवतीति भावः । **न चेति** । न च न जानीथ । किंतु जानीथ एवेत्यर्थः । **मदयन्तिका** । अत्र किल प्रसिद्धौ । तारामैत्रकं प्रेम । तत्र माधवे । अतिभूमिमतिदूरम् । **तत्खल्विति** । माधवानुरक्ता मालतीयस्यानुशय इत्याशयः । विजृम्भते प्रकाशते । अपक्षे मालती माधवपरेत्यसत्पक्षे । अभिनिवेशो रोपः । निरवशेषमिति क्रियाविशेषणम् । दोष इत्यस्या दौर्भाग्यं त्यागो वा नित्यशङ्कानुकुलतया स्यादिति भावः । **निष्कम्पेति** । सततपरपुरुषालोकनेन लज्जाहीनतया दा-

---

१ अह्महे. २ दट्ठुं. ३ दौर्मनस्यरा ( टी. ) ४ वि एसो. ५ वालम्भस्स. ६ वाप्तातं. ७ **कहं** अह्मे असन्तं जाणीमो. ८ उपतापयन्ति.

ज्ञादिति । मैनां भणिष्यथ मदयन्तिकया कथितमिति । ( जं दाणिं तस्सिं महाणुहावे माहवे किं वि किल मालदीए तारामेत्त[1]अं आसी तस्सिं सव्वलोअस्स अदिभूमिं गदो पवादो । तं क्खु एदं विअम्भदि । ता पिअसहि जधा एसो भत्तुणो अवे[3]क्खाहिणिवेसो णिरवसेसं हिअआदो उद्धरीअदि तधा क[4]रेध । अण्णह महा[5]दोसो त्ति जाणीदं होद । णिक्कम्पदारुणा[6] अम्मकाओ दूमावेन्ति हिअअं मणुस्साणं ईरिसादो दुरहिसंगादो त्ति । मा णं भणिस्सध मदअन्तिआए कधिदं त्ति । )

लव०—अयि असंबद्धलोकप्रवादमोहिते अपेहि । न त्वया सह जल्पिष्यामि । ( अइ असंबद्धलोअप्पवादमोहिदे अवेहि । ण तुए सह जप्पिस्सं । )

मद०—सखि प्रसीद प्रसीद । अथवा न यूयमस्फुटं भणितास्तिष्ठथ । किं च वयं सत्यमेव माधवैकमयजीवलोकां मालतीं जानीमः । केन वा कठोरकेतकीगर्भविभ्रमावयवदौर्बल्यनिर्वाहितसुन्दरत्वविशेषं माधवस्वहस्तनिर्मितबकुलावलीविरचितकण्ठावलम्बमात्रसंधारितजीवनं मालत्या माधवस्य च प्रभातचन्द्रमण्डलापाण्डुरपरिक्षामरमणीयदर्शनं न विभावितं शरीरम् । किं च तद्दिवसे कुसुमाकरोद्यानपर्यन्तरथ्यामुखसमागमे सविभ्रमोल्लसितकौतूहलोत्फुल्लप्रसरन्नयनोत्पलबहलविलासमसृणसंचारतारकाविराजमानविभ्रमा अनङ्गनाट्या[10]चार्यसर्वाकारोपदेशनिर्मितवैदग्ध्यमुग्धमधुरास्त्वयापि न निरूपिता अनयोर्दृष्टिसंभेदाः । किं च मम भ्रातुर्दानवृत्तान्तं श्रुत्वा तत्क्षणो-

---

ष्णत्वमत एवेयं कुलटा न वेति परेषां संदेह इति भावः । **लवङ्गिका** । अत्रापेहि दूरं गच्छ । **मदयन्तिका** । अत्र न यूयमिति त्वदस्फुटवादे मेऽवसाद इत्यर्थः । न खलु न जानीमः । अपि तु जानीम एव । तथा च त्वमपह्नवं किंकरोषीत्यर्थः । कठोरः परिणतो जातपाण्डिमेत्यर्थः । यद्वा अकठोरा बाला केतकीत्यर्थः । तादृशी सातिपाण्डुरेव भवति । न विभावितं न ज्ञातम् । अपि तु सर्वैरेव ज्ञातमित्यर्थः । तत्किमपह्नवं करोषीति भावः । विभ्रमो विलासः । स च स्त्रियां यथा—'यानस्थानासनादीनां नेत्रवक्त्रादिकर्मणाम् । उत्पद्यते विशेषो यः स विलास इति स्मृतः ॥' पुरुषे यथा—मन्दसंचारिणी दृष्टिर्गतिश्च वृषभायिता । तिपूर्वस्तथालापो विलासः कथ्यते यथा ॥ किं न त्वया निरूपिता येनापह्नुष

---

१ वाआमेत्तं. २ सा एसो. ३ उवेक्खा. ४ करेहि. ५ महन्तो पमादो ६ दारुणासु कुलकण्णकासु…दूमोवदि. ७ अइ असावधाणे. ८ किंवि मन्तइस्सं; मन्तिदव्वं. ९ न खलु न जा०. १० नृत्यायित.

च्छलितगम्भीरावेगव्यतिकरम्लायमानदेहशोभयोरुद्धर्तमानमूलबन्धनमिव न लक्षितं हृदयम् । किं चैतदप्यपरं स्मृतं मया । ( सहि पसीद पसीद । अहवा ण तुह्म अफुडं भणिदाओ चिट्ठध । किं अ अह्मे सव्वं जेव्व माहवेक्कमअजीअलोअं मालदिं जाणीमो । केण वा कठोरकेदईगब्भविब्भमावअवदोब्बलणिव्वाहिदैंसुन्दरत्तणविसेसं माहवसहत्थणिम्मविदबउलावलीविरहदकण्ठावलम्बमेत्तसंधारिदजीवणं मालदीए माहवस्स अ पभातचन्दमण्डलापाण्डुरपरिक्खामरमणीअदंसणं ण विभाविदं सरीरं । किं अ तहिंअसे कुसुमाअरुज्जाणपेरन्तरच्छामुहसमागमे सविब्भमुल्लसिदकोदूहलुप्फुल्लपसरन्तणअणुप्पलबहलविलाससमसिणसंचारचारुतारआविराअन्तविब्भमा अणङ्गणट्ठाआरिअसव्वाआरोवदेसणिम्मविदविअड्ढमुद्धमहुरा तुए वि ण णिरूविदा इमाणं दिट्ठिसंभेदा । किं अ मम भादुणो दाणवुत्तन्दं सुणिअ तक्खणुच्छलिदगम्भीरावेअव्वइअरमिलाअन्तदेहसोहाणं उव्वत्तमाणमूलबन्धणं विअ ण लक्खिअं हिअअं । किं अ । एदं अवरं वि सुमरिदं मए । )

लव०—किमिदानीमपरम् । ( किं दाणि अवरं । )

मद०—यत्खलु मम जीवितप्रदायिनस्तस्य महानुभावस्य चेतनाप्रतिलम्भप्रियनिवेदिकाया मालत्या भगवतीविदग्धवचनोपन्यासबोधितेन हृदयं जीवितं च माधवेन पारितोषिकत्वेन स्वयंग्राहसाहसे नियुक्तम् । अथ च लवङ्गिके तत्र त्वयैव भणितं प्रतीष्टः खलु नः प्रियसख्या अयं प्रसाद इति । ( जं क्खु मह जीविदप्पदाइणो तस्स महाणुहावस्स चेदणापडिलम्भपिअणिवेदिआए मालदीए भअवदीविअड्ढवअणोवण्णासबोधिदेण हिअअं जीविदं अ माहवेण पारिदोसिअत्तणेण सअंगाहसाहसे णिउत्तं । अह अ लवङ्गिए तहिं तुए जेव्व भणिदं पडिच्छिदो क्खु णो पिअसहीए अअं पसादो त्ति । )

---

इत्यर्थः । आवेगोऽप्राप्तिदुःखम् । अङ्कारितं सुतप्तम् । उद्वर्तमानमुत्पतत् । आवेगोऽयमिष्टानाप्तिजः । यदाह—' आवेगश्च भवेत्पुंसामिष्टानावाप्तिसंभवात् । ' **लवङ्गिका** । किमिदानीमपरम् । त्वया स्मृतमिति शेषः । **मदयन्तिका** । अत्र चेतनाप्राप्तिरूपमेव प्रियम् । पारितोषिकं यद्बयालवणितेत्यादिश्लोके दर्शितम् । नि-

---

१ जीविदं. २ केदअ. ३ णिवट्टिद. ४ वलम्बणमेत्तसंजीवणं. ५ तस्सिं. ६ परिसरुव्वेल्लमाणसविलास. ७ मसिणसिणिद्धसंचरण. ८ तारआविअम्भमाणाणङ्गसिङ्काराआरिअ ९ मणहरा. १० णुव्वत्तगम्भीरुव्वेअवइअरन्धआरिअ; न्वइअरंगारिदमि०. ( व्यतिकराङ्गारितम्ला० टी.). ११ उक्खण्डिअमाण. १२ मूलं विअ. १३ चोदिदेण. १४ सअंगाहे. १५ तुए क्खु एव्वं.

**लव०**—सखि[1] कतमः पुनः स महाभाग इति विस्मृतं मया। ( सहि कदमो उण सो महाभाओ[2] त्ति विसुमरिदं मए। )

**मद०**—सखि स्मर स्मर येन तस्मिन्दिवसे विकटदुष्टश्वापदापदेश[3]-कालगोचरं गताशरणा तत्कालसंनिहितेन जीवितप्रदायिना पीवरभुजस्तम्भेन[4] निष्कारणबान्धवेन सकलभुवनैकसारनिजदेहोपहारसाहसं कृत्वा परिरक्षितास्मि। येन च दृढदंष्ट्राविदारितविकटमांसलोत्तानपरिणाहिवक्षःस्थलेन[5] जरठजर्जरितजपापीडहारिणा करुणैकमनसा मम कृते विसोढा अतिदुष्टशार्दूलनखशिखावज्रप्रहारा मारितश्च स दुष्टश्वापदमहाराक्षस इति। ( सहि सुमर सुमर जेण तस्सिं दिअसे विअडदुट्ठसावदावदेसकाल[6]गोअरं गदा असरणा तक्का[7]-लसण्णिहिदेण जीविदप्पदाइणा पीअरभुअत्थम्भेण णिक्कारणबन्धवेण सअलभुवणेक्कसार-णिअदेहोवहारसाहसं कदुअ परिरक्खिदह्मि। जेण अ दिढदाढा[9]विदारिअविअडमंसुल्लुत्ताणपरिणाहिवक्ख[10]त्थलेण जरठजज्झरिदजवापीडहारिणी[11] करुणेक्क[12]मणेण मम किदे[13] विसहिदा अतिदुट्ठसद्दूलणहसिहावज्जप्पहारा मारिदो अ सो दुट्ठसावदमहारक्खसो त्ति। )

**लव०**—हुं मकरन्दः। ( हुं मअरन्दो। )

**मद०**—( सानन्दम्। ) प्रियसखि किं किं भणसि। ( पिअसहि किं किं भणासि। )

---

युक्तं दत्तम्। तच्चितानुरागं विना नोपपन्नमिति भावः। **लव०**—अर्थान्तरोक्तिप्रसङ्गेन प्रकृतापह्नवार्थमाह—आं सखि इति। आमिति पूर्वस्मरणार्थः। विस्मृतमिति। ज्ञात्वापि तत्कथाकथनायायं प्रश्न इति भावः। **मदयन्तिका**। अत्र स्मर इति मकरन्दमिति भावः। विकुष्टो रुष्टः। श्वापद इति व्याघ्रव्याजेन यम इत्यर्थः। अवलग्नसंनिहितेति पाठेऽवलग्नं कण्ठः। संभावितः स्यातः। कर्मधारयोऽत्र। विकटं विशालम्। मांसलं स्थूलम्। उत्तानमुच्छ्रितम्। जरठं कठिनं जर्जरितं विध्वंसितं यदोड्रपुष्पमुकटं तदिव हरति। कर्तर्युपमान इति णिनिः। हरणमिह समीकरणम्। रक्ताक्तदेहतया साम्यम्। शिखा अग्रम्। **लवङ्गिका**। अत्र हुं वितर्के। 'हुं वितर्के विस्मये' इत्यमरः। **मदयन्तिका**। अत्राह्लादातिशयात्पुनः पुनः प्रश्नः। प्रियनाममधुपानेऽपि न

---

१ आं सखि...पुनरसौ ( टी. ). २ महाणुहावो. ३ विकुष्ट ( टी. ). ४ स्तम्भसंभावितनिष्कारण०. ५ स्थललाञ्छनेन ( टी. ), ६ सावद्दविणिवादगो०. ७ सुलग्ग. ८ म्भेण संभाविदा. ९ दिढविअडमंसु०. १० वक्खत्थललञ्छणेण; वच्छत्थललञ्छणजज्झरिद. ११ धारिणा. १२ करुणाधणेण; णाअरेण; करुगम०. १३ किदे वि णिमज्जन्तसअलणहणिआअवज्जपञ्जरप्पहारो ( निमज्जत्सकलनखनिकायवज्रपञ्जरप्रहारः ).

लव०—ननु भणामि मकरन्द इति । ( णं भणामि मअरन्दो त्ति ) ( सस्मितं शरीरमस्याः स्पृशन्ती संस्कृतमाश्रित्य । )

वयं तथा नाम यथात्थ किं वदा-
म्ययं त्वकस्माद्विकलः कथान्तरे ।
कदम्बगोलाकृतिमाश्रितः कथं
विशुद्धमुग्धः कुलकन्यकाजनः ॥ १ ॥

मद०—( सलज्जम् । ) सखि किं मामुपहससि । ननु भणामि निर्वापयन्ति मां तादृशस्यात्मनिरपेक्षव्यवसायिनः कृतान्तकवल्यमानजीवितबलात्कारप्रत्यानयनगुरुकोपकारिणो जनस्य संकथासु नामग्रहणस्मरणानि । तथा च स त्वयापि गाढप्रहावेदनारम्भविस्मारितशरीरसंगलितस्वेदसलिलोत्पीडो मोहमुकुलायमाननेत्रनीलोत्पलयुगलो भूमिविलग्नासिलताविष्टम्भधैर्यधारितशरीरभारः प्रत्यक्षीकृत एव मदयन्तिकानिमित्तमात्रविच्छर्दितमहामहार्घजीवलोको महाभाग इति । ( स्वेदादीन्विकारान्नाटयति ।)

( सहि किं मं उवहससि । णं भणामि णिव्वावेअन्ति मं तारिसस्स अप्पणिरवेक्खव्ववसाइणो किदन्तकवलिज्जन्तजीविदबलामोडिअपच्चाणअणगुरुओवआरिणो जणस्स

---

तृप्तातोऽश्रुलेवाहेति भावः । **लवङ्गिका** । ननुशब्द आशयाविष्कारे । **वयमित्यादि** । यथात्वमात्थ तत्तथा । मालती माधवानुरक्तेति स्वीकृतमित्यर्थः । अहं किं नाम वदामीत्यांभनिवेशमात्रम् । अयं पुनः कुलकन्यकाजनः कथामध्ये कथमकस्मात्कदम्बगोलकाकारमाश्रितः बहलपुलकशालित्वात् । विकलो विह्वलः सन् । कीदृशः । विशुद्धो निष्कलङ्कः । कामाभिषङ्गदोषशून्य इति यावत् । मुग्धो रसानभिज्ञः । सर्वमिदं सोल्लुण्ठम् । अत एव वैदग्ध्यतया शिल्पकारिणीत्वेन संस्कृताश्रयणम् ॥ १ ॥ **मदयन्तिका** । अत्र उपहससीति नाहं मकरन्दानुरक्ततया हृष्टा किंतु तद्वीरत्वमभिनन्दामीति न हासस्थानमिति भावः । अत एव चित्तचोरिकयाह—**नन्विति** । एवं स्वहर्षस्यान्यथासिद्धिमुक्त्वा निजाङ्गसङ्गजं स्वेदादिकं मकरन्देऽन्यथयति—तथा चेति । विस्मारितशरीरेति मूर्च्छाकथनम् । संगलितो मिलितः । उत्पीडः पूरः । कन्दोट्टं नीलोत्पलम् । मोहेति मोहेन नेत्रमीलनं न तु मदङ्गसङ्गादिति भावः । यदाह—'व्यसनाभिघातभयपूर्ववैरस्मरणजो भवति मोहः ।' इति । प्रहारमूर्छने कथमयं भूमौ न पतितोऽत आह—भूमीति । विष्टम्भः संबन्धः । विच्छर्दितः परित्यक्तः । महामहार्घमतिदुर्लभम् । जीवलोको

---

१ सद्यूहं. २ अहं. ३ च कस्मात्. ४ गुरुनरो० ( टी० ). ५ णिव्वावेदि...सुमरणं.

संकधासु णामग्गहणसुमरणाइं । तधा अ सो तुए वि गाढ[2]प्पहारवेअणारम्भविह्ला[3]रिदसरीरसंगलिदसेअसलि[4]लुप्पीलो मोहमउलाअन्तणेत्तकन्दोट्टजुअलो भूमिवि[5]लोग्गिदासिलदाविट्टम्भधीरधारिअसरीरभारो पच्चक्खीकिदो एव्व मदअन्तिआणिमित्तमेत्ताविच्छाइ[6]अमहामहग्घजीवलोओ त्ति । )

**बुद्ध०**—( शरीरमस्याः स्पृशन्ती । ) व्यवसितं प्रियसख्याः शरीरेण । ( विवँसिदं पिअसहीए सरीरेण । )

**मद०**—( सलज्जम् । ) प्रियसखि अपेहि । उद्भिन्नास्मि सहवासिन्या विस्रम्भेण । ( पिअसहि अवेहि । उब्भिण्णह्मि सहवासिणीएँ वीसम्भेण । )

**लव०**—सखि मदयन्तिके वयमपि ज्ञातव्यं जानीमः । तत्प्रसीद । विरम व्यपदेशात् । एहि विस्रम्भगर्भकथाबन्धसदृशं सुखं तिष्ठामः । ( सहि मदअन्तिए अह्मे वि जणिदव्वं जाणीमो । ता पसीद । विरम व्यवदेसादो । एहि विस्सम्भगब्भकहाबँन्धसरिसं सुहं चिट्ठह्म । )

**बुद्ध०**—सखि शोभनं लवङ्गिका भणति । ( सहि सोहणं लवङ्गिआँ भणादि । )

**मद०**—विधेयास्मि सांप्रतं प्रियसख्योः । ( विधेआह्मि संपदं पिअसेहीणं । )

**लव०**—यद्येवं तत्कथय कथं नु ते कालो गच्छतीति । ( जइ एव्वं ता कधेहि कहं णु दे कालो गच्छदि त्ति । )

---

मर्त्यभुवनम् । प्रियालिङ्गनस्मरणादिना स्वेदादिकम् । स्वेदादीनित्यनेन किलकिंचितभावाविष्करणम् यदाह—'यदन्तर्निहितस्याङ्गैः सन्यापारैर्मनोभुवः । सव्रीडाविष्कृतिः स्त्रीणां तदाहुः किलकिंचितम् ॥' अत्र स्वेदादिमता तव शरीरेण मकरन्दसंभोगोऽभिलषित इत्यर्थः । **मदयन्तिका** । अत्र सहवासिन्याः सख्याः । नाहं कामजस्वेदादिनोद्भिन्ना किं तु त्वद्विस्रम्भकथयेति भावः । अभिण्णह्मीति पाठेऽभिज्ञातास्मीत्यर्थः । **लव०** । अत्र जानीम एवेति कामन्दक्यादिद्वारा तव मकरन्दस्य चेष्टितं ज्ञातमेव । तत्कथमपह्नव इति भावः । व्यपदेशाच्छलात् । सदृशमिति मकरन्दे स्नेहानुबन्धमपि कथयेत्याशयः । उभयमपि क्रियाविशेषणम् ॥ **बुद्धरक्षिता** । अत्र शोभनं कथयितुमर्हसीत्यर्थः । **लवङ्गिका** । अत्र मकरन्दवियोगेन कथं वर्त-

---

१ संकहामेत्तस्स० णं सुमरणं अ. २ गाढगुरुप्पहर ( नख ). ३ विह्वलाविअ ( विह्वलित ). ४ लुग्गमो. ५ विगालिदासिअट्ठि ( विगलितासियष्टि ). ६ विच्छादिअमहग्घजीविदो. ७ अस्सत्थसरीरे किं वाआ । दंसिदं सरीरेण मअरन्दसमाअमोच्छुकं ( अस्वस्थशरीरे किं वाचा । दर्शितं शरीरेण मकरन्दसमागमोत्सुक्यम् । ). ८ आपि विसंवादसीले प्पिअ०. ९ णीए मालदीए; विस्रं० विस्रंभतया ( टी. ). १० एअन्धसुरसं. ११ ०आए भणिद. १२ ०सहीओ.

**मद०**—निशामय प्रियसखि। मम बुद्धरक्षितापक्षपातप्रत्ययेन प्रथममेव तस्मिञ्जने भृतोद्वृत्तकौतूहलोत्कण्ठामनोरथं हृदयमासीत्। ततो विधिनियोगानिर्वृत्तदर्शना भूत्वा दुर्वारदारुणानङ्गदुःखसंतापितकथंचिच्चत्तविघटमानजीविता संभावितास्मि। विजृम्भितापूर्वसर्वाङ्गप्रज्वलितमदनहुतवहोद्दामदाहदुःसहायासदुर्मनायमानपरिजना प्रत्याशाविमोक्षमात्रसुलभमृत्युनिर्वाणप्रतिकूलबुद्धरक्षितावचनविवर्धितावेगव्यतिकरविसंष्ठुलेमं जीवलोकपरिवर्तमनुभवामि।

(णिसामेहि पिअसहि। मम बुद्धरक्खिदापक्खवादप्पच्चएण पढमं ज्जेव्व तस्सिं जणे भरिदुव्वरन्तकोदूहलुक्कण्ठामणोरहं हिअअं आसी। तदो विहिणिओआणिउत्तदंसणा भविअ दुव्वारदारुणाणङ्गदुक्खसंदाविदकड्ढन्तचित्तविहडन्तजीविदा संभाविआह्मि। विअम्भिआपुव्वसव्वङ्गप्पज्जलिदमअणहुदवहुद्दामदाहदूसहाआसदुम्मणाअन्तपरिअणा पच्चासाविमोक्खमेत्तसुलहमित्तुणिव्वाणपडिऊलबुद्धरक्खिदावअणविवड्ढिआवेअवइअराविसंठुला इमं जीवलोअपरिवत्तं अणुभवामि।)

संकल्पस्वप्नान्तरेषु च मनोरथोन्मादमोहिता प्रेक्षे तं जनम्।
सोपि प्रियसखि मुहूर्तनिर्व्यूढविस्मयविसंष्ठुलोद्वेल्लविस्तीर्यमाणललितेन-

---

स इति भावः। **मदयन्तिका**। अत्र . निशामय शृणु। एकवचनमिह लवङ्गिकापेक्षया। बुद्धरक्षिताया विदितवृत्तान्तत्वात्। कथाकथनं तु रागवृद्धये यदाह—यात्रा पुरस्कन्दनमुत्सवो वा स्वप्नोऽथ चित्रं रतिसंकथा च। भवत्युपायाः प्रथमावलोके यूनोर्यतो वृद्धिमुपैति रागः॥' पक्षपात इति बुद्धरक्षितापक्षपातो गुणबाहुल्यं विना न भवतीति विश्वास इति भावः। भृतोद्वृत्तमतिरिक्तीभवत्। कौतूहलमुत्कण्ठा च मनोरथश्चेति विग्रहः। ततो बहुव्रीहिः। यद्वा अतिरिक्तीभवत् कौतूहलमुत्कण्ठा च यत्र मनोरथे तादृशो मनोरथो यत्र तत्तथा। सर्वाङ्गदाहो व्याध्यवस्थायाम्। यदाह—मनःसंमोहसर्वाङ्गदाहवृत्त्यादिभिस्तथा। शिरसो वेदनाभिश्च व्याधेरभिनयो यथा॥' मरणमेव निर्वाणं मोक्षः सर्वदुःखापहारकत्वात्। मद्यलादिष्टसङ्गस्तव स्यादिति बुद्धरक्षितावचनम्। विसंष्ठुला संशयितचित्ता। जीवलोकस्य परिवर्तोऽन्यथात्वं मूर्छेत्यर्थः। यद्वा मूर्छानन्तरं पुनर्जीवलोकप्रवेशोऽत्र परिवर्तनम्। संकल्पान्तरे भावनाबलजज्ञानमध्ये स्वप्नज्ञानमध्ये चेत्यर्थः। निर्व्यूढ उपचितः।

---

१ भृतोद्वृत्त (टी.) २ मदन. ३ पितोत्कण्ठितचित्त. ४ तस्सिं जणे अदिभूमिं गदो अणुराओ। अवि अ तस्सिं जणे. ५ अविरलको०-मणहरं. ६ णिओइअचिर (नियोजितचिर). ७ दारुणाआसदुक्खसंदावडज्झन्त (संतापदह्यमान). ८ जीविदासा दूरविअम्भिआ० (दूरविजृम्भिता०). ९ पज्जलण.

त्रपुण्डरीकताण्डवोद्भटप्ररूढमैरेयमदघूर्णितामिव चिरं निर्ध्यायति माम् । किं च कवलितारविन्दकेसरकषायकण्ठकलहंसघोषघर्घरस्खलितगम्भीरभारतीभरितकर्णविवरं प्रिये मदयन्तिके इति मां व्याहरति । अथ च प्रस्फुरत्पयोधरोच्छलदुत्तरीयांशुकाञ्चलावलम्बनपरिभवेन ससंभ्रमोत्तराङ्गिधमधमायमानहृदयां मां समुत्त्रासयति । (संकप्पंसिविणन्तरेसु[1] अ मणोरहुम्मादमोहिदा पेक्खामि तं जणं । सो वि[2] पिअसहि मुहुत्तणिव्वूढविह्मअविसंठुलुव्वेल्लवित्थरन्तलेलिदणेत्तपुण्डरीअताण्डवुब्भटप्परूढमैरेअमदघुण्णिदं[6] विअ चिरं णिज्झाअदि मं । किं अ कवलिआरविन्दकेसरकसाअकण्ठकलहंसघोसघग्घरक्खालिअगम्भीरर्भारदीभरिदकण्णविवरं पिए मदअन्तिए त्ति मं वाहरदि । अध[9] अ पप्फुरन्तपओधरुच्छलदुत्तरीअअंशुअञ्चलावलम्बणपरिभवेण ससंभमुत्तरङ्गिधमधमाअन्तहिअअं मं समुत्तासेदि ।)

सहसा विसर्जितांशुकप्रसृतां च तत्क्षणकठोरकमलदण्डायमानबाहुबन्धनापवारितपयोधरोद्गमां विघटमानविकलमेखलावलयसंदानितपीवरोरुप्रतिषिद्धविप्रतीपगमनां प्रतिकूलवादिनीमपि[10] प्रत्यादरप्रयत्ननिर्वर्तितमुहु-

उद्वेल्लत्सभ्रूक्षेपम् । प्ररूढमैरेयं प्रसन्नमद्यम् । तस्य मदो मत्तता । 'मैरेयमासवः सीधुः' इत्यमरः । घूर्णितमितिक्रियाविशेषणम् । निर्ध्यायति चिन्तयति । कषायः सुरभितः । कलहंसो राजहंसः । घोषः शब्दः । घर्घरमस्फुटम् । स्खलितं च्युतम् । एतदुभयं साध्वसवशात् । हर्षसंजातस्वरभेदाद्वा । यदाह—'स्वरभेदो भयक्रोधमदहर्षादिभिर्भवेत् ।' भरितकर्णविवरमिति क्रियाविशेषणम् । वस्त्राञ्चलग्रहणेन स्त्रीप्रसादनम् । यदाह—'रहसि ग्रहणेनापि हस्ते वस्त्रे च मूर्धनि । कार्यं प्रसादनं नार्या अपराधं समीक्षता ॥' परिभवेन प्रतिकारबुद्ध्या । सभयं पूर्वाननुभवात् । अत्र किं स्यादित्युत्तरंगि कम्पवत् । आतङ्काद्धमधमायमानमुष्णमिव चित्तं यस्यास्ताम् । यद्वा उत्तरङ्गयुद्गतकल्लोलम् । धमधमायमानं सकम्पम् । कल्लोलश्च कम्पस्योत्तरोत्तरप्रकर्षः । उत्त्रासयति चकितां करोति । शीघ्रं त्यक्तवस्त्रा च सा प्रसृता गमनोद्यता च । कर्मधारयः । पुलकितत्वेन दण्डायमानता । अपवारितोऽपिहितः । उद्गमो विस्तारः । आलिङ्गनविघटनं कृत्वापसरणे कुचालोकनादिकं नायकस्य जायते । नायिका च तदा संवरणाय न प्रभवतीति भावः । तर्हि पलायते किमिति नेत्यत आह—**विघटमानेति** । विघटमानालिङ्गनजरोमाञ्चसंचयात् । विकला स्वस्थानचलनात् । संदानं बन्धनम् । तत्प्रापिताभ्यामित्यर्थः । प्रतीपं प्रतिकूलम् । गमनाभावे पुनः का-

१ संकप्पचिन्ताए. २ नह अ. ३ मुहुत्तं उद्गूढ. ४ वित्थारिपेरन्तणाल (विस्तारिप्रान्तनाल). ५ रत्त (रक्त) टी०. ६ तण्डवुप्पीडडम्बरपढिरूढ. ७ मेरेअवप्पं; मदघुम्मन्तसीलं णिव्वण्णेदि (घूर्णनशीलं निर्वर्णयति). ८ नारधीरणादभरिद. ९ अध पहावन्तो (प्रभवन्) विअ उत्तरीअ; उत्तरिअअंचल. १० मपि मामत्या० (टी.).

र्तकोपोपरागदुःखपरुषीकृतहृदयां स्निग्धपुनरुक्तपर्यस्तलोचनविभावितशेष-चित्तसारामुपहसति । द्विगुणबाहुदण्डावेष्टननियन्त्रितां प्रियसखि प्ररूढ[1]-शार्दूलकठोरकररुहाक्रमणविकटपत्रावलीप्रसाधनोत्तानवक्षःस्थलनिष्ठुरनिवेश-निःसहां कृत्वा सावेगविधुतमस्तकाविद्धकबरीनिहितकरपरिग्रहपुञ्जीकृतो-न्नमितनिश्चलमुखावयवस्वच्छन्दविकासविदग्धवदनकमलो वामगण्डमूलचिर-निहितप्रस्फुरत्पुञ्जिताधरसमुद्गतमनोहरस्पर्शनिर्भरोद्धर्षितशरीरशोभामुल्लसि-तसाध्वसानन्दविषमसंभ्रमवलनमोहमन्थरभ्रमल्लोचनां किमपि दुर्विनयसाह-सानुरूपव्यवसायो मामनभ्यर्थनीयमभ्यर्थयति ।

( सहसा विसज्जि[2]अअंसुअप्पसारिदं अ तक्खणकठोरकमलदण्डाअमाणबाहुबन्धणाववारि-अपओहरुग्गमं विहडन्तविअल[3]मेहलावलअसंदा[4]णिज्जन्तपीवरोरुप्पडिसिद्धविप्पदीवगमणं पडिऊलवादिणिं वि अव्वो[5]अरपअत्तणिव्वत्तिदमुहुत्तकोवोवराअदुक्खपरुसीकिदहिअअं सिणिद्ध[6]पुणरुत्तपल्हत्थलोअणविहाविदासेसचित्तसारं मं उवहँसदि[7] । दिउणबाहु-दण्डावेढ्ढ[8]णाणिअन्तिदं पिअसहि प्परूढसद्दूलकठोरकररुंहो[9]रम्फविअडपत्तावलीपसाहणु-त्ताणवच्छत्थलणिट्ठुरणिवेसणीसहं कदुअ सावेअविहुअमत्थं[10]आविद्धकबरीणिहिदक-रपरिग्गहोवग्गिदुण्णमिअणिच्चलमुहावअवसच्छन्दविओ[11]सविअड्ढवअणकमलो वाम-

---

न्तावरुद्धतया हूं हूमित्यादिनिषेधमाह--**प्रतिकूलेति** । उपरागः संबन्धः । निषि-द्धपुनरुक्ते पुनः पुनर्निषेधवाक्ये पर्यस्तं निषेधविपरीतं स्निग्धत्वादिधर्मत्वात् । यद्वा पर्यस्तं विश्रान्तम् । चित्तसारः संभोगेच्छापरता । उपहासः परिहासः । स च हृदि संभोगेच्छा वाचि परं ते निषेध इत्येवंरूप इत्यर्थः । स्निग्धपुनरुक्तेतिपाठे स्निग्धपुनरुक्तं पुनः पुनः स्निग्धं पर्यस्तं क्षिप्तं लोचनमित्यर्थः । आवेष्टनमावेष्टः तेन गाढालिङ्गनमु-क्तम् । कररुहो नखः । ओरम्फ आक्रमणम् । प्रौढव्याघ्रनखवत्कठोरं यत्कररुहमि-ति भावः । निष्ठुरं निबिडम् । निवेशोऽर्पणम् । निःसहां वचनाद्यक्षमाम् । अत्र कररुहाक्रमणमेव पत्रावलीति रूपकम् । चुम्बनमाह—**सावेगेति** । ओवग्गिदं पुञ्जीकृतं लम्बितमित्यर्थः । मुखावयवा ललाटादयः । विकासितं चुम्बनादिनियुक्त-म् । वदनस्य वैदग्ध्यं चुम्बनचातुर्यात् । इह कन्यायास्त्रिविधं चुम्बनम् । ललित-कच्छुरितकघटितकभेदात् । तत्र ललितकमाह–प्रस्फुरितेति । घटितकमाह-

---

१ प्रौढ ( टी० ). २ विसज्जिअओसरिअ; विसज्जिअंसुअमोसरिअ० ( ०तांशुकामप-सृत्य टी० ). ३ विह्मल, विअड ( विकट–टी०. ). ४ संधाणिज्जन्त. ५ सव्वादर. ६ निसिद्ध ( निषिद्ध–टी० ); रुत्तपह्मलविलोअण. ७ ०सारं उवहासिअ ( उपहस्य ). ८ वेढ्ढणनिच्चेढ्ढाणि-आमिअं; णिव्वतिअं. ९ रुहप्पहार. १० आवत्तिद्ध. ११ विअसिद, विलसिद.

गण्डमूलचिरणिहिदप्पप्फुरन्तपुञ्जिदाहरसमुग्गदमणुहरप्फंसणिब्भरुद्धंसिदसरीरसोहं उल्ल-सिदसद्धसाणन्दविसमसंभमंवलणमोहमन्थरभमन्तलोअणं किं वि दुव्विणेअसाहसाणुरूववसाओ मं अब्भत्थेदि । )

एवं नाम प्रियसखि समक्षं सर्वमनुभूय ततो झटिति प्रतिबुद्धा शून्यारण्यसंनिभं पुनरपि मन्दभाग्या विभावयामि जीवलोकमिति । ( एव्वं णाम पिअसहि समक्खं सव्वं अणुभविअ झत्ति पडिबुद्धा सुण्णारण्णसंणिभं पुणो वि मन्दाभाइणी विभावेमि जीअलोअं त्ति । )

**लव०**—( विहस्य । ) सखि मदयन्तिके स्फुटमाख्याहि । अथ तस्मिन्नवसरे स्नेहविभ्रमोन्मिश्रहासविकसद्बुद्धरक्षितालोचननिरूपितं परि-जनाद्गोपनीयं त आसनमचूडकं शयनीयप्रच्छदपटापवारितं भवति किं न वेति । ( सहि मदअन्तिए फुडं आचक्खेहि । अध तस्सिं अवसरे सिणेह-बिब्भमुम्मीसहासविअसन्तबुद्धरक्खिदालोअणणिरूविदं परिअणादो गोवणिज्जं दे आसं-णमच्चूलअं सअणिज्जपच्छदवडावारिदं भोदि किं ण वेत्ति । )

**मद०**—अयि असंबद्धपरिहासशीले अपेहि । ( अइ असंबद्धपरिहा-सशीले अवेहि । )

**बुद्ध०**—सखि मदयन्तिके मालतीप्रियसखी खल्वीदृशान्येव मन्त्रयितुं जानाति । ( सहि मदअन्तिए मालदीपिअसही क्खु ईदिसाइं ज्जेव्व मन्तिदुं जाणादि । )

---

पुञ्जितं योजितम् । ईषत्परिगृह्य मीलितनेत्रा जिह्वाग्रेण घटयति करेण नेत्रे तस्या-च्छादयतीति घटितकम् । छुरितकं तु प्रागेवोक्तम् । समुद्गम उद्रेकः । एवं च सर्वाङ्गीणनायकस्पर्शोत्प्रमोदमाह मनोहरेति । उद्धर्षितमुद्गतरोमाञ्चम् । नायि-काया वामाङ्गे सकलोपचारव्यवस्थापनाद्वामकपोलेत्युक्तम् । वर्धमानां सुरतावस्था-माह समुल्लसितेति । समुल्लसिताभ्यां साध्वसानन्दाभ्यां विषमो यः संभ्रमः संवेगस्तत्र मोहेन किंकर्तव्यतामूढतया मन्थरत्वमेकतरपक्षाव्यवस्थितिः । साध्वसेन प्रवृत्तिरानन्देन च निवृत्तिरित्याशयः । अनभ्यर्थनीयं सुरतादिकम् । ततो झटितीति जागरावस्थाकथनम् । **लवङ्गिका** । अत्र मचूडकं विधावीति ख्यातम् । निःसहत-नुत्वेनासनमचूडकेऽपि धातुत्यागप्रश्नवैदग्धीयमिति भावः । पुष्पवतीशङ्कया परिजन-

---

१ कपोल; मूलोषारिणि०. २ मणहरसहअसारस्सदमणहरुकस्सिद ( सहजसाररवतमनोहरोत्कर्षित ). ३ रुब्भमाविद ( रोद्भ्रामित ). ४ संभममणहरसंवलण...चेअणं ( चेतनां ). ५ दुव्विणीद. ६ एवं नाम इति नास्ति बहुपुस्तकेषु. ७ तदोझत्ति. ८ विब्भमुज्जिअ (विभ्रमोर्जित). ९ णिअम्बस्स मूलं सअणिज्जं पच्छदवडो वा भोदि. १० ०सही एव्व इअं ईरिसाणि जा०.

**मद०**—सखि मा खल्वेवं मालतीमुपहस। ( सहि मा क्खु एव्वं मालदिं उवहस। )

**बुद्ध०**—सखि मदयन्तिके पृच्छामीदानीं ते किमपि यदि न मे विश्वासभङ्गं करोषि। ( सहि मदअन्तिए पुच्छिस्सं दाणिं दे किं वि जइ ण मे विस्सासभङ्गं करेसि। )

**मद०**—सखि किं पुनरपि प्रणयभङ्गेन कृतापराधोऽयं जनो येनैवं मन्त्रयसे। प्रियसखि त्वं लवङ्गिका च सांप्रतं मे हृदयम्। ( सहि किं पुणो वि पणअभङ्गेण किआवराहो अअं जणो जेण एव्वं मन्तेसि। पिअसहि तुमं लवङ्गिआ[1] अ संपदं मे हिअअं। )

**बुद्ध०**—यदि ते कथमपि मकरन्दः पुनरपि दर्शनपथमवतरति तदा किं त्वया कर्तव्यम्। ( जइ दे कधं वि मअरन्दो पुणो वि दंसणपहं ओदरदि तदो किं तुए कादव्वं। )

**मद०**—एकैकावयवनिःसङ्गलग्ननिश्चले चिरं लोचने निर्वापयिष्यामि। ( एक्केक्कावअवणीसङ्ग[2]लग्गणिच्चले चिरं लोअणे णिव्वावइस्सं। )

**बुद्ध०**—अथ सोपि मन्मथबलात्कारितो यदि कंदर्पजननीं त्वां रुक्मिणीमिव पुरुषोत्तमः स्वयंग्राहसहधर्मचारिणीं करोति ततः का प्रतिपत्तिः। ( अध[3] सोवि मम्महबलक्कारिओ जइ कंदप्पजणणिं तुमं रुक्किणिं विअ पुरुसोत्तमो सअंगाह[4]सहधम्मचारिणिं करेइ तदो का[5] पडिवत्ती। )

**मद०**—( निःश्वस्य। ) किं मामेतावदाश्वासयसि। ( किं मं एत्तिअं आसासेसि[6]। )

---

हासानिवारणाय गोपनम्। **बुद्ध०**। अत्र पृच्छामि यदि हृद्गतं रहस्यं कथयसीति भावः। **मदय०**। अत्र कृतापराध इत्यत्र शिरश्चालनगतिः। **बुद्ध०**। अत्रात्मसमर्पणमेव त्वया कार्यमिति भावः। **मदय०**। अत्र तद्दर्शनामृतसेकशीतला भविष्यामीति भावः। निःसङ्गः सर्वाङ्गव्यापी। **बुद्ध०**। अत्राथशब्दो यद्यर्थे। बलात्कारितो बलात्कारेण प्रवर्तितः। रुक्मिणी काममाता प्रद्युम्नमातृत्वात्। पक्षे कामावस्थाकारिणीम्। पुरुषोत्तमः कृष्णः। अथ च पुरुषेषूत्तमो मकरन्दः। स्वयंग्राहेण

---

१ ०ङ्गिआए समं. २ निसग्ग ( निसर्ग ). ३ जइ. ४ ग्गाहसाहसेण. ५ कीरिसी. ६ किं एत्तिअं आसासिदाम्हि.

**बुद्ध०**—सखि कथय । ( सहि कहेहि । )

**लव०**—सखि कथितमेव हृदयावेगसूचकैर्दीर्घनिःश्वासैः । ( सहि कधिदं ज्जेव्व हिअआवेअसूअएहिं दीहणीसासेहिं । )

**मद०**—सखि काहमस्य तेनैवात्मानं पणीकृत्य दुष्टशार्दूलकवलनादाकृष्टस्य तस्यैव कृत्यकरस्यात्मनः शरीरस्य । ( सहि का अहं इमस्स तेण ज्जेव्व अत्ताणअं पणीकदुअ दुट्ठसद्दूलकवलणादो कड्ढिअस्स तस्स ज्जेव्व केरअस्स अत्तणो सरीरस्स । )

**लव०**—सदृशं खलु महानुभावतायाः । ( सरिसं क्खु महाणुभावदाए ।

**बुद्ध०**—स्मरिष्यस्येतद्वचनम् । ( सुमरेसि एदं वअणं )

**मद०**—कथं द्वितीयप्रहरनाडिकाविच्छेदपटहस्ताड्यते । तद्यावन्नन्दनं निर्भर्त्स्य सपादपतनमभ्यर्थ्य मालत्या उपर्यनुकूलयिष्यामि । ( कधं दुदीअपहरनाडिकाविच्छेदपडहो ताडीअदि । ता जाव णन्दणं णिब्भच्छिअ सपाअदपडणं अब्भत्थिअ मालदीए उवरि अणुऊलइस्सं । ) ( इत्युत्थाय गन्तुमिच्छति । )

( मकरन्दो मुखमुद्घाट्य हस्तेन गृह्णाति । )

**मद०**—सखि मालति प्रतिबुद्धासि । ( विलोक्य सहर्षसाध्वसम् । ) अम्मो अन्यदेव किमप्येतद्वर्तते । ( सहि मालदि पडिबुद्धासि । अम्मो अण्णं जेव्वं किं वि एदं वट्टदि । )

---

गान्धर्वेण । स्वधर्मचारिणी भार्या । प्रवृत्तिर्वार्ता । **मदयन्तिका** । इह ममाभाग्येन किं स्यादिति निःश्वास इति भावः । **मदयन्तिका** । अत्र काहमात्मशरीरस्य किं तु न कापि । मकरन्दस्यैव मच्छरीरमिति भावः । केरकशब्दः कृत्यकरवाची । पणीकृत्य मूल्यतया यो व्यवस्थाप्यते स कृत्यकरः । **लवङ्गिका** । अत्र महानुभावता कृतज्ञता । **बुद्धरक्षिता** । सांप्रतमेवैतद्वचनस्योपयोगं स्थिरीकृत्याह । स्मरिष्यसीदं वचनम् । **मदयन्तिका** । अत्र ' नाडी कालेऽपि षट्क्षणे ' इत्यमरः । षट्क्षणावच्छिन्नः कालो नाडी । द्वितीया नाडी द्वादशक्षणात्मकः कालः । मदयन्तिकामकरन्दसंघट्टनविषयस्य समाप्तिपटहोऽयमित्यर्थः । यद्वा द्वितीयनाडी द्वितीयभगिनी मालती तया सह विच्छेदो वियोगो यथोपक्रान्तसंबन्धविघटनामित्यर्थः । **मकरन्दः** । गृह्णाति मदयन्तिकामित्यर्थः । **मदयन्तिका** । अत्राम्मो इति स्वच्छंदप्रलपितस्वा-

---

१ मिच्चु० (मृत्यु) कवलादो. २ परकेर०, एव्व परएअस्स (परकीयस्स) किच्चकिंकरस्स. ३ सुमरेहि. ४ दुदिअआमवि०. ५ पडणं वा. ६ हत्थे. ७ सहरिसं ससाध्वसं च. ८ अम्हहे. ९ एदं एव्व व०.

मक०—

रम्भोरु संहर भयं क्षमते विसोढु-
मुत्कम्पितं स्तनभरस्य न मध्यभागः।
इत्थं त्वयैव कथितप्रणयप्रसादः
संकल्पनिर्वृतिषु संस्तुत एष दासः ॥ २ ॥

बुद्ध०—(मदयन्तिकामुखमुन्नमय्य संस्कृतमाश्रित्य।)

प्रेयान्मनोरथसहस्रवृतः स एष
सुप्तप्रमत्तजनमेतदमात्यवेश्म।
प्रौढं तमः कुरु कृतज्ञतयैव भद्र-
मुक्षिप्तमूकमणिनूपुरमेहि यामः ॥ ३ ॥

मद०—सखि बुद्धरक्षिते क्व पुनरिदानीमस्माभिर्गन्तव्यम्।
(सहि बुद्धरक्खिदे कहिं पुणो दाणिं अह्मेहिं गन्दव्वं।)

बुद्ध०—यत्रैव मालती। (जहिं जेव्व मालदी।)

---

भिप्रायानुतापे। रम्भेत्यादि। हे रम्भोरु भयं त्यज। यतस्तव स्तनभारस्योत्कम्पं सोढुं मध्यभागो न क्षमते समर्थो न भवति। अतिकृशो मध्यदेशः कुचयोर्भयकम्पस्य भारं न सहत इति भावः। भयमिहापरिचितदर्शनात्। विकारमिति पाठे तत्र सकम्पस्य स्तनभारस्य विकारं मध्यभागो न क्षमते। संकल्पसुखेष्वनेनोक्तप्रकारेण त्वयैव कथितप्रार्थनासंपत्तिरेषोऽहं संस्तुतः परिचितो दासो विधेयः। प्रणयः प्रेम तद्रूपो वा प्रसादः ॥ २ ॥ प्रेयानित्यादि। प्रेयान् प्रियतमो मनोरथसहस्रैर्वृतः प्रार्थितो यस्त्वया संकल्पादिष्वनुभूतः स एष सोऽयमित्यर्थ इति प्रागनुरागोद्भेदः। अतः कृतज्ञतया पूर्वोपकारस्य स्मरणेनैव भद्रमभीष्टं विवाहरूपं कुरु। तत्र सामग्रीमाह—एतदमात्यगृहं केचित्सुप्ताः केचित्प्रमत्ता जना यत्र तादृशम्। गाढं तमः। अन्धमिति पाठेऽन्धं करोतीत्यन्धम्। तम इत्यर्थः। उत्क्षिप्तमुत्तोलितमत एव मूकमशब्दं मणिप्रधानं नूपुरं यथा तथैहि यामः। विवाहसंपादनायेति भावः। तत्र सुप्तादिना गृहलोकानामदर्शनं प्रौढान्धकारतया बहिर्लोकानामदर्शनम्। नूपुरस्याप्यशब्दतया परवितर्काभाव इति गमनमप्रत्यूहं स्यादिति दर्शितम्। प्रमत्त इति रदाभ्यां निष्ठातो न इति नत्वं न भवति। न ध्याख्यापृमूर्छिमदामिति निषेधात् ॥ ३ ॥ मदयन्तिका। अत्रानेन मकरन्दसंमतिमाह—यत्रैव मालती। वर्तेत

---

१ विकारमुत्कम्पिनः स्तनतटस्य; उत्कम्पनं. २ संस्कृत. ३ लवङ्गिका. ४ उत्क्षिप्य. ५ मालदी गआ.

मद०—किं निर्वृत्तसाहसा मालती । ( किं णिव्वुत्तसाहसा मालदी । )

बुद्ध०—अथ किम् । अन्यच्च । त्वं भणसि । ( अध ई । अण्णं अ तुमं भणासि । ) ( ' काहं इमस्य ' इत्यादि पठति । मदयन्तिकाश्रूणि पातयति । )

बुद्ध०—महाभाग दत्तः खलु स्वयमात्मा प्रियसख्या । ( महाभाअ दिण्णो क्खु सअं अप्पा पिअसहीए । )[1]

मक०—

अद्योर्जितं विजितमेव मया किमन्य-
द्द्योत्सवः फलवतो मम यौवनस्य ।
यस्य[2] प्रसादसुमुखेन समुद्धृतेयं[3]
देवेन बान्धवधुरा मकरध्वजेन ॥ ४ ॥

तदनेन पक्षद्वारेण निर्गत्य[4] साधयामः ।

( निभृतं परिक्रामन्ति । )

मक०—अहो निशीथनिःसंचाररमणीयता राजमार्गस्य । तथा हि संप्रति ।

प्रासादानामुपरि वलभीतुङ्गवातायनेषु[5]
भ्रान्त्वावृत्तः[6] परिणतसुरागन्धसंस्कारगर्भः ।

---

इति शेषः । एतेनागामिनोऽङ्कस्यावतारः सूचितः । **मदयन्तिका** । अत्र पितृनैरपेक्ष्येण मालत्यात्मनिवेदनं यदि तदा ममापि तत्स्यादित्याशयः । **बुद्धरक्षिता** । अत्र च तथा प्रागेव मत्समक्षं त्वया मकरन्दायात्मा दत्तः । इदानीं कुतस्तेऽपास्यमित्याशयः । स्वगृहत्यागदुःखादश्रुपातेन सूचितात्मदानां मदयन्तिकामाह [बुद्ध०]—अत्र तुभ्यमिति शेषः । **अद्येत्यादि** । अद्योर्जितं सातिशयं कृत्वा मया विजितम् । सर्वकार्यसंपादनात् । सफलस्य मम यौवनस्याद्योत्सवः । अत एवान्यत्किम् । अपि तु न किमपि । साध्यमस्तीति शेषः । यस्य मम बान्धवधुरा मित्रकृत्यं कामदेवेन सम्यग्धृता । प्रसन्नतया सुमुखेन । एवकारोऽप्यत एव । यदि माधवसंगतेयं स्यात्तदा मया सर्वाकारं जितं न स्यादिति भावः । कन्यावरणे बान्धवा एव भवन्ति । यदाह—' कन्याया वरणे माता पितरौ बान्धवा अपि । ' पक्षद्वारं खडिक्किका ॥ ४ ॥ ' अर्धरात्रनिशीथौ द्वौ ' इत्यमरः । **प्रासादानामिति** । अयं वायुस्तरुणानां नूतनस्त्रीसमागमं प्रकाशयति । अनेन मदयन्तिकाप्रोत्साहनमुक्तम् । कीदृशः

---

१ दिण्णं क्खु अत्ताणं पिअसहीए पडिवज्जस्स ( प्रतिपद्यस्व ). २ यन्मे. ३ समुद्यता. ४ एतन्नास्ति क्वचित्. ५ जाल. ६ भ्रान्त्या, प्राप्तामोदः.

मा॒लयामोदी मुहुरुपचितस्फारकर्पूरवासो
वायुर्यूनामभिनववधूसंनिधानं व्यनक्ति ॥ ५ ॥
( इति निष्क्रान्ताः सर्वे । )

**इति नन्दनाविप्रलम्भो नाम सप्तमोऽङ्कः ।**

---

उक्तस्थानेषु भ्रान्त्वावृत्तः । आदौ भ्रान्तः पुनरावृत्त आयातः । अनेन मन्दत्वम् । भ्रान्त्या भ्रमणेनायात इति वा । परिणतपुष्परसगन्धसमूहबन्धुः । पुष्पस्रजा हृष्टः सुरभिर्वा । मुहुरुपचितोऽत्यर्थं प्रवृद्धः । स्फारो दीर्घतया बृहत्तरः । कर्पूरसंपर्की च । पश्चात्कर्मधारयः । यद्वा कर्पूरविशेषणमेव द्वयम् । एभी रतिसौगन्ध्ये ध्वनिते । यतोऽतिमनोहरोऽत एव स्त्रीसांनिध्यकर इति भावः । उपहितमल्लेति पाठेऽपि कर्मधारयः ॥ ५ ॥

प्रासोष्ट यं रत्नधरो द्विजेशो द्विजेशवन्द्या दमयन्तिकापि ।
जगद्धरं तत्कृतटिप्पणेऽङ्कोऽगमन्मनोहारिणि सप्तमोऽयम् ॥

**इति सप्तमोऽङ्कः ।**

---

१ स्फीत. २ वातो यूनामभिमत.

## अष्टमोऽङ्कः ।

( ततः प्रविशत्यवलोकिता । )

**अवलोकिता**—वन्दिता मया नन्दनावासप्रतिनिवृत्ता भगवती । तद्यावन्मालतीमाधवसकाशं गच्छामि । ( परिक्रम्य । ) एतौ तौ निर्वर्तितग्रीष्मदिवसावसानमज्जनौ दीर्घिकातटशिलातलमलंकुरुतः । तद्यावदुपसर्पामि । ( वन्दिदा मए णन्दणावासं[1]पडिणिउत्ता भअवदी । ता जाव मालदीमाहवसआसं[2] गच्छह्मि । एदे दे णिव्व[3]त्तिदगिह्मदिअहावसाणमज्जणा दीहिआतं[4]डसिलातलं अलंकरेन्ति[5] । ता जाव उपसप्पा[6]मि । ) ( निष्क्रान्ता[7] । )

**प्रवेशकः ।**

---

( ततः प्रविशत उपविष्टौ मालतीमाधवाववलोकिता च । )

**माधवः**—( सानन्दम्[8] । ) वर्तते[9] हि मन्मथप्रौढसुहृदो निशीथस्य[10] यौवनश्रीः । तथा हि ।

> **दलयति परिशुष्यत्[11]प्रौढतालीविपाण्डु-**
> **स्तिमिरनिकरमुद्यन्नैन्दवः प्राक्प्रकाशः ।**
> **वियति पवनवेगादुन्मुखः केतकीनां**
> **प्रचलित इव सान्द्रो मन्दमन्दं[12] परागः ॥ १ ॥**

( स्वगतम् । ) तत्कथं वामशीलां मालतीमुपावर्तये । भवत्वेवं तावत् । ( प्रकाशम् । ) प्रिये मालति प्रत्यग्रसायंतनस्नानसविशेषशीतलामत्र भवतीं निदाघ[13]संतापशान्तये किंचिद्विज्ञापयामि । तत्किमित्यद्यानिमित्तमन्यथैव मां संभावयसि ।

---

तदेवं मदयन्तिकामादाय मकरन्दे माधवान्तिकं चलिते मालतीमादाय निर्गतस्य माधवस्य कामन्दकीगृहस्थितस्य वार्ताप्रस्तावनायावलोकिताप्रवेशः । सूचनं च पूर्वाङ्के । जहिं ज्जेव्व मालतीति वचनेन मालतीमाधवयोरेकत्र वासः सूचितः । तत्र च यद्यपि तयोरेव प्रवेशोऽर्हति तथापि कन्याप्रलोभने सख्यानुकूल्ये तत्प्रवेश इति पूर्वाङ्के कृतमेव । **अवलोकिता** । अत्र 'सरो वापी तु दीर्घिका' इत्यमरः । **दलयतीत्यादि** । अयं चान्द्र उद्योत उद्गच्छन्नत एव शुष्यत्प्रगल्भतालीपत्रवत्पाण्डुरस्तिमिरसंघं खण्डयति । प्रथमतो व्योम्नि वायुवेगेनोर्ध्वमुखीभूय प्रचलितो घनः केतकीपराग इव । इन्दोरयमैन्दवः । मन्दमन्दमिति प्रचलनक्रियाविशेषणम् । उपावर्तये संमुखीकु-

---

१ णावसथ. २ आसं ज्जेव. ३ परिणिव्व०. ४ तीर. ५ ०न्ति मालदीमाहवा. ६ उवसप्पिस्सं [ उपसर्प्स्यामि ]. ७ इति नि०. ८ स्वगतं स्व० सा०. ९ वर्धते. १० निशीथिनीनाथस्य. ११ शुष्क. १२ ०न्द्रः; माकरन्दः; स्फारस्फारश्. १३ निदाघशा०.

निश्चोतन्ते सुतनु कबरीबिन्दवो यावदेते
यावन्मध्यः स्तनमुकुलयोर्नार्द्रभावं जहाति ।
यावत्सान्द्रप्रततनुपुलकोद्गेदवत्यङ्गयष्टि-
स्तावद्गाढं वितर सकृदप्यङ्कपालीं प्रसीद ॥ २ ॥

अयि निरनुरोधे

जीवयन्निव समूढसाध्वसस्वेदबिन्दुरधिकण्ठमर्प्यताम् ।
बाहुरैन्दवमयूखचुम्बितस्यन्दिचन्द्रमणिहारविभ्रमः ॥ ३ ॥

अथ वा दूरे तावदेतत् । कथमालापसंविभागस्याप्यभाजनमयं जनो भवत्याः ।

दग्धं चिराय मलयानिलचन्द्रपादै-
र्निर्वापितं तु परिरभ्य वपुर्न नाम ।
आमत्तकोकिलरुतव्यथिता तु हृद्या-
मद्य श्रुतिः पिबतु किंनरकण्ठि वाचम् ॥ ४ ॥

---

रोमि ॥ १ ॥ **निश्चोतन्त इत्यादि** । हे सुशरीरे यावदेते कबरीजलबिन्दवः स्रवन्ति यावत्कुचकलिकयोर्मध्य आर्द्रतां न त्यजति यावच्च निबिडव्यापि रोमाञ्चं प्रकाशयन्ती काययष्टिस्तावद्गाढं यथा तथा सकृदपि मेऽङ्कपालीं क्रोडप्रदेशं देहि । अतः प्रसीद । तदिह निदाघतापशान्तये जलबिन्दवः । कुचार्द्रता पुलकोद्गमश्च सर्वाङ्गशैत्यापत्तये । यावत्तावच्छब्दाववध्यर्थौ । सान्द्रेत्यादिपदे कर्मधारयमत्वर्थीयाद्बहुव्रीहिरेवेष्टो लघुत्वादिति न्यायेन बहुव्रीहिसंभवे कथं मत्वर्थीय इति न देश्यम् । एतद्वचनस्य प्रायिकत्वात् । तथैव नानाप्रयोगदर्शनादिति दिक् । 'पालिः पङ्क्तिप्रदेशयोः' इति शाश्वतः ॥ २ ॥ **जीवयन्नित्यादि** । बाहुः कण्ठेऽर्प्यताम् । कीदृशः । समूढं सद्योजातं पुञ्जितं वा यत्साध्वसं भयं तेन स्वेदबिन्दुर्यत्र सः । अननुभूततया भयम् । चान्द्रकरस्पृष्टोऽत एव स्यन्दी क्षरन्बालचन्द्रकान्तहारस्तत्तुल्यः । घर्मविघातकत्वात् । अत एव सौहित्याज्जीवयन्निव । 'समूढः पुञ्जिते भुग्ने सद्योजाते सुनिश्चिते ।' इति विश्वः । ससाध्वसश्रमेति पाठे ससाध्वसो भयवान्यः श्रम इत्यर्थः । संविभागो भेदः । अभाजनमस्थानम् । अजहल्लिङ्गोऽयम् । अयं जन इत्यनेन दीनतोद्भावनेनानुकूल्यं स्वीयमाह । भवत्या इत्यनेन नायिकोत्तेजनम् ॥ ३ ॥ **दग्धमित्यादि** । चिरं दक्षिणवायुचन्द्रकरैस्तापितं मे वपुरालिङ्ग्य न चेन्निर्वापितमतसीकृतं तदा समदकोकिलरवपीडिता मे श्रुतिः कर्णोऽद्येदानीं हृद्यां वाचं पिबतु । सादरं शृणोत्वित्यर्थः । अत एव वाङ्माधुर्यद्योतनाय किंनरकण्ठि इति संबोधनम् । किंनरस्येव कण्ठः स्वरो यस्यास्तादृशि

---

१ युगलयोः; कलशयोः; मुकुलयोरा० २ प्रतत. ३ अङ्ग. ४ अयि मालति निरनुक्रोशे. ५ स्यन्द. ६ पुनर्न. ७ कर्णरसायनानि.

**अव०**—( उपसृत्य ) अयि अनिर्वहणशीले यदिदानीं मुहूर्त[1]मात्रान्तरितमाधवा दुर्मनायमाना मम पुरतो भणसि चिरयत्यार्यपुत्रोऽपि नाम कियच्चिरेण प्रेक्षिष्ये येन पुनर्विच्छर्दि[2]ताशेषसाध्वसा विस्मृतनिमेषविघ्नमवलोकयन्त्येवं भणिष्यामि द्विगुणावेष्टनपरिरम्भेण संभावयेरिति तस्य ते सांप्रतमयं परिणामः । ( अइ अणिव्वहणसीले जं दाणिं मुहुत्तमेत्तन्दरिदमाहवा दुम्मणाअन्ती मह पुरदो भणासि चिराअदि अज्जउत्तो अवि णाम किअच्चिरेण पेक्खिस्सं जेण पुणो विच्छडिआसेससज्झसा विसुमरिअणिमेसविग्घं ओलोअन्ती[3] एव्वं भणिस्सं दुउण[4]वेढणपरिरम्भेण संभावअसि त्ति तस्स[5] दे संपदं अअं परिणामो । )

( मालती सासूयमिव तां पश्यति । )

**माधवः**—( स्वगतम्[6] । ) अहो भगवती[7]प्रधानान्तेवासिन्याः सर्वतोमुखं वैदग्ध्यमक्षर्य[8]श्च सुभाषितरत्नकोषः । ( प्रकाशम् ) प्रिये[9] सैत्यमवलोकिता वदति ।

( मालती मूर्धानं चालयति । )

**माधवः**—शापितासि मम लवङ्गिकावलोकितयोश्च जीवितेन यदि वाचा[10] न कथयासि ।

---

हे । 'स्वरे कण्ठः प्रकीर्तितः' इति रत्नकोशः । अङ्ककण्ठगात्रेषूपसंख्यानान्डीष् । पूर्वार्धे तुशब्दो यद्यर्थः । द्वितीये पुनरर्थः । यदि नालिङ्गनं देयं तदा मधुरमालपेति भावः । नाम संभावनायाम् । आलिङ्गनादानं संभाव्यते यतः । त्वयि वदन्त्यां कलकोकिलरवोऽपि कर्णकटुरित्यनुरागाधिक्यमात्मन उक्तम् । इहाद्यपदमिदानीमर्थे । अन्यथा निशीथवर्णनेऽद्यास्मिन्नहनीत्यस्यानर्थक्यापत्तेः । एवं चाद्यास्मिन्नहनीति व्युत्पत्तिः प्रायिका ॥ ४ ॥ **अवलोकिता** । अत्र यदिदानीमिति वाक्यभूषायाम् । भणनस्वरूपमेवाह–चिरयतीति संभावयेरित्यन्तम् । सांप्रतमिति शिरश्चालनकाकौ । चिरयति विलम्बते । विच्छर्दितं त्यक्तम् । विघ्नमिति क्रियाविशेषणम् । **परिणाम इति** । या त्वं चिरविरहमसहमाना माधवार्थिनी सा कथमधुना तत्र वाग्यमनमालम्बस इति भावः । असूया गुणेषु दोषारोपः । सा चेह हास्यनिवेदनादिति भावः । **माधवः** । सर्वतोमुखं सर्वतोगामि । सुभाषितान्येव रत्नानि तेषां कोषः पात्रम् । 'कोषोऽस्त्री कुड्मले पात्रे' इति मेदिनीकरः । प्रियेत्यादिप्रश्नवाक्यम् ॥ मूर्धकम्प उक्तनिषेधाय । **माधवः** । शापितासि शपथीकृतासि ।

---

१ मुहुत्तंतरिदमाहवा; महावेवि. २ विवाड्डिआ. ३ आलोअअन्ती. ४ वेट्टणं, विउणवेढ [ द्विगुणवेष्ट ]०; दुउणिआवे–म्भणेण संभावइस्सं. ५ स एव्व अअं परि०. ६ अपवार्य. ७ भगवत्याः प्रथमा०. ८ एतद्वाद्दे नास्ति क्वचित्; अक्षय्यः, अक्षय्यं '०रत्नसंचारसंस्करणम्' इ. पा. ९ प्रिये अपि सत्य०. १० मे

**मालती**—नाहं किमपि जानामि। (णाहं किं वि जाणामि।)

(इत्यर्धोक्ते लज्जां नाटयति)

**माधवः**—अहो अनवसितार्थमन्थरस्य वचसश्चारुता। (सहसा निरूप्य।) अवलोकिते किमेतत्।

**बाष्पाम्भसा मृगदृशो विमलः कपोलः**
**प्रक्षाल्यते सपदि राजत एष यस्मिन्।**
**गण्डूषपेयमिव कान्त्यमृतं पिपासु-**
**रिन्दुर्निवेशितमयूखमृणालदण्डः॥ ५॥**

**अव०**—सखि किमिदानीमुच्छलितबाष्पोत्पीडमन्थरं रोदिषि। (सहि किं दाणिं उच्छलिअबाहुप्पीडमन्थरं रोदिसि।)

**मालती**—सखि कियच्चिरं प्रियसख्या लवङ्गिकाया असंनिधानदुःखमनुभविष्यामि। प्रवृत्तिलाभोऽप्यस्या दुर्लभः। (सहि केच्चिरं पिअसहीए लवङ्गिआए असण्णिधाणदुक्खं अनुहविस्सं। पउत्तिलम्भो वि से दुल्लहो।)

**माधवः**—अवलोकिते किं नामैतत्।

**अव०**—तवैव शपथोपन्यासेनैषा लवङ्गिकां स्मृत्वा तस्याः प्रवृत्तिनिमित्तमुत्ताम्यति। (तुह ज्जेव्व सवधोवण्णासेण एसा लवङ्गिअं सुमरिअ ताए पउत्तिणिमित्तं उत्तम्मदि।)

**माधवः**—नन्विदानीमेव तत्र मया कलहंसकः प्रेषितः प्रच्छन्नमुपगम्य नन्दनावासप्रवृत्तिमुपलभस्वेति। (साशंसम्।) अवलोकिते अपि नाम बुद्धरक्षिताप्रयत्नः सफलोदर्क एव मदयन्तिकां प्रति स्यात्।

---

अनवसितोऽनिश्चितः। किमेतदिति वक्ष्यमाणवाक्यार्थस्य प्रश्नः। **बाष्पेत्यादि**। हरिणाक्ष्या एव कपोलो बाष्पजलेन सपदि प्रक्षाल्यते। अत एव विमलः। किमेतत्। यत्र चन्द्रो राजते। कीदृक्। गण्डूषेण मुखपूरणेन पातव्यं दीप्त्यमृतं पातुमिच्छुरिव निहितः किरण एव मृणालदण्डो येन सः। किरणरूपमृणाललतिकया पातुमिच्छतीत्यर्थः। अनेन कपोलस्य चन्द्राधिककान्तिमत्त्वमुक्तम्। 'गण्डूषो मुखपूर्तौ स्यात्' इति शाश्वतः॥ ५॥ **अवलोकिता**। अत्रोच्छलितो बहुलीभवन्। मन्थरमिति क्रियाविशेषणम्। **मालती**। अत्रासंनिधानदुःखमसंगमेन जनितक्लेशम्। प्रवृत्तिलम्भो वार्ताप्राप्तिः। 'वार्ता प्रवृत्तिर्वृत्तान्त उदन्तः स्यादथा-

---

१ ०र्थरम्यवच०; र्थमन्दधर्षव०. २ अवलोक्य. ३ उच्च०. ४ ०पीडं रोदिआदि. ५ लाहो वि मे. ६ वअणो ७ पउत्तिलाहे—लम्भ. ८ एव हि. ९ प्रेषितः गच्छ त्वं...नावसथं प्र०; प्रच्छन्नः संनिपत्य नन्दनावासं प्र०.

**अव०**—कुतः संदेहो महानुभावस्य । महाभाग प्रथममेव शार्दूलनखरालंकृतस्य मकरन्दस्य मोहविराममहोत्सवं निवेदयन्त्यै भगवत्या नियुक्तेन भवता मालत्यै जीवितेन समं प्रसादीकृतं हृदयम् । यदि कोऽपि त्वां सांप्रतं मदयन्तिकालाभेन वर्धयति किमिदानीं तस्य पारितोषिकं भविष्यति । ( कुदो संदेहो महाणुभाअस्स । महाभाअ पुढमं ज्जेव्व सद्दूलणहरालंकिदस्स मअरन्दस्स मोहविराममहूसवं णिवेदअन्तीए भअवदीए णिउत्तेण भवदा मालदीए जीविदेण समं पसादीकिदं हिअअं । जइ को वि तुमं संपदं मदअन्तिआलम्भेणं वड्ढावेदि तदा किं दाणिं तस्स पारितोसिअं भविस्सदि । )

**माधवः**—अनुयोक्तव्यमेवानुयुक्तोऽस्मि । ( हृदयमवलोक्य । ) इयमस्ति मालतीप्रथमदर्शनाभिषङ्गसाक्षिणः कामकाननालंकारस्य लक्ष्मीवतः केसरतरोः प्रसूनमाला ।

> प्रेम्णा मद्ग्रथितेति यां प्रियसखीहस्तोपनीतानया
> विस्तारिस्तनकुम्भकुड्मलभरोत्सङ्गेन संभाविता ।
> संप्राप्ते त्वथ पाणिपीडनविधौ मां प्रत्यपेताशया
> या मय्येव लवङ्गिकेत्यवगते सर्वस्वदायीकृता ॥ ६ ॥

**अव०**—सखि मालति वल्लभा खलु त इयं बकुलमाला । ततोऽवहिता भव मेदानीमेषा सहसैव परहस्तगता भविष्यतीति । ( सहि मालदि वल्लहा क्खु दे इअं वउलमाला । तदो अवहिदा भव मा दाणिं एसा सहसज्जेव्व परहत्थगदा भविस्सदित्ति । )

---

ह्वयः ।' इत्यमरः । **अवलोकिता** । अत्र निवेदयन्त्या मालत्या इत्यन्वयः । मालत्या इति षष्ठ्यन्तम् । मालत्याः कृत इत्यर्थः । **माधवः** । अनुयुक्तः पृष्टः । स्वकीयहृदयालोकनमागामिश्लोकस्य रसद्योतनाय । प्रसवः पुष्पम् ॥ **प्रेम्णेत्यादि** । या माला प्रियसख्या लवङ्गिकया हस्तेनोपनीता मद्ग्रथितेति हेतोः प्रेम्णानया मालत्या पीनकुचघटमुकुलस्य भरो यत्र तेन क्रोडेन सह संभाविता संभावनां नीता । ततो नन्दनेन सह विवाहे संप्राप्ते मां प्रति निरस्तप्रत्याशया लवङ्गिकेयमित्यधिगते मय्येव यया सर्वस्वदानं कृतम् । अनेन पूर्वानुरागकथनेन नायिकाविस्रम्भ उक्तः । विस्तारः परिणाहः । कुम्भपदेनोन्नतता कुड्मलपदेन मृदुता भरशब्देन प्रौढिरुक्ता । पाणिपीडनं विवाहः । दीयत इति दायः ॥ ६ ॥ **अवलोकिता** । अत्र

---

१ एतन्नास्ति क्वचित्. २ मोहाविच्छेअं. ३ लाहेण. ४ करेसित्ति. ५ अनया अनु०. ६ साक्षिणी ७ प्रसव. ८ वा...नीतेति वा. ९ तेप्यथ. १० दायः. ११ एसा दाणिं परस्स हत्थं गमिस्सदि-

**मालती**—प्रियं प्रियसखी मे उपदिशति । ([1]पिअं पिअसही मे उवदिसदि ।)

**अव०**—कथं पदशब्द इव । (कधं पदसद्दो विअ ।)

**माधवः**—(नेपथ्याभिमुखमवलोक्य ।) अये कलहंसकः प्राप्तः ।

**मालती**—दिष्टया वर्धसे मदयन्तिकालाभेन । (दिट्ठिआ वड्ढसि मदअन्तिआल[2]म्भेण ।)

**माधवः**—(सहर्षं परिष्वज्य ।) प्रियं प्रियं नः । (आत्मनः[3] कण्ठादवतार्य बकुलमालां ददाति ।)

**अव०**—निर्व्यूढः खलु भगवत्याः संभावनाभारो बुद्धरक्षितया । (णिव्वूढो क्खु भअवदीए संभावणाभारो बुद्धरक्खिदाए ।)

**मालती**—(सहर्षम् ।) अम्महे प्रियसखि लवङ्गिकापि दृश्यते । (अ[4]म्महे पिअसही लवङ्गिआ वि दीसइ ।) (इत्युत्तिष्ठति ।)

(त[5]तः प्रविशन्ति संभ्रान्ताः कलहंसकबुद्धरक्षितामदयन्तिकालवङ्गिकाः ।)

**स[6]र्वाः**—परित्रायतां परित्रायतां महाभागः । अर्धमार्गे खलु नगररक्षिपुरुषाभियोगो मकरन्दस्य जातः । ततस्तत्कालमिलितेन कलहंसकेन समं वयमनुप्रेषिताः । (परित्ताअदु परित्ताअदु महाभाओ । अद्धमग्गे क्खु णअररक्खिपुरिसाभिओओ मअरन्दस्स जादो । तदो तक्कालमिलिदेण कलहंसएण स[7]मं अह्मे अणुप्पेसिदाओ ।)

**कलहंसः**—यथेतोमुखागतैरपि महान् कलकलः श्रुतोऽस्माभिस्तथा तर्कयाम्यन्यदपि पारक्यं बलमुपगतमिति । (जधा इदोमुहा[8]गदेहिं पि महन्तो कलअलो सुदो अम्हेहिं तधा तक्केमि अण्णं वि पारक्कअं बलं उव[9]गदं त्ति ।)

---

येनैव मकरन्दस्य मदयन्तिकालाभः कथनीयस्तेनैवेयं प्राप्या । अतस्त्वमेव तं कथयेति गुप्त्या माधवेन सहात्मानं संभावयेत्याशयः । **मालती** । तथा चाहमेव कथयामीति भावः । **अवलोकिता** । अत्र श्रूयत इति भावः । **मालती** । अत्र मकरन्दस्य मदयन्तिकाविवाहेनेत्यर्थः । इदं वचनं मालत्या माधवं प्रति । **माधवः** । प्रियं न इति । आलापलाभेनातिप्रियमित्यर्थः । **अवलोकिता** । अत्र निर्व्यूढो निर्वाहं नीतः । खलु निश्चये । संभावना प्रतिष्ठा । **मालती** । अम्महे विस्मये । **सर्वाः** । अत्राभियोगः अवस्कन्दः । **कलहंसकः** । अत्र

---

१ सहि पिअं मे उवदिसासि; अस्मात्परं–अवलोइदे उभअं वि तुमं एव्व उवदिस । इत्यधिकमेक० पु०. २ लाहेण. ३ इति बकुलमालां कण्ठे ददाति. ४ अह्मेहिं वि (अस्माभिरपि). ५ प्रविश्य संभ्रान्ताः कल० बु० मद० ल० च. ६ लव०. ७ सहिदा. ८ गदेहिं अम्हेहिं कल०. ९ उवागदं.

**मालत्यवलोकिते**—हा धिक् हा धिक् सममेव हर्षोद्वेगसंभेद उपनतः । ( हद्धी हद्धी । [1]समं ज्जेव्व हरिसुव्वेअसंभेदो उवणदो । )

**माधवः**—सखि मदयन्तिके स्वागतमेह्येहि । अनुगृहीतमस्मद्गृहं भवत्या । ननु स[2] एवासौ किमित्यस्वस्था भवती । एकाकिनो[3] बहुभिरभियोग इति यत्किंचिदेतद्वयस्यस्य ।

**हरेरतुलविक्रमप्रणयलालसः[4] साहसे**
**स एव भवति क्वणत्कररुहप्रचण्डः सखा ।**
**स्फुट[5]त्करटकोटरस्खलितदानसिक्तानन-**
**द्विपेश्वरशिरःस्थिता[6]स्थिदलनैकवीरः करः ॥ ७ ॥**

तदहमपि विक्रान्तप्लुतं[7] विलसतः प्रियसुहृदः प्रत्यनन्तरो भवामि ।

( इति विकटं परिक्रम्य कलहंसकेन सह निष्क्रान्तः । )

**अर्व० लव० बुद्धरक्षिताः**—अपि नामानाहतौ प्रतिनिवर्तिष्येते एतौ महानुभावौ । ( अवि णाम अणाहदा पडिणिव्वट्टिस्सन्दि एदे महाणुहावा । )

**मालती**—सख्यावलोकिताबुद्धरक्षिते त्वरितं गत्वा भगवत्या एतं वृत्तान्तं निवेदयतम् । त्वमपि प्रियसखि लवङ्गिके त्वरितं विज्ञापयार्यपुत्रं यदि तावद्युष्माकं वयमनुकम्पनीयास्ततोऽप्रमत्ताः परिक्रामतेति । ( सहिओ [8]अवलोइदाबुद्धरक्खिदाओ तुरिदं गदुअ भअवदीए एदं उत्तन्दं णिवेदेह[9] । तुमं वि पिअसहि लवङ्गिए विण्णावेहि अज्जउत्तं जइ दाव तुह्माणं अह्मे अणुकम्पणीआओ तदो अप्पमत्ता[12] परिक्कमेद्धत्ति । )

( निष्क्रान्ता[13] लवङ्गिकाबुद्धरक्षितावलोकिताः । )

---

पारक्यं परकीयम् । **माधवः** । स्वागतं कुशलम् । स एव प्रसिद्धपौरुषः । असौ मकरन्दः । यत्किंचिदिति न गणनीयमित्यर्थः । **हरेरित्यादि** । हरेः सिंहस्य स उक्तगुणः कर एव सखा द्वितीयो भवति । विक्रमे कर्तव्ये । नान्यमत्रापेक्षत इत्यर्थः । करः कीदृशः । अतिपराक्रमप्रश्रये सतृष्णः । शब्दायमाननखैः प्रचण्डः । स्फुटतः करटस्य गण्डस्थलस्य मध्याच्च्युतेन मदजलेन सिक्तमुखहस्तिराजमस्तकस्थितास्थिविदारणे श्रेष्ठवीरः । तथा च सखा मकरन्दः सिंह इव साहसे द्वितीयानपेक्ष इत्यर्थः । 'काकेभगण्डौ करटौ' इत्यमरः । 'निष्कुहः कोटरं वा ना इत्यपि ॥ ७ ॥ विक्रान्तस्य वीरस्य प्लुतं गतिविशेषम् । विलसतः कुर्वतः । प्रत्यनन्तरो द्वितीयः ।

---

१ समकालं. २ स्वस्था भवन्तु भवत्यः. ३ ०नोऽपि. ४ सस्याहवे. ५ स्फुरत्. ६ स्थिरा; कदनास्थिरेकः ७ विक्रान्तिपूतं-र्वं; विक्रमानुरूपं; न्तिपूतः सुहृदः प्रत्यन्तरो०. ८ अवलोकितादयः. ९ अप्पाडिहदा. १० बुद्ध० वलो० ११ कहेध. १२ ०मत्तं. १३ मालतीमदयन्तिकावर्जं सर्वास्तयेति निष्क्रान्ताः ।

**मालती**—हा धिक् हा धिक् । न ज्ञायते कथं वेला गम्यतामिति । भवतु । प्रियसख्या लवङ्गिकायाः प्रतिनिवृत्तिमार्गमवलोकयन्ती स्थास्यामि । ( परिक्रामति । सातङ्कम्[1] ) स्फुरितं मे वाममवामलोचनेन । ( हद्धी हद्धी । ण जाणीअदि कधं[2] वेला गमिअदि[3] त्ति । होदु । पिअसहीए[4] लवङ्गिआए पडिणिउत्तिमग्गं ओलोअन्ती चिट्ठिस्सम् । फुरिदं[5] मे वामं अवामलोअणेन । ) ( उपविशति । )

( प्रविश्य[6] )

**कपालकुण्डला**—आः पापे तिष्ठ ।

**मालती**—( सत्रासम् । ) हा आर्यपुत्र । ( हा अज्जउत्त । ) ( इत्यर्धोक्ते वाक्स्तम्भं नाटयति । )

**कपाल०**—( सक्रोधहासम् । ) नन्वाक्रन्द[7] ।

**त्वद्वत्सलः क्व स[8] तपस्विजनस्य हन्ता**
**कन्याविटः पतिरसौ परिरक्षतु[10] त्वाम् ।**
**श्येनावपातचकिता वन[11]वर्तिकेव**
**किं चेष्टसे[12] ननु चिरात्कवलीकृतासि ॥ ८ ॥**

यावच्छ्रीपर्वतमुपानीय[13] लवशो[14] लवश एनां निकृत्य दुःखमरणां करोमि । ( इति मालतीमाक्षिप्य[15] निष्क्रान्ता । )

---

**मालती** । [ स्फुरितमिति ] अत्र वाममनिष्टम् । अवामो दक्षिणः । दक्षिणाक्षिस्पन्दनं स्त्रीणामनिष्टसूचकमिति भावः । अनेन कपालकुण्डलाप्रवेशोऽपि सूचितः ॥ **त्वदि-त्यादि** । ननु हे स त्वत्प्रियः क्व वर्तते । तापसजनस्याघोरघण्टस्य घातकः । कन्याया विटोऽतिकामुकोऽसौ त्वां रक्षतु । अत एव पातीति पतिः । यच्चिराय कवलितासि किं चेष्टसे वनवर्तिकेव । श्येनः 'सैवान' इति ख्यातः पक्षी । तस्याव-पातोऽतिवेगस्तेन त्रस्तारण्यवर्तिका यथेत्यर्थः । 'वर्तको वर्तिकादयः' इत्यमरः । अत्र वनग्रहणेन वर्तिकायाः स्वकुलवेष्टितत्वमुक्तम् । एतस्यास्तद्वैपरीत्यमिति भावः । यद्वा वनेनारक्षितत्वेन वर्तिकाया अतिभीरुत्वमुक्तम् । यद्वा वनावस्थानेन वर्तिकाया एकाकिनीत्वमुक्तम् । अत एव मालत्यपि तथेति साम्यम् । नववर्तिकेत्यपि पाठः ॥ ८ ॥ लवशो लवशोऽनेककणान् कृत्वा । आक्षिप्य गृहीत्वा ।

---

१ साशंकम्. २ कधं इयदी; लवंगिका किं चिराअदि कधं एदावदी. ३ अतिक्कमेम. ४ पिअसहिम्द०. ५ फुरिदं क्खु मे वामेदरेण; लोअणेण अणेन. ६ ततः प्रविशति कपा०. ७ अक्रन्द आक्रन्द. ८ वल्लभः. ९ नु. १० रक्षति-क्षिता. ११ नव, ०तानन. १२ नेक्षसे ननु मया. १३ उत्तीर्य. १४ प्रतिपर्व तिलशः १५ आदाय; मालत्यासह.

मद०—अहमपि मालतीमेवानुगमिष्यामि । (परिक्रम्य) सखि मालति । (अहं वि मालदीं जेव्व अणुगमिस्सं । सहि मालदि ।)

लव०—(प्रविश्य ।) सखि मदयन्तिके लवङ्गिका खल्वहम् । (सहि मदअन्तिए लवङ्गिआ क्खु अहं)

मद०—अपि संभावितस्त्वया महाभागः । (अवि संभाविदो तुए महाभाओ ।)

लव०—नहि नहि । स खलूद्यानवाटोपनिर्गमादेव कलकलं श्रुत्वा सावक्षेपापविद्धविकटोरुदण्डनिष्ठुरं प्रधाव्य परानीकं प्रविष्टः । ततः प्रतिनिवृत्तास्मि मन्दभागिनी । शृणोमि च गृहे गृहे गुणानुरागनिर्भरस्य पौरलोकस्य हा माधव महानुभाव हा मकरन्द साहसिकेति परिदेवनाः । महाराजोपि किल मन्त्रिदुहित्रोर्विप्रलम्भवृत्तान्तं श्रुत्वा संजातमत्सराधिक्षेपस्तत्क्षणविसर्जितानेकप्रौढपदातिनिवहश्चन्द्रातपेन सौधशिखरस्थितः प्रेक्षत इति मन्त्र्यते । (णहि णहि । सो क्खु उज्जाणवा[1]डोवणिग्गमादो ज्जेव्व कलअल सुणिअ सावक्खेवावविद्धवि[2]अडोरुदण्डणि[3]ट्ठुरं पधा[4]विअ पराणीअं पविट्टो । तदो पडिणिउत्तह्मि मन्दभाइणी । सुणेमि अ घरे घरे गुणाणुराअणिब्भरस्स पोरलोअस्स हा माहव महाणुभाव हा मअरन्द साहसिअ त्ति परिदेवणाओ । महाराओ वि किल मन्तिधीआणं विप्पलम्भवुत्तन्तं सुणिअ संजादमच्छेराधिक्खेवो तक्खणविसज्जिदाणेअप्पोढपदाइणिवहो च[11]न्दादवेण सोहसिहरट्ठिदो पेक्खदित्ति मन्तीअदि ।)

मद०—हा हतास्मि मन्दभागिनी । (हा हदह्मि मन्दभाइणी ।)

लव०—सखि मालती पुनः क्व । (सहि मालदी उण कहिं ।)

---

मदयन्तिका । अत्रापिः प्रश्ने । संभावितो लब्धः । लवङ्गिका । अत्र उपनिर्गमः समीपगमनम् । एतेन मार्गस्य शून्यत्वमुक्तम् । अवक्षेपोऽवहेला । अपविद्धमःक्रान्तम् । विशालोरुयुगलदण्डाभ्यां निर्भरं गाढं यथा तथा धावित्वेत्यर्थः । अनीकं सैन्यम् । धिआ दुहिता । विप्रलम्भो वञ्चनम् । चन्द्रातपश्चन्द्रप्रकाशः । मालत्या वियोगदशायां तापकत्वेनानुभवादातप इत्युक्तम् । मन्त्र्यते पौरलोकेनैव । मदयन्तिका । अत्र

---

१ अणुवट्टिस्सं. २ पिअसहि. ३ अइ. ४ वाडणि०. ५ साधिक्खेवं दूरणिक्खेवा०. ६ विअडणिजोरु (निजोरु). ७ णिब्भरं. ८ महाभाअ. ९ मच्छरावेओ. १० पाइक्क. ११ चन्दादवमोहिद(शोभित)सोह०.

मद०—सखि सा खलु प्रथममेव ते मार्गवमलोकयितुं प्रसृता । पश्चादहं तां न प्रेक्षे । अपि नामोद्यानगहनं प्रविष्टा भवेत् । ( सहि सा क्खु पढमं एव्व दे मग्गं ओलोइदुं पसरिदा । पच्चादो अहं तं ण पेक्खामि । अवि णाम उज्जाणगहणं पविट्ठा भवे । )

लव०—सखि त्वरितमन्विष्यावः । अतिकातरा मे प्रियसखी उपस्थितानर्थेऽस्मिन्नवसरे सा न धारयत्यात्मानम् । ( त्वरितं परिक्रम्य । ) सखि मालति ननु भणामि सखि मालतीति । ( सहि तुरिदं अण्णेसह्म । अदिकातरा मे पिअसही उवट्ठिदानत्थे इमस्सिं अवसरे सा न धारेदि अत्ताणं । सहि मालदि णं भणामि सहि मालादि त्ति । ) ( इतस्ततः परिक्रामतः । )

( प्रविश्य प्रहृष्टः )

कलहंसकः—दिष्ट्या कुशलेन वयं निर्गताः संघट्टदुर्गमात् । हीमाणहे प्रक्ष्यामीव निर्मलनिरन्तरोद्धूतधौततरवारिधारापरिस्फुरितचन्द्रकिरणोज्ज्वल-भीषणदर्शनं मदलीलाकलितकामपालविकटभुजदण्डाविद्धहलहेलाविक्षुभितो-द्वेल्लिततरगकलिन्दतनयास्रोतःसंनिभंविकटविश्रृङ्खलोत्पतितनिर्दयामन्दमक-रन्दव्यतिकरक्षोभविकलप्रतियोधपरिवर्तनोद्गतसमस्तगगनाङ्गनावकाशविशं-कलितकलकलं पारक्यबलसमूहम् । स्मरामि च भीषणभुजवज्रजर्जरित-पञ्जरावसन्नसुभटहस्तावलुप्तविविधायुधनिवहघातिताशेषरिपुसैन्यदत्तविकटा-पसाररिक्तमार्गसंचारनिर्वर्तितविषमसमरसाहसं नाथमाधवम् ।

---

प्रसृता निर्गता । अहं प्रसृतेत्यन्वयः । अपीत्यादि शङ्कायाम् । **लवङ्गिका** । अत्र नन्वहम् । अव्ययत्वादनेकार्थत्वम् । तथा च मद्वचनमपि न शृणोषीत्यर्थः । **कलहंसकः** । अत्र हीमाणहे इति हे मातरिरितिवन्नीचस्य हर्षाश्चर्ये । पश्यामीव परबलमित्यन्वयः । धौतो निशितः । तरवारिः खड्गः । विधुरिलं भीषणम् । कलितः स्वीकृतः । 'कलिवली कामधेनू' इति शाब्दिकाः । 'कामपालो हलायुधः' इत्यमरः । आविद्धा वक्रं प्रेरिता । हेला क्रीडा । कलिन्दतनया यमुना । संनिभमिति यथा बलेन हलाकृष्टा यमुना प्रतीपमागता तथा परबलमपीति भावः । विस्तारेण वा बलस्य तादृग्यमुनासाम्यम् । विकटं विस्तीर्णं यथा तथा । विश्रृङ्खलः आपतितः संमुखागतः । निर्दयो निष्करुणः । अमन्दः सत्वरः । व्यतिकरेण मिलनेन क्षोभः । परिवर्तनेन पलायनेन । उद्गत उत्थितः । विशङ्कलितो व्याप्तः । 'दोर्दोषा भुजा भुजः' इति शब्दप्रकाशः । जर्जरितपञ्जरा अत एवापसृताः पलायिताः । ओअल्लोऽपसृतः । हस्तेभ्योऽवलुप्त आच्छे-

---

१ सा. २ उवत्थणट्ठिद्ग इम०. ३ अस्मात्परं लव-न्तिके-( त्वरितं परिक्रामन्त्यौ ) सहि इ०. ४ विच्छुरित.

( दिट्ठिआ कुसलेण [1]अह्मे णिग्गदा संघट्टदुग्गमादो । हीमाणहे पेक्खामि विअ णिम्मलणिरन्तर[2]रुद्धदधोदतरवारिधारापरि[3]प्फुरिदचन्दकिरणु[4]ज्जलविड्डुरिल्लदंसणं मदलीलाकलिदकामवालविअडभुअदण्डाविद्धहलहेलाविक्खुभिदुव्वेल्लिदतरंगकालिन्दतणआसोतसंणिहं विअडविसङ्कलुप्पाडिदणिद्दआमन्दमअरन्दव्वइअरक्खोभविअलपडिजोहपरिवत्तणुग्गदसमत्थगअणङ्गणावआसविसंकलि[5]दंकलअलं पारक्कबलस[6]मूहं । सुमरामि अ भीसणभुअवज्जजज्जरि[7]दपञ्जरावस[8]ण्णसुभटहत्थावलुत्तविविहा[9]उहणिअहघातिदासेसरिपुसेण्णदत्ताविअडापसाररिक्कमग्गसंचारणिव्वत्तिदविसमसमरसाहसं णाहमाहवम् । )

अहो गुणानुरागो नरेन्द्रस्य यदिदानीं सौधशिखरावतीर्णप्रतीहारविनयोपन्यासप्रशामितविरोधसंकट उपनीतमाधवमकरन्दमुखचन्द्रयोर्वारंवारं संचारितस्निग्धलोचनः कलहंसकादभिजनं ज्ञात्वा निर्वर्तितमहार्घगुरुबहुमानः प्रस्फुरन्मत्सरवैलक्ष्यमसीमलिनितमुखौ भूरिवसुनन्दने मधुरवचनोपन्यासेन किमिदानीं युवयोर्भुवनाभोगभूषणाभ्यां महानुभावाभ्यां नवयौवनगुणाभिरामाभ्यां जामातृभ्यामपरितोष इति प्रतिबोध्य गतोऽभ्यन्तरं राजा । इमावपि माधवमकरन्दावागच्छतः । अहमपि भगवत्या इमं वृत्तान्तं निवेदयामि । ( अहो गुणाणुराओ णरिन्दस्स जं दाणिं सोधसिहरावदिण्णपडिहारविणओवण्णासपसमिदविरोहसंक[10]डो उवणीदमाहवमअरन्दमुह[11]चन्दे वारंवारं सं[12]चारिदसिणिद्धलोअणो कलहंसआदो अहिजणं जाणि[13]अ णिव्वत्तिअमहग्घगुरुबहुमाणो पप्फुरन्तमच्छरवेलक्खमसीमलिणिदमुहे भूरिवसुणन्दणे म[14]हुरवअणोवण्णासेण किं दाणिं तुह्माणं भुवणाभोअभूसणेहिं महाणुहावेहिं णवजो[15]व्वणगुणाभिरामेहिं जामादुकेहिं अपरितोसो त्ति पडिबोधिअ गओ अब्भन्दरं राआ । इमे वि माहवमअरन्दा आअच्छन्दि । अहं वि भअवदीए इमं उत्तन्दं णिवेदेमि । ) ( इति निष्क्रान्तः । )

---

दितः । विकटो विषमः । अपसारः पलायनम् । रिक्तः शून्यः । **सौधेति ।** प्रतीहारेण सौधाग्रादवतीर्य तयोः स्वरूपं ज्ञात्वा तदुपन्यासः कृत इत्यर्थः । अभिजनो वंशः । बहुमानः संमानः । तावानीय दृष्ट्वा तयोः सापराधयोरपि गुणानुरागा-

---

१ ह्मि णिग्गदो...दुग्गमादो. २ रुद्धुत्त ( रोद्धृत्त. ) ३ पडिफलि ( प्रतिफलित–टी० ). ४ ज्जलरमणीयभीभण; ज्जुलन्तपिअरिअभीसण. ५ ओसरन्त ( अवसरत् ); विअसन्दकोलाहलम्. ६ पाइक्कसमूहं.. अस्मात्परं–दाणिं वि पेक्खामि विअ. इत्यधिकं क्वचित्. ७ रोवसण्ण; भुजवज्जखचितपञ्जरपज्जत्थसमरविग्गह. ८ उद्दामदसमोसारिअसेणिअणिअरं पाइक्करिक्क ( युधोपमर्दममवसारितसैनिकनिकरं पदातिरिक्त ). ९ सिहरंतारिदात्र. १० विरोहो सोभेक्करसोवणीद. ११ चन्दे ओलोइअ. १२ पसारिद. १३ सुणिअ. १४ महुरोवण्णासेण,–सेहिं. १५ दर्शन; नव–अभिजन.

( ततः प्रविशतो माधवमकरन्दौ । )

मक०—अहो प्रेयसः सर्वपुरुषातिशायि निर्व्याजमूर्जितं तेजः । तथा हि ।

दोर्निष्पेषविशीर्णसंचयवलत्कङ्कालमुन्मथ्नतः
प्राग्वीराननुपत्य तत्प्रहरणान्याच्छिद्य विक्रामतः ।
उद्वेल्लद्धनरुण्डखण्डनिकराकीर्णस्य संख्योदधे-
र्द्वेधास्तम्भितपत्तिपङ्क्तिविकटः पन्थाः पुरस्तादभूत् ॥ ९ ॥

माधवः—नन्वनुशयस्थानमेतत् । पश्य ।

अद्यैवेन्दुमयूखखण्डखचितं पीतं निशीथोत्सवे
यैर्लीलापरिरम्भदायिदयितागण्डूषशेषं मधु ।
संप्रत्येव भवद्भुजार्गलगुरुव्यापारभग्नास्थिभि-
र्गात्रैस्ते कथयन्त्यसारविधुरान्प्रायेण संसारिणः ॥ १० ॥

स्मर्तव्यं तु सौजन्यमस्य नरपतेर्यदपराद्धयोरप्यनपराद्धयोरिव नौ सांप्रतं चेष्टितवान् । तदेहि । मालतीसमक्षमधुना मदयन्तिकाहरणवृत्तान्तं विस्तरतः कथ्यमानं श्रोतुमिच्छामि । तथा च ।

कथयति त्वयि सस्मितमालतीवलितलोलकटाक्षपराहतम् ।
वदनपङ्कजमुल्लसितत्रपास्तिमितदृष्टि सखी नमयिष्यति ॥ ११ ॥

---

दतिगौरवमेव राज्ञा कृतमिति भावः । न परितोष इति नः शिरश्चालने । **मकरन्दः** । प्रेयसः प्रीतस्य । माधवस्येत्यर्थः । निर्व्याजं वास्तवम् । ऊर्जितं बलवत् । **दोरित्यादि** । प्रेयसो युद्धार्णवस्य पन्था अग्र एवमभूत् । द्वेधा पार्श्वद्वये स्तम्भितया पत्तिपङ्क्त्या भयंकरः । प्रेयसः कीदृशस्य । बाहुसंचूर्णनत्रुटितसंधिस्फुटत्कङ्कालं यथा तथा प्रथमं वीरानुन्मथ्नतोऽभिभवतः । इतरत्र तदीयायुधानि गृहीत्वा पराक्रमं कुर्वतः । इदं विशेषणद्वयं योग्यतया प्रेयस इत्यस्य । संख्योदधेः कीदृशस्य । स्फुरन्नरमुण्डखण्डसमूहव्याप्तस्य ॥ ९ ॥ **अद्येत्यादि** । यै रात्र्युत्सवे चन्द्रकिरणखण्डखचितं क्रीडालिङ्गनदातृवनितागण्डूषावशिष्टं मधु पीतमद्यैव ते संप्रत्येव लोकान्बाहुल्येन तुच्छविकलाञ्शरीरैः कथयन्ति । कीदृशैः । त्वदीयभुजार्गलप्रबलताडनात्त्रुटितास्थिभिः । तथा च क्षणदृष्टमुग्धचेष्टिताः प्राक्तनकर्मायत्ता जना इति भावः ॥ १० ॥ **कथयतीत्यादि** । त्वयि कथयति सति वदनपद्मं सखी मालत्या एव मदयन्तिका नमयिष्यति । कीदृशम् । सहासमालतीचञ्चलपक्ष्मकटाक्षैः पराहतम् । उद्गतलज्जानिश्चलदृष्टि च । मदयन्तिकानिमित्तयुद्धश्रवणेन

---

१ गलत्. २ अनुपात्य. ३ लुन्नरिरुण्ड; रुण्ड-तु-मु-ण्ड. ४ वयस्य ननु. ५ निचितं. ६ तैः. ७ भिदुरान्. ८ अपराधिनोः. ९ कृतोपसदनं, कृतप्रसादम्. १० चलित. ११ त्रपं, सितभ्रु ततः.

( इति परिक्रामतः । ) अयमसावुद्यानवटः । ( प्रविशतः । )

**माधवः**—कथं शून्य[1] एव दीर्घिकाप्रदेशः ।

**मकरन्दः**—वयस्य नूनं[2] मस्मद्व्यतिकरोद्वेगपर्याकुलत्वादितस्ततः परिभ्रमन्त्य आत्मानमत्रैवोद्यानगहने विनोदयन्त्यो[3] भविष्यन्ति । तदेहि पश्यावः ।

( उभौ परिक्रामतः । )

**लवङ्गिकामदयन्तिके**—सखि मालति । ( सहसावलोक्य[4] सहर्षम् । ) दिष्ट्या पुनरप्येतावनाहतौ महानुभावौ दृश्येते । ( सहि मालदि । ) ( दिट्ठिआ पुणो वि एदे अणाहदा महाणुभाआ दीसन्ति । )

**माधवमकरन्दौ**—भवत्यौ क्व[5] मालती ।

**उभे**—कुतो मालती । पदशब्देनावां विप्रलब्धे मन्दभागिन्यौ । ( कुदो मालदी । पदसद्देण अह्मे विप्पलद्धाओ मन्दभाइणीओ । )

**माधवः**—भवत्यौ कथं[6] कथमपि सहस्रधैव विध्वंसते मे[7] हृदयमतः स्पष्टमभिधीयताम् ।

> **मम हि कुवलयाक्षीं प्रत्यनिष्टैकबुद्धे-**
> **र्भृशमयमनुबद्धोत्कम्प एवान्तरात्मा[8] ।**
> **स्फुरति च[9] खलु चक्षुर्वाममेतच्च कष्टं**
> **वचनमिह[10] भवत्योः सर्वथा हा हतोऽस्मि ॥ १२ ॥**

**मद०**—तया खल्वितो निर्गते महानुभावे बुद्धरक्षितामवलोकितां च भगवतीसकाशं विसृज्याप्रमादनिमित्तं विज्ञापयार्यपुत्रमिति लवङ्गिकानुप्रेषिता । तत उत्ताम्यमानैतस्या मार्गमवलोकयितुमग्रतः

---

मालत्या हासः ॥ ११ ॥ **लवङ्गिकामदयन्तिके** । अत्रानेनावाभ्यां समर्थिता मालती । अधुना तु युवयोरवलोकनेनावां वञ्चिते इत्यर्थः । **माधवः** । कथमिति त्रासे । कथमप्यनिर्वचनीयेन रूपेण ध्वंसते । स्थितिं न बध्नाति । **ममेत्यादि** । यतोऽयं ममान्तरात्मात्यर्थमनुगतोत्कम्प एवास्ति । कीदृशस्य । पद्माक्षीं प्रत्यनिष्टैकमतेः । मम वामं चक्षुः स्फुरति च । इह भवत्योर्वचनम् । कष्टमेतद्दुःखदायि । हा कष्टे । सर्वथा हतोऽस्मि । अन्तरात्मनोऽशकुनस्य भवद्वचनस्य चैकमत्यादिति भावः ॥ १२ ॥ **मदयन्तिका** । अत्र पश्चादाद्यां प्रसृते इत्यन्वयः । विचितान्य-

---

१ शून्या इवामी–इदानीमिमे–प्रदेशाः. २ नूनं शङ्के आवयोः समरसंकटोद्वेगेन व्याकुलत्वात्. ३ विनोदयन्ति. ४ विलोक्य. ५ क्वासौ, क्व सा. ६ कथमिव सहसैव. ७ नो. ८ द्रवति हृदयमन्तर्भ्रंशयती० ९ हि…चक्षुः स्पष्टमेतच्च वामं. १० नमपि.

प्रसृता । पश्चादहम् । ततो न प्रेक्षे । तत आवाभ्यां यावद्विट-पान्तराणि विचितानि तावद्युवां दृष्टाविति । ( तए क्खु इदो णिग्गदे महाणुहावे बुद्धरक्खिदं अवलोइदं अ भअवदीसआसं विसज्जिअ अप्पमादणिमित्तं विण्णवेहि अज्ज-उत्तं त्ति लवङ्गिआ अणुप्पेसिदा । तदो उतम्ममाणा एदाए मग्गं ओलोइदुं अग्गदो पस-रिदा[1] । पच्छादो[2] अहं । तदो ण पेक्खामि । तदो अह्मेहिं[3] जाव विडवन्दराइं विजिणिदाइं ताव तुह्मे दिठ्ठत्ति । )

माधवः—हा प्रिये मालति

किमपि किमपि[4] शङ्के मङ्गलेभ्यो यदन्य-
द्विरमतु परिहासश्चण्डि पर्युत्सुकोऽस्मि ।
कलयसि[5] कलितोऽहं वल्लभे देहि वाचं
भ्रमति हृदयमन्तर्विह्वलं निर्दयासि ॥ १३ ॥

उभे—हा प्रियसखि कासि । ( हा पिअसहि कहिं सि[6] । )

मक०—वयस्य किमित्यविज्ञाय वैक्लव्यमवलम्ब्यते ।

माधवः—सखे त्वमपि किं न जानासि माधवस्नेह[7]दुःखितायास्तस्याः कातर्यचेष्टितानि ।

मक०—अस्त्येतत् । किं तु भगवतीपादमूलगमनमप्याशङ्क्यते[8] । तदेहि तत्र तावत्पश्यावः[9] ।

उभे—एतदपि संभाव्यते । ( इदं वि संभावीअदि । )

माधवः—एवं नामास्तु । ( इति परिक्रामति[10] । )

मकरन्दः—( विचिन्त्य स्वगतम् । )

---

न्विष्टानि । **किमपीत्यादि** । मङ्गलेभ्योऽन्यदनिष्टं किमप्यनिर्वचनीयं यद्यस्मा-त्परिहासादहं शङ्के स परिहासो विरमतु । परिहासेन तव निह्नवेऽनिष्टं शङ्केऽतस्तं मुञ्चेति भावः । हे चण्डि कोपने समुत्सुकोऽस्मि यतः । तथा च कोपेनापि निह्नवं मा कुर्वित्याशयः । अथ मामनेन प्रकारेण कलयसि जिज्ञाससे तर्हि कलितो ज्ञातो ऽहम् । हे वल्लभे वाचं देहि । त्वमेव वल्लभा । अतो वदेत्यर्थः । विह्वलमधीरं सन्मम चित्तमन्तर्भ्रमति स्थितिं न लभते । अत एव सोपालम्भमाह निष्करुणासि ॥ १३ ॥ **मकरन्दः** । वैक्लव्यं दुःखितत्वम् । **माधवः** । कातर्यं कातरत्वं तेन चेष्टितानि

---

१ °रिदा मालती. २ पच्छादो अह्मे न तां पेक्खामो. ३ अह्मेहिं मग्गिदा एत्थ विड° जाव तुह्मे. ४ मनसि. ५ कलय विक°. ६ गदा।।से. ७ मत्स्नेह. ८ गच्छाव. ९ एवं. १० सर्वे परिक्रामन्ति.

याता भवेद्भगवतीभवनं सखी नो[2]
जीवन्त्युपेष्यति[3] न वेत्यभि[4]शङ्कितोऽस्मि ।
प्रायेण बान्धवसुहृत्प्रियसंगमादि
सौदामनीस्फुरणचञ्चलमेव सौख्यम् ॥ १४॥

( इति निष्क्रान्ताः सर्वे । )

इति मालत्यपहारो नामाष्टमोऽङ्कः ।

---

प्राणत्यागादीनि । **यातेत्यादि** । अस्माकं सखी भगवतीगृहं यदि गता भवेत्तदा जीवन्ती समागमिष्यति । न वा गता तदा नागमिष्यतीत्याशङ्कितोऽस्मि । तत्र हेतुः । बन्धुजनमित्रप्रियाणां संगम आदौ यस्य तत्सौख्यं बाहुल्येन विद्युत्स्फुरणचञ्चलमेव भवति । तदिह भगवतीपादमूलेति साधारणपदोल्लेखेन मालत्या भविष्यत्सौदामिनी-पार्श्वगमनस्य सूचनेन नवमाङ्कावतारोऽपि सूचितः । अत एवाङ्कावतारोऽयम् । यदाह—'समाप्यमान एकस्मिन्नङ्केऽन्यस्य च सूचनम् । समासतो हि नाट्यज्ञैरङ्कावतार उच्यते' ॥ सुहृन्मित्रम् । प्रियं प्रीतिविषयं मनोज्ञं वस्तु ॥ १४ ॥

सूते स्म यं रत्नधरोऽतिमान्यो मान्यातिमान्या मदयन्तिकापि ।
जगद्धरं तत्कृतटिप्पणेऽङ्को गतोऽष्टमोऽयं रसरम्यरूपः ॥

इत्यष्टमोऽङ्कः ।

---

१ सद्नं. २ सा. ३ त्यथैष्यति. ४ चेत्य., त्युपश०

# नवमोऽङ्कः ।

( ततः प्रविशति सौदामिनी । )

**सौदामिनी**—एषास्मि सौदामिनी भगवतः श्रीपर्वतादुत्पेत्य[1] पद्मावतीमुपाश्रिता । [2]मालतीविरहिणः संस्तुतप्रदेशदर्शनासहिष्णोः संस्त्यायं परित्यज्य सह सुहृद्वर्गेण बृहद्द्रोणीशैलकान्तारप्रदेशम[3]धितिष्ठतो माधवस्याधुनान्तिकं प्रयामि । भोस्तथाहमुत्पतिता यथा सकल एष गिरिनगरग्रामसरिदरण्यव्यतिकरश्चक्षुषा परिक्षिप्यते[4] । ( पश्चाद्विलोक्य । )

> **पद्मावती विमले[5]वारिविशालसिन्धु-**
> **पारासरित्परिकरच्छलतो बिभर्ति ।**
> **उत्तुङ्गसौधसुर[6]मन्दिरगोपुराट्ट-**
> **संघट्टपाटितविमुक्तमिवान्तरिक्षम् ॥ १ ॥**

अपि च ।

> **सैषा विभाति लवणा[7] ललितो[8]र्मिपङ्क्ति-**
> **रभ्रागमे जनपदप्रमदाय यस्याः ।**
> **गोगर्भिणीप्रियनवोलपमालभारि-**
> **सेव्योपकण्ठविपिनावलयो भवन्ति[9] ॥ २ ॥**

---

अधुना पूर्वसूचितसौदामिन्या मालतीजीवननिवेदनेन माधवप्रत्युज्जीवनाय प्रवेशमाह—**तत इति** । नानासिद्धिस्थानत्वेन देवतात्मकतया भगवत्पदं श्रीपर्वते । संस्तुतः परिचितः द्रोणी नद्या मध्यम् । तथेत्यनेनोत्पतनस्य दूरत्वमुक्तम् । व्यतिकरः समूहः । परिक्षिप्यत इव नेत्रमण्डले प्रविष्टीक्रियत इव । **पद्मावतीत्यादि** । पद्मावती पुरी गगनमिव धारयति । विमलवारिरच्छजला महती सिन्धुश्च पारा च सरितौ तयोः परिकरो वेष्टनं तद्व्याजात् । उच्छ्रितप्रासाददेवकुलपुरद्वाराट्टालिकानां घर्षणेनादौ विदीर्णं ततो विशेषेणोभयतस्त्यक्तम् । उत्तुङ्गसौधादय आकाशं पाटयित्वा निर्गताः । अथ नदीच्छलेन तदाकाशं पतितमिवेत्यर्थः ॥ १ ॥ **सैषेत्यादि** । सैषा लवणा नदीभेदो विभाति । मनोज्ञकल्लोलावलिः । वर्षासु यस्या गवां गर्भिणीनां प्रिया नवा योलपमाला तृणविशेषराजिस्ता बिभ्रति । ताच्छील्ये णिनिः । अत एव सेव्याः परिशीलकसुखदाः समीपवनपङ्क्तयो लोकहर्षाय भवन्तीति । सैषेत्यनेन पूर्वदृष्टत्वमुक्तम् । अपो बिभर्तीत्यभ्रम् । अभ्रति गच्छति ।

---

१ दुपेत्य. २ तत्र मा०. ३ शमुपश्रुत्याधुना; प्रवेशो माधवस्य तदन्तिकमनुप्रयामि. ४ परिक्षिप्यंते. ५ विपुल. ६ पुरगोपुरमन्दिरा. ७ वरदा. ८ चलितो०, वलितो. ९ बिभान्ति.

( अन्यतोऽवलोक्य । ) अयमसौ भगवत्याः सिन्धोर्दारितरसातलस्तटप्रपातः ।

यत्रत्य एष तुमुलध्वनिरम्बुगर्भ-
गम्भीरनूतनघनस्तानितप्रचण्डः ।
पर्यन्तभूधरनिकुञ्जविजृम्भमाणो
हेरम्बकण्ठरसितप्रतिमानमेति ॥ ३ ॥

एताश्च चन्दनाश्वकर्णकेसरपाटलाप्रायतरुगहनाः परिणतमालूरसुरभयोऽरण्यगिरिभूमयः स्मारयन्ति खलु तरुणकदम्बजम्बूवनावनद्धान्धकारगुरुनिकुञ्जगम्भीरगह्वरोद्गारगोदावरीमुखरितस्निग्धविशालमेखलाभुवो दक्षिणारण्यभूधरान् । अयं च मधुमतीसिन्धुसंभेदपावनो भगवान्भवानीपतिरपौरुषेयप्रतिष्ठः सुवर्णबिन्दुरित्याख्यायते । ( प्रणम्य । )

जय देव भुवनभावन जय भगवन्नखिलवरद निगमनिधे ।
जय रुचिरचन्द्रशेखर जय मदनान्तक जयादिगुरो ॥ ४ ॥

---

वेत्यत्रम् । अतो बकारयुक्तं तत् । अयुक्तं चेदं पदमित्यवधेयम् । चतुष्पादो गर्भिण्येति समासः । 'उलपो नाम तृणान्तरे' इति मेदिनीकरः । मालभारीत्यत्र 'इष्टकेषीकमालानां चिततूलभारिषु' इति ह्रस्वः ॥ २ ॥ रसातलतटः पृथ्वीतटः । तलशब्दः स्वरूपे । प्रपातोऽतटम् । यद्वा तटे प्रपातोऽतिशयितं पतनम् ॥ **यत्रत्येत्यादि** । यदीय एष महाध्वनिः सिन्धोः पर्यन्तगिरिकुञ्जेषु वर्धमानो विघ्नेशगलध्वनिसाम्यं गच्छति । तस्य गजास्यत्वेन गभीरध्वनित्वात् । कीदृशः । जलपूर्णगभीरनवमेघध्वनिवत्प्रचण्डः । 'तुमुलो महति स्मृतः' इति विश्वः ॥ ३ ॥ चन्दनं रक्तचन्दनं देवदारु वा । उपचारात् । अन्यथास्य मलयजत्वविरोधात् । अश्वकर्णो वृक्षभेदः । प्रायःशब्दः प्रभृत्यर्थो बाहुल्यार्थो वा । परिणतं पक्वम् । मालूरं बिल्वफलम् । तरुणो वृक्षभेदः । अवनद्धो धृतः । उद्गारः प्रतिशब्दः । गोदावरीनदीभेदः । मेखला नितम्बः । भूधरान्मलयादीन् । सौदामिन्या दक्षिणदेशवासित्वेन स्मरणम् । मधुमतीसिन्ध्वोर्नद्योः संभेदः संगमस्तस्य पावनः पावित्र्यहेतुः । स्वयंभूसंनिधानस्य महातीर्थहेतुत्वात् । अपरिमिताज्ञाता पुरुषकृता प्रतिष्ठा स्थितिर्यस्य । एतेन स्वयंभूतत्वमुक्तम् । आख्यानं प्रसिद्धिः ॥ अदृष्टार्थं शिवनुतिमाह—**जयेति** । भुवनानां कार्यजातानां भावन उत्पादक । दीव्यतीति देव द्युतियुक्त । भगवन् भगं तत्वज्ञानं तद्युक्त । तथा च रागद्वेषादिरहित इत्यर्थः । स्तुतिफलमाह—अखिलवरान्भुक्तिमुक्त्यादीन्ददाति तादृशो निगमो वेदस्तन्निधे तत्कर्तः । यद्वा निगम आविर्भावस्तदाश्रय । तथा च । वेदद्वाराविर्भावेन जगदुपकारक इत्यर्थः ।

---

१ विलोक्य. २ स एष. ३ तुमुलः ४ स्वनेन. ५ रणित. ६ सरल. ७ बद्ध. ८ गुरुगिरिनिकुञ्जगुञ्जद्गम्भीरगह्वरोद्गारघोरघोषणगोदा. ९ सकल. १० न्निखिल०, निखिलवाङ्निगम. ११ जय जया.

( गमनमभिनीय । )

अयमभिनवमेघश्यामलोत्तुङ्गसानु-
मदमुखरमयूरीमुक्तसंसक्तकेकः ।
शकुनिशबलनीडानोकहस्निग्धवर्ष्मा
वितरति बृहदश्मा पर्वतः प्रीतिमक्ष्णोः ॥ ५ ॥

अपि च ।

दधाति कुहरभाजामत्र भल्लूकयूना-
मनुरसितगुरूणि स्त्यानमम्बूकृतानि ।
शिशिरकटुकषायः स्त्यायते सल्लकीना-
मिभदलितविकीर्णग्रन्थिनिष्यन्दगन्धः ॥ ६ ॥

( ऊर्ध्वमवलोक्य । ) अये कथं मध्याह्नः । तथा ह्यत्र संप्रति

काश्मर्याः कृतमालमुद्गतदलं कोयष्टिकष्टीकते
तीराश्मन्तकशिम्बिचुम्बिनमुखा धावन्त्यपः पूर्णिकाः ।
दात्यूहैस्तिनिशस्य कोटरवति स्कन्धे निलीय स्थितं
वीरुन्नीडकपोतकूजितमनुक्रन्दन्त्यधः कुक्कुभाः ॥ ७ ॥

---

मनोज्ञचन्द्रभूषण । तथा च वेदकारणाय कृतशरीरपरिग्रह इत्यर्थः । तर्हि पौरुषेयत्वाद्वेदाप्रामाण्यं स्यादित्यत आह–मदनेति । सर्वदोषनिधेः कामस्य नाशन निर्दोष । अत एव भगवन् । तथा च नोक्तदोषः । आदौ सर्गादौ गुरो । ब्रह्मादीनामित्यर्थात् । तथा च वेदस्य भगवत्कर्तृत्वमायातीति ॥ ४ ॥ **अयमित्यादि** । अयं गिरिर्नेत्रयोर्हर्षं ददाति । कीदृशः । नवीनमेघश्यामतुङ्गसानुः । हर्षप्रीतमयूरस्त्रीकृता संसक्ता मिलिता केका मयूरवाणी यत्र सः । शकुनिभिः पक्षिभिः शबला कर्बुरा ये नीडानोकहाः पक्षिवासवृक्षास्तैः स्निग्धं वर्ष्म शरीरं यस्य सः । तरूणां पक्षिव्याप्तत्वेनाशेषपक्षिणो नीड एव वसन्तीति भावः । बृहदश्मा विपुलशिलः । ' केका वाणी मयूरस्य ' इत्यमरः । ' शबलैताश्च कर्बुरः ' इति च । कुलायो नीडमस्त्रियाम् ' इति च । ' अनोकहः कुटः शालः ' इति च । ' शरीरं वर्ष्म विग्रहः ' इति च ॥ ५ ॥ **दधतीत्यादि** । अत्र गिरौ गुहावासिनां तरुणभल्लूकानामम्बूकृतानि सश्लेष्मकथूत्कारध्वनयोऽनुरसितेन प्रतिरवेण स्थूलानि स्त्यानं घनतां दधति । शल्लकीनां वृक्षभेदानां गजखण्डितविस्तीर्णसंधिपर्वनिर्गतगन्धः स्त्यायते निबिडीभवति । निष्यन्दः स्पर्शाच्छिशिरः शीतो रसतः कटुः कषायः । स्त्यानमिति भावप्रधानो निर्देशः । ' अम्बूकृतं सनिष्ठीवम् ' इत्यमरः ॥ ६ ॥ **काश्मर्या इत्यादि** । गम्भार्याः सकाशात्कृतमालमारग्वधवृक्षमुद्भूतपत्रम् । घनच्छायमिति यावत् ।

---

१. मयूरा०. २ नीला. ३ स महीयान्. ४ भाजां मत्तभ०. ५ शल्ल०. ६ तीरान्तंबिक, तीराश्मा०; श्मान्तरकच्छ०. ७ तिनिशस्य ८ कुक्कुटाः.

तद्भवतु[1] । माधवमकरन्दावन्विष्य यथाप्रस्तुतं साधयामि । ( इति निष्क्रान्ता । )

विष्कम्भकः[2] ।

( ततः प्रविशतो[3] माधवमकरन्दौ । )

**मक०**—( सकरुणं निःश्वस्य । )

**न यत्र प्रत्याशामनुपतति नो वा[4] रहयति**
**प्रविक्षिप्तं[5] चेतः प्रविशति च मोहान्धतमसम् ।**
**अकिंचित्कुर्वाणाः पशव इव तस्यां[6] वयमहो**
**विधातुर्वामत्वाद्विपदि परिवर्तामह इमे ॥ ८ ॥**

कोयष्टिकः 'कोवा' इति ख्यातः पक्षी टीकते गच्छति । गम्भार्यां अल्पपत्रत्वात् । यद्वा कृता संपन्ना माला वृक्षपङ्क्तिर्यत्र तं प्रदेशं गच्छतीत्यर्थः । तीरस्थोऽश्मन्तकस्तीराश्मन्तकः । शाकपार्थिवादिः । 'अश्मन्तकोल्लकोला' इति ख्यात आम्रातको वा वीरणं वा । तस्य शिम्बिः शिखा लताभेदो वा तस्याश्चुम्बिनं चुम्बनकरणं मुखं यासां तादृशाः पूर्णिकाः पक्षजातयः अपः पानीयानि धावन्ति गच्छन्ति । ग्रीष्मतप्तास्ता नीडं विहाय जलमनुगच्छन्तीत्यर्थः । यद्वा तीराश्मन्तकं तीरवर्ति वीरणमपःपूर्णिकाः कुम्भीरमाक्षिका धावन्ति व्रजन्ति । ग्रीष्मतप्तजलं त्यक्त्वा तीरवीरणादिच्छायामनुसरन्तीत्यर्थः । यद्वा अश्मन्तकं शिंशिपावृक्षस्तस्य शिम्बिरग्रमित्यर्थः । तिनिशस्यातिमुक्ताख्यवृक्षस्य छिद्रवति स्कन्धे प्रकाण्डे छायासेवनार्थं दात्यूहैः पक्षिभेदैः 'कोण्डाडाडक' इति ख्यातैर्निलीय स्थितम् । वीरुल्लता नीडं वासो यस्य कपोतस्य पाण्डुनामपक्षिणः शब्दितं लक्षीकृत्य कुक्कुभा अधस्तरूणां रुदन्ति । ग्रीष्मतापात्कपोता निजनीडवासिनः कुक्कुभाश्च तृषार्ता रुदन्तीत्यर्थः । जातिस्वभाव एवासौ । यद्वा कुक्कुभाः क्रन्दन्त्याह्लादयन्ति । अहो कपोतरुतमित्यभिलषन्तीत्यर्थः । 'गम्भारी सर्वतोभद्रा काश्मरी मधुपर्णिका । ' इत्यमरः । 'आरग्वधे राजवृक्षशम्याकचतुरङ्गुलाः । आरेवतव्याधिघातकृतमालसुवर्णकाः । ' ॥ इति च । 'कोयष्टिकष्टिट्टिभकः' इत्यपि । आम्रातकेऽम्लिकायामश्मन्तको वीरणेऽपि च । शिंशिपाश्मन्तकं प्राहुः' इति धरणिः । शिम्बिः शिखा लताभेदः' इति विश्वः । 'नासाच्छिन्न्यां तु पूर्णिका' इति च । पूर्णिका पल्लीति ख्याता पतविङ्गेति ख्याता वा । 'अपःपूर्णिका कुम्भिरमाक्षिका' इत्यपि धरणिः । दात्यूहः कालकण्टकः' इत्यमरः । 'तिनिशे स्यन्दनो नेमी रथद्रुरतिमुक्तकः । ' इति च । 'अस्त्री प्रकाण्डः स्कन्धः स्यात्' इति च । 'तित्तिरिः कुम्कुभो लावः' इति च । मयूरप्रमाणोऽयं पक्षी ॥ ७ ॥ तदित्युपसंहारे । **विष्कम्भक इति** । शुद्धविष्कम्भकोऽयम । यदाह—'शुद्धो मध्यमपात्रेण संस्कृतोक्त्या निबध्यते' ॥ इति । **न यत्रेत्यादि** । यैरस्माभिस्तादृशं राजसैन्यं जितमिमे वयं स्रष्टुर्वाम्याद्विपत्तौ पुनःपुनर्वर्तामहे ।

१ यावत. २ शुद्धावि०. ३ प्रविशति मा० मकरन्दश्च. ४ वाहयति च. ५ प्रतिक्षिप्तं. ६ तस्याः.

**माधवः**—हा प्रिये मालति क्वासि । कथमविज्ञाततत्त्वमद्भुतं झटिति पर्यवसितासि । मन्दकरुणे प्रसीद । संभावय माम् ।

प्रियमाधवे किमसि मय्यवत्सला
ननु सोऽहमेव यमनन्दयत्पुरा ।
स्वयमागृहीतकमनीयकंकण-
स्तव मूर्तिमानिव महोत्सवः करः ॥ ९ ॥

वयस्य मकरन्द दुर्लभः पुनर्जगति तावतः स्नेहस्य संभवः ।

सरसकुसुमक्षामैरङ्गैरनङ्गमहाज्वर-
श्चिरमविरतोन्माथी सोढः प्रतिक्षणदारुणः ।
तृणमिव ततः प्राणान्मोक्तुं मनो विधृतं तया
किमपरमतो निर्व्यूढं यत्करार्पणसाहसम् ॥ १० ॥

---

यत्र विरतौ चित्तम् । कर्तृ । प्रत्याशां नानुगच्छति न वा त्यजति । अन्वयव्यतिरेकानिश्चयात् । तथा च सा जीवति न वेति न ज्ञायत इति भावः । रहत्यागे स्वार्थे णिच् । प्रतिक्षिप्तं पुनः पुनः प्रेरितं सच्चेतः पुनर्मोहरूपगाढान्धकारं प्रविशति । किं कर्तव्यमिति न जानीम इति भावः । अत एव कामप्यर्थक्रियामकुर्वाणाः पशव इव ॥ ८ ॥ **माधवः** । यत एवाविज्ञातं तत्त्वमत एवाश्चर्यम् । पर्यवसिता समाप्तिं गता । संभावयाश्वासय । **प्रियेत्यादि** । हे प्रियमाधवे मयि किमस्निग्धासि । माधवान्यशङ्कामपनयति—ननु हे अहमेव स यं पूर्वं तव करः स्वयमनन्दयत् । तथा च माधवान्यशङ्कामपि मा कृथा इति भावः । आगृहीतमीषद्गृहीतं सात्त्विककम्पादिना चपलतया मनोज्ञसूत्रं येन सः । यद्वा आगृहीतमभिगृहीतं करसमर्पणात् । अत एव मूर्तिमान्कृतदेहपरिग्रहो महोत्सव इव । सोऽपि गृहीतमण्डनो नन्दकश्च भवति । उद्गृहीतमिति पाठ उच्चैर्गृहीतमित्यर्थः । 'कङ्कणं मण्डने सूत्रे' इति विश्वः । तादृशस्येत्यनुस्मृतिः करग्रहणमहोत्सवानुध्यानस्वास्थ्यात्तदभ्यासाद्वा । यदाह—'स्वास्थ्याभ्याससमुत्था श्रुतिदर्शनसंभवानुस्मृतिः' ॥ इति ॥ ९ ॥ **सरसेत्यादि** । तया काममहाज्वरोऽवस्थादशको बहुकालं सोढः । अनङ्ग एव महाज्वर इति वा । नवपुष्पमृदुभिरङ्गैः । कीदृशः । संततमर्मव्यथाकारी । अत एव प्रतिमुहूर्तमुन्मूलनोद्यतः । एतेन दुःसहत्वमुक्तम् । ततः प्राणांस्त्यक्तुं तया मनो विशेषेण निरपेक्षतया धृतम् । अत एव तृणमिव । सारमाह-इतः करार्पणसाहसादपरं किमस्ति । अपि तु न किमपीत्यर्थः । यत्कंरस्यार्पणं स्वयमेव दानं तदेव साहसं निर्व्यूढं निःशेषेण दोषमपहाय वृत्तम् । कुलकन्यकानां तन्निषेधात्साहसत्वम् । तृणमिवेत्यत्र लिङ्गवचनभेदे नोपमादोषो भवति ।

---

१ क्वासि देहि मे प्रतिवचनं क०. २ पुनरमं. ३ अयमा. ४ पुनस्तादृशस्य स्नेहस्य, पुनः खलु. ५ सरल. ६ मितो.

अपि च ।

मयि विगलितप्रत्याशत्वाद्विवाहविधेः पुरा
विकलकरुणैर्मर्मच्छेदव्यथाविधुरैरिव ।
स्मरसि रुदितैः स्नेहाकूतं तथा व्यतनोदसा-
वहमपि यथाभूवं पीडातराङ्गितमानसः ॥ ११ ॥

( सावेगम् । ) अहो नु खलु भोः ।

दलति हृदयं गाढोद्वेगं द्विधा तु न भिद्यते
वहति विकलः कायो मोहं न मुञ्चति चेतनाम् ।
ज्वलयति तनूमन्तर्दाहः करोति न भस्मसा-
त्प्रहरति विधिर्मर्मच्छेदी न कृन्तति जीवितम् ॥ १२ ॥

मक०—वयस्य निरवग्रहं दहति दैवमिव दारुणो विवस्वान् । इयं च ते शरीरावस्था । तदस्य पद्मसरसः परिसरे मुहूर्तमास्यताम् । अत्र हि

रसान्तर्गतत्वेन धीमतामनुद्वेगात् । 'यत्रोद्वेगो न धीमताम्' इति दण्डिवचनात् ॥ १० ॥ मयीत्यादि । सखे असौ प्रिया स्नेहेङ्गितं रुदितैस्तथा विस्तारयामास यथा पीडाचपलचित्तोऽहमप्यभूवं भूतोऽस्मीति स्मरसि । इतिरध्याहार्यः । अन्यथा कर्माप्राप्तिः । रुदितस्य करुणजन्यत्वात्करुणहेतुमाह—विवाहविधेः पूर्वं मयि नैराश्याद्विकलानि स्वविषयव्यावृत्तानि करणानीन्द्रियाणि तैर्लक्षिता । अनेन मोह उक्तः । लक्षणे तृतीया । कीदृशैः । मर्मच्छेदव्यथादीनैरिव । अनेन विश्वासवत्त्वमुक्तम् । निःश्वासेन मर्मच्छेदोन्नयनात् । तथा च निःश्वासरुदितमोहैः करुणरस उक्तः । यद्वा विकलकरणैर्व्यतनोद्रुदितैरिव । इतरत्समम् ॥ ११ ॥ अहो नु खलु भो इत्याश्चर्ये ॥ दलतीत्यादि । मम हृदयं दलति विदीर्यते । सवेदनत्वात् । दृढोद्वेगम् । नैव द्विधा भिद्यते द्विधा भिन्नं न भवति । स्फुटिते पीडोपशान्तिरिति भावः । तुशब्द एवार्थे पुनरर्थे वा । पुनर्न भिद्यत इत्यर्थात् । भिद्यत इति कर्मकर्तरि तङ् । अथ च दलति तन्न भिद्यत इति विरोधाभासः । एवमुत्तरत्रापि । विह्वलः कायो मोहं दधाति न तु चेतनां त्यजति । पुनश्चैतन्ययोगात् । स्थिरे मोहे दुःखाज्ञानात्कृतार्थः स्यामिति भावः । तदिहाध्यात्मिकविपद्द्वयमुक्तम् । अन्तर्दाहः शरीरं दीपयति न भस्मसात्करोति । कार्त्स्न्येन भस्मरूपं न करोतीत्यर्थः । सातिः कार्त्स्न्ये । तथात्वे दुःखाज्ञानमेव स्यादित्याशयः । अनेनाधिभौतिकी विपदुक्ता । तदिह व्याधिदशायां मोहादय उक्ताः । यदाह—'मनःसंमोहसर्वाङ्गदाहवृत्त्यादिभिस्तथा । शिरसो वेदनाभिश्च व्याधेरभिनयो भवेत्' ॥ इति । इह कायावच्छिन्न आत्मा कायपदेनोक्तः । अन्यथा मोहस्यात्मधर्मतया कायेऽसम्भव इत्यवधेयम् । 'स्त्रियां मूर्तिस्तनुस्तनूः' इत्यमरः ॥ १२ ॥ जडतानिवृत्त्यर्थं माधवमन्यचित्तं कर्तुमाह—वयस्य इति । निरवग्रहं निष्प्रतिबन्धं यथा ॥ उपवेशफ-

१ करुणैः. २ सोद्वे०. ३ भज्यते. ४ वयस्य माधव; निरवग्रहः, दैवं—शवः. इ. पा. ५ अत्र.

उन्नालबालकमलाकरमाकरन्द-
निष्यन्दसंवलनमांसलगन्धबन्धुः ।
त्वां प्रीणयिष्यति पुरः परिवर्तमान-
कल्लोलशीकरतुषारजडः समीरः ॥ १३ ॥
( परिक्रम्योपविशतः । )

मक०—( स्वगतम् । ) भवतु । एवं तावदाक्षिपामि । ( प्रकाशम् । )
वयस्य माधव

एतस्मिन्मदकलमल्लिकाक्षपक्ष-
व्याधूतस्फुरदुरुदण्डपुण्डरीकाः ।
बाष्पाम्भःपरिपतनोद्गमान्तराले
दृश्यन्तामविरहिताश्रियो विभागाः ॥ १४ ॥
( माधवः सावेगमुत्तिष्ठति । )

मक०—कथं प्रतिपत्तिशून्यमुत्थायान्यतः प्रवृत्तः । ( निःश्वस्योत्थाय च । ) सखे प्रसीद । पश्य पश्य

---

त्माह--**उन्नालेत्यादि**। समीरो वायुरिह त्वां प्रीणयिष्यति प्रीतं करिष्यति। तद्योग्यतामाह-ग्रीष्मान्तेऽल्पोदकतयोद्गतनाला बाला ये पद्मसंघास्तेषां पुष्परसक्षरणेन यन्मिश्रणं तेन मांसलः पुष्टो यो गन्धस्तन्मित्रम् । अग्रे दोलायमानकल्लोलशीकरैः शीतलो जडो मन्दः । यद्वा शीकरा एव तुषारास्तैर्जडः शीत इत्यर्थात् । 'आकरो निवहोत्पत्तिस्थानश्रेष्ठेषु कथ्यते।' इति मेदिनीकरः। माकरन्दः। 'तस्येदम्' इत्यण् ॥ १३ ॥ आक्षेपोऽन्यमनस्कता । **एतस्मिन्नित्यादि**। अत्र सरसि भुवः प्रदेशा दृश्यन्ताम् । अश्रुपूर्णनेत्रतयादर्शनमाशङ्क्याह--एकस्य नेत्रजलस्य परिपतनमन्यस्योत्थानं तयोर्मध्ये । कीदृशाः । हर्षाव्यक्तमधुररवहंसविशेषपक्षकम्पितचलद्दीर्घनालपद्माः । नीलोत्पलयुक्ताश्च । पूर्वं विशिष्टपद्ममुक्तमिह तु नीलपद्ममात्रमित्यपौनरुक्त्यम् । यद्वा पूर्वं श्वेतपद्ममुक्तम् । इह तु नीलं तदित्यदोषः । श्वेतश्यामकमलसंवलनेनातिरम्यतोक्ता । अविरहिताश्रिय इति पाठे श्रीः शोभा लक्ष्मीर्वा । सरसि तस्याः सतताधिवासात् । तथा च श्रीयुक्ता इत्यर्थः । 'मलिनैर्मल्लिकाक्षास्ते' इत्यमरः । 'मल्लिको हंसभिद्यपि' इति मेदिनीकरान्मल्लिक आख्या यस्येति ज्ञायते । अनुप्रासश्च नागरागेति समानश्रुत्यापि संभवतीत्यवधेयम् । सोद्वेगं शीतवातादिदुःसहत्वादिति भावः ॥ १४ ॥ 'प्रतिवाक्यप्रदानादिश्रुत्यालोकनवर्जनम् । तूष्णीम्भावो विचेतस्त्वं जडतायां भवन्ति हि ॥ इति जडताचिह्नं माधवे सचमत्कारमाह--**कथमिति**। निरूप्य नेयं जडता किं त्वनुस्मृतिरित्याह--**शून्यमिति** । शून्यं निर्लक्ष्यमन्यतो गमनेनानुस्मृतिः । यद्वा

---

१ उच्चाल. २ संचलन, संवलित. ३ प्राणयि०. ४ परिवर्तमानः. ५ इति परि०. ६ मल्लिकाख्य, काक्षि. ७ कुवलयिनो भुवो. ८ सोद्वेगम्. ९ निष्पाति०.

वानीरप्रसवैर्निकुञ्जसरितामासक्तवासं पयः
पर्यन्तेषु च यूथिकासुमनसामुज्जृम्भितं जालकैः ।
उन्मीलत्कुटजप्रहासिषु गिरेरालम्ब्य सानूनितः
प्राग्भारेषु शिखण्डिताण्डवविधौ मेघैर्वितानाय्यते ॥ १५ ॥

अपि च ।

जृम्भाजर्जरडिम्बडम्बरघनश्रीमत्कदम्बद्रुमाः
शैलाभोगभुवो भवन्ति ककुभः कादम्बिनीश्यामलाः ।
उद्यत्कन्दलकान्तकेतकभृतः कच्छाः सरित्स्रोतसा-
माविर्गन्धशिलीन्ध्रलोध्रकुसुमस्मेरा वनानां ततिः ॥ १६ ॥

---

अन्यतः शून्यं मालतीव्यतिरिक्तवस्त्वज्ञानात् । अत एव प्रद्वेषादन्यकार्याणां कथितानुस्मृतिरिति । अप्रतिपत्तिशून्यमिति पाठेऽनवधानेन चैतन्यविरहो यथातथोत्यायेत्यर्थः ॥ **वानीरेत्यादि** । सखे कुञ्जसंबन्धि नदीनां पयः पश्य । वेतसपुष्पैर्लग्नसौरभम् । तासामेवोपान्तेषु च यूथिकाकुसुमानां जालकैः कोरकैर्विकासितम् । यद्वा यूथिकाश्च सुमनसश्च तासां जालकैः । यूथिका जूहीति प्रसिद्धा । सुमनसो जात्यः । 'सुमना मालती जातिः' इत्यमरः । तथा गिरेः सानूनेकदेशानालम्ब्येह प्राग्भारेषु शिखरेषु वर्तमानैर्मेघैर्वितानाय्यते । वितानाचारः क्रियते । मयूरनृत्यविधाननिमित्तम् । निमित्तसप्तमीयम् । कीदृशेषु । विकसत्कुटजपुष्परूपहासवत्सु । तदिह मयूरनृत्यार्थं मेघैर्वितानं कुटजैर्हास इति यत्तत्पश्येत्यर्थः । एवं च कुटजवृक्षा द्रष्टारो मयूरा नर्तका मेघो वितानमिति नृत्यसामग्री । ध्वनिस्तु शिखण्डिपदेन पञ्चचूडोपेतशिरस्कत्वेन विदूषक उक्तः । प्राग्भारपदेन च प्राञ्चतीति प्राक् प्रकृष्टज्ञानवान्भारो दुःसहो यस्य स मूर्खो द्रष्टोक्तः । तस्य च हास उचित एव । यद्वा शिखण्डिपदेन त्रिशिखण्डयोगितया बाल उक्तः । तस्य च नृत्ये मूर्खो हसत्येव । 'बालानामपि कर्तव्यं त्रिशिखण्डविभूषणम्' ॥ इति बालानां शिखण्डित्वे मानम् । 'वानीरवञ्जुलाः' इत्यमरः । 'क्षारको जालकं क्लीबे कलिका कोरकः पुमान् ।' इति च । वितानमाचरतीत्यर्थे क्यङन्ताण्णिचि वितानाय्यत इति रूपम् ॥ १५ ॥ **जृम्भेत्यादि** । सखे शैलपर्यन्तभूमयो जृम्भया विकासेन जर्जरः पृथग्भूतो यो डिम्बो गोलकस्तस्य डम्बरेणारम्भेण व्याप्ता अत एव श्रीमन्तो नीपवृक्षा यत्र तादृश्यो भवन्तीति यत्तत्पश्येत्यर्थः । एवं सर्वत्र दिशो मेघमालाश्यामा भवन्ति । यद्वा कादम्बानां कलहंसानां स्त्रियः कादम्बिन्यस्ताभिः श्यामाः । नदीप्रवाहाणां कच्छाः कूलान्युद्यद्भिर्विकासितैः कन्दलैर्नवाङ्कुरैः कान्ता मनोज्ञा ये केतकवृक्षास्तद्धारका भवन्ति । यद्वा उद्यन्कन्दलः कन्दो यस्य कान्तकेतकस्येत्यर्थः ।

---

१ नीवार. २ निह. ३ भागेषु. ४ झर्झर. ५ आविर्भूत.

**माधवः**—सखे पश्यामि । किं तु दुरालोकरमणीयाः संप्रत्यग्रण्यागिरिभूमयः । तत्किमेतत् । ( सास्रम् । ) अथवा किमन्यत् ।

**उत्फुल्लार्जुनसर्जवासितवहत्पौरस्त्यझञ्झानिल-**
**प्रेङ्खोलस्खलितेन्द्रनीलशकलस्निग्धाम्बुदश्रेणयः ।**
**धारासिक्तवसुंधरासुरभयः प्राप्तास्त एतेधुना**
**घर्माम्भोविगमागमव्यतिकरश्रीवाहिणो वासराः ॥ १७ ॥**

हा प्रिये मालति

---

यद्वा उद्यन्त्यः कन्दलां मल्लीवृक्षस्तं कान्तकेतकं च बिभ्रतीत्यर्थः । वनानां मालाविर्गन्धानि व्यक्तीभवत्सौरभानि यानि शिलीन्ध्रलोध्रकुसुमानि तैः स्मेरा सहासेव । मनोज्ञा वा । 'शिलीन्ध्रं कन्दलीपुष्पम्' इति विश्वः । शिलीन्ध्रं 'सूल' इति ख्यातम् । वनमिह पद्मं जलं विपिनं वा । 'जृम्भा विकासजृम्भयोः' इति विश्वः । डिम्बोऽण्डेऽपि च गोलके ' इति धरणिः । 'डम्बरोऽस्त्री समारम्भः' इति विश्वः । 'कादम्बिनी मेघमाला कादम्बर्त्री च कथ्यते ।' इति शाश्वतः । 'कन्दलः कलहे कन्दे मल्लयामङ्करसङ्घयोः ।' इति मेदिनीकरः । 'पुंसि कच्छस्तथाविधः' इत्यमरः । वनं नीरेऽम्बुजे क्लीबं काननेऽप्यालये वनम् ' । इति मेदिनीकरः ॥ १६ ॥ **उत्फुल्लेत्यादि** । अधुना त एते दिवसाः प्राप्ता ये मनोराज्येन मया धृता इत्यर्थः । इह त एत इति सर्वनामभ्यां दिनानामत्युत्कण्ठाहेतुत्वं ध्वनितम् । कीदृशाः । उत्फुल्लाभ्यामर्जुनशालाभ्यां वासितः सुरभीकृतो वहन् पौरस्त्यः प्राच्यो यो झञ्झानिलः प्रचण्डवायुः प्रावृषेण्यवातो वा तस्य प्रेङ्खोल आन्दोलनं तेन स्खलिताः स्वस्थानच्युता इन्द्रनीलमणिखण्डा इव श्यामा मेघपङ्क्तयो येषु ते । अत्रार्जुनग्रहणेऽपि द्वितीयतरोः सर्जस्य ग्रहणं कदम्बाद्युपलक्षणार्थम् । तथा ग्रीष्मोष्मतप्तमहीसेकसौरभवन्तः । ईषद्वृष्टौ तदुद्गमात् । घर्मस्य ग्रीष्मस्य विगमोपगमोऽम्भस आगम आगमनं तयोर्व्यतिकरः संबन्धस्तेन श्रियं शोभां वोढुं शीलं येषां ते । यद्वा घर्माम्भसः स्वेदजलस्य यौ विगमागमौ तयोर्व्यतिकरः संभेदः । वर्षारम्भ इत्यर्थः । तस्य श्रीः सम्पत्तिस्तद्वाहिन इत्यर्थः । पौरस्त्य इति पुरसस्त्यक् । 'झञ्झा ध्वनिविशेषे स्यात्' इति मेदिनीकरः । तदन्वितोऽनिलो झञ्झानिलः । यद्वा 'झञ्झानिलः प्रावृषेण्यः' इति रत्नकोशः । अत्र वास्यमानेति कर्तव्ये संपूर्णक्रियात्वपरनिष्ठाप्रत्ययान्तवासितपदोपादानात्समस्तपुष्पसौरभसंक्रान्तिर्वायोर्ध्वनिता । अत एव मलयानिलाज्झञ्झानिलोत्कर्षः कटाक्षितः । उन्मादावस्थो माधवः । उन्मादश्चेष्टवियोगात् । यदाह—'इष्टजनस्य वियोगादुन्मादो विभवनाशाच्च ' ॥ १७ ॥

---

१ दुग. २ तटभू०. ३ मरुत. ४ ०लत्स्खलि०; ०तेन्द्रशेखरमणिस्नि०. ५ एवा.

**तरुणतमालनीलबहुलोन्नमदम्बुधराः**
**शिशिरसमीरणाधूतनूतनवारिकणाः।**
**कथमवलोकयेयमधुना हरिहेतिमती-**
**र्मदकलनीलकण्ठकलहैर्मुखराः ककुभः॥ १८॥**

( शोकातिं नाटयति। )

**मकरन्दः**—कोऽप्यतिदारुणो दशाविपाको वयस्यस्य संप्रति। ( सास्त्रम्। ) मया पुनर्वज्रायमाणेन विनोद आरब्धः। ( निःश्वस्य। ) एवं च पर्यवसितप्रायैव नो माधवं प्रति प्रत्याशा। ( सभयं विलोक्य। ) कथं प्रमुग्ध एव। ( आकाशे। ) मालति मालति किमपरं निरनुक्रोशासि।

**अपहसितबान्धवं त्वया विहितं साहसमस्य तृष्णया।**
**तदिहानपराधिनि प्रिये सखि कोऽयं करुणोज्झितः क्रमः॥ १९॥**

कथमद्यापि नोच्छ्वसिति। हन्त मुषितोऽस्मि दैवेन।

**मातर्मातर्दलति हृदयं ध्वंसते देहबन्धः**
**शून्यं मन्ये जगदविरतज्वालमन्तर्ज्वलामि।**
**सीदन्नन्धे तमसि विधुरो मज्जतीवान्तरात्मा**
**विष्वङ्मोहः स्थगयति कथं मन्दभाग्यः करोमि॥ २०॥**

---

**तरुणेत्यादि**। कथमधुना दिशोऽहमवलोकयेयम्। तरुणतमालान्नीलास्तद्वद्बहु नीलाः प्रचुरा उद्गच्छन्तो मेघा यासु ताः। शीतवातक्षिप्तनवजलकणाः। हरेरिन्द्रस्य हेतिरस्त्रं धनुस्तद्वतीः। मदकलमयूरकोलाहलैः शब्दवतीः। 'कलहं कलकलेऽपि च' इति विश्वः। सरित इति पाठे प्रतिबिम्बेन मेघत्वम्। हरेः कृष्णस्य हेतिश्चक्रं तन्नामकपक्षियुक्ताः। दुःखितेनर्तुज्ञानं दुःखमयत्वेनैव। यदाह 'ऋतून्पश्यति दुःखार्तः सर्वान्दुःखसमाश्रितान्।' इति। तदनेन प्रबन्धेन वर्षाकाल उक्तः। यदाह—'कदम्बनीपकुटजैः शाद्वलैः सेन्द्रगोपकैः। मेघवातैः सुखस्पर्शैः प्रावृट्कालं प्रदर्शयेत्' ॥ १८॥ **शोकेति**। मूर्च्छितः पततीति भावः। **मकरन्दः**। विनोदश्चित्तस्वास्थ्यम्। **प्रमुग्धः** संज्ञाशून्यः। अनुक्रोशोऽनुकम्पा तद्विपरीतासि। **अपेत्यादि**। अगणितमात्रादिके हे सखि अस्य लोभेन त्वया साहसं कृतम्। तदिह प्रिये प्रीते निरपराधेऽपि निर्दयः क्रमः कोऽयम्। केयं परिपाटिस्तवेत्यर्थः। कथमीदृशं पतिं त्यक्त्वा निर्दयासीति भावः॥१९॥ उच्छ्वासः संज्ञालाभः। **मातरित्यादि**। मातर्मातरित्यावेगः। द्विधा भवति हृदयमिति पीडा।

---

१ येहम०. २ इति निःश्वस्य शो०. ३ क्रोयम०, कोप्यतिशयदा०. ४ संप्रति वर्तते. ५ वज्रमयेन. वज्रायमाणेन पुरो विनोदनमारब्धं, पुनरज्ञानेन वज्रमयेन किल विनोदः प्रारब्धः। ६ प्रायेष, ७ माधवप्रत्या. ८ हा सखि मा०. ९ मय्यधृष्टया. १० ०तक्रमः. ११ अविरल, अविकल.

कष्टं भोः कष्टम् ।

बन्धुताहृदयकौमुदीमहो मालतीनयनमुग्धचन्द्रमाः ।
सोऽयमद्य मकरन्दनन्दनो जीवलोकतिलकः प्रलीयते ॥ २१ ॥

हा वयस्य माधव ।

गात्रेषु चन्दनरसो दृशि शारदेन्दु-
रानन्द एव हृदये मम यस्त्वमासीः ।
तं त्वां निकाममकमनीयमकाण्ड एव
कालेन जीवितमिवोद्धरता हतोऽस्मि ॥ २२ ॥

( स्पृशन् । )

अकरुण वितर स्मितोज्ज्वलां
दृशमतिदारुण देहि मे गिरम् ।
सहचरमनुरक्तचेतसं
प्रियमकरन्द कथं न मन्यसे ॥ २३ ॥

( माधवः संज्ञां लभते )

---

अवयवसंधिः शिथिलीभवतीत्यस्वस्थता । विश्वं शून्यं मन्य इति बाह्यासंवेदना निर्वेदः । अविरतं ज्वालं यथा तथान्तर्ज्वलामीति चिन्ताजनितो दाहः । अन्तरात्मा निरालम्बः सीदन्नवसादं गच्छन्गाढान्धकारे मज्जतीवेति ग्लानिः । विष्वक्सर्वतो मोहश्छादयतीति मोहः । मन्दभाग्योऽहं किंकरोमीति दैन्यम् । कथं शब्दः किमित्यर्थे । सर्वनामत्वान्नानार्थता । विष्वगित्यत्र सुषमादित्वात्षत्वम् ॥ २० ॥ परिदेवितमाह—**कष्टमिति**। **बन्धुतेत्यादि** । सोऽयं बन्धुसमूहचित्तकार्तिक्युत्सवो मालतीनेत्रबालचन्द्रो मकरन्दहर्षजनकः सर्वजनतिलकोऽद्य प्रलयमापद्यत इत्यर्थः । ' मह उद्धव उत्सवः ' इत्यमरः ॥ २१ ॥ **गात्रेष्वित्यादि** । यस्त्वं मम काये चन्दनरस आसीः । सुखस्पर्शत्वात् । नेत्रे शरत्कालीनचन्द्रः । आनन्दजनकत्वात् । चित्त आनन्द एव साक्षाद्धर्ष एवासीः । तं त्वामतिकान्तमकस्मादेव मम जीवनमिवोद्धरतोन्मूलयता कालेन समयेन यमेन वा हतोऽस्मि । यथा जीवनोद्धारेऽहं हतस्तथा त्वदुद्धारेऽपीति भावः ॥ २२ ॥ सोन्मादो विलपति—**अकरुणेत्यादि** । हे निर्दय हासमनोज्ञां दृशं देहि । हासपूर्वं पश्येत्यर्थः । यद्वा स्मितेन विकासेनोज्ज्वलां विकसितामित्यर्थः । वचनादानादतिदारुण हे मे वाचं देहि । मित्रमनुरक्तचित्तं हे प्रियमकरन्द कथं न मन्यसे । कथं नाङ्गीकरोषि । इष्टावेगादीनां सत्वात्करुणो रसः । यदाह—' इष्टनाशधनापायबन्धुव्यसनताडनैः । शापक्लेशोपघातैश्च जायते करुणो रसः । अश्रुनिश्वासवैवर्ण्यस्रस्ताङ्गैश्च स्मृतिक्षयैः । परिदेवितशोकाद्यैरभिनेयः स सूरिभिः ' ॥ २३ ॥

---

१ पूर्ण, बाल. २ माधवेऽथ. ३ हृदि. ४ गात्रमस्य संस्पृशन्. ५ अविनष्ट.

**मक०**—( सोच्छ्वासम् । ) अयमचिरधौतराजपट्टरुचिरमांसलच्छविर्नवजलधरस्तोयसीकरासारेण प्रियवयस्यं मे संजीवयति । दिष्ट्या समुच्छ्वसितस्तावत् ।

**माधवः**—तत्किमत्र विपिने प्रियावार्ताहरं करोमि । ( विलोक्य । ) साधु साधु ।

**फलभरपरिणामश्यामजम्बूनिकुञ्ज-**
**स्खलनतनुतरङ्गामुत्तरेण स्रवन्तीम् ।**
**उपरि विघटमानः प्रौढतापिच्छनीलः**
**श्रयति शिखरमद्रेर्नूतनस्तोयवाहः ॥ २४ ॥**

( सरभसमुत्थायोन्मुखः कृताञ्जलिः । )

**कच्चित्सौम्य प्रियसहचरी विद्युदालिङ्गति त्वा-**
**माविर्भूतप्रणयसुभगाश्चातका वा भजन्ते ।**
**पौरस्त्यो वा सुखयति मरुत्साधुसंवाहनाभि-**
**र्विष्वग्विभ्रत्सुरपतिधनुर्लक्ष्म लक्ष्मीं तनोति ॥ २५ ॥**

---

**मकरन्दः** । अचिरधौतत्वेन राजपट्टस्य नीलत्वस्निग्धत्वे उक्ते । राजपट्टं खडीति ख्यातम् । रुचिरा दीप्तिमती मांसला घना छविः कान्तिर्यस्य सः । **माधवः** । वार्ताहरो दूतः । अतिप्रवृद्धकालतया दूतप्रेषणम् । यदाह–' प्रसह्यमानकामार्तो बहुस्थानसमुत्थितः । स्वावस्थादर्शनार्थं तु प्रेषयेद्दूतमात्मनः ' ॥ **फलेत्यादि** । नवमेघो गिरेरग्रं श्रयति । फलभारपाकश्यामजम्बूनिकुञ्जात्स्खलनेनाल्पकल्लोलां नदीमुत्तरेण नद्या उत्तरसमीपे । एनपा द्वितीया । कीदृशः उपरि विघटमान ऊर्ध्वस्थानं त्यजन् । विकासितमालपुष्पान्नीलस्तद्वद्वा नीलः । उपचितघनमालेति पाठ उपचिता घना च माला येषामित्यर्थः । घने नूतनत्वेनातिश्यामता । यद्वा स्रवन्तीमुपरि विघटमानो विविधप्रकारेण श्रयन् । उत्तरेणोत्तरदेशे । उत्तरेणेति विभक्तिप्रतिरूपको निपातः । किंचिदेवोत्तरेणेतिवत् । आश्रयार्थकतया घटेः सकर्मकता । ' स्रवन्ती निम्नगापगा ' इत्यमरः । कृताञ्जलिरित्यनेन विनय उक्तः । विनयपूर्वकश्च संदेशः कार्यः । यदाह–' संदेशं चैव दूत्यास्तु प्रदद्यान्मदनाश्रयम् । तस्येयं समवस्थेति कथया विनयेन हि ' ॥ २४ ॥ **कच्चिदित्यादि** । प्रार्थनोचितं सुभगप्रश्नमाह—हे सौम्य सुन्दर प्रिया वल्लभा सहचरी सततानुगता विद्युत्त्वामालिङ्गति कच्चित् । कथयेत्यर्थः ॥ ' कच्चित् कामप्रवेदने ' इत्यमरः । विरहित्वेन कान्ताभिलाषात्प्रथमं कान्तासंगमप्रश्नः । ' चारुचन्द्र-

---

१ जलदः. २ कथमत्र, किमिवात्र. ३ परिणाह. ४ स्खलितः; तनुशरीराम्. ५ उपचितघनमालप्रौढ ६ सादर०. ७ चर. ८ सुमुखाः, मुखराः, सुखिताः. ९ लक्ष्मीषदेतत्.

(आकर्ण्य ।) अये[1] प्रतिरवभरितकन्दरानन्दितोत्कण्ठनीलकण्ठकलकेकानुबन्धिना मन्द्रहुंकृतेन मामनुमन्यते[2] । यावदभ्यर्थये । भगवन् जीमूत[3] ।

**दैवात्पश्येर्जगति विचरन्निच्छया मत्प्रियां चे-**
**दाश्वास्यादौ तदनु कथयेर्माधवीयामवस्थाम् ।**
**आशातन्तुर्न च कथयतात्यन्तमुच्छेदनीयः**
**प्राणत्राणं कथमपि करोत्यायताक्ष्याः स एकः[5] ॥ २६ ॥**

---

जयोः सौम्यः' इति शाश्वतः । प्रियालिङ्गने सुखं तद्विरहे दुःखमिति त्वमपि जानासीति ध्वनिनम् । यद्वा कच्चिदेवमभिमतं ममेत्यर्थः । उत्पन्नस्नेहेन सुभगाः सुमुखाश्चातकास्त्वां सेवन्ते । वा समुच्चये । अनेनार्थिसंपात्तिरुक्ता । पुरोवातश्च मृदुप्रेरणाभिस्त्वां सुखयति । अन्योऽपि सहायश्चरणमुष्टिग्रहणादिरूपसंवाहनां कुरुत इति ध्वनिः । अनेन सहायसंपत्तिरुक्ता । विष्वक्सर्वतो लक्ष्मीं शोभां बिभ्रादिन्द्रधनुः । कर्तृ । लक्ष्म चिह्नं तव तनोति । अनेन प्रसाधनमुक्तम् । विश्वं बिभ्रदिति पाठे हे विश्वं बिभ्रद्भुवनं दधान । वर्षेण शस्यादिसमृद्धया जगदुपकारकत्वमुक्तम् । प्रसाधनमाह । इन्द्रधनूरूपं चिह्नं तव शोभां तनोति । बिम्बं बिभ्रदिति पाठे तु बिम्बं मण्डलं शोभां तनोति । कीदृशम् । इन्द्रधनुश्चिह्नं बिभ्रद्धानम् । तदिह जगदुपकारकतया ममाप्युपकारं करिष्यसीति भावः ॥ २५ ॥ गर्जितेनानुमतिमाह—**अये इति** । प्रतिशब्दभरितकन्दरत्वेनानन्दिता समृद्धोत्कण्ठा यस्य सः । यद्वा आनन्दिता हृष्टा उत्कठा उद्ग्रीवा इत्यर्थः । मन्द्रं गभीरम् अनुमन्यते स्वीकरोति । आर्तिवशाद्देवत्वारोपणेन भगवन्निति । अवधारणे यावत् । जीमूत मेघ ॥ **दैवादित्यादि** । इच्छया जगति विचरंस्त्वं मत्प्रियां यदि दैववशात्पश्येर्द्रक्ष्यसि तदा प्रथमं तां प्रबोध्याथ माधवदशां कथयिष्यसि । अवस्थानिवेदनेन तन्मरणमाशंक्याह—कथयता त्वयाशा पुनःसंगमप्रत्याशा सैव तन्तुः । जीवनबन्धहेतुत्वात् । नैवात्यर्थमुच्छेद्यः । चैवार्थे । अत्र हेतुमाह—स आशातन्तुरेकस्तस्याः प्राणत्राणं कष्टाकष्टया करोति नाहमित्यर्थः । इह तावत्कालं सा जीवति न वेति संभावना दर्शनस्य दैवादित्यनेनोक्ता । प्रसङ्गतो मत्कार्यमिति जगति विचरन्नित्यनेनोक्तम् । मत्प्रियामित्यनेन सुकुमारत्वादिना विरहदुःखासहिष्णुतोक्ता । आदावाश्वासनं वार्ताश्रवणपटुत्वार्थम् । अत्यन्तमित्यनेन मध्यमविधया दशाकथनम् । तेन च तन्नैराश्यनिषेध इत्युक्तम् । कथमपीत्यनेनाशातन्तुमात्रं तद्रक्षणाय कल्पत इत्युक्तम् । आयताक्ष्या इत्यनेन कटाक्षादिस्मरणेन गुणकीर्तनम् । माधवस्येयं माधवीया । वृद्धाच्छः । उन्मादावस्थेयम् ।

---

१ अयं, अथ किमयं. २ कण्ठे कान्तेन ध्वनिना मामनमन्यते. ३ जीमूतनाथ. ४ पश्येर्यदि जगति तां मत्प्रियां मालतीं चेत् विचरन्मत्प्रियां मालतीं. ५ एव.

( सहर्षम् । ) अये प्रचलितः । तदन्यतः संचरामि[1] ( इति परिक्रामति । )

**मक०**—( सोद्वेगम्[2] । ) कथमिदानीमुन्मादोपरागो[3] माधवेन्दुमास्कन्दति । हा तात हा अम्ब हा भगवति परित्रायस्व[4] परित्रायस्व । पश्य माधवस्यावस्थाम् ।

**माधवः**—धिक्[5]प्रमादः ।

**नवेषु लोध्रप्रसवेषु कान्तिर्दृशः कुरङ्गेषु गतं[6] गजेषु ।**
**लतासु नम्रत्वमिति प्रमथ्य व्यक्तं[7] विभक्ता विपिने प्रिया[8] मे ॥ २७ ॥**

हा प्रिये मालति[9] ।

**मक०**—

**सुहृदि गुणनिवासे प्रेयसि प्राणनाथे**
**कथम्[10]अपि सहपांसुक्रीडनप्रौढसख्ये ।**
**प्रियजनविरहाधिव्याधि[11]वेगं दधाने**
**हतहृदय विदीर्य त्वं द्विधा न प्रयासि ॥ २८ ॥**

**माधवः**—सुलभा[12]नुकारः खलु जगति वेधसो निर्माणसंनिवेशः ।

---

असंवद्धप्रलापात् ॥ २६ ॥ सहर्षत्वं मद्वचनमङ्गीकृत्य प्रचलित इति । **मकरन्दः** । उपरागो राहुग्रासः । शैशवे संकटप्रदेशे पित्रादीनां स्मरणस्य स्वभ्यस्ततया विरहसंकटेऽपि तदाह हा तातेति । **माधवः** । प्रमादोऽनिष्टम् । **नवेष्वित्यादि** । नूतनलोध्रपुष्पेषु कान्तिः पाण्डिमा गौरत्वं वा । इह नवपदेन स्निग्धतोक्ता । दृशो विलोकितानि हरिणीषु । गमनं हस्तिषु । नम्रत्वं लतासु । इतिशब्द आद्यर्थे । 'हेला लीलेत्यमी हावाः' इतिवत् । प्रमथ्य मारयित्वा मे प्रिया विपिने विभक्ता खण्डखण्डीकृत्य धृता । यद्वा । इति प्रकारार्थः । तेन लोध्रप्रसवादिभिर्मे प्रिया विभागीकृता । कान्त्यादिविभागद्वारा प्रियाविभाग एवोन्नीयत इत्यवधेयम् । विपिन इति प्राणिवधस्थानाभिप्रायम ॥ २७ ॥ **सुहृदीत्यादि** । हे हतहृदय कथमपि विदीर्य द्विधा त्वं न प्रयासि । हतेति निन्दायाम् । मित्रे गुणनिधानेऽतिप्रेमवति जीवेश्वरे सहधूलिक्रीडागाढमैत्रे कान्तावियोगमनोव्यथाव्याधिमन्तर्दधाने सति । सुहृदित्यादौ हेतुहेतुमद्भावः । 'धूलिः क्लियां पासुर्ना' इत्यमरः ॥ २८ ॥ प्रियाविभागाशङ्कां निरस्यति—**सुलभेति** । संनिवेशः प्रकारः । अनुकारः सादृश्यम् । तथा च लोध्रप्रसवादीनि प्रियाका-

---

१ संभावयामि. २ साकूतम्. ३ ०राग एव. ४ ०स्व मां. ५ (द्विपदिकया सर्वतोवलोक्य) ६ गजेषु यातं. ७ स्फुटं. ८ प्रियास्मिन्. ९ अस्मात्परं इति मूर्च्छांति इत्यधि. ए. पु. १० कथमिव. ११ ०खेदं. १२ ( आश्वस्योत्थाय ) सुल०.

भवतु। एवं तावत्। (उच्चैः।) अयमहं भोः प्रणिपत्य भूधरारण्यवासिनः सत्त्वान्विज्ञापयामि। मुहूर्तमवधानदानेन मामनुगृह्णन्तु भवन्तः।

भवद्भिः सर्वाङ्गप्रकृतिरमणीया कुलवधू-
रिहस्थैर्दृष्टा वा विदितमथ वास्याः किमभवत्।
वयोऽवस्थां तस्याः शृणुत सुहृदो यत्र मदनः
प्रगल्भव्यापारश्चरति हृदि मुग्धश्च वपुषि ॥ २९ ॥

कष्टं भोः कष्टम्।

केकाभिर्नीलकण्ठस्तिरयति वचनं ताण्डवादुच्छिखण्डः
कान्तामन्तःप्रमोदादभिसरति मदभ्रान्ततारश्चकोरः।
गोलाङ्गूलः कपोलं छुरयति रजसा कौसुमेन प्रियायाः
कं याचे यत्र तत्र ध्रुवमनवसरग्रस्त एवार्थिभावः ॥ ३० ॥

अयं च

दन्तच्छदारुणिमराजितकान्तदन्त-
मुन्नम्य चुम्बति वलीवदनः प्रियायाः।
काम्पिल्लकप्रसवपाटलगण्डपालि
पाकारुणस्फुटितदाडिमकान्ति वक्त्रम् ॥ ३१ ॥

---

न्त्याद्यनुकारीणि न तु सा विभक्तेति भावः। सत्त्वान्प्राणिनो विज्ञापयामीति सानुनयं वचनम् ॥ **भवद्भिरित्यादि**। भवद्भिरिहस्थैः सर्वाङ्गेषु स्वभावरम्या सा कुलवधूर्दृष्टा वा। अथवास्या भवद्भिः किं विदितमभवत्। शुभमशुभं वा किं विज्ञातमित्यर्थः। ननु तस्याः किं वय इत्याह—हे सुहृदस्तस्या वयोवस्थां शृणुत। यत्र वयोवस्थायां हृदि मदनः प्रगल्भव्यापारो वपुषि मुग्धो बालश्चरति। एतेन वयःसन्धिरुक्ता। सर्वाङ्गेत्यनेनाभिज्ञानप्रकाशनम्। कुलवधूत्वेन चाञ्चल्याभावः। इहस्थैरित्यनेन परिचयचातुरी। वाकारद्वयेन दर्शनवृत्तान्तयोः सफलत्वं दर्शयति। ' सुरते निःसाध्वसता प्रागल्भ्यं समुदाहृतम् ॥ इति भरतः ॥ २९ ॥ **केकाभिरिति**। किं यत्र तत्र याचे। अपि तु न किमपि प्रार्थये। यतोऽप्रस्तावग्रस्तोऽर्थिभावोऽर्थित्वम्। अनवसरमाह—नृत्यादुद्गतपिच्छभारो मयूरः केकाभिर्वचनं छादयति। चकोरः पक्षिभेदो मत्ततया भ्रमत्तारकः संश्रित्तहर्षात्प्रियामभिसरति। गोलाङ्गूलः श्याममुखो वानरः पुष्पजधूल्या कान्तायाः कपोलौ चित्रयति। अतः सत्वानामन्यत्रासक्ततयार्थित्वानवसर इति भावः। 'प्लवङ्गकीशप्लवगगोलाङ्गूलवलीमुखाः।' इत्यमरमाला। कं याच इति पाठे कं प्राणिनं प्रार्थय इत्यर्थः ॥ ३० ॥ **दन्तेत्यादि**। वलीवदनो वानरोऽयं कान्ताया मुख-

---

१ प्रकाशं. २ चारिणः. ३ खलु. ४ स्थगयति. ५ कान्तामत्तः. ६ कौंकुमेन. ७ दन्तमाल. ८ ल्यक. ९ पाकान्तर.

एषं[1] प्रियतमास्कन्धविश्रान्तकरः करी । कथमत्राप्यनवसरः ।

**कण्डूकुड्मलितेक्षणां सहचरीं[2] दन्तस्य कोट्या लिख-**
**न्पर्यायव्यतिकीर्णकर्णपवनैराह्लादिभिर्वीजयन् ।**
**जग्धार्धैर्नवसल्लकीकिसलयैरस्याः स्थितिं कल्पयं[3]-**
**न्धन्यो[4] वन्यमतङ्गजः परिचयप्रागल्भ्यमभ्यस्यति ॥ ३२ ॥**

( अन्यतोवलोक्य ) अयं तु

**नान्तर्वर्तयति ध्वनत्सु जलदेष्वामन्द्रमुद्गर्जितं**
**नासन्नात्सरसः करोति कवलानावर्जितैः शैवलैः ।**
**दानज्यानिविषादमूकमधुपव्यासङ्गदीनाननो**
**नूनं प्राणसमावियोगविधुरः स्तम्बेरमस्ताम्यति ॥ ३३ ॥**

अलमनेनार्याँसितेन । एँष सानन्दसहचरीसमाकर्ण्यमानमधुरगम्भीरकण्ठ-गर्जितध्वनिरपरो मत्तमातङ्गयूथेपालः प्रत्यग्रविकसितकदम्बसंङ्घातसुरभि-

---

मुत्क्षिप्य चुम्बति । कीदृशम् । अधररागेण रक्ता मनोज्ञा दशना यत्र तत् । काम्पिल्लो रोचनीवृक्षः । स्वार्थे कन् । तस्य प्रसवेन पुष्पेण फलेन वा रक्तगण्डप्रदेशः । पाकान्त-रमन्तिमपाकस्ततः स्फुटितं विदीर्णं यद्दाडिमफलं तत्कान्ति । तत्सममित्यर्थः । तदिहा-प्यनवसर एव । ' शाखामृगवलीमुखाः ' इत्यमरः । ' काम्पिल्लः कर्कशश्चन्द्रो रक्ताङ्गो रोचनीत्यपि । ' इत्यमरः । रोहिणानोकहो रोहणवृक्षः ॥ ३१ ॥ **कण्डूरित्यादि** । अयं सुकृती वन्यहस्त्यस्याः प्रियायाः परिचयप्रागल्भ्यं सुरतनिःसाध्वसतामनुतिष्ठति । कीदृशः । कण्डूतिमुद्रितेक्षणां प्रियां दन्ताग्रेणालिखन्नीषदुल्लिखन् । कण्डूयन्नित्यर्थः । अत एव कण्डूकाले कुड्मलितेक्षणत्वं जातिः । पर्यायेण क्रमेण निक्षिप्तौ कर्णौ तयोर्वातैः मुदैर्वीजयन् । कवलितार्धैर्नवशल्लकीपल्लवैरस्याः प्राणधारणं कल्पयन् ॥ ३२ ॥ **नान्त-रित्यादि** । अयं स्तम्बेरमो हस्ती ताम्यति ग्लानो भवति । नूनं निश्चितं प्रेयसीवि-श्लेषेण विह्वलः । जलदेषु ध्वनत्सु सत्स्वीषद्गम्भीरमुद्गतकण्ठगर्जनं नान्तर्वर्तयति न करोति । समीपस्थात्सरस आवर्जितैर्मिलितैः शैवलैः कवलान्न करोति । मदहान्या यो विषादस्तेन मूकानां भ्रमराणां व्यासङ्गेनान्यचित्ततया शोच्यमुखः । यद्वा व्यासङ्गो विशेषेणासङ्ग इत्यर्थः । तदिह मदहानिश्चिन्तया संतापात् । दीनत्वमधोमुखचिन्तनात् । एतेनानुस्मृतिसंजाता विषयव्यावृत्तिरुक्ता ॥ ३३ ॥ अहमिवायमपि कान्तातिरिक्तमन्यन्न वेत्तीत्यत आह—**अलमिति** । रतौत्सुक्यान्मधुरकण्ठगर्जितश्रवणाद्वा सानन्देति । मातङ्गो

---

१ अग्रतोवलोक्य; अये एष; अयं च रोहिणानोकहस्कन्ध०; करः—कण्ठ; विभ्रान्तकरः. २ अनुचरीं. ३ कारयन्. ४ अन्यः, मन्ये. ५ प्रारम्भ. ६ नाप्या०. ७ ( सानन्दम् ) एष. ८ गम्भीरधीरकंण्ठध्वनिः प्रवृद्धनवयौवनोन्मादप्रस्तुतामंदसप्तपर्णप्रसूनमकरंदसुंदरमदवारिसंस्वा-ददत्तचित्तोन्मत्तानुरक्तेंदिंदिरनिकरझणझणायमानरणत्कारझंकारसंभारश्रवणालंबितकर्णो गो-दावरींदीवरवासितामंदमकरन्दतुंदिलमलयानिलोल्लासितामलाविदलितललितकमलपरंपरापुंज-परिमलप्राग्भारघ्राणसुखितेंद्रियवर्गापरो मत्तमातंगवर्गपालः. ९ वर्गपालकः. १० संवादि, संपात.

शीतलामोदबहलसंग[1]लितमांसलकपोलनिष्यन्दकर्दमित[2]कषायमुद्दलितकमलिनीखण्डविप्रकीर्णपर्णकमलकेसरमृणाल बिसकन्द कोमलाङ्कु[3]रनिकरमनवरतप्रवृत्तकमनीयकर्णतालताण्डवप्रच[4]लजर्जरितजलतरङ्गविततनीहा[5]रमुत्रस्तकुररसारसं सरोऽवगाह्य विहरति । भवत्वेनमाभाषे । महाभाग नागपते श्लाघ्ययौवनः खल्वसि । कान्तानुवृत्तिचातुर्यमप्यस्ति भवतः । किंतु ( सापवादम् । )

**लीलोत्खातमृणालकाण्ड[6]कवलच्छेदेषु संपादि[7]ताः**
**पुष्यत्पुष्करवासितस्य पयसो गण्डूषसंक्रान्तयः ।**
**सेकः सीकरिणा करेण विहितः कामं विरामे पुन-**
**र्न स्नेहादनरालनालनलिनीपत्रातपत्रं धृतम् ॥ ३४ ॥**

[8]कथमवधीरणानीरसं व्रजति । हन्त मूढ एवास्मि योऽस्मिन्वनच[9]रे वयस्यमकरन्दोचितं [10]व्यवहरामि । हा प्रियवयस्य[11] ।

**धिगु[12]च्छ्वसितवैशसं मम[13] यदित्थमेकाकिनो**
**धिगेव रमणीयतां त्वदनुभा[14]वभावादृते ।**

हस्ती । संपातः संपर्कः । संगलितो मिलितः । मांसलः पीनः । निस्यन्दो मदः । कषायः सुगन्धिः । करटो गण्डदेशः ॥ 'सुरभौ च कषायः स्यात्' इति शाश्वतः । समुद्दलितमुन्मूलितम् । पर्णं पत्रम् । 'तालो गीतक्रियामाने मध्यमाङ्गुलिसंमिते ।' इत्यमरमाला । 'नीहारस्तु कुहेलिका' इति हारावली । कुररः पक्षिभेदः । अनुवृत्तिः सेवा । सापवादं सदोषम् ॥ **लीलेत्यादि** । क्रीडोन्मूलितबिसदण्डकवलसमाप्तिषु विकसत्पद्मसुरभितस्य जलस्य गण्डूषसंक्रान्तयः संबन्धाः संपादिता दत्ताः । पुष्यदिति पाठे पुष्टीभवदित्यर्थः । अम्भःकणवता स्थूलहस्तेन सेकः कृतः । तदिदं द्वयं कामं युक्तमेव । दोषमाह—विरामे सरोऽवगाहविरतौ गमनकाले पुनरकुटिलनालपद्मपत्रच्छत्रं न स्नेहाद्धृतम् । एतदयुक्तमित्यर्थः । अतः कान्तानुवृत्तिं न जानासीति भावः । 'पुष्कराम्भोरुहाणि च' इत्यमरः । गण्डूषपदेन स्वयं पीत्वा जलादानं ध्वनितम् । 'नलिनी पद्मिनी पद्मम्' इत्यमरमाला । 'अरालः कुटिले मतः' इति मेदिनीकरः । आतपात्त्रायत इत्यातपत्रमित्युचितं पदम् ॥ ३४ ॥ चलचित्तत्वेन पार्श्वस्थं मित्रमपश्यन् सखेदमाह—**कथमिति धिगित्यादि** । इत्थमेकाकिनो मम यदुच्छ्वसितवैशसं प्राणधारणदुःखं तद्धि वृथा । एकाकित्वमत्र

१ संव०, संक०. २ तीरं समुद्धतकम० प्रकीर्णकेसरमृणालकन्दाङ्कुर०; कषायकरटः. ३ ०रमनोहरम्; ०ङ्कुरमाहरन्ननवरत. ४ प्रचलकर्णजर्जरिततरलतर. ५ नीहारवित्रस्त. ६ खण्ड. ७ संपातिताः. ८ (निरूप्य) कथं. ९ चरेऽपि. १० व्याहरामि. ११ वयस्य मकरन्द- १२ गुंच्छ्वसिमि. १३ समघटीऽय०. १४ ०त्वनुभवं वृथा भाविनम्, विरोधिरमणी. यवस्त्वनुभवाद् द्विधाभाविनः; वस्त्वनुभवान्यथाभाविनः ।

**त्वया सह न याति[1] योत्र दिवसोपि स ध्वंसतां**
**प्रमोद[2]मृगतृष्णिकां धिगपरत्र या[3] जायते ॥ ३५ ॥**

**मक०**—अये उन्मादमोहान्तरितोऽपि मां[4] प्रति कुतश्चिद्व्यञ्जका[5]त्प्रबुद्ध एवास्य सहजस्नेहसंस्कारः । त[6]दसंनिहितमेव मां मन्यते । ( पुरः[7] स्थित्वा । ) एष पार्श्वचर एव ते म[8]करन्दो मन्दभाग्यः ।

**माधवः**—हा प्रियवयस्य संभावय परिष्वजस्व माम् । प्रियां तु मालतीं प्रति निराशः[9] परिश्रान्तोस्मि । ( इति मूर्च्छति । )

**मक०**—( सहर्षम् । ) ए[10]ष संभावयामि जीवितेश्वरम् । ( विलोक्य सकरुणम् । ) हा कष्टम् । आ[11]विर्भूतमत्परिष्वङ्गोत्कण्ठ एव निश्चेतनः संवृत्तः । तत्कृतमिदानीं [12]जीविताशाव्यसनेन । सर्वथैव मे नास्ति वयस्य इति युक्तः परिच्छेदः । हा वयस्य

**यत्स्नेहसंज्वरवता हृदयेन नित्य-**
**माबद्धवेपथु विनापि निमित्तयोगात् ।**
**[13]त्वद्व्यापदो गणयता भयमन्वभावि**
**तत्सर्वमेकपद एव मम प्र[14]शान्तम् ॥ ३६ ॥**

---

हेतुः । धिगेव रमणीयवस्त्वनुभवान्वृथाभाविन इति मुख्यः पाठः । रम्यपदार्थविषयानुभवान्निष्फलोत्पादशीलान्धिक् । रमणीयवस्त्वनुभवादिति पाठे वृथाभाविनोऽनुभवाद्रम्यवस्तु धिक् । निष्फलं तज्ज्ञानमित्यर्थः । धिगेव रमणीयतां त्वदनुभावभावादृत इति पाठे मम सौन्दर्यादिकं धिक् । कुतः । तवानुभावः सहभावस्तत्र भावोऽभिप्रायस्तं विना । यद्वा अनुभावो वागङ्गसत्त्वाभिनये भावः सत्त्वं तं विना । 'वागङ्गसत्त्वाभिनयेऽनुभावस्तु स्मृतो बुधैः' ॥ इति भरतः । भावादित्यृतेयोगे पञ्चमी । त्वया मकरन्देन तया मालत्या च सह यो दिवसो नास्ति सोऽपि दिवसो विलीयताम् । अन्यत्र मालतीमकरन्दाभ्यां या प्रमोदमृगतृष्णा मम जायते तामपि धिक् । युवाभ्यां विना दैवान्मे हर्षोऽप्याभासीभूत इति भावः । अत एव प्रमोदस्य मृगतृष्णाया रूपकेणालीकत्वमुक्तम् ॥ ३५ ॥ **मकरन्दः** । उन्माददशायामनिश्चयाद्यतः कुतश्चिदित्युक्तम् । व्यञ्जकात्संस्काराभिव्यञ्जकात् । प्रबुद्धः उद्बुद्धः ॥ **माधवः** । संभावय पालय । श्रमाद्वैराग्याच्च मूर्च्छत्येतदर्थं निराश इत्युक्तम् । **मकरन्दः** । जीवितेश्वरमित्यनेन तुल्या जीवनसामग्र्युक्ता । निश्चेष्टः प्रलययुक्तजनाकृतिः । परिच्छेदो निश्चयः । **यदित्यादि** । स्नेहरूपसंतापवता

---

१ भाति; यस्तया च दिवसः स विध्वंसताम्. २ प्रमोह. ३ का मानुषे. ४ संप्रत्ययं मां प्रत्यप्रतिकूलो यतः कु;० मां प्रत्यविकलः. ५ व्यञ्जनात्. ६ तत्संनि०...मां न. ७ पुरतः. ८ स मक०. ९ ०श एव, निराशपरिश्रमः संवृत्तोस्मि. १० एषोहं. ११ कथमा०, निश्चेष्टः सं०. १२ आशा०. १३ त्वय्यां०. १४ प्रणष्टम्.

सखे वरं त एवातिक्रान्ता मुहूर्तास्तथाविधमपि भवन्तं येषु चेतयमानमनुभूतवानस्मि। इदानीं तु

> भारः कायो जीवितं वज्रकीलं
> काष्ठाः शून्या निष्फलानीन्द्रियाणि।
> कष्टः कालो मां प्रति त्वत्प्रयाणे
> शान्तालोकः सर्वतो जीवलोकः॥ ३७॥

(विचिन्त्य।) तत्किं नु खलु माधवास्तमयसाक्षिणा मया भवितव्यमिति जीवामि। भवत्वमुष्माद्गिरिशिखरात्पाटलावत्यां निपत्य माधवस्य मरणाग्रेसरो भवामि। (किंचित्परिक्रम्य सकरुणं निवृत्यावलोक्य च।) कष्टं भोः कष्टम्।

> तदेतदासितोत्पलद्युति शरीरमस्मिन्नभू-
> न्ममापि तिदृढपीडनैरपि न तृप्तिरालिङ्गनैः।

---

हृदा विनापि भयकारणेन सकम्पं भयं नित्यमन्वभाव्यनुभूतं यत्तत्सर्वं मम भयं त्वदीयविपत्तीर्गणयतः संभावयत एकस्मिन्क्षणे परिसमाप्तम्। कदा ते किं स्यादित्यादिभयं प्रकृतदशया प्रशान्तमिति भावः। एतत्पक्षे गणयतेति पाठे विधिनेत्यर्थात्। यद्वा त्वय्यापदो गणयता हृदा यद्भयमनुभूतं तदधुना गतामित्यर्थः। तथा च त्वन्निमितमधुना तु सहेतुकैव विपदिति भावः॥ ३६॥ वरं मनागिष्टे। 'मनागिष्टे वरं यत्तु कश्चिदाह तदव्ययम्।' इति शाश्वतः। अव्ययानामनेकार्थत्वादुक्तोऽर्थः सुलभ एव। चेतयमानं चेतनावन्तम्। **भार इत्यादि**। कायो भारो धर्तुमशक्यः। धारणाशक्यतया व्याधिः। जीवनं वज्रकीलकमनुच्छेदात्। अनेन मर्मच्छेदः। मर्मच्छेदेन चिन्ता। दिशः शून्या इति जडता। इन्द्रियाणि नेत्रादीन्यफलानि कार्याक्षमाणि। बाह्यविषयाग्रहाद्दैन्यम्। कालः कष्टो दुःखदः। दैन्येन जीवनाक्षमता। संसारः सर्वत्र प्रशान्तदर्शनः। तथा च त्वां विना न मज्जीवनमिति भावः। त्वत्प्रयाणे तव गमने विनाश इति यावत्। सतिसप्तमीयम्। मां प्रतीति सर्वत्र योज्यम्। यद्वा। पृथिव्यादिद्रव्यनवके प्रधानद्रव्यदूषणेन दोषमाह तत्र काय इति पृथिव्या जीवनमित्यात्मनः काष्ठा इति दिश इन्द्रियाणीतीन्द्रियाणां काल इति कालस्य लोक इति विषयाणां दोष उक्तः। शान्तालोकोऽनुपभोग्य इत्यर्थः॥ ३७॥ अस्तमयो विनाशः। व्याधिदशायामयम्। यहाह—'निर्वेदश्चैव चिन्ता च दैन्यं ग्लानिः श्रमस्तथा। जडता मरणं चैव व्याधौ तु करुणेऽपि च॥' पाटलावती नदीभेदः। प्रियदर्शनार्थं निवर्तनम्। मूर्च्छां दृष्ट्वा सकरुणम्॥ तादृशं दृष्ट्वा सखेदमाह—**तदित्यादि**। सखे

---

१ अथवा. २ शल्यभूतम्. ३ संप्रति. ४ इत्यतो. ५ माधवमर०. ६ सकरुणं परिवृत्या०. ७ ममापि. ८ पीडितैः.

**यदुल्लसितविस्मया[1] बत निपीतवत्यः पुरा**
**नवप्रणयविभ्रमाकुलितमालतीदृष्टयः ॥ ३८ ॥**

आश्चर्यम्[2] । एतस्यां[3] तनावचरमे वयसि तावतो गुणसमाहारस्य संनिवेशः कथमिवाभूत् । सखे माधव

**आपूर्णश्च कलाभिरिन्दुरमलो यातश्च राहोर्मुखं**
**संजातश्च घनाघनो जलधरः शीर्णश्च वायोर्जवात् ।**
**निर्वृत्तश्च फलेग्रहिर्द्रुमवरो दग्धश्च दावाग्निना**
**त्वं चूडामणितां गतश्च जगतः[4] प्राप्तश्च[5] मृत्योर्वशम् ॥ ३९ ॥**

तत्परिष्वजेहं[6] तावदेवं गतमपि प्रियवयस्यम् । अर्थितश्चानेन संप्रत्ययमेवार्थः । (परिष्वज्य) हा वयस्य विमलविद्यानिधे गुणगुरो र्मालतीस्वयंग्राहजीवितेश्वर कामन्दकीमकरन्दानन्दनमुखचन्द्र माधव अयमत्रं[10] ते जन्मन्यपाश्चिमः पश्चिमावस्थाप्रार्थितो मकरन्दबाहुपरिष्वङ्गः । सखे संप्रति मुहूर्तमपि मकरन्दो जीवतीति मैव मंस्थाः[11] ।

**आ जन्मनः सहनिवासितया[12] मयैव**
**मातुः पयोधरपयोऽपि समं निपीयं[13] ।**
**त्वं[14] पुण्डरीकमुख बन्धुतया निरस्त-**
**मेको निवापसलिलं पिबसीत्ययुक्तम् ॥ ४० ॥**

---

यत्तवाङ्गं नीलनलिनश्यामं तदेतत् । अस्मिन्नङ्गे गाढासङ्गनैरप्यालिङ्गनैर्मम तृप्तिर्नाभूत् । यदङ्गं नवस्नेहविलासव्याकुलमालतीदृष्टय उपचिताद्भुताः । पूर्वं निपीतवत्यो नित्यादरेणावलोकितवत्य इत्यर्थः । बत खेदे ॥ ३८ ॥ अचरमे नूतने । समाहारो मेलकः । **आपूर्ण इत्यादि** । सखे त्वं संसारस्य चूडामणीभूतश्च मरणं प्राप्तश्च । अत्र तुल्ययोगितया दृष्टान्तमाह—निर्मलश्चन्द्रः कलाभिः पूर्णश्च राहुग्रस्तश्च । मेघो घनाघनो वर्षुकाब्दश्च वातवेगाद्विशकलितश्च । द्रुमश्रेष्ठः फलेग्रहिः फलभारवान्निर्वृत्तो जातश्च वनाग्निना दग्धश्च । यथा तथा त्वमपीत्यर्थः । 'घनाघनो मत्तगजे वर्षुकाब्दमहेन्द्रयोः' । इत्यमरमाला । यद्वा घनाघनोऽतिनिबिडः । घनशब्दस्यैवावृत्त्या प्रयोगाद्द्रवद इतिवत् । फलेग्रहिर्निपातनात् । फलानि गृह्णाति धारयतीति फलेग्रहिः । 'स्यादवन्ध्यः फलेग्रहिः' इत्यमरः ॥ ३९ ॥ एवं गतं मूर्च्छितम् । अयमर्थ आलिङ्गनरूपः । मया सहेति शेषः । अपश्चिमो दुर्लभः । पश्चिमावस्था शेषावस्था । **आ जन्मेत्यादि** । हे पद्मास्य जन्मन आरभ्य मयैव समं तुल्यगृहतया मातुः स्तन्यं पीत्वाधुना त्वमेको निवाप-

---

१ विभ्रमाः; ० विभ्रमं मधु; विस्मयं. २ हन्त भोः. ३ एकस्यां तनावेतावतो. ४ जगतां. ५ प्राप्तोसि. ६ अस्मात्प्राक्-विचिन्त्य इत्य०. ७ फला. ८ हा मा०. ९ हा का० नन्दजनक; नन्दचन्द्र. १० अयं स. ११ मैवं; मैवावमंस्थाः । कुतः. १२ ०सतया; मयैव—सहैव. १३ निपीतं. १४ तत्त्वं.

( सकरुणं विमुच्य परिक्रम्य च । ) इयमधस्तात्पाटलावती । भगवत्यापगे

**प्रियस्य सुहृदो यत्र मम तत्रैव संभवः ।**
**भूयादमुष्य भूयोऽपि भूयासमनुसंचरः ॥ ४१ ॥**

( इति पतितुमिच्छति । )

( प्रविश्य सहसा । ) **सौदामिनी**—( वारयित्वा । ) वत्स कृतं साहसेन ।

**मक०**—( विलोक्य । ) अयि कासि । किमहं त्वया प्रतिषिद्धः ।

**सौदा०**—आयुष्मन् । किं[2] त्वं मकरन्दः ।

**मक०**—मुञ्च[3] । स एवास्मि मन्दभाग्यः ।

**सौदा०**—वत्स योगिन्यस्मि मालत्यभिज्ञानं च धारयामि ।
( इति बकुलमालां दर्शयति । )

**मक०**—( सोच्छ्वासं[4] सकरुणम् । ) आर्ये अपि जीवति मालती ।

**सौदा०**—अथ किम् । अपि च वत्स किमत्याहितं माधवस्य । यदनिष्टं व्यवसितोऽसीत्याकम्पितास्मि[5] ।

**मक०**—आर्ये तमहं प्रमुग्धमेव वैराग्यात्परितत्यज्यागतः । तदेहि[6] । तूर्णं संभावयावः । ( इति त्वरितं परिक्रामतः । )

**माधवः**—( आश्वस्य ) अये प्रतिबोधित एवास्मि केनापि । ( विचिन्त्य । ) नूनमस्यायमभिनवजीमूतजलबिन्दुवाहिनः प्रभञ्जनस्यानवेक्षितास्मदवस्थो व्यापारः ।

**मक०**—( विलोक्य । ) दिष्ट्या पुनः प्रत्यापन्नचेतनो वयस्यः ।

**सौदा०**—( विलोक्य । ) संवदत्युभयो[11]र्मालतीनिवेदितः शरीराकारः ।

---

सलिलं प्रेतोदकाञ्जलिं बन्धुसमूहेन दत्तं पिबसीत्येतदयोग्यम् । सहपानार्थमहमप्यागच्छामीत्यर्थः । ' निवापः पितृदेये स्यात् ' इत्यमरः ॥ ४० ॥ आपगा नदी । **प्रियस्येत्यादि** । मित्रस्य संभव उत्पत्तिर्यत्र ममापि तत्रैव भूयात् । अमुत्रापरस्मिँल्लोके पुनरप्यस्यानुचरो भूयासमित्यर्थः । भूयादित्यादौ प्रार्थनायां लिङ् ॥ ४१ ॥ **सौदामिनी** । अत्याहितं प्रमोहोऽभूत् । **माधवः** । प्रभञ्जनो वायुः । **सौदा०**-

---

१ अम्ब; किमर्थम०; प्रति०-प्रतिहतः. २ अये. ३ मुञ्च मां. ४ सोच्छ्वासकरुणम्. ५ ०त्याशंकितास्मि, भीत्याकम्पि०, अस्मात्परं-अथ माधवः क्व इत्यधिकं क्वचित्. ६ सौदा०-तदेहि. ७ आश्वासितः; प्रतिबोधितवानस्मि. ८ उत्थायोपविश्य वि०. ९ स्यायं नवजलधरप्रभ०, मयमस्य नवजलधरपवनस्या०. १० दृष्ट्वा सोच्छ्वासं. ११ अनयोः

**माधवः**—भगवन् पौरस्त्यपर्वन

**भ्रमय जलदानम्भोगर्भान्प्रमोदय चातका-**
**न्कलय शिखिनः केकोत्कण्ठान्कठोरय केतकान् ।**
**विरहिणि जने मूर्च्छां लब्ध्वा विनोदयति व्यथा-**
**मकरुण पुनः संज्ञाव्याधिं विधाय किमीहसे ॥ ४२ ॥**

**मक०**—सुविहितमनेनाखिलजन्तुजीवनेन मातरिश्वना ।

**माधवः**—देवं वायो तथापि भवन्तमेवं प्रार्थये ।

**विकसत्कदम्बनिकुरुम्बपांसुना**
**सह जीवितं वह मम प्रिया यतः ।**
**अथ वा तदङ्गपरिवासशीतलं**
**मयि किंचिदर्पय भवान्हि मे गतिः ॥ ४३ ॥**

---

उभयोर्माधवमकरन्दयोः । **माधवः** । मूर्च्छयैव तं सोपालम्भमाह । **भगवन्निति** । पौरस्त्येत्यनेन भिन्नदेशकथनम् । तेन सहजकृत्रिमवैरशङ्का निरस्ता । तव विरहिदुःखमेव न कृत्यम् । अपि त्वन्यदपीत्याह—**भ्रमयेत्यादि** । जलपूर्णान्मेघांश्चालय । कोकिलान्हर्षय । केकयोत्कण्ठानूर्ध्वगलान्सेच्छान्वा मयूरान्कलय नर्तय । कलेरनेकार्थत्वात् । केतकान्केतकीवृक्षान्कठोरय कोरकितान्कुरु । कोरकितत्वेन निम्नोन्नततया कठोरत्वम् । 'केतक्यामपि केतकः' इति शब्दभेदः । अत एव 'केतकाधानहेतोः' इति मेघदूते । यद्वा केतकीपुष्पाणि कठोरय विकासय । तत्करोतीति णिच् । अस्मिन्पक्षे लिङ्गमाशिष्यम् । लोकाश्रयत्वाल्लिङ्गव्यत्यय इत्यवधेयम् । विरहिजने मूर्च्छां प्राप्य व्यथां स्फोटयति सति पुनः संज्ञाव्याधिं चेतनारूपं रोगं कृत्वा किं त्वमिच्छसि । महता दुःखितदुःखशान्तिः क्रियते । त्वं प्रबोध्य दुःखयसीत्यनर्हम् । अत एवाकरुण इत्युक्तम् । प्रमोदय चातकानीत्यपि पाठः । प्रथमपाठे तु कोकिलप्रमोदो वर्षास्वपि कविसंप्रदाये वर्ण्यत इत्यवधेयम् ॥ ४२ ॥ **मकरन्दः** । मातरिश्वा वायुः । वातीति वायुरित्युचितपदन्यासेन जीवनयोग्यतोक्ता । **माधवः** । तथाप्यनिष्टकरणादपि । **विकसदित्यादि** । मम प्रिया यतो यत्र तं देशं मम जीवितं प्रफुल्लकदम्बसमूहधूल्या सह प्रापय । घटय मे इति वा पाठः । सा विरहदीना म्रियेतातस्तज्जीवनाय मज्जीवितं नयेति भावः । पांसुना

---

१ वायो. २ कोकिलान्–मौलिकान्. ३ केतकं. ४ सुविहित०, हितमनेन: ५ अस्मात्परं—अपि च ।

**एते (के) तकसूनसौरभजुषः पौरप्रगल्भाङ्गना-**
**व्यालोलालकवल्लरीविलुठनव्याजोपभुक्ताननाः ।**
**किं चोन्निद्रकदम्बकुड्मलपुटीधूलीलुठत्षट्पद-**
**व्यूहव्याहतिहारिणो विरहिणः कर्षन्ति वर्षानिलाः ॥४३॥** इत्यधिकं क्वचित

६ भगवन् देव; एवं–एव, एतावत्. ७ घटय मे. ८ अपि वा. ९ भवांस्तु.

( कृताञ्जलिः प्रणमति । )

**सौदा०**—सुसमाहितः[1] खल्वभिज्ञानार्पणस्यावसरः ।

( अञ्जलौ बकुलमालां मुञ्चति[2] । )

**माधवः**—( साकूतविस्मयहर्षम्[3] । ) कथमियमस्मद्विरचिता प्रियतमास्त[4]-नोन्नाहदुर्ललितमूर्तिरनङ्गमन्दिराङ्गनबकुलप्रसव[5]माला । ( निरूप्य[6] सहर्षम् । ) कः संदेहः । तथा हि स एवायमस्याः

**मुग्धेन्दुसुन्दरतदीयमुखावलोक-**
**हेलाविशृङ्खलकुतूहलनिह्नवाय ।**
**दुर्न्यस्तपुष्परचितोऽपि[7] लवङ्गिकाया-**
**स्तोषं ततान विषमग्रथितोपि भागः[8] ॥ ४४ ॥**

---

सहेत्यनेन परमाणुरूपं मे मनोऽपि तत्समूहे गमिष्यतीति न ते प्रयासोऽपि स्यादित्युक्तम् । नो वा प्रियाङ्गसदावस्थितिहिमं यत्किञ्चिद्वस्तु मयि तदर्पय देहि । ईरयेति पाठे प्रेरयेत्यर्थः । तदेव मे तापशान्त्यै स्यादिति भावः । अत्र हेतुमाह-यतो मम भवान्गतिराश्रयः । आश्रयस्याश्रितजीवनं युक्तमेवेति भावः । अपि वेति पाठेऽपि संभावनायाम् ॥ ४३ ॥ **सौदामिनी** । समाहितो युक्तः । वायुप्रार्थनाप्रकरणात् । **माधवः** । प्रियाङ्गसङ्गिमालालोकात्सहर्षत्वम् । यदाह—' प्राप्ये वाप्यप्राप्ये लब्धेऽर्थे प्रियसमागमे वापि । हृदयमनोरथलाभे हर्षः संजायते पुंसाम् ॥ ' उन्नाह उत्सेध उपरिवहनं वा । दुर्ललितातिप्रिया । अनङ्ग एव मन्दिरमनङ्गस्य वा मन्दिरम् ॥ **मुग्धेत्यादि** । अस्या मालायाः स एवायं भागो यो लवङ्गिकाया अपि संतोषमकरोत् ॥ अपिपदान्मालत्या अपीत्यर्थः । विषमं ग्रथितं ग्रन्थना यत्र सः । विषमेण ग्रथित इति वा । अत्र हेतुमाह—मुग्धं मनोज्ञमिन्दुकान्तं यन्मालतीमुखम् ॥ यद्वा विरहात्क्षामत्वादिना बालेन्दुवत्कान्तं यत्तदास्यं तदालोके सति हेलया शृङ्गारचेष्टया विशृङ्खलं सर्वत्र वर्तमानं यत्कौतुकं तद्गोपनाय दुर्न्यस्तैः पूर्वग्रथनादन्यथा दत्तैः पुष्पै रचितः । एतत्तु प्रथमाङ्क एव व्यक्तम् । ननु हेला स्त्रीविषया । यदाह भरतः—' यौवने त्रिदश स्त्रीणां विकारा नेत्रपातजाः । आदौ त्रयोऽङ्गजास्तेषां दश स्वाभाविकास्तथा ॥ ' तत्राङ्गजेषु हावहेलालक्षणम्—' अक्षिभ्रुवोर्विकाराद्याः शृङ्गारस्य च सूचकाः । सग्रीवारेचका भावा हावास्तेभ्यः समुत्थिताः ॥ य एव हावः सैवासौ शृङ्गाररससंभवा । समाख्याता बुधैर्हेला ललिताभिनयात्मिका । ' अतो माधवे हेलेत्ययुक्तम् । मैवम् । स्त्रीणामित्यस्योपलक्षणत्वात्पुरुषेऽपि कामावस्थासाम्याद्धेलावचनात् । यदाह—' हेला

---

१ समीहितः, ज्ञानस्यार्पणावसरः. २ अर्पयति. ३ साकूतं सहर्षं सविस्मयं च विलोक्य सा०. ४ प्रियास्तनो. ५ पादपकुसुम. ६ सम्यङ्निरूप्य. ७ रचनोपि. ८ ग्रथितैकभागः; ०तो विभागः.

(सहर्षोन्मादमुत्थाय।) प्रिये[1] मालति इयं वीक्ष्यसे[2]। (सकोपमिव।) अयि मदवस्थानभिज्ञे[3]

**प्रयान्तीव प्राणाः सुतनु हृदयं ध्वंसत इव**
**ज्वलन्तीवाङ्गानि प्रसरति समन्तादिव तमः।**
**त्वराप्रस्तावोऽयं न खलु परिहासस्य विषय-**
**स्तवक्ष्णोरानन्दं वितर मयि मा भूरकरुणा ॥ ४५ ॥**

(सर्वतो[4] दृष्ट्वा सनिर्वेदम्।) कुतोऽत्र मालती। (बकुलमालामुद्दिश्य[5]।) अयि प्रियाप्रणयिनि[6] बकुलमाले उपकारिण्यसि। अतः स्वागतं भवत्याः।

**निष्प्रत्यूहाः[7] प्रियसखि यदा दुःसहाः संबभूवु-**
**र्मोहोद्दाहव्यसनगुरवो[8] मन्मथोन्मादवेगाः।**
**तस्मिन्काले कुवलयदृशस्त्वत्समाश्लेष[9] एव**
**प्राणत्राणं प्रगुणमभवन्मत्परिष्वङ्गकल्पः[10] ॥ ४६ ॥**

---

हावश्च भावश्च व्याजो विश्रम्भभाषणम्। चाटुः प्रेमाभिसंधानं चकितं च विलासितम्'॥ तत्र रागतः सहसा प्रवृत्तौ हेतुश्चित्तोल्लासो हेलेति। यद्वा अवलोक्यत इत्यवलोकः। कर्मणि घञ्। इन्दुसुन्दरमालतीमुखेऽवलोक्या दृश्या या हेला तया विशृङ्खलं यन्माधवस्य कुतूहलं तद्व्रोपनायेत्यर्थः॥ ४४॥ संकल्पलिखितप्रियादर्शनाद्धर्षः। दर्शनाप्राप्त्या पुनराह—नन्विति। अत्राप्यलाभादुपालभ्यते। **अयीति**। परिहासाददर्शनमाशङ्क्य तदनवसरमाह—**प्रयान्तीत्यादि**। प्राणाः प्रयान्तीव सर्वतः शून्यत्वात्। हे सुतनु मनो ध्वंसत इव मोहात्। अङ्गज्वलनमतिदाहात्। एतेन व्याधिरुक्तः। सर्वतस्तमः प्रसरतीव। अनेन जडता। सकलेन्द्रियाणामग्रहात्। जडतानन्तरं मरणशङ्कायामाश्वास एव युक्त इत्याह—त्वरेति। खलु निश्चये। यत एवं ततो नेत्रप्रीतिं देहि। स्वं दर्शयेत्यर्थः। मद्विषये निर्दया मा भविष्यसि। यद्वा अकरुणा मा भूर्न भवसि। माङिति कालसामान्ये लुङ्। पूर्वकरुणेदानीमपि निर्वाह्यतामित्यर्थः। इव शब्द उत्प्रेक्षायाम्॥ ४५॥ **निरित्यादि**। यदा माल्त्याः पद्माक्ष्याः कामोन्मादोद्वेगा निर्विघ्ना अत्यर्थं दुःसहा अङ्गदाहदुःखमहान्तस्तद्दुःखोपदेशकाराः संबभूवुः संभूयोद्गतास्तत्र काले तस्यास्त्वदालिङ्गनमेव शीघ्रं प्राणरक्षकमभूत्। अत एव मदालिङ्गनतुल्यः। उन्माथ उन्मथनमुद्वेग इति यावत्। प्रगुणमिति पाठे प्रकृष्टगुणमित्यर्थः। क्रियाविशेषणं वा। कामदुःखोद्वेगस्य प्रियसङ्गस्यालाभादविघ्नत्वम्। मालतीप्रणयित्वात्प्रियसखि इति। दुःसहत्वमधृतिकरणात्। उद्दाह उद्गतदाहः। व्यसनस्थाने 'व्यथन' इति पाठे व्यथनं

---

१ चण्डि. २ विलोक्यसे; नन्वियं वी०. ३ मदनावस्था०. ४ इति दिशोवलोक्य. ५ मालां प्रति. ६ ०यिनि परमोपका०. ७ ०त्यूहं. ८ मोहोद्दाम. ९ षणं वा. १० ञाणप्रगुण; प्रगुणनमभून्म०, त्वरितमभवन्म०.

( सकरुणं निर्वर्ण्य । )

आनन्दमिश्रमदनज्वरदीपनानि
गाढानुरागरसवन्ति तदा तदा च ।
स्नेहाकराणि मम मुग्धदृशश्च कण्ठे
कष्टं स्मरामि तव तानि गतागतानि ॥ ४७ ॥

( हृदये निधाय मूर्च्छति । )

**मक०**—( उपसृत्य वीजयन् । ) सखे समाश्वसिहि समाश्वसिहि ।

**माधवः**—( समाश्वस्य । ) मकरन्द किं न पश्यसि कुतोऽपि सहसैव मालतीस्नेहं वहतो बकुलदाम्नो लाभः । तत्कथं नु मन्यसे कुत एतदिति ।

**मक०**—वयस्य इयमार्या योगीश्वर्यस्य मालत्यभिज्ञानस्योपनेत्री ।

**माधवः**—( विलोक्य सकरुणं कृताञ्जलिः । ) आर्ये प्रसीद कथय जीवति मे प्रियतमा ।

**सौदा०**—वत्स समाश्वसिहि समाश्वसिहि । जीवति सा कल्याणी ।

**माधवमकरन्दौ**—( समुच्छ्वस्य । ) आर्ये यद्येवं तत्कथय क एष वृत्तान्त इति ।

**सौदा०**—पुरा किल करालायतने मालतीमुपहरन्नघोरघण्टः करवालपाणिर्माधवेन व्यापादितः ।

---

पीडा । अधुना मालां विनास्याः कथं जीवनं भविष्यतीति भावः ॥ ४६ ॥ निर्वर्ण्य निरूप्य । **आनन्देत्यादि** । मम मालत्याश्च कण्ठे तव गतागतानि स्मरामि । स्मरणस्यातिदुःखदत्वात्कष्टम् । तदा तदा तस्मिंस्तस्मिन्काले । तत्र चोरिकाविवाहात्पूर्वं मालतीकण्ठगतेति गतं लवङ्गिकाबुद्धया माधवकण्ठमागतेत्यागतमित्येकम् । चोरिकाविवाहे मालत्या माधवकण्ठे नीतातो गतमथ तन्मुखदर्शनात्स्वकण्ठेऽर्पितेत्यागतमिति द्वितीयम् । पुनस्तत्र प्रणयवशान्माधवेन मालत्यै दत्तेति गतमिदानीं तु सौदामिन्या मालतीसकाशादानीय दत्तेति त्रीणि गतागतानि । अत एव बहुवचनम् । कीदृशानि । तद्दशायामन्तरान्तरा हर्षलाभादानन्दमिश्रितकामतापप्रकाशनानि । दृढानुरागरसयोगीनि । स्नेहस्याकरो येषु तानि । स्नेहं प्रीतिमाकुर्वन्ति व्याकुर्वन्तीति स्नेहकराणि । कृञो हेत्वित्यादिना टप्रत्ययः । तदा चेति चकारात्कालान्तरपरिग्रहः ॥ ४७ ॥ **मकरन्दः** । आर्या मान्या ।

---

१ निःश्वस्य. २ आनन्दनानि. ३ च तस्याः. ४ स्नेहाङ्कनानि. ५ इति हृ०; मूर्च्छितः पतति. ६ वयस्य. ७ स्नेहस्वहस्तस्य लाभः. ८ अञ्जलिं बध्वा. ९ अपि जीवति, प्रिय०-प्रिया. १० अस्ति पुरा करालायतनेऽघोरघण्टः कृपाणपाणिर्व्यापा०.

**माधवः**—( सावेगम् । ) आर्ये विरम विरम । विज्ञातो वृत्तान्तः ।

**मक०**—सखे क इव ।

**माधवः**—सखे किमन्यत् । सकामा कपालकुण्डलेति ।

**मक०**—आर्ये अप्येवम् ।

**सौदा०**—एवं यथा विदितं वत्सेन ।

**मकरन्दः**—कष्टं भोः कष्टम् ।

> **कुमुदाकरेण शरदिन्दुचन्द्रिका**
> **यदि रामणीयकगुणाय संगता ।**
> **सुकृतं तदस्तु कतमस्त्वयं विधि-**
> **र्यदकालमेघवितर्तिर्व्ययूयुजत् ॥ ४८ ॥**

**माधवः**—हा प्रिये मालति कष्टमतिबीभत्समापन्नासि ।

> **कथमिव तदाभवस्त्वं कमलमुखि कपालकुण्डलाग्रस्ता ।**
> **उत्पातधूमलेखाक्रान्तेव कला शशधरस्य ॥ ४९ ॥**

भगवति कपालकुण्डले

> **निर्माणमेव हि तदादरलालनीयं**
> **मा पूतनात्वमुपगाः शिवतातिरेधि ।**

**माधवः** । सकामा मदपकारेण सिद्धप्रतिज्ञेत्यर्थः । **कुमुदेत्यादि** । कुमुदसमूहेन यदि शरच्चन्द्रचन्द्रिका सौन्दर्यगुणार्थं संगता प्राप्ता सत्सुकृतं शोभनकरणमस्तु । द्वयोरपि रम्यत्वात् । अयं पुनः कः प्रकारः कुत्सितप्रकारो वा यदकालमेघपाङ्क्ति-र्व्ययूयुजद्वियोजयामास । विच्छेदं कृतवतीत्यर्थः । ध्वनिनात्र कुमुदाकरो माधवश्च-न्द्रिका मालती मेघसंततिः कपालकुण्डलेत्युक्तम् ॥ ४८ ॥ **अतिबीभत्स-मिति** । उद्वेगहेतुकपालकुण्डलादर्शनाद्बीभत्सः । यदाह—' उद्वेजनैश्च बहुभिर्बी-भत्सरसः समुद्भवति ' । **कथमित्यादि** । तत्कवलिता हे पद्ममुखि तदा त्वमपि कथमभवः । भयात्कथं त्वमासीः किं त्वयोक्तं कस्ते त्राताभूदित्यादि-ज्ञापनाय कथमिति सामान्यनिर्देशः । केतुकवलिता चन्द्रकलेव । एतदुपमया बीभ-त्सजविषादसंभवा ग्लानिरप्युक्ता । यदाह—' अपस्मारस्तथोन्मादो विषादो मद एव च । मृत्युर्व्याधिर्भयं चैव भावा बीभत्ससंभवाः ॥' ४९ ॥ ' स्त्रीबालं नैव घातयेत्' इति निजधर्मं जानत्या त्वया सा घातितेति सोल्लुण्ठमाह—भगवति इति । **निर्माणमित्यादि** । तन्निर्माणं मालतीरूपादिकमेव तदादरेण रक्षणीयं

१ सोद्वेगम्. २ निवेदितं. ३ भोः क०. ४ गुणेन. ५ सुकृते यदस्तु. ६ वितर्तिं त्वयू. ७ कथमपि. ८ रेखा. ९ तदा तव. १० पूतनत्व०. ११ ०तातिरेव.

नैसर्गिकी सुरभिणः कुसुमस्य सिद्धा
मूर्ध्नि स्थितिर्न मुसलैरवताडनानि ॥ ५० ॥

सौदा०—वत्स अलमावेगेन ।

अकरिष्यदसौ पापमतिनिष्करुणैव सा ।
नाभविष्यमहं तत्र यदि तत्परिपन्थिनी ॥ ५१ ॥

उभौ—( प्रणम्य । ) अतिप्रसन्नमार्यापादैः । तत्कथय का पुनस्त्वस्माकमेवंविधो बन्धुः ।

सौदा०—ज्ञास्यथः खल्वेतत् । ( उत्थाय । ) इयमहमिदानीम्

गुरुचर्यातपस्तन्त्रमन्त्रयोगाभियोगजाम् ।
इमामाक्षेपिणीं सिद्धिमातनोमि शिवाय वः ॥ ५२ ॥

( इति समाधवा निष्क्रान्ता । )

मक०—आश्चर्यमाश्चर्यम् ।

व्यतिकर इव भीमस्तामसो वैद्युतश्च
क्षणमुपहतचक्षुर्वृत्तिरुद्भूय शान्तः ।

---

भवति । रम्यत्वादेव । पूतनात्वं राक्षसीत्वं तन्नाशेन मोपगा मा गमिष्यसि । यद्वा मांसं मे ततो भक्षयितव्यं किमिति चिन्तकत्वं पूतनात्वम् । 'पूतनत्वम्' इति पाठे राक्षसत्वमित्यर्थः । पूतना राक्षसीभेदे हरीतक्यां च पूतना ।' इति विश्वः । शिवतातिः कल्याणकर्येधि भव । 'शिव इत्यबोधीः' इति पाठे तन्निर्माणं शिवे कल्याणनिमित्तमित्यज्ञासीः । 'शिवतामुपैति' इति पाठे तन्निर्माणम् । कर्तृ । शिवतां कल्याणत्वं गच्छति । अतः पालनमस्य । भद्रवस्तुपुरस्कारः स्वभावादेवेत्याह—मनोहरस्य ख्यातस्य सुगन्धस्य वा पुष्पस्य मस्तके धृतिः स्वभावसिद्धा । न पादैः [अवताडितानि] पीडनानि स्वभावसिद्धानीत्यर्थः ॥ ५० ॥ **अकरिष्यदिति** । असौ कपालकुण्डला पापं तद्वधरूपमकरिष्यदेव । अतिनिष्करुणा यतः सा । यदि तत्र स्थाने वधे वा तस्या विरोधिनी नाहमभविष्यम् । क्रियातिपत्तौ लृङ् । बुद्धिप्रत्यक्षतयासाविति ॥ ५१ ॥ **उभौ** । अतिप्रसन्नं प्रसादः कृतः । **सौदामिनी** । ज्ञास्यथः । युवामित्यर्थात् । **गुर्वित्यादि** । गुरुचर्या गुरुसेवा गुर्वी चर्या विशिष्टमनुष्ठानम् । तपश्चान्द्रायणादि । तन्त्रं मण्डलवर्तनादि । मन्त्रस्ताराप्रभृतिदेवीनां तन्त्रस्य वागमस्य वा मन्त्रः । योगः समाधिः । एष्वभियोगादभ्यासाज्जातामिमामाकर्षणीं सिद्धिं युष्माकं कल्याणाय विस्तारयामि ॥ ५२ ॥ **व्यतिकर इति** । मालतीवार्ताया अप्यज्ञानादयं तामसोऽन्धकारजः अत एव भीमः । तज्जीवनज्ञानाद्वैद्युतश्चायं वि-

---

१ चरणैः; लैर्बन कुट्टनानि. २ दुष्क०; यतो निष्करुणेष. ३ माधवमक० ४ विधः, अस्माकमकारणब०. ५ ०थ, ज्ञास्यते. ६ चर्याभियोगतः; सिद्धयामि०. ७ माकर्षिणीं. ८ विद्यां. ९ मुपगत.

( विलोक्य सभयम् )

**कथमिह[1] न वयस्यस्तात्किमेतत्** ( विचिन्त्य ) **किमन्य-**
**त्प्रभवति हि महिम्ना[2] स्वेन योगीश्वरीयम्** ॥ ५३ ॥

( सवितर्कम् । ) किमयमर्थो[3]नर्थ इति संप्रति प्रमुग्धोऽस्मि । अपि च ।

**अस्तोकविस्मयमप[4]स्मृतपूर्ववृत्त-**
**मुद्भूतनूतनभयज्वरजर्जरं नः ।**
**एकक्षणत्रुटितसंघटितप्रमोह[5]-**
**मानन्दशोकशबल[6]त्वमुपैति चेतः** ॥ ५४ ॥

तदत्र[7] कान्तार[8]गहने सहास्मद्वर्गेण प्रविष्टां भगवतीमन्विष्य[9] तस्या वृत्तान्तमेनं कथयामि ।

( इति **निष्क्रान्ताः[10] सर्वे** । )

**माल[11]त्यन्वेषणं नाम नवमोऽङ्कः ।**

---

युत्संबन्धी । व्यतिकरः संपर्कः । अत एवानन्दाश्रुसंभारेणोपहतनेत्रवृत्तिः । कीदृशः । क्षणमुद्भूय शान्तः । अत एव विद्युद्विद्योतवितर्कः । कथमिह स्थाने वयस्यो माधवोऽपि नास्ति । तत्किमिदं क्व गतः केन वा स नीत इति विचिन्त्येत्यर्थः । निर्णयमाह—अन्य-त्किम् । यत इयं योगीश्वरी निजतपःप्रभावेण प्रभवति । अनया नीत इति भावः ॥ ५३ ॥ संशय्याह—**किमयमिति** । सौदामिनीनयनेऽर्थः प्रयोजनं कपालकुण्डलान-यनेऽनर्थ इति भावः । **अस्तोकेत्यादि** । अस्माकं चित्तम् । कर्तृ । हर्षशोकाभ्यां शबलत्वं मिश्रत्वं गच्छति । कीदृशम् । अनल्पाश्चर्यम् । एकदैव नानारससंभवात् । अप-स्मृतं विस्मृतं पूर्ववृत्तं मालतीहरणरूपं यत्र अत एवानन्दः । उद्भूतं नवं भयं माधवाप-कारशङ्काकृतं तेन ज्वरेण जीर्णम् । अत एव शोकः । यद्वा । माधवानवलोकनेनोद्भूतनव-शङ्काज्वरजर्जरतया शोकः । एकक्षण एव त्रुटितो घटितश्च प्रमोहो यत्र तत् । मालती-लाभसंभावनया त्रुटितो माधवापकारसंभावनया घटित इति भावः । अत एवात्याश्चर्यम् । स्तोकशब्दोऽल्पपर्यायः । अस्मद्वर्गेण मदयन्तिकालवङ्गिकाभ्याम् । 'विप्रनष्टाम्' इति कस्मिंश्चित्पुस्तके पाठो दृश्यते तत्रादृश्यमानामित्यर्थः ॥ ५४ ॥ भगवतीं कामन्दकीम् । अनेनाग्रिमाङ्कावतारस्यापि सूचनादङ्कावतारोऽयम् ॥

प्रासूत यं रत्नधरोऽतिविद्यो विद्योतिविद्या दमयन्तिकापि ।
जगद्धरं तत्कृतटिप्पणेऽङ्कोऽगलन्नवीने नवमोऽनवद्यः ॥

**इति नवमोऽङ्कः ।**

---

१ इव. २ किमन्यत्स्वेन. ३ ०यमनर्थ इति मुढोऽस्मि. ४ मविस्मृत. ५ प्रबोध, प्रमोद. ६ लं समु०. ७ दत्रैव. ८ राक्षसाने. ९ तीमनुसृत्य वृत्ता. १० निष्क्रान्तः. ११ सौदामिनीदर्शनः.

## दशमोऽङ्कः ।

( ततः प्रविशति कामन्दकी लवङ्गिका मदयन्तिका च । )

**कामन्दकी**—( सकरुणं सास्रम् । ) हा वत्से मालति मदङ्कालंकारिणि क्कासि देहि मे प्रतिवचनम् ।

आ जन्मनः प्रतिमुहूर्तविशेषरम्या-
ण्याचेष्टितानि तव संप्रति तानि तानि ।
चाटूनि चारुमधुराणि च संस्मृतानि
देहं दहन्ति हृदयं च विदारयन्ति ॥ १ ॥

अपि च । पुत्रि

अनियतरुदितस्मितं विराज-
त्कतिपयकोमलदन्तकुड्मलाग्रम् ।
वदनकमलकं शिशोः स्मरामि
स्खलदसमञ्जसमुग्धजल्पितं ते ॥ २ ॥

**इतरे**—( सास्रम् । ) हा प्रियसखि सुप्रसन्नमुखचन्द्रसुन्दरि क्क गतासि । को वा शिरीषकुसुमसुकुमारस्य ते शरीरस्य दैवदुर्विनय-

---

सहास्मद्वर्गेणेत्यव्यवधान एव सूचनात्तत्प्रवेशमाह–**तत इति** । कामन्दकी मालतीविश्लेषं श्रुत्वा विलपति–**हेत्यादि । आ जन्मन इत्यादि** । जन्मन आरभ्य प्रतिक्षणाधिक्यमनोज्ञानि तव तानि तानि पूर्वानुभूतान्याचेष्टितानि विनयादीनि संस्मृतानि सन्ति मेऽङ्गं दहन्ति चित्तं च दारयन्ति । अनेन बाह्या मानसी च पीडोक्ता । तथा चाटूनि वाक्कौशलानि स्मृतानि दाहादिकं कुर्वन्ति । विनयादीनामद्वेषकारितया रम्यत्वम् । चाटूनि कीदृशानि । चारूणि शोभावन्ति मधुराण्यनुल्बणानि च । यदाह—'सर्वावस्थाविशेषेषु दीप्तेषु ललितेषु च । अनुल्बणत्वं चेष्टानां माधुर्यमिति संज्ञितम्' ॥ १ ॥ **अनियतेत्यादि** । बालायास्तवास्यपद्मं स्मरामि । कीदृशम् । अस्थिरे क्रन्दनहास्ये यत्र तत् । शोभमानकिंचिन्मृदुदशनकलिकाग्रम् । सम्यक्स्थानप्रयत्नाभावात्स्खलत् । तत्त्वहान्यासमञ्जसं संख्यातिक्रमादज्ञानाद्वासमञ्जसम् । मुग्धमर्थाभावात् । जल्पितं मन्दोक्तिर्यत्र तत् । सर्वत्र शैशवमेव हेतुः । कमलकमित्यत्राल्पार्थे कन् । सम्यगञ्जसा तत्त्वेन वर्तत इति समञ्जसमिति । 'अञ्जसा तत्त्वतूर्णयोः' इति विश्वः । मंजु जल्पितमिति मञ्जु मनोहरम् ॥ २ ॥ **इतरे** । अत्रैकाकिन्या एकमात्रस्वरूपायाः । आदावुपस्थितोऽथा-

---

१ मदलंकारका०. २ प्रभृति यानि. ३ वचनानि च चारुनेत्रे. ४ चाति. ५ ( आकाशे ) अपि. ६ रुचिर. ७ मञ्जु,–तं तत्. ८ मद० लवङ्गिके.

परिणाम एकाकिन्या उपनतः । महाभाग माधव उपस्थितास्तमित-महोत्सवस्ते जीवलोकः संवृत्तः । ( हा पिअसहि सुप्पसण्णमुहचन्दसुन्दरि कहिं गदासि । को वा सिरीसकुसुमसुउमारस्स दे सरीरस्स देव्वदुव्विणअपरिणामो एकाकिणीए उवणदो । महाभाअ माहव उवत्थिदत्थमिदमहूसवो दे जीअलोओ संउत्तो । )

**काम०**—( सविशेषखेदम् । ) हा वत्सौ

**अभिनवरागरसोऽयं भवतोः कृतकौतुकः परिष्वङ्गः ।**
**लवलीलवङ्गयोरिव नियतिमहावात्ययाभिहतः ॥ ३ ॥**

**लव०**—( सोद्वेगम् । ) हताश वज्रमय सर्वथा नृशंसमसि हृदय । ( हदास वज्जमअ सव्वहा णिसंसं सि हिअअ । ) ( इति हृदयमाहत्य पतति । )

**मद०**—सखि लवङ्गिके ननु भणामि क्षणमात्रमपि तावत्समाश्वसिहि । ( सहि लवङ्गिए णं भणामि क्खणमेत्तं वि दाव समस्सस । )

**लव०**—सखि किं करोमि दृढवज्रलेपप्रतिबद्धनिश्चलमिव जीवितं न मां परित्यजति । ( सखि किं करोमि दिढवज्जलेवपडिवद्धणिच्चलं विअ जीविदं ण मं परिच्चअदि । )

**काम०**—वत्से मालति जन्मनः प्रभृति वल्लभा ते लवङ्गिका । तत्किमेनामुज्जिहानजीवितां वराकीं नानुकम्पसे । इयं हि

---

स्तमितो महोत्सवो यत्र सः । **अभिनवेत्यादि** । अभिनवे रागेऽनुरागे रस इच्छा यत्र । यद्वा । अभिनवरागो नूतनासक्तो रसः शृङ्गारो यत्र । कृतं कौतुकं हर्षो नर्मोत्सवो वा यत्र । सोऽयं भवतोर्युवयोः परिष्वङ्ग आलिङ्गनं नियतिर्दैवं सैव महावात्या तयाभिहतः । लवली लताभेदः । लवङ्गो वृक्षभेदः । तयोः परिष्वङ्गः संपर्क इव । अभिनवौ लौहित्यरसौ यत्र सः । रसः आर्द्रता । कृतं कौतुकं कुतूहलं दृष्टॄणां येन सः । 'रागोऽनुरागे लौहित्ये' इति विश्वः । 'शृङ्गारादौ द्रवे चापीच्छायामप्ययं रसः ।' इति धरणिः । कौतुकं त्वभिलाषे स्यादुत्सवे नर्महर्षयोः । कुतूहलेऽपि तत्प्रोक्तम्' इति मेदिनीकरः । तदिहाचेतनोपमया तयोरपि बाल्यो-र्वृक्षविवाह इव मया विवाहोऽप्यकारि । दैवेन स न सोढ इत्युक्तम् । देशान्तरनयनान्नियतेर्वात्यया सह रूपकम् ॥ ३ ॥ **लवङ्गिका** । अत्र नृशंसं नाशकम् ॥ **लवङ्गिका** । अत्र प्रतिबद्धं घटितमत एव निश्चलम् । **कामन्दकी** ।

---

१ दुर्विलास. २ हा महा०; महाणुभाअ. ३ उवत्थिअत्थ०. ४ रतो. ५ विहतः. ६ सावेगम् ७ हदाहि०. ८ मदअंतिए. ९ जन्मतः. १० ०भवरा-तमा.

उज्ज्वलालोकया स्निग्धा त्वया त्यक्ता न राजते।
मलीमसमुखी वर्तिः प्रदीपशिखया यथा ॥ ४ ॥

कथं च[1] कल्याणि कामन्दकीं त्यजसि। नन्वकरुणे मदीयचीवरोष्मणैव ते प्रगुणीकृतान्यङ्गानि।

स्तन्यत्यागात्प्रभृति सुमुखी दन्तपाञ्चालिकेव
क्रीडायोगं तदनु विनयं प्रापिता वर्धिता च।
लोकश्रेष्ठे गुणवति वरे स्थापिता त्वं मयैव
स्नेहो मातुर्मयि समधिकस्तेन युक्तस्तवापि ॥ ५ ॥

( सवैक्लव्यम्। ). चन्द्र[3]मुखि संप्रति निराशास्मि संवृत्ता।

अकारणस्मेर[4]मनोहराननः
शिखाललाटार्पितगौरसर्षपः[5]।
तवाङ्क[6]शायी परिवृत्तभाग्यया
मया न दृष्टस्तनयः स्तनंधयः ॥ ६ ॥

---

उज्जिहानमूर्ध्वं गतम्। कण्ठोपगतमिति यावत्। **उज्ज्वलेत्यादि।** लवङ्गिकामुद्दिश्य। त्वया त्यक्तेयं न शोभते प्रदीपशिखया त्यक्ता वर्तिरिव दशेव। उज्ज्वल आलोको दर्शनं यस्यास्तया। शिखापक्ष आलोक उद्योतः। स्निग्धा प्रीता। स्नेहवती तैलादियोगात्। मलीमसं म्लानं मुखमाननं यस्याः सा। मलीमसं दग्धतया श्यामं मुखमग्रं यस्याः सा च ॥ ४ ॥ प्रगुणीकृतानि ऋजूकृतानि। उत्पत्त्यनन्तरं नाडीनां शुद्धद्रव्येणर्जुकरणात्। यद्वा प्रगुणता पुष्टिः। **स्तन्येत्यादि।** तेन हेतुना मातुः सकाशादधिकः स्नेहोऽयं मयि तव युक्तः। यद्वा तेन हेतुनायं वियोगस्तव युक्त इति सोल्लुण्ठम्। यतः स्तनपानत्यागादारभ्य क्रीडायोगं खेलम्। यद्वा क्रीडा कला योगो विद्याप्रयोगस्तं प्रापिता। ततः पश्चाद्विनयमनौद्धत्यं प्रापिता वृद्धिं प्रापिता च। दन्तपाञ्चालिकेव दन्तमयकृत्रिमपुत्रिकेव। जनेषु श्रेष्ठे शोभादिगुणयुक्ते जामातरि त्वं स्थिरीकृता। परिणयात्। मयैव न तु पित्रादिनेत्यर्थः। बाल्य एव कान्तिमत्त्वात्सुमुखीत्युक्तम्। 'पाञ्चालिका पुत्रिकायाम्' इति विश्वः। पाञ्चालिकापि क्रीडादिकं कार्यत इति प्रसिद्धमेव। विद्याभ्यासौ बाल्य एव स्त्रीणाम्। यदाह—'बाल्येऽधीयीत विद्यां स्त्री कामशास्त्रादिकं पुनः।' पुरुषगुणा अपि भरते—'शोभा विलासो माधुर्यं स्थैर्यं गाम्भीर्यमेव च। ललितौदार्यतेजांसि पौरुषेया गुणा अपि' ॥ ५ ॥ करुणस्नेहाद्विक्लवता। **अकारणेत्यादि।** विगतभाग्यया मया तव पुत्रो न दृष्टः। कीदृशः।

---

[1] त्वं; जहासि, परित्य०. [2] राञ्चलो०; प्रगुणितानि. [3] हा चन्द्र०. [4] स्नेह. [5] शेखरः. [6] तवाङ्क-ङ्क-गामी.

**लव०**—भगवति प्रसीद। निःसहास्मि सांप्रतं जीवितोद्वहनेन। साहमस्माद्गिरिशिखरादात्मानमवधुत्य निर्वृता भविष्यामि। तथा मे भगवत्याशिषं करोतु येन जन्मान्तरेऽपि तावत्प्रियसखीं प्रेक्षिष्ये। (भअवदि पसीद। णिस्सहम्मि संपदं जीविदुव्वहणेण। साहं इमादो गिरिसिहरादो अत्ताणं अवधुणिअ णिव्वुदा भविस्सं। तहा मे भअवदी आसिसं करेदु जेण जम्मन्तर वि दाव पिअसहिं पेक्खिस्सं।)

**काम०**—ननु लवङ्गिके कामन्दक्यपि नातःपरं वत्सावियोगेन जीविष्यति। समश्चायमुत्कण्ठावेग आवयोः। किं च।

> **संगमः कर्मणां भेदाद्यदि न स्यान्न नाम सः।**
> **प्राणानां तु परित्यागे संतापोपशमः फलम्॥ ७॥**

**लव०**—यथा यूयमाज्ञापयथ। (जहा तुह्मे आणवेध।) (उत्तिष्ठति।)

**काम०**—(सदयं वीक्ष्य।) वत्से मदयन्तिके।

**मद०**—किमाज्ञापयथ अग्रेसरी भवेति। अवहितास्मि। (किं आणवेध अग्गेसरी होहि त्ति। अवहिदह्मि।)

---

अकारणेनालक्षितहेतुतया स्मेरमीषद्धसनं तेन मनोज्ञं मुखं यस्य सः। शिखायां ललाटे च दत्तश्वेतसर्षपः। एतत्तु रक्षार्थे। क्रोडे सुप्तः। स्तनपायी च॥ ६॥ **लवङ्गिका।** अत्र जीवितेति। तां विना जीवनमनर्हमिति भावः। निर्वृतेति। मरणे तद्वियोगदुःखापनयादिति भावः। **कामन्दकी। उत्कण्ठेति।** जन्मान्तरे तां द्रक्ष्यामीत्युत्कण्ठा ममापीत्यर्थः। तत्कथं मयापि स्वतोऽसिद्धतया त्वय्याशीर्दातव्येति भावः। **संगम इत्यादि।** कर्मणां वैचित्र्यादस्माकं मालत्या सह संगमो न स्यात्। अनागमो निर्युक्तिको यतः सः। मालत्या मम च कर्मणां साम्ये मानाभावाज्जन्मान्तरे संगमो निर्युक्तिक इति भावः। तर्हि प्राणत्यागेनालमत आह—प्राणत्यागः पुनस्तापशान्तिफलः। तथा च तदर्थं स क्रियत इति भावः। संगमाभावे तु मानम्—'मृतोऽपि मानुषः शक्तो नानुगन्तुं मृतं जनम्। जायावर्जं च सर्वस्य याम्यः पन्था विभिद्यते॥' इति स्मृतिः॥७॥ **मदयन्तिका।** भाविवाक्यमुन्नीयाह—**किमिति।** अत्राग्रेसरी मरणे

---

१ व्वहणे, णस्स. २ गिरिवरादो, प्पपादादो. ३ आसिप्पसादं; आसिसं पसादीकरेदु. ४ क्यापि...जीवितव्यं. ५ समानश्चायमावयोरुत्कण्ठाप्रसंगः. ६ न स्यादनागमः; न स्यात्ततो तु मा; कर्मणां योगान्न हि स स्यादनागमः. ७ संतापोपरमः, ८ मदयन्तिकाम्.

**लव०**—सखि प्रसीद। विरमैतस्मादात्मनो व्यापादनात्। मा खल्वेतं जनं विस्मरिष्यसि। (सहि पसीद। विरम एत्तो अत्तणो वावादणादो। मा क्खु एदं जणं विसुमरेसि।

**मद०**—(सकोपमिव।) अपेहि। नास्मि ते वशंवदा। (अपेहि। णह्मि दे वसंवदा।)

**काम०**—हन्त निश्चितं वराक्या।

**मदय०**—(स्वगतम्।) नाथ मकरन्द नमो नमस्ते। (णाह मअरन्द णमोणमो दे।)

**लव०**—भगवति अयमेव मधुमतीस्रोतःसंदानितपवित्रमेखलो महीधरविटङ्कः। (भअवदि अअं ज्जेव्व मधुमदीसोत्तसंदाणिदपवित्तमेहलो महीहरविटङ्को।)

**काम०**—कृतमिदानीं प्रस्तुतान्तरायेण। (सर्वाः पतितुमिच्छन्ति।)

(नेपथ्ये।)

आश्चर्यमाश्चर्यम्।

व्यतिकर इव भीमस्तामसो वैद्युतश्च
क्षणमुपहितचक्षुर्वृत्तिरुद्भय शान्तः।

**काम०**—(विलोक्य साद्भुतहर्षम्।)

कथमिह मम वत्सस्तत्किमेतत्

**मक०**—(प्रविश्य।)

किमन्य-
त्प्रभवति हि महिम्ना स्वेन योगीश्वरीयम्॥८॥

(नेपथ्ये।)

कथमतिदारुणो जनसंमर्दो वर्तते।

---

प्रथमा। अवहिता मर्तुम्॥ **लवङ्गिका**। अत्राहं प्रिय इत्याशयः। **मदयन्तिका**। अत्र वशंबदायत्ता। ते वचो न करिष्यामीत्यर्थः। **कामन्दकी**। निश्चितं निश्चयः कृतः। **मदयन्तिका**। स्वगतं गुरुसमीपे प्रियस्मरणस्यायुक्तत्वात्। अत्र जन्मान्तरेऽप्ययं प्रियः स्यादिति तत्कालेऽस्य स्मरणमिति भावः॥ **लवङ्गिका**। अत्र मधुमती नदी। संदानितं बद्धम्। विटङ्को निर्गतोन्नतप्रदेशः। 'विटङ्क उन्नते देशे' इति रत्न-

---

१ गदा. २ उपगत. ३ पुनर्नेपथ्ये-कथ०. ४ योगे. ५ जनावमर्दः संप्रवर्तते.

**मालत्यपायमधिगम्य विरक्तचेताः**
**सांसारिकेषु विषयेषु च जीविते च ।**
**निश्चित्य वह्निपतनाय सुवर्णबिन्दु-**
**मभ्येति भूरिवसुरित्यधुना हताः स्मः ॥ ९ ॥**

**मद०** ङ्गिंके—झटिति मालतीमाधवयोर्दर्शनाभ्युदयो झटित्यत्या-हितं च । ( झत्ति मालदीमाहवाणं दंसणब्भुदओ झत्ति अच्चाहिदं अ । )

**काम०मकरन्दौ**—दिष्ट्या—हा धिक्कष्टं भोः । आश्चर्यमाश्चर्यम् ।

**किमयमसिपत्रचन्दनरसच्छटासारयुगपदवपातः ।**
**अनलस्फुलिङ्गकलितः किमयमनभ्रः सुधावर्षः ॥ १० ॥**
**संजीवनौषधिविषव्यतिकरमालोकतिमिरसंभेदम् ।**
**अद्य विधिरशनिशशधरमयूखसंवलनमनुकुरुते ॥ ११ ॥**

( नेपथ्ये । )

हा तात विरम विरम दर्शनोत्सुकास्मि ते वदनकमलस्य । प्रसीद संभावय माम् । कथं मम कारणात्समस्तलोकालोकान्तरालविख्यातनिर्मलकुलैकमङ्गलप्रदीपभूतमात्मानं परित्यजसि । मया पुनरनार्यया निरनुक्रोशा

---

कोशः ॥ ८ ॥ सकरुणः कश्चिद्वनेचर आह-**मालतीत्यादि** । भूरिवसुर्निश्चित्य निश्चयं कृत्वा वह्निपतनायाग्निं प्रवेष्टुं सुवर्णबिन्दुं शिवं लक्ष्यीकृत्यागच्छति । कीदृशः । मालतीमरणं ज्ञात्वा संसारविषयेष्वैश्वर्यादिषु जीवितेषु प्राणधारणेषु च । विविक्तं विवेकशालि । निर्विण्णमिति यावत् । चेतो यस्य सः । विरक्तेति पाठः सुगम एव । जीवितेष्विति बहुवचनं प्राणधारणक्रियाणां बहुत्वात् । अधुना भूरिवसुवियोगे सति हताः स्मः ॥९॥ **मदय०** अत्रात्याहितं महाभीतिः । **किमित्यादि** । असयः खड्गाः पत्राणि यस्य वृक्षस्य । दारकत्वात् । चन्दनरसच्छटा । आश्चर्यात् । आसारो वृष्टिः । तयोरेकदावपातः पतनं किमयम् । भूरिवसुगतानर्थश्रवणादसिपत्रपातः । मालतीमाधवयोर्जीवनाच्चन्दनरसासार इति भावः । किमयं मेघहीनोऽमृतवर्षोऽग्निस्फुलिङ्गमिश्रः ॥ १० ॥ **समित्यादि** । संजीवनौषधेर्विषस्य च व्यतिकरं मेलकं तेजसस्तिमिरस्य च मेलकं वज्रस्य चन्द्रकरस्य च मिलनं विधाताद्य सदृशीकरोतीत्यर्थः । आर्याच्छन्दः ॥ ११ ॥ **नेपथ्ये** । अत्र लोको जगत् । अलोकः स्वर्गः । तयोर्मध्य इत्यर्थः । मङ्गलं श्रेयः । अनार्यया बाल्या ।

---

१ ०तेषु. २ मह्लसवो. ३ छटाभिसार, सारयोर्यु०. ४ अपि च । सं०. ५ संदर्शन समु०.

यूयामिति संभावितमासीत् । ( हा ताद विरम दंसेणूसुआह्मि दे वअणकमलस्स । पसीद संभावेहि मं । कधं मम कारणादो समत्थलोआलोआन्तरालविक्खादणिम्मलकुले-कमक्कलप्पदीवभूदं अत्ताणं परिच्चअसि । मए उण अणज्जाएँ णिरणुक्कोसा तुह्मेति संभाविदं आसि । )

**कामन्दकी**—हा वत्से मालति ।

**जन्मान्तरादिव पुनः कथमपि लब्धासि यावदयमपरः ।**
**उपराग इव शशिकलां कवलयितुमुपस्थितोऽनर्थः ॥ १२ ॥**

**इतरे**—हा प्रियसखि । ( हा पिअसहि । )

( ततः प्रविशति प्रमुग्धां मालतीं धारयन्माधवः । )

**माधवः**—कष्टं भोः कष्टम् ।

**एषा प्रवासं कथमप्यतीत्य**
**याता पुनः संशयमन्यथैव ।**
**को नाम पाकाभिमुखस्य जन्तो-**
**र्द्वाराणि दैवस्य पिधातुमीष्टे ॥ १३ ॥**

**मक०**—( सहसोपसृत्य माधवं प्रति ) सखे अथ सा योगिनी क्व ।

**माधवः**—

**श्रीपर्वतादिहाहं सत्वरमपतं तयैव सह सद्यः ।**
**करुणवनेचरवचनादनन्तरं तां न पश्यामि ॥ १४ ॥**

---

निरनुक्रोशा निर्दयाः । नन्दनाय दानोपक्रमात् । **जन्मेत्यादि** । उपरागो राहुग्रहः । यथा कृष्णपक्षाज्जन्मान्तराच्चन्द्रस्यैका कलोपलभ्यते तां च कवलयितुं राहुरुपस्थितस्तथा तावकीनमिदं वृत्तान्तस्वरूपमिति भावः ॥ १२ ॥ प्रमुग्धा पितृशोकजनितमोहात् । **माधवः** । अनर्थपरंपरायोगादतिकष्टम् । **एषेत्यादि** । इयं मालती प्रवासमतीतापि राक्षसीहस्तमतिक्रान्तापि पुनरन्यथैव कथं संशयं प्राप्ता । पितृशोकात् । अत्रोपपत्तिमाह—फलदानाभिमुखस्य भाग्यस्य द्वाराणि सुखदुःखोपनयनानि निवारयितुं को नाम जन्तुरीष्टे समर्थो भवति । अपि तु न कोऽपीत्यर्थः । 'प्रवासः परहस्ते च परदेशेऽपि कथ्यते' इति नानार्थः । नामानवक्लृप्तौ । द्वाराणीति बहुत्वेन निवारणेऽशक्यतोक्ता ॥१३॥ **श्रीपर्वतादिति** । श्रीपर्वतादहमिह सत्वरमतिशीघ्रमपतमागतोऽस्मि । तया मालत्या सह । करुणाप्रधानवनेचरवचनादनन्तरं तां मालतीं न पश्यामि । मालत्यपायमधिगम्ये-

---

१ ऊसुआह्मि दे वअणकमलदंसणस्स. २ विक्खम्भाणिम्मलेक्क (विष्कम्भनिर्मलैक.) ३ अलज्जाए णिरणुक्कोसाए ( शया ) तुह्मे परिच्चना. ४ दपि. ५ भीरु यावदयम्. ६ विकलयितुं. ७ सहसोपेत्य. ८ नादहं सत्वरमापतितस्तयेव. ९ वन्तरितां.

**काम० मकरन्दौ**—( सप्रणयमाकाशे ) महाभागे पुनः परित्रायस्व नः । किमर्थमन्तर्हितासि ।

**लव० न्तिके**—सखि मालति ननु भणामि सखि मालतीति । ( सोत्कम्पम् । ) भगवति परित्रायस्व । चिरनिरुद्धनिश्वासनिःस्फुरमस्या हृदयम् । हा अमात्य हा प्रियसखि द्वावपि युवां परस्परावसानस्य कारणं जातौ । ( सहि मालदि णं भणामि सहि मालदि त्ति । भअवदि परित्ताहि । चिरणिरुद्धणिस्सासणिप्फुरं से हिअअं । हा अमच्च हा पिअसदि दुवे वि तुम्हे परप्परावसाणस्स कारणं जादा । )

**कामन्दकी**—हा वत्से मालति ।

**माधवः**—हा प्रिये ।

**मकरन्दः**—हा प्रियसखि ।

( सर्वे मोहमुपगम्य पुनः संज्ञां लभन्ते )

**कामन्दकी**—( ऊर्ध्वमवलोक्य । ) तत्किमेष झटिति पात्यमाना-दिवाम्बुदादम्बुनिवहः परिस्खलन्नस्मान्प्रीणयति ।

**माधवः**—(सोच्छ्वासम् । ) अये प्रत्यापन्नचेतना मालती । तथा ह्यस्याः

**भवति विततश्वासोन्नाहप्रणुन्नपयोधरं**
**हृदयमपि च स्निग्धं चक्षुर्निजप्रकृतौ स्थितम् ।**
**तदनु वदनं मूर्च्छाच्छेदात्प्रसादि विराजते**
**परिगतमिव प्रारम्भेऽह्नः श्रिया सरसीरुहम् ॥ १५ ॥**

( नेपथ्ये । )

---

त्यादि करुणवनेचरवचनम् । आर्याच्छन्दः ॥ १४ ॥ **लवङ्गिकामदयन्तिके** । सखि मालति ननु भणामि सखि मालति इति प्रलापक्रमोऽयम् । अत्र निः-स्फुरं चलनशून्यम् । **कामन्दकी** । सौदामिनीप्रभावकृतवृष्टयाश्चर्यमाह—किमि-ति । मेघाभावाद्वृष्टेराश्चर्यहेतुतयेवकारः संगच्छते । **माधवः** । प्रत्यापन्नं पुनरा-यातम् । **भवतीत्यादि** । अस्या नासा दीर्घश्वासा भवति । चलनादेव । प्रसन्न-स्तनं हृदयमपि भवति । चक्षुश्च स्निग्धं सन्निजप्रकृतिस्थिरं भवति । तदनु-तत्पश्चान्मुखम् । कर्तृ । मूर्च्छापगमात्प्रसन्नं शोभते शोभया सर्वतो व्याप्तं पद्म-मिव । परिणतमिति पाठे विकसितमित्यर्थः । विततश्वासोन्नाहप्रणुन्नपयोधरमिति पाठे

---

१ अत्रैवान्त; किमित्यन्तारितासि. २ सोत्कण्टम्. ३ निश्चलं. ४ ०रासासणस्स. ५ प्रिये मालति. ६ पात्यमान इव. ७ स्रवन्नस्मान्प्रीणाति. ८ चेतनेव. ९ श्वासानासा प्रसन्नपयो.

**अविगणय्य नृपं सहनन्दनं चरणयोर्नतमग्निचये पतन् ।**
**सपदि भूरिवसुर्विनिवर्तते मम गिरा गुरुसंमदविस्मयः ॥ १६ ॥**

**माधवमकरन्दौ**—( ऊर्ध्वमवलोक्य सहर्षम् ) भगवति दिष्ट्या वर्धसे ।

**सा योगिन्यम्बरतो विघटितजलदाभ्युपैत्ययं यस्याः ।**
**वागमृतजलासारो जलदजलासारमतिशेते ॥ १७ ॥**

**कामन्दकी**—प्रियं नः प्रियं नः ।

**मालती**—दिष्ट्या चिरस्य प्रत्युज्जीवितास्मि । ( दिट्ठिआ चिरस्स पच्चुज्जीविदह्मि । )

**कामन्दकी**—( सहर्षबाष्पम् । ) एह्येहि पुत्रि मालति ।

**मालती**—हा कथं भगवती । ( कथं भअवदी । ) ( इति पादयोर्निपतति । )

**कामन्दकी**—( उत्थाप्यालिङ्ग्य मूर्ध्न्याघ्राय । )

**जीवं जीवितसमाय जीवितं देहि जीवतु सुहृज्जनश्च ते ।**
**अङ्कैस्तुहिनसङ्गशीतलैः पुत्रि मां प्रियसखीं च जीवय ॥ १८ ॥**

**माधवः**—वयस्य मकरन्द संप्रत्युपादेयो माधवस्य जीवलोकः संवृत्तः ।

**मकरन्दः**—( सहर्षम् ) एवमेतत् ।

**मद० लवङ्गिके**—प्रियसखि मनोरथातिक्रान्तदर्शने संभावयावां परिष्वङ्गेण । ( पिअसहि मणोरहातिक्कन्तदंसणे संभावेहि अह्मे परिसङ्गेण । )

---

दीर्घश्वासस्योत्साहेनोद्गमेन प्रेरितौ स्तनौ यत्र तदित्यर्थः ॥ १५ ॥ **अवीत्यादि** । तत्क्षणं मद्वाष्पाभ्यामात्यो निवर्तते । कीदृशः । नन्दनसहितं नृपं पादनतमपि तिरस्कृत्याग्निसमूहे पतन् । गाढहर्षाश्चर्यश्च । सहभावस्य विकल्पात्सहनन्दनमिति ॥ ॥ १६ ॥ **सेत्यादि** । सेयं योगिनी भिन्नमेघा संप्रत्यायाति यस्या अयं वागमृतजलसारो वचनामृतजलधारा जलधरजलधारामप्यतिक्रामति । सौहित्यादिना ततोप्यधिका भवतीत्यर्थः ॥ १७ ॥ **मालती** । अत्र चिरस्य बहुकालेन । **जीवेत्यादि** । हे पुत्रि त्वं जीव । ततो वल्लभाय जीवितं देहि । त्वज्जीवनाद्बन्धवोऽपि ते जीवन्तु । प्रशस्ताङ्कैः । प्रशस्तार्थे कन् । हिमसंबन्धशीतलैर्मां लवङ्गिकां च जीवय ॥ १८ ॥ **मदयन्तिकाल०** । संभावय योजय

---

१ मुखे. २ वर्तितः. ३ सविस्मयम्. ४ योगिनीयमतिरयाविघ०, पेति नौ. ५ (सहर्ष) प्रियं. ६ एतन्नास्ति क्वचित्. ७ सहर्ष सबाष्पं च. ८ ०यच; उपाघ्राय. ९ एहि. १० एवैतत्. ११ इतरे.

**मालती**—हा प्रियसख्यौ । (हा पिअसहिओ ।) (इत्युभे आलिङ्गति ।)

**कामन्दकी**—वत्सौ किमेतत् ।

**माधवमकरन्दौ**—भगवति

**कपालकुण्डलाकोपदुर्जातजनितापदः ।**
**वयमभ्युद्धृताः कृच्छ्रान्निर्बन्धादार्ययानया ॥ १९ ॥**

**कामन्दकी**—कथमघोरघण्टवधाविजृम्भितमेतत् ।

**मद० लवङ्गिके**—अहो आश्चर्यम् । पुनरुक्तदारुणस्य परिणामरमणीयत्वं विधेः । (अहो अच्चरिअं । पुणरुत्तदारुणस्स परिणामरमणिज्जत्तणं विहिणो ।)

(प्रविश्य ।)

**सौदामिनी**—(उपसृत्य) भगवति कामन्[1]दाकि स एष वश्चिरंतनोऽन्तेवासी जनः प्रणमति ।

**कामन्दकी**—अये भ[2]द्रा सौदामिनी ।

**माधवमकरन्दौ**—(सविस्मयम् ।) कथमियं सा भगवत्याः पक्षपातस्थानमाद्यशिष्या सौदामिनी । तत्सर्वमधुना संगच्छते ।

**कामन्दकी**—

**एह्येहि भूरिजन[3]जीवितदानपुण्य-**
**संभारधारिणि चिरा[4]दसि हन्त दृष्टा ।**
**दत्तप्रमोदमपि न[5]न्दय मे शरीर-**
**मालिङ्ग्य सौहृदनिधे विरम प्रणामात् ॥ २० ॥**

---

**कपालेत्यादि** । अनया सौदामिन्या कपालकुण्डलारोषाद्दुर्जातं मालत्यपहरणरूपं तज्जनितविपत्तेः सकाशात्कृच्छ्रात्संकटान्निर्बन्धेनातिप्रयत्नेन वयमुद्धृताः ॥ १९ ॥ **मदयन्तिकाल०** । अत्र पुनःक्लेशकारितया पुनरुक्तदारुणत्वम् । प्रतिकूलस्यैव विधेरधुनानुकूलत्वमित्याश्चर्यम् । **एहीत्यादि** । मालतीरक्षणेन बहुजनरक्षणजन्यपुण्यनिवहधारिके हे चिरेण त्वं दृष्टासि । अतो हेतोस्त्वमेह्यागच्छ । हन्त हर्षे । ममाङ्गमालिङ्ग्य हर्षय । शरीरं कीदृशम् । दत्तानन्दमपि मालतीदर्शनेनेति भावः । हे सौहृदाश्रये नतेर्विरम । त्वमेव नमस्या यतः ॥२०॥ तदेवाह—**वन्द्येत्यादि** । त्वमेव संसारस्य नमस्या एवंविधै-

---

१ एतन्नास्ति क्वचित्. २ भद्रम्. ३ वसु. ४ चिराय मयासि. ५ मभिनन्दय.

अपि च ।

वन्ध्या त्वमेव जगतः स्पृहणीयसिद्धि-
रेवंविधैर्विलसितैरतिबोधिसत्त्वैः ।
यस्याः पुरापरिचयप्रतिबद्धबीज-
मुद्भूतभूरिफलशालि विजृम्भितं ते ॥ २१ ॥

**मद० लवङ्गिके**—इयं सार्या सौदामिनी । ( इअं सा अज्जा सौदामिणी ।

**मालती**—बाढम् । अनया खलु भगवतीसम्बन्धपक्षपातिन्या निर्भर्त्स्य कपालकुण्डलामात्मन आवसथमुपनीय भगवतीस्नेहनिर्विशेषं समाश्वासितास्मि । किं च केसरावलीसाभिज्ञानहस्तयेहागत्य सर्वे यूयं संधारिताः । ( बाढम् । इमाए क्खु भअवदीसंबन्धपक्खवादिणीए णिब्भच्छिअ कपालकुण्डलं अत्तणो आवसधं उवणीअ भअवदीसिणेहनिव्विसेसं समासासिदह्मि । किं अ केसरावलीसाभिण्णाणहत्थाए इह आगत्तूण सव्वे तुह्मे संधारिदाँ । )

**मद० लवङ्गिके**—सुप्रसन्ना नः कनिष्ठा भगवती । ( सुप्पसणा णो कणिट्ठा भअवदी । )

**माधवमकरन्दौ**—अहो नु खलु भोः ।

---

विलसितैराकाशक्रमरूपैर्वा श्लाघनीयासिद्धिस्त्वं यतः । कीदृशैः बोधिसत्वा जीमूतवाहनादयः तानप्यतिक्रामन्ति तैः । तेषामेकैकजीवनात्त्वया त्वनेकजीवनादतिशय इति भावः । यद्वा बोधिसत्वो बुद्धविशेषः तदतिक्रमवर्तिभिः । अनेकपुण्यकारित्वात् । यस्यास्तव विजृम्भितं चेष्टितं पूर्वपरिचयेन प्रतिबद्धमङ्कुरितं बीजं करणं यत्र तत् । उद्भूतप्रचुरफलयुक्तं च भवति । तथा च त्वदुपकरणेन कृतार्थास्मीति भावः । अन्यदपि कलमाद्यङ्कुररूपं विजृम्भितं पूर्वप्रतिबद्धबीजमुद्भूतप्रचुरफलशालि भवतीति ध्वनिः ॥ २१ ॥ **मालती** । अत्र समासादिता प्रापिता । केसरावली बकुलमाला सैवाभिज्ञानं प्रत्ययचिह्नं हस्ते यस्याः । तथा संधारिता रक्षिता । मज्जीवनेनेति भावः । **मदयन्तिकालवङ्गिके** । अत्र त्वज्ज्येष्ठा कामन्दकी यथास्माकं सुप्रसन्ना तथा त्वमपि भवेत्यर्थः । सौदामिनीज्येष्ठत्वादपि भगवत्या गुरुत्वात्तस्यामत्यादरसूचनम् । यद्वा सौदामिन्या एव भगवतीकनिष्ठत्वेनादर उक्तः ।

---

१ जग–नां–ति. २ अविरोधिस०. ३ भ्भितेन, तं नः. ४ सादिना ( टी० ). ५ वल्यभि० ( टी० ) ६ मरणादूय ( टी० ) ७ मरणादो सा एसा जीविदप्पदाहइणी सो० इत्य० क्वचित्. ६ इतरे.

**अपि चिन्तामणिश्चिन्तापरिश्रममपेक्षते ।**
**इदं त्वचिन्तितं मन्ये कृतमाश्चर्यमार्यया ॥ २२ ॥**

**सौदा०**—( स्वगतम् । ) हन्त लज्जयति मामत्यन्तसौजन्यमेतेषाम् । ( प्रकाशम् । ) भगवति एतत्प्रहृष्टनन्दनाभिनन्दितेन राज्ञा पद्मावतीश्वरेण भूरिवसोः प्रत्यक्षमभिलिख्य पत्रमायुष्मतो माधवस्य प्रेषितम् । ( लेखमर्पयति । )

**कामन्दकी०**—( गृहीत्वा वाचयति । ) स्वस्त्यस्तु वः । परमेश्वरः समाज्ञापयति यथा

**श्लाघ्यानां गुणिनां धुरि स्थितवति श्रेष्ठान्वये च त्वयि**
**प्रत्यस्तव्यसने महीयसि परं प्रीतोऽस्मि जामातरि ।**
**तेनेयं मदयन्तिकापि भवतः प्रीत्यै तव प्रेयसे**
**मित्राय प्रथमानुरागघटिताप्यस्माभिरुत्सृज्यते ॥ २३ ॥**

( माधवमुद्दिश्य ) वत्स श्रूयताम् ।

**माधवः**—श्रुतम् । इदानीं सर्वथा कृतार्थोऽस्मि ।

**मालती**—दिष्ट्येदानीमपहृतं हृदयस्याशङ्काशल्यम् । ( दिट्ठिआ एत्तहिं अवहदं हिअअस्स आसङ्कासल्लं ।)

**लव०**—सांप्रतं निरवशेषं श्रीमाधवस्य मालत्याश्च फलिता मनोरथाः । ( संपदं णिरवसेसं माहवसिरिणो मालदीए अ फलिदा मणोरहा ।)

---

**अपीत्यादि** । चिन्तामणिरपि चिन्तारूपं परिश्रममपेक्षते । अचिन्तितप्रदाने चिन्तामणित्वव्याघातादिति भावः । इदं पुनराश्चर्यं मन्ये यदार्यया सौदामिन्याचिन्तितं कृतमिति । तथा चात्रानुकारोऽपि नेति भावः । अत एवात्यन्ताश्चर्यम् ॥ २२ ॥ **सौदामिनी** । नन्दने प्रहर्षो मकरन्दमदयन्तिकानुरूपघटनात् । वरगुणानाह—**श्लाघ्यानामिति** । यदिह त्वयि जामातर्यत्यर्थं प्रीतोऽस्मि तेनेयं मदयन्तिका तव प्रीत्यै त्वत्प्रीतिं कर्तुं भवतः प्रेयसे मित्राय सुहृदे मकरन्दायाद्यास्माभिरपि दीयते । पूर्वमनुरागेण दत्ता । प्रीतिहेतुमाह—सच्चरितानां गुणिनां च गणनीये स्थिते प्रशस्तवंशे । पाठान्तरे ख्यातवंशे । प्रत्यस्तं क्षिप्तं व्यसनमशुभं यत्र तत्र । सातिशये । प्रत्युत्पन्नमताविति पाठेऽभिनवोत्पन्नबुद्धौ प्रतिभावतीत्यर्थः ॥ २३ ॥ **माधवः** । कृतार्थता नृपनन्दनाविरोधात् । **मालती** । आशङ्का विरोधादिविषया । मर्मभेदित्वाच्छल्यम् । **लवङ्गिका** ।

---

१ इदं त्वकृतमन्येन कृताश्चर्यमाचिन्तितम्. २ आलिख्य. ३ ०न्ववाये त्वयि. ४ कापि. ५ ०श्य सहर्षम्. ६ सर्वतः. ७ दाणिं, णो हिअ. एदं वि पाव अदगदं. ८ णिरवसेसा पूरिदा ०सिरिणो मणो.

**मक०**—( पुरोऽवलोक्य । ) कथमवलोकिताबुद्धरक्षिते कलहंसकेन सह प्रमोदनिर्भरं नृत्यन्त्याविव एवागच्छतः ।

( ततः प्रविशतोऽवलोकिताबुद्धरक्षिते कलहंसकश्च । )

**सर्वे**—( विविधं नृत्यं कृत्वोपसृत्य सप्रणामं कामन्दकीं प्रति ) जय भगवति कार्यनिधाने । ( माधवं प्रति । ) जय मकरन्दनन्दन माधव पूर्णचन्द्र दिष्ट्या वर्धसे । ( जअ भअवदि कज्जणिहाणे । ) ( जअ मअरन्दणन्दण माहव पुण्णचन्द दिट्ठिआ वड्ढसि । ) ( सर्वे सस्मितं पश्यन्ति )

**लव०**—को वास्मिन्संपूरितसर्वप्रकारमहोत्सवे न परिहाससंपूर्णो भवति । ( को वा ईमस्सिं संपूरिदसव्वप्पआरमहूसवे ण परिहाससंपुण्णो होइ । )

**काम०**—एवमेतत् । अस्ति वा कुताश्चिदेवंभूतमद्भुतं विचित्ररमणीयोज्ज्वलं प्रकरणम् ।

**सौदा०**—इदमत्र रमणीयतरं यदमात्ययोर्भूरिवसुदेवरातयोश्चिरात्पूर्णोऽयमितरेतरापत्यसंबन्धात्मा मनोरथः ।

**मालती**—( स्वगतम् । ) कथमिव । ( कहं विअ । )

**माधवमकरन्दौ**—( सकौतुकम् । ) भगवति अन्यथा वस्तुवृत्तमन्यथा वचनमार्यायाः ।

---

अत्र श्रीमाधवस्येति प्राकृते पूर्वनिपातानियमत्वात् । फलिता मनोरथाः । एतयोरायातिशुद्धविवाहादिति भावः । **सर्वे इति** । भगवति कार्यनिधाने । अत्र जयेति शेषः । **लवङ्गिका** । अपि तु सर्वोऽपीत्यर्थः । **कामन्दकी** । अद्भुतमित्यादिनोपगूहनमाह । यदाह—'अद्भुतस्य तु संप्राप्तिर्भवतादुपगूहनम् ।' इति । प्रकरणं मालतीमाधवाख्यम् । कथमिव । अत्र पित्राद्यनुमत्या नाहं दत्ता तत्कथमियमेवमाहेति भावः । अन्यथेति । चोरिकया वृत्तं वस्तु विवाहकृत्यम् । आर्यायाः सौदा-

---

१ बु०नावलोकिताकलहंसा दूरतः समुद्गतानस्मान्वीक्ष्य तत्रैव हर्षनिर्भरं प्रनृत्ताः; हंसश्च दूरतः समागतानस्मान्वीक्ष्य तत्रैव हर्षनिर्भरं नृत्यन्त इत एवागच्छन्ति । २ परिपूरिद सव्वमहू०, सव्वप्पआरपरिपू०; को वा. होइ इत्यस्यस्थाने तदीअकज्जं वि अ एतास्सिं संपूरिदम् । अदो सव्वप्पआरमहूसवे णच्चइ । ( तदीयकार्यमपि चैतस्मिन्संपूर्णम् । अतः सर्वप्रकारमहोत्सवे नृत्यति । ) इ.पा.३ एवमद्भु. ४ महाप्र०. भूतं महाद्भुतं. ५ रामणीयकं, रमणीयान्तरं. ६ संपूर्णः. ७ न्धरूपः. ८ तं कहं. ९ वस्तु प्रवृत्तमन्यथा वचनपर्यायः.

**लव०**—( जनान्तिकं ) भगवति किं प्रतिपत्तव्यम् । ( भअवदि ) किं[1] पडिवज्जिदव्वं । )

**काम०**—( स्वगतम्[2] । ) संप्रति मदयन्तिकासंबन्धे[3]न्नन्दनोपग्रहात्प्रत्यस्तशङ्काः खलु वयम् । ( प्रकाशम् । ) वत्सौ न खल्वन्यथा वस्तु[4]वृत्तं यतः श्रावकावस्थायामस्मत्सौदामिनीप्रत्य[5]क्षमनयोर्वृत्तेयं प्रतिज्ञावश्यमावाभ्यामपत्यसंबन्धः कर्तव्य इति । प्रधानप्रकृतिकोपस्त्वेवं परिहृत[6]ः ।

**मालती**—अहो संवरणम् । ( अहो संवरणं[7] । )

**माधवमकरन्दौ**—आश्चर्यम् । जयन्ति[8] महतां संस्तुतापलापिन्यः कल्याणिन्यो नीतयः ।

**कामन्दकी**—वत्स[9]

**यत्प्रागेव मनोरथैर्वृतमभूत्कल्याणमायुष्मतो[10]-**
**स्तत्पुण्यैर्मदुपक्रमैश्च फलितं क्लेशो[11]ऽपि मच्छिष्ययोः ।**
**निष्णा[12]तश्च समागमोऽपि विहितस्त्वत्प्रेयसः कान्तया**
**संप्रीतौ नृपनन्दनौ यद[13]परं प्रेयस्तदप्युच्यताम् ॥ २४ ॥**

---

मिन्या वचनमन्यथा । अमात्यागोचरेणेत्यर्थः । **लवङ्गिका** । अत्र सौदामिनीवचनं किंरूपमित्याशयः । **कामन्दकी** । श्रावकेति पाठकदशायाम् । प्रकृतिः शिष्टः । **मालती** । अहो संवरणम् । अत्र मन्त्रिणो मत्पितुरिति शेषः । **माधवमकरन्दौ** । कल्याणिन्यो मम संपन्ना यत इति भावः । **यदित्यादि** । यदायुष्मतोर्युवयोः । कल्याणमन्योन्यलाभरूपं पूर्वं मनोरथैरेव वृतमाकाङ्क्षितमभूत्तत्पुण्यैर्मदुपक्रमैश्च निसृष्टार्थदूतीकल्पकपटैः फलितम् । मच्छिष्ययोरवलोकितासौदामिन्योः क्लेशोऽपि फलित इति लिङ्गविपरिणामो योग्यत्वात् । क्लेशेनेति पाठे ताभ्यामेव फलितमित्यर्थः । तथा त्वन्मित्रस्य मकरन्दस्य मदयान्तिकया सह संबन्धोऽपि निष्णातो निःशङ्कं विहितः । नृपनन्दनावतिप्रीतौ विहितौ । अत एव निःशङ्कता ।

---

१ किं एत्थ. २ अपवार्य. ३ संम्बन्धेन नन्दनावग्रहात्. ४ वस्तु प्रवृत्तमन्यथा वचनमस्याः । ५ समक्षं तयोः. ६ प्रातिहतः. ७ ०रणं उपाअस्स. ८ जयन्ति खलु महतां विसंवादिन्यः प्रत्यायिन्यः कल्याणाः, जयन्ति खलु महतामविसंवादिन्यः कल्याणनीतयः, महतां विसंष्ठुलाः प्रतीपिन्यः कल्याणिन्यः, महतामेव संस्तुतप्रलापिण्यः. ९ वत्स माधव. १० ०ष्मता. ११ क्लेशैश्च, क्लेशेऽपि. १२ निष्ठातश्च, संपूर्णश्च, विस्तीर्णश्च. १३ किम०.

**माधवः**—( सहर्षं प्रणमन्[१] । ) भगवति अतःपरमपि प्रियमस्ति । तथापीदमस्तु[२] भगवतीपादप्रसादात् ।

**सन्तः सन्तु निरन्तरं सुकृतिनो विध्वस्तपापोदया**
**राजानः परिपालयन्तु वसुधां धर्मे[३] स्थिताः सर्वदा ।**
**काले संततवर्षिणो जलमुचः सन्तु क्षितौ[४] पुण्यतो**
**मोदन्तां घनबन्धु[५]बान्धवसुहृद्गोष्ठीप्रमोदाः प्रजाः[६] ॥ २५ ॥**

( इति निष्क्रान्ताः सर्वे । )

**इति मालतीमाधवे दशमोऽङ्कः ।**

**इति मालतीमाधवं नाम प्रकरणं समाप्तम् ।**

---

अपरमतःपरं यत्प्रेयः प्रियं कर्तव्यमस्ति तदप्युच्यताम् ॥ तत्करोमीत्यर्थः ॥ २४ ॥

**सन्त इत्यादि** । सज्जना निरन्तरं धार्मिकाः सन्तु । अत्र हेतु । विनष्टपापोद्रेकाः । तथा च सतां पुण्यमुज्जृम्भतां पापं नश्यतामित्यर्थः । राजधर्मे रक्षणादौ सदा स्थिता नृपा भुवं रक्षन्तु । धनं दधातीति वसुधेत्यनेन विपुलधनवत्त्वं भुव उक्तम् । काले वर्षादौ शस्याविरोधि सम्यक् ततं व्यापकं यथा तथा वर्षणशीला मेघाः सन्तु । अकालवृष्ट्या शस्यनाशात्काल इत्युक्तम् । अत्र हेतुमाह–प्रजानां लोकानां पुण्यात् । प्रजा हृष्यन्ताम् । घनबद्धो निरन्तरकृतो बान्धवानां संबन्धिनां सुहृदां मित्राणां गोष्ठीषु प्रकृष्टहर्षो याभिस्ताः । तदनेन प्रशस्तिरुक्ता । काव्योपसंहारोऽप्यनेनैव कृतः । यदाह—'वरदानस्य उक्तिर्या सा काव्य उपसंहृतिः । इति ॥ २५ ॥

लब्धं दुर्लभशासनं सुरगणग्रामश्च कैवर्तिका-
द्विद्यावंशविभूषिते अपि शुभे छत्रे उभे धारिते ।
येनायं समभूद्विजातितिलकश्चण्डेश्वरः पण्डितो
मीमांसैकरहस्यवश्यहृदयो दातावदाताशयः ॥ १ ॥
देवेशे समसूत सोऽयममले मीमांसकं सत्कविं
सोऽप्युच्चैरजनिष्ट जैमिनिमते रामेश्वरं सद्बुधम् ।
सूते स्मायमपि प्रतीपजयिनं मीमांसयालंकृतं
शुद्धं धीरगदाधरं कविवरं पुत्रं पवित्राशयम् ॥ २ ॥

---

१ प्रणमति. २ भरतवाक्यम् ।

**शिवम ( भीर ) स्तु सर्वजगतां परहितनिरता भवन्तु भूतगणाः ।**
**दोषाः प्रयान्तु शान्तिं सर्वत्र सुखी भवतु लोकः ॥ २५ ॥**

३ वृत्तौ. ४ स्थिराः. ५ बद्ध; गोष्ठी–भोग. ६ अतःपरं–काम०–एवमस्तु इत्यधिकम् ।
७ इति श्रीभवभूतिविरचितं समाप्तमिदं मा० प्र०

विद्याधरं वरमजीजनदेष धीरं
हीरं जनेषु जयिनं गुरुणोक्तशास्त्रे ।
प्रासूत सोऽयममलं गुणिनं सुपुत्रं
तं रत्नपूर्वधरमेष जगद्धरं च ॥ ३ ॥

येनापाठि कठोरगोतममणेर्वैशेषिकं खण्डनं
येनाश्रावि सकोषकाव्यनिवहं तत्पाणिनीयं मतम् ।
छन्दोऽलंकरणं च भव्यभरतं येनाध्यगायि श्रुति-
स्तस्यामुष्य जगद्धरस्य कवितुष्टीकेयमुज्जृम्भताम् ॥ ४ ॥

असूत यं रत्नधरोऽतिभव्योऽतिभव्यरूपा दमयन्तिकापि ।
जगद्धरं तत्कृतटिप्पणेऽङ्कः समाप्तिमापद्दशमोऽनवद्यः ॥ ५ ॥

**इति श्रीमन्महोपाध्यायपण्डितराजमहाकविराजधर्माधिका-रिश्रीरत्नधरपण्डितात्मजश्रीजगद्धरविरचितायां मालतीमाधवटीकायां दशमोऽङ्कः ।**

१ कृतश्रीकण्ठपदलाञ्छनभवभूतिवाग्विलासमाल०

# अनुक्रमणी ।